Handbook of
Cross-Cultural Psychology

Handbook of Cross-Cultural Psychology
Second Edition

Edited by John W. Berry, Ype H. Poortinga, Janak Pandey,
Pierre R. Dasen, T. S. Saraswathi, Marshall H. Segall,
and Cigdem Kagitçibasi

VOLUME 1
Theory and Method

VOLUME 2
Basic Processes and Human Development

VOLUME 3
Social Behavior and Applications

性相近　　習相遠

**Basic human nature is similar at birth;
Different habits make us seem remote.**

From the *San Zi Jing*

Second Edition

Handbook of
Cross-Cultural Psychology

VOLUME 2
BASIC PROCESSES AND
HUMAN DEVELOPMENT

Edited by

John W. Berry
Queen's University, Canada

Pierre R. Dasen
University of Geneva, Switzerland

T. S. Saraswathi
M. S. University of Baroda, India

Allyn and Bacon
Boston • London • Toronto • Sydney • Tokyo • Singapore

This volume is dedicated to
the memory of Ruth H. Munroe
1930–1996

First edition published under the titles *Handbook of Cross-Cultural Psychology,*
Volume 3, *Basic Processes,* edited by Harry C. Triandis and Walter Lonner,
copyright © 1980 and *Handbook of Cross-Cultural Psychology,* Volume 4,
Developmental Psychology, edited by Harry C. Triandis and Alastair Heron,
copyright © 1981, by Allyn & Bacon.

Library of Congress Cataloging-in-Publication Data

Handbook of cross-cultural psychology. -- 2nd ed.
     p.   cm.
   Includes bibliographical references and index.
   Contents: v. 1. Theory and method / edited by John W. Berry, Ype
H. Poortinga, Janak Pandey.
   ISBN 0-205-16075-1 (v. 2)
   1. Ethnopsychology.   I. Berry, John W.
GN502.H36   1996
155.82—dc20   96-16261
                                                      CIP

Printed in the United States of America
10 9 8 7 6 5 4 3 2   01 00 99 98

CONTENTS

VOLUME 2: BASIC PROCESSES AND HUMAN DEVELOPMENT
Edited by J. W. Berry, P. R. Dasen, & T. S. Saraswathi

VOLUME 1: THEORY AND METHOD
Edited by J. W. Berry, Y. H. Poortinga & J. Pandey

VOLUME 3: SOCIAL BEHAVIOR AND APPLICATIONS
Edited by J. W. Berry, M. H. Segall & C. Kagitçibasi

FOREWORD

Humans have been interested in how culture influences "naive psychology" (beliefs, customs, ways of life) from the time when they had the leisure to do so, and they have been recording their impressions since Herodotus. The scientific study of the link between culture and psychology started in the 19th century, perhaps with Comte's *Cours de philosophie positive* (6 volumes, 1830 to 1842). Much of the knowledge that had accumulated between the 19th century and the mid-1970s was presented in the first edition of the *Handbook of Cross-Cultural Psychology* (6 volumes, 1980 to 1981).

But science provides an ever-changing panorama. Between 1975 and today some of the ideas about what culture and psychology are have changed. Culture has become a less static, more dynamic, and "constructed" conception. Psychology has finally realized that culture has a major role to play in the way psychology is shaped.

That is so because we humans are all ethnocentric. This is a fundamental reality, reflecting that we all grow up in a specific culture (even when it is cosmopolitan and a mixture of other cultures) and learn to believe that the standards, principles, perspectives, and expectations that we acquire from our culture are *the* way to look at the world. Unexamined assumptions are one of the central aspects of culture. When we construct psychological theories, the more the subject matter deviates from biological and physiological phenomena, the more our culture intrudes in the shaping of the theories that we construct. In social and clinical psychology, for instance, much of what we present as "the truth" reflects our culture. The only way to correct the "false consensus" we perceive as "the truth" is to compare our ideas with the ideas that have been generated in other contexts. This can be done by emphasizing general issues of how culture influences psychological processes, as is done in "cultural psychology." It can also be revealed very sharply when we study different "indigenous psychologies." Much can be learned, in addition, by comparing data from several cultures, as is done in "cross-cultural psychology," and by examining how cultures interact with each other, as is done in "intercultural psychology."

John Berry has wisely included many of these perspectives in the *Second Edition*. He has done this by including more editors and authors from different cultures, traditions, and theoretical perspectives, and by broadening the definition of what is to be included in this edition. Thus, the second edition is broader, with authors who are more diverse in age, culture, and theoretical perspectives, than the first edition.

In this edition there are chapters on indigenous and evolutionary psychologies that were not included in the first edition. The research methods covered in chapters of the *First Edition* have not changed much, so these chapters are "archived" in the *Second Edition;* but two new methodological chapters have been added. Relatively new research areas—the examination of the developmental niche, the construction of identity, individualism and collectivism, intergroup relations, sex and gender issues, aggression, crime, and warfare, cross-cultural training, and health—now have separate chapters.

Some of these topics had a minor presence in 1972, when the first edition was formulated. For instance, the individualism and collectivism theme was not yet a focus of cross-cultural research, but became quite important after the first edition was published. I should have included a chapter on cross-cultural training in the first edition, but I was so concerned that the *Handbook* might include too much material reflecting my own interests that I went too far in holding back such material. It is gratifying that the *Second Edition* corrects this mistake.

The constellation of editors and authors of the *Second Edition* consists of about one-fifth old and four-fifths new writers, of diverse ages and cultures. I am delighted to see that the new generation of cross-cultural psychologists is moving the field forward.

Summer of 1995

Harry C. Triandis
Champaign, Illinois

Harry Triandis is Professor of Psychology at the University of Illinois. His recent books include *Culture and Social Behavior* (1994, New York: McGraw-Hill) and *Individualism and Collectivism* (1995, Boulder, CO: Westview Press). He edited (with W. W. Lambert, J. W. Berry, W. J. Lonner, R. Brislin, A. Heron, & J. Draguns) the first edition of the *Handbook of Cross-Cultural Psychology* (1980–81), and the international volume of the *Second Edition of the Handbook of Industrial and Organizational Psychology* (M. D. Dunnette and L. M. Hough 1990–1994, Palo Alto, CA: Consulting Psychologists). In 1994 he received the Otto Klineberg Award for his work on cultural syndromes, and the American Psychological Association's Award for Distinguished Contributions to the International Advancement of Psychology.

PREFACE

Cross-cultural psychology is the systematic study of relationships between the cultural context of human development and the behaviors that become established in the repertoire of individuals growing up in a particular culture. The field is diverse: some psychologists work intensively within one culture, some work comparatively across cultures, and some work with ethnic groups within culturally plural societies; all are seeking to provide an understanding of these culture-behavior relationships. This inclusive view about the diversity of the field has guided the editing of this second edition of the *Handbook of Cross-Cultural Psychology*.

The field of cross-cultural psychology has greatly evolved and expanded since the publication of the first edition of the *Handbook* in 1980. Under the general editorship of Harry Triandis, the six volumes of the first edition established the field as a wide-ranging but focused and coherent approach to understanding human experience and behavior in cultural context. The fifty-one chapters covered a vast territory, exploring virtually every corner of the discipline of psychology. The focus was consistently on how cultural factors influence psychological development and guide behavioral expression, and the integration was achieved through editorial coordination and collegial exchanges among authors.

Usually, second editions must exhibit both continuity and change. In this edition of the *Handbook*, continuity is represented by similar organization and coverage of materials to those in the first edition. More specifically: the present Volume 1 (Theory and Method) is a sequel to first edition Volumes 1 and 2 (Perspectives, and Methodology); the present Volume 2 (Basic Processes and Human Development) stems from Volumes 3 and 4 (Basic Processes, and Developmental); and the present Volume 3 (Social Behavior and Applications) follows mostly from Volumes 5 and 6 (Social, and Psychopathology). However, in this edition there has been no attempt to replicate the original compendium. Instead, the current editors decided to "archive" many of the earlier chapters, letting them stand as important and comprehensive statements of contemporary knowledge; where appropriate, present chapters refer readers to these earlier treatments. Chapters in the first edition that are considered as "archived" should be consulted by readers who want to have a comprehensive view of the field. These include: in Volume 1, a consideration of psychological universals and of the politics and ethics of cross-cultural research; in Volume 2, presentations of various methods (ethnographic, observational, surveying and interviewing, psychometric assessment, projective testing, experiments, unobtrusive measures, translation and content analysis, and holocultural methods); in Volume 3, surveys of research on motivation; in Volume 4, overviews of Piagetian theory, personality development and games and sports; in Volume 5, examinations of exchange theory, and small group behavior; and in Volume 6, reviews of alienation and depression. The topics of all other chapters in the first edition have, in one way or another, been updated and incorporated in the various chapters in this second edition.

This *Handbook*, in fewer chapters (34), focuses on topics for which there have been important theoretical and empirical advances since the late 1970s. Some chapters are true sequels to earlier ones; authors who are continuing earlier topics were asked to assume that readers have (or can) read the original chapter, and to start their review where the other chapter left off (usually around 1978). Other chapters attend to new topics that were barely evident in 1980; authors of these were asked to develop their material from earlier and more basic sources. The overall results, we hope, is a *Handbook* that can be used alone, or in sequence with the first edition.

The field of cross-cultural psychology has changed considerably over the past two decades. Four changes in particular have been important. One substantial change is in diversification in the concept of *culture* and how it may be related to psychology. Some of this change has followed a move in cultural anthropology away from a view of culture as objectively knowable and describable, providing a relatively stable context for individual human development, to a more interactive and creative relationship between individuals and their sociocultural surroundings. This move in anthropology has led to a parallel shift in cross-cultural psychology, stimulating the emergence of a subfield known as "cultural psychology." This aspect of diversification is represented particularly in Volume 1 by pairs of chapters on Theory and on Method that portray these contrasting perspectives on the concept of culture. A final chapter in Volume 1 attempts to provide an integrative framework within which this recent diversification can be viewed.

There can be no doubt that for many years cross-cultural psychology was done mostly by those in Western, economically and politically powerful nations; the objects of their attention were usually "others." When these others lived elsewhere, they were "tribes," and when they were closer at hand they were "subcultures" or "minorities." Recognizing the ethnocentrism in this arrangement, two other changes have occurred that represent moves away from this position. In the first emergent subfield, cross-cultural psychology has been increasingly carried out with cultural groups that co-reside in culturally plural societies, influencing each other, and being influenced in common by the many institutions that are widely shared in the larger society (e.g., public education, mass media, justice). This new subfield itself has a number of variants, and many terms have been used to describe them: "acculturation psychology," "ethnic psychology," and, in the French language tradition, "psychologie interculturelle." Much of this work has been accomplished by psychologists whose ethnic heritage is within the groups being studied.

In the second emergent subfield there has been increasing interest among the "others" in understanding themselves in their own terms, drawing upon their own culturally-rooted concepts and intellectual traditions. This move has brought about new approaches, known variously as "indigenous psychology," or "ethnopsychology." In these, a single cultural tradition is the locus of interest, and leadership is being provided by psychologists whose cultural backgrounds are also from within the cultural groups being studied, and which cumulatively span an ever-widening range. This search for indigenous origins and outcomes has been advocated both as a valuable activity in its own right, and as an important step towards achieving a more inclusive, panhuman psychology: it is argued that only when the universe of indigenous psychologies has been sampled can a universal psychology be achieved.

A last change has involved a shift away from the search for, and cataloging of, differences in psychological phenomena toward an interest in also identifying similarities. This interest in similarities has been present for many decades but recent developments in human ethology have begun to influence psychology, and are providing a base for this increasing interest in similarities. At the same time, the field has been increasingly clear in its conceptualization of the difference–similarity contrast as a dimension ranging from *relativism* at one pole to *universalism* at the other. All positions on this dimension are represented in this *Handbook*.

Given this diversification, it is no longer possible to give a single definition of key concepts (such as *culture*), to characterize the typical method used (such as the comparative method), or even to provide one definition of the field of cross-cultural psychology that the editors (never mind all the authors) would find to their liking. However, it is possible to identify what does hold the field, and this *Handbook*, together: the field rejects the long-standing exclusion of *culture* by the discipline of psychology; in contrast, it seeks to incorporate cultural aspects of human life as a major factor in behavior. The various ways in which cultural factors are conceptualized and linked to behavior constitutes the diversity of the field. In a sense, this combination of an underlying communality, but with variation in expression, corresponds to the perspective of *universalism,* which makes the assumption that basic psychological processes are shared panhuman characteristics of the species, but that culture provides an opportunity to develop and express these processes in highly variable ways.

In many respects, these changes in the field correspond to the sequence of three methodological orientations to the field outlined in 1969 and later elaborated as three goals of cross-cultural psychology in 1974. As outlined in Chapter 2 in Volume 1, the first goal was to *transport* current hypotheses and conclusions to other cultural contexts in order to *test* their validity. This goal was associated with the *imposed etic* methodological approach, and it has now resulted in a massive amount of data on psychological differences across cultures. For some critics of the field it has also become identified (somewhat erroneously) as the whole of cross-cultural psychology. The second goal was to *explore* new cultural systems to *discover* psychological phenomena not available in the first culture. This goal was associated with the *emic* methodological approach and it can be identified with the moves toward "cultural," "indigenous," and "ethnic" psychologies that we have witnessed over the past decade. The third was to *integrate* psychological knowledge gained from these first two activities, and to *generate* a more panhuman psychology that would be valid for all people. This goal was associated with the *derived etic* methodological approach, and it can be identified with the increased contemporary interest in psychological similarities and the search for a universal psychology. Cross-cultural psychology thus appears to be evolving in a sensible and understandable way.

Cross-cultural psychology is fundamentally concerned with understanding human diversity. As we have just noted, a basic proposition of the field is that cultural factors affect human behavior; it thus follows that cultural factors must also affect the psychology that we do, including the way we conceive of behavior, study it, interpret it, and apply it. In recognition of this cultural impact on psychology, one goal of this second edition of the *Handbook* is to incorporate as much cultural diversity as possible, both by the selection of editors and authors, and by the coverage of the literature. In this endeavor, we have succeeded to some extent: the editors have different cultures of origin, representing Asia, Europe, and North America; their teaching and research experience also include Africa and Oceania (but not South America). Chapter authors include those whose cultural origins are in all continents, representing over twenty mother tongues and with access to psychological literature in all major languages. However, there are evident failures to represent all cultural diversity: research rooted in Western Academic Scientific Psychology (W.A.S.P.), and written in English, overwhelms this *Handbook* as it does any other contemporary psychological work, although hopefully not as much. Moreover, within chapters, there are obvious cultural perspectives taken, and selections made, that result in coverage that falls well short of a pan-cultural treatment. Despite these shortcomings, this *Handbook* represents a serious and honest attempt to engage human diversity where it exists in the psychological literature.

Cross-cultural psychology, while still dominated by Western views and psychologists, is no longer their exclusive preserve. What started as a Western-based attempt to understand the "others" is now a field well-populated by these "others." In part, this has come about by many developing world psychologists having experienced Western psychology (as graduate students, as research collaborators, or as "consumers"), and being both attracted to, and wary of it. The attraction has brought them to the field, while the wariness has brought critical and culturally-rooted alternative perspectives. This process of enrichment by cultural diversification has had a major impact on the field, and continues at an accelerating pace.

The institutions of cross-cultural psychology reflect this growth and diversification. Almost thirty years ago, a meeting of social psychologists concerned with cultural influences took place in Nigeria, and led to the initiation of the *Cross-Cultural Social Psychology Newsletter* (edited by Harry Triandis). A year later (1968) the first of a series of a *Directory of Cross-Cultural Psychological Research* (edited by John Berry) was published in the *International Journal of Psychology* (which was founded in 1966 in part to promote the cross-cultural point of view). Walt Lonner established the *Journal of Cross-Cultural Psychology* in 1970, and John Dawson pulled these various activities and people together in 1972 to found the International Association for Cross-Cultural Psychology (IACCP). This Association has met every two years in a different country since its inaugural meeting in Hong Kong. In 1984, the French-language Association pour la Recherche Interculturelle (ARIC) was founded, primarily through the efforts of Pierre Dasen. These two associations held a joint meeting in Liège in 1992 in an effort to establish closer ties. Conference proceedings of both associations are a core resource in the field.

Other publications in the field have appeared with increasing frequency. For example, in 1974 Walt Lonner and John Berry initiated the Sage Series on Cross-Cultural Research and Methodology, publishing eighteen volumes on a wide variety of topics in psychology and cognate disciplines; this series has been reconstituted (in 1996) as the Sage Series on Cross-Cultural Psychology. Another series, *Cross-Cultural Psychology Monographs* was established by the IACCP in 1991, under the editorship of Fons van de Vijver and Ype Poortinga. Chapters in the *Annual Review of Psychology* focusing on cross-cultural research have appeared at regular intervals since 1973. In addition to these publications, there has been a virtual explosion of textbooks in the field, some covering all domains in which cross-cultural psychologists are active, and some focusing on specific domains, such as social or developmental psychology.

The three volumes of this *Handbook* attempt to extend these publications in two ways. First, the most recent ideas and information in an area have been incorporated in the chapters; the treatment should thus be the most up-to-date available. Second, the writing has been pitched at a level suitable for graduate students and professionals who have a substantial background in psychology, but not necessarily in cross-cultural psychology. All authors were asked to provide basic definitions and descriptions of their area, and then move on to the main tasks of evaluating and integrating the area.

In Volume 1, theoretical and methodological issues are presented as an initial orientation to the broad features of cross-cultural psychology. In Volumes 2 and 3 the field is reviewed and evaluated in the more or less conventional categories used by general psychology. Readers may prefer to use the *Handbook* by beginning with the chapter that comes closest to their own substantive area, move to cognate areas of interest, and then delve into the broader issues addressed in Volume 1. Whatever your approach to the materials in these volumes, we hope that your understanding of the myriad ways in which culture and behavior can be intertwined will be enriched, and that you will be more convinced than ever about the importance of culture as a factor in the production and display of human diversity.

The process of developing an outline for this *Handbook*, and suggesting appropriate chapter authors, was primarily the responsibility of the team of co-editors. However, we were assisted by an editorial advisory group made up of the Editors of the First Edition of this *Handbook,* including Harry Triandis, Bill Lambert, Walt Lonner, Alastair Heron, Rich Brislin, and Juris Draguns. The task of reviewing drafts of chapters, recommending revisions, and keeping authors on track and on schedule largely fell to my volume co-editors. And, of course, the main work of any writing project has fallen to the chapter authors themselves. Najum Rashid has managed the chapter texts and their numerous revisions with accuracy and diligence. I thank all of them for their efforts, and for their contribution to this *Handbook.*

J. W. Berry
Department of Psychology
Queen's University
Kingston, Ontario
Canada

ABOUT THE EDITORS

John W. Berry

John Berry is a Professor of Psychology at Queen's University, Kingston. He received his B.A. from Sir George Williams University (Montreal) in 1963, and his Ph.D. from the University of Edinburgh in 1966. He has been a lecturer at the University of Sydney for three years, a Fellow of Netherlands Institute for Advanced Study and a visiting Professor at the Université de Nice and the Université de Genève. He is a past Secretary-General, past President and Honorary Fellow of the International Association for Cross-Cultural Psychology, and has been an Associate Editor of the *Journal of Cross-Cultural Psychology* and co-editor of the first edition of this *Handbook.* He is the author or editor of over twenty books in the areas of cross-cultural, social, and cognitive psychology, and is particularly interested in the application of cross-cultural psychology to public policy and programs in the areas of acculturation, multiculturalism, immigration, health, and education.

Pierre R. Dasen

Pierre R. Dasen is Professor of Anthropology of Education at the Faculty of Psychology and Education of the University of Geneva.

He studied developmental psychology in Geneva, was an assistant to J. Piaget, and received a Ph.D. from the Australian National University. He studied the cognitive development of Aboriginal children in Australia, Inuit in Canada, Baoulé in Côte d'Ivoire, and Kikuyu in Kenya; he has also contributed to research in cognitive anthropology among the Yupno of Papua-New-Guinea, and in Bali. His research topics have included visual perception, the development of sensori-motor intelligence, the causes and effects of malnutrition, the development of concrete operations as a function of ecocultural variables and daily activities, definitions of intelligence, number systems, and spatial orientation. His current interests are in everyday cognition, informal education, and parental ethnotheories.

In the last few years, he has directed a research team working on intercultural education, which is currently concerned with the access of migrant adolescents to professional training.

P. Dasen is the co-author or co-editor of several volumes and textbooks on cross-cultural psychology and intercultural education.

T. S. Saraswathi

T. S. Saraswathi is Professor and Chair in the Department of Human Development and Family Studies at the Maharaja Sayajirao University of Baroda, India. She is a recipient of numerous professional awards and international fellowships for her contributions to the field of developmental psychology and has published several articles in reputed journals and edited books. Her books and monographs on child development and related fields include *Trends & Issues in Child Development, Invisible Boundaries: Grooming for Adult Roles, Developmental Psychology in India: An Annotated Bibliography, Human Development & Family Studies: An Agenda for Research & Policy* (co-edited with B. Kaur), *Capturing Complexities: A Methodological Study of Women, Households and Development* (co-edited with an international team).

ABOUT THE CONTRIBUTORS

Lewis Aptekar Lewis Aptekar is Professor of Counselor Education at San Jose State University in San Jose, California. He has also been affiliated with the University of Nairobi's Institute of African Studies, University of Swaziland, Johns Hopkins University, and the Universidad del Valle, Cali Colombia. His research focuses on children in the developing world who are in particularly difficult circumstances. He is the author of *Street Children of Cali* (1988) and *Environmental Disasters in Global Perspective* (1994), as well as numerous scholarly articles in such journals as *Anthropology & Education Quarterly, Child Abuse & Neglect, Cross-cultural Research, International Journal of Mental Health, Journal of Adolescent Research, Journal of Comparative Family Studies,* and *World Development.* His research has been supported by the International Red Cross, the National Science Foundation of the United States, and the United Nations. He has served as Secretary/Treasurer of the Society for Cross-cultural Research, and has been the recipient of numerous academic awards including two Fulbright Scholarships and a Kellogg-Partners of the Americas Fellowship in International Development.

Carmel Camilleri Carmel Camilleri, Doctor of the University of Paris-Sorbonne (1971), has been an Associate Professor of Social Psychology at University of Tunis (Tunisia), and a Professor at the University of Tours (France) and at University of Paris–Sorbonne. He has been editor of the review *Psychologie Française,* and vice-president of the Association pour la Recherche Interculturelle (ARIC). He specializes in the areas of cross-cultural and cross-cultural educational psychology.

David W. Carraher David W. Carraher received his Ph.D. in social psychology from the City University of New York and spent 19 years teaching and researching in cognitive psychology at the Federal University of Pernambuco. He has authored articles and books on everyday cognition, on critical thinking, and on mathematics education, with special emphasis on ratio and proportions, as well as award winning educational software published in Brazil and the United States. He is currently Senior Researcher at TERC, in Cambridge, Massachusetts.

Stephen J. Ceci Stephen J. Ceci is the Helen L. Carr Professor of Psychology at Cornell University. He teaches and conducts research in developmental, social, cognitive, quantitative, and clinical psychology. His awards include a Senior Fullbright-Hayes fellowship, a NIH Research Career Scientist Award, the 1994 Robert Chin Prize from SPSSI for his 1993 article in *Psychological Bulletin* (this same article was named one of the 20 outstanding articles by Hertzig and Farber in the 1994 *Annual Progress in Psychiatry and Psychology*), the IBM Supercomputing Prize for research in the social sciences, a Senior MRF Prize for his 1991 article in *Developmental Psychology,* and the Arthur Rickter Award in 1990 for his work on children's testimony. He is the president-elect of Division 1 of APA.

J. B. Deregowski J. B. Deregowski, Anderson Professor of Psychology at the University of Aberdeen, Fellow of the Royal Society of Edinburgh, was born in Poland and through no effort on his part, educated in a variety of cultures. He began his studies of cultural differences in perception in Zambia in 1965, as a Ministry of Overseas Development Fellow at (now defunct) Rhodes-Livingstone Institute, and has continued taking interest in this and related fields ever since.

Lutz H. Eckensberger Lutz H. Eckensberger is more a cultural psychologist than a cross-cultural psychologist. He got his Diplom degree in psychology in 1964, and, after applied studies on the evaluation of technical schools in Afghanistan, he finished his Doctorate in 1970. After his Habilitation in 1973 he became a Professor at the University of the Saarland (Saarbruecken), where he has been a full professor since 1976 (Development and Culture). In 1996, he moved to Frankfurt, where he is head of the psychology section of the German Institute of International Educational Research, and has the Chair of Psychology at the Johann Wolfgang Goethe University. In 1985–86 he was fellow of the Center for Advanced Studies in Berlin. Besides his focus on methods and methodology, his interest is in moral development but also in the relation between affects and cognitions, which he studies in environmental and health contexts. He has published over seventy articles in journals and books and he is editor of fifteen books. He is a member of IACCP, and was a member of the Executive Committee from 1984 to 1986, representing Western Europe.

Nico Frijda Nico Frijda was born in Amsterdam, the Netherlands, in 1927. He studied psychology at the University of Amsterdam (1945–1951), and graduated at this same university on "Understanding Facial Expressions." He became a full professor in experimental psychology at the University of Amsterdam in 1965, and remained so till 1992. His early research interests were also in the domain of cross-cultural psychology: In 1960 he published (together with H. C. J. Duijker) the book *National Character and National Stereotypes;* in 1966 a publication appeared (co-authored with G. Jahoda) entitled *On the Scope and Methods of Cross-Cultural Research* (International Journal of Psychology). Frijda is well-known for his outstanding and encompassing work on emotions, culminating in the book *The Emotions* (Cambridge University Press, 1986). Since 1992 he has occupied a special chair in the psychology of emotions.

Sara Harkness Sara Harkness is Professor in the School of Family Studies at the University of Connecticut. She received a B.A. in Comparative Literature from Brown University and a Ph.D. in Social Anthropology from Harvard, where she also was an NIMH Postdoctoral Research Fellow, earned a Master of Public Health degree, and taught at the School of Public Health. She has carried out research on culture, health, and human development in Guatemala, Kenya, the Netherlands, and the United States. She is co-editor (with Charles M. Super) of *Parents' Cultural*

Belief Systems: Their Origins, Expressions, and Consequences (1995), of *New Directions for Child Development: Anthropological Perspectives* (1985), and of the *Culture and Human Development* series published by Guilford Press.

Giyoo Hatano Giyoo Hatano is a Professor of Educational Psychology at Keio University, Mita, Tokyo. He has been interested in both cognitive and sociocultural aspects of conceptual development, expertise, and literacy acquisition. He is an editorial board member of numerous journals, including the *British Journal of Developmental Psychology, Cognition, Cognition and Instruction, Cognitive Psychology, European Journal of Psychology of Education, Journal of Mathematical Behavior, Learning and Instruction,* and *Mind, Culture and Activity.* He was elected as a foreign associate of National Academy of Education (U.S.) in 1992.

P. R. Kinnear Paul Kinnear graduated from the University of Edinburgh and has worked at the University of Aberdeen for many years. His original research was concerned with the color vision losses of diabetics, but he has also done research into genetic color vision losses. More recently he has been interested in spatial ability, especially people's capacities to visualize topographical maps and drawings, whether they be students of architecture, engineering, or taking part in the outside recreation of orienteering. He has also monitored the performance of telephone operators working from home in a year's project on teleworking sponsored by British Telecommunications.

Jeanette Lawrence Jeanette Lawrence is an associate professor in developmental psychology in the School of Behavioral Science, The University of Melbourne. Formerly she was a senior lecturer in the School of Education at Murdoch University in Western Australia. Her research interests include the study of development within culture, especially adult and adolescent development, and applications of social cognitive models to personal and social issues. She has been prominent in developing models of how people make decisions and solve problems in settings other than the traditional laboratory, especially judicial sentencers' reasoning processes, adolescents' and professionals' reasoning about shoplifting events. Her pursuit of interactions between cognition and the social environment have involved the use of microgenetic methods of investigation.

Hanna Malewska-Peyre Hanna Melewska-Peyre is Professor at the Institute of Philosophy and Sociology and at the Institute of Political Studies, Polish Academy of Sciences in Warsaw. She received her Ph.D. from the University of Warsaw in 1959. She taught at the Universities of Warsaw and Lodz, presented her habilitation thesis (docent) in social psychology and became director of the Laboratory of Social Psychology in Warsaw. She was expert of UNESCO in Paris and Research Director at Centre National de la Recherche Scientifique (France)–Center for Interdisciplinary Research in Vaucresson. She has been Visiting Professor at the University of Montréal. She specializes in cross-cultural social psychology.

Batja Mesquita Batja Mesquita was born in Amsterdam, the Netherlands, in 1960. She studied psychology and philosophy at the University of Amsterdam from 1980 to 1987, and graduated from there in 1993 with a focus on cultural variations in emotions. She worked as a visiting researcher at the Institute for Social Research of the University of Michigan from 1993 to 1995, and as a consultant for UNICEF from 1993 to 1995. Research was carried out among Surinamese, Turkish, and Dutch people in the Netherlands; European Americans and Mexicans in the United States; and Bosnian women in Central Bosnia. Batja Mesquita is a fellow of the Royal Dutch Academy of Science and as such is currently working as a researcher at the division of Social Psychology.

R. C. Mishra   R. C. Mishra is Reader in Psychology at Banaras Hindu University. He obtained a D. Phil. from Allahabad University. He has been post-doctoral research fellow and Shastri research fellow at Queen's University in Canada. Cultural influence on human development represents his main research interest. He has contributed numerous articles to professional journals and books both in India and abroad in the fields of cognition, acculturation, schooling, and cross-cultural studies. He is the co-author of *Ecology, Acculturation, and Psychological Adaptation.*

Ajit K. Mohanty   Ajit K. Mohanty is a Professor of Psychology at the Centre of Advanced Study in Psychology, Utkal University, Bhubaneswar, India since 1983. He completed his doctoral work at the University of Alberta, Canada, where he was a Killam Scholar. As a Fulbright Fellow, he did his post-doctoral research at the University of Wisconsin, Madison. A psycholinguist working on multilingualism and reading and language acquisition, his research publications include a book, *Bilingualism in a Multilingual Society.* Mohanty has been a Senior Fellow in the Central Institute of Indian Languages, Mysore, and a Visiting Scholar in several international institutions.

Christiane Perregaux   Christiane Perregaux is a Professor at the University of Geneva, Faculty of Psychology and Educational Sciences. She was previously a preschool teacher in a multicultural school for ten years. She now does research and teaching on the questions of cultural and linguistic diversity of migrations in European society, the contacts between learners of different cultures and languages in multicultural and multilinguistic contexts. Previous publications are "Enfant cherche Ecole" (Zoé, 1989); "Transits" (Syros, 1993); "Odyssea, accueils et approches interculturelles (COROME, 1994); "Les enfants à deux vois: des effets du bilinguisme sur l'apprentissage de la lecture" (Lang, 1994).

P. A. Russell   Phil Russell graduated in psychology and received a Ph.D. in comparative psychology from the University of Hull, England. He is a lecturer in psychology at the University of Aberdeen. His early research was in the area of curiosity and exploratory behavior in animals. More recently he has researched mainly in human experimental aesthetics, working particularly on the aesthetics of music and paintings. He has also published in the areas of children's play, social prejudice, animal models of human psychopathology, and evolutionary psychology.

Klaus Scherer   Klaus Scherer was born in Leverkusen, Germany, in 1943. He studied economics, sociology, and psychology at the University of Cologne and at the

London School of Economics and Political Sciences (1962–1965). He graduated in social psychology at Harvard University in Cambridge, Massachusetts. He was professor in psychology subsequently at the University of Pennsylvania (1970–1972), at the Institut für Psychologie of the University of Kiel, Germany (1972–1973), at the University of Giessen, Germany, and has been professor in psychology at the University of Geneva, Switzerland from 1985 till now. Some of his major research interests are in the areas of emotion, stress and coping, communication and interaction, and intercultural comparison. He is initiator of one of the first large-scale cross-cultural studies on emotions, resulting in the book *Experiencing Emotion: A Cross cultural Study* (1986).

Analucia D. Schliemann   Analucia Schliemann graduated in education at the Federal University of Pernambuco, Brazil, and in psychology at the University of Paris, France. She obtained her doctoral degree in psychology from University College London, University of London, England, for a thesis inspired by Piaget's theory and methods. Since then, while at the Federal University of Pernambuco, she developed and published many studies on the use and understanding of mathematical concepts among children and adults at work and in schools. In 1986 she was a Fulbright Scholar at the Learning Research and Development Center, University of Pittsburgh. Since 1994 Analucia moved to the United States where she works at Tufts University teaching and conducting research on cognitive development and learning.

Robert Serpell   Robert Serpell has conducted research on children's cognitive development, intelligence, socialization, education, and literacy in rural and urban communities in Zambia and in Baltimore, Maryland, U.S.A. Formerly Professor of Psychology and Director of the Institute for African Studies (1977–83) at the University of Zambia, he is currently Professor and Director of Applied Developmental Psychology at the University of Maryland–Baltimore County. He received his basic education at the Lycée Français in London, followed by studies at Westminster (an English "public school"), at the University of Singapore, and at Oxford University, England. He received his Ph.D. from the Department of Experimental Psychology at the University of Sussex, England, based on research conducted in Zambia from 1965 to 1968.

Daniel Stöcklin   Daniel Stöcklin is an assistant at the Seminar of Sociology of Fribourg University, Switzerland. He is currently preparing his doctoral dissertation on street children in China. His publications include parts of this dissertation, mainly on aspects such as socialization of Chinese children, and children born outside China's restriction policy on births. He is member of the Centre International de l'Enfance (Paris) and of Defence of Children International (Geneva), and of the Goran Aijmer European China Anthropology Network (Oxford).

Charles M. Super   Charles M. Super is Professor at the University of Connecticut and Dean in the School of Family Studies. He earned a B.A. in psychology from Yale University and a Ph.D. in developmental psychology from Harvard University. He has carried out research on children and families in Kenya, Colombia, Guatemala, Bangladesh, the Netherlands, and the United States, and served as consultant in Haiti, India, and Bangladesh for the United Nations Development Program, the U.S. Agency for International Development, and UNICEF. He is editor (with Sara Harkness) of the *Culture and Human Development* series published by Guilford Press, which includes their edited volume *Parents' Cultural Belief Systems: Their Origins, Expressions, and Consequences.*

Jaan Valsiner   Jaan Valsiner received his education at Tartu University, in Estonia. Since 1981 he has been on the faculty at the department of psychology of the University of North Carolina at Chapel Hill, U.S.A. He is one of the founding members of the Carolina Consortium on Human Development and a member of the Center of Developmental Science. Valsiner is the editor of the journal *Culture & Psychology.* His interests are in cultural developmental psychology, historical development of ideas in psychology, and theory and methodology of psychology. He is a winner of the 1995 Alexander-von-Humboldt Research Prize. His books include *Culture and the Development of Children's Action* (1987, 1997) and *The Guided Mind* (1997).

Roderick Fulata Zimba   Roderick Fulata Zimba has a doctorate from Purdue University, West Lafayette, Indiana, U.S.A., and is an Associate Professor of Educational Psychology at the University of Namibia. One of his primary areas of research is moral development as expressed by non-Western populations of the world. He also has conducted considerable research in the area of child care and development in African settings. In addition to being a deputy dean of the Faculty of Education at the University of Namibia and teaching postgraduate students, he is currently exploring the moral dimensions of discipline problems in secondary schools.

INTRODUCTION TO VOLUME 2

Structure of the Volume

In the first edition of the *Handbook*, one volume was devoted to "basic processes" (Volume 3) and another to "developmental psychology" (Volume 4), which explains, historically and pragmatically, the title of the present volume. We could have stayed closer to the previous structure in subdividing the book correspondingly into two sections. We purposefully avoided doing this, if only because we believe that this is an artificial distinction. All of psychology deals, in some sense, with basic processes; and all psychology should be, or should become, developmental. To quote Heron (Heron & Kroeger, 1981, p. 1) from the introduction to previous Volume 4 of the *Handbook*, "Any serious attempt to study human behavior and experience must, in the very nature of things, be both developmental in depth and cross-cultural in breadth." Because the integration of culture and the individual is a long and gradual process, a developmental methodology is absolutely essential in (cross-)cultural psychology (Eckensberger, 1979; Cf. also chapter by Greenfield, Volume 1, this *Handbook*).

Despite the different structure, most of the topics covered in the first edition are also found, in one form or another, in this second edition. Basic processes that were covered then included perception and aesthetics, now treated in a single chapter; cognition is featured again, although it was not deemed necessary to distinguish explicitly between psychological and anthropological approaches.[1] The new development in this edition is a chapter on so-called "everyday cognition." Emotion also appears prominently in both editions, while the topics covered under the category of "motivation" in the previous edition are now included in Volume 3 covering social psychology, in particular the topic of aggression, which has become even more important today, and need for achievement, which has been replaced with the study of other value dimensions such as individualism–collectivism.

Volume 4 in the previous edition, on developmental psychology, included two chapters on language development (language acquisition) and bilingualism, now treated in a single chapter, and chapters on memory and Piaget's theory, now covered under cognition. The specific, detailed treatment of infancy and the socialization through play, toys, and games, have not been carried over, but the topics are covered, albeit with a more theoretical stance, in the first chapter on the cultural structuring of child development. The previous edition included a chapter on schooling and the development of cognitive skills, while this volume treats schooling as one aspect of education, and takes a more macro-social and sociohistorical approach. The first edition included a chapter on personality development, which is not featured again, but was related to topics such as moral development and identity, two topics that are now given chapter-length treatment. Among interesting innovations is the coverage of the life-span perspective, and an inroad into more applied issues, in the form of a chapter on children "growing up in particularly difficult circumstances."

Thus, the reader will notice that the topics of research have not changed fundamentally, although a few have disappeared and a few new ones are now fashionable, but the approach has become more dynamic, constructivist, and sociohistorical, a trend that is explicitly developed in terms of theory and methods in Volume 1 of this edition, and to which we will return briefly below. The most important change between the two editions is no doubt a wider, more global coverage, that is reflected in the countries of origin and/or residence of the authors and co-editors. The two corresponding volumes in the first edition reflected a 2 to 1 ratio of North Americans to Europeans; we now have more Europeans, half of whom use French as their first language (possibly a reflection of the ethnocentrism of one of the co-editors!), only approximately a quarter from North America, and, most importantly, another quarter from Asia, Latin America, and Africa combined. Even though there is still an overwhelming Western bias, we take this to be a welcome step in the right direction.

The first three chapters are broad overviews of theoretical frameworks in (cross-) cultural developmental psychology. Super and Harkness set the stage, in their introductory chapter to the volume, for viewing the cultural structuring of human development. The interface wherein culture and the individual meet and evolve is deduced from a broad sweep across historical and disciplinary traditions. Their concept of "developmental niche" is a significant contribution that not only theoretically integrates the two open systems, namely, the culture and the individual, but also attempts to account for developmental changes that are mutually adaptive. It is, in our view, the natural complement of the ecocultural framework used in the textbooks by Segall, Dasen, Berry, and Poortinga, (1990) and Berry, Poortinga, Segall, and Dasen (1992). It deals more specifically with one of the processes that links ecology and culture to individual behavior: cultural transmission. At the same time, this chapter also covers issues of interactions (co-evolution, co-construction) between biology and culture (see also chapter by Keller, Volume 1, this *Handbook*).

The chapter documents the current historical period of paradigm dialogue. In the search for the interface of culture and mind, the meeting of theoretical and methodological ideas from allied disciplines perhaps heralds what Super and Harkness describe as synonymous to the differentiation–integration paradigm for organismic development put forward by Heinz Werner.

Camilleri and Malewska-Peyre further put the concepts of socialization and enculturation into a sociohistorical perspective. In complex industrial societies, marked by the co-existence of several social subgroups stemming from migration, these concepts become linked to processes of acculturation (cf. Chapter by Berry

& Sam in Volume 3, this *Handbook*). In Camilleri and Malewska-Peyre's views, socialization is not the passive soaking up of social influences, but the active co-construction of identity by developing individuals and other members of their culture.

Valsiner and Lawrence extend the idea of the continuity of culture–individual co-construction across adulthood and the life span by providing an integration of what Bronfenbrenner (1993) terms the person-context-process-time model. The chapter is highly theoretical and makes frequent reference to anecdotal "evidence" to illustrate its many interesting arguments. The chapter thus shows a paradigm shift in what is considered to be appropriate "data," and a shift from the positivist's conception of culture as an independent variable, to that of interdependency of culture and person in explaining behavior and development (cf. Chapters by Miller and Greenfield, Volume 1, this *Handbook*).

A second part of the volume is devoted to chapters more specifically focused on various domains of "basic processes": perception, visual communication, and aesthetics (Russel, Deregowski & Kinnear), cognition (Mishra), and everyday cognition (Schliemann, Carraher & Ceci). While there seems to have been, in the authors' own assessment, only modest progress in research on perception, Mishra concludes that "with the availability of new data, the relationship between culture and cognition has appeared to be more complex than was generally thought in previous years. Hence, all theoretical positions have shown signs of revision in order to accommodate the newer data in their framework." (p. 168) He agrees with Russell, Deregowski, and Kinnear in their criticism of "safari style" research, and in their conclusion that "cross-cultural work is likely to be most fruitful when the cultures examined are chosen to permit the testing of specific hypotheses bearing on psychological theory." (p. 136) The most rapidly expanding field is no doubt that of "everyday cognition," and the three chapters should be considered together as a review of the state of the art in the field of culture and cognition.

Language acquisition and bilingualism constitute a very active area of current research, covered here by Mohanty and Perregaux. In addition to presenting new theoretical developments, their chapter has also useful educational implications. As regards emotions, the universality of facial expression used to be the single cross-cultural "fact" most often quoted in mainstream psychology textbooks (Lonner, 1989). This over-simplification is questioned in the chapter on emotions by Mesquita, Frijda, and Scherer, who present a much more balanced view of universal and culturally relative aspects of emotions. The chapter also contains a new componential theory, viewing emotion as process, that is, a transaction with the environment. The topic of morality and moral development, that had not been covered in the first edition of the *Handbook,* is here fully reviewed by Eckensberger and Zimba. These authors also present their own theoretical paradigm, and conclude that cross-cultural research should begin with the study of "a culture's metaethical assumptions," rather than starting at the empirical level.

In each of these chapters, developmental aspects are covered as far as the available literature permits. Thus, while the themes follow the classical division of labor within mainstream psychology, the coherence with a more global approach is maintained both through the developmental outlook and the inherently interdisciplinary cross-cultural perspectives.

The volume ends with two chapters of a more applied character, one on education, schooling, and literacy (Serpell & Hatano), and one on children who grow up in especially difficult circumstances (Aptekar & Stöcklin), providing a link between research, theory, and policy issues. This third part could, of course, have given rise to a full volume in itself.

In this introduction, we will not comment further on each of these chapters individually, but raise some issues relevant to all or most of them.

Basic Processes

What do we mean when we speak of "basic processes," and how do we distinguish these from the apparently less basic ones that are covered in Volume 3, namely social behavior, personality and psychopathology? One way to attempt a distinction is to see basic processes as more linked to biology and less to cultural transmission; basic processes are hence expected to be more universal than less basic ones. Poortinga, Kop, and van de Vijver (1990) propose such a dimension of increasing cultural influence, starting with the psychophysical and psychophysiological domain, through perception and cognition, to personality and social behavior. The former are subject to organismic structural constraints and learning processes such as habituation and conditioning, while the latter occur through rule and norm-governed learning under external, cultural constraints. For these authors (and also for Berry et al., 1992), however, even social interaction processes show a high degree of similarity between cultures, while Jahoda (1988) goes to the extreme of arguing that no universals can be found in social psychology.

Another way to consider basic processes employs the distinction between deep and surface phenomena. Psychologists search beyond manifest behavior for the underlying, inferred, psychological structures, mechanisms, processes, processors, or whatever these may be called in different theoretical schools. Of relevance to the cross-cultural approach is the general conclusion that these underlying basic processes are generally found to be strongly universal, while their manifestation in surface phenomena is only weakly universal or culturally relative (Dasen, 1981; Dasen, 1993).

Both of these views about basic processes contain some truth, and are illustrated in numerous ways in the chapters of this volume. Yet the world is not that simple. Even the most basic processes occur in a web of social interactions, are socially and culturally situated, or even culturally co-constructed. The embeddedness of each of the basic processes in the cultural context is best illustrated by the following quote from the chapter by Schliemann et al. on everyday cognition: "Thinking is regarded as a truly social and cultural enterprise: thought, communication, and action are not unconstrained free productions of the individual. They must be understood in terms of the symbolic systems (. . .) people draw upon in acting and interpreting events, including those involving the actions of others." (p. 179) The same could be said not only of thinking, but of all the other basic processes studied by psychologists.

Be it socialization processes, emotion expression, bilingualism, or any other "basic process" covered in this book, it has become obvious that none of them is really basic, if that is taken to mean simple, less complex. Furthermore, some of the chapters explicitly deal with research in social psychology (e.g., Camilleri & Malewska), or are clearly linked to what is often called personality (lifespan development, emotions, etc.), so that we can draw no clear and absolute border between the contents of Volumes 2 and 3 of this *Handbook*.

Developmental Psychology

A standard way to structure contributions to developmental psychology would have been to distinguish age periods, such as infancy, childhood, adolescence, adulthood, and old age. However, the developmental contributions in this volume are not so much geared to a description of behavior at various ages or stages, but are more process-oriented. While they provide a wealth of information, they cannot possibly cover all of the recent research, and the reader may want to turn to other sources in the field. After the publication of the previous edition of the *Handbook* (Volume 4), the important *Handbook of Cross-Cultural Human Development* edited by Munroe, Munroe, and Whiting (1981), and the only but outstanding manual in French by Bril and Lehalle (1988), several other book-length treatments appeared (Bornstein, 1980; Stevenson & Wagner, 1982; Wagner, 1983; Fishbein, 1984; Dasen & Jahoda, 1986; Super, 1987; Lamb, Sternberg, Hwang, & Broberg, 1992) as well as a series of volumes by Valsiner (1987; 1988a; 1988b; 1988c; 1989a; 1989b; 1994), and last but not least Kagitçibasi's (1996) most recent book.[2] A few volumes specialize in infancy (Field, Sostek, Vietze, & Leiderman, 1981; Nugent, Lester, & Brazelton, 1989/1990) or adolescence (Esman, 1990; Schlegel & Barry III, 1991), and a few volumes deal more specifically with human development in specific cultural areas, particularly Asia (Saraswathi & Dutta, 1988; Stevenson, Azuma, & Hakuta, 1986; Suvannathat, Bhanthumnavin, Bhuapirom, & Keats, 1985; Saraswathi & Kaur, 1993) and Africa (Nsamenang, 1992; Ohuche & Otaala, 1981). Of interest also is a textbook of developmental psychology that is not cross-cultural as such, but takes culture seriously (Cole & Cole, 1989), and there are a few chapters on developmental issues in two recent textbooks of cross-cultural psychology (Berry, et al., 1992; Segall, et al., 1990).

After all this effort, has mainstream developmental psychology started to take culture seriously? Not really, we fear. There is little evidence that new developmental theories are systematically put to a cross-cultural test, and this applies even to theoretical strands such as life-span development, neo-Piagetian theories, or co-constructivism, that include sociocultural dimensions from the start. Just as was the case with more traditional theories, there is an enormous time lag between the development of a theory, usually in a monocultural setting, and its cross-cultural expansion. If an explicit claim to universality without empirical test has become rare, it remains implicit in most cases. Thus, it is not useless, we feel, to provide once more, in this volume, a compendium of what a cross-cultural approach to human development has to offer. Neither is the so-called "indigenization" of developmental psychology very far advanced; some of the references listed previously reflect this trend (see also chapter by Sinha, Volume 1, this *Handbook*) and we think that the most interesting future development will no doubt occur mainly in this area.

If cross-cultural research is no longer the preserve of expatriates, it has taken a strong foothold within multicultural societies. There are numerous examples of research with ethnic groups, migrants, and refugees at various age levels from infancy to adolescence. A particularly interesting special issue of the *International Journal of Behavioral Development*, and a book, both edited by Greenfield and Cocking (1993; 1994) link research on minority groups in the United States to research in the contexts where they or their parents originated. It is illustrative of the multidisciplinary nature of a cross-cultural approach, particularly in linking anthropology and psychology. If these new developments are particularly interesting for theory development, they also carry with them a promising potential for applications. The significance of cross-cultural issues in applied developmental psychology is increasingly evident in a "shrinking globe" with the need to deal with multicultural groups in trade and commerce, educational and work settings. The problems and achievements of non-voluntary and voluntary migrants (Ogbu & Gibson, 1991) reiterate the need for understanding human development in terms of the cultural context of the host society as interacting with the cultural background and meaning the migrant groups bring with them (see chapter by Berry & Sam, Volume 3, this *Handbook*). The impact of expanding the horizons of developmental psychology to encompass cross-cultural variations cannot be overemphasized. As different groups come together setting the stage for conflict situations in educational, residential, or community settings, then undoubtedly, the knowledge, sensitivity, and appreciation of the different worldviews that people bring into the situation will be useful in conflict resolution. We will come back to the issues of applied research in the last part of this introduction.

Conflict or Convergence? The Paradigm Dialogue

Volume 1 of this *Handbook* has focused on epistemological considerations of the paradigms that guide research and theory development, in particular on the contrast between the so-called cross-cultural and cultural approaches, akin to the distinction between "Naturwissenschaften" and "Geisteswissenschaften" (Krewer, 1993), absolutism and relativism (Berry, et al., 1992) or, to follow Guba's (1990) and Lincoln's (1990) classification, the positivist and post-positivist paradigms, on the one hand, and the constructivist paradigm on the other. For the positivist outlook, reality exists "out there" and is driven by immutable natural laws that can be subjected to empirical tests under carefully controlled conditions. Compared to this extreme position, post-positivism is more moderate in its claim to be able to fully and objectively apprehend reality, and methodologically, it leads to research in more natural settings, using more qualitative methods. Often linked to this option is critical theory that is ideologically and politically oriented, and rejects the possibility of value free research; instead of seeking to predict or to control, this research is geared to transform the world. These approaches taken together can be contrasted with the constructivist paradigm that seeks multiple realities, existing in the form of local and specific social constructions. The corresponding methodology is hermeneutic and dialectic, that is, descriptive of the ways the various actors in the scene (co-)construct their respective perspectives. In the constructivist approach, qualitative rather than quantitative methods are preferred, and relevance rather than rigor is the quality criterion. (See chapters by Miller and Greenfield, Volume 1, this *Handbook*).

Among the various chapters in Volume 2, those dealing with perception and cognition come closest to a positivist position, while Valsiner and Lawrence represent the hermeneutics of constructivism most clearly, followed closely by Serpell and Hatano, who take a clear sociohistorical stance; the latter is also reflected in much of the work reviewed by Schliemann, Carraher, and Ceci on everyday cognition.

Most chapters seem to take the mid-line of a post-positivist position, with a slight leaning towards the relativist side of the dimension. The dynamics of a co-constructivist socialization that leads to various identity strategies, presented by Camilleri and Malewska-Peyre, is a case in point that leans toward constructivism but is mainly based on a post-positivist social psychology. In Mohanty and Perregaux's treatment of bilingualism, critical theory comes through; they show that the study of bilingualism is always related to sociolinguistics, insofar as the social valuation of the languages has to be taken into account.

In this paradigm dialogue, between conflict and convergence, we believe that the conflict, if it indeed exists, will be an intermediate stage on the way to convergence; but to shake up the absolutism that still dominates mainstream psychology, an extreme form of relativism may be needed for a while.

Gender Issues

The issue of gender differences in human behavior and development has engaged the attention of developmental psychologists, anthropologists, and cross-cultural psychologists for several decades. Surprisingly, the study of sex or gender differences has not been singled out for special attention in any of the chapters in Volume 2 of the *Handbook*. However, gender is implicit in theorizing related to developmental niche, life-course development, and the development of social identity, as well as in the applied issues related to education and consequences of political and social turmoil. Judging by the explosion of feminist literature on gender issues and varied response to the same, a prediction that the issue will remain alive and active for decades to come is likely to be highly valid. The issue of gender should be singled out for special mention in this Introduction because characterization by gender is perhaps the most powerful variable to impact the developing child. A book length treatment by Best and Williams (1993), and their chapter in Volume 3 of the present *Handbook,* provide more comprehensive reviews on the topic. Recent work in the area of neuropsychology and behavior genetics (see Plomin & McClearn, 1993) calls attention to interesting interfaces between biological sex and sociocultural gender.

According to Beall (1993), two kinds of biases predominate in the study of gender in psychology, namely, the alpha and beta biases. The former refers to the exaggeration of the observed differences between males and females. The history of psychology is laced with references to intellectual giants of yester years who believed women had smaller brains, were less intelligent, and that higher education would be injurious to their reproductive health! Subtler versions of this bias are evident even today. The second type of bias refers to the tendency to minimize or understate the differences between the two genders, a tendency generally less prevalent in the field and most evident in some of the early feminist literature.

The glaring patriarchal perspective in contemporary psychology was dramatically highlighted by Gilligan (1982; 1993; 1994; see also the debate in the special issue of *Feminism and Psychology,* 1994, vol. 4, no. 3) in the by now well-known but controversial book, *In A Different Voice.* Two significant points form the central thesis of Gilligan's arguments and merit attention here: (1) The major theories (psychoanalysis, cognitive-developmental, ego identity, moral development) from which cross-cultural and developmental psychology draw heavily, are based predominantly on the study of males, and (2) a decontextualized analysis of perceived gender differences, when both genders are included in empirical studies, leads to a hierarchical organization of qualitative differences emphasizing the alleged superiority of the male in various aspects of development (e.g. morality, personal–social characteristics, locus of control, cognitive skills, and so on).

In this context, Sternberg's (1993) analysis of the nature of research questions and their intricate relation with the kind of answers obtained illustrates the social construction of science as applicable not only to the study of gender but to the general field of psychology and that of cross-cultural psychology in particular.

The point that needs reiteration relates to the fallacy of viewing biologically determined sex and culturally shaped gender separately. As is evident from the quotations to follow, neither biological nor social scientists view pancultural universalities to imply biological predispositions, or biological determinism of some characteristics to imply fixed gender related characteristics:

> *Whereas the sex-differentiated aspects of human biology are relatively constant, the cultural context varies a great deal, sometimes exaggerating the influence of biology, sometimes counteracting it, and sometimes in a more neutral fashion simply letting the influence of biology shine through without either exaggerating or counteracting it. (Bem, 1984, p. 179).*

Advocating an interactional model, Ehrhardt (1984, p. 54) comments:

The study of gender-related behavior has been hampered in the past by the narrowly defined main-effect model that posits biology versus learning. Instead, a biosocial perspective that includes constitutional as well as environmental factors needs to be applied if we want to make progress in our understanding of complex phenomena such as gender identity development and other aspects of gender-related behavior.

There can be little argument that the issue of gender warrants more attention than has been accorded to it at present in cross-cultural developmental psychology.

Knowledge-Driven versus Problem-Oriented Research: The Twain Must Meet

Remember Neisser's (1982) lamentation of the "thundering silence" of psychology regarding questions of interest and importance to our everyday lives. We believe that the evidence presented in this volume represents a quantum leap in this respect, although a lot still remains to be done (see also chapter by Poortinga on convergence, Volume 1, this *Handbook*). Noteworthy, in particular, is the interest evinced in the study of everyday problems. Also interesting are the applications of the knowledge available regarding each of the basic processes : consequences of stability and change in social identity for multicultural societies and migrant populations; differential competence and transfer evident in everyday cognition as opposed to cognitive skills acquired in schools; the positive or negative outcomes of bi- or multi-lingualism depending upon the larger context from which the language and its people derive meaning and "prestige." Many more could be mentioned. While practically all the chapters offer ideas with scope for application, the last two chapters, one on education, schooling, and literacy (Serpell & Hatano), and one on children who grow up in particularly difficult circumstances (Aptekar & Stöcklin), focus on application as a central theme and provide a link between research, theory, and policy issues, as well as a transition to Volume 3.

Education (more specifically formal school education) continues to be (and will continue to be) a subject of central interest to researchers, and policy and program planners in both developed and developing regions of the world. The great divide in economic prosperity, technological advancement, and the rapid spread of the market economy have generated mind-boggling controversies ranging from the hegemony of Western imposition to the conservatism of religious fundamentalism. With the shrinking globe and the pressing need for distance communication regarding population, health, human rights, environment and other related issues, education does seem to be *the* answer to improving people's quality of life. Yet, as is evidenced in the successful and not-so-successful interventions cited in the Serpell and Hatano chapter, the light at the end of the tunnel is not yet visible.

In their rich review of literature related to children growing up under difficult circumstances, Aptekar and Stöcklin have still touched only the tip of the iceberg. In a world filled with never abating violence, the traumatic consequences of war and its aftermath undoubtedly demand priority attention of international organizations, governments, social workers, and researchers. In this dark abyss of hopelessness and pain, the research findings that children and youth are "vulnerable but resilient," if not "invincible" (Tizard & Varma, 1992; Werner & Smith, 1982) provides for some optimism. The latter study of children in Hawaii indicated that even among children who faced serious risk of developmental disturbance due to a host of family and community related factors such as poverty, marital disharmony, low birth weight, and so forth, risk was buffered and resilience increased by factors such as smaller family size, child spacing, availability of alternative caregivers, access to close emotional bonding, and social support. (For a review related to risk factors and resilience, see Bronfenbrenner, 1986.)

As mentioned by Aptekar and Stöcklin in their chapter, children confronting violence and absence of home/family represent only a fraction of children living under difficult circumstances. A vast array of other groups that could well be included under this blanket include children faced with domestic violence; malnutrition; sexual abuse; gender discrimination and the all encompassing poverty and child labor, to mention only a few. Each of these find a prominent place in the agenda for action of program and policy makers around the world. Yet, substantive research data of a cross-cultural nature is either unavailable or inaccessible, a lacuna that has far-reaching consequences both in terms of informed program and policy planning and of social accountability of the psychological sciences.

What do we know? How confident are we to advise the policymakers on the basis of what we know? What does cross-cultural psychology have to inform us regarding the contextual meaning of grave social problems related to children and youth? For example, does child labor have the same meaning in different social contexts ? What are the glaring gaps in our knowledge concerning children growing up in adverse circumstances? Does psychology in general and cross-cultural psychology in particular have a social accountability? Answers to these and related questions are imperative if the contributions of cross-cultural psychology are to gain credibility with decisionmakers who plan policies and programs to help children and youth actualize their potentials.

Any effort to extend the application of available knowledge in the area of cross-cultural psychology draws attention to the fact that (a) real life problems call for a broader perspective than afforded by sub-specializations in the discipline of psychology, such as social, clinical, and so forth, (b) multiplicity of causal factors (macro- to micro-level) that interact with each other in producing a positive or buffering a negative effect, (c) age and gender differentials in consequences, and (d) the contextualization of the problem. It also points to the possibility that the challenge of dealing with real-life problems and their solutions in varied cultural contexts may enrich and facilitate theory construction in place of testing theories developed in a different cultural context.

In sum, the incorporation of cultural issues in the field of developmental psychology, be it in theory building or in its application to field situations, can serve as a mutually enriching experience for expanding the theoretical horizons as well as the extension of knowledge to promote the well-being of children in cultural contexts where the need for intervention is pressing. Furthermore, such a perspective is likely to strengthen the voice of advocacy of the developmental psychologists who are with increasing frequency being called upon by international organizations to assist in formulating policies for promoting the well-being of children and adolescents worldwide.

T. S. Saraswathi[3]

P. R. Dasen

Endnotes

1. This means that cognitive anthropology, which had been given a full treatment by D. Price-Williams, is no longer covered explicitly. The reader interested in the most recent developments in this field can find an overview in Wassmann (1993).

2. Gardiner, Mutter, and Kosmitzki (1997) provide a textbook of cross-cultural human development across the life span with a focus on Bronfenbrenner's theory.

3. Grateful thanks and appreciation to the Johann Jacobs Foundation, whose funding made my (T. S. Saraswathi's) participation possible; to my colleague Baljit Kaur, who devoted time for careful copy editing amidst several pressures on her time and energy; to my friend Kaushalya Rana, for her meticulous checking of the references; to the UGC-DCA staff of the M.S. University of Baroda, Mahesh, Deepak, Anil, and Mukesh who helped in several ways and kept me going with their friendly cheer; and Mr. Kumar for his e-mail services despite the inevitable technological problems.

References

Beall, A. E. (1993). The social constructionist view of gender. In A. E. Beall & R. J. Sternberg (Eds.), *The psychology of gender* (pp. 127–147). New York: Guilford Press.

Bem, S. L. (1984). Androgyny and gender schema theory: A conceptual and empirical integration. In T. B. Sonderegger (Ed.), *Psychology and gender. Nebraska Symposium on Motivation 32* (pp. 179–226).

Berry, J. W., Poortinga, Y. H., Segall, M. H., & Dasen, P. R. (1992). *Cross-cultural psychology: Research and applications.* Cambridge: Cambridge University Press.

Best, D. L. & Williams, J. W. (1993). A cross-cultural view point. In A. E. Beall & R. J. Sternberg (Eds.), *The psychology of gender* (pp. 215–248). New York: Guilford Press.

Bornstein, M. H. (1980). *Comparative methods in psychology.* Hillsdale: Lawrence Erlbaum.

Bril, B. & Lehalle, H. (1988). *Le développement psychologique est-il universel? Approches interculturelles.* Paris: Presses Universitaires de France.

Bronfenbrenner, U. (1986). Ecology of the family as a context for human development : Research perspectives. *Developmental Psychology, 22,* 723–742.

Bronfenbrenner, U. (1993). The ecology of cognitive development: Research models and fugitive findings. In R. Wozniak & K. W. Fischer (Eds.), *Development in context* (pp. 3–44). Hillsdale, NJ: Erlbaum.

Cole, M. & Cole, S. R. (1989). *The development of children.* New York: W. Freeman.

Dasen, P. R. (1981). 'Strong' and 'weak' universals: Sensori-motor intelligence and concrete operations. In B. B. Lloyd & J. Gay (Eds.), *Universals of human thought: Some African evidence* (pp. 137–156). Cambridge: Cambridge University Press.

Dasen, P. R. (1993). Schlusswort. Les sciences cognitives: Do they shake hands in the middle? In J. Wassmann & P. R. Dasen (Eds.), *Alltagswissen/Savoirs quotidiens/Everyday cognition. Les sciences cognitives dans le dialogue interdisciplinaire* (pp. 331–349). Fribourg: Presses de l'Université de Fribourg.

Dasen, P. R. & Jahoda, G. (Eds.). (1986). Cross-cultural human development: Special issue. *International Journal of Behavioral Development, 9*, 417–437.

Eckensberger, L. H. (1979). A metamethodological evaluation of psychological theories from a cross-cultural perspective. In L. H. Eckensberger, W. J. Lonner, & Y. H. Poortinga (Eds.), *Cross-cultural contributions to psychology* (pp. 255–275). Lisse: Swets & Zeitlinger.

Ehrhardt, A. A. (1984). Gender differences: A biosocial perspective. In T. B. Sonderegger (Eds.), *Psychology and gender. Nebraska Symposium on Motivation 32* (pp. 179–226).

Esman, A. H. (1990). *Adolescence and culture.* New York: Columbia University Press.

Field, T. M., Sostek, A. M., Vietze, P., & Leiderman, P. H. (1981). *Culture and early interactions.* Hilldale: Lawrence Erlbaum.

Fishbein, H. (1984). *The psychology of infancy and childhood: Evolutionary and cross-cultural perspectives.* Hillsdale: Lawrence Erlbaum.

Gardiner, H. W., Mutter, J. D. & Kosmitzki, C. (1997). *Lives across cultures: A cross-cultural perspective on human development.* Boston: Allyn and Bacon.

Gilligan, C. (1982). *In a different voice: Psychological theory and women's development.* Cambridge, MA: Harvard University Press.

Gilligan, C. (1993). *In a different voice: Psychological theory and women's development,* 2nd edition. Cambridge, MA: Harvard University Press.

Gilligan, C. (1994). Afterword: The power to name. *Feminism & Psychology, 4*(3), 420–424.

Greenfield, P. M. & Cocking, R. R. (Eds.). (1993). International roots of minority child development. *International Journal of Behavioral Development, 16*(3).

Greenfield, P. M. & Cocking, R. R. (Eds.). (1994). *Cross-cultural roots of minority child development.* Hillsdale: Lawrence Erlbaum.

Guba, E. G. (1990). The alternative paradigm dialog. In E. G. Guba (Ed.), *The paradigm dialog* (pp. 17–30). Newbury Park: Sage.

Heron, A. & Kroeger, E. (1981). Introduction to developmental psychology. In H. C. Triandis & A. Heron (Eds.), *Handbook of cross-cultural psychology* (Vol. 4, pp. 1–15). Boston: Allyn and Bacon.

Jahoda, G. (1988). J'accuse. In M. H. Bond (Ed.), *The cross-cultural challenge to social psychology* (pp. 86–94). Newbury Park: Sage.

Kagitçibasi, C. (1996). *Family and human development across cultures: A view from the other side.* Hillsdale: Lawrence Erlbaum.

Krewer, B. (1993). Psychologie transculturelle ou psychologie culturelle: L'homme entre une nature universelle et des cultures spécifiques. In F. Tanon & G. Vermès (Eds.), *L'individu et ses cultures* (pp. 79–90). Paris: L'Harmattan.

Lamb, M. E., Sternberg, K. J., Hwang, C. P., & Broberg, A. G. (Eds.). (1992). *Child care in context: Cross-cultural perspectives.* Hillsdale: Lawrence Erlbaum.

Lincoln, Y. S. (1990). The making of a constructivist: A remembrance of transformations past. In E. G. Guba (Ed.), *The paradigm dialog* (pp. 67–87). Newbury Park: Sage.

Lonner, W. J. (1989). The introductory psychology text and cross-cultural psychology. Beyond Ekman, Whorf and biased IQ tests. In D. M. Keats, D. Munro, & L. Mann (Eds.), *Heterogeneity in cross-cultural psychology* (pp. 4–22). Amsterdam: Swets & Zeitlinger.

Munroe, R. H., Munroe, R. L., & Whiting, B. B. (Eds.). (1981). *Handbook of cross-cultural human development.* New York: Garland STPM.

Neisser, U. (Ed.). (1982). *Memory observed. Remembering in natural contexts.* San Francisco: W. H. Freeman.

Nsamenang, B. (1992). *Human development in cultural context.* Beverly Hills: Sage.

Nugent, J. K., Lester, B. M., & Brazelton, T. B. (Eds.). (1989/1990). *The cultural context of infancy. Vol. 1: Biology, culture and infant development. Vol. 2: Multicultural and interdisciplinary approaches to parent-infant relations.* Norwood: Ablex.

Ogbu, J. & Gibson, M. (1991). *Minority status and schooling: A comparative study of immigrant and involuntary minorities.* New York: Garland.

Ohuche, R. O. & Otaala, B. (Eds.). (1981). *The African child and his environment.* Oxford: Pergamon Press.

Plomin, R. & McClearn, G. E. (1993). *Nature, nurture and psychology.* Washington, DC: American Psychological Association.

Poortinga, Y. H., Kop, P. F. M., & van de Vijver, F. J. R. (1990). Differences between psychological domains in the range of cross-cultural variation. In P. J. D. Drenth, J. A. Sergeant, & R. J. Takens (Eds.), *European perspectives in psychology, vol. 3* (pp. 355–376). Chichester: Wiley.

Saraswathi, T. S. & Dutta, R. (Eds.). (1988). *Developmental psychology in India, 1975–1986.* New Delhi: Sage.

Saraswathi, T. S. & Kaur, B. (Eds.). (1993). *Human development and family studies in India.* New Delhi: Sage.

Schlegel, A. & Barry III, H. (1991). *Adolescence: An anthropological enquiry.* New York: Free Press (Macmillan).

Segall, M. H., Dasen, P. R., Berry, J. W., & Poortinga, Y. H. (1990). *Human behavior in global perspective: An introduction to cross-cultural psychology.* Boston: Allyn and Bacon.

Sternberg, R. J. (1993). What is the relation of gender to biology and environment? An evolutionary model of how what you answer depends on just what you ask. In A. E. Beall & R. J. Sternberg (Eds.), *The psychology of gender* (pp. 1–6). New York: Guilford Press.

Stevenson, H., Azuma, H., & Hakuta, K. (1986). *Child development and education in Japan.* London: W. Freeman.

Stevenson, H. & Wagner, D. (Eds.). (1982). *Cultural perspectives on child development.* San Francisco: W. Freeman.

Super, C. (1987). *The role of culture in developmental disorder.* New York: Academic Press.

Suvannathat, C., Bhanthumnavin, D., Bhuapirom, L., & Keats, D. M. (1985). *Handbook of Asian child development and child rearing practices.* Bangkok: Behavioral Science Research Institute.

Tizard, B. & Varma, V. (Eds.). (1992). *Vulnerability and resilience in human development: A Festschrift for Ann and Alan Clarke.* London: J. Kingsley.

Valsiner, J. (1987). *Culture and the development of children's action: A cultural-historical theory of developmental psychology.* Chichester: J. Wiley.

Valsiner, J. (Ed.). (1988a). *Child development within culturally structured environments. Vol. 1: Parental cognition and adult–child interaction.* Norwood: Ablex.

Valsiner, J. (1988b). *Culture and developmental psychology.* Bern: Hogrefe.

Valsiner, J. (1988c). *Developmental psychology in the Soviet Union.* Indianapolis: Indiana University Press.

Valsiner, J. (Ed.). (1989a). *Child development in cultural context.* Toronto: Hogrefe and Huber.

Valsiner, J. (1989b). *Human development and culture.* Toronto: Lexington Books.

Valsiner, J. (1994). Culture and human development: A co-constructivist perspective. In P. van Geert, L. Mos, & W. J. Baker (Eds.), *Annals of theoretical psychology, Vol. X* (pp. 247–298). New York: Plenum.

Wagner, D. A. (Ed.). (1983). *Child development and international development: Research-policy interfaces.* San Francisco: Jossey-Bass.

Wassmann, J. (1993). Der kognitive Aufbruch in der Ethnologie. [The cognitive revolution in anthropology.] In J. Wassmann & P. R. Dasen (Eds.), *Alltagswissen-Les savoirs quotidiens-Everyday cognition* (pp. 95–133). Freiburg, Switzerland: Universitätsverlag Freiburg.

Werner, E. & Smith, R. S. (1982). *Vulnerable but invincible. A longitudinal study of resistant children and youth.* New York: McGraw-Hill.

1

THE CULTURAL STRUCTURING
OF CHILD DEVELOPMENT

CHARLES M. SUPER
University of Connecticut
United States

SARA HARKNESS
University of Connecticut
United States

Contents

Introduction

Perhaps the time will come when a psychology that treats humans as iso-
lated, timeless organisms, and fails to take account of culture and history,
will seem like a Hamlet *with the Prince of Denmark as the only character*
(Jahoda, 1993, p. 194).

Jahoda voiced this hope at the close of his intellectual history of "culture" and "mind" in Western philosophy and social science. In this work he traced the long-standing debate between the positivist determination to treat the human mind as a part of nature and subject to fixed laws that can be discerned through the scientific method, and the more romantic objection that the mind is separate from nature, creating and always being recreated by culture. The experimental, nomothetic approach to the individual, Jahoda argued, is but one aspect of mankind's larger adventure of understanding. He speculated that its domination in modern academic psychology is probably a "temporary aberration" (Jahoda, 1993, p. 189), already challenged by a lively and growing concern with the role of culture and context. (See also chapters by Jahoda & Krewer, and Miller in Volume 1, this *Handbook*).

The literature reviewed in this chapter provides two reasons to hope that scholarship in the late 20th century may progress to a new synthesis rather than merely oscillate between these two philosophical extremes. First, most of the scholars now working at the interface of culture and mind operate within a framework of systematic science—empirical though not experimental—which can hold both the positivist and the romantic to a common, broader reality check. The methodology of learning about ourselves has progressed dramatically since the days of Locke and Rousseau, Wundt and Boas, even Skinner and Erikson. Now more sophisticated and rigorous techniques for both qualitative understanding and quantitative knowledge are available, and there is a growing appreciation that both kinds of tools are needed for the endeavor.

Second, our understanding of human development itself has also progressed in recent decades. The notion that individuals are not born full members of any culture but learn to become such is not new. The idea was well developed by the ancient Greeks as it applied to their own children's education (see Borstelmann, 1983), although the implications for understanding other adult groups were not widely appreciated (see Jahoda, 1993). Certainly by the time of the Enlightenment, Locke and others were explicit in emphasizing the malleability of the child's mind as an important element in their philosophies. Today it is common to see questions of "culture and mind" in a developmental perspective. Framing the issues in terms of human growth, rather than differences among groups of adults, contributes significantly to a scientific resolution of at least some questions that formerly belonged only to philosophy. Rapid advances in the developmental sciences (both biobehavioral and psychological) therefore provide us with a substantial opportunity to move forward in the discussion.

The status of the current research enterprise also provides reasons to be concerned that the potential for progress will not be fully realized. Most salient is a discouraging continuation of disciplinary isolation. Ten years ago, not long after the previous edition of this *Handbook,* we outlined problems of disciplinary provincialism resulting from the diverging histories of psychology and social anthropology, as personified in the departure of the young anthropologist Franz Boas from Wundt's brass-fitted psychometric laboratory to search for an understanding of human behavior through field studies of the Kwakiutl (Harkness & Super, 1987; Super & Harkness, 1986a). Since that formative event, we argued, the two fields of inquiry have each acquired a century of methods, core facts, theories, paradigms, and even mythic origin stories; these typically function to protect each field's integrity, to keep it together, and thus to keep it separate from others. Despite theoretical shifts and a broadening of paradigms in both disciplines, however, there remains a significant parochialism regarding accumulated knowledge as well as current methods.

This continuing insularity is especially problematic because there is a paradox to be resolved in developing a science of the individual-in-context, namely that the two systems to be integrated are fundamentally discontinuous. The human skin is a perceptual marker between the two, as well as a biological barrier that works to maintain the integrity of the organism. At first glance, this observation does not seem problematic: we do not, except in rare historical instances, have trouble distinguishing a horse from its rider, much less a living figure from his or her environmental ground. Yet, as the term "individual-in-context" itself suggests, recent thinking has emphasized the cultural structuring of child development as an integrated process precisely because of problems in the decontextualized approach. Attempts to reconcile the competing needs for analysis and synthesis, for differentiation and integration, can be seen in the several disciplines concerned with individual and environment. In these efforts to relate culture and development, some core ideas recur time and again.

A broad consideration of both anthropological and psychological research reveals three frequent conceptualizations of the cultural environment and how it relates to the developing child. First is the idea of the child's environment as a stage peopled by a cast of characters with their assigned roles and tasks, all within a given frame of the routines of daily life. Second is the environment as defined by commonly shared practices relevant to children, a "community of practice" in which the person and environment are woven together, inseparably and holistically, into a multistranded fabric. Third is the environment as a reality not only of manifest settings and actions but also of guiding ideas, particularly culturally shared ideas held by parents and other caretakers, that inform the ways children are cared for. Although there is considerable conceptual overlap among these three approaches, each is associated primarily with a group of researchers who have their own particular history and disciplinary affiliations.

It is our belief that sufficient information about culturally structured variations in human development has been accumulated to support a new understanding of how both development and cultural transmission take place. We argue that the most effective theoretical models draw on the interdisciplinary conceptual and methodological tools that surround the three core concepts, and that when properly integrated these models help resolve the child-in-context paradox. In the first section of this chapter we review recent studies that are concerned with culture and development, focusing on the three distinctive approaches just mentioned. We then turn to integrative frameworks that model salient principles from each of these approaches in order to talk about integration of child and context. Finally, we conclude by noting several broad themes in the literature and prospects for the future.

The Cultural Organization of Settings

The first major approach to culture and child development, focusing on settings, derives from the seminal work of John and Beatrice Whiting and has been further developed by several generations of scholars whom they trained. It is notable, however, that the initial impetus for the Whitings' theoretical approach was not to understand child development *per se*, but rather to delineate a model for the cultural formation of adult personality, a central concern of the "culture and personality" school in social anthropology at mid-century. In this formulation, the physical ecology, cultural history, and "maintenance systems" (e.g., economy, social and political structure) form the structures to which parenting must adapt; these in turn shape children's development, promoting culture-specific patterns of personality in the adult, including anxieties, conflicts, and defensive systems. The shared need to express and resolve these conflicts is played out at the cultural level through "projective–expressive systems" such as rituals and beliefs (Whiting & Child, 1953; Whiting, 1977). Thus, the hypothesized sequence of causes and consequences in the Whiting model begins and ends with culture, but these are linked together by individual developmental processes through culturally structured environments of childbearing. Work by J. Whiting and colleagues used this framework to examine possible relationships between aspects of experience in early childhood (such as mother–child sleeping arrangements or parental socialization practices) and cultural customs or beliefs (such as adolescent circumcision ceremonies or beliefs about the causes of illness) that might reflect underlying shared psychological dispositions in adulthood (see Whiting, 1977).

In subsequent work by the Whitings and their colleagues, however, the nature and developmental effects of these childhood environments have become the primary focus of research. Of particular importance are the Six Culture Study (B. Whiting & J. Whiting, 1975) and further analyses of the "different worlds" of childhood (B. Whiting & Edwards, 1988). In the Six Culture Study, the Whitings addressed the question of how children's social behavior is affected by the cultural environments in which they are reared. Extensive analysis of observational data collected on samples of children in each community led to the identification of two dimensions of contrast: Dimension A contrasted nurturance and responsibility to dependence and dominance, and Dimension B distinguished social–intimate behavior from authoritarian–aggressive behavior. In each case, the six cultures could be divided into two equal and contrasting sets, with variation in societal complexity corresponding to Dimension A, whereas household type (nuclear versus extended) covaried with Dimension B. For both dimensions of contrast, the Whitings suggested that children's social behavior is a product of its immediate settings, including the people with whom children routinely interact, the places where they spend time together, and the roles they are assigned. It is through the creation of settings for everyday life that multifaceted constructs such as "societal complexity" are translated into the proximate determinants of behavior for children and their caretakers.

The Whitings' analysis of societal complexity, women's workload, children's household tasks, and the development of social behavior made effective use of John Whiting's (1977) theoretical model linking aspects of cultural "maintenance systems" to the environments of child life, but went beyond the model in relating these features of the cultural environment to individual behavioral and developmental outcomes in both parents and children. It also led to Beatrice Whiting's novel formulation of culture as a "provider of settings" (Whiting, 1980) and of parents as organizers of settings for their children's development, an idea elaborated by B. Whiting and Edwards (1988) in a sequel analysis of data from the Six Culture Study and several related projects. As B. Whiting and Edwards (1988, p. 35) state:

> *Our theory holds that patterns of social behavior are learned and practiced in interaction with various types of individuals in a variety of settings. In part, the effect of culture on these patterns in childhood is a direct consequence of the settings to which children are assigned and the people who frequent them. Socializing agents orchestrate children's participation in these learning environments by assigning children to some and proscribing others.*

Viewed from this perspective, the power of settings to shape social behavior can even transcend the influence of the particular culture, leading to cross-culturally generalized patterns for certain categories of people. For example, the Whitings and their associates suggested that differences in social behavior between boys and girls may be due at least in part to universal patterns of difference in the settings to which they are assigned by their mothers and other caretakers. B. Whiting and Edwards (1988) found that girls were more apt to be close to home, involved in activities directed by their mothers, in the company of adult females, in the presence of babies and toddlers, and more involved in child care than were boys. Similar differences have been found for the social settings of adolescent boys and girls (Schlegel & Barry, 1991).

Other researchers working in this tradition have studied several aspects of culturally regulated social settings for children and their effects on behavior and development. For example, Seymour (1976; 1988) found that children of lower-class or lower-caste families in an Indian community were more involved in household chores, reflecting the differences in maternal workload. B. Whiting and Edwards (1988, p. 119) cite Weisner's data from families who divided their time between their farmsteads in western Kenya and urban dwellings in Nairobi; mothers were more nurturant with their young sons when in town, where they spent more time together in crowded apartments and had fewer other children around to care for. Weisner has particularly developed the concept of "activity settings" to highlight behavioral consequences for children (Gallimore, Goldenberg, & Weisner, 1993; Weisner, 1984). The effects of household density on mothers' behavior were also demonstrated by the Munroes' (1971) research on infant caretaking patterns in a Logoli community of western Kenya. They found that infants in households with more potential caretakers were held more and were responded to more quickly when they cried. However, these infants received *less* care by their mothers, who were more apt to be busy with gardening and other tasks. These results underline the importance of regarding the infant's caretaking environment as a system rather than as a function of a single caretaker's behavior. A related analysis, among the Efe foragers of the Ituri forest in Zaire, describes a pattern of "multiple caretaking" where, in a technologically primitive as well as dense living situation, other women as well as fathers share with mothers in the care and feeding of young infants (Tronick, Morelli, & Ivey, 1992). Other recent studies of the settings of childhood continue to add to our knowledge of the ecologies of child development around the world (e.g., Nsamenang, 1992; Saraswathi & Dutta, 1988).

The ecocultural model of Berry (1975, 1995) is another descendant of the approach taken by the Whitings. In that model, human development and behavior are viewed as adaptive to cultural and biological features of populations, which themselves are adaptive to ecological context. This ecocultural model has been used both in developmental studies in Africa (e.g., Berry, Van de Koppel, Sénéchal, Annis, Bahuchet, Cavalli-Sforza, & Witkin, 1986) and as an organizing framework for textbooks in cross-cultural psychology (e.g., Berry, Poortinga, Segall, & Dasen, 1992).

The Six Culture Study and related work spanned more than three decades, and the changes that are evident in the development of this school both reflected and contributed to larger intellectual currents of the times. From a theoretical model of culture and personality was derived a framework for the study of children's cultural environments. From an explanatory framework based on Freudian theory and learning theory grew a perspective that gave a more active role to the child as learner. From a general recognition of children's environments came ultimately a more focused conceptualization of settings and the cultural routines that take place within them as proximate sources of socialization. Recent research in several different subdisciplines has expanded on this awareness in its focus on practices and activities, and the communication of cultural meaning systems to the participating child.

Culture, Communication, and Practices

An enduring theme in studies of child development across cultures has been the idea of the environment as a communicative medium. In this metaphorical conceptualization, two systems—the individual and the contextual—interact, each sending "messages" that are assimilated into the other's respective internal organizations. Historically, cultural researchers, like early developmentalists, focused their attention on messages from the environment to the child; only more recently have cultural theorists, following trends in developmental psychology, recognized the agency of the individual and the bidirectionality of influence (see chapter by Miller, Volume 1 of this *Handbook*).

The traditional theme of cultural messages sent to the child is evident in the classic works of Ruth Benedict and Margaret Mead, as described by LeVine (1973, p. 54):

> *The transmission of culture from generation to generation is, in Mead's view, a process of communication in which many aspects of the growing individual's cultural environment relay the same messages to him, messages reflecting the dominant configurations of his culture. He acquires his "cultural character" by internalizing the substance of these messages.*

The theme of culture as a conveyer of messages is echoed again in Shweder and associates' analysis of moral socialization in Indian and U.S. communities (Shweder, 1982; Shweder, Mahapatra, & Miller, 1990; Shweder & Much, in press). They suggest that moral socialization results from the fact that children "discern the moral order as it is dramatized and made salient in every day practices" (Shweder, Mahapatra, & Miller, 1990, p. 195); for example, Indian children learn about "pollution" through the implicit and explicit messages contained in daily activities and events, and in verbal interaction, including adult comments on children's behavior and statements of rules.

Goodnow (1990, p. 281–282) emphasizes the particular importance of tacit messages (in contrast to verbalized ones) that are conveyed by aspects of the cultural environment, as these may be more likely to be perceived as reality itself:

> *When clocks abound in public space, for instance, and most adults wear watches, the message is clear that keeping track of time is important. . . . Regardless of the name given, I would like to see us pay particular attention to these less verbal ways of conveying messages. I would also like to raise the possibility that messages conveyed in this tacit, uncommented-upon form may have a particular impact. For instance, they may appear to have a particular objective validity and be the least likely to be reflected upon and recognized as being matters of custom and value rather than of nature.*

Thus important sources of cultural messages in this view include the ordinary behavioral routines and everyday organization of living that are regarded as customary. The importance of habitual, automatic, and preconscious (even subconscious) social behaviors—often called customs when referring to their cultural organization—has been emphasized by scholars from a broad array of intellectual traditions (e.g., Bourdieu, 1977; Quinn & Holland, 1987).

P. Miller and Hoogstra (1992) relate the two themes of implicit, nonverbal messages and those conveyed by language through the concept of indexicality, the property of language to "provide a map" to the social terrain through systematically varied patterns of language use. They suggest (p. 86) that:

The indexical property of language thus provides a link to models of socialization that emphasize the powerful socializing impact of tacit organizations of time and space, with their associated routines and distributions of persons (Goodnow, 1990; Harkness & Super, 1983; Super & Harkness, 1986; B. Whiting, 1980). To the extent that language forms and functions are distributed contrastively across the various settings to which the child is habitually assigned, they help to define the "cast of characters, activities, and standing rules of the setting[s]"; (B. Whiting, 1980, p. 106). In this way language contributes to the implicit, unintentional delivery of socializing messages.

The metaphor of "messages" conveyed by the environment to the child naturally leads to the question of what processes are involved in the child's assimilation of these messages. Child language researchers have suggested a linguistic conceptualization of this process: rather than "being socialized," the child is seen as "acquiring culture" in a process analogous to the acquisition of a first language (Harkness, 1992; Schwartz, 1981). Further, the child's acquisition of language is seen as integral to the process of becoming a competent member of the culture (Ochs & Schieffelin, 1984; see also Mohanty & Perregaux, this volume). Within the process of language socialization and acquisition, researchers have identified particular routines that seem to be important for the dual processes of language and culture acquisition. For example, Watson-Gegeo and Gegeo (1977) demonstrate how Samoan children learn about both rules of social interaction and the structure of the language through "calling-out" and repeating routines. Schieffelin (1990) likewise describes how Kaluli mothers in New Guinea teach their children not only how to speak but also how to feel through verbal practices such as the *"elema* routine," in which the mother directs her young child "say like that" to a third person who is present.

A major and consistent finding across these studies is that not only does the *content* of cultural routines vary, but also the *nature* of children's participation in them (e.g., Blount, 1982; Harkness, 1988; Harkness & Super, 1977; Ochs & Schieffelin, 1984; Rabain-Jamin, 1994). At one extreme is the Western, educated, middle-class model of mother-initiated, child-directed talk marked by special features ("baby talk'" or "motherese") thought to make it more engaging and easy to understand for young children. At the other are language communities in pre-industrial, non-Western communities in Africa and the Pacific, as well as some non-middle-class communities in the United States, where children are either expected to learn language without benefit of special instruction or, at the very least, to accommodate themselves to the linguistic demands of the environment (Rogoff, 1990). Communication may be diadic, as in the former model, or triadic as in the *elema* routines as described by Schieffelin (1990) for the

Kaluli, or as in mother–child–infant interactions among the Kipsigis as described by Harkness (1988), in which the mother issues verbal directives to the toddler about taking care of the baby, which the toddler echoes in talk with the baby. Children may also participate in a variety of ways—e.g. as observer—in verbal routines, such as storytelling among primarily adult speakers (P. Miller & Moore, 1989).

This research has raised important questions about the nature and significance of language input to acquisition and the development of language-related skills or later adaptation to school, but its significance for present purposes lies in the identification of routines involving communication within a cultural meaning system as a framework for understanding the cultural structuring of child development. This approach has also been elaborated by researchers who focus on "practices" or "activities" (P. Miller & Goodnow, 1995).

The study of children's involvement in cultural practices is rooted in anthropological observations of children's learning (especially in non-Western settings, e.g., Fortes, 1938/1970), as well as from studies of "informal learning" in apprenticeship situations (e.g., Greenfield & Lave, 1982). Recent developments in this approach have been more theoretical than empirical, with much scholarly effort devoted to the elucidation of what is meant by "practices" and how the study of children's involvement in practices differentiates this approach from others (e.g., P. Miller & Goodnow, 1995). Although this approach (or constellation of approaches) has much in common with the study of cultural settings and is to some extent derived from that tradition, researchers in the "practices" school often trace their own intellectual genealogy to Marx and the Russian psychologists such as Vygotsky, the American educational philosopher John Dewey, and contemporary French theorists, especially Bourdieu. There are variations among different scholars in the field as to exactly what constitutes "practices" as opposed to "activities" or even "contexts" (Cole, 1995), but this approach is unified by several core assertions. As recently summarized by P. Miller and Goodnow (1995, p. 8–13), these are:

1. Practices provide a way of describing development-in-context, without separating child and context and without separating development into a variety of separate domains.
2. Practices reflect or instantiate a social and moral order.
3. Practices provide the route by which children come to participate in a culture, allowing the culture to be "reproduced" or "transformed."
4. Practices do not exist in isolation.
5. The nature of participation has consequences.

The first assertion, on the child-in-context, is a key philosophical commitment in the "practices" school, and it has been used to reconceptualize development as "stretching to accomplish something together during participation in activities" (P. Miller & Goodnow, 1995, p. 53) rather than as a process of individual growth. This perspective, it is argued, makes it reasonable to avoid the assumption of a boundary between the mind and the environment. As Rogoff, Baker-Sennett, Lacasa, and Goldsmith (1995, p. 53–54) state:

> *Viewing development as participation challenges the idea of a boundary between internal and external phenomena (for example, between arithmetic knowledge and the availability of order forms listing pricing information)—a boundary that is derived from use of the isolated individual as the unit of analysis. A person is a part of an activity in which he or she participates, not separate from it. Our perspective discards the idea that the social world is external to the individual and that development consists of acquiring knowledge and skills. Rather, a person develops through participation in an activity, changing to be involved in the situation at hand in ways that contribute both to the ongoing event and to the person's preparation for other involvement in other, similar events.*

How, and how tightly, an individual's skilled behavior is tied to specific activities and contexts is a core issue, as illustrated by the sequence of studies carried out by Cole and his associates. In their research in Liberia in the 1970s, they noted differences in cognitive test performance among schooled and unschooled children in Liberia and set out to devise psychological tests that would index the knowledge that unschooled people have, and the extent to which their knowledge, gained in the context of everyday activities, might generalize to solving other intellectually similar problems (Cole, Gay, Glick, & Sharp, 1971). Later research among the Vai, carried out with Sylvia Scribner, sought to understand the effects of literacy on thinking in a context where literacy training was provided in traditional settings apart from Western schooling (Scribner & Cole, 1981). In more recent research on children in school and non-school activity settings, Cole and his associates have attempted to identify and analyze cognitive processes as observed in naturally occurring behavior, and to compare these across settings and in test situations. They found that it is possible to construct cognitive tests that reflect local cultural knowledge, and that people's performance on an array of tasks reflects the degree of synchrony between the task and their prior experience. Equally interesting, however, was the discovery that many kinds of cognitive processes that can be readily observed in a school setting are difficult to capture for individuals in other settings. Much of the problem solving observed in naturalistic settings was found to be subtly negotiated or shared among group members, both child and adult. The shared nature of cognitive tasks in everyday life is poignantly illustrated by the story of two boys in the club, Reggie and Archie, whose abilities and deficiencies complemented each other: Archie had severe learning disabilities that made it very difficult for him to read, but had good social and organizational skills, while Reggie could read but had a hard time staying with a designated activity. Alone, each of the boys was unable to function effectively in the club, but together they made a successful team—so successful that the adults running the club were unaware of Archie's learning disabilities (Cole, in press).

The example of Reggie and Archie again brings us back to the issue of how development is viewed from the perspective of "practice" or activity theory. Whereas Vygotsky proposed that participation in shared activities, especially guided activity with a more knowledgeable partner, enabled the child to perform beyond his own individual abilities, he also believed that eventually this experience would be transformed into the child's own individual level of achievement which could be assessed, for example, in tests. What research on children's participation in practices has shown, however, is that this is not necessarily the case. On the positive side, Saxe (1990), working with child candy vendors in Brazil, has provided a detailed description of the spontaneously organized mentoring and use of graded tasks that enable young children to acquire the mathematical skills needed to survive in the market place. On a larger scale, Lancy (in press) has presented an ethnography of the Kpelle practices that lead up to the pattern of success and failure in test situations first delineated by Cole and his colleagues (Cole et al., 1971).

However, Nunes and colleagues, also working with child vendors in Brazil, showed that abilities demonstrated in the market context were not expressed in school or test situations (Nunes, 1995). Similarly Lave (see Greenfield & Lave, 1982) studied Liberian tailors and found that generalizability of skills learned through apprenticeships was limited: tailoring experience did not predict the ability to estimate the lengths of sticks of wood nearly as well as it predicted the ability to estimate the circumference of waistbands on trousers. Greenfield and Childs (see Greenfield & Lave, 1982) studied Mayan girls' and boys' ability to recognize and reproduce patterns similar to those used in backstrap weaving, which the girls (but not the boys) were taught by their mothers. They found that girls, compared to unschooled boys, were able to represent the patterns more accurately thread by thread, but boys who had been to school did better at replicating the general visual impression of patterns and at imitating novel patterns.

This kind of evidence leads some scholars to insist on the inseparability of the person from the activity context. Shweder, a strong advocate of this position, argues that reality itself resides in the "intentional worlds" in which "subject and object cannot possibly be separated and kept apart because they are so interdependent as to need each other to be" (Shweder, 1990, p. 3). Lave (1990), in this same spirit, takes the position that testing of the individual, removed from the original context of practice, is inherently illegitimate as a means of assessing development. This emphasis on embeddedness complicates comparative research, as evidenced by the difficulty Rogoff, Mistry, Göncü, and Mosier (1993) had in finding tasks to use for a cross-cultural study which were both objectively the same and, viewed from within the experience of participating mothers and children, equally representative of their everyday experiences. The extreme position also ignores the many circumstances in which skills and knowledge are available out of the initial context of acquisition. In Greenfield and Child's study of weaving (cited earlier), for example, the boys' better performance at completing novel patterns was hypothesized to be due to their greater experience with the world beyond the village, where they would have the opportunity to observe a wider variety of cloth patterns; evidently they somehow acquired a more general, internalized model of cloth patterns that was not tied to the actual practice of weaving.

The central challenge for researchers interested in the relationships among culture, practices, and human development, Cole (1995, p. 106) notes, "is to attain greater precision in our ability to communicate about [a supra-individual sociocultural entity that is] the unit of analysis and the forms of interaction by which individual psychological functioning and its socioculturally structured environments are intertwined." The first part of this challenge is to understand the practices of the child-in-context; the second part is to find a way of talking about "individual psychological functioning" and "socioculturally structured environments" that allows us to see the two strands that are interwoven; or, to return to the opening metaphor of this section, to see the two systems that so intimately communicate. Paradoxically, in the more extreme versions of the "practices" approach both the individual and the culture disappear into the nexus of the interactive context. When the reality of individual knowledge apart from its context of usage is denied, the reality of a shared culture—whether consisting of knowledge or customs and practices—also cannot be considered apart from the individuals who constantly create and transform it. Thus this approach does not ask how certain activities come to be carried out or understood the way they are in particular cultural communities, but rather it begins with their presence in individual experience. Similarly, the approach is singularly nondevelopmental in that it has no way of representing development within the child beyond the accretion of further "practices." As Rogoff (1990, p. 28–29) has noted, the practices approach in its pure form is a version of what Pepper (1942) termed "contextualism," a philosophy characterized by complete relativism of the historical moment and the denial of any general principles. This would make both comparative and developmental studies exceedingly difficult.

Thus, as an emerging perspective, the practices approach illustrates both the promise and the problems of studying the cultural structuring of child development. It has made an important contribution to a better understanding of how psychological skills—particularly cognitive skills—are used in everyday life. The fine-grained ethnographic accounts of individual behavior in specified activity contexts show vividly how skills are used transactionally. This research has not yet answered the question of how cognitive development takes place in "practice" or in the child, but it does suggest that some kinds of thinking are rarely done by individuals alone in real-life situations (see also Schliemann, Carraher, & Ceci, this volume). In addition, the attention to practices themselves has highlighted a valuable point of entry into studying the cultural structuring of child development. Practices index cultural meaning systems that shape the agenda of child development in any given context, and this agenda can be expected to have important consequences for what and how children learn. The study of children's participation in cultural practices, then, complements research on parents' cultural belief systems, the third area to be discussed here.

Parents' Cultural Belief Systems

Parental beliefs have attracted increasing attention from researchers in human development in recent years, as attested by the rapid growth of published work in this area (Goodnow & Collins, 1990; Sigel, 1985; Sigel, McGillicuddy-De Lisi, & Goodnow, 1992). The emergence of parents' *cultural* belief systems or "parental ethnotheories" as a topic of study has been made possible by parallel trends in psychology, social anthropology, and related new interdisciplinary approaches to culture and human development (Harkness & Super, 1996).

For much of psychology's history, parents' ideas about children were generally considered to be a pragmatic matter of education, to which developmental science could make an appropriate contribution of knowledge. At the same time, attempts to relate specific beliefs and attitudes to actual behavior proved disappointing. Subsequently, parents' beliefs were rediscovered as "naive psychology" and as epigenetic stuctures in their own right (e.g., Sameroff & Feil, 1985).

Anthropological interest in how parents think dates back at least to classics such as Mead's studies of childrearing in Pacific societies (see Mead, 1972). The Whitings' cross-cultural studies of children's environments are also permeated with interpretations (based on interviews as well as observations; see Minturn & Lambert, 1964) of parental beliefs as they inform behavior. In discussing cross-cultural variation in children's chores, for example, Whiting and Edwards present the following picture of mothers in Khalapur, India:

> *The Khalapur mothers make a clear distinction in the chores that they assign to sons and daughters; they consider housework to be women's work. They ask their daughters to help but assign comparatively little work. They know that their daughters will do much household work when they become married (as arranged by their parents) and go to live in a new village. As daughters-in-law, the new wives will cook and keep house under the supervision of their mothers-in-law. Parents, therefore, feel that as children, girls should be treated as "visitors." This is obviously a cultural ideal—in fact, the girls do some child care and housework and run errands, but comparatively speaking, they have more free time for undirected activities (Whiting & Edwards, 1988, p. 110).*

The idea that parental action is motivated not only by immediate concerns such as the need to accomplish household work, but also by anticipations of the future, is the cornerstone of LeVine's theory of "parental goals" as they relate to subsistence patterns and health conditions, the organization of parenting strategies, and child health and development (LeVine, 1974; LeVine, Dixon, LeVine, Richman, Leiderman, Keefer, & Brazelton, 1994; LeVine, Miller, & West, 1988; Richman, Miller, & LeVine, 1992). LeVine suggests that "what parents want for their children" can be conceptualized in terms of a universal hierarchy of goals, ranging from ensuring basic survival to the acquisition of economic capabilities, and finally to the attainment of locally relevant cultural values. In traditional agrarian societies with high infant mortality rates such as have been prevalent in sub-

Saharan Africa, he argues, parents' caregiving behavior is organized by the most basic goal of ensuring survival past infancy. This approach is part of a "quantitative" strategy of bearing as many children as possible in order that at least some will survive to adulthood and care for aging parents. In urbanized industrial societies with low infant mortality rates, on the other hand, LeVine and his colleagues suggest that parents take a "qualitative" approach and their goals are oriented around the child's acquisition of skills and cultural values for a competitive adult future. The different parental goals may be expressed in differential rates of soothing, proximal caregiving behavior (such as holding the baby) versus more distal and stimulating (such as talking to the baby) (LeVine, et al., 1994; Richman, Miller, & LeVine, 1992).

It is important to note that in LeVine's framework parental goals are mostly unconscious, shared assumptions rather than beliefs that are either "taught" in a didactic sense or ordinarily discussed among members of a culture. Thus, parents in societies with high infant mortality rates, such as the Gusii, may not consciously feel anxious about the immediate well-being of their infants but their practices of care are designed to monitor the infant's physical status and to respond quickly to signs of distress (LeVine et al., 1994). In contrast, Swedish mothers, in a society with low-infant mortality, may express considerably more overt anxiety about the physical well-being of their unborn or newborn infants, but they nevertheless orient their child care practices around the infant's assumed physical survival and focus their energies on developing affective bonds (Welles-Nyström, 1988).

LeVine's view of parental goals as a set of culturally shared assumptions is compatible with the concept of "cultural models," which Quinn and Holland (1987, p. 4) described as "presupposed, taken-for-granted models of the world that are widely shared (although not necessarily to the exclusion of other, alternative models) by the members of a society and that play an enormous role in their understanding of that world and their behavior in it." As such, cultural models are a kind of schema, characterized not only as representations of reality but also as motivators of human action by virtue of their representation of what states of the world can and should be pursued (D'Andrade, 1992). This overlap of schemas and motivation, according to D'Andrade, is linked to culture by the fact that many (though not all) schemas are culturally constituted. He offers the example of "achievement" as a construct, often used in motivation research, but whose meaning is based in cultural definitions of what it is to "achieve" something.

As socially shared, implicit models of the world, cultural models are often "transparent" to their users. Scholars from a variety of traditions (e.g., Bril & Lehalle, 1988; Goodnow, 1990; Hutchins, 1980) have noted that such models not only shape a person's perception of reality but may also be experienced as reality itself. This feature of cultural models is well exemplified by provocative research on parents' "developmental timetables," or expectations of the timing of children's development. Although biologically based maturation processes would suggest that children everywhere should achieve developmental skills at similar ages, cross-cultural comparisons have shown that there are systematic patterns of variation in parental expectations, which can be related to larger cultural patterns on the one hand and on childrearing practices and (sometimes) developmental outcomes on the other. Ninio's (1979) seminal study of mothers in Israel found that those of European background had earlier expectations for their infants' cognitive development than did mothers of African or Asian background. A pattern of ethnically based variation among coresidents of the same geographic area was also found in Australia, where Anglo-Australian mothers had earlier expectations than did Lebanese-Australians (Goodnow, Cashmore, Cotton, & Knight, 1984). Similarly, varying expectations have been shown among Vietnamese, Haitian, and French-Canadian parents in Montréal (Pomerleau, Malcuit, & Sabatier, 1991; Sabatier, Pomerleau, Malcuit, St.-Laurent, & Allard, 1990). In this latter study the authors draw links from their findings about maternal beliefs and patterns of communication to issues in education and health for the more recent immigrant families, a concern that occurs frequently in the broader literature on families' expectations for their children and conditions of migration and culture change. There are now a number of studies demonstrating cross-cultural variation in parental expectations and beliefs about development (e.g., Bril & Sabatier, 1986; Bril, Zack & Hombessa-Nkounkou, 1989; Hopkins & Westra, 1989; Keller, Miranda, & Gauda, 1984; Palacios & Moreno, 1996).

One important finding from this body of work is that developmental expectations may vary widely depending on the domain. For example, Hess, Kashiwagi, Azuma, Price, and Dickinson (1980) showed in a cross-cultural comparison of American and Japanese mothers that whereas mothers in San Francisco had earlier expectations for achievement of social skills with peers and verbal communication, Japanese mothers expected earlier development of emotional control, compliance with authority, and courtesy.

It appears that not only cultural membership but also professional role or experience as a parent or early chilhood teacher may contribute to group differences in developmental timetables, as Edwards, Gandini, and Giovaninni's (1996) study of Italian and American parents and teachers illustrates. They found that while the American and Italian parents held divergent expectations (with the Americans expecting earlier achievement), teachers from the two communities were more similar to each other, occupying a common ground between the two cultural extremes of parents in each place. Parents' (and teachers') developmental expectations would appear to reflect cultural values as well as beliefs, and they should logically be associated with cultural differences in socialization pressures. It is also possible, as Edwards, Gandini, and Giovaninni (1996) suggest, that parental expectations are the *result* rather than the instigator of real group differences in children. In this case, we might hypothesize that other aspects of children's settings or daily routines—for example, being a member of a large family, or being expected to sit through family dinners or to tolerate the affectionate attentions of visiting relatives—may contribute to real developmental differences without the involvement of "socialization pressures" in the usual sense.

As illustrated by the research on "developmental timetables," there are several related questions to address in understanding parents' cultural belief systems: What are the nature and sources of parental ethnotheories? How do parents' cultural belief systems vary both across and within cultures, and what are the roles of culturally appointed "experts" and individual experience? What is the relationship between parents' cultural belief systems and behavior? And finally, through what mechanisms do parental ethnotheories affect the health and development of children? Recent studies are beginning to shed light on some of these questions.

Nature and Sources

Parents' cultural belief systems are related both to more general cultural belief systems and to the particular experiences of raising individual children in a specific time and place; they represent a convergence of the public and the private, the shared and the personal. The sources of parental ethnotheories, thus, include more general ideas prevalent in the social environments of parents, both present and past. For example, Lightfoot and Valsiner (1992) have described "social suggestion complexes" represented in advertisements for children's toys and clothing that carry a multitude of shared meanings. They note that an advertisement for super-hero underwear beginning with the statement, "Team up with their favorite characters and you'll be the hero" conveys several messages to parents: that mothers can take a role in providing their children with fun and excitement; that mothers will thereby be included in children's fantasy world; and that the image of superheroes is a positive one supported by mothers as well as children. More generally, this advertisement also implicitly communicates the American middle-class idea of a fun-based, egalitarian relationship between parents and young children. One could further add that the advertisement also suggests that mothers should *work* to build a close positive emotional relationship with their children, rather than taking this relationship for granted, a distinctive cultural orientation that has been contrasted with, for example, Indian beliefs about relationships (J. Miller & Bersoff, in press).

Parental ethnotheories can also be derived from more general cultural models: they are an example of what Quinn and Holland (1987, p. 11) describe as "general-purpose cultural models which are repeatedly incorporated into other cultural models developed for special purposes." Harkness, Super, and Keefer (1992) have discussed American parents' ideas about "stages" and "independence" in relation to young children as an example of this principle. Both constructs are pervasive in American thinking about a variety of domains, from the global to the individual; they are used by parents to interpret particular child behaviors—for example, a child's intransigence at being strapped into a car seat—as well as informing parental responses to these behaviors. The substantial literature on cultural concepts of "intelligence" can also be examined in this light, for the way it organizes parental and societal responses to children (e.g., Berry & Bennett, 1992; Dasen, Dembélé, Ettien, Kabran, Kamagate, Koffi, & N'Guessan, 1985; Harkness & Super, 1992b; Serpell, 1977; Super, 1983; Sternberg, Conway, Ketron, & Bernstein, 1981; see also Mishra, this volume). These more general cultural models may be formalized to varying extents. For example, Welles-Nyström (1996) discusses the role of "equality ideology" in Sweden as it is expressed in official government family policies (e.g., parental leave) as well as in mothers' cultural beliefs about parenting. These examples illustrate D'Andrade's (1987) observation that cultural models are organized in hierarchical relationships with other more general ideas such as independence, intelligence, or equality, as well as more specific ideas such as schemas of what a two-year-old tantrum means. It is important to recognize, however, that these hierarchical arrangements are constantly growing and changing in the context of parental experience, and that they are apt to include elements that are contradictory as well as mutually supportive. These features are particularly apparent in situations of rapid social change, such as Gilbert has described for rural areas in South Africa (Gilbert, Nkwinti & van Vlaenderen, submitted for publication).

Cross-Cultural and Intra-Cultural Variation

Cross-cultural variation in parental ethnotheories bears a complex relationship to intra-cultural variability and change; both are active areas of research. A central question about cross-cultural variation is whether there are any general principles guiding the kinds of ethnotheories characteristic of different types of socio-cultural contexts, or whether both ethnotheories and their cultural contexts are best seen as unique manifestations of shared human life at a particular historical moment. Some general principles have been proposed, but it is clear that further work is needed to develop conceptualizations that more closely fit the complex realities of cultural patterns. For example, based on detailed ethnographic studies in Tahiti and Nepal, Levy (1996) proposes that "simple" societies (small, egalitarian communities with little occupational specialization) may have predictably different views on children's ways of learning from "complex" ones (larger, socially differentiated, etc.). Specifically, he suggests that parents in simple societies (like the villagers he studied in Tahiti) may expect children to learn on their own, with little specific instruction but against a general backdrop of social expectation to conform to community norms; while in more complex settings, like the cities of Nepal, there are explicit rules and practices for teaching and learning. In another contrast drawn by various researchers, Western societies are contrasted to non-Western societies, or to ethnic minorities within Western societies, in terms of individualism or independence versus collectivism, interdependence or a socio-centric orientation as developmental scripts and endpoints (e.g., Greenfield, 1994; see also chapter by Kagitçibasi, Volume 3 of this *Handbook*).

Although both these contrasts capture cultural differences that have been noted by many observers, there are complexities that suggest caution in moving too quickly to large generalizations. For example, Schieffelin's research on the *elema* verbal routines in a simple society in New Guinea (see earlier), shows that mothers in at least some simple societies *do* believe in the importance of teaching their children. Super's (1976) research on "African infant precocity" likewise illustrates the point that some aspects of development such as learning to sit and to walk may be supported by *more* parental instruction in some "simple" societies than is generally the case in complex societies such as the United States and Europe. In relation to the independence–interdependence contrast, Greenfield—who has proposed this as a useful way to think about the dilemmas of ethnic minorities living in the United States—states that "there is more than one variety of individualism or independence orientation and more than one variety of collectivism or interdependence orientation across cultures" (Greenfield, 1994, p. 7).

In this context, understanding the nature of variability in parental ethnotheories *within* cultural settings is emerging as a major focus of study. One approach is to map variability within a cultural sample, as Palacios has done in his study of parental beliefs in the region of Seville, Spain (Palacios & Moreno, 1996). Palacios' strategy reversed the usual procedure of identifying different groups of parents on the basis of socioeconomic indicators and then studying differences among them; instead, the three groups of parents in Palacios' research are defined in terms of their differing profiles of beliefs, which he characterizes as traditional, modern, and paradoxical. Further, Palacios and his colleagues have demonstrated that the developmental roots of these different parental belief profiles can be found as far back as early adolescence, and that educational experience may play an important role. Formal education as a source of intra-cultural variability has also been investigated by LeVine and his colleagues in their studies of mothers in an urban Mexican community, where they found that more educated mothers expected earlier development of verbal communication skills in their infants (LeVine, Miller, Richman, & LeVine, 1996).

Other research has highlighted the influence of differing social roles in the genesis of variation both across and within cultural communities. For example, Harkness, Super, Keefer, Raghavan, and Kipp-Campbell (1996) studied differences in the use of "root metaphors" of development (Pepper, 1942) by parents and pediatricians in a U.S. Health Maintenance Organization. They found that although both pediatricians and parents favored the use of "organicist" metaphors over "mechanist" metaphors to explain children's behavior, the pediatricians favored the organicist metaphors even more than the parents, whereas parents preferred mechanist metaphors more than did the pediatricians. The research by Edwards, Gandini, and Giovaninni (1996) on preschool parents' and teachers' developmental timetables, discussed earlier, also provides some insights into the ways that social roles may create commonalities in ethnotheories of people in different societies. They suggest that the relative similarities among teachers' expectations, compared to parents', may stem from the shared training and job experience of teachers. They conclude (p. 285):

> . . . *teachers have expectations that in part reflect their particular cultural traditions and societal ideologies (and which they share with the families with whom they work) but equally reflect a sort of professional culture shared internationally with other practitioners of parallel or equivalent education and training and experience with children.*

Thus one aspect of understanding variability in cultural belief systems within and across settings is the recognition that individual people may belong to more than one cultural group. Harwood and her colleagues (Harwood, Miller, & Irizarry, 1995) address this issue in suggesting a definition of culture as including hierarchical "levels of shared discourse" (p. 120) in which individuals may maintain numerous group memberships based on the common discourse and practices of ethnicity, parenthood, religious affiliation, social class, or other characteristics. Harwood's findings on patterns of cultural and social class differences in Anglo American and Puerto Rican mothers' beliefs are consistent with this view. Specifically, social class differences among Puerto Rican and Anglo American mothers' beliefs about desirable developmental end points (e.g., a greater emphasis on the development of independent versus obedient behavior) are not replicated as cross-cultural differences between the two groups; rather, each cultural group presents its own distinctive profile of beliefs, but social class differences are apparent within these shared profiles. Thus, just as similarities among preschool teachers in different cultural communities can be ascribed to their membership in a supranational culture of teacher education and experience, so can similarities based on social class also reflect the generalized differing realities to which families with differing socioeconomic constraints must adapt.

The Instantiation of Parental Ethnotheories

Inherent in much of the research on parents' cultural belief systems is a concern with how such systems are manifested, or instantiated, in behavior. Researchers interested in cultural belief systems have taken several different approaches to this question. The most general one is to look for group-level correspondence (e.g., Caudill & Weinstein, 1969). However, an expectation for such linear relations can be misleading, as there are many other, more dynamic possibilities. Pomerleau, Malcuit, and Sabatier (1991) provide one example from their Québec study: both Haitian and Vietnamese (immigrant) mothers stress the value of social conformity, but they differ significantly in their directive, conformity-producing behaviors in a teaching task.

A second strategy is to use knowledge of parental belief systems, drawn from ethnographic and cross-cultural studies, to formulate hypotheses about expected cross-cultural variation in parental behavior. Bornstein and his colleagues take this approach in analyzing differences in patterns of maternal responsiveness to infants in the United States, France, and Japan (Bornstein, Tamis-LeMonda, Tal, Ludemann, Toda, Rahn, Pecheux, Azuma, & Vardi, 1992). Drawing from a variety of previous research in these countries, they derived a general characterization of beliefs and behavior in the three settings, such as "the American mother is believed to be interested in promoting autonomy in her infant, and organizes her interactions so as to foster physical and verbal independence in the child" (p. 809). Based on such general premises, Bornstein et al. predicted specific differences in maternal behavior: for example, they predicted that American mothers would emphasize "environment-oriented responsiveness by incorporating the world outside the dyad into their interactions" (p. 810). Analysis of videotaped home observations did show some culturally varied patterns in maternal behavior, although not entirely in the predicted ways. In addition, however, there were similarities in rates of nurturant and imitative responses, leading the authors to suggest that patterns of similarity may relate to infant behaviors that demand more specific responses (e.g. infant distress signals), whereas variability may reflect domains of culturally constituted discretion.

A third approach to the question of relationships between cultural beliefs and behavior is to focus on behavior that is codified in cultural practices as an entry point to the understanding of parental beliefs. This approach can be most fruitful, according to Goodnow (1996, p. 317), when practices are chosen for analysis that involve long-term goals and that are perceived as part of a larger "developmental project." In addition, practices that are not easily explained on purely rational or economic grounds—such as children's participation in household work—may be especially rich sources. Practices related to household work are also a fruitful domain for cross-cultural research on parental beliefs, as Goodnow notes, because families everywhere must deal with this issue.

Another presumably universal domain that has proved particularly rich for the study of parental ethnotheories is the organization of sleep, including sleeping arrangements, scheduling, and caretaker involvement in children's transitions between wakefulness and sleep. Beginning with the work of Caudill and Plath (1966) on Japanese sleeping arrangements, the question of "who sleeps by whom" has been recognized as reflecting deeply held cultural convictions about the self, the family, and the nature of human development. More recently, Shweder and colleagues (Shweder, Jensen & Goldstein, 1995) have applied this perspective to a comparative study of cultural preference patterns and actual sleeping arrangements in Indian and U.S. families; they find that choices made by Indian respondents correspond to a different set of moral principles than those made in the United States (e.g., respect for hierarchy vs. autonomy). Research by Abbott (1992) on sleeping arrangements in an American Appalachian community highlights the cultural theme of autonomy versus social cohesion as a key component in sleeping arrangements. Like Abbott, Morelli and her colleagues (Morelli, Rogoff, Oppenheim, & Goldsmith, 1992) find that parents' ideas about independence or separation are at the core not only of beliefs but also of related parental emotions about sleep management in children—although in the case of American parents who favor sleeping alone as a practice to foster healthy independent development, culturally constructed moral conviction may sometimes conflict with the emotional impulse to respond to a crying child alone in its bed. As research by Wolf and his colleagues (Wolf, Lozoff, Latz, & Paludetto, 1996) has shown, the cultural structuring of sleeping arrangements for young children is also systematically related to other sleep management practices including where the child falls asleep, establishment of a regular bedtime and related routines, presence of adults while the child falls asleep, and use of a bottle or "transitional object" for the child to sleep with. They note that this constellation of practices reflects central cultural beliefs:

How a child is allowed to fall asleep is one of the earliest forms of culturally determined interaction with the child. Sleep practices are embedded in a set of child rearing behaviors that reflect values about what it means to be a "good" parent and how the parents are to prepare the child for entry into the family and the community (p. 377).

Despite the fact that practices may be accurate *expressions* of cultural belief systems, however, Wolf and Lozoff (1989) raise the possibility that the cultural message from the child's point of view may be somewhat different. For example, practices emphasizing separation, rather than fostering a healthy sense of independence, "may be teaching children not to rely on other people as a way of handling stress, but to rely on objects for comfort" (p. 292).

Developmental Consequences of Parental Ethnotheories

Although there has been a great deal of research on the effects of *individual* belief systems on children's development, the effects of culturally shared belief systems are just beginning to be explored empirically. As evident from the previous discussion, however, parents' cultural belief systems, in both their explicit and their less conscious aspects, are assumed to influence developmental outcomes through a variety of pathways involving customary practices, modes of interaction, and parental responsivity. At times the identification of these pathways in the literature seems almost haphazard, but the multiplicity of routes leads to an important insight: Parental ethnotheories have a "directive force" (D'Andrade, 1992); that is, their primary function is to motivate and organize a potentially disparate array of actions, events, and situations.

One fairly direct consequence of parents' belief systems can be identified in the area of nutrition research in developing countries, where the outcomes of interest literally include life and death. There is a large literature on specific cultural beliefs about weaning foods, for example, and their link to patterns of malnutrition and infection (Engle, 1992, provides a summary). In much of this work, the measurement of beliefs and especially their realization in feeding behavior provides only a general characterization of the community, although there are exceptions. More useful still, from a theoretical point of view, is Zeitlin's conceptualization of "positive deviance" (Zeitlin, Ghassemi, & Mansour, 1990) as intra-cultural variation in mothers' beliefs that yield differing developmental outcomes for children even in the face of similar sociocultural and economic circumstances (see also Dasen & Super, 1988). Engle and her colleagues (Engle, Zeitlin, Medrano, & Garcia, 1996) have pursued this line of thinking in their study of Nicaraguan mothers' beliefs about infant feeding practices, as they relate to maternal feeding practices and children's nutritional status. They demonstrate that mothers who have more "active" feeding beliefs—contrary to the dominant culture—have children who have better developmental status. It was difficult in the Engle et al. study to demonstrate the direct behavioral routes for this effect, although a related study in

Bangladesh was more successful in this regard (Zeitlin, Super, Beiser, Gulden, Ahmed, Ahmed, & Sockalingham, 1990).

Thus, as several scholars (e.g., Bornstein et al., 1992; McGillicuddy-De Lisi, 1985) have suggested, the developmental effects of cultural belief systems may derive from a variety of specific practices as they relate to and reinforce each other over time. Our analysis of the "three R's" of Dutch childrearing and the socialization of infant states of arousal demonstrates this principle (Super, Harkness, van Tijen, van der Vlugt, Dykstra, & Fintelman, 1996). The "three R's"—a widely shared belief in the importance of *rust* (rest), *regelmaat* (regularity), and *reinheid* (cleanliness)—are instantiated in a diverse but culturally meaningful constellation of practices, including the imposition of generous sleep regimens, maintenance of regular bedtimes, and a lower level of interpersonal stimulation (e.g., touching and talking to the baby), when compared to U.S. practices. Evidently as a result of these differences, the Dutch babies they studied, compared to an American sample, slept more and in longer bouts, and they were calmer while awake.

All of this research demonstrates that the cultural structuring of child development is a function of coordinated systems of settings, beliefs, and behavior rather than being predictable from specific kinds of isolated environmental inputs. As just mentioned, parental ethnotheories probably play a special role in the coordination through their directive qualities. This insight from culturally comparative research applies as well to monocultural studies (some of which assume that individual differences are uniquely personal rather than organized within that culture). It might be applied, for example, to Scarr's (1985) demonstration that children's developmental outcomes are better predicted by maternal education and vocabulary knowledge than by observed parenting behaviors. That is, it may well be that parental education, in this context, is a meaningful index to belief systems that can, in turn, be instantiated through a variety of specific practices; the practices themselves, in contrast, may not be associated with developmental outcomes unless they are connected to other practices and environmental features in culturally meaningful ways. Thus to understand how children's development is shaped by their cultural environments, there is a need to consider the organization of the environment itself as a system. In recent years, several researchers have attempted to accomplish this heuristic goal through the elaboration of theoretical frameworks for understanding the child's developmental or ecocultural niche, and it is to these that we now turn.

Integrative Frameworks

The foregoing review of current research and its historical antecedents has focused on three distinctive but complementary conceptualizations of the cultural environment as it relates to the developing child: As a social setting for daily life; as a collection of customary practices that convey messages to the child; and as a reality fashioned by the caretakers' shared beliefs about children and child care. We have pointed out that each of these bodies of research provides a critical perspective on the larger problem of culture and individual development. It is also evident, however, that each neglects important insights, and further that none of them accommodates sufficiently two core issues that are well articulated in the broader disciplines of social anthropology and developmental psychology. These are, respectively, the integration of various elements in the child's cultural environment with each other and with the wider cultural ecology; and endogenous aspects of individual development that necessarily alter the specifics of the individual–environment interactions.

There have been several attempts in recent years to formulate a model that highlights these issues, both in order to understand the cultural regulation of development, and also to guide future research. The three models to be discussed— Weisner's ecocultural niche, Worthman's developmental microniche, and our conceptualization of developmental niche—vary in their focus, but each of them emphasizes the structured, dynamic and integrative nature of the environment.

The Ecocultural Niche

The ecocultural model used by Weisner and his colleagues (Gallimore, Goldenberg, & Weisner, 1993; Weisner, 1984; Weisner, in press; Weisner, Gallimore, & Jordan, 1988; Weisner, Matheson, & Bernheimer, 1996) draws on all three research traditions reviewed earlier. They emphasize "the activities and practices of the daily routine as the locus for contextual influence" (Weisner, in press: 5), and suggest that "activity settings are in part social constructions of the participants"; thus "the subjective and objective are intertwined [and] are the setting for the individual" (Gallimore, Goldenberg, & Weisner, 1993, p. 541). To this integration the model contributes a unique emphasis on the task of family adaptation in constructing daily routines, and it identifies twelve ecocultural domains (such as family domestic workload, supports for mothers, gender role training, and peer and child activity groups) that constitute resources and constraints in that task. This model has been used to examine family interventions, the home–school interface, families with developmentally delayed children, and families who intentionally adopt nonconventional childrearing values and practices (Bernheimer, Gallimore, & Weisner, 1990; Gallimore & Goldenberg, 1993; Gallimore, Goldenberg, & Weisner, 1993; Weisner & Garnier, 1992; Weisner, Matheson, & Bernheimer, 1996). Methodologically, Weisner and his colleagues have emphasized that to understand how cultural-level factors influence the lives of individuals, it is necessary to identify and observe at least five constituent factors (stated here in the context of their research on learning: Weisner, Gallimore, & Jordan, 1988, p. 329):

1. The *personnel* present who teach and influence children; their availability in activities throughout the child's daily routine.
2. The *motivations* of the actors.
3. *Cultural scripts for conduct* commonly used by participants in teaching/learning contexts that arise in natal [i.e., home] cultural and school settings.

4. The nature of *tasks and activities in the daily routine*, and the frequency and distribution of their performance.
5. The *cultural goals and beliefs* of those present in the activity setting.

Through assessment of these factors using interviews and behavior observations, researchers have demonstrated that Hawaiian children, in their natal settings, spontaneously produced most literacy-related behavior during child-generated activities carried on without adult supervision, and correspondingly, classroom learning activities that were successful with these children were child-generated interactions "in which children are able to use scripts similar to those observed in natal settings" (Weisner, Gallimore, & Jordan, 1988, p. 327). In contrast, most other activities in the home context were found to be dissimilar to classroom activities. The topic of school success in children whose home cultures differ from the "culture of the classroom" has received considerable attention in recent years (e.g., Eldering & Leseman, 1993; Mistry & Martini, 1993; Serpell, 1993; see also Brislin & Horvath, Volume 3 of this *Handbook*), and the ecocultural approach described here has been successful in identifying and describing many of the cultural issues related to children's learning.

The Developmental Microniche

The developmental microniche has recently been introduced as an organizing concept by Worthman (1994; 1995; Worthman, Stallings, & Jenkins, 1993) in order to model relationships of biology, behavior, and culture in shaping human development. Physical development is the primary outcome in Worthman's application of the microniche idea, and she points out that most models of growth treat environmental features as "traits" of the individual child. Rejecting this theoretical limitation, Worthman posits the microniche as a "spatiotemporal envelope of states and conditions experienced in the course of development" (Worthman, 1994, p. 210). This enables her to consider contextual variables as dynamic, shaped by both exogenous and endogenous factors. The latter factors—growth dynamics within the individual child—are generally neglected in the kind of studies reviewed in this chapter, often because of the deliberate focus on cultural factors. Worthman's work, however, highlights qualitative transformations in developmental patterns due to the interaction (not just "exchange") between individual characteristics and cultural reality. In a study of Hagahai (New Guinea) adolescents, for example, Worthman, Stallings, and Jenkins (1993) demonstrate the importance of examining the specific biosocial environment assigned to individuals rather than taking general measures of the environmental quality. They found that the relative nutritional and developmental status of adolescents in some highland areas shifted when health services were introduced: the status of boys improved, while that of girls deteriorated as sex-biased care and differential use of parental resources increased. Within the same general context, therefore, boys and girls came to occupy different specific environments because of the way their personal characteristics (gender) led to the organization of their microniches.

The Developmental Niche

The developmental niche is a theoretical framework generated specifically to foster integration of concepts and findings from multiple disciplines concerned with the development of children in cultural context (Harkness & Super, 1992a; Super & Harkness, 1986a). Two overarching principles reflect its origins in social anthropology and developmental psychology: First, that a child's environment is organized in a non-arbitrary manner as part of a cultural system, including contingencies and variable flexibility, thematic repetitions, and systems of meaning; and second, that the child has an inborn disposition, including a particular constellation of temperament and skill potentials as well as species-specific potentials for growth, transformation, and the organization of experience into meaning. Both the environment and the individual are seen as open systems in the formal sense, that is, ones that participate in structured interchanges with external systems.

At the center of the developmental niche (see Figure 1–1) is the individual child. In one sense the niche can be described only for a single child with his or her particular set of inherited dispositions and family composition; thus it can be usefully applied to the clinical analysis of developmental psychopathology (Super &

FIGURE 1–1   A schematic representation of the developmental niche

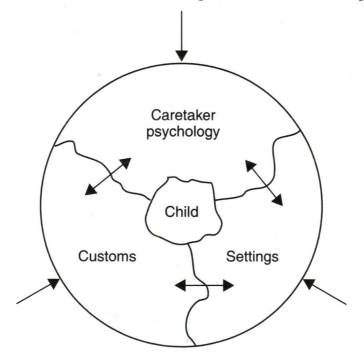

Harkness, 1993). Nevertheless, the framework is equally useful in deriving a generalized description of the recurring patterns within a single cultural community, and that is the sense in which it is applied here. Surrounding the child are the three major subsystems of the developmental niche:

Subsystem 1: The physical and social settings in which the child lives. As reviewed above, the people who frequent the settings of a child's daily life influence the kind of interactions in which the child has the opportunity and the need to participate. Similarly, the physical setting provides a particular combination of dangers and affordances (Super, 1987). Opportunities to enter or leave particular settings are a major structuring feature of the culture, as life-course theorists have noted (and as Valsiner and Lawrence discuss in this volume).

Subsystem 2: The culturally regulated customs of child care and childrearing. Customs in this sense are sequences of behavior or institutional arrangements so commonly used by members of the community and so thoroughly integrated into the larger culture that individuals need not particularly rationalize them. They usually seem to members of the culture as obvious and natural solutions to everyday problems, developmental requirements, or social needs.

Subsystem 3: The psychology of the caretakers. This component includes parental ethnotheories of child behavior and development as well as the affective orientations that parents bring to their experience of parenting. Most important among the ethnotheories are beliefs concerning the nature and needs of children, parental and community goals for rearing, and shared understandings about effective rearing techniques.

These three subsystems share the common function of mediating the individual's developmental experience within the larger culture. Of particular significance for integrating research on these individual components are three corollaries that derive in part from the two overarching principles indicated earlier:

Corollary 1: The three components of the developmental niche operate together with powerful though incomplete coordination as a system. There are homeostatic mechanisms that promote consonance among elements of the niche, but typically there are also inconsistencies so that internal dynamics as well as external influences can be a force for change. In principle, one would expect that parents and communities would arrange daily care and activities for children that are consistent with beliefs and goals, and that such care would be customary under conditions of relative stability in a society. However, parents rarely have adequate resources and freedom to achieve this state fully.

Corollary 2: Each of the three subsystems of the niche is functionally embedded in other aspects of the human ecology in specific and unique ways; in other words, the three subsystems act as the primary channels through which the niche, as an open system, is influenced by outside forces. Connections between subsystems of the niche, on the one hand, and outside systems, on the other, may be most evident under conditions of change. This corollary indicates that any one of the three components may be a primary route of influence. Economic or social change may lead to new settings for children; religious persuasion, scientific discovery, personal experience, or didactic instruction in "parenting" may alter caretakers' ethnotheories; and new customs may emerge in response to new technology or intercultural contact. Any such change will likely cause instability in the niche and activate internal adjustments as indicated in Corollary 1.

Corollary 3: Each of the three subsystems of the niche is involved in a process of mutual adaptation with the individual child. The child's adaptation to the environment has long been explored under the topic of socialization, but there is a complementary environmental adaptation in which the child's personal qualities such as age, sex, abilities, personality, and temperament influence the parents and other actors in the niche. The general principle of mutuality has been made widely in psychology over the past two decades (see Camilleri & Malewska-Peyre, this volume), and has been most powerfully applied in theories of environment-genetic interaction through shared and non-shared environments (Plomin, Chipuer, & Neiderhiser, in press; Scarr & McCartney, 1983).

The developmental niche framework has been used by several scholars to direct their research efforts and to construct an explanation for similarities and divergences in development in different cultural settings. In the Kenyan study for which it was originally developed, it has proven useful in the domains of motor skills (Super, 1976, 1981), emotional expression (Harkness & Super, 1983, 1985; Super & Harkness, 1982), cognitive development (Super, 1991), goodness of fit between child temperament and environmental demands (Super & Harkness, 1986b, 1993, 1994), and health risks for infectious disease (Super, Keefer, & Harkness, 1994). More generally, it has been applied by ourselves and others to language development (Blount, 1990; Harkness, 1988, 1990), literacy (Harkness & Super, 1993), mathematical skills (Pellegrini & Stanic, 1993), patterns of developmental dysfunction (Super, 1987), and the household production of health (Harkness & Super, 1992a). Gauvain (1995) has elaborated portions of the approach to focus on cognitive development in diverse settings, and Eldering (in press) has applied it to the study of immigrant children and families.

The Systematic Power of Culture

Each of the corollaries specified in the developmental niche framework reflects an important characteristic of the cultural structuring of development. When several of these principles are seen to operate together, however, the systematic power of culture becomes evident. Corollary 3, regarding the environment's responsiveness to individual differences, simply reiterates a principle already established in monocultural studies of development. The other two corollaries, however, suggest that any pattern of differential responsiveness will reflect both the specific links between the niche's subsystems and the larger cultural ecology, and also the relationships among the three subsystems. In this light, the pattern of environmental adaptation to individual differences is seen to be itself a construct of culture and can be expected to vary.

Chen and his colleagues provide one example in their comparative study of peer relationships in Canada and China. In their Shanghai sample, they found that shyness (as opposed to social boldness) in 8- and 10-year-old children is associated with higher peer acceptance and positive teacher ratings of competence, opposite to the relationship generally found in European and North American settings (Chen, Rubin, & Sun, 1992). At age 12, however, the relationship in their Chinese sample reversed in part, such that shyness-sensitivity became associated with peer rejection (Chen, Rubin, & Li, 1995), consistent with findings in Western samples. The authors explain the initial difference with reference to the positive evaluation in Chinese culture generally of the soft-spoken, well-mannered, school-achieving child, while the later similarity across samples may reflect a declining influence of adult social standards, compared to the influence of peers. Thus the differential responsiveness of the developmental niche in the Chinese and Canadian contexts is constructed by a combination of the values and beliefs of the teachers and peers, their customary responses to desirable and undesirable behavior, and the change with age in the dominant and valued settings. Other examples are provided by Super and Harkness (Harkness & Super, 1990; Super & Harkness, 1994), concerning differential consequences of irregular temperament in infancy in rural Africa and metropolitan America; by deVries (1984), concerning survival rates of infants under conditions of drought and famine among the Masai; by Korn and Gannon (1983), concerning adjustment patterns of Puerto Rican and white American children in New York City; and by van den Boom (1991), concerning Dutch and American mothers' patterns of interaction with irritable babies. In all these cases, components of the niche and their interrelations influence the pattern of environmental response to, and hence the developmental consequences of, individual differences in temperament. A similar analysis can be carried out for differential responsiveness to gender, as illustrated by the New Guinea study cited previously (Worthman, Stallings, & Jenkins, 1993) and a large literature on gender differences in malnutrition, morbidity, and mortality in many parts of north India and Bangladesh. In a broader framework, young females are known to suffer unusually high rates of malnutrition, morbidity, and mortality, compared to young males in many areas of north India and Bangladesh; ethnographic, observational, and other evidence demonstrates the social settings, customs of care, and social beliefs and values that create the phenomenon (see, for example, Das Gupta, 1987).

In these and other examples, the power of the culturally regulated environment (whether differential or not) comes from the coordinated action of the three subsystems of the niche, that is, from how actions of the three subsystems relate to each other, to outside forces, and to the individual child. These aspects of development in context cannot be accounted for by models of the environment that overlook its systematic structure, or by individualistic models of the child. It is the coordination of settings, customary practices, and caretaker psychology that create the cultural structuring of child development.

Themes and Prospects

This review has focused primarily on recent theory and research related to three distinctive conceptualizations of culture's influence on child development, and has described efforts by ourselves and others to forge a new, more powerful framework based on a synthesis of several approaches. Three recurring themes emerge from this review, issues that have been of concern to many scholars and that we believe will continue to occupy a central place in the work that lies ahead: how best to conceptualize variability within and across cultural settings, to characterize activities of the child's mind, and to improve methodological rigor in research in culture and development.

Variability within and across cultural settings is at the heart of the matter. Converging evidence from several traditions suggests both unique aspects of each cultural configuration, and also supra-cultural dimensions of contrast. We are still only beginning to understand the nature of cross-cultural variation, and some suggested dimensions of contrast (e.g., sociocentric versus individualistic) capture important differences. We also have knowledge of how some features, such as social class or patterns of experience, create a basis for similarity and contrast. There remains much to do, however, before we fully understand these systematic differences and can conceptualize them in a way that is universally applicable. Likewise, the understanding of intra-cultural variation is an important but not yet achieved goal. This is true regarding how we conceptualize differences between cultural settings as children move among them (e.g., home and school, migration) and also individual variability within a cultural framework. Wallace's (1961) oft-cited statement that one role of culture is to organize internal variation remains an unmet challenge to research. Can we find efficient ways to characterize the cross-cultural differences in internal variation? The research on "positive deviance," already discussed, can make a significant contribution to this quest in that "positive deviants" do not differ from the dominant ethos of their culture in idiosyncratic or accidental ways; rather, it seems likely that their ideas and behavior represent departures that are systematically framed in terms of locally constructed cultural understandings. Both kinds of variability—within and between cultures—will remain high on the research agenda, for they hold keys to fundamental issues in human behavior.

A second theme that emerges from our review is the idea of the child as an active learner, engaged in receiving and somehow assimilating information from the environment, and also influencing the cultural surround. There is a high level of consensus among researchers from varying traditions that an active child is essential to conceptualizing child–environment interactions, regardless of the specific metaphor used. But exactly how this process takes place, and what specific regularities in the environment form the basis of the child's learning, will be the object of discussion and research for some time to come. This effort will be enhanced by the now generally shared recognition that cultural meaning systems, although elusive, are a critical reality that must be taken into account in order to understand the child. Part of the challenge is to include in our understanding a recognition that there is also internally organized change ("development") going on in the actively learning child.

The third theme that emerges from our consideration of the literature is methodological: settings, practices, and ethnotheories can all provide useful points of entry to research on the cultural structuring of child development. Researchers have varied considerably, however, in the extent to which their work incorporates systematic information on all three aspects of children's environments. Frameworks such as the developmental niche remind us to look in all subsystems as well as to examine their interrelationships, for these are often the source of culture's influence. Research methods, both qualitative and quantitative, from several traditions are needed to accomplish this, but the increase in rigor and explanatory power should justify the effort. The influence of parental ideas on mother–child interaction can really only be demonstrated by using data on the ideas of the mothers who are observed; likewise, interpretations of children's behavior in particular interactional settings can be more persuasively related to aspects of their daily lives if both behavior and settings are systematically studied for the same children. Comparative studies remind us that even in our own cultures we too often assume we know—or we overlook entirely—what kinds of settings, customs, and ideas characterize our children's lives. In this sense we cannot understand the development of our own children until we can understand the children of others.

An emerging challenge for cultural studies of development, one that must be described as a prospect, not yet a theme, is to focus on applications of the cultural perspective to improving the lives of children in our changing world. As a few examples cited in this review illustrate, delineating cultural factors in development can often reveal places or moments for effective intervention. This is true as young children move from home to school, as their families migrate to cities or other countries, and in the campaigns for improved health behaviors in the home. Such studies also return exceptional contributions to our general understanding; as previously noted, conditions of change often make visible the dynamics of cultural structuring not easily seen otherwise.

There is a progression over the past few decades in the research on culture and human development, regardless of theoretical orientation, that is worth a final comment. In the 1960s and early 1970s the major contribution of comparative research was to demonstrate what kinds of variations in behavior and development existed beyond the then traditional research sphere of middle-class Euro-Americans and Europeans. In the following decade theoretical attention turned appropriately to questions of causality, or independent variables, and broad, inclusive dimensions of cultural variation were examined for their covariation with group differences in developmental outcome. More recently the existence of profound cultural regulation of development has become widely accepted and most of the studies reviewed here have been concerned with how such regulation takes place. In this context, and related to more general theoretical change, all manner of assumptions have been questioned and new perspectives added. By focusing on the process of development we have come closer to reframing and resolving historical debates about culture and mind. It remains the case, however, that part of what we are doing is relearning what we—or more often, someone in another discipline—already knew. An important contribution to the full enterprise reviewed here, therefore, will be continued efforts to transcend the disciplinary barriers that make it difficult for scholars to understand the methods and knowledge that have been contributed already. Each part of our science makes most sense in the context of contributions from other methods and perspectives; as in *Hamlet*, the meaning derives from how the pieces fit together. Only when the whole scene is laid before us, with all the players present, do we have a story to tell.

References

Abbott, S. (1992). Holding on and pushing away: Comparative perspectives on an Eastern Kentucky child-rearing practice. *Ethos, 20,* 33–65.

Bernheimer, L. P., Gallimore, R., & Weisner, T. S. (1990). Ecocultural theory as a context for the Individual Family Service Plan. *Journal of Early Intervention, 14,* 219–233.

Berry, J. W. (1975). An ecological approach to cross-cultural psychology. *Nederlands Tijdschrift voor de Psychologie, 30,* 51–84.

Berry, J. W. (1995). The descendents of a model. *Culture & Psychology, 1,* 373–380.

Berry, J. W. & Bennett, J. A. (1992). Cree conceptions of cognitive competence. *International Journal of Psychology, 27,* 1–16.

Berry, J.W., Poortinga, Y. H., Segall, M. H., & Dasen, P. R. (1992). *Cross-cultural psychology: Research and applications.* New York: Cambridge University Press.

Berry, J. W., van de Koppel, J. Sénéchal, C., Annis, R., Bahuchet, S., Cavalli-Sforza, L. & Witkin, H. (1986). *On the edge of the forest: Cultural adaptations and cognitive development in Central Africa.* Lisse: Swets & Zeitlinger.

Blount, B. (1982). Culture and the language of socialization: Parental speech. In D. A. Wagner & H. W. Stevenson (Eds.), *Cultural perspectives on child development* (pp. 54–76). San Francisco: Freeman.

Blount, B. (1990). Parental speech and language acquisition: An anthropological perspective. *Pre- and Perinatal Psychology, 4,* 319–337.

Bornstein, M. H., Tamis-LeMonda, C. S., Tal, J., Ludemann, P., Toda, S., Rahn, C. W., Pecheux, M., Azuma, H., & Vardi, D. (1992). Maternal responsiveness to infants in three societies: The United States, France, and Japan. *Child Development, 63,* 808–821.

Borstelmann, L. J. (1983). Children before psychology: Ideas about children from antiquity to the late 1800s. In W. Kessen (Ed.), *Handbook of child psychology, volume 1: History, theory, and methods (fourth edition)* (pp. 1–40). New York: John Wiley & Sons.

Bourdieu, P. (1977). *Outline of a theory of practice.* New York: Cambridge University Press.

Bril, B. & Lehalle, H. (1988). *Le développement psychologique est-il universel? Approches interculturelles.* Paris: Presses Universitaires de France.

Bril, B. & Sabatier, C. (1986). The cultural context of motor development: postural manipulations in the daily life of Bambara babies (Mali). *International Journal of Behavioral Development, 9,* 439–453.

Bril, B., Zack, M., & Hombessa-Nkounkou, E. (1989). Ethnotheories of development and education: A view from different cultures. *European Journal of Psychology of Education, 4,* 721–735.

Caudill, W. & Plath, D. W. (1966). Who sleeps by whom? Parent–child involvement in urban Japanese families. *Psychiatry, 29,* 344–366.

Caudill, W. & Weinstein, J. (1969). Maternal care and infant behavior in Japan and America. *Psychiatry, 32,* 12–43.

Chen, X., Rubin, K. H., & Li, Z. (1995). Social functioning and adjustment in Chinese children: A longitudinal study. *Developmental Psychology, 31,* 531–540.

Chen, X., Rubin, K. H., & Sun, Y. (1992). Social reputation and peer relationships in Chinese and Canadian children: A cross-cultural study. *Child Development, 63,* 1336–1343.

Cole, M. (1995). The supra-individual envelope of development: Activity and practice, situation and context. In J. J. Goodnow, P. J. Miller & F. Kessel (Eds.), *Cultural practices as contexts for development. New Directions for Child Development, Vol. 67* (pp. 105–118). San Francisco: Jossey-Bass.

Cole, M. (in press). *Culture in mind.* Cambridge, MA: Harvard University Press.

Cole, M., Gay, J., Glick, J. S., & Sharp, D. W. (1971). *The cultural context of learning and thinking.* New York: Basic Books.

D'Andrade, R. G. (1987). A folk model of the mind. In D. Holland & N. Quinn (Eds.), *Cultural models in language and thought* (pp. 112–148). New York: Cambridge University Press.

D'Andrade, R. G. (1992). Schemas and motivation. In R. G. D'Andrade & C. Strauss (Eds.), *Human motives and cultural models* (pp. 23–44). Cambridge: Cambridge University Press.

Das Gupta, M. (1987). Selective discrimination against female children in rural Punjab, India. *Population Development Review, 13,* 77–100.

Dasen, P. R., Dembélé, B., Ettien, K., Kabran, K., Kamagate, D., Koffi, D. A., & N'Guessan, A. (1985). N'glouêlé, l'intelligence chez les Baoulé [N'glouêlé, intelligence among the Baoulé]. *Archives de Psychologie, 53,* 295–324.

Dasen, P. R. & Super, C. M. (1988). The usefulness of a cross-cultural approach in studies of malnutrition and psychological development. In P. R. Dasen, J. Berry, & N. Sartorius (Eds.), *Health and cross-cultural psychology: Towards applications* (pp. 112–139). Newbury Park: Sage.

deVries, M. W. (1984). Temperament and infant mortality among the Masai of East Africa. *American Journal of Psychiatry, 141,* 1189–1194.

Edwards, C. P., Gandini, L., & Giovaninni, D. (1996). The contrasting developmental timetables of parents and preschool teachers in two cultural communities. In S. Harkness & C. M. Super (Eds.), *Parents' cultural belief systems: Their origins, expressions, and consequences* (pp. 270–288). New York: Guilford Press.

Eldering, L. (in press). Child rearing in bicultural settings: A cultural ecological approach. *Psychology and Developing Societies: A Journal.*

Eldering, L. & Leseman, P. (Eds.). (1993). *Early intervention and culture: Preparation for literacy— the interface between theory and practice.* The Hague: UNESCO Publishing.

Engle, P. L. (1992). *Care and child nutrition* [Theme paper presented at International Nutrition Conference]. New York: UNICEF.

Engle, P. L. Zeitlin, M., Medrano, Y., & Garcia M., L. (1996). Growth consequences of low-income Nicaraguan mothers' theories about feeding 1-year-olds. In S. Harkness & C. M. Super (Eds.), *Parents' cultural belief systems: Their origins, expressions, and consequences* (pp. 428–446). New York: Guilford.

Fortes, M. (1938/1970). Social and psychological aspects of education in Taleland. *Africa* (Supplement to Vol. 11). Reprinted in J. Middleton (Ed.), 1970, *From child to adult: Studies in the anthropology of education* (pp. 14–74). New York: The Natural History Press.

Gallimore, R. & Goldenberg, C. (1993). Activity settings of early literacy: Home and school factors in children's emergent literacy. In E. Forman, N. Minick & C. A. Stone (Eds.), *Contexts for learning: Sociocultural dynamics in children's development* (pp. 315–335). Oxford: Oxford University Press.

Gallimore, R., Goldenberg, C. N., & Weisner, T. S. (1993). The social construction and subjective reality of activity settings: Implications for community psychology. *American Journal of Community Psychology, 21,* 537–559.

Gauvain, M. (1995). Thinking in niches: Sociocultural influences on cognitive development. *Human Development, 38,* 25–45.

Gilbert, A. J., Nkwinti, G., & van Vlaenderen, H. (submitted for publication). *Planting pumpkins: Socialization and the role of local knowledge in rural South Africa.*

Goodnow, J. J. (1990). The socialization of cognition: What's involved? In J. W. Stigler, R. A. Shweder & G. Herdt (Eds.), *Cultural psychol-*

ogy: Essays on comparative human development (pp. 259–286). Cambridge: Cambridge University Press.

Goodnow, J. J. (1996). From household practices to parents' ideas about work and interpersonal relationships. In S. Harkness & C. M. Super (Eds.), *Parents' cultural belief systems: Their origins, expressions, and consequences* (pp. 313–344). New York: Guilford Press.

Goodnow, J. J., Cashmore, J. A., Cotton, S., & Knight, R. (1984). Mothers' developmental timetables in two cultural groups. *International Journal of Psychology, 19,* 193–205.

Goodnow, J. J., & Collins, W. A. (1990). *Development according to parents: The nature, sources, and consequences of parents' ideas.* London: Erlbaum.

Greenfield, P. M. (1994). Independence and interdependence as developmental scripts: Implications for theory, research, and practice. In P. M. Greenfield & R. R. Cocking (Eds.), *Cross-cultural roots of minority child development* (pp. 1–37). Hillsdale, NJ: Erlbaum.

Greenfield, P. & Lave, J. (1982). Cognitive aspects of informal education. In D. A. Wagner & H. W. Stevenson (Eds.), *Cultural perspectives on child development* (pp. 181–207). San Francisco: Freeman.

Harkness, S. (1988). The cultural construction of semantic contingency in mother–child speech. *Language Sciences, 10,* 53–67.

Harkness, S. (1990). A cultural model for the acquisition of language: Implications for the innateness debate. *Developmental Psychobiology, 27,* 727–740.

Harkness, S. (1992). Human development in psychological anthropology. In T. Schwartz, G. M. White, & C. A. Lutz (Eds.), *New directions in psychological anthropology* (pp. 102–121). New York: Cambridge University Press.

Harkness, S. & Super, C. M. (1977). Why African children are so hard to test. In L. L. Adler (Ed.), *Cross-cultural research at issue* (pp. 145–152). New York: Academic Press.

Harkness, S. & Super, C. M. (1983). The cultural construction of child development: A framework for the socialization of affect. *Ethos, 11,* 221–231.

Harkness, S. & Super, C. M. (1985). Child-environ-ment transactions in the socialization of affect. In M. Lewis & C. Saarni (Eds.), *The socialization of emotions* (pp. 21–36). New York: Plenum.

Harkness, S. & Super, C. M. (1987). The uses of cross-cultural research in child development. *Annals of Child Development, 4,* 209–244.

Harkness, S. & Super, C. M. (1990). Culture and psychopathology. In M. Lewis & S. Miller (Eds.), *Handbook of developmental psychopathology* (pp. 41–52). New York: Plenum.

Harkness, S. & Super, C. M. (1992a). The developmental niche: A theoretical framework for analyzing the household production of health. *Social Science and Medicine, 38,* 217–226.

Harkness, S. & Super, C. M. (1992b). Parental ethnotheories in action. In I. E. Sigel, A. V. McGillicuddy-De Lisi & J. J. Goodnow (Eds.), *Parental belief systems: The psychological consequences for children* (2nd ed.) (pp. 373–392). Hillsdale, NJ: Erlbaum.

Harkness, S. & Super, C. M. (1993). The developmental niche: Implications for children's literacy development. In L. Eldering & P. Leseman (Eds.), *Early intervention and culture: Preparation for literacy* (pp. 115–132). Paris: UNESCO.

Harkness, S. & Super, C. M. (1996). Introduction. In S. Harkness & C. M. Super (Eds.), *Parents' cultural belief systems: Their origins, expressions, and consequences* (pp. 1–24). New York: Guilford.

Harkness, S., Super, C. M., & Keefer, C. H. (1992). Learning to be an American parent: How cultural models gain directive force. In R. G. D'Andrade & C. Strauss (Eds.), *Human motives and cultural models* (pp. 163–178). New York: Cambridge University Press.

Harkness, S., Super, C. M., Keefer, C., Raghavan, C., & Kipp-Campbell, E. (1996). Ask the doctor: The negotiation of cultural models in American parent-pediatrician discourse. In S. Harkness & C. M. Super (Eds.), *Parents' cultural belief systems: Sociocultural origins and developmental consequences* (pp. 289–310). New York: Guilford.

Harwood, R. L., Miller, J. G., & Irizarry, N. L. (1995). *Culture and attachment: Perceptions of the child in context.* New York: Guilford.

Hess, R. D., Kashiwagi, K., Azuma, H., Price, G. G., & Dickinson, W. P. (1980). Maternal expectations for mastery of developmental tasks in Japan and the United States. *International Journal of Psychology, 15*, 259–271.

Hopkins, B. & Westra, T. (1989). Maternal expectations and motor development: Some cultural differences. *Developmental Medicine and Child Neurology, 31*, 384–390.

Hutchins, E. (1980). *Culture and inference: A Trobriand case study.* Cambridge:,MA: Harvard University Press.

Jahoda, G. (1993). *Crossroads between culture and mind: Continuities and change in theories of human nature.* London: Harvester Wheatsheaf.

Keller, H., Miranda, D., & Gauda, G. (1984). The naive theory of the infant and some maternal attitudes: A two-country study. *Journal of Cross-Cultural Psychology, 15*, 165–179.

Korn, S. J. & Gannon, S. (1983). Temperament, cultural variation and behavior disorder in preschool children. *Child Psychiatry and Human Development, 13*, 203–212.

Lancy, D. F. (in press). *Playing on the mother ground: Cultural routines for children's development.* New York: Guilford.

Lave, J. (1990). The culture of acquisition and the practice of understanding. In J. W. Stigler, R. A. Shweder & G. Herdt (Eds.), *Cultural psychology: Essays on comparative human development* (pp. 309–327). Cambridge: Cambridge University Press.

LeVine, R. A. (1973). *Culture, behavior, and personality.* Chicago: Aldine.

LeVine, R. A. (1974). Parental goals: A cross-cultural view. *Teachers College Record, 76*, 226–239.

LeVine, R. A., Dixon, S., LeVine, S., Richman, A., Leiderman, P. H., Keefer, C. H., & Brazelton, T. B. (1994). *Child care and culture: Lessons from Africa.* Cambridge: Cambridge University Press.

LeVine, R. A., Miller, P. M., Richman, A. L., & LeVine, S. (1996). Education and mother–infant interaction: A Mexican case study. In S. Harkness & C. M. Super (Eds.), *Parents' cultural belief systems: Their origins, expressions, and consequences* (pp. 254–269). New York: Guilford.

LeVine, R. A., Miller, P. M., & West, M. M. (Eds.). (1988). *Parental behavior in diverse societies. New Directions for Child Development, Vol. 40.* San Francisco: Jossey-Bass.

Levy, R. (1996). Essential contrasts: Differences in parental ideas about learners and teaching in Tahiti and Nepal. In S. Harkness & C. M. Super (Eds.), *Parents' cultural belief systems: Their origins, expressions, and consequences* (pp. 123–142). New York: Guilford.

Lightfoot, C. & Valsiner, J. (1992). Parental belief systems under the influence: Social guidance of the construction of personal cultures. In I. E. Sigel, A. V. McGillicuddy-De Lisi & J. J. Goodnow (Eds.), *Parental belief systems: The psychological consequences for children* (2nd Ed.) (pp. 393–414). Hillsdale, NJ: Erlbaum.

McGillicuddy-De Lisi, A. (1985). The relationship between parental beliefs and children's cognitive level. In I. E. Sigel (Ed.), *Parental belief systems: The psychological consequences for children* (pp. 7–24). Hillsdale, NJ: Erlbaum.

Mead, M. (1972). *Blackberry winter: My earlier years.* New York: Simon & Schuster.

Miller, J. G. & Bersoff, D. M. (in press). Development in the context of everyday family relationships: Culture, interpersonal morality and adaptation. In M. Killen & D. Hart (Eds.), *Morality in everyday life: A developmental perspective.* Cambridge: Cambridge University Press.

Miller, P. J. & Goodnow, J. J. (1995). Cultural practices: Toward an integration of culture and development. In J. J. Goodnow, P. J. Miller & F. Kessel (Eds.), *Cultural practices as contexts for development. New Directions for Child Development*, vol. 67 (pp. 5–16). San Francisco: Jossey-Bass.

Miller, P. J. & Hoogstra, L. (1992). Language as tool in the socialization and apprehension of cultural meanings. In T. Schwartz, G. M. White & C. A. Lutz (Eds.), *New directions in psychological anthropology* (pp. 83–101). Cambridge: Cambridge University Press.

Miller, P. J. & Moore, B. B. (1989). Narrative conjunctions of caregiver and child: A comparative perspective on socialization through stories. *Ethos, 17*, 428–449.

Minturn, L. & Lambert, W. W. (1964). *Mothers of six cultures: Antecedents of child rearing.* New York: Wiley.

Mistry, J. & Martini, M. (1993). Preschool activities as occasions for literate discourse. In R. Roberts (Ed.), *Coming home to preschool: The socio-cultural context of early education. Advances in Applied Developmental Psychology,* Vol. 7 (pp. 220–245). New York: Ablex.

Morelli, G. A., Rogoff, B., Oppenheim, D., & Goldsmith, D. (1992). Cultural variation in infants' sleeping arrangements: Questions of independence. *Developmental Psychology, 28,* 604–613.

Munroe, R. H. & Munroe, R. L. (1971). Household density and infant care in an East African society. *Journal of Social Psychology, 83,* 3–13.

Ninio, A. (1979). The naive theory of the infant and other maternal attitudes in two subgroups in Israel. *Child Development, 50,* 976–980.

Nsamenang, B. (1992). *Human development in cultural context.* Newbury Park, CA: Sage.

Nunes, T. (1995). Cultural practices and the conception of individual differences: Theoretical and empirical considerations. In J. J. Goodnow, P. J. Miller & F. Kessel (Eds.), *Cultural practices as contexts for development. New Directions for Child Development,* Vol. 67 (pp. 91–104). San Francisco: Jossey-Bass.

Ochs, E. & Schieffelin, B. (1984). Language acquisition and socialization: Three developmental stories and their implications. In R. A. Shweder & R. A. LeVine (Eds.), *Culture theory: Essays on mind, self, and emotion* (pp. 276–322). Cambridge: Cambridge University Press.

Palacios, J. & Moreno, M. C. (1996). Parents' and adolescents' ideas on children: Origins and transmission of intracultural diversity. In S. Harkness & C. M. Super (Eds.), *Parents' cultural belief systems: Their origins, expressions, and consequences* (pp. 215–253). New York: Guilford Press.

Pellegrini, A. D., & Stanic, G. M. (1993). Locating children's mathematical competence: Application of the developmental niche. *Journal of Applied Developmental Psychology, 14,* 501–520.

Pepper, S. C. (1942). *World hypotheses: A study in evidence.* Berkeley, CA: University of California Press.

Plomin, R., Chipuer, H. H., & Neiderhiser, J. (in press). Behavioral genetic evidence for the importance of the nonshared environment. In E. M. Hetherington, D. Reiss, & R. Plomin (Eds.), *Separate social worlds of siblings: Impact of the nonshared environment on development.* Hillsdale, NJ: Erlbaum.

Pomerleau, A., Malcuit, G., & Sabatier, C. (1991). Child-rearing practices and parental beliefs in three cultural groups of Montréal: Québécois, Vietnamese, Haitian. In M. H. Bornstein (Ed.), *Cultural approaches to parenting* (pp. 45–68). Hillsdale, NJ: Erlbaum.

Quinn, N., & Holland, D. (1987). Culture and cognition. In D. Holland & N. Quinn (Eds.), *Cultural models in language and thought* (pp. 3–42). Cambridge: Cambridge University Press.

Rabain-Jamin, J. (1994). Language and socialization of the child in African families living in France. In P. M. Greenfield & R. R. Cocking (Eds.), *Cross-cultural roots of minority child development* (pp. 147–166). Hillsdale, NJ: Erlbaum.

Richman, A., Miller, P., & LeVine, R. (1992). Cultural and educational variations in maternal responsiveness. *Developmental Psychology, 28,* 614–621.

Rogoff, B. (1990). *Apprenticeship in thinking: Cognitive development in social context.* New York: Oxford University Press.

Rogoff, B., Baker-Sennett, J., Lacasa, P., & Goldsmith, D. (1995). Development through participation in sociocultural activity. In J. J. Goodnow, P. J. Miller & F. Kessel (Eds.), *Cultural practices as contexts for development. New Directions for Child Development,* Vol. 67 (pp. 45–66). San Francisco: Jossey-Bass.

Rogoff, B., Mistry, J., Göncü, A., & Mosier, C. (1993). *Guided participation in cultural activity by toddlers and caregivers. Monographs of the Society for Research in Child Development,* Vol. 58 (8), (serial no. 236).

Sabatier, C., Pomerleau, A., Malcuit, G., St.-Laurent, C., & Allard, L. (1990). Comment les mères montréalaises se représentent-elles le développement du nourrisson? Une comparaison de trois cultures [Montreal mothers' representation of infant development: A comparative study of three ethnic groups]. In D. Dansereau, B. Terrisse & J. Bouchard (Eds.), *Education familiale et intervention précoce.* [Family education and early intervention.] (pp. 87–102). Montréal: L'Agence d'Arc.

Sameroff, A. J. & Feil, L. A. (1985). Parental concepts of development. In I. E. Sigel (Ed.), *Parental belief systems: The psychological consequences for children* (pp. 83–106). Hillsdale, NJ: Erlbaum.

Saraswathi, T. S. & Dutta, R. (1988). *Invisible boundaries: Grooming for adult roles.* New Delhi: Northern Book Centre.

Saxe, G. (1990). *Culture and cognitive development: Studies in mathematical understanding.* Hillsdale, NJ: Erlbaum.

Scarr, S. (1985). Constructing psychology. *American Psychologist, 40*, 499–512.

Scarr, S. & McCartney, K. (1983). How people make their own environments: A theory of genotype $\rightarrow$ environment effects. *Child Development, 54*, 424–435.

Schieffelin, B. B. (1990). *The give and take of everyday life: The language socialization of Kaluli children.* New York: Cambridge University Press.

Schlegel, A. & Barry, H. III (1991). *Adolescence: An anthropological inquiry.* New York: Free Press.

Schwartz, T. (1981). The acquisition of culture. *Ethos, 9*, 4–17.

Scribner, S. & Cole, M. (1981). *The psychology of literacy.* Cambridge, MA: Harvard University Press.

Serpell, R. (1977). Strategies for investigating intelligence in its cultural context. *Quarterly Newsletter of the Institute for Comparative Human Development, 1*, 11–15.

Serpell, R. (1993). *The significance of schooling: Life-journeys in an African society.* Cambridge: Cambridge University Press.

Seymour, S. (1976). Caste/class and child-rearing in a changing Indian town. *American Ethnologist, 3*, 783–796.

Seymour, S. (1988). Expressions of responsibility among Indian children: Some precursors of adult status and sex roles. *Ethos, 16*, 355–370.

Shweder, R. A. (1982). Beyond self-constructed knowledge: The study of culture and morality. *Merrill-Palmer Quarterly, 28*, 41–69.

Shweder, R. A. (1990). Cultural psychology: What is it? In J. W. Stigler, R. A. Shweder & G. Herdt (Eds.), *Cultural psychology: Essays on compara-*

tive human development (pp. 1–43). Cambridge: Cambridge University Press.

Shweder, R. A., Jensen, L. A., & Goldstein, W. M. (1995). Who sleeps by whom revisited: A method for extracting the moral goods implicit in practice. In J. J. Goodnow, P. J. Miller, & F. Kessel (Eds.), *Cultural practices as contexts for development. New Directions for Child Development,* Vol. 67 (pp. 21–39). San Francisco: Jossey-Bass.

Shweder, R. A., Mahapatra, M., & Miller, J. G. (1990). Culture and moral development. In J. W. Stigler, R. A. Shweder & G. Herdt (Eds.), *Cultural psychology: Essays on comparative human development* (pp. 130–204). Cambridge: Cambridge University Press.

Shweder, R. A. & Much, N. C. (in press). Determinations of meaning: Discourse and moral socialization. In W. Kurtines & J. Gewirtz (Eds.), *Moral development through social interaction.* New York: Wiley.

Sigel, I. E. (Ed.). (1985). *Parental belief systems: The psychological consequences for children.* Hillsdale, NJ: Erlbaum.

Sigel, I. E., McGillicuddy-De Lisi, A., & Goodnow, J. J. (Eds.). (1992). *Parental belief systems: The psychological consequences for children* (2nd Ed.). Hillsdale, NJ: Erlbaum.

Sternberg, R. J., Conway, B. E., Ketron, J. L., & Bernstein, J. (1981). People's conceptions of intelligence. *Journal of Personality and Social Psychology, 41*, 37–55.

Super, C. M. (1976). Environmental effects on motor development: The case of African infant precocity. *Developmental Medicine and Child Neurology, 18*, 561–567.

Super, C. M. (1981). Behavioral development in infancy. In R. H. Munroe, R. L. Munroe, & B. B. Whiting (Eds.), *Handbook of Cross-Cultural Human Development* (pp. 181–270). New York: Garland Press.

Super, C. M. (1983). Cultural variation in the meaning and uses of children's intelligence. In J. G. Deregowski, S. Dziurawiec & R. C. Annis (Eds.), *Explications in cross-cultural psychology* (pp. 199–212). Lisse: Swets & Zeitlinger.

Super, C. M. (1987). The role of culture in developmental disorder: Introduction. In C. M.

Super (Ed.), *The role of culture in developmental disorder* (pp. 1–8). New York: Academic Press.

Super, C. M. (1991). Developmental transitions of cognitive functioning in rural Kenya and metropolitan America. In K. Gibson, M. Konner & J. Lancaster (Eds.), *The brain and behavioral development: Biosocial dimensions* (pp. 225–257). Hawthorne, NY: Aldine.

Super, C. M. & Harkness, S. (1982). The development of affect in infancy and early childhood. In D. A. Wagner & H. W. Stevenson (Eds.), *Cultural perspectives on child development* (pp. 1–19). San Francisco: Freeman.

Super, C. M. & Harkness, S. (1986a). The developmental niche: A conceptualization at the interface of child and culture. *International Journal of Behavioral Development, 9*, 545–569.

Super, C. M. & Harkness, S. (1986b). Temperament, culture, and development. In R. Plomin & J. Dunn (Eds.), *The study of temperament: Changes, continuities, and challenges* (pp. 131–150). Hillsdale, NJ: Erlbaum.

Super, C. M. & Harkness, S. (1993). Temperament and the developmental niche. In W. B. Carey & S. A. McDevitt (Eds.), *Prevention and early intervention: Individual differences as risk factors for the mental health of children—a Festschrift for Stella Chess and Alexander Thomas* (pp. 115–125). New York: Brunner/Mazel.

Super, C. M. & Harkness, S. (1994). The cultural regulation of temperament-environment interactions. *Researching Early Childhood, 2*, 59–84.

Super, C. M., Harkness, S., van Tijen, N., van der Vlugt, E., Dykstra, J., & Fintelman, M. (1996). The three R's of Dutch childrearing and the socialization of infant arousal. In S. Harkness & C. M. Super (Eds.), *Parents' cultural belief systems: Their origins, expressions, and consequences* (pp. 447–466). New York: Guilford Press.

Super, C. M., Keefer, C. H., & & Harkness, S. (1994). Child care and infectious respiratory disease during the first two years of life in a rural Kenyan community. *Social Science and Medicine, 38*, 227–229.

Tronick, E. Z., Morelli, G. A., & Ivey, P. K. (1992). The Efe forager infant and toddler's pattern of social relationships: Multiple and simultaneous. *Developmental Psychology, 28*, 568–577.

van den Boom, D. C. (1991). The influence of infant irritability on the development of the mother–infant relationship in the first 6 months of life. In J. K. Nugent, B. M. Lester & T. B. Brazelton (Eds.), *The cultural context of infancy (Vol. 2)* (pp. 63–89). Norwood, NJ: Ablex.

Wallace, A. F. C. (1961). *Culture and personality.* New York: Random House.

Watson-Gegeo, K. & Gegeo, D. (1977). From verbal play to talk story: The role of routines in speech events among Hawaiian children. In S. Ervin-Tripp & C. Mitchell-Kernan (Eds.), *Child Discourse* (pp. 67–90). New York: Academic Press.

Weisner, T. S. (1984). A cross-cultural perspective: Ecocultural niches of middle childhood. In A. Collins (Ed.), *The elementary school years: Understanding development during middle childhood* (pp. 335–369). Washington, DC: National Academy Press.

Weisner, T. S. (in press). The 5-to-7 transition as an ecocultural project. In A. J. Sameroff & M. M. Haith (Eds.), *Reason and responsibility: The passage through childhood.* Chicago: Chicago University Press.

Weisner, T. S., Gallimore, R., & Jordan, C. (1988). Unpackaging cultural effects on classroom learning: Native Hawaiian peer assistance and child-generated activity. *Anthropology and Education Quarterly, 19*, 327–351.

Weisner, T. S. & Garnier, H. (1992). Nonconventional family life-styles and school achievement: A 12-year longitudinal study. *American Educational Research Journal, 29*, 605–632.

Weisner, T. S., Matheson, C. C., & Bernheimer, L. P. (1996). American cultural models of early influence and parent recognition of developmental delays: Is earlier always better than later? In S. Harkness & C. M. Super (Eds.), *Parents' cultural belief systems: Their origins, expressions, and consequences* (pp. 496–531). New York: Guilford.

Welles-Nyström, B. (1988). Parenthood and infancy in Sweden. In R. A. LeVine, P. M.

Miller & M. M. West (Eds.), *Parental behavior in diverse societies. New Directions for Child Development*, Vol. 40. San Francisco: Jossey-Bass.

Welles-Nyström, B. (1996). Scenes from a marriage: Equality ideology in Swedish family policy, maternal ethnotheories, and practice. In S. Harkness & C. M. Super (Eds.), *Parents' cultural belief systems: Their origins, expressions, and consequences* (pp. 192–214). New York: Guilford.

Whiting, B. B. (1980). Culture and social behavior: A model for the development of social behavior. *Ethos, 8*, 95–116.

Whiting, B. B. & Edwards, C. P. (1988). *Children of different worlds: The formation of social behavior.* Cambridge, MA: Harvard University Press.

Whiting, B. B. & Whiting, J. W. M. (1975). *The children of six cultures: A psychocultural analysis.* Cambridge, MA: Harvard University Press.

Whiting, J. W. M. (1977). A model for psychocultural research. In P. H. Leiderman, S. R. Tulkin & A. Rosenfeld (Eds.), *Culture and infancy: Variations in the human experience* (pp. 29–48). New York: Academic Press.

Whiting, J. W. M. & Child, I. L. (1953). *Child training and personality: A cross-cultural study.* New Haven: Yale University Press.

Wolf, A. W. & Lozoff, B. (1989). Object attachment, thumbsucking, and the passage to sleep. *Journal of the American Academy of Child and Adolescent Psychiatry, 28*, 287–292.

Wolf, A. W., Lozoff, B., Latz, S., & Paludetto, R. (1996). Parental theories in the management of young children's sleep in Japan, Italy, and the United States. In S. Harkness & C. M. Super (Eds.), *Parents' cultural belief systems: Their origins, expressions, and consequences* (pp. 364–384). New York: Guilford Press.

Worthman, C. M. (1994). Developmental microniche: A concept for modeling relationships of biology, behavior, and culture in development. *American Journal of Physical Anthropology Suppl., 18*, 210.

Worthman, C. M. (1995). Biocultural bases of human variation. *ISSBD Newsletter, 27*(1), 10–13.

Worthman, C. M., Stallings, J. F., & Jenkins, C. L. (1993). Developmental effects of sex-differentiated parental care among Hagahai foragers. *American Journal of Physical Anthropology Suppl., 16*, 212.

Zeitlin, M., Ghassemi, H., & Mansour, M. (1990). *Positive deviance in child nutrition.* Tokyo: United Nations University.

Zeitlin, M., Super, C. M., Beiser, M., Gulden, G., Ahmed, N., Ahmed, M., & Sockalingham, S. (1990). *A behavioral study of positive deviance in young child nutrition and health in Bangladesh.* [Report to the Office of International Health, USAID].

2

SOCIALIZATION AND IDENTITY STRATEGIES[1]

C. CAMILLERI
Université de Paris V-Sorbonne
France

H. MALEWSKA-PEYRE
Centre de Recherches Interdisciplinaires de Vaucresson, France
and Polish Academy of Sciences, Poland

Contents

Introduction

This chapter reviews the concept of socialization and its evolution in socio-historical context, and how its transformation in modern societies has given rise to problems of identity. The social universe of children is changing more rapidly now than at the time of Durkheim, Freud, or Piaget, the forerunners of socialization theory, due to the decline of the influence of religion, a reorientation of values, and a shift from collective to individual morality. The new interest in identity is partly related to these changes. Furthermore, the study of socialization and identity is now less Eurocentric, due to recent developments in cross-cultural research that have widened the available perspectives. It is also more interdisciplinary in nature, now dealing with concepts and instruments of anthropology, sociology, and even with some historical data (e.g., the work of Lipiansky, 1991a, on French identity). Finally, phenomena related to rapid social change (such as immigration, or the construction of the European Union) involve a modification of the concept of national identity. For all these reasons, there is a revival of interest in identity.

From Socialization to Identity Strategies

Concepts of Socialization and Enculturation

Socialization concerns the relations of individuals with their social environment. These are not random, but are guided by general factors that act on the individual. There are biological factors, and interacting with them, a host of social influences from other individuals and groups. In its most basic definition, *socialization* means the totality of modifications produced in the individuals' relationships with their environment (material, social, mental) as a result of interaction with others. These modifications affect all that individuals receive and express, globally as well as at the level of basic processes (e.g., perceptual, emotional, and cognitive functions).

There are two processes by which one internalizes the social world. In the first, individuals form a general mental picture of others, which becomes a permanent internal reference (Mead,1934 a and b). Individuals also internalize whatever allows them to identify with a particular society, with its own characteristics, by which they become members of this particular group. This leads to a more narrow definition of socialization, in relation to which we shall define the concept of culture. In the broadest sense of culture, everything that is social is also cultural, because it is created by human beings and cannot be reduced to a fixed configuration of imposed biological elements. But there is also culture in a more narrow sense, as the configuration of constructed elements that specify human groups and distinguish one group from the other (Brown, 1965; Bronfenbrenner, 1969; Danziger, 1970; Malewska-Peyre & Tap, 1991).

Despite the many characterizations of culture, there is one central idea : Among the various models that circulate in the social domain (from those that govern institutions to those that determine opinions, styles, fashions, and fads) and that influence individuals in all their relations with the environment, culture designates the most durable, shared, and valued ones. The processes by which individuals acquire the culture that is specific to their society is designated by different terms, one of which is *enculturation*. The place and the importance of enculturation in the dynamics of socialization, of which it constitutes a dimension, varies according to the type of society. But first we have to specify the relations that exist between these two close concepts: socialization and education.

Our second definition of socialization is that socialization appears to be adaptive (Malrieu, Baubion-Broye & Hajjar, 1991). The functional and normative traits of socialization have been particularly stressed by Durkheim and his followers, who looked for the ultimate goals of the socialization processes in the contribution individuals make to the efficient functioning of their society.

This functionality appears also in the traditions of Wallon, Piaget, and Freud who emphasized the fundamental role society plays in the development of personality. These theorists have studied the modalities and stages according to which individuals incorporate social norms in order to follow a life course that is considered normal. The functional character of this internalization appears here even more profoundly than in Durkheim's school of thought. For sociologists, maladjustment to society will lead to sanctions that come from the lack of external adaptation, while for psychologists there will be a hindrance in inner development, preventing full development as a human being (Malewska, 1972).

In both approaches however, there is a justification of the prescriptive dimension of socialization, which also links it to the concept of *education*. Education may be viewed as an effort to draw to the attention of individuals, and to stimulate them to acquire those values that allow them to attain what is considered to be best for them. However, some authors, such as Muszynsky (1970) do not view the two concepts as synonymous. They hold that socialization implies "actions that are not intentional," while "actions that are deliberate constitute education" (p. 41).

Socialization occurs through a host of specific means, namely through imitation, identification, play, role taking, language acquisition, contact with books, media, and all of the other means of learning. For a long time, especially in the early sociology of Durkheim, socialization was envisaged as a set of unilateral actions of the group on individuals, who found themselves thus "marked" as an object by the initiatives of others. Now the field has moved to a more interactive perspective, which takes into account the effects of individuals on their surroundings just as much as the impact of these surroundings on individuals; in fact, the two influence each other. This is particularly obvious in the observations of psychologists on the development of children and adolescents. They show how, even when they seem to be soaking up social messages, individuals in reality involve themselves actively with their contents and ultimate goals (Rabain, 1989; Malewska-Peyre & Tap, 1991).

Socialization and Social Evolution

We must also take into account the impact of sociological variables, and consider the type of environment in which these interactions occur. Despite its obvious limitations, we will use the distinction between "traditional" and "industrial" societies. The former, especially the small and less complex societies, are characterized by the consensus of the entire group on collective "models," including values and other important aspects of interaction between individuals. Furthermore, social change being slow, these models prove to be particularly stable. They have had the time to crystallize into an extended traditional heritage, usually respected to the point of being sacred, and are transmitted from one generation to another. In this case, socialization will be particularly obvious, formalized, and socially controlled. In these societies, cultural characteristics tend to be all powerful. This has two consequences: First, this mode of sociological functioning prevents the appearance of these relatively more free, partial, and fluid extra-cultural models that we have mentioned before. For this reason, enculturation tends to absorb the totality of socialization. One might say that culture is like the envelope of society and enculturation the envelope of socialization. Second, the cultural models completely control all situations in life, from the broadest values to the very details of every situation. Thus, these societies tend to be saturated by rules and regulations. The totality of these prescriptions generally have to be respected by everyone in order to become respected group members and at the same time, to attain the very essense of "humanity." In this case, enculturation is indistinguishable from both socialization and from education.

In industrialized societies, with their rapid change, subgroups have become increasingly numerous and fluid. They show marked independence from the models that govern the larger society. For this reason, one no longer deals with simple subsystems (e.g., sub-groups of sex, age), but with real sub-cultures. Differences between subgroups, which used to be complementary, tend to become disparate and conflict-ridden. This is seen in Western society, for example, in the generation gap between young and old. Knowledge of the culture at the level of the society is no longer sufficient to predict and interpret the representations of these subgroups, such as socioeconomic subgroups. Thus in this new context "culture cannot be assumed to be the main independent variable if social class is not dealt with adequately" (Kagitçibasi, 1989, p. 138). It is necessary to articulate the knowledge of their specific subcultures.

There is thus a structural change: Culture in modern societies ceases to be the total integrating system, becoming that which the subgroups recognize as what they have in common in spite of the differences. Culture has a tendency to exhibit fewer specific features, but instead shows more general attitudes, principles of conduct, and global schemes of actions. To this extent one passes from a "microscopic" socialization to a broad "framework of socialization" (Camilleri, 1989). In addition, the reduction of the importance of the position occupied by global culture in society is due not only to the development of different subcultures, but also the acceleration of change renders difficult the crystallization of representations, values, and knowledge into traditions. On the contrary, rapid change favors transitory collective meanings that become more important than cultural heritage. That is why, in the socialization process, their importance increases at the expense of enculturation.

In complex traditional societies (for example the ancient societies of Europe, Asia, and the Arab World) and even more so in the industrialized societies, individuals are never confronted with the society as a whole, but only with subgroups that they enter simultaneously or successively. In so far as subgroups represent stable subsystems of the general cultural system, social mobility has the dominant effect of validating their position in the system and thus confirming the primary socialization. In contrast, in industrial societies, mobility from one disparate subgroup to another leads to socialization practices that are themselves disparate. The common element provided by enculturation tends to diminish. And, because culture itself undergoes rapid and important transformations, the agents of socialization increasingly tend to operate with models that change during the individuals' life course. Thus one can no longer say that individuals only internalize their native culture, because they necessarily have to be confronted with different models. In the midst of a single society enculturation is now combined with acculturation. (See chapter by Berry and Sam in Volume 3). Hence, individuals have to be ready for desocializations and successive resocializations in the course of their life span. It is therefore true, when one considers the life course of the migrants in the industrialized societies, that "the immigrant children are raised with diverging fragments of a world image and with diverging experiences" (Roosens, 1989, p. 90). But it is important to avoid seeing a gap between the socialization of these children of migrants and that of the local population. Although the clashes, the divergences and conflicts occur only at the level of the subcultures and not at the level of the general culture, the problems that the local population have to solve are not qualitatively different from the ones faced by the migrants, even though they may be not quite as strong. Thus a new type of education has to teach both groups of the population to cope with the changes and the cultural turning points which await them (Abdallah-Pretceille, 1988).

Individuality will take on a new importance. The passage through two or more subcultures will allow individuals to make comparisons, to become aware of the totality of the representations and values of these subcultures, and thus to distance themselves from both of them. This gives them the possibility not to be, like before, simply immersed in the social and cultural field, but to "emerge" as actors in a social and cultural context that becomes a conscious object of knowledge. This new mental state will give them a new power that they will use to a greater or lesser degree depending on their personalities and the circumstances, the power of a personal manipulation of the diversified materials provided by their society. One will understand that, under these conditions, the culture that is experienced differs notably from the culture that is given (Chombart de Lauwe, 1989).

These processes, while not impossible, are not facilitated nor encouraged in traditional societies. This leads to some reservations regarding the interactionist thesis. As noted earlier, when individuals appear to receive social messages passively, this means only that their active involvement produces conformity; but in traditional societies, the collective models greatly encourage conforming at all times and for all purposes, the reproduction of tradition being the prevalent norm. On the other hand, in industrial societies, individuals not only benefit from the possibility of manipulating a diversified social subject matter, but they are even encouraged to do so. They will need to choose between concurrent models that they come across every day including in the most important institutions of socialization and education: family, school, and church. This they carry out by different processes, particularly by the interplay of selective identifications. In fact, from the moment society permanently accomodates subdivisions, conflict structurally takes a firm hold in the process of socialization (Kourganoff-Duroussy & Mollo, 1981) and should be treated as a positive element. This may be necessary in achieving a qualitatively superior state, and for this reason, education should deal with conflict and conflict resolution (Abdallah-Pretceille, 1988).

Through the media, individuals are confronted with worldwide models, from which they develop a "social imagination" that was earlier non existent or rarely present and now becomes important and competes with "social reality." Thus from infancy onwards, as M. J. Chombart de Lauwe (1981) has shown, individuals are confronted with problems of sorting out values and knowledge, in fact, to choose their socialization. This develops their internal control at the expense of the traditional external control (Kagitçibasi, 1989).

This choice between divergent social norms, all of which can be attractive, forces individuals to question the collective norms and leads them to want social change, to envisage new social and cultural goals, and to provide their own socialization plans (Malrieu et al., 1991, p. 184). In this case, socialization itself undergoes a significant change: at the same time that a person adapts to society (which was the only preoccupation of Durkheimian sociology), the society now adapts to the person. The consequence of these new attitudes on social interactions is obvious: in the appropriation of social norms, it is the processes of transformation and innovation that take over from conformity. Individuals can now formulate their own socialization and enculturation prescription from what Goodenough (1976) has called the "cultural pool." Processes become more important than products.

Under these circumstances, when observing individuals who communicate with each other, it becomes difficult to predict and understand what is happening between them from knowing the general culture, because individuals interact with others each according to their own particular pattern. We therefore have to study the relationships and processes that occur in the contacts between individuals who are the bearers of these cultures, and go beyond the established science of culture and cultural learning to a theory of the concrete processes of intercultural interactions.

And, finally, beyond a certain threshold of disparity between the socialization sequences, attained in modern cultural contexts, individuals must furnish an exceptional effort to manage these disparities while maintaining their unity. In these cases the problems of identity, as we shall see, become particularly acute.

Identity and its Dynamics

The Structure of Identity

When individuals are asked what their identity is they answer that "it is me" or "myself." The most common procedure to clarify what they mean by this dates back to Kuhn and McPhartland (1954): it is to ask them to respond repeatedly to the question "Who am I?." Three categories of identity descriptions are obtained:

1. Values that they cherish ("I think that," "I believe that"), based on representations of what things are or should be, and on the implicit meanings that they attribute to life.
2. Categorical attributes by which they define themselves as members of social groups ("I'm a human being," "a woman," "a young man," "a father," "a student") and which are usually related to the roles and statuses occupied in society (status characteristics).
3. Personality traits ("ambitious," "authoritarian," "cheerful").

On the basis of these three kinds of answers, one can describe the main characteristics of identity structures:

Individuals can be pleased with these personality traits that form a part of their *real identity*, or they may wish to change them, more or less, as a function of a certain image they value for themselves. This produces a *value identity* that reflects what psychoanalysts have termed the *ideal self*. These two dimensions of identity can be close or far apart from each other; in the latter case, efforts are usually made to reduce the gap.

But if we believe that we can do away with our traits or change them, it means that we do not think that we are stuck with them. That implies our belief in the *ontological function* of the identity processes, that is, their function of constructing what we are and desire to be. In this effort at identity building many obstacles emerge from within us, and even more so from our environment, that force us to become aware of reality and to negotiate who we are or wish to be within the constraints imposed by that reality; this is the *pragmatic*, instrumental, or utilitarian function.

Two other fundamental dimensions of identity arise from the individuals' descriptions: a *social identity*, formulated in detail by Tajfel (1978) and cognitive psychologists, and a *personal identity*. The latter was first postulated by James (1890), followed by Mead (1934b), who analyzed the connection between the "me," sociologically constituted by the interiorization of social roles, and the "I" that forms a more personal component.

Social identity implies categorical attributes that refer to social groups to which individuals belong, in which individuals invest their energy, and with which they identify themselves. By that we mean that individuals perceive themselves as resembling other group members, sharing with them the most salient features, values, meanings, and goals. Because these pre-exist in society, social identity is always, to some degree, assigned or prescribed.

Nevertheless, social identity is neither simple nor the same for all; for each person, there will be a configuration of sub-identities bound to groups to which they belong, a different combination being mobilized in different circumstances (Zavalloni & Guérin, 1984). This is why, as Oriol (1984, 1988, 1989) has stressed, our social belonging should not be considered as having its roots in one single group to the exclusion of others, and is not experienced as "I am this and not anything else," except when individuals lock themselves into a simplified identity in reaction to particular events or situations. The problem is to cope with this diversity without being divided by it. These identity dynamics are being studied by the "contextualist" and "interactionist" theories that are presently popular (Lipiansky, 1991b; Kastersztein, 1990; Taboada-Léonetti, 1990a; Clanet, 1990; Oriol, 1984, 1993; Vinsonneau, 1996; Denoux, 1995).

A review of the literature shows that personal identity consists of three levels:

1.   Individuals feel they resemble the members of the "in-group" while feeling separate from those of the "out-group." Tajfel and his school of thought had a tendency to exaggerate this feeling of separation to the point of creating a feeling of opposition between "we" and "they," and this feeling was supposed to be a necessary condition for the development of a positive "in-group" identity and thus of a positive personal identity. Such an initial distinction between two regions in the social sphere can be considered as an intermediary level in the definition of the "self."

2.   In addition to the objective sequence and hierarchy of past and present subgroups to which individuals belong, their choices and differential investments lead them to establish a subjective hierarchy among subgroups. As Doise (1988) has shown, while there has been extensive research on the consequences of the individuals' membership in a social category, much less attention has been paid to the processes that lead them to utilize one system of categories rather than another, or lead them to transform the existing systems. Tajfel and his followers "do not take into account the way in which individuals themselves define social reality" (Deschamps, 1991, p. 55). But it is this particular way in which each one of us internalizes the group that leads to the individual dimension of identity.

3.   The third level deals with the personal characteristics that distinguish individuals from others within the same group. However, even at the level of individual differences, the social and individual dimensions are always closely linked. While individuals may have personal qualities and faults, their values are at least partly those that prevail in their group; this is particularly true, as psychoanalysis has shown, of those that constitute the super-ego.

One cannot therefore speak of a dichotomy between these two fundamental dimensions of identity. They should rather be considered like the two poles of the same axis, with a variable emphasis on one or the other according to the situation. One thus remains faithful to the conception of Mead and "his idea of dialogue between an "I" and the "self," the individual becoming the product of society and the society a continuous creation of individuals" (Deschamps, 1991, p. 51). This conversation follows different modalities, from dialogue and negotiation to confrontation. The same social items or influences can be adopted by individuals, and can be used as building blocks of their identities, or they can be perceived as opposing this construction. We can accept all or a part of the identity assigned to us, or we can diversely reject it. When we accept it, as Saraswathi and Pai (in press) show in relation to traditional Indian society, the social groups "are in the position to influence an individual's educational, marriage and occupational life without it being perceived as an act of invasion into personal privacy" (p. 10).

The dynamics of identity lead individuals not only to construct a "self" in which they distinguish themselves from others, but also to perceive their continuity throughout their life span. But this affirmation does not fit easily with the contextualist or interactionist theories, according to which particular identity profiles occur in different situations. For example, for Lipiansky (1991b), identity is not a set of characteristics attached to the individual, but "an interactive process of assimilation and differentiation, where the definition of the self constantly interferes with the definition of the other" (p. 90).

Furthermore, the thesis of identity constancy or continuity through space and time clashes with the contradictions often manifested by subjects when affirming their identity. While carrying out a series of experiments in a university setting with male and female students, Vinsonneau (1996) found that the females all stated that they considered themselves equal to men. But when they had some tasks to accomplish as a team with the male students, their behavior showed that they would systematically submit to the boys, who were left with the leadership role. Thus, while adopting a feminist identity as far as the expression of principles was concerned, their behavior showed a traditional feminine identity. Another series of experiments was carried out with young people from the Maghreb, aged 15 to 23; they were asked to choose between symbolic objects or situations, some of which marked a preference for Muslim culture or religion, and the other rejected them. While all of them expressed their attachment in principle to Islam, many of them (sometimes even a majority of them) chose objects or situations that contradicted this assertion. In view of these results, Visonneau (1996) wondered if identity unity and constancy are not merely cultural norms interiorized in various ways, or not at all, by the individual: this would explain why some subjects accept these contradictions without any apparent embarrassment, whereas others feel sufficiently disturbed to seek psychotherapeutic help. However, it is difficult to believe that a person could accept feeling split into a series of unattached "I's." People who do not show any disturbance when expressing these contradictory identities make use consciously or unconsciously of multiple strategies (some of which will be described below) to justify these contradictions or to ignore them.

If one adopts the thesis of identity constancy and unity maintained through space and time, one must admit that it is not obtained by the simple permanence of elements such as attitudes, feelings, and representations and habits that repeat themselves. Even if these are partly routine they are open to change. Our individual future is made of novelty as well as of stability. In other words, although identity is constant, its content varies; it is a "dialectical" integration of the different in the same, of change in continuity. The construction of identity is a permanent effort in order to harmonize opposites, in a combination that we find acceptable (Camilleri, 1991).

Thus, identity is not given at the outset, but its construction requires much effort. Individuals have to acquire and maintain the basis of this identity, in particular the meanings and the global values that help them to adjust to their environment, and to achieve a self-image backed by self esteem.

Identity and Social Change

The kind and extent of effort required in identity construction depends on the social context, but in every context there will be pressure from social expectations and the cultural system. The interiorization of culture allows an almost effortless identity construction. It satisfies the ontological function of providing a system of meanings and values that automatically give them a satisfactory cohesion. The more individuals identify with the group, the more they emerge with a typical social personality common to all members of the group. This enables them to relate to a common cultural identity, which serves as a shared reference point in order to construct and evaluate their own identity, so that each individual relates to this cultural identity in his or her own fashion, according to his or her own adhesions and identifications (Clanet, 1990). Therefore, we are not dealing with the "basic personality" of Kardiner, based on psychoanalytical views that are not widely accepted and that many authors blame for confining the subject to a single fixed collective identity (Oriol, 1993). At the same time, in as much as individuals interiorize culture, they satisfy the pragmatic function of adapting to the environment.

There are two other advantages. Because the cultural system is coherent, the values accepted by individuals and those that allow adaptation to the environment are the same; this coherence minimizes the risks of contradictions and of internal conflicts. Second, because the configuration of value representations are shared by the members of a cultural group, they agree on the manner in which they must think of themselves and of the world. Thus, the identity that they choose for themselves tends not to differ from the prescribed one, and merges also with the identity of belonging and of participation. This strongly reduces the risks of conflict between individuals.

As noted earlier, this description has to be adapted to the sociocultural context. These advantages manifest themselves fully in traditional groups. Their members participate most profoundly in the culture that tends to be systematic and coherent, to occupy the ideological space without competition, and to be accepted without reservations, because it is considered as originating in the transcendent and absolute truth. Communion in this type of culture tends to render useless, or to greatly reduce, the individual negotiations required by identity dynamics because the difficult management of the relationships with themselves and the environment has been taken care of by the group. This strong feeling of security reinforces an almost fusional identification to the social group. This powerful articulation of individuals to their group develops a "culture of relatedness" (Kagitçibasi, 1985) and in liaison with it, builds a type of education in which "the child would constantly refer to others for control of his actions, acceptance, evaluation and approval" (Kagitçibasi, 1989, p. 141).

It is therefore in these societies that the possibility for members to "individualize" themselves is reduced to a minimum. The social categorization is strong and stable, and bound to the cultural system that prescribes a place for every individual according to defined criteria. Individuals, placed into subgroups in which they can foresee easily the sequence in the course of their existence, within very limited margins of mobility, receive a combination of assigned sub-identities, but that are largely accepted and internalized. They are unlikely to be frustrated by the gap between their actual roles and the imaginary ones, unlike what happens in the West, especially in key moments like adolescence, with the well-known difficulties that this produces (cf. Tap & Malewska-Peyre, 1993).

While it cannot be said that the members of traditional societies are purely community oriented, (i.e., that they would have only a social identity and belonging, and no individual identity), the sociocultural conditions permitting the singularization of the individual are reduced. For example, if a child shows a predisposition to be different, parents may be worried and take him or her to consult a traditional healer. The dominant process is therefore that the members of the group distinguish themselves from others mainly by their belonging to prescribed networks in which the statuses and roles are different.

However, some singularization does occur through certain behavior patterns. For example, at the lowest level one can find it in what Codol (1975) has identified as the phenomenon of "ultimate conformity of self." In strongly conformist groups, individuals may want to distinguish themselves by interpreting and applying the norms in an even narrower way than the others. Singularization also exists in complex traditional societies, where individuals can choose their social categories when they begin to take part in freely constituted subgroups, based on leisure activities, companionship, or friendship. Last, it occurs via personality traits (qualities, faults, various peculiarities, personal styles, etc.) that set apart individuals in all social contexts.

Singularity, an extreme form of personal identity, is thus not absent in traditional societies, but is allowed to manifest itself only in a small number of contexts. In particular, it is not permitted at the ideological level, that is, at the level of values and general norms of behavior. Conformity and singularity are not mutually exclusive but are at the ends of a single dimension; one can move from one to the other within the limits of societal constraints.

In Western industrialized societies, social categorization is weakened. At the level of cultural representations, there is little justification for it. This has two consequences. First, social roles are more open to individual variations because they are not strongly formalized. Second, there is a wide choice of categorizations because the importance of self-selected subgroups increases at the expense of those in which one is required to be involved. Given this more extensive choice, individuals take part in a variety of more mobile and differentiated subgroups. They identify themselves more with one group, less with another, more permanently with one group, only sporadically with another, diversifying thereby their sub-identities. Social mobility becoming a real possibility, they can identify more with the outside reference groups in addition to the groups to which they belong. The conditions are thus available for a free, critical identification to take over from conditional, fusional identification.

The individual coefficient in identity processes increases notably as their socio-cultural base, (i.e., all that is socially prescribed) is weakened in the Western world (Baumeister, 1986). The traditionally collective "identity markers" (being rooted in and belonging to a place, marriage, profession, social status, genealogy, conditions linked to age and gender) are becoming more problematic. That which was formerly assigned becomes henceforth an individual responsibility. As the collective support of identity weakens, individuals have to take over. The coherence of one's behavior and its predictability by others may no longer be assured by external means, so one has to establish internally a coherence and a continuity that will seem adequate to oneself and to others. Of course we do not speak here about totalitarian societies.

One can then understand the change that has occurred in the experience and representation of identity process. Taboada-Léonetti (1990a), commenting on some observations made by Lévi-Strauss, writes that "none of the so-called 'primitive' people seem to take for granted a substantial identity; they divide it up into numerous elements, the combination of which is always problematic. In many cultures the identity is split into several 'souls,' or recomposed through the means of emblems and of social positions. Identity appears then as an unstable combinatorial function and not as an unchangeable essence" (Taboada-Léonetti, 1990a, p. 19). It is only when the collective code that guarantees the development of "functional life-span sequences" becomes blurred, as it does in Western societies, that identity becomes a means to ensure personal unity. Identity should be solid enough to integrate situations rather than splitting because of disparities, and constant enough to ensure sufficient predictability of behavior.

The individual coefficient in identity construction is further reinforced through another aspect of culture change, namely the narrower base of common values that is linked to the appearance of diversified and even conflicting subcultures. Consider, for example, the variety of opinions expressed in Western societies on the management of procreation, education, allegiance to authority, work, nature, and death. On all such fundamental themes, one can no longer rely on the cultural system. Hence individuals are not only given a choice, they are encouraged to choose. Modern life increases the possibilities and difficulties of choice (Baumeister, 1986). Under these conditions individualization of identity extends to singularization in an increasing number of domains, raising it to the rank of a social value. However, this experience sometimes produces strong insecurities.

On the one hand, in Western societies, assignment of identity is weak but it has not disappeared. The possibility not to obey social pressures increases with the expanding singularization, and increases the gap between situations that one expects "for oneself" or "for others." This leads to the development of a "polemic identity" geared toward self-realization. One seeks to be taken for what one is rather than what others want to make of us, or want to make us believe that we are. And we know that these efforts have to be maintained and repeated endlessly. This is the first aspect of the increasing uncertainty of identity when it becomes a process mainly under the control of the individual.

On the other hand, modern societies create and reinforce a crisis of meanings, because social mobility brings individuals into contact with different or conflicting representations and values, that constantly test the unity of meanings on which they live. Furthermore, the cultural system having changed, individuals must themselves reestablish this unity, and conduct the negotiations required by the identity dynamics. The process is difficult and the results obtained more fragile, because they are less backed by social confirmation (Tap, 1980). Given the possibilities of social mobility and the intense competition in all aspects of Western societies, the self-image of individuals is constantly being threatened more than in traditional groups.

The increasing problems and numerous uncertainties linked to identity dynamics enhances the probability of accidents and crises throughout the lifespan and especially in its more sensitive phases. This leads to the emergence and diversification of strategies invented by individuals, that is, to behavior targeted consciously or unconsciously to avoid the intrasubjective and intersubjective tensions caused by identity problems.

More or less indirect and dispersed analyses of such strategies can be found, in so far as threats to the unity of meaning are concerned, in the literature on the theory of "cognitive dissonance" (Festinger, 1957), or on problems of self-esteem, and in the observations on various forms of stigmatization. Our attention is now drawn to culturally peripheral minority groups within multicultural Western societies, because, there, the challenges are dramatic and the strategies more obvious.

Minorities' Identity Strategies

Culture Contact and Identity Strategies

Ethnic or national identity is not usually activated in everyday experience. Consciousness of it is revived in situations like migration or mixed marriage, and in situations of change or threats to cultural values or national identity, like in war. Similarly, religious identity is never so strong as in times of religious wars.

In this part of the chapter, we shall mainly examine the attitudes and behaviors of minorities toward a dominant culture. Berry (1984) asked some pertinent questions concerning individuals engaged in lasting contact with a new and dominant society, leading to a typology of modes of acculturation (see Berry & Sam chapter in Volume 3 of this *Handbook*).

Integration is considered the most favorable strategy to cope with cultural change (Berry, Kim, & Boski, 1987). Studying Canadian populations, these authors observed that integration was a good predictor of psychological well-being and low acculturative stress. But integration is only possible in some conditions: The person should have sufficient skills to learn a new culture and a new language in order to participate fully in the new society. The values and habits of the culture of origin should not be in strong contradiction with the values of the dominant society. And the "new" society should be open to the "newcomers" and avoid discrimination (Boesch, 1983).

The distance between two cultures is one of the crucial factors of successful or unsuccessful integration. For example, migrants of Polish origin in the United States were much better integrated than migrants of Muslim culture coming to France from North Africa (Boski, Jarymowicz, & Malewska-Peyre, 1992). There were more disparities between the fundamental values of Muslim countries and those of the French Christian society (and even more, of French lay society) than there were between Polish and American values.

Some traditional Muslim values, attitudes, and norms are in contradiction with everyday French culture. This was confirmed by research on a large sample of adolescents of second generation migrants from Maghreb countries and from Portugal and Spain, compared to French youth (Malewska-Peyre and Zaleska, 1980; Zaleska, 1982). The results show major differences between the choice of values of the adolescents and those of their parents. Second generation migrant adolescents tended to share the values of their French peers rather than those of their parents. This was particularly significant for the young girls from Maghreb countries. In their own ethnic group, the male occupies a dominant position, while the woman is deprived of independence. On witnessing the apparent equality between men and women in France, the North African girls become aware of their low status. They are, more than boys, confronted with the problem of whether to maintain their religious and ethnic identity. For these young people, the main problem consists in reconciling their parents' traditional values and their participation in the cultural community of their peers. This is sometimes impossible. To a lesser degree, this is also true for adolescents from Portugal living in France.

Serious cultural conflicts can lead to cognitive dissonance and difficulties in the construction of a coherent identity. The construction of identity is a process of conciliation between the "sameness" of the person in time and space and the integration of new experiences, values, and representations. The term "sameness" not only pertains to physical and psychological traits but also to the coherence of the value system, what Camilleri (1990) calls "unity of meaning." Incongruence of identity could be the result of a conflict between the pragmatic need for adaptation to a dominant culture and the "ontological" need for self-loyalty. This is what Malewska-Peyre (1978; Malewska-Peyre & Zaleska, 1980) described as "constancy of central values," based on early learning, individual experience and resistance to change.

Normally, culture provides an equilibrium between the pragmatic and ontological needs of an individual. This does not occur in the case of rapid social change. When cultural discrepancies occur, which is often the case for migrants, individuals will have to choose between different contradictory norms and attitudes. To preserve the congruity of their identity, they develop cognitive strategies to avoid or reconcile contradictions.

In this chapter, when analyzing the possible conflicts between cultural rules, we shall refer to our own research on migration, mainly from North Africa to France, as well as to research on conflicts between modern and traditional values and representations in Muslim societies (Camilleri 1973, 1979, 1980, 1984a; Malewska-Peyre, 1978; Malewska-Peyre & Zaleska, 1980; Malewska-Peyre, 1988). We cannot provide here all the details of the empirical procedures and results, but will illustrate this research program with a few examples.

Camilleri (1973) worked in Tunisia with a sample of nearly 1,500 young people (17 to 30 years old) with a survey using questionnaires, the content analysis of letters sent to a radio station for a program on youth problems, and the analysis of court proceedings in divorce cases; he also produced case studies. Having started with the hypothesis that major conflicts would be found between these young people and their parents, this research not only confirmed the occurrence of conflicts, but also showed the invention of strategies that allowed them to be moderated or suppressed, to preserve the family cohesion. Another of Camilleri's studies (1980) was based on a questionnaire adressed to 100 young people (16 to 25 years old) of North African origin living in or near Paris. In addition to confirming the previous findings, it showed how these young people adapt through combining in various ways features of French and North African cultures.

Malewska-Peyre, working at an interdisciplinary research center attached to the French Ministry of Justice, directed a research program for more than a decade on the topic of "crisis of identity and social deviance." In the research reported by Malewska-Peyre (1982), socialization, identity, and deviance, as dependent variables, were studied in relation to the independent variables of migration, culture and socioeconomic status. The empirical data were based on a comparison between about 500 young boys and girls who came into contact with the juvenile court and protection system and a group of youngsters who never appeared in court. The adolescents from North African and Portugese families were compared to those of French origin of the same (low) socioeconomic status. The data came from several sources: non-directive, biographical interviews, an adapted version of the "Who am I" test (Kuhn and McPhartland, 1954), a questionnaire presenting alternative choices of cultural values, and a sentence completion test. Malewska-Peyre (1988) reports on action-oriented research carried out jointly by researchers and social workers in a multiethnic suburb of Paris. The central topic was the study of identity problems (negative identity formation) due to racism and discrimination, with a view towards the prevention of social problems. A group of fifteen teenagers were observed repeatedly over a period of six months.

Strategies to Preserve Coherence of Identity

Camilleri (1990, 1991) formulated a typology of these strategies, which is based on two main axes: first, the prevalence of pragmatic versus ontological concerns; second, the relative need for preserving a coherent identity. We can thus distinguish a strategy of *simple coherence,* by which the individual suppresses one of two contradictory statements, and strategies of *complex coherence,* when the person tries to elaborate rationalizations that help reconcile two contradictory statements, taking into account all elements of opposition.

Conflict Avoidance by Simple Coherence

A first strategy is the valorization of "ontological" preoccupations, which occurs when individuals consider the conflictual values to be crucial for the construction of their identity, when the self is vested in the conflict. This is the case for many religious fundamentalists. They try to avoid conflict by clinging to their own values, and if their intransigence is likely to provoke a situation of maladjustment, they delegate the pragmatic functions to somebody else. Fundamentalism, in its usual forms, rejects pragmatism. Every contradiction with dogma must be rejected or ignored. It is a classic case of total coherence of values.

Another possibility is to minimize the moral transgressions required by the modern world. A good example of this is the attitude of parents toward the schooling of their daughters. In a traditional Muslim family, girls should not attend school after puberty, but, on the other hand, an educated girl has a better chance to make a good marriage. Therefore, parents tolerate the minimum of independence necessary to the girl's education, but once the diploma is obtained, she will be again subjected to strict parental supervision. She might even be put through a sort of traditional "purification." The parents feel that they have respected Muslim law and "a minimum of pragmatism" is preserved (Camilleri, 1990).

A second strategy is the valorization of "pragmatism," which occurs when individuals are under pressure to adapt to their social environment. Our research on migrants and North African cultures (Camilleri 1979, 1980, 1984b; Malewska 1970, Malewska-Peyre, 1984) has demonstrated frequent changes of behavior according to social situations. In everyday life, children maintain the traditional style of relations with their parents and adopt a "modernist" style with their peers at school. In professional situations or during lunch with colleagues, many migrants would drink wine, even if they would never do so at home. The private and public universe are governed by different laws. But such behavior is not fully opportunistic. Indeed, in more important situations such as marriage, or the education of children, real values are revealed: the minimum of "ontological" or traditional norms are preserved.

Situations of greater or lesser prevalence of pragmatic or ontological preoccupations lead to such an alternation of cultural codes. In the case of girls from the Maghreb, we sometimes witnessed astonishingly rapid shifts from traditional to modernist codes and vice versa. Coming home, the girl would change her appearance, makeup would be washed away and hair covered: she would become a good daughter. We called this "the chameleon identity" (Malewska-Peyre, 1988). In fact, the girl has a sort of "circumstantial" identity (Kastersztein, 1990). This behavioral technique allows her to survive in a multicultural environment while avoiding permanent conflicts and quarrels with parents and others.

People are seldom completely opportunistic. Cynical opportunism is possible only when people are indifferent to their reputation and do not feel any guilt when transgressing norms. Evidently, a certain "fluidity of identity" could facilitate opportunistic behavior as well as situations of social anomie or biculturalism.

Conflict Avoidance by Complex Coherence

Avoidance of conflict by way of suppressing one of two contradictory statements is not always satisfying for a person. Some people, when confronted with such conflicts, elaborate complex rationalizations to reduce the contradiction. Festinger (1957) described this as reduction of cognitive dissonance. Camilleri (1990) observed two types of "complex coherence" to deal with these situations:

First, we can sometimes observe the simple addition or *superposition of the rules* from traditional and modern cultural codes: many people do not think about logical implications but they build "subjective arrangements." The most widespread case is the "strategy of maximization of advantages" (Camilleri, 1973). The person chooses the most advantageous traits of each cultural system, ignoring any logical inconsistencies. For instance, many men, when looking for a wife, adopt the Western system and choose their wife freely without their parents' permission. But after marriage they return to the traditional code because it allows them to exercise more power over their wife and children. This kind of "egocentric manipulation" does not respect the internal logic of any system, but satisfies personal needs.

Second, other people try to reduce the contradictions of both cultural codes using three different rational means (Camilleri, 1990). One is by *reappropriation*. It is usual to reappropriate fundamental religious texts such as the Koran, the Sunna, or commentaries of law, asserting that some new ideas (for instance, more liberalism in education, less orthodoxy in patterns of family life, more rationalism in different fields, etc.) already existed in the scriptures, at least implicitly. This strategy permits a rational reappropriation—the integration of social change in the cultural heritage without touching the "authenticity" of ethnic tradition. The Tunisian government often used this strategy to introduce social change. For example, in its modernization efforts, it recalled some pre-Islamic traditions to justify the introduction of family planning (Malewska, 1970) or the "Roman heritage" of North Africa to justify some changes in political life (Camilleri, 1983).

Another way to reduce contradictions is by *dissociation*. Many strategies of dissociation can be observed. For instance, an effort is made to avoid criticism of ancestors for utilizing some irrational method of education by dissociating these practices from their persons: "in their time it was understandable." The respect of older parents, one of the major rules of Islam, is then preserved.

A third way is by *deducing modern values from traditional ones*. We can find some reasoning demonstrating that some modern behavior is the best way to serve some traditional values. For example, modern education of women allows them to become, in the present environment, more useful wives for their husbands and better educators for their children; that is, better education of women facilitates better education of children.

Finally, many young people claim to be able to preserve some traditional values, like "honor of the women" without obeying old prescriptions blindly. These reasonings tend to value the meaning of a rule more than the rule itself.

To save the unity of the family and mutual attachment, adolescents frequently avoid the expression of their differing opinions, especially on minor issues. All these efforts try to synthesize traditional and modern systems of values, by creating new unities of meaning, to avoid contradictions and a dogmatic closing of the mind. In consequence they serve to preserve the family, social ties, and the community.

Strategies to Avoid Stigmatization and Depreciation of Identity

Consistency is an important dimension of identity, especially in Western societies. Valorization is another important constitutive dimension. Several authors (Codol, 1979; Rogers, 1959) have stressed the fact that seeing oneself in a positive way is a major characteristic of mankind. An exclusively negative self-image, such as an inconsistent or shattered self-image, is considered a symptom of psychological disturbance. By positive identity we mean a feeling of possessing certain qualities, of being able to influence people and situations (Codol, 1975), of at least partially controlling one's environment and of having a rather good image of self as compared to others. Positive identity is considered as a sign of good mental health and of social adjustment. Evidently these feelings and images pertaining to the self do fluctuate; these fluctuations and the building up process are dependent upon one's experiences and, in particular, one's interaction with others (Rodriguez-Tomé, 1972), as well as upon one's social group and its rank (Tajfel, 1978).

Conversely, negative identity is a feeling of ill-being, of helplessness, of being thought badly of; it is having a poor image of one's activity and self. This feeling is painful, especially when the perceptions others have of us are not related to our actions. These unfavorable interactions and stigmatizations play a key role in the construction of negative identity. Positive or negative assessment of a given person depends largely on the social expectations, related to social roles. The person will be judged all the more negatively if his/her behavior does not meet social expectations (Malewska-Peyre, 1978, 1982, 1990). For migrants educated in a different culture, it is sometimes difficult, if not impossible, to conform to these expectations, especially when they are unfamiliar with them.

Furthermore, we must take into account that merely belonging to certain social categories means *a priori* that the individual will suffer from rejection and negative judgments based on negative social stereotypes and prejudices. Whatever their actual behavior, ethnic minorities, members of low socioeconomic groups, and marginalized individuals are often labelled with negative tags. The crucial decision of labelling rests with the group and its organs of social control. When the messages one gets from others is persistently negative, one's self image deteriorates (Malewska-Peyre, 1978, 1982). We call "crises of identity" the situations in which individuals are unable to construct a coherent and valorized identity that would define their belonging to a new social group, making social insertion impossible.

For the interactionist approach, judgments by others will thus influence self-image in two ways: first, in the interpersonal situation when the individual's behavior does not meet the other's expectations as prescribed by social role, and second, in social situations where the individual belongs to a group or fulfills a social role associated with stereotyped negative images. In our analysis, we focus mainly on messages, exchanges, and interactions in the framework of a socio-psychological approach, but we do not forget that repeated failure and setbacks, or serious health problems and handicaps could play a key role in self-depreciation.

In our research (Malewska-Peyre, 1982; 1988), we examined negative judgments imposed on certain groups and, in particular, racist and xenophobic stereotypes that provoke a depreciation of migrants' collective and individual identities. We looked at related strategies developed in order to avoid negative self-image. We could have chosen other stereotypes, but it seems that the psychological consequences of racial and ethnic prejudice are of great importance and impact; they are also more tangible and therefore easier to study than for other groups such as women or the elderly. The mechanisms involved are nevertheless identical.

Some Empirical Studies

Most of the data presented are derived from two studies, already mentioned (Malewska-Peyre, 1982). One of the important and significant results of our research is the frequency of racist attitudes experienced by second generation migrants in France. Seven out of ten adolescents stated during interviews that they felt deeply affected by racist prejudice and discrimination, boys less than girls, and Portuguese and Spanish less than Arabs. Note that in France, migrants do not have the same civil rights as nationals, which emphasizes their unequal status.

The experience of racism at school is particularly serious. It provokes conflicts, truancy, dropping out, and finally results in short school careers with all their consequences. In our data, failure at school is strongly related to the self-image of adolescents. Short schooling handicapped their chances to find employment and favored marginalization, which is more frequent among second generation migrants than among French adolescents.

In general, there is a strong correlation between negative identity and experience of racism and xenophobia, and a weaker one between having the status of second generation migrant and depreciation. We observed a higher frequency of negative self-image in these populations than in populations of nationals (Malewska-Peyre, 1982). It is also probable that this negative self-image discourages efforts to look for solutions to situations of failure, namely efforts to adopt behavioral patterns or strategies that would help overcome obstacles and change the situation (Malewska-Peyre & Ioannides, 1990).

A recent publication on the history of the notion of "Maghrebian mentality" in French psychiatry (Berthelier, 1994) reviews the theories on Maghrebian psychological differences and inferiority as compared to Europeans. This kind of social representations justified French colonialism and certainly contributed to depreciate the image of nationals from Arabic countries in France.

The starting point for an analysis of identity strategies was the recognition that depreciation of one's self-image is a painful experience which, when repeated or lasting, induces an even more dramatic state of negative identity. In consequence, the individual develops defense mechanisms or even patterns of behavior (which we call strategies) to lessen or avoid suffering. These strategies can be individual or collective.

Individual Strategies

There are now millions of children and adolescents either born in Western Europe of migrant parents, or who come early in life from Third World countries to join them. Public opinion stigmatizes them as troublemakers, illiterates, and deviants (Costa-Lascoux, 1985, 1988). The development of these young people's identity is mainly threatened by the internalization of the depreciating and stereotyped image projected by society (Algan & Néry, 1968).

This reaction implies self-effacing behavior, or submission, or even a guilt feeling for being what one is. During the interviews, migrant girls expressed this submissive attitude quite often. They would say such things as: "I am from Portugal but I am nice" and another said "I do not mix with guys from my country (West Indies), they are all stupid or mad," but "I do not date French boys much because my mother tells me not to make trouble and to know my place." The strategy they accept is one of unobtrusiveness, "to avoid being noticed," to be like others, preferably like the French, but without aspiring to the same social position. Not to provoke, not to disturb, not to ask for too much, but to live quietly in one's corner. In accordance with our observations (Malweska-Peyre, 1984), these strategies are used by relatively isolated youngsters, whose families are rather poorly integrated.

Another reaction is the repression of racist experiences, through their very negation: "I've never met a racist." They refuse to be concerned by racism or tend to play down its effects. The expressions drawn from our interviews show it: "When they say 'dirty wog,' they mean it as a joke. Me and my friends we don't listen, we try to forget it." Indeed, they repress the experience or avoid talking about how they had been rejected. One young man who maintained during the interview that he had never encountered racism told us later, when other topics were discussed, how he had been refused entry in a cafe, because of his "Arab face." Repression of these negative occurrences makes anxiety more tolerable. The strategy of transformation of reality allows one to bear it better; not seeing things or playing them down permits one to avoid feeling pain.

There are more sophisticated, because more conscious, variations of this strategy: We can also observe a conscious decision to suppress this sort of humiliating experience. One respondent said: "We can't do anything about racism in France, so we'd better live with it, behave like it did not exist. It's my choice. I do not fight racism, I ignore it; I do not worry about the conversations of lunatics." Another respondent, a student of Asian origin, said, "In fact I despise racists just as much as they despise me, but I do not show it. My culture teaches me to be polite." These illustrations of the various strategies show a certain passivity toward the social environment. The problem is resolved in an internal way. The actor does nothing to change his personal situation or the situation of his social group.

Another individual strategy is that of *assimilation*. The aim is then to become assimilated with the dominant group, to try to resemble them to the point of internalizing the dominant culture and denying one's own difference; this strategy is what is sometimes called "passing." This implies renouncing one's own identity and trying to resemble the dominant population as much as possible, both physically and culturally. This strategy may entail various operations to erase one's physical differences, such as straightening one's hair or dyeing it blond or red, modifying slanting eyes, utilizing a skin-lightening cream, and erasing one's cultural origins by changing one's first name. By behaving according to the dominant patterns, a person might go as far as scorning his or her original community. These young people, more often than others, say that they have a French mentality, or simply that they are French (Taboada-Léonetti, 1982). However, this strategy is not always possible because its psychological cost is very high.

Galap (1986) shows this clearly in his research on students from the French West Indies. Administratively and legally, they are French. When they come to France they wish, more or less consciously, to be similar to the French and to embrace French culture. After experiencing racism, many of them start emphasizing the value of their own culture and valorizing their own identity. Galap quotes a few examples of unconscious racism that hurt even more than more overt racism: Expressions such as "You are like us," or "You are quite light-skinned," which are intended as compliments, have racist connotations. They show that the person who uses them adheres, possibly unconsciously, to a system of prejudices in which the belief in the superiority of the white skin ranks high. Half-caste persons thus addressed have no alternative but to take a stand against a part of themselves, which implies a mental suppression or disowning of all or part of their culture; this is no less than a mutilation. Galap stresses that the dominant culture's ideology generates ethnicity and even, as we will see later, a backlash of racism. Certain West Indian students went back to reasserting the value of their "négritude" and the difficult history of their community.

In fact, the best way to avoid disparagement is, in our opinion, to accept or even increase the value of one's differences. This is the strategy of *valorization*. This strategy of opposition to racism leads individuals to dismiss the image of themselves projected by a xenophobic society, sometimes to overvalue their own differences and to adopt an attitude of protest. There are some striking examples in the works of some West Indian authors whose endeavors to revalorize Africa imply a parallel derrogation of colonialist Europe. Widespread ideological associations of meanings are reversed. Africa becomes synonymous with gentleness, culture, and civilization, while Europe represents savagery, war, and barbarism. This strategy could be as much individual as collective.

Aggression could be another active response to disparagement. This seems to be more of an active reaction to a painful stimulus than a full-fledged strategy. When someone says "Whenever I hear the words 'dirty wog,' I hit out," it is a violent emotional reaction, but one which is rooted in the Arab tradition of defending one's honor, of taking revenge. Violence can also take the form of collective action.

Collective Strategies

The active and collective strategies (Taboada-Léonetti, 1990b) can lead to a deeper political commitment as well as to an idealization of one's own culture and the development of a critical attitude toward Western civilization. This could also partly explain the success of Muslim fundamentalism.

In France, adolescents of second generation migrants from North Africa created a strong movement, (the "Beur" movement), which has played an important historical role to increase their standing in French society. They tried to dissociate themselves from their parents—they wanted to do "better," to find a better place in society than their parents, because they were better educated. Their political commitment found expression in their claim to the right to vote, to have easier access to French nationality (being born in France), but to keep their cultural roots.

Strategies that call upon values common to both French and migrant children are sometimes supported by large political movements, not only leftist groups, but also by movements for human rights and against racism. A Moroccan girl said, "I'm fed up with all this harassment about nationality; we are all workers, nationality is of little relevance." These young people often build up an identity and find reasons for living by transcending the narrow references of a nation and stressing supranational values such as egalitarianism or human rights. It is easier to share values based on equality and human rights, values which are common to the French and migrants, rather than values mainly based on national culture and history.

Youth could also be a means to assert one's similarity to the French without attempting assimilation. This was recently expressed by protests by French citizens and migrants against unemployment and the precariousness of life for young people. The most violent protests have taken the form of riots in the suburbs of big cities, where the relative deprivation of youth from lower socioeconomic classes, migrants and French alike, is strongly felt (Dubet & Lapeyronnie, 1992).

These latter strategies go beyond individual strategies while providing, at times, a solution to individual problems of identity, to disparagement or negation of one's own singularity and one's difference. Sometimes, they provide an opportunity to become integrated in society with "a similar but different status," which is more difficult when society is in crisis.

The "choice" of a strategy depends on the individual as well as on the societal situation. The social and cultural context is here a factor of primordial importance. In situations of great cultural distance, of social exclusion and discrimination, of rapid social change, of threat to personal or national identity, people will develop different strategies. These strategies depend also on personal resources. This last point could be an interesting topic for research.

Conclusion

The processes of socialization and of identity strategies present themselves as two complementary aspects of the same phenomenon. When the social context is stable, as it tended to be in traditional societies, this would strongly fashion the individuals, fixing their identity with so much stability that individuality would be viewed as an essence, a substance contained in the subject. In this limited case, socialization and identity are one and the same thing. But when the social context breaks up into a diversity of different segments, identity will set itself in motion. It becomes a dynamic process by which individuals attempt from the inside to compensate for and to control the events of the exterior, so as not to break up themselves. Socialization and identity then diverge strongly, the latter tending to become a reactional activity of regulation of the former. Thus identity will be expressed by the use of a set of strategies, localized processes by which individuals search for regulation through daily interactions.

How will things evolve in the future? Saraswathi and Pai (in press) have observed in India that, in view of the problems caused by modernization, a return to older behaviors considered more adaptive, could be seen, which brings them to state that "change often is of a circular nature" (p. 35). This will probably be the case for a number of issues, as one can already see in societies in the process of modernization. As a whole, however, one can imagine that the change will become both more radical and more rapid, because the turbulence of modern social contexts can only increase with the growing interaction between contemporary societies, that superimposes the disparities of their cultures on that of the local subcultures. We have to draw all the consequences of this structural interference, especially for the control of these ever more changing processes of socialization and of these identity dynamics. This will be the main task of tomorrow's education.

Endnote

1. Translated by A. Anugraham, C. Dasen, and
   P. Dasen.

References

Abdallah-Pretceille, M. (1988). Quelques points d'appui pour une formation des enseignants dans une perspective interculturelle.In F. Ouellet (Ed.) *Pluralisme et école* (pp. 495–509). Québec: Institut québécois de recherche sur la culture.

Algan, A. & Néry, M. (1968). L'image de soi chez l'adolescente délinquante: étude bibliographique. *Annales de Vaucresson.* Vaucresson: Centre de Formation et de Recherche.

Baumeister, R. F. (1986). *Identity, cultural change and the struggle for life.* New York: Oxford University Press.

Berry, J. W. (1984). Cultural relations in plural societies. In M. Brewer & N. Miller (Eds.), *Groups in contact* (pp. 11–27). New York: Academic Press.

Berry, J. W., Kim, U. & Boski, P. (1987). Acculturation and psychological adaptation. In Y. Y. Kim & W. B.Gudykunst (Eds.), *Cross-cultural adaptation,* (pp. 62–89). Newbury Park, CA: Sage.

Berthelier, R. (1994). *L'homme maghrébin dans la littérature psychiatrique.* Paris: L'Harmattan.

Boesch, E. (1983). From expulsion to hospitality. A psychologist looks at the refugee problem. In E. Boesch and A. Goldschmidt (Eds.), *Refugees and development* (pp.53–74). Baden-Baden: Nomos-Verlag.

Boski, P., Jarymowicz, M. & Malewska-Peyre, H. (1992). *Identity and cultural difference* (in Polish). Warsaw: Polish Academy of Science, Institute of Psychology.

Bronfenbrenner, U. (1969). On making the new man: Some extrapolation from research. *Canadian Journal of Behavioral Sciences, 1,* 4–24.

Brown, R. (1965). *Social Psychology.* New York: The Free Press.

Camilleri, C. (1973). *Jeunesse, famille et développement: Essai sur le changement socioculturel dans un pays du Tiers-Monde (Tunisie).* Paris: Editions du Centre National de la Recherche Scientifique.

Camilleri, C. (1979). Crise socioculturelle et crise d'identité dans des sociétés du Tiers-Monde: l'exemple des sociétés maghrébines. *Psychologie Française, 3–4,* 259–268.

Camilleri, C. (1980). Les immigrés maghrébins de la seconde génération. *Bulletin de Psychologie,* tome 33, *347,* 985–995.

Camilleri, C. (1983). Images de l'identité et ajustements culturels au Maghreb. *Peuples Méditerranéens, 24,* 127–152.

Camilleri, C. (1984a). Changements culturels, problèmes de socialisation et construction de l'identité. In *Socialisation et déviance des jeunes immigrés* (pp.35–66). Vaucresson: Centre de Recherches Interdisciplinaires.

Camilleri, C. (1984b). Problèmes psychologiques de l'immigré maghrébin. *Les Temps Modernes, 452-453-454,* 1877–1901.

Camilleri, C. (1989). Réflexion d'ensemble sur la socialisation. In C. Clanet (Ed.), *Socialisations et cultures* (pp. 433–445). Toulouse: Presses Universitaires du Mirail.

Camilleri, C. (1990). Identité et gestion de la disparité culturelle: Essai d'une typologie. In Camilleri, C., Kastersztein, J., Lipiansky, E.M., Malewska-Peyre, H., Taboada-Léonetti, I., Vasquez, A., *Stratégies identitaires* (pp.85–110). Paris: Presses Universitaires de France.

Camilleri, C. (1991). La construction identitaire: Essai d'une vision d'ensemble. *Les Cahiers Internationaux de Psychologie Sociale, 9-10 ,* 91–104.

Chombart de Lauwe, M. J. (1981). *Un monde autre, l'enfance: De ses représentations à son mythe.* Paris: Payot.

Chombart de Lauwe, P. H. (1989). Transformations, cultures et socialisation. In C. Clanet (Ed.), *Socialisations et cultures* (pp. 31–40). Toulouse: Presses Universitaires de Toulouse-le-Mirail.

Clanet, C. (1990). *L'interculturel.* Toulouse: Presses Universitaires du Mirail.

Codol, J. P. (1975). On the so called "superior conformity of the self" behavior: Twenty experimental investigations. *European Journal of Experimental Social Psychology, 5,* 457–501.

Codol, J. P. (1979). *Semblables et différents.* Thèse de doctorat d'Etat. Toulouse: Université de Toulouse-le-Mirail.

Costa-Lascoux, J. (1985). A propos de la

délinquance immigrée. In *Immigration, multiethnicité et socialisation des jeunes* (pp. 181–195). Actes des Vèmes Journées Internationales du Centre de Recherches Interdisciplinaires de Vaucresson.

Costa-Lascoux, J. (1988). *De l'immigré au citoyen.* Paris: La Documentation Française.

Danziger, K. (Ed.). (1970). *Readings in child socialization.* Oxford: Pergamon Press.

Denoux, P. (1995). L'identité interculturelle. *Bulletin de Psychologie, 48,* 264–270.

Deschamps, J. C. (1991). Identités, appartenances sociales, différenciations individuelles. *Les Cahiers Internationaux de Psychologie Sociale, 9–10,* 49–61.

Doise, W. (1988). Individual and social identities in intergroup relations. *European Journal of Social Psychology, 18,* 99–111.

Dubet, F., & Lapeyronnie, D. (1992). *Les quartiers d'exil.* Paris: Seuil.

Festinger, L. (1957). *A theory of cognitive dissonance.* New York: Row, Peterson.

Galap, J. (1986). *Ethnicité et sociétés: L'exemple antillais.* Paris: Colloque de l'Association Française d'Anthropologie (multigraphié).

Goodenough, W. H. (1976). Multiculturalism as the normal human experience. *Anthropology and Education Quarterly, 7,* 4–7.

James, W. (1890). *Principles of psychology.* New York: Holt.

Kagitçibasi, C. (1985). Culture of separateness-Culture of relatedness. *Papers in Comparative Studies, 4,* 91–99.

Kagitçibasi, C. (1989). Child rearing in Turkey: Implications for immigration and intervention. In L. Eldering & J. Kloprogge (Eds.), *Different cultures, same school* (pp. 137–152). Lisse: Swets & Zeitlinger.

Kastersztein, J. (1990). Les stratégies des acteurs sociaux: Approche dynamique des finalités. In Camilleri, C., Kastersztein, J., Lipiansky, E.M., Malewska-Peyre, H., Taboada-Léonetti, I., Vasquez, A. *Stratégies identitaires* (pp. 27–42). Paris: Presses Universitaires de France.

Kourganoff-Duroussy, M., & Mollo, S. (1981). La socialisation. In M. Hurtig & J. A.Rondal (Eds.), *Introduction à la psychologie de l'enfant,* (vol. 3, pp. 33–54). Liège: Mardaga.

Kuhn, M. & McPhartland, T. S. (1954). An empirical investigation of self attitudes. *American Sociological Review, 19,* 68–75.

Lipiansky, E. M. (1991a). *L'identité française. Représentations, mythes, idéologies.* Paris: Editions de l'Espace Européen.

Lipiansky, E. M. (1991b). Identité, communication interculturelle et dynamique des groupes. *Connexions, 58,* 59–69.

Malewska, H. (1970). *Rapport sur la planification familiale en France, Pologne, Suède et Tunisie.* Paris: UNESCO (multigraphié).

Malewska, H. (1972). Les mécanismes de la socialisation. In S. Nowak (Ed.), *Théorie des attitudes* (pp. 235–256). Varsovie: Panstwowe Wydawnictwo Naukowe (in Polish).

Malewska-Peyre, H. (1978). La crise d'identité chez les jeunes immigrés. *Annales de Vaucresson.* Vaucresson: Centre de Formation et de Recherche.

Malewska-Peyre, H. (1982). L'expérience du racisme et de la xénophobie chez les jeunes immigrés. In H. Malewska-Peyre (Ed.), *Crise d'identité et déviance chez les jeunes immigrés* (pp. 53–73). Paris: La Documentation Française.

Malewska-Peyre, H. (1984). Crise d'identité, problèmes de déviance chez les jeunes immigrés. *Les Temps Modernes, 452-453-454,* 1794–1811.

Malewska-Peyre, H. (1988). Les stratégies identitaires des jeunes. In H. Malewska-Peyre & C. Gachon (Eds.), *Le travail social et les enfants de migrants: racisme et identité* (pp. 203–223). Paris: Centre d'Information et d'Etudes des Migrations Internationales & L'Harmattan.

Malewska-Peyre, H. (1990). Le processus de dévalorisation de l'identité et les stratégies identitaires. In Camilleri, C., Kastersztein, J., Lipiansky, E.M., Malewska-Peyre, H., Taboada-Léonetti, I., Vasquez, A., *Stratégies identitaires* (pp.111–142). Paris: Presses Universitaires de France.

Malewska-Peyre H. & Ioannides, C. (1990). Stratégies identitaires des adolescentes dans les situations d'échec. *Enfance, 44,* 263–284.

Malewska-Peyre, H. & Tap, P. (Eds.). (1991). *La*

socialisation, de l'enfance à l'adolescence. Paris: Presses Universitaires de France.

Malewska-Peyre, H. & Zaleska, M. (1980). Identités et conflits de valeurs chez les jeunes immigrés. *Psychologie Française, 25,* 125–138.

Malrieu, P., Baubion-Broye, A. & Hajjar, V. (1991). Le rôle des oeuvres dans la socialisation de l'enfant et de l'adolescent. In H. Malewska & P. Tap (Eds.), *La socialisation de l'enfance à l'adolescence* (pp. 163–191). Paris: Presses Universitaires de France.

Mead, G. H. (1934a). *On social psychology.* Chicago: The University of Chicago Press.

Mead, G. H. (1934b). *Mind, self and society.* Chicago: The University of Chicago Press.

Muszynsky, H. (1970). *Introduction à la méthodologie de la pédagogie.* Varsovie: Panstwowe Wydawnictwo Naukowe.

Oriol, M. (Ed.). (1er vol.: 1984, 2ème vol.: 1988). *Les variations de l'identité. Etude de l'évolution de l'identité culturelle des enfants d'immigrés portugais en France et au Portugal.* Nice-Strasbourg: IDERIC et Fondation Européenne de la Science.

Oriol, M. (1989). Les devenirs possibles de l'identité des Portugais dans la France et l'Europe de demain. In B. Lorreyte (Ed.), *Les politiques d'intégration des jeunes issus de l'immigration* (pp. 352–365). Paris: L'Harmattan.

Oriol, M. (1993). De l'impossibilité de formaliser la définition des identités collectives. *Psychologie-Europe, 2,* 49–53.

Rabain, J. (1989). Premiers apprentissages moteurs, premiers apprentissages sociaux (Sénégal). In C. Clanet (Ed.), *Socialisations et cultures* (pp. 99–108). Toulouse: Presses Universitaires du Mirail.

Rodriguez-Tomé, H. (1972). *Le moi et l'autre dans l'inconscient.* Neuchâtel: Delachaux et Niestlé.

Rogers, C. R. (1959). *A theory of therapy, personality and interpersonal relationship in psychology: A study of a science.* New York: McGraw-Hill.

Roosens, E. (1989). Cultural ecology and achievement motivation: Ethnic minority youngsters in the Belgian system. In L. Eldering & J.

Kloprogge (Eds.), *Different cultures, same school* (pp. 85–106). Lisse: Swets & Zeitlinger.

Saraswathi, T. S. & Pai, S. (in press). Socialization in the Indian context. In H. S. R. Kao & D. Sinha (Eds.), *Asian perspectives of psychology.* New Delhi: Sage.

Taboada-Léonetti, I. (1982). Identité nationale et liens avec le pays d'origine. In H. Malewska-Peyre (Ed.), *Crise d'identité et déviance chez les jeunes immigrés* (pp. 205–247). Paris: La Documentation Française.

Taboada-Léonetti, I. (1990a). Introduction à la problématique de l'identité. In Camilleri, C., Kastersztein, J., Lipiansky, E. M., Malewska-Peyre, H., Taboada-Léonetti, I., Vasquez, A., *Stratégies identitaires* (pp. 7–26). Paris: Presses Universitaires de France.

Taboada-Léonetti, I. (1990b). Stratégies identitaires et minorités: Le point de vue du sociologue. In Camilleri, C., Kastersztein, J., Lipiansky, E. M., Malewska-Peyre, H., Taboada-Léonetti, I., Vasquez, A., *Stratégies identitaires* (pp. 43–84). Paris: Presses Universitaires de France.

Tajfel, H. (1978). Social categorization, social identity and social comparison. In H. Tajfel (Ed.), *Differentiation between social groups: Studies in social psychology of intergroup relations* (pp. 60–76). London: Academic Press.

Tap, P. (Ed.). (1980). *Identités collectives et changements sociaux.* Toulouse: Privat.

Tap, P. & Malewska-Peyre, H. (Eds.). (1993). *Marginalités et troubles de la socialisation.* Paris: Presses Universitaires de France.

Vinsonneau, G. (1996). *L'identité des jeunes en société inégalitaire. Le cas des maghrébins en France.* Paris: L'Harmattan.

Zaleska, M. (1982). Identité culturelle des adolescents issus des familles de travailleurs immigrés. In Malewska-Peyre H. (Ed.), *Crise d'identité et déviance chez les jeunes immigrés* (pp. 177–188). Paris: La Documentation Française.

Zavalloni, M., & Guérin, C. L. (1984). *Identité sociale et conscience: Introduction à l'ego-écologie.* Toulouse: Privat; Montréal: Presses de l'Université.

3

HUMAN DEVELOPMENT
IN CULTURE ACROSS THE LIFE SPAN

JAAN VALSINER
University of North Carolina at Chapel Hill
United States

JEANETTE A. LAWRENCE
The University of Melbourne
Australia

Contents

Introduction: Unifying Life-Span Development and Culture

Human development occurs throughout the entire time that a person is alive, although this truism is not always recognized by psychologists. Somehow, it has been tacitly assumed that issues of development are relevant for those considered to be "less developed" than the researcher, either in terms of being younger and less experienced, or by coming from a society with fewer of the trappings of occidental societies than the researcher's own social background. The researcher faces two basic hurdles of understanding: to overcome one's ethnocentrism in looking at the "others"and to overcome one's particular socialized perspective of looking at persons of other ages—younger, or older.

To consider life-span developmental and cross-cultural psychologies is a complex task because developmental psychology has been neither consistently culture inclusive (Jahoda, 1986; Schwartz, 1981) nor generally life-long in its investigations (Dowd, 1990; Packer, 1994). The traditional focus of developmental psychology on childhood (rather than the whole life course) has made it easy to neglect cultural meaningfulness of psychological phenomena as those exist in individual personal forms. Knowledge about those individual forms has been habitually lumped together into aggregated data of large samples, with the belief that large numbers of subjects guarantee generalizability of the findings to populations. The logical inconsistency and epistemological futility of such practices have been known for a long time (Allport, 1937, 1962, 1966; Valsiner, 1986).

In its turn, cross-cultural psychology has not been specifically developmental in its approach. As an outcome of comparative psychology, its usual treatment of culture has drawn on traditional group comparisons, where groups can be labelled as "cultures" because of their ethnic and/or geographical habitats (Valsiner, 1989b). As Lonner (1993, p. v) argued, "an intransigent mainstreamer might view culture as no more than a nominal category in which can be found different manners of dress, different foods, different languages, different religions, and so on." Such a perspective easily leads to the neglect of cultural meaningfulness by reducing it to category membership. Both the life-span focus within developmental psychology and comparative cross-cultural psychology have advanced without giving sufficient attention to the mechanisms of human development by which culture and life-long personal development constrain each other.

Precisely because of the reciprocal and parallel blindspots of developmental and cross-cultural psychologies, and with due recognition of the partial advances each has made, in this chapter we consider how human beings develop throughout life within culture. Culture here amounts to generic semiotic organization of both intra-psychological and inter-psychological functions. Human psychological processes are made possible by the construction and use of signs. These signs regulate both intra-personal (or intra-mental) processes, and those of the person's relations with the surrounding world. The world of human beings is a *personally meaningful* world, where that meaningfulness is a result of joint construction by the person and the social world. This general orientation to meaning-regulated psychological development is sometimes called a "co-constructionist" perspective

(Valsiner, 1994a, 1994b, 1994c; see also chapter by Miller, Volume 1 of this *Handbook*). People construct their own psychological development by meaningful actions at certain moments in their personal lives that entail "branching off" (or bifurcation) of their possible life course.

Life-Span Developmental Psychology

Together with the sociological companion approach of life-course development (e.g., Elder, 1991; Featherman & Lerner, 1985), life-span developmental psychology is filled with assertions that development is a fundamental characteristic of the total human condition, and does not belong to any one period.

The life-span approach is not confined to a single assumption. Baltes (1987, p. 612) specified a "family of perspectives" that extend its investigations beyond childhood. In self-consciously drawing links between different theoretical approaches and specializations, Baltes claimed that life-span developmental psychology is exemplified by shared assumptions that development is a life-long process, involving different directions of change in different dimensions of experience. These assumptions are worked out in loosely related specialized research interests. The focus on development in the latter years of the human life course has been a major contribution of Baltes and his group as well as other contemporary developmentalists (e.g., Salthouse, 1991; Schaie, 1990; 1994).

Antecedents of Contemporary Life-Span Issues

Historical primacy in employing in-depth analyses to the psychology of the life course belongs to the Vienna Psychological Institute of the 1920s (Ash, 1988), and Charlotte Bühler and her collaborators (Bühler, 1933; Frenkel, 1936), although life-span concerns had a substantial early history in 18th and 19th century European thought (See Baltes, 1979; Reinert, 1979 for historical overviews). With changes in psychology after World War II, life-span issues were under-emphasized, except for Erikson's persistent focus (1946, 1963; 1976; 1992). This interest re-emerged in the early 1970's in North America, and continues strongly into the nineties (Adler, 1989; Baltes, 1987; Baltes & Reese, 1984; Dannefer, 1992; Dannefer & Perlmutter, 1990; Featherman, & Lerner, 1985; Labouvie-Vief, 1989; Salthouse, 1984, 1991; Schaie, 1994; Thompson, 1988; Waterman & Archer, 1990; Willis & Schaie, 1986). Yet in these later accounts, there are distinctive traces of early perspectives about how the human life-course can be analyzed in order to understand changes in personal life as parts of larger systems in which person and culture work upon each other.

Charlotte Bühler's Account of the Dynamics of Adults' Lives
Charlotte Bühler's research group made significant inroads into life-span studies, by searching for the principles that would characterize systemic functioning of psychological processes at different periods of life (Bühler, 1933; Frenkel, 1936;

Schramek, 1934). Bühler's creative methods for describing individuals' life course changes, productivity, and subjective retrospection set the stage for a major research program in life-span developmental psychology, with particular emphasis on development in mid-life. Charlotte Bühler took her research further into explorations of adults' personal goals under the somewhat confusing label of "humanistic psychology" (Bühler & Massarik, 1968).

For Bühler, the biological phases of the life-course constituted the foundational conditions for psychological and social change. Five phases of life were characterized in psychological terms, with younger and later (mid-adulthood and onward) periods contrasted by changes in dominance relations, such that the needs that dominated thinking in younger periods were later replaced by duties. Thus, adult life entails periods of change that are filled with the individual's search for meaning. Such meanings were closely intertwined with familial and vocational roles, so that the structure of successive person-environment relationships included many reorganizations in the hierarchy of dominant concerns, even when external manifestations of those reorganizations seemingly remained the same.

In addition to intra-individual variability in periods of productivity, Bühler and her colleagues found evidence of professional specialization. They discovered that older workers compensated for the physical superiority of younger workers by relying on their experience, familiarity, and mental stability. Nearly 60 years later, Perlmutter, Kaplan, and Nyquist (1990) were to demonstrate how older waiters used their heads and their social skills to save their tired legs, confirming the earlier findings. Thus, long before cognitive psychology's emphasis on the domain specificity of expertise (Chi, Glaser & Farr, 1988), Bühler's investigations emphasized the dominance of experience and specialization over inexpert effort in vocational development.

Personally unique psychological development was seen as ". . . an irreversible process . . . unique with each and every individual" (Bühler & Massarik, 1968, p. 6), the inevitable consequence of goal-setting and meaning-construction that allows the person to become an autonomous psychological being. For example, contrary to commonsense assumptions that early secure attachments had continuing positive outcomes throughout life, Bühler demonstrated empirically that early positive identification with parents could be followed by constructions of artificial self-identities that crumbled in mid-life (e.g., in Bühler & Massarik, 1968, pp. 185–186). Although Bühler linked her person-centered life-course focus to cultural and educational influences, under the guidance of the culture and personality school of anthropology, she conceptualized cultural influences in terms of unidirectional transmission. Cultural influences were seen as "effects" rather than as components of a developing system.

In general, this early work pointed to the significance of choice points and branching pathways that could not be adequately explained in terms of early experiences. Culture and adult experience were important. In addition, Bühler's emphasis on individualized goals and changes in direction paved the way for later approaches that would give greater attention to person/culture interactions at specific points of change.

Erikson's Psychodynamic Approach to the Life Span

Erikson has long promoted his view of human development as a lifelong process, with his delineation of age-related life stages. Given that Erikson's (1963) work linked his psychodynamic background with concerns of the "culture and personality" school of thought, it is easy to relegate his work to the domain of personality theories (e.g., Baltes, 1987), or to focus on the ego-identity concept in terms of different identity statuses within adolescence (e.g., Marcia, 1966). However, if it is reconsidered from a comparative–cultural perspective, Erikson's work is important, because he consistently emphasised the dynamic, synthetic nature of developmental transformation. He insisted on viewing personality, biology, and culture as mutually integrating parts of the same system. Thus, while Erikson claimed that Sioux child training entailed a firm basis for trust, he saw that trust as emerging in a systemic way, instead of being caused by specific encounters:

> We believe we are dealing here, not with simple causality, but with a mutual assimilation of somatic, mental, and social patterns which amplify one another [emphasis added] and make the cultural design for living economical and effective. Only such integration provides a sense of being at home in this world (Erikson, 1963, p. 156).

Not only did Erikson emphasize interactions between the individual and the culture at different periods of the life cycle, but he also stressed the developmental significance of periodic interactions between individuals. Thus, the assumption of social roles by mature adults permits the development of other members of the group, and the development of adults is inherently interdependent with the development of their elders and their youngers. Hareven (1986) illuminated this point by showing the relative significance of intergenerational interactions within a changing culture. Her comparison of interdependence between generations in 19th and 20th century families is important for understanding how the changing pressures on economically responsible adults influence transitions and experiences for their children and their parents.

Erikson, likewise, had already avoided the neglect of the middle adult years and the social embeddedness of the person in many inter-generational kinship and relationship ties. Furthermore, he understood that the social context within which the individual develops itself undergoes change, usually resulting in the types of role conflicts and confusions that he encountered for himself during his guided anthropological field trips (Erikson, 1963, pp. 120–133). He came to believe that development is not fixed for the individual or the social group. Both change, so that individuals find varying degrees of support (or suppression) of their personal development under different conditions within their changing society. Consequently, development in culture involves a constant encounter of heterogeneous and often contradictory social expectations from the different institutions and persons surrounding any given individual. From the outset of life, oppositions of actions and meanings need to be coordinated so that a new developmental transformation can occur:

> *Parents must not only have certain ways of guiding by prohibition and permission; they must also be able to represent to the child a deep, an almost somatic conviction that there is a meaning to what they are doing. [emphasis added] Ultimately, children become neurotic not from frustrations, but from the lack or loss of societal meaning in these frustrations* (Erikson, 1963, pp. 249–250).

Erikson's theoretical constructions were enriched by his field excursions into Sioux and Yurok life contexts, as well as by his personological life-course analyses of Mahatma Gandhi (Erikson, 1969) and Martin Luther (Erikson, 1958). He consistently saw culture as one integrated and inseparable part of the complex causal system operating in the life of any person developing within any cultural context. Although his examples were drawn from extreme cultural contexts (e.g., those of Sioux and Yurok were set up by him as extreme comparisons—see Erikson, 1963, pp. 166–170), the comparisons were not designed to produce a description of cross-cultural differences per se. Rather, they were chosen to indicate the ways in which the role of extreme versions of culture in the developmental system can be organized. Similarly, Erikson's comparisons of the personages of Dr. Borg (from Ingmar Bergman's film *Wild Strawberries*) and Praneshacharya (from P. R. Reddy's *Samskara*) were directed at finding the general–(cultural)–psychological mechanisms that operate in the personality systems of diametrically contrasting forms (Erikson, 1976, 1992).

In this respect, Erikson's interests were similar to those of modern cultural psychologists (e.g., Shweder, 1990) who seek to understand how person and culture "constitute each other". Further, his approach of uniting psychodynamic theorizing with cultural phenomenology continues to be relevant in different societies (Kakar, 1992; Marcia, Waterman, Matteson, Archer & Orlofsky, 1993; Waterman & Archer, 1990), and to be supported by calls for neo-Eriksonian links between culture and psychoanalysis (Coté, 1993). Interests in age-related models of ego-identity and personality development have taken some of Erikson's ideas into middle and later adult years, but with less of Erikson's intense concern with specific transactions between person and culture.

Modern Approaches to Life-Span Development

A revival of interest in the whole of life within its social settings emerged in Europe and North America in the seventies (see Baltes, 1979; Reinert, 1979). Interest in life-span development has taken several distinct routes, focusing on gerontological issues, structural concerns with age periodization or continuations of Erikson's concerns with critical periods. Overall, there is little to link some of these lines of research except the assumption that development is not an exclusive property of childhood, and the conviction that new models of development are needed to explain significant changes in mature person's lives.

Dialectical Life-Span Perspective
The reassessment of child-focused models of intellectual development was partly provoked by cross-cultural critiques of Piaget's universalist claims for universal

sequences of stages in cognitive development, and partly by dissatisfaction with Piaget's (e.g., 1972) assumptions of the sufficiency of formal thought as a model of adult cognition (e.g., Kramer, 1983; Labouvie-Vief & Chandler, 1978). Concurrently, Riegel (1973; 1976; 1979) attacked the structuralist, organismic assumptions of developmental psychology by emphasizing the dialectical nature of developmental progress, and by advocating searches for post-formal manifestations of adult reasoning. His notions, that developmental change (in the form of dramatic leaps) would be more likely to emerge from asynchronies between the physical, historical, social, biological, and psychological dimensions of people's lives, flew in the face of assumptions of synchronous, structured, person-oriented change.

Riegel's approach constituted a radical departure from traditional psychology and its methods, because of its insistence on the uniqueness of individual persons, the concreteness of their life circumstances in time and history, and the possibility of novelty in development that ensued from dialectical contradictions between these persons and external forces. Although Riegel's death and reformulations of his basic dialectical approach allowed life-span developmental psychology to proceed in the direction of less radical methodologies (See Baltes & Cornelius, 1977), his emphasis on contextualization of the individual is a continuing feature of theorizing in the area (Dannefer, 1992; Featherman & Lerner, 1985).

Life-Span Development as Selective Optimization

Given his agenda of explaining what development can involve in later life, Baltes' (1987) account of life-span perspectives is most concerned with showing that aspects of life where people experience decline (e.g., in "fluid intelligence") can be compensated for by other abilities. Specifically, his proposal calls for expansion of the concept of development to include not only phenomena of growth (gain), but other directions of change as well. Development comes to be defined as any change in the adaptive capacity of the organism, whether positive or negative (Baltes, 1987, p. 616).

The addition of an "end-of-the-life-span" to the "beginning-of-the-life-span" perspective carries with it the need to modify concepts of development to account for decline as well as gain. Assuming that all developmental change involves adaptive specialization (Baltes & Baltes, 1990, p. 16), makes it is possible to interpret that adaptive process as a trade-off between gains and losses, with life period differences. Childhood development is mostly marked by gains in excess of losses, and old age, vice versa.

This dual pathway of development allowed Baltes to move to his central theme of selective optimization with compensation as the mechanism for successful aging. The combinatory processes of selection and compensation give the individual some executive control over the processes of adaptation. One compensates for loss in one area of functioning by exercising one's capacities in another area to a greater extent. In terms of cognitive development, Salthouse (1991) as well as Baltes (1987; Baltes & Baltes, 1990) has shown how failing fluid intelligence is given adaptive compensation by personal adaptation or intervention. For example, Kleinig, Smith, and Baltes (1989) demonstrated that older adults could be trained to use compensation strategies that increased their failing memory capacity. Most older adults without brain-related diseases are able to raise their levels of performance with simple programs of cognitive training (Baltes, 1991; Schaie & Willis, 1986). Baltes and Baltes (1991, p. 8) are ready to admit that the selective optimization concept is utopian, and their extensive research program is aimed at testing the limits of reserves that can be used in the service of intentionally canalized options. Although Baltes (1990, p. 851) acknowledges the significance of society in the creation of a positive culture of old age, this acknowledgment emphasizes specific interventions for compensatory change, where a "rich number of opportunities permitting individuals to select means and ends commensurate with their course of life." We lack a more general account of how social and physical factors are likely to interact with personal choice to induce the diversity that the Baltes' team observed in their aged subjects.

Predispositional and environmental influences on decline in old age have been traced for 36 years in Schaie's longitudinal study (see Schaie, 1994). Schaie's (1994, p. 310) documentation of seven factors that reduce the risk of cognitive decline in old age lists environmental input (the absence of chronic disease, favorable demographic circumstances, intellectually stimulating environment, an intellectually able spouse) and personal lifestyles (flexibility and life satisfaction at mid-life, and maintained perceptual speed). Schaie's approach is interventionist, seeking to redress some of the natural signs of cognitive degeneration. Central to these interventionist approaches is the efficacy of socially originated action in strategy training programs (e.g., Schaie & Willis, 1986).

Whereas non-deliberate adaptation seems to fit uneasily with the Baltes and Schaie models, Dannefer and Perlmutter (1990) allow for different change processes, with varying degrees of intention and purpose. Along with their concept of "cognitive generativity" or "minded activity" (p. 110) that is akin to selective optimization, they specify other processes of change, such as physical ontogeny that accounts for the natural aging process, and what they call "habituation" or the regularized response set by which people are predisposed to behave in predictable ways.

Structuralist and Stage Traditions in Adult Development
With change in fashion away from structuralist models, and with criticisms of Piaget's claims for universal formal thought (e.g., Keating, 1980; Kramer, 1983), different venues for the search for adults' logical operations emerged. Studies of everyday reasoning followed some early investigations of logicial thinking in the supermarket (for instance, Capon & Kuhn, 1979), leading to studies in non-laboratory settings (e.g., Poon, Rubin & Wilson, 1989; Sternberg & Wagner, 1986; also Schliemann, Carraher & Ceci, this volume). Pitt (1983) proposed a general problem-solving model that linked Piagetian-type developmental interests to analyses of the information processes by which adult logic is applied to specific problems. In many respects, cognitive psychology's growing interest in professional exper-

tise took up the slack that accompanied the demise of developmental structuralist models (see Chi, Glaser & Farr, 1988). It has mainly been in the specialized domain of university student development that age-related, stage-like models have persisted, and these have been mostly geared to North American conditions (King, Kitchener, Davison, Parker & Wood, 1983; Mines & Kitchener, 1986). Along with the preoccupation with aging, this meant that middle adulthood represented a gap in developmental psychologists' analyses that was substantially filled by sociologists' concerns with adult socialization (Dowd, 1990; Elder, 1991).

Several attempts at periodization of the adult years from a different perspective followed the popular North American and European sectioning of adulthood into series of transitions and changing directions. Levinson (1986; Levinson, with Darrow, Klein, Levinson, & McKee, 1978) used intensive biographical interviews to trace remembered changes in men's early dreams for their future lives, marriage, family, and mentor relationships and age-periodized life courses. He described middle-aged men's development in terms of a series of eras, examining the organization of their lives at particular points in time. Looking for influential factors that were general across white-collar and blue-collar workers, he found evidence of the relevance of a dream of a life trajectory in adolescence and facilitation of life opportunities by a mentor who can foster the young man's entry into vocational and social groups.

Roberts and Newton (1987) followed up the male stories by reviewing several dissertation studies of the lives of females in different professions. They found that life courses of women were less influenced by early dreams of the self in later years. Women were less likely to have entry into social roles facilitated by mentors, and they were more concerned with social factors than simply following personal career goals.

It is possible that some of the gender differences observed in these studies were related to the actual professions and groups into which individuals are socialized. Therefore, Darling and Lawrence (1994) examined the life courses of a group of 26 successful Australian women whose profession of writing novels is personally involving. Half of these women writers had been motivated by early visions of themselves as writers from the time of leaving school, even when social events (such as World War II) gave them little encouragement for their dreams. Like Roberts and Newton's (1987) lawyers, few experienced the assistance of specific professional mentors. Rather, most found support for their writing in informal groups and among friends. This analysis necessitates an examination of the choice points leading to branching directions in writers' life courses, moving the age-periodization approach to an intensive look at the specific times when personal aspiration and social conditions either hindered or facilitated professional development. For some, family demands led to reactivations of mostly dormant dreams, for example, by writing stories for a child. For others, writers' support groups faciltiated their redefinitions of themseves as writers.

In one sense, this life-structure line of research is not strictly "life-span," because it commences with adolescence and early adulthood, and in Levinson's case, seems to depend on describing the structures at successive periodizations of men's adult years, without critical analysis of the mechanisms of change. Nevertheless, if the life structure is interpreted within the frame of transactions between culture and individual, then it holds out a promise for redressing some gaps in the contemporary life-span approach. It may be most suitable to examine individuals' development within the productive middle years in terms of the roles a society assigns to specific persons, and their interpretations of those roles. It is necessary to take into account the continuing transactions that occur between persons and social structures (institutions) if we are to understand what development means and how it is effected over the whole of life and within specific cultures.

Contemporary Perspectives on Culture in Relation to Life-Span Development

Within the contemporary scene of context-related approaches to psychology, both cross-cultural and cultural psychological traditions have been moving toward culture-inclusive life-span developmental psychology. In their recent discussion of the contributions of cross-cultural psychology, Segall, Dasen, Berry, and Poortinga (1990, p. 349) criticized popular "safari-style research" in which favorite tests are taken to exotic cultures, and results compared with homeland norms. The burden of their argument is that cross-cultural psychology is primarily a method of doing research that is as valuable for investigating development, as it is for any other area of human psychology (Berry, Poortinga, Segall, & Dasen, 1992). Cross-cultural psychology is often oriented toward testing the universal claims to which models of development have been susceptible. It also borrows heavily from traditional psychology's methodological repertoire of quantification, samples-to-population generalizations, and the use of linear statistical models.

Deconstructing and Reconstructing Methodology

The meaning of methodology has become reduced to the question of methods, and separated from the texture of human construction of knowledge (see Branco & Valsiner, in press). This makes it possible to separate the set of data-analytic methods (or statistical procedures as a whole) from the framework of the ideas that lead the research questions. The methods begin to dominate empirical research in psychology, rather than theoretical issues that are of interest. Cross-cultural psychology may be particularly affected by this change because the use of ever-more-sophisticated methods in cross-cultural data construction and analyses often turns the most illustrious cultural phenomena into some "measure" of an uninterpretable kind.

It has been argued (Gigerenzer et al., 1989) that most uses of statistical methods in psychology are social-conventional constructions. Most uses of statistics in psychology are based on the belief in the objectivity-granting nature of statistics. Such beliefs abound in contemporary psychology at large, including cross-cultural psychology as a part of psychology. That those beliefs are based on inadequate understanding of the nature of the statistical knowledge-construction system has been argued (Gigerenzer, 1993). Yet the belief in the objectivity-granting power of "the statistical method" (often considered to be the synonym of "the scientific method") keeps its stronghold in contemporary psychology. As a result, systematic construction of homogeneous categories of phenomena that are notable for their homogeneity takes place in psychology (Valsiner, 1984, 1986, 1989c).

When psychologists are interested in the study of development, the quantitative orientation that has dominated psychology over the last 50 years is particularly out of touch with the phenomena (Baldwin, 1930; Valsiner, 1987; Van Geert, 1994). Development is a phenomenon of structuration, and structures cannot be measured by reducing them to a conglomerate of linear dimensions. A similar issue confronts psychologists who study culture; cultural complexity is likewise not reducible to quantified dimensionality. Further, in the case of systemically organized phenomena—and both culture and development can safely be assumed to be of that kind—the separation of "independent" and "dependent"-labelled "variables" is a mental construction of psychologists of questionable usefulness (Anandalakshmy, 1974).

While it can be suggested that the tradition of cross-cultural comparisons of "variables" is a conceptual impasse, it is no easy task to point to viable alternatives that exist in contemporary psychology. Possibly a clear understanding of the metathoretical frames of reference (see Valsiner, 1987, 1989a, chapter 2) can be helpful. Cross-cultural psychology has usually made use of the inter-individual reference frame: "cultures" (treated as entities) are compared (on the basis of "variables"), with a result of making statements about their differences. This research tactic undoubtedly produces an accumulation of empirically-based claims about differences, but it bypasses the central question of how each culture serves as an organizational framework for persons who "belong to it." Answering that latter question is in principle impossible when researchers adopt the inter-individual frame of reference.

In contrast, the *individual-socioecological frame of reference* provides access to the systemic organization of culture (and of the person). It entails a direct empirical focus on the relationship between person and the immediate life context, which is culturally regulated by internalized cultural meanings and social suggestions by the "social others" (Valsiner, 1989a, pp. 36–38). In contemporary cultural psychology (which emerged to some extent on the basis of the cross-cultural research traditions) the shift from the use of an inter-individual to an individual–socio-ecological reference frame can be noted.

Cultural Psychology: New and Old

Cultural psychology has a time-honored tradition in human sciences (see chapter by Jahoda & Krewer in Volume 1, this *Handbook*). Historically, the first chair in psychology was established in the area that is the direct antecendent of contemporary cultural psychology. Moritz Lazarus was appointed to the *Lehrstuhl* of

Völkerpsychologie at the University of Bern in 1860 (see Jahoda, 1993, p. 146) long before the social institutional beginnings of psychology as such in 1879. Aside from different versions of the *Völkerpsychologie*-tradition in German-speaking countries (Stern, 1991), the emphasis on culture as intricately intertwined with personal psychological functioning has been visible in anthropology and linguistics (Sapir, 1924). What distinguishes different versions of cultural psychology from cross-cultural psychology is the focus on systemic processes that make person and culture unified as the persons function in their social worlds. This is an example of the use of the individual–socioecological frame of reference. In contrast, if cross-cultural comparisons (i.e., use of inter-individual frame of reference) are used in cultural psychologies, then the information obtained from such comparisons functions merely as background evidence that demarcates an interesting phenomenon, yet leaves its investigation to systemic analysis efforts.

The German tradition of symbolic action theory and its sequels is a good example of this kind of methodological perspective taking. Initiated by Ernest E. Boesch (1991) over the last forty years, and borrowing from the traditions of Pierre Janet, it has been developed in different conceptual directions by his disciples (Eckensberger, 1995; Krewer, 1992; see also chapter by Miller in Volume 1, this *Handbook*). Eckensberger (1979, 1990, 1995; Eckensberger, & Kornadt, 1977; Eckensberger, & Burgard, 1983; Eckensberger, Krewer & Kasper, 1984; Eckensberger & Zimba, this volume) has developed a sophisticated, dynamic theoretical perspective for a cultural psychology of human action and thinking (Eckensberger, 1990; 1992). Within that perspective, the use of psychology's traditional methods would be counterproductive to the theoretical aims of the system. Starting from a focus on goal-directed actions and emerging reflexive abstraction, Eckensberger's (1992, 1995) cultural view of mental processes carefully retains the notion of agency. It is the active person who constructs "action barriers" and negotiates them—at the levels of action, reflexive abstraction, and self-reflection (Eckensberger, 1995). Development of the person is interdependent with the culture, yet the person's subjective world retains its idiosyncratic nature exactly as the person constructs one's psychological system. Therefore it is only natural that Eckensberger (1993; 1995) takes an interest in the moral reasoning processes as cultural phenomena, through methods of analyzing ordinary language material collected from single cases. This effort brings his theoretical orientation to bear upon issues of life-span cultural development. For example, investigations of how life crises and subjective self-reconstruction by cancer patients revealed how cultural means are put to use in a person's transaction with the life-world (Eckensberger & Kreibich-Fischer, 1994). This approach is deeply phenomena-oriented in its basis, and systemic in its constructive efforts.

North-American versions of cultural psychology usually combine the interests of cultural anthropology and psychology. Cole's work in the area of culture and cognition spans more than the last two decades (e.g., Cole 1975, 1981, 1990, 1991, 1992; Cole & Bruner, 1971; Laboratory of Comparative Human Cognition, 1983). Starting from the cultural-historical school of psychology (of Luria and Vygotsky), Cole (1990, 1992) has been looking for ways in which person and culture are unified in a systemic organizational form. Thus, he considers the metaphor of "mutual interweaving" as the main mechanism by which culture and person are related (see Cole, 1992, p. 26 for the metaphor of "intermingling of threads from two ropes," specifically, those of biological "modules" and cultural contexts). This interweaving reflects the general process in which ". . . the culture becomes individual and the individuals create their culture" (Laboratory of Comparative Human Cognition, 1983, p. 349), or, how culture and cognition are mutually constituted. The locus of this mutual constituting process is the concrete activities carried out in everyday life (Cole, 1985; Newman, Griffin & Cole, 1989). Cognitive processes that are established within such contexts can be transferred to other contexts under the social facilitation of the transfer. In applying his version of cultural psychology directly to life-span thought, Cole (1995) illustrates how the interactions between mind and culture enter into the process of development in different periods of life.

Shweder's (1984, 1992; Shweder & Much, 1987; Shweder & Sullivan, 1993) claims of recent years underscore the influence of culture as a primary factor in the constitution of the self. From a perspective dependent on contemporary North American cultural antropology, Shweder (1990, p. 25) explains his cultural psychology within the study of "subject-dependent objects" (intentional worlds) and "object-dependent subjects" (intentional persons) who interpenetrate each other's identities, and set the conditions for each other's existence and development. Intentional persons live in the context of culturally organized environments, take over different aspects from those environments (for instance, cultural myths), and use those in the organization of their personal worlds.

The emphasis on semiotic mediation of thinking persons that Wertsch (1985, 1991, 1995) brings to cultural psychology directs attention to the dynamic process of situation redefinition as the primary means of development. Interaction partners are constantly in some relation of intersubjectivity. They share similar situation definitions that they then transcend by the process of situation redefinition. Wertsch (1990, 1991) makes Bakhtin's concept of dialogicality work within his system, where the analysis of "voices" affords the revelation of complexity of messages. The result is a consistent return to the study of ambivalences embedded in communicative messages in the form of a "polyphony of voices." Different voices can be seen in utterances, in ways that "interanimate" or dominate each other in the act of speaking within situated activity contexts. Wertsch's perspective affords the analysis of heterogeneity of culture in both the external and internal worlds of the person (Smolka, 1992, 1993). In his recent turn to the study of adult identity formation, Wertsch's dynamic voicing perspective becomes directly applicable to the study of life-course development.

In summary, the main feature that separates cultural psychologies from cross-cultural traditions is the effort to provide a systemic account of how culture participates in the psychological functioning of human beings. Each theoretical formulation of cultural psychology emphasises transactions between the person and the social world. From that orientation, the traditional methodological directions taken by cross-cultural psychology do not allow them to deal with these significant microgenetic transactions. Instead, the strong concern with cultural contexts that is evident in these contemporary cultural psychologies contains the potential for building a conceptual bridge to life-span developmental psychology as it has established itself today. The two disciplines converge in their interests in the contextualization of the person's life course. Each carries with it the potential for treating person–cultural contextual interactions as central units of analysis for understanding how lives change.

Relocating Life-Span Development within the Culture

It is appropriate to locate accounts of life-span development within this general approach, because contextualism is so definitely emphasised by modern life-span theorists (e.g., Dannefer, 1992; Featherman & Lerner, 1985; Labouvie-Vief, 1982, 1994; Labouvie-Vief & Chandler, 1978; Thomae, 1979). There appear to be two directions by which culture-propagating approaches can become integrated with the life-span tradition.

First, in principle, traditional cross-cultural psychology could easily expand to study comparisons between life-course periods (in early, middle, and late adulthood) between different national and ethnic groups. That such studies would unearth a wealth of empirical data is guaranteed by the different age periodizations espoused in different societies. However, this essentially empiricist attempt at integration would merely enrich the existing cross-cultural tradition by making comparisons in larger numbers of smaller scale life-course categories. For example, in addition to the existing comparisons of how adolescents in Society X differ from their counterparts in Society Y, similar questions would be asked about adults in substages of development. How would menopausal women or retired men in Societies X and Y differ? Such studies could not be expected to inform the study of life-span developmental psychology because they would simply borrow cross-cultural psychology's nondevelopmental perspective, and expand it to cover more periods of the human life-span and more societies.

The second direction is more promising. It entails a systemic inspection of person–culture interactions along the lines suggested by the cultural psychologies we have mentioned, in what Lonner (1993, p. vi) called the relativist's "study (of) culture deeply in the singular and explicitly non-comparative sense." This direction focuses on how human development is organized in general by observing it closely in the particular. The life-span developmentalist's attention to social structural constraints has to be addressed in terms of how cultural phenomena actually guide processes of human development. In addition to being mentioned by authors who propagate their specific versions of cultural psychology, this question is implicit in Berry et al's (1992) general framework for cross-cultural psychology. They argued that the ecological context provides a setting in which individuals and contextual factors interact. Furthermore, they acknowledged the significant role of the individual within society.

> *We also accept that individuals can recognize, screen, appraise and* alter all of
> these influences, *[emphasis added] (whether direct or mediated) and as a result
> there are likely to be wide individual differences in the psychological outcomes.
> (Berry et al, 1992, p. 13).*

Thus, cross-cultural psychologists agree substantially with life-span theorists
(e.g., Baltes, 1987; Dannefer & Perlmutter, 1990) in characterizing development as
primarily contextualized phenomena that carry with them the possibility of individually unique multidirectional routes. What is needed in both approaches is a
way of conceptualizing how unique personal–cultural experiences become formed,
and subsequently change within interactions between social–cultural and individual psychological transactions. That missing link between personal uniqueness and social experience needs to be conceptualized by a perspective that recognizes active roles of both the person and the society, is formulated in non-
deterministic ways, and allows for development of novelty.

Cultural Canalization of Personal Development

The use of the cultural canalization metaphor belongs within the domain of co-
constructionist approaches in contemporary developmental psychology. The term
"canalization" characterizes the "bounded indeterminacy" that development entails. Co-constructing agents (the person and the social world) set up *mutual* constraints that delimit the set of next steps possible for developmental change. Constraints may be temporary, transitory, and heterogeneous (see Valsiner, 1987, chapter
4), yet their function is to reduce the unmanageable excesses of uncertainty in
person–environment relationships, and to specify routes that development might
follow. Actual courses of development are constructed by developing persons
within the set of presently functioning constraints set up by the collective culture
and the person (see Valsiner, 1989a). Thus a co-constructionist perspective speci-
fies that personal development is guided by constraints upon acting, feeling, and
reasoning. Such constraints nevertheless only direct—rather than strictly determine—the construction of a personal life course. Consequently, this perspective
on direction recognizes the jointly active roles of persons and their cultural worlds
in human development.

The idea of canalization has had a productive history in developmental biology. Starting from the wider contexts of field theories in human sciences (e.g.,
Bühler, 1990/1934, Köhler, 1928, Lewin, 1935; see also Bourdieu, 1991, p. 239–251;
Bourdieu & Wacquant, 1992, pp. 94–140, for recent versions of field theory in sociology), canalization mostly reached developmental psychology through the theoretical biological heritage of Waddington (see an analysis by Gilbert, 1991).

Acting upon each other dialectically, social and personal constraining forces
lead to new syntheses in the development of person and social context. Mutual
constraining is a process jointly created by the person and the social world that
organizes the person's development throughout the life span in irreversible time
(Valsiner, 1993, 1994d). Cultural meanings are intricately interwoven with the con-

straining forces being exerted upon the person, and they too are remade through development. Psychological processes are simultaneously narrowed in scope and expanded in possibilities for novelty by the constraining functions of meanings. Even physiological, maturation-governed aspects of development are given cultural meaning as they become functional in social contexts.

All development is regulated by boundaries that are continually being constructed by social structures (institutions, informal groups) that exist in present time. As Mayer (1986) pointed out, different social structures create specific roles for the person to fulfill, laying down time schedules dictated by institutional logic. The boundaries survive over time because of their relative environmental stability and utility, for example, family and work are reorganized, or through people's internally reconstructed versions of their meanings for the boundaries in their values and beliefs. Canalizing social structures guide the person towards always unpredictable, but ever imagined future states (Valsiner, 1993, Van Geert, 1994). Effectively, they provide the person with distinctions between acceptable events and their alternatives.

From this perspective, constraining does not simply involve repression of freedom. Rather, it includes simultaneous limiting and enabling devices that narrow the arena of further activity for a developing person, all the while setting up the very arena in which that person may perform in novel ways. For instance, decisions and events pertaining to the life of one family member can constrain outcomes for relatives in the social roles they are expected to fulfil. Some of the most extreme of cultural practices depend upon the actualization of specific social role expectations at transition periods, for instance, the tradition of sati (widow burning) in India (Datta, 1990).

Synchronic and Diachronic Constraining

The multitude of constraints that guide a person's acting, feeling, and thinking can be described in terms of their synchronic and diachronic characteristics. Synchronic constraints are multilevel and systemic organizers of personal lives that concur at the given time and context. Diachronic devices entail "feed-forward" constraining of the person's possible future acting or thinking.

Synchronic constraining devices entail external constraints of social class membership, external constraints of social suggestions from others and internalized constraints such as personal ideas of "behaving properly," These external and internal devices complement each other in the given context. For example, the external marking of a caste, social class, or profession limit a person's possible ways of acting and feeling in a public context (e.g., by special publicly displayed symbols such as dress and demeanor). However, that external canalization device is complemented by marked persons' internalized reconstructions of what the class membership means to them personally, and as they actively transform social roles and rules by their novel actions (Freeman, 1979, 1981).

Some active constraints bring special dimensions from family and collective cultural history to a person's here-and-now construction of personal culture knowledge. The cultural canalization function of any prescribed ritual antedates the life course that is being dramatically altered by it at the culturally appointed time. Thus, an adolescent's entrance into a cycle of transitional rites of passage is pre-scheduled, even before the child is born. These types of cultural canalization devices are called diachronic, because they operate over historical time, and are made available by the collective memory that transmits them across generations. The diachronic constraints pre-organize the psychological development of a person over one's life course, thus acting as feed-forward devices for making the future predictable at least in the sense of general schematic depictions.

The interests of anthropologists and sociologists in social class, caste, and roles provide rich accounts of the functioning of diachronic cultural devices in many societies (Anandalakshmy, 1974; Barnett, 1976; Marriott & Inden, 1977; Mohapatra & Mohapatra, 1979; Vincentnathan, 1993). Any collective–cultural ritualistic event maintained by transferring it across generations fulfils this function. Religious texts also set the stage for varied kinds of activities by persons in their everyday lives, ranging from efforts to re-educate others towards repression of sensuality in the name of religion (Grimshaw, 1989), to reification of sensuality in the service of religious beliefs (Marglin, 1985).

Diachronic canalization devices set up the collective–cultural structural background for the functioning of the synchronic canalization processes. They also set up socially shared knowledge about human development as it is manifest in specific cohorts. In these terms, cohorts are not subpopulations. Rather, these represent age-sets within a whole society, differentiated by being confounded with the vocational and familial roles attached to them (Talle, 1988).

Life-Cycle Periodization as a Diachronic Canalization Device

Every society uses some general scheme of life-cycle categorization for defining similarity groups. Meanings linked with these groups entail value-laden expectations that are made visible through the prescription of social rituals at culturally expected life transition points (e.g., births, birthdays, initiation rites, weddings, funerals). Illustrating how specific cultural meanings can be attached to transitions, Doi (1991) reported that second generation Japanese Americans had transformed a traditional Japanese rite of passage to old age *(kanreki)* at 60 years of age into an American-style birthday party.

Categorization by age may coincide with accentuated biological development periods (e.g., beginning to walk independently, emergence of permanent teeth, puberty, etc.), or it may take into account cognitive developmental factors (e.g., the perceived "trustworthiness" of children at the six- to seven-year age level that coincides with the emergence of concrete operations). Goodnow, Cashmore, Cotton, and Knight's (1984) finding of different developmental timetables in Anglo and Lebanese Australian mothers' expectations for their children's activities provides clear evidence of cultural differences in the meanings attached to different ages.

Any kind of semiotic basis can be arbitrarily used to segment the life course, for instance, the use of magic symbolism of number 7 in medieval Europe (Kon, 1988), or relative estimations of age (e.g., "fathers" are always older than "sons";

the latter become fathers and have sons, etc.). When relative time estimations are used, they may be irreversible (e.g., grandfather is relative to father as father is relative to son). They may be cyclical. For instance, in cases where ancestors—obviously older than their living adult sons or daughters—are believed to be reborn as little children, one can talk about intransitivity in the organization of age periods (formally: A < B < C < A). Such collective cultural models of intransitive age periodization lead to situations where young children are assumed to have elevated social relevance for the well-being of adults, as in the case of the Ijaw in the Niger Delta (Leis, 1982). Children are believed to have supernatural powers, they come from the spirit world populated by ancestors, may return to that world (by dying), and can communicate directly with the spirits.

Viewed cross-culturally (as well as across the history of an individual culture), age stages are likely to be differently represented. As Kakar (1992, p. 11) pointed out, the Hindu *ashrama* periodization of the life course does not distinguish the first three stages of life charted out by Erikson (infancy, early childhood, and play age). Likewise, the separate age period of adolescence that is so important in European and North-American cultures has been identified as a cultural invention of the turn of the 20th century. Historians of childhood who have tried to delineate the cultural construction of the adolescence period have reached a difficult paradox. On one hand, features of psychological conduct usually characteristic of adolescence (e.g., heightened search for moral values, concentration on one's own role in social contexts) are found in historical descriptions over centuries and societies (Weinstein & Bell, 1982). On the other hand, symbolic recognition (by semiotic labelling) of adolescence as a special age period is not always found. For example, Hareven (1986) discovered that 19th century American mill families expressed little consciousness of distinct life stages of adolescence and middle age. Instead of concentrating on the normative transitions that concern 20th century cohorts, they were concerned with the external critical events of migration, economic crises, strikes, and mill shutdowns that defined their lives.

In contemporary India, Ramanujam (1992, p. 49) directly attributed the differentiation of adolescence as a separate and developmentally relevant age period to urbanization. Of course, verbal naming is only one way of recognizing the uniqueness of adolescence or any other age periodization. Schlegel and Barry (1991) found that an adolescent stage of life was named for boys by only 36 percent of 175 societies, and for girls by only 46 percent. Yet some other symbolic points of recognition (e.g., dress, ornament, hair style) and some form of social adolescence were evident in most societies they studied.

Constructing a Life-Course: A Constraining Perspective

For developing persons, constraining processes occur in time and space through their own lived-through experiences. People construct personal meanings for the events they experience, with the assistance of the meanings and boundaries provided by the social structures and other individuals. Each person's internal version of the social meaning attached to an experience can be said to constitute "personal culture" (Valsiner, 1989a), and this personal sense of the life course agrees to a greater or lesser degree with a narrative form that fits the expectations circulating within social discourse (Gergen & Gergen, 1986; 1988). Thus, a woman in a closed religious community may give her open assent to sanctions against reading secular newspapers, but within the confines of her children's threatened rebellion, actually supervise their secret reading of the evening newspaper (Lawrence, Benedikt & Valsiner, 1992).

New settings for personal development are likely to be pre-organized by externally given lifecycle markers (e.g., "graduation ceremony" or "initiation rite"), and they would be governed by the specific action constraints the social structure lays down as appropriate (e.g., dress and action codes for proper conduct). Nevertheless, a subjective construction of an upcoming event influences a person's conduct. For instance, if a graduating student sees the ceremony as a ritualized joke designed to impress people about academic superiority, he (or even she!) may decide to arrive for graduation wearing drag rather than sober clothes covered by an academic gown. Under the conditions of bidirectional culture transmission, the person may elect to follow the socially pre-organized and personally constraining organization of the event, or s/he may transform that event into a novel, personalized form. From the perspective of life-span developmental psychology, it is at moments of relevant change in the life course that cultural tools are used to reorganize the whole future of the life course (Devereux, 1963).

Given the multiple possibilities that are available at any temporal moment at the population level, the set of possible individual life trajectories is highly heterogeneous. No two life courses are exactly similar. The range for a variety of individual life courses is specified by its outer limits, and further organized by the society's currently maintained constraining system (e.g., social class or caste differentiation), along with the society's strictness or flexibility in the face of individuals' actions. Examples of differentiations within societies include vocational roles (Dumont, 1980), special castes of saints and holy people (Weinstein & Bell, 1982), and structures of family and marriage organization (Bhatt, 1991; Kapadia, 1990; Levine, 1988; Valsiner, 1989a, chapter 4). Therefore, when viewed from the vantage point of a specific person, the actual unilinearity is being constructed in irreversible time, out of the set of possible mulitilinear trajectories that are made available at the population level.

An Account of Development through Culture

Human development is potentially multidirectional and necessarily contextualized. From the multitude of possible life-course trajectories, persons active in their specific contexts construct their individually unique life courses. It is claimed here that this construction process is based on mutual constraining of the person by the environment, and of the environment by the person.

Our account of canalization owes something to earlier elaborations of Waddington's "epigenetic landscape" model (Valsiner, 1987), and borrows from the work of the Russian evolutionist Severtsov who was concerned with explanation of different routes and levels of evolutionary change (see Sewertzoff, 1929). We also preserve early life-span concern with dialectics (Baltes, 1979; Labouvie-Vief & Chandler, 1978; Riegel, 1979), by emphasizing the mutual constraining interactions that occur between social structure and individual.

An account of life-span development within our constraining perspective is given in Figure 3–1. This account is built on the contrast between "collective culture" and "personal culture" (see Valsiner, 1989a). The parts of Figure 3–1 that are conceptually relevant include the boundaries of the life-course possibilities (constraints set up by society), and personal branching-off points (or bifurcation points).

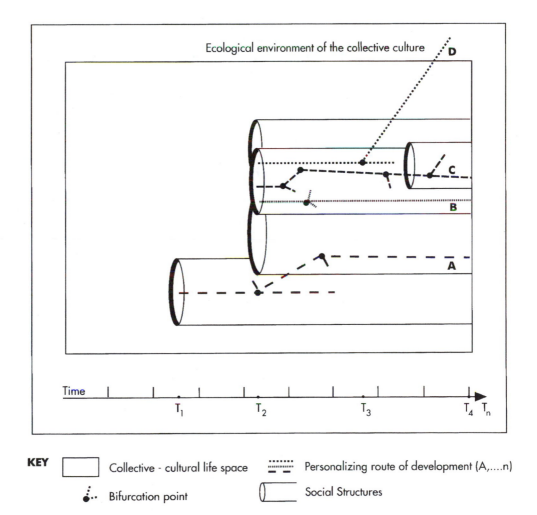

FIGURE 3–1   Elements of a co-constructionist account of life-span development within culture

The Collective-Cultural Life Space

The whole human developmental process is worked out within a specific collective-culture that sets historical and ideological parameters around its social structures (e.g., families, schools), groups of people (e.g., age-sets), and individuals as they exist and develop. It provides the conceptual frame and tools with which the person constructs personal meanings, as illustrated in the figure by the rectangular frame that defines the life space.

Religious beliefs, expectations of what is valuable and desirable, and cultural norms of behavior place ideological and conceptual parameters on patterns of development within a specific culture (Berger & Luckmann, 1966; Erikson, 1946). A distinguishing feature of any culture is what its members take for granted. They do not need to have everyday conventions explained to them, because the culture provides stories and narratives, according to which they can assign meanings to objects, events, and relationships. For instance, beliefs about the cyclical nature of existence in Hindu culture give a frame of reference to cultural members' interpretations of what their development means for them at a given time, in terms of death and reincarnation. Such a view of human existence within the natural and supernatural world is different from views that belong to a secularist view of Western medicine and from Christian doctrines of continuing, transformed personal life beyond death (LeGoff, 1984).

A culture itself is open to environmental influence and able to undergo change, because of its temporal/historical and ecological location, respectively denoted in the figure by the time line and the identification of the ecological environment in which the collective-culture is located. Development of the collective-culture, its social structures and members cannot extend beyond the present time (shown at T_4, with time continuing on to a presently unknown time (T_n). Outside, other collective cultures exist in the phenomenological world, and they may impinge on its development, as cultural members travel in and out.

Social Structures Constraining Personal Development

Within the ideological and normative boundaries of the collective-culture, specific social structures define the roles and developmental tasks that are appropriate for age-sets and other classes of persons. In Figure 3–1, these social structures are illustrated as cylinders that canalize development for individuals. Social structures have different sizes and different times of commencement over the life span (e.g., family, school, work). In addition, since human existence is concurrently organized within various kinds of social institutions, as Bronfenbrenner (1979; 1989; 1993) has demonstrated in his ecological theory of development, different social structures simultaneously operate to constrain a cultural member's development (illustrated in Figure 3–1 at T_2).

Consider the life of a youth in an isolated village, constrained by a few social structures (e.g., family, religion). At a point in time, a 20th-century traveller (anthropologist, freedom fighter) enters the village and introduces new life possibilities, such as urban migration or life in a guerilla unit. He creates a potential bifurcation point for the youth. If the youth takes up the introduction as a personal choice, then his pathway of development takes a new route, moving into a new set of social structures (e.g., unattached male group, political party). He leaves his community and family behind, but if he sends his wages back home, the family continues as an influential social structure in his life, albeit one that now is given new meaning and significance. Regardless of the nature of new social structures, they function in a similar way, by imposing their constraints on the youth by rules (e.g., when he can return to the village), special practices (e.g., secret ceremonies and oaths) and other features that define life within the group. They also allow regularity of experience (by their constraining processes), and access to collective ideologies and beliefs.

While emphasizing the personalized significance of such social structures, the life-span premise of contextualized development does not always specify how contexts impose constraints on the development of individuals. (Dowd, 1990; Featherman & Lerner, 1985). In our account, these social structures that set up socially defined boundaries also provide opportunities for people to construct individualized life pathways along those normalized routes. The social obligations of the daughter-in-law in Hindu society impose limitations on her personal aspirations, while allowing her access to family privileges (Narain, 1970). Similarly, family obligations to provide care for elderly members pervade British family life in ways that demand that daughters rearrange their lives to allow time for caregiving (Finch & Mason, 1993). Nevertheless, these very obligatory roles simultaneously hold out ways of interpreting events and feelings that allow daughters to redefine themselves (e.g., as professional caregivers, Pearling & Aneshensel, 1994) or to expect rewards for roles fulfilled (e.g., religious merit or a special inheritance).

Personalizing Routes of Development

Regardless of the strictness of cultural norms and roles expected by social structures, individualized acceptance of socially approved routes of development is neither automatic nor inevitable, even among small children. The reciprocal personally constraining (canalizing) activities that we have described can either lead a person along pathways of development acceptable to the social structure (e.g., fulfilling the obligations of one's filial responsibilities), or it can lead the person away from the socially acceptable routes, toward others. For example, by refusing to take up the family responsibility and instead pursuing a personal career goal, a person may leave the village to become a guerilla fighter or a prostitute. In both of these new routes he or she will find a social context that supports and canalizes further life-course construction.

Individualized life courses are constructed with different bifurcation points and different possible branching pathways within the same social structure. In Figure 3–1, the personalizing developmental route shown as (A) reaches a bifurcation point (at T_2). At that point, the person moves into another set of social structures rather than continuing along the original possible route. The permissible change may involve culturally defined adult roles (e.g., political necessities for school leavers), a new career or a dramatic change in lifestyle (e.g., entering a Buddhist monastery).

Another personalized route (B) continues in a set of social structures with little disturbance, and yet another (C) in the same social structures has multiple bifurcation points and moves into a subsequent structure, containing still permissible possibilities. Abilities, goals, and actions influence personal constraining that is exerted back onto the social structures to make the C route a reality. For example, adult students' personal goals conflicted with lecturers' stated objectives for a university course of study, but enabled the students to redefine their university experience in terms of other constraining structures in their lives (Lawrence & Volet, 1991). Such goals do not always precede the interaction as fixed intentions. Saxe and Gearhart (1990) observed how young Brazilian straw weavers selected specific adults as teachers because of their own goals for mastering different weaves. Other goals emerged for the same children within the tutorial interchange, although the verbal instructions of their tutors were focused on specific activities and not on the larger goals for the work that the children developed.

Some social structures are less flexible than others in the developmental routes that they tolerate. People find and exploit some latitude in even the most rigid systems, as Wikan (1982) discovered in a strict Sohari Muslim community. Despites customs that severely restricted women's roles, wives maneuvered arrangements to create physical and mental space for themselves (e.g., by persuading an authoritarian husband to change houses or jobs). Novel routes for development are forced back onto the social structure by persons' efforts to change their life courses.

In contrast to socially permissible routes, the personalized route shown as (D) in Figure 3–1 follows a socially acceptable pathway until a bifurcation point is reached (at T_3). Here a personal change in direction takes the person right out of current social structures and, in fact, out of the given collective cultural life space. In Lawrence et al's (1992) case history, a mother secretly disobeyed her orthodox religious culture's rules against reading secular material. She provided a bifurcation point for herself and her daughter by allowing the children to read newspapers and listen to the radio. The mother's changed behavior could remain hidden within the structure. The daughter went much further out of the culturally acceptable conduct, reading library books and overtly contravening cultural dress codes. After many years, she moved out of the closed culture's social structures altogether, finding her cultural and ethnic expression in a liberal community.

Other individuals who move physically away from a certain collective-cultural setting, usually attempt to transport its ideals with them. Missionary wives who migrated to Hawaii in the 19th century tried to recreate their collective-culture and its norms in the Pacific, changing the new social environment in what they saw as utopian directions (Grimshaw, 1989). Still others who travel return to the original collective-culture and bring back new ideas with them, initiating what Bartlett (1923, p. 163) called "borrowing," whereby new elements are introduced into the culture and result in changes not only in the carrier but the collective-culture itself (see chapter by Berry & Sam, Volume 3, this *Handbook*). Bartlett's illustration of the introduction of peyote into the rituals of Winnebago Native Americans demonstrated the ways in which the new element gradually became part of the culture via a sequence of reactions to the old ways that were provoked by the new element. Eventually, the culture itself was transformed.

It is not difficult to find individualized choices that take the person out of socially constrained canals, and into different life-course pathways. For instance, people frequently experience role conflict when socially defined roles cannot be coordinated (e.g., being a professional woman and a wife and mother, Finch & Mason, 1993). Persons can "fail" in their assigned roles, and there is some leeway in most societies for those who do not meet socially defined obligations (Sherif, 1936). Specifically, the multiplicity of role assignments may lead the person to construct a heterogeneous form of role-coordination, starting relatively early in their ontogeny (Oliveira & Rossetti-Ferreira, 1995).

The heterogeneity of social canalization in societies guarantees synchronic coexistence of specializations. Deviations from general norms are collective-culturally sanctioned for people with the specific semiotic markings of socially recognized special life courses (e.g., saints: Weinstein & Bell, 1982; temple dancers: Marglin, 1985; teachers: Wolcott, 1974). Furthermore, at times of social upheaval, individual people's efforts to reconstruct the constraint system lead to partial (or total) change of the local norms. In such circumstances, the irreversibility of time functions to weld microgenetic changes into ontogenetic pathways for both person and culture. Negotiations between persons and structures at constraint boundaries (Valsiner, 1987) may succeed, or fail. In either case, the active co-construction of conduct can be represented in this canalization scheme.

Personal Reconstructing of the Constraint System

The social worlds of any society are filled with cases of persons of specific social backgrounds moving into vocational activities that are possible but actively discouraged. To illustrate how the discouraging messages of the social structure can be ignored and new possibilities taken up by the individual, we refer to an incident in a recent autobiographical narrative. The Delany Sisters for a century lived as African Americans in the United States (Hearth, Delany, & Delany, 1993). Sadie Delany at 103 told of her trials as a "colored" teacher (p. 119) in a New York school system. Colored teachers were not permitted to teach in white schools. If she were to progress from elementary to high school teaching, Sadie realized that she must act in a way not permitted by the structure. She explained, "I had to be a little clever—Bessie (her 101-year-old sister) would say sneaky—to find ways to get around these brick walls set up for colored folks" (p. 119). Her plan was to apply for a high school position, and when her name reached the top of the list, to avoid the personal interview. A face-to-face encounter would have meant that she would be automatically "bounced down the list," ostensibly for a number of reasons, but really because of her race. Sadie "skipped the appointment, and sent a letter, acting like there was a mix-up" (p. 119). She arrived on the first day of classes, confronting the authorities with the reality of her appearance, and incidentally a choice of their own:

> It was risky, but I knew what a bureaucracy it was, and that in a bureaucracy
> it's easier to keep people out than to push them back down. Child, when I
> showed up that day . . . they just about died when they saw me. . . . Once I
> was in, they couldn't figure out how to get rid of me. (Hearth, Delany &
> Delany, 1993, pp. 119–120).

Sadie made a deliberate choice to use the occasion as a bifurcation point where
her life would either take a pathway out of the norm while nevertheless continuing to exist within the social structure, or be further confined by confrontational
prejudice.

Once Sadie's social defiance actually occurred, a new phenomenon had
emerged in her life and in the life of the school. Its effect could not be removed.
Even if Sadie were immediately dismissed, her act would stand and retain its significance for her and all observers. The construction and dissemination of a "Sadie
myth" would function as a diachronic constraining device for persons in subsequent generations.

When events are filled by personal–cultural content they can become significant for the culture. An analysis of Nepali women's songs (Skinner, Basnet, &
Valsiner, 1993) demonstrated how collective cultural forms may be retained as
new content is inserted into them, thus leading to the reconstruction of the collective cultural complex. This is similar to changes in ongoing rituals with accommodation to new practices (Bartlett, 1923). Within Christian Church contexts, once
some women took upon themselves the priestly role, the institution was forced to
deal with the new phenomenon of the woman priest. Denial of its legitimacy by
conservatives introduced yet another phenomenon into the culture that provoked
further cycles of change (Lawrence & Dodds, 1994). Collective culture is never
harmonious, but includes a multitude of differentiated "voices" that attempt to
canalize personal cultures in institutionally designated directions. However, thanks
to the active role of individuals, such efforts often fail, or backfire.

In a similar vein, potent moments for demonstrating the bidirectional nature
of relations between personal and collective cultures can be found where established rituals fail (e.g., see the description of failure of fire-walking ceremony in
Freeman, 1981), or where persons volunteer to move through experiences of bodily
invasive religious rituals for reconstructing their personal cultures (Obeyesekere,
1981). People must make sense of unexpected and extreme happenings. The existing collective-cultural system is constantly being tested at its boundaries and reconstructed through such testing.

We can observe the ways in which a person can change society when personal
ontogenetic change follow from microgenetic life events. The person's ontogenetic
change leads to cultural transformation in local social norms and meanings. Hence,
observations of ontogenetic changes across the life span within a culture naturally
shift attention to microgenetic changes that have participated in their emergence.
The focus on contextualized aspects of development espoused by life-span theorists (e.g., Baltes, 1987; Dannefer & Perlmutter, 1990) requires an account of the
transactions that occur in concretized points of time and cultural location, as Riegel

(1979) argued so cogently. Further, the psychological processes involved in this personal construction process need to be elaborated.

The Nature of the Internalization/Externalization Process

Internalization and externalization involve reciprocal cyclical processes by which the person operates on semiotic material, the signs that stand for objects and events within the meanings the collective-culture constructs and uses to represent its realities. By "internalization," we understand the process by which meanings that are held out for the individual by social structures and social others are brought over into the individual's thinking. This process of bringing over meanings is bidirectional (from outer to inner world, and back), and constructive. What originally had collective-cultural meaning in the inter-personal (or inter-mental) domain, under the guidance of socially defined interpretations of reality becomes intra-personal (intra-mental) (Lawrence & Valsiner, 1993).

This transposition occurs during social interactions, for example, when two persons are engaged in dyadic problem solving, during explicit teaching episodes, or implicitly while persons engage in the normal activities of life. The reciprocal process of "externalization" connotes activities in the injection back into the social environment of material that once was social in character and had become personal (Semin, 1989; Valsiner, 1989a). In order to go beyond general statements about these concepts, it is necessary to specify the "materials" that are "brought over" from the social to the personal world of any individual, and how the "bringing over" process operates. The first question can be answered in generic terms. The "materials" are semiotic. Signs that can be cognitively manipulated are constructed to represent realities. They involve the transformation of collective-cultural meanings into systems of personal sense. For instance, rituals of initiation and graduation ceremonies are supposed to carry the sense of both the social and the personal significance of the occasion. Forms of conduct, tattoo (Fellman & Thomas, 1986; TeRiria & Simmons, 1989), or dress (Enninger, 1985) convey unity with past generations and provide the individual with transitional markers to which they can refer in times of doubt.

In relation to the co-constructionist, mutually canalizing account of human development, focal activities are mental interpretive actions (operations) by which each person creates a personal sense of the ideals, roles, and relationships presented within the collective culture's meanings, propagated by social structures. External signs become internal as social meaning is taken up by the individual, to be either accepted in a generally agreed-upon way, or transformed by the internal conceptual system that actively brings it in. Knowledge and affective structures in the individual's mind are both the locus of transformation, and the means for effecting construction and reconstruction (transformation) of future input and expressable output. Thus, each person builds a unique mental construction of reality, even when social others are engaged in the building activities.

Social contributions to the mental construction work revolve around the manner in which significant people and structures organize and give meaning to phenomena in the social environment. They make available the appropriate individual pieces for incorporating in the construction. They also provide the frames within which individual pieces can be built into the uniquely constructed personal culture of meaning, or *bricolage* of different pieces of meaning (to use Lévi-Strauss' terminology, see also Hatton, 1989; Lawrence et al, 1992). While constrained by this *bricolage* of meanings, the person's intra-mental construction has a highly dynamic structure, so that it is being constantly rearranged. It is never complete, but changes as it receives sufficient support in the person's new encounters in social settings. Different internalization/externalization encounters across the life span occur at the microgenetic level. They explain how individuals are active in constructing and re-constructing their own personal cultures at different moments in time, and how their activities at significant bifurcation points can lead them into unknown pathways that influence their own development and that of the social structures in which they live.

Internalization/Externalization Cycles: An Example
In her autobiographical account of finding her Australian Aboriginal identity, Sally Morgan (1987) reported a series of incidents that illustrate the internalization–externalization cycle in the communication of meanings between the person and others in her immediate social structure (the extended family). Sally's mother and grandmother had persistently told the children that their skin was darker than their friends' because they had an Indian background. Sally knew there was some mystery, because her even darker grandmother Nan, would hide when friends came home. Although she accepted the story into adulthood, her sister Jill had already constructed a different personal interpretation. She believed that they were Aboriginal, but that the older women felt they needed to perpetuate the constructed myth. In racially prejudiced Western Australia, to have come from India was more socially acceptable than to be part Aboriginal.

As a grown woman, Sally became more demanding in her requests for details about her racial origins. One day she simply asked her mother, " 'We're Aboriginal, aren't we Mum?' 'Yes dear,' she replied, without thinking" (Morgan, 1987, p. 135). With the long-term lie admitted, new possibilities arose for all of them, and this is where we see the cycles of changing conceptions and expressions (meanings) working between people. Morgan reports the effect on herself and her sister.

> *I was very excited by my new heritage. Jill, it does mean something, to have admitted it. Now she might tell us more about the past. But the way I look at it, it's a beginning. Before we had nothing. At least now we've got a beginning. (Morgan, 1987, p. 136)*

From that beginning point, Sally acted upon and institutionalized her acceptance of the new status (in culturally defined social structures) by applying for a government scholarship for Aboriginal students. The implicit was accepted, incorporated into her personal identity and acted upon socially. "It wasn't the money

I was after . . . I desperately wanted to do something to identify with my new-found heritage, and that was the only thing I could think of" (p. 137).

The scholarship in turn brought differences in the personal identity of other members of the family, and their sense of being in the world. Nan slowly began to change her social behaviors. She started to take explicit interest in the news about black people, and adopted a self-label of Nyoogah (the Aboriginal people of South Western Australia), that she then generalized to all black people. She gradually became less furtive, and made open comments about the treatment of Nyoogahs. For the whole family, the revelation led to an intense search for relatives and their stories.

Sally's changed inner meanings were externalized into her immediate social and institutionalized social environments, and the injection of her changes provoked further changes, in individuals in the family, and even beyond. For instance, friends complained to the government that she was falsifying her past in order to obtain the benefits, and she reasserted even more strongly her aboriginality.

Thus, in this case history, and in our account of the internalization/externalization process, we go inside socially constraining and canalizing processes, to describe the character of person–culture transactions in terms of meanings and constructed versions of personal sense. Meanings are attached to roles (e.g., caring family member, fully-functioning Islamic adult); activities (e.g., rituals); and group and person labels (saint, colored person, Nyoogah). Social structures are constraining persons within their social roles, they are using these meanings to allow each person to discern the activities that are available, and the expectations and beliefs that are offered for assent.

The internalization/externalization processes are not confined to the exceptional. They are applicable to many points of change, large or small in significance. In relation to cultural values, Briggs (1979) described how values and valued behaviors are conveyed to Canadian Inuit children by means of routine interpersonal games that adults play with them. By locating their interactions within a game structure, adults are able to use pretense, ambiguity, and contradiction to allow children to internalize values in emotionally charged experiences that give them entry to stereotypic and novel actions. Children could try out different versions of everyday activities within their cultural frameworks, and the limits of approved actions are conveyed by adults by constructive use of conflict.

From the perspective of co-constructed personal meaning, we can take a fresh look at the frequently quoted statement by Bakhtin:

> . . . *the language as living social–ideological concreteness, as multivoicedness of opinion [Russian: raznorechivoe mnenie], lies for the individual consciousness on the boundary between one's own and of the foreign. The word of a language is a half-foreign word. It becomes "one's own" when the speaker inhabits it with his intention, his accent, masters the word, links it to his senseful and expressive efforts. Until that moment of appropriation [Russian: prisvoenie] the word [exists] not in neutral and faceless language . . . but in others' speech, foreign con-*

texts, in service of foreign intentions: from here one has to take it and make it one's own (Bakhtin, 1975, p. 106).

Bakhtin's views on language and thought processes have usually been interpreted in terms of "social sharing" of language and other semiotic means. Yet even if language is half "foreign" to the person, it becomes one's own cultural tool through making it one's own. The supposedly "shared" meanings (see Berger & Luckmann, 1966, for a sociological account) are interpreted and instantiated in new constructions. In some cases, the meanings that are assumed to be shared are sufficiently vague to allow individual interpretations to coexist without disrupting the activity. For example, there will be a range of interpretations of the graduation ceremony, from belief in the valedictory speeches, through socially constrained participation by bored family members, to skepticism by graduates who participate for the sake of family appearances. The show can proceed, until perhaps our student arrives in drag and forces everyone to reassess the vague meanings on which they were operating.

In these terms, potential multidirectionality of development across the life span is constantly being actualized at a given point in irreversible time by constant semiotic construction of personal sense. The inclusion of such constructed personal sense in the decision processes at bifurcation points has consequences for the subsequent development of that person, both intra-mentally (e.g., how she socially defines herself), and in the actual conduct by which she makes her stand. Thus, we submit that efforts to elaborate the nature of internalization/externalization processes fills the gap in the account of how cultural canalization and individual life-span trajectories meet and diverge.

Conclusions

We have proposed a view of life-span development for the person in the culture in terms of routes through different experiences over the whole of lifetime. While the route that is lived out by a given person may seem unidirectional from the viewpoint of that individual at any given time, multiple possibilities for a person's development always exist. From the viewpoint of possible future life-course pathways, these possibilities arise because previous actualities are constrained by activities of both the society and the person. For a life-span researcher, the life of the person is not only lived within a collective culture, but it is constrained and provided with non-random directions. Within that constraining process, the person is an active co-constructor all through life, operating with the help of self-generated goals, intentions, and interpretations.

Collective culture and person are seen as mutually open to change. Their interactions at specific periods in personal life courses have potential for changing both of them. It is during these bifurcation points that microgenetic change can drive ontogenetic transformation, and reorganization of some aspects of the collective culture. The mechanisms for effecting changes in person–culture transactions involve exchanges and transformations of semiotic meanings in internalization/externalization processes.

In general, this account permits developmentalists to put the life-span of the individual back into the center of psychological concerns, in the tradition of Bühler's emphasis on the uniqueness of the life course of each individual (Bühler, 1933; Bühler & Massarik, 1968). It also provides a way of explaining the workings of the multidirectional emphasis that Baltes (1979, 1987) argued so effectively is fundamental to a life-span approach. Multidirectionality is given its proper meaning in a culture inclusive, life-span developmental psychology.

Human development is not an all promising and forever progressing tendency, as European and North American child development paradigms have habitually assumed, to the chagrin of cross-cultural psychologists. Human development also is not a downward slide, as biological models of aging have suggested. Cross-cultural psychologists were able to see the significance of the culture-bound nature of human psychology and its varied routes. They did not easily give up nondevelopmental general assumptions and associated comparative methodological concerns in order to theorize about the ongoing place of the person in a cultural context. Modern cultural theorists have proposed that developmental and cross-cultural psychologists alike could look again at person–culture transactions, and posit ways of describing these interactions and their effect on change. We too have examined these transactions, arguing that a cultural view of development holds out the greatest promise for understanding how development moves over a life time.

The present life-span perspective leads to demands that persons not be plucked out of their collective cultures for decontextualized comparisons. Rather, it requires that we take up the call for culture-inclusive, open-systemic whole-life approaches to the study of development. Of course, this is not a simple order, for it means making interacting person–culture systems the object of analysis, and focusing on analyses of ontological change over 90 years or more. It also means microgenetically investigating the interactions between mutually constraining systems along the way, in order to observe the microgenetic changes that influence ontogenetic pathways. Human beings remain self-constructing persons within their cultural worlds, and they construct those worlds through internalization and externalization.

References

Adler, L. L. (Eds.). (1989). *Cross-cultural research in human development.* New York: Praeger.

Allport, G. W. (1937). *Personality: a psychological interpretation.* New York: Henry Holt and Co.

Allport, G. W. (1962). The general and the unique in psychological science. *Journal of Personality, 30,* 405–422.

Allport, G. W. (1966). Traits revisited. *American Psychologist, 21,* 1-10.

Anandalakshmy, S. (1974). How independent is the independent variable? In J. L. M. Dawson &. W. Lonner (Eds.), *Readings in cross-cultural psychology* (pp. 79–89). Hong Kong: University of Hong Kong Press.

Ash, M. G. (1988). Die Entwicklung des Wiener Psychologischen Instituts 1922–1938. In A. Eschbach, K. Mulligan, & W. W. Schmitz (Eds.), *Viennese heritage, Vol. 2. Karl Bühler's theory of language* (pp. 303–325). Amsterdam: John Benjamins.

Bakhtin, M. (1975). *Voprosy literatury i estetiki [Problems of literature and aesthetics].* Moscow: Khudozhestvennaya Literatura.

Baldwin, J. M. (1930). James Mark Baldwin. In C. Murchison (Ed.), *A history of psychology in autobiography* (Vol. 1, pp. 1–30). New York: Russell & Russell.

Baltes, P. B. (1979). Life-span developmental psychology: Some converging observations on history and theory. In P.B. Baltes (Ed.), *Life-span development and behavior* (Vol 2, pp. 255–279). New York: Academic Press.

Baltes, P. B. (1987). Theoretical propositions of life-span developmental psychology: On the dynamics between growth and decline. *Developmental Psychology, 23* (5), 611–626.

Baltes, P. B. (1991). The many faces of human ageing: Toward a psychological culture of old age. *Psychological Medicine, 21:* 837–854.

Baltes, P. B., & Baltes, M. M. (Eds.). (1990). *Successful aging: Perspectives from the behavioral sciences.* Cambridge: Cambridge University Press.

Baltes, P. B. & Cornelius, S. W. (1977). The status of dialectics in developmental psychology: Theoretical orientation versus scientific method. In N. Datan and H. W. Reese (Eds.), *Life-span developmental psychology* (pp. 121–134). New York: Academic Press.

Baltes, P. B. & Reese, H. W. (1984). The life-span perspective in developmental psychology. In M. H. Bornstein, & M. E. Lamb (Eds.), *Developmental psychology: An advanced textbook, Vol. 23* (pp. 493–531). Hillsdale, NJ: Erlbaum and Associates.

Bartlett, F. C. (1923). *Psychology and the primitive culture.* New York: Macmillan.

Barnett, S. (1976). Coconuts and gold: Relational identity in a south Indian caste. *Contributions to Indian Sociology, 10* (1), 133–156.

Berger, P. & Luckmann, T. (1966). *The social construction of reality: A treatise in the sociology of knowledge.* New York: Doubleday.

Berry, J. W., Poortinga, Y. H., Segall, M. H., & Dasen, P. R. (1992). *Cross-cultural psychology: Research and applications.* Cambridge: Cambridge University Press.

Bhatt, G. S. (1991). *Women and polyandry in Rawain-Jaunpur.* Jaipur: Rawat.

Boesch, E. E. (1991). *Symbolic action theory and cultural psychology.* Berlin: Springer.

Bourdieu, P. (1991). *Language and symbolic power.* Cambridge, MA: Harvard University Press.

Bourdieu, P. & Wacquant, L. J. D. (1992). *An invitation to reflexive sociology.* Chicago: University of Chicago Press.

Branco, A. U. & Valsiner, J. (in press). Changing methodologies: a co-constructionist study of goal orientations in social interactions. In G. Misra (Ed.), *Cultural construction of social cognition.* Cambridge: Cambridge University Press.

Briggs, J. L. (1979). The creation of value in Canadian Inuit society. *International Social Science Journal, 31* (3), 393–403.

Bronfenbrenner, U. (1979). *The ecology of human development.* Cambridge, MA: Harvard University Press.

Bronfenbrenner, U. (1989). Ecological systems theory. *Annals of Child Development, 6,* 185–246.

Bronfenbrenner, U. (1993). The ecology of cognitive development: Research models and fugitive findings. In R. H. Wozniak & K. W. Fischer (Eds.), *Development in context* (pp. 3–44). Hillsdale, NJ: Erlbaum and Associates.

Bühler, C. (1933). *Der menschliche Lebenslauf als psychologisches Problem.* Lepzig: Hirzel.

Bühler, C. & Massarik, F. (Eds.). (1968). *The course of human life.* New York: Springer.

Bühler, K. (1990). *Theory of language: The representational function of language.* Amsterdam: John Benjamins. [original in German in 1934].

Capon, N. & Kuhn, D. (1979). Logical reasoning in the supermarket: Adult females' use of a propositional reasoning strategy in an everyday context. *Developmental Psychology, 15* (4), 450–452.

Chi, M. T. H., Glaser, R., & Farr, M. (Eds.). (1988).

The nature of expertise. Hillsdale, NJ: Erlbaum and Associates

Cole, M. (1975). An ethnographic psychology of cognition. In R. W. Brislin, S. Bochner, & W. Lonner (Eds.), *Cross-cultural perspectives on learning* (pp. 157–175). New York: Wiley.

Cole, M. (1981). Society, mind, and development. In F. S. Kessel & A. W. Siegel (Eds.), *The child and other cultural inventions* (pp. 89–123). New York: Praeger.

Cole, M. (1985). The zone of proximal development: Where culture and cognition create each other. In J. V. Wertsch (Ed.), *Culture, communication, and cognition: Vygotskian perspectives* (pp. 146–161). Cambridge: Cambridge University Press.

Cole, M. (1990). Cultural psychology: A once and future discipline? In J. Berman (Ed.), *Nebraska Symposium on Motivation, Vol. 37* (pp. 279–336). Lincoln: University of Nebraska Press.

Cole, M. (1991). On putting Humpty Dumpty together again: A discussion of the papers on the socialization of children's cognition and emotion. *Merrill-Palmer Quarterly, 37* (1), 199–208.

Cole, M. (1992). Context, modularity and the cultural constitution of development. In L. T. Winegar & J. Valsiner (Eds.), *Children's development within social context, Vol 2: Research and methodology* (pp. 5–31). Hillsdale, NJ: Erlbaum.

Cole, M. (1995). Culture and cognitive development: From cross-cultural research to creating systems of cultural mediation. *Culture & Psychology, 1*, 25–54.

Cole, M. & Bruner, J. S. (1971). Cultural differences and inferences about psychological processes. *American Psychologist, 26*, 867–876.

Côté, J. E. (1993). Foundations of a psychoanalytic social psychology: neo-Eriksonian propositions regarding the relationship between psychic structure and cultural institutions. *Developmental Review, 13*, 31–53.

Dannefer, D. (1992). On conceptualization of context in developmental discourse: Four meanings of context and their implications. In D. L. Featherman, R. M. Lerner, & M. Perlmutter (Eds.), *Life-span development and behavior* (Vol 11, pp. 83–110). Hillsdale, NJ: Erlbaum and Associates.

Dannefer, D. & Perlmutter, M. (1990). Development as a multidimensional process: Individual and social constituents. *Human Development, 33*, 108–137.

Darling, J. & Lawrence, J. A. (1994). *Australian women writers' experience of early career dreams and mentoring*. Paper presented at Eighth National Human Development Conference, Melbourne, July.

Datta, V. N. (1990). *Sati: A historical, social and philosophical enquiry into the Hindu rite of widow burning*. Delhi: Manohar.

Devereux, G. (1963). Two types of modal personality models. In B. Kaplan (Ed.), *Personality viewed cross-culturally* (pp. 227–241). New York: Norton.

Doi, M. L. (1991). A transformation of ritual: The Nisei 60th birthday. *Journal of Cross-Cultural Gerontology, 6*, 2, 153–163.

Dowd, J. J. (1990). Ever since Durkheim: The socialization of human development. *Human Development, 33*, 138–159.

Dumont, L. (1980). *Homo hierarchicus: The caste system and its implications*. Revised Edition. Chicago: University of Chicago Press.

Eckensberger, L. (1979). A metamethodological evaluation of psychological theories from a cross-cultural perspective. In L. H. Eckensberger, W. J. Lonner, & Y. H. Poortinga (Eds.), *Cross-cultural contributions to psychology* (pp. 255–275). Lisse: Swets & Zeitlinger.

Eckensberger, L. H. (1990). From cross-cultural psychology to cultural psychology. *The Quarterly Newsletter of the Laboratory of Comparative Human Cognition, 12*, 1, 37-52.

Eckensberger, L. H. (1992). Agency, action and culture: Three basic concepts for psychology, in general and for cross-cultural psychology, in specific. *Arbeiten der Fachrichtung Psychologie*, Universität des Saarlandes. No. 165. Saarbrücken.

Eckensberger, L. H. (1993). Normative und deskriptive, strukturelle und empirische Anteile in moralischen Urteil. In L. H. Eckensberger & U. Gähde (Eds.), *Ethische Norm und empirische Hypothese* (pp. 328–379). Frankfurt-am-Main: Suhrkamp.

Eckensberger, L. H. (1995). Activity or action: Two different ways towards an integration of culture into psychology. *Culture & Psychology, 1,* 1, 67–80.

Eckensberger, L. H. & Burgard, P. (1983). The cross-cultural assessment of normative concepts: Some considerations on the affinity between methodological approaches and preferred theories. In S. H. Irvine & J. W. Berry (Eds.), *Human assessment and cultural factors* (pp. 459–480). New York: Plenum.

Eckensberger, L. H. & Kornadt, H. J. (1977). The mutual relevance of the cross-cultural and the ecological perspective in psychology. In H. McGurk (Ed.), *Ecological factors in human development* (pp. 219–227). Amsterdam: North-Holland.

Eckensberger, L. H. & Kreibich-Fischer, R. (1994). Affektive und kognitive Verarbeitung des Krankheitsgeschehens bei krebskranken Patienten [The affective and cognitive coping process of cancer patients]. *Jahrbuch der Psychoonkologie* (pp. 41–76). Wien: Springer.

Eckensberger, L. H., Krewer, B., & Kasper, E. (1984). Simulation of cultural change by cross-cultural research: Some metamethodological considerations. In P. Baltes (Ed.), *Life-span developmental psychology: Historical and generational effects* (pp. 73–107). New York: Academic Press.

Elder, G. H. Jr. (1991). Lives and social change. In W. R. Heniz (Ed.), *Theoretical advances in life course research: Status passages and the life course,* (Vol. I, pp. 58–86). Weinheim: Deutscher Studien Verlag.

Enninger, W. (1985). The design features of clothing codes—the function of clothing displays in interaction. *Kodikas, 8,* 1–2, 81–110.

Erikson, E. H. (1946). Ego development and historical change. *Psychoanalytic Studies of the Child, 2,* 359–396.

Erikson, E. H. (1958). *Young man Luther: A study of psychoanalysis and history.* New York: Norton.

Erikson, E. H. (1963). *Childhood and society, 2nd edition.* New York: Norton.

Erikson, E. H. (1969). *Gandhi's truth: On the origins of militant nonviolence.* New York: Doubleday.

Erikson, E. H. (1976). Reflections on Dr. Borg's life cycle. *Daedalus. Spring,* 1–28.

Erikson, E. H. (1992). Report to Vikram: Further perspectives on the life cycle. In S. Kakar (Ed.), *Identity and adulthood* (pp. 13–34). Dehli: Oxford University Press.

Featherman, D. L. & Lerner, R.M. (1985). Ontogenesis and sociogenesis: Problematics for theory and research about human development and socialization across the life-span. *American Sociological Review, 49,* 659–676.

Fellman, S. & Thomas, D. M. (1986). *The Japanese tattoo.* New York: Abbeyville Press.

Finch, J. & Mason J. (1993). *Negotiating family responsibilities.* London: Tavistock/Routledge.

Freeman, J. M. (1979). *Untouchable: An Indian life history.* Stanford: Stanford University Press.

Freeman, J. M. (1981). A firewalking ceremony that failed. In G. R. Gupta (Ed.), *The social and cultural context of medicine in India* (pp. 308–336). Delhi: Vikas.

Frenkel, E. (1936). Studies in biographical psychology. *Character & Personality, 5,* 1–34.

Gergen, K. J. & Gergen, M. M. (1986). Narrative form and the construction of psychological science. In T. R. Sarbin (Ed.), *Narrative psychology: The storied nature of human conduct* (pp. 22–44). New York: Praeger.

Gergen, K. J. & Gergen, M. M. (1988). Narrative and the self as relationship. In L. Berkowitz (Ed.), *Advances in experimental social psychology,* Vol. 21 (pp. 17–56). New York: Wiley.

Gigerenzer, G. (1993). The Superego, the Ego, and the Id in statistical reasoning. In G. Keren & C. Lewis (Eds.), *A handbook for data analysis in the behavioral sciences: Methodological issues* (pp. 311–339). Hillsdale, NJ: Erlbaum.

Gigerenzer, G., Swijtink, Z., Porter, T., Daston, L., Beatty, J. & Krüger, L. (1989). *The empire of chance.* Cambridge: Cambridge University Press.

Gilbert, S. F. (1991). Epigenetic landscaping: Waddington's use of cell fate bifurcation diagrams. *Biology and Philosophy, 6,* 135–154.

Goodnow, J.J., Cashmore, J., Cotton, S., and Knight, R. (1984). Mothers' developmental time-tables in two cultural groups. *International Journal of Psychology, 19,* 193–205.

Grimshaw, P. (1989). New England missionary wives, Hawaiian women, and 'the cult of true womanhood.' In M. Jolly & M. Macintire

(Eds.), *Family and gender in the Pacific* (pp. 19–44). Cambridge: Cambridge University Press.

Hareven, T. (1986). Historical changes in the social construction of the life course. *Human Development, 29,* 171–178.

Hatton, E. (1989). Lévi-Strauss's Bricolage and theorizing teachers' work. *Anthropology and Education Quarterly, 20,* 2, 74–96.

Hearth, A. H., Delany, S., & Delany, A. E. (1993). *Having our say: The Delany Sisters' first 100 years.* New York: Kodansha International.

Jahoda, G. (1986). A cross-cultural perspective on developmental psychology. *International Journal of Behavioral Development, 9,* 417–437.

Jahoda, G. (1993). *Crossroads between culture and mind.* Cambridge, MA: Harvard University Press.

Kakar, S. (1992). Setting the stage: The traditional Hindu view and the psychology of Erik H. Erikson. In S. Kakar (Ed.), *Identity and adulthood* (pp. 2–12). Delhi: Oxford University Press.

Kapadia, K. M. (1990). *Marriage and family in India.* Calcutta: Oxford University Press.

Keating, D. P. (1980). Thinking processes in adolescence. In J. Adelson (Ed.), *Handbook of adolescent psychology* (pp. 211–246). New York: Wiley.

King, P. M., Kitchener, K. S., Davison, M. L., Parker, C. A., & Wood, P. K. (1983). The justification of beliefs of young adults: A longitudinal study. *Human Development, 26,* 9106–116.

Kleinig, R., Smith, J., & Baltes, P. B. (1989). Testing-the-limits and the study of adult age differences in cognitive plasticity of a mnemonic skill. *Developmental Psychology, 25,* 247–256.

Köhler, W. (1928). Bemerkungen zur Gestalttheorie. *Psychologische Forschung, 11,* 188–234.

Kon, I. S. (1988). *Rebenok i obshchestvo [Child and society].* Moscow: Nauka.

Kramer, D. (1983). Post-formal operations? A need for further conceptualization. *Human Development, 26,* 91–105.

Krewer, B. (1992). *Kulturelle Identität und menschliche Selbsterforschung.* Saarbrücken: Breitenbach.

Laboratory of Comparative Human Cognition. (1983). Culture and cognitive development.

In W. Kessen (Ed.), *Handbook of child psychology, Vol. 1: History, theory & methods* (pp. 295–356). New York: Wiley.

Labouvie-Vief, G. (1982). Dynamic development and mature autonomy: A theoretical prologue. *Human Development, 25,* 141–161.

Labouvie-Vief, G. (1989). Logic and self-regulation from youth to maturity: A model. In M. L. Commons, F. A. Richards, & C. Armon (Eds.), *Beyond formal operations* (pp. 158–179). New York: Praeger.

Labouvie-Vief, G. (1994). *Psyche and eros: Mind and gender in the life course.* Cambridge: Cambridge University Press.

Labouvie-Vief, G. & Chandler, M. (1978). Cognitive development and life-span developmental theory. In P. B. Baltes (Ed.), *Life-span development and behavior* (Vol 1, pp. 181–210). New York: Academic Press.

Lawrence, J. A., Benedikt, R., & Valsiner, J. (1992) Homeless in the mind: A case-history of personal life in and out of a close orthodox community. *Journal of Social Distress and Homelessness, 1* (2), 157–176

Lawrence, J. A. & Dodds, A. E. (1994). Women homeless in the church. In D. Haskell (Ed.), *Tilting at Matilda* (pp. 89–96). Fremantle, WA: Fremantle Arts Centre Press.

Lawrence, J. A. & Valsiner, J. (1993). Conceptual roots of internalization: From transmission to transformation. *Human Development, 36,* 150–167.

Lawrence, J. A. & Volet, S. (1991). The significance and function of students' goals. In L. Oppenheimer & J. Valsiner (Eds.), *The origins of action: Inter-disciplinary and international perspectives* (pp. 133–152). New York: Springer-Verlag.

LeGoff, J. (1984). *The birth of purgatory.* Chicago: University of Chicago Press.

Leis, N. B. (1982). The not-so-supernatural power of Ijaw children. In S. Ottenberg (Ed.), *African religious groups and beliefs* (pp. 151–169). Meerut, India: Folklore Institute.

Levine, N. (1988). *The dynamics of polyandry.* Chicago: University of Chicago Press.

Levinson, D. (1986). A conception of adult development. *American Psychologist, 41,* 3–13.

Levinson, D., with Darrow, C. N., Klein, E. B.,

Levinson, M. H., & McKee, B. (1978). *The seasons of a man's life.* New York: Knopf.

Lewin, K. (1935). *A dynamic theory of personality.* New York: McGraw-Hill.

Lonner, W. J. (1993). Foreword. In J. Altarriba (Ed.), *Cognition and culture* (pp. v–viii). Amsterdam: North-Holland.

Marcia, J. (1966). Development and validation of ego-identity status. *Journal of Personality & Social Psychology, 3*, (55), 551–558.

Marcia, J., Waterman, A. S., Matteson, D. R., Archer, S. L., & Orlofsky, J.L. (1993). *Ego-identity: A handbook for psychosocial research.* New York: Springer-Verlag.

Marglin, F. A. (1985). *Wives of the god-king.* Delhi: Oxford University Press.

Marriott, M. & Inden, R. (1977). Toward an ethnosociology of South Asian caste systems. In K. David (Ed.), *The new wind: Changing identities in South Asia* (pp. 227–238). The Hague: Mouton.

Mayer, K. U. (1986). Structural constraints on the life course. *Human Development, 29*, 162–170.

Mines, R. A. & Kitchener, K. S. (1986). *Adult cognitive development: Methods and models.* New York: Praeger.

Mohapatra, M. & Mohapatra, S. (1979). Untouchability and the untouchables in an Indian state. *Journal of Social Research, 22*, 72–83.

Morgan, S. (1987). *My place.* Fremantle: Fremantle Arts Centre Press.

Narain, D. (1970). Interpersonal relationships in the Hindu family. In R. Hill & R. König (Eds.), *Families in East and West* (pp. 545–480). Paris: Mouton.

Newman, D., Griffin, P., & Cole, M. (1989). *The construction zone: Working for cognitive change in school.* Cambridge: Cambridge University Press.

Obeyesekere, G. (1981). *Medusa's hair.* Chicago: University of Chicago Press.

Oliveira, Z. M. & Rossetti-Ferreira, M. C. (1995). Understanding of co-constructive nature of human development: Role coordination in early peer interaction. In J. Valsiner & H. G. W. Voss (Eds.), *The structure of learning processes* (pp. 177–204). Norwood, NJ: Ablex.

Packer, M. (1994). Cultural work on the kindergarten playground: Articulating the ground of play. *Human Development, 37* (5), 259–276.

Pearling, L. I. & Aneshensel, C. S. (1994). Caregiving: The unexpected career. *Social Justice Research, 7* (4), 373–390.

Perlmutter, M., Kaplan, M., & Nyquist, L. (1990). Development of adaptive competence in adults. *Human Development, 33*, 185–197.

Piaget, J. (1972). Intellectual evolution from adolescence to adulthood. *Human Development, 5*, 1–12.

Pitt, R. B. (1983). Development of a general problem-solving schema in adolescence and early adulthood. *Journal of Experimental Psychology: General, 112* (4), 547–584.

Poon, L. W., Rubin, D. C., & Wilson, B. A. (1989). *Everyday cognition in adulthood and later life.* Cambridge: Cambridge University Press.

Ramanujam, B. K. (1992). Toward maturity: Problems of identity seen in the Indian clinical setting. In S. Kakar (Ed.), *Identity and adulthood* (pp. 37–55). Delhi: Oxford University Press.

Reinert, G. (1979). Prolegomena to a history of life-span developmental psychology. In P. B. Baltes (Ed.), *Life-span development and behavior* (Vol 2, pp. 205–243). New York: Academic Press.

Riegel, K. F . (1973). Dialectic operations: The final period of cognitive development. *Human Development, 16*, 346–370.

Riegel, K. F. (1976). The dialectics of human development. *American Psychologist, 31*, 689–700.

Riegel, K. F. (1979). *Foundations of dialectical psychology.* New York: Academic Press.

Roberts, P. & Newton, P. M. (1987). Levinsonian studies of women's adult development. *Psychology and aging, 2* (2), 154–163.

Salthouse, T. A. (1984). Effects of age and skill in typing. *Journal of Experimental Psychology: General, 113*, 345–371.

Salthouse, T. A. (1991). *Theoretical perspectives on cognitive aging.* Hillsdale, NJ: Erlbaum and Associates.

Sapir, E. (1924). Culture, genuine and spurious. *American Journal of Sociology, 29*, 4, 401–429.

Saxe, G. B. & Gearhart, M. (1990). A developmental analysis of everyday topology in unschooled straw weavers. *British Journal of Developmental Psychology, 8*, 251–258.

Schaie, K. W. (1990). Intellectual development in adulthood. In J. E. Birren & K. W. Schaie (Eds.), *Handbook of the psychology of aging*, 3rd ed. (pp. 291–309). New York: Academic Press.

Schaie, K. W. (1994). The course of adult intellectual development. *American Psychologist, 49*, 304–313.

Schaie, K. W. & Willis, S. L. (1986). Can adult intellectual decline be reversed? *Developmental Psychology, 22*, 223–232.

Schlegel, A. & Barry III, H. (1991). *Adolescence: An anthropogical enquiry*. New York: Free Press.

Schramek, R. (1934). Franz Liszt: Eine psychologische Untersuchung über Leben und Werk. *Archiv für die Gesamte Psychologie, 92*, 45–84.

Schwartz, T. (1981). The acquisition of culture. *Ethos, 9*, 4–17.

Segall, M. H., Dasen, P. R., Berry J. W., & Poortinga, Y. H. (1990). *Human behavior in global perspective*. Boston: Allyn and Bacon.

Semin, G. R. (1989). On genetic social psychology: A rejoinder to Doise. *European Journal of Social Psychology, 19*, 401–405.

Sewertzoff, A. (1929). Direction of evolution. *Acta Zoologica, 10*, 59–141.

Sherif, M. (1936). *The psychology of social norms*. New York: Harper & Brothers.

Shweder, R. (1984). Anthropology's romantic rebellion against the enlightenment, or there is more to thinking than reason and evidence. In R. Shweder & R. A. LeVine (Eds.), *Culture theory* (pp. 27–66). Cambridge: Cambridge University Press.

Shweder, R. (1990). Cultural psychology—what is it? In J. W. Stigler, R. A. Shweder & G. Herdt (Eds.), *Cultural psychology* (pp. 1–43). Cambridge: Cambridge University Press.

Shweder, R. (1992). Ghost busters in anthropology. In R. D'Andrade & C. Strauss (Eds.), *Human motives and cultural models* (pp. 45–57). Cambridge: Cambridge University Press.

Shweder, R. & Much, N. (1987). Determinations of meaning: Discourse and moral socialization. In W. M. Kurtines & J. L. Gewirtz (Eds.), *Moral development through social interaction* (pp. 197–244). New York: Wiley.

Shweder, R. & Sullivan, M. (1993). Cultural psychology: Who needs it? *Annual Review of Psychology, 44*, 497–523.

Skinner, D., Basnet, B., & Valsiner, J. (1993). Singing one's life: An orchestration of personal experiences and cultural forms. *Journal of South Asian Literature, 26*, 1 & 2, 15–43.

Smolka, A. L. B. (1992). *Towards the co-constructive methodology in the study of human development*. Paper presented at the First Conference on Socio-Cultural Studies, Madrid, September 15–18.

Smolka, A. L. B. (1993). A dinamica discursive no ato de escrever: relações oralidade escitura. In A. L. B. Smolka & M. C. Goés (Eds.), *A linguagem e o outro no espaco escolar: Vygotsky e a construção do conhecimento*. Campinas: Papyrus.

Stern, E. (1991). Problems of cultural psychology. *The Quarterly Newsletter of the Laboratory of Comparative Human Cognition, 12*, 1, 12–24.

Sternberg, R. J. & Wagner, R. K. (Eds). (1986). *Practical intelligence: Origins of competence in the everyday world*. Cambridge: Cambridge University Press.

Talle, A. (1988). *Women at loss: Changes in Maasai pastoralism and their effects on gender relations*. Stockholm: Stockholm University Press.

TeRiria, K. & Simmons, D. (1989). *Maori tattoo*. Auckland: The Bush Press.

Thomae, H. (1979). The concept of development and life-span developmental psychology. In P. B. Baltes & O. G. Brim, Jr. (Eds.), *Life-span development and behavior* (Vol. 2, pp. 282–312). New York: Academic Press.

Thompson, R. A. (1988). Early development in life-span perspective. In P. B. Baltes, D. L. Featherman, & R. M. Lerner (Eds.), *Life-span development and behavior* (Vol. 9, pp. 129–172). Hillsdale, NJ: Erlbaum and Associates.

Valsiner, J. (1984). Two alternative epistemological frameworks in psychology: The typological and variational modes of thinking. *Journal of Mind and Behavior, 5*, 4, 449–470.

Valsiner, J. (1986). Between groups and individuals: Psychologists' and laypersons' interpretations of correlational findings. In J. Valsiner (Ed.), *The individual subject and scientific psychology* (pp. 113–152). New York: Plenum.

Valsiner, J. (1987). *Culture and the development of children's action*. Chichester: Wiley.

Valsiner, J. (1989a). *Human development and culture.* Lexington, MA: D.C. Heath.

Valsiner, J. (Ed.). (1989b). *Cultural context and child development.* Toronto: C. J. Hogrefe and H. Huber.

Valsiner, J. (1989c). From group comparisons to knowledge: A lesson from cross-cultural psychology. In J. P. Forgas & J. M. Innes (Eds.), *Recent advances in social psychology: An international perspective* (pp. 501–510). Amsterdam: North-Holland.

Valsiner, J. (1993). Irreversibility of time and the construction of historical developmental psychology. Paper presented at the XII Biennial Meetings of the International Society for the Study of Behavioural Development, Recife, Pernambuco, Brazil. July 19–23, 1993.

Valsiner, J. (1994a). Bi-directional cultural transmission and constructive sociogenesis. In W. de Graaf & R. Maier (Eds.), *Sociogenesis re-examined.* New York: Springer.

Valsiner, J. (1994b). Culture and human development: A co-constructionist perspective. In P. van Geert & L. Mos (Eds.), *Annals of theoretical psychology* (Vol. 10, pp. 247–298). New York: Plenum.

Valsiner, J. (1994c). Co-constructionism: What is (and is not) in a name. In P. van Geert & L. Mos (Eds.), *Annals of theoretical psychology* (Vol. 10, pp. 343–368). New York: Plenum.

Valsiner, J. (1994d). Irreversibility of time and the construction of historical developmental psychology. *Mind, Culture and Activity, 1,* 1–2, 25–42.

Van Geert, P. (1994). Vygotskian dynamics of development. *Human Development, 37,* 346–365.

Vincentnathan, L. (1993). Untouchable concepts of person and society. *Contributions to Indian Sociology, 27,* 1, 53–82.

Waterman, A. S. & Archer, S. A. (1990). A life-span perspective on identity formation: Developments in form, function, and process. In P. B. Baltes, D. L. Featherman, & R. M. Lerner (Eds.), *Life-span development and behavior* (Vol 10, pp. 29–57). Hillsdale, NJ: Erlbaum and Associates.

Weinstein, D. & Bell, R. M. (1982). *Saints and society.* Chicago: Chicago University Press.

Wertsch, J. (1985). *Vygotsky and the social formation of mind.* Cambridge, MA: Harvard University Press.

Wertsch, J. (1990). The voice of rationality in a sociocultural approach to mind. In L. C. Moll (Ed.), *Vygotsky and education* (pp. 111–126). Cambridge: Cambridge University Press.

Wertsch, J. V. (1991). *Voices in the mind.* Cambridge, MA: Harvard University Press.

Wertsch, J. V. (1995). Sociocultural research in the copyright age. *Culture & Psychology, 1,* 1, 81–102.

Wikan, U. (1982). *Behind the veil in Arabia.* Chicago: University of Chicago Press.

Willis, S. L. & Schaie, K. W. (1986). Practical intelligence in later adulthood. In R. J. Sternberg & R. K. Wagner (Eds.), *Practical intelligence: Origins of competence in the everyday world* (pp. 236–268). Cambridge: Cambridge University Press.

Wolcott, H. F. (1974). The teacher as an enemy. In G. D. Spindler (Ed.), *Education and cultural process* (pp. 411–425). New York: Holt, Rinehardt & Winston.

4

PERCEPTION AND AESTHETICS

P. A. RUSSELL, J. B. DEREGOWSKI **and** *P. R. KINNEAR*
Department of Psychology, King's College
University of Aberdeen
Scotland

Contents

Introduction

Given the *prima facie* central and fundamental role of perception in cognition, the potential importance of cross-cultural studies of perception scarcely needs emphasis. Comparisons of the way people from different cultures perceive the world should provide several kinds of insights. At a relatively specific level, cross-cultural studies can illuminate the functioning and development of the perceptual systems themselves. Central to this aspect is the expectation that cross-cultural similarities and differences in perception will be linkable to similarities and differences in the experiences provided by different cultures. Furthermore, cross-cultural research enables us to establish the nature and extent of cultural universals in perception, an issue which bears upon the possibility that some aspects of perception reflect fundamental and universal characteristics of the human nervous system. On a wider level, the central importance of perception means that cross-cultural perceptual studies may be able to contribute to our understanding of cultural similarities and differences in many other aspects of cognition, motivation, and behavior.

A wide-ranging review of cross-cultural studies of perception published prior to mid-1976 was contributed to the first edition of the *Handbook of Cross-Cultural Psychology* by Deregowski (1980a). Of the topic areas included in that review, some, such as studies of constancies, time perception and visual, olfactory, and auditory acuity, have since seen little significant development and so are omitted here. The present chapter focuses on three main topics. Of these topics, pictorial perception (reviewed here by Deregowski) and color perception (reviewed by Kinnear), were covered by Deregowski (1980a). The third topic, aesthetics (reviewed by Russell, with a contribution on color preferences by Kinnear), was previously covered by Berlyne (1980) in a separate chapter of the first edition of the *Handbook*. As a general rule, work in these three areas covered in the first edition of the *Handbook* is not discussed again here, except where some coverage is necessary for an understanding of the more recent work. Given the broad nature of the area denoted by the term perception, and the indistinct nature of its boundaries, any review of this area must necessarily be somewhat selective. It has been necessary, therefore, to exclude some topics which, in the wider scheme, may be seen as having an equal claim to attention.

Pictorial Perception

Studies of pictorial perception can be conveniently summarized under three main headings: the perception of pictures, the act of depicting (drawing and painting), and visual illusions. The potential importance of cultural artefacts as a source of evidence on cultural similarities and differences in perception is also briefly considered.

The Perception of Pictures

The perception of pictures is associated with a number of theoretical issues which have continued to attract the attention of researchers. In the cross-cultural context, difficulties in pictorial perception, especially, are of particular interest. Although difficulties in pictorial perception experienced by certain cultural groups were reported in the last century and were confirmed by further reports in both psychological and non-psychological literature, the first systematic investigations in this area were carried out by Hudson (1960, 1962). Selected aspects of the research inspired by Hudson's work are presented here. More comprehensive treatments can be found in Deregowski (1980a, 1980b, 1980c, 1989, 1990).

Perception of what a picture depicts, and indeed the perception that it depicts anything at all, depends on both the picture and the perceiver. This point is driven home cogently by pictures that are perceptually puzzling to even pictorially sophisticated populations, such as those pictures that require disentanglement of the meaningful element from general 'noise,' or those that are capable of evoking several mutually exclusive percepts. Perceptual difficulties are also evident in the considerable effort required to learn how to interpret radiographic photographs for medical diagnosis. It follows that investigations of pictorial perception in pictorially unsophisticated cultures are not concerned with phenomena unique to those cultures and affecting every member of those cultures in an equal measure but rather with phenomena that are more abundant, and therefore more readily observable, in those cultures.

Perceptual difficulties of the most fundamental nature, wherein the subject fails to recognize a depiction as a depiction, are relatively rare. Some apparent instances of this are evidently actually related to unfamiliarity with the context of the depiction. Muldrow working in Ethiopia (Deregowski, Muldrow, & Muldrow, 1972) observed that when the Me'en (Mekan), most of whom were unfamiliar with pictures, were given a page from a children's coloring book they would smell it, examine its texture, listen to it while flexing it, even attempt to taste it, but they would entirely ignore the picture. To evaluate the hypothesis that this reflects the tendency of the Me'en, when presented with a novel material, paper, to examine it thoroughly but ignore surface markings, large pictures about 50cm x 100cm in size were printed on coarse cloth, a material with which the Me'en were familiar. Two of the pictures showed single animals, the dik-dik and the leopard. When these pictures were used, only a small number of people responded "I don't know" when asked what they saw in the picture (five such responses out of 68). Such a response could, therefore, no longer be thought of as modal in the population. A further nine of the responses attributed wrong names to the animals, for example, calling a leopard a giraffe. The remaining responses were correct.

It therefore appears that although the Me'en did not respond to pictures on paper, a majority did recognize an indigenous animal clearly depicted on familiar material. This is consistent with Nadel's (1939) observation that young Yoruba boys could readily identify outline figures of common objects on native leather work (i.e., in their culturally familiar context), but were unable to identify the same objects drawn on paper. It is worth noting, however, that in the case of the Me'en there was a proportion of subjects for whom even pictures on cloth seemed obscure.

Because the observations on the Me'en concerned the most pictorially unsophisticated population that, as far as is known, has been hitherto studied systematically, its findings suggest that acceptance of the concept that patterns on a flattish surface may represent three-dimensional entities is fairly automatic if the circumstances are appropriate. It must be stressed that the Me'en subjects did not mistake depictions for real objects—they would not have stood patiently within a foot or two of a foraging leopard; they recognized their significance. It must also be noted, however, that, for unknown reasons, two of the subjects attempted to leave, and only one could be cajoled back before the experiment was completed.

Pars pro toto responses, such as those made by Kenyan subjects to a picture of a tortoise displayed by Shaw (1969), or responses in which diverse parts are named but the subject does not name the entire object (and this was also the case with some Me'en subjects), suggest that cultural differences in naming fragmented pictures may be linked to differences in the ability to integrate such pictures. There is evidence that, within some Western cultures, younger children find the task of integrating fragmented depictions much more difficult than older children (Gollin, 1965; Spitz & Borland, 1971). Bentley (1986) tested Zulu schoolchildren from an urban primary school as well as a group of preschoolers. He found that ability to perform the task increased markedly with age and was much influenced by the extent of deletions. He used two kinds of deletion: in one, 75 percent of the undeleted segments represented "distinctive features"; in another, 25 percent of the undeleted segments did so. He found that stressing the distinctive features did not make the task easier for the children from the four youngest groups (preschool and grades 1–3), but it did facilitate recognition by the older, fourth-grade pupils. Bentley interpreted the results as showing that Gibson's (1969) idea that invariant distinctive features of objects are used for their recognition, and that children learn to recognize objects by learning to differentiate between distinctive and nondistinctive features, is questionable. Conclusions here, however, rest ultimately upon the definition of the distinctive features of an object and the relationship between these and their depiction. It is possible to argue that the features of an object thought to be distinctive by the experimenter (e.g., a bird's beak) might not be critical for recognition if the "nondistinctive" features of the object are sufficiently characteristic of it to ensure recognition of the picture. For example, the shape of a bird as a whole may be such that, when portrayed, correct recognition is assured even though distinctive features, in the sense of "points of concentration of information" (Attneave, 1954), are lacking.

An extension of Bentley's study (Bentley & Deregowski, 1987) to embrace a cross-cultural comparison showed cultural differences. The experimental groups were Kwengo Bushman children, urban Zulu children, and urban White South African children. Of these groups, contrary to the expectations based on pictorial exposure and environmental conditions, the Kwengo were the outstanding performers. They were unmatched by either the White or the Zulu children on stimuli with 80 percent deletion, and on stimuli with 50 percent they did not differ from the White children but were superior to the Zulus. Bentley speculated that the result may reflect the tendency of the Kwengo to integrate the perceptual elements more efficiently, as hunters are likely to do (Berry, 1971). He also speculated that some of the Zulus might be more prone to seek the experimenter's approval. The suggestion that the integration of pictorial elements varies cross-culturally is also supported by the reports of significant cross-cultural differences on implicit-shape constancy tasks (Deregowski, 1976).

The correct naming of elements of a picture does not predicate ability to correctly perceive their mutual relationships. These relationships may be confined within the plane of the picture but may also extend into the illusory third dimension. In connection with the latter, Hudson's (1960) study of pictorial depth has proved seminal to a whole school of research. The essence of the findings is that there are marked differences among various cultural groups in the manner in which they perceive pictures. The reasons for these differences remain obscure, but their very existence has important practical implications. Some of the investigations prompted by Hudson's study were intended to investigate the generality of the findings, others to analyze the problem further and to place it within the established framework of perceptual phenomena. Some of the latter will be reviewed here.

The pictures of Hudson's test show certain naturalistic settings and require verbal responses from subjects. This raises several obvious questions. Do the procedures of the test measure perception of pictorial depth or only the ability to describe pictorial depth? Do they measure perception of pictorial depth in general or only in a certain narrow setting? In order to probe these questions, a variety of tests can be used.

The most direct and intuitively convincing measure of pictorial depth perception is provided by Gregory's (1973) "Pandora's Box," a device so made that while an image of an object is projected into one eye, a moving point-light is seen by both eyes and its apparent distance from the observer can, therefore, be judged. This device was used by Deregowski and Byth (1970) to determine the apparent depth in Hudson's pictures. Data obtained from two of Hudson's pictures yielded a significant difference between Bantu and European subjects on one of the pictures, that incorporating overlap cues as well as the cue of familiar size, but not on the picture which incorporated only the latter cue. The Bantu sample drawn from a population expected, in virtue of Hudson's observations, to show a low incidence of pictorial depth perception did, in the case of the first picture, show lower incidence of depth than the European sample.

In another study (Deregowski, 1968), responses of subjects to Hudson's test and to simple geometric stimuli were compared. The subjects were shown the geometric drawings, and required to build the models shown. The models built were judged to be either 3D or 2D. Comparison of the responses made to Hudson's test and to the construction task showed that Hudson's test is more difficult, many of the responders scoring 2D on Hudson's test but 3D on the construction test, whereas the reverse combinations of scores practically did not obtain. On the other hand, subjects scored as 3D on Hudson's test tended to be scored as 3D on the construction task. Therefore, detection of perceptual difficulties concerning pictorial depth depends on the method used.

This work also made use of drawings, such as that shown in Figure 4–1, which have become known as impossible figures. Strictly speaking, these figures might be more appropriately called "figures showing impossible objects" because the impossibility relates to the difficulties that observers have when trying to visualize the represented three-dimensional objects. As patterns of lines on a flat page, these "impossible figures" are entirely legitimate. The time for which such a figure has to be displayed to enable the observer to copy it appears to depend on the extent of the self-contradictory nature of the figure, and so upon the perception of pictorial depth. Indeed, it was found that when subjects classified as either 2D or 3D perceivers by means of the construction task just described, were asked to copy such a figure, the 2D perceivers found the task markedly easier. The results were thought to suggest that 2D perceivers see the figure merely as a flat pattern and hence do not see it as impossible at all (Deregowski, 1980b).

This explanation is, however, an oversimplification, as Young and Deregowski (1981) have shown. They used the same task with English Primary School children and found that the difficulties of copying impossible figures increased with age, a result entirely compatible with the above findings. Careful questioning revealed, however, that the developmental changes were not a consequence of younger children's inability to see pictorial depth, but of their not being disturbed by the perceptually contradictory nature of the "impossible" figures. The same techniques were used among the Kwengo (Kxoe) Bushmen of the Caprivi Strip (Deregowski & Bentley, 1987). Young and Deregowski's findings suggest that subjects who find the impossible figures confusing do so because they do not integrate the figures strongly. One would accordingly expect such subjects to be more "careless" when building models shown in drawings, and the resulting models to be less well integrated. To test this, rural Kwengo children drawn from a newly established primary school were requested to build models and to copy an impossible figure. It was found that those schoolchildren who built well integrated 3D models took significantly longer to copy the impossible figure than did those whose 3D models were not well integrated. There was no such difference between the two groups who built 2D models. Therefore, the results support Young's observa-

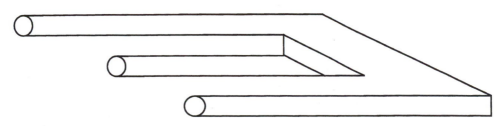

FIGURE 4–1   An impossible figure (figure showing an impossible object).

tions about the relationship between perceptual integration and the tolerance of mutually contradictory elements in impossible figures.

It should be noted that the Deregowski and Bentley results were obtained from a sample of subjects that performed better on pictorial perception tasks than the environmental conditions would lead one to anticipate. This was demonstrated by comparisons of Kwengo (Kxoe), Sekele (!xu), and Zulu children on yet another task measuring perception of pictorial depth. The two Bushmen groups were chosen because, while they live in the same environment, they are serogenetically (Nurse & Jenkins, 1977) and linguistically (Traill, 1985) quite distinct. As psychological functioning of these populations has not been investigated, a datum population was thought desirable and to this end a sample of Zulu children (an accessible and much studied group) was also drawn. The task (Deregowski & Bentley, 1986) required subjects to set a pair of wooden calipers (subsequently called the Kwengo calipers) so as to match the angle of a depicted figure. It was assumed that perceived three-dimensionality of a figure will affect the setting and that, therefore, the responses to Figure 4–2a will be set at a greater angle than those to Figure 4–2b, although the angles as measured in the plane of the paper are equal. This expectation was confirmed. Furthermore, significant cross-cultural differences were found: Kwengo children, who showed themselves most responsive to pictorial depth cues, differed significantly from Sekele children but did not differ from Zulu children. Simple environmental considerations would lead one to expect not an absence of a significant difference between urbanized Zulus and remotely rural Kwengo but greater sensitivity to pictorial depth cues in the latter. The same considerations would lead one to expect no difference between the Kwengo and the Sekele, yet a significant difference was observed. In another, already described, experiment carried out by Bentley and Deregowski (1987), Kwengo children

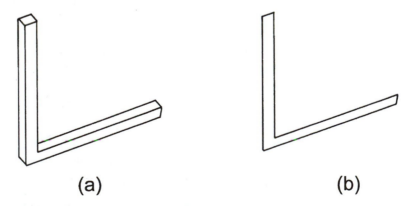

(a)   (b)

FIGURE 4–2   **Figures to which subjects respond by setting calipers to match the depicted angle: a) 3D, b) 2D. (Deregowski & Bentley, 1986).**

sampled from the same population were found to recognize incomplete figures more efficaciously than either middle-class urban White children or Zulu children from an urban school.

The previous research was selected for review because it employed new methods. In parallel with such work, a large body of other research using either Hudson's test or its derivatives, or using other pictorial material and with questions similar to those of Hudson's test, has been carried out by diverse researchers. Because it does not contradict the findings just reported, it will not be reviewed, but we shall examine briefly research pertaining to the applied aspects of the problem after presenting a global conclusion that cultural groups, for reasons that are at present unidentified, differ in their ability to perceive pictures. Furthermore, it appears that it might be erroneous to assume that pictures form a single category spanning the continuum of representativeness. According to this single-category assumption, each individual picture occupies a position on the representativeness continuum determined by the effectiveness with which it incorporates various monocular cues. Pictures incorporating more pervasive cues are more likely to be mistaken for the depicted objects, and are more likely to be correctly identified and seen in depth. The findings suggest that there are certain perceptual characteristics of linear pattern, such as obliquity of straight segments, which evoke pictorial depth even though the picture that they create has no representative value, and indeed may, as is the case with impossible figures, be self-contradictory. In contrast, there are pictures that are readily recognizable as representations of three-dimensional objects but which are seen as flat pictures. Silhouettes of objects and pin-figures fall into this category. These two types of pictures can be thought of as representing another continuum. This continuum (defined by Conley, 1985 and Deregowski, 1990 as stretching from eidolic to epitomic) is subject to cultural influences. Indeed, striking cross-cultural differences in artistic styles suggest that this is so, that certain "liberties" which some cultures take with monocular cues are found unacceptable by other cultures. The use of so-called inverse perspective in Byzantine art (see following) is a clear instance of this. Pictures incorporating this perceptually justifiable device (Bartel 1958; ten Doesschate 1964; Deregowski & Parker 1992, 1994) are seen as distorted by many Western viewers.

The motive of Hudson's investigations into perception of pictures was entirely pragmatic: it was to elucidate the nature of difficulties encountered by some populations when interpreting safety posters. It is, therefore, not surprising that in parallel with the analytic theme relating to perceptual processes involved in pictorial perception, there has run another theme (which can perhaps be termed pedagogic) concerning the use of pictures for instruction, and instruction on the use of pictures. The importance of this theme is considerable because pictures are one of the main channels of communication within the Western societies. Hudson (1962) conducted some of the earliest studies of the problem and reverted to the issue later in an intensive study of Bantu and White primary schoolchildren in South Africa (Duncan, Gourlay & Hudson, 1973).

In the context of this theme, two distinct experimental pursuits are taking place.

The goal of one of them is the development of a method of instruction whereby such perceptual difficulties as have been found can be remedied. The second, more modest in its ambition, seeks to determine the kind of pictures that are easily understood and hence can be used in a particular population. Simultaneously, attempts are being made to relate the observed difficulties to broader theoretical frameworks. For example, Colomb and Dasen (1986) attempted to place the difficulties observed in the Ivory Coast within the framework of Piagetian theory. Because such broad theories fall outside the scope of this chapter, such attempts will not be discussed here.

If difficulties with pictorial perception are the result of misdirected attention, as Serpell and Deregowski (1980) suggest, they should be reduced by instructional methods that enhance the observers' tendency to interpret pictorial cues as if they signified pictorial depth. Seddon and Shubber (1984), Seddon, Eniaiyeju, and Jursho (1984), Seddon, Tariq, and Dos Santos Veiga (1984), Seddon, Eniaiyeju, and Chia (1985), Seddon and Nicholson (1985), and Nicholson, Seddon, and Worsnop (1977), working in schools in a variety of cultures, including Nigeria, Bahrain, Pakistan, and Cape Verde, have endeavored to develop methods for achieving this, paying special attention to the use of diagrams for teaching chemistry. Leach (1975) has explored allied problems among Shona schoolchildren. Investigations of the effects of difficulties in pictorial perception upon classroom performance have been carried out by several workers (e.g., Modiano, Macdonaldo, & Villasana, 1982) and confirm the existence of cross-cultural differences.

Indian researchers (Mishra,1982; Sinha, 1977; Sinha & Mishra, 1982) have introduced a distinctive approach to the comprehension of pictorial materials, especially of symbols. Their samples of subjects are unique in that they are categorized on three dimensions: caste, urban contact, and education. The effects of the first two variables in their studies of symbols (Mishra, 1987; Sinha & Mishra, 1982) showed that familiarity of symbols had significant impact upon responses. It would appear that pictorial symbols have to be learned, presumably by association with the objects that they signify (e.g., the symbol for "Deep Water" is learned by being found near deep water), in order to be correctly interpreted when placed out of context, as in Mishra's test. This learning is of immediate practical interest because it is the foundation of the usefulness of symbols. Ideally, symbols should be such as to require no learning at all. Are such symbols possible? Tzeng, Trung, and Rieber (1990) examined some aspects of this issue by means of semantic scales, the theoretical underpinnings of which are outside the psychology of perception and so are not discussed here.

Another interesting investigation from Sinha's school is that of Mishra (1988) concerning the interpretation of actions depicted in two pictures, though this task falls outside the bounds of the definition of perception adopted here.

The Act of Depicting (Painting or Drawing)

The act of depicting comprises two linked elements: perception of the object and the abstraction therefrom of those features that will constitute the depiction, and the representation of those features on a surface by means of lines and/or patches of color. The resulting depiction, therefore, testifies to a variety of perceptual and motor skills, only the former of which are of interest in the present context. In addition, the depiction is generally greatly influenced not only by the appearance of the object being drawn, but also by the appearance of depictions of similar objects previously encountered, that is, by the established cultural practice. In consequence, the consideration of pictures as indices of perceptual functioning is hazardous, but it is nevertheless a meaningful task which, in the case of some extinct cultures, offers the sole insight into cognitive functioning of a cultural group. This is notably so in the case of palaeolithic paintings, which are practically the only source of evidence that our ancestors did make attempts to communicate with each other. The study of such paintings by modern scholars is a cross-cultural endeavor spanning cultures separated by a time gap of about 15,000 years. Although much speculation about such paintings has taken place, much of it concerning psychological functioning, purely perceptual considerations have been, by and large, ignored in favor of such issues as the motivation behind the paintings (the suggestions ranging from magical beliefs to "art for art"), the psychical condition of the artist when drawing, and the possibility that this condition was a result of a trance or intake of opiates (Lewis-Williams & Dowson, 1988; Marshack, 1989), or the relationship between artistic ability and other functions, most notably language (Davidson & Noble, 1993).

Such perceptual analysis as has been attempted (Clegg, 1995; Deregowski, 1995; Halverson, 1987, 1992, 1995) suggests that the perceptual devices used by palaeolithic depictors were identical with those identified by the Gestalt scholars and commonly employed by Western artists. An obvious and embarrassing question can, however, be asked. Had the perceptual devices used by the artists been of an essentially different kind from those used by the Western artists, would a modern scholar have been able to recognize them?

Jahoda (1991) presents a thorough review of the speculations on the significance of the apparent similarities between palaeolithic art, drawings made by children from Western cultures and drawings by members of certain remote populations. These speculations involve the hypothesis that the drawings reflect general mental development (a stance directly contrary to that taken by Serpell, 1979), a hypothesis that allows the intellectual capacity of the authors of drawings obtained from non-Western cultures to be readily measured by reference to the scale set by Western children's drawings. The hypothesis is, as Jahoda pointed out, an extrapolation from Haeckel's (1866) "Biogenic law." In fact, the enterprise has proved largely unfruitful, mainly because support for the hypothesis has been sought in collections of drawings obtained in a rather unsystematic manner from a variety of exotic cultures, leading, inevitably, to selective presentations of evidence.

The idea of using scales based on drawings derived in a Western culture for psychological assessment in other cultures reappears in applications of the Draw-a-Man Test and its derivatives (Goodenough 1926; Harris, 1963), wherein a scale based on drawings of a human figure by Western children of various ages is used to assess intellectual development. The scale is not, however, cross-culturally valid, as shown by data collected by Fortes (1940, 1981) from the Tallensi, whose cultural artifacts did not, at the time of data collection, include pictures and whose contact with pictorial cultures was minimal. The data clearly demonstrate a selective depiction of features by subjects whose performance could not have been affected by an established "cultural" style. Two characteristics of the results obtained are particularly noteworthy. First, no great difficulties were encountered in inducing the Tallensi to draw. Second, the drawings do not fit the Goodenough scale because the representations of men drawn by the Tale are essentially stick-like, with exaggerated navels and penises. The navels are about as large as the heads and the facial features (the central elements of the Goodenough scale) are entirely missing. Similar abstractions were reported by Reuning and Wortley (1973) in their study of Bushmen who were required to draw by using their fingers in a sand tray. This technique was also used by Berry, Van de Koppel, Sénéchal, Annis, Bahuchet, Cavalli-Sforza, and Witkin (1986) in their study of Biaka Pygmy and Bangandu villagers in Central Africa, but scored for "body proportioning" rather than intelligence or abstraction.

There is a tendency to regard a style of drawing prevailing in a certain group as a "convention" and Golomb (1992) suggests that Fortes did so, but this statement obscures, rather than clarifies, the issue. A convention is a practice based on general consent. There could not have been such consent between Tale draughtsmen who drew pin figures because the draughtsmen were not in contact with each other. There could, however, have been such an agreement in the case of the Western-style drawings obtained by Fortes from the same population over a quarter of a century later. In the latter case, the agreement could have arisen through the tacit acceptance of the Western usage by Tale schoolchildren. Thus, the prevalence of a certain behavior may be a result of a convention, but it need not be. The important fact about the earlier set of drawings collected by Fortes is that drawings of this kind do not figure as the first, or even the early, drawings on such scales as that of Goodenough, indicating the lack of cross-cultural validity of this scale.

An earlier review (Deregowski, 1980c) listed other scattered and nonconclusive cross-cultural studies of drawings. It is surprising that so little systematic work has been done on the topic of free drawing, which calls for negligible experimental resources, and yet is likely to bring rewards. A closely related and equally neglected topic is that of copying drawings. The use of this task to investigate the perception of impossible figures has already been mentioned. Other interesting results have been obtained by comparing copying performance in response to simple models (such as a cube) and to drawings of such models. When both types of stimuli are copied with the stimuli on display, the responses to them differ markedly and can fairly be described as "drawings" and "copies" respectively. When, however, the stimuli are hidden after a brief display, similar responses are obtained to models and to drawings of models (Deregowski, 1976), suggesting that the stimulus drawing is encoded as if it were a model, with its implied three-dimensionality taken into account.

Broderick and Laszlo (1989) investigated the ability of Swazi children to copy squares oriented uprightly (i.e., with two of their sides in subjects' fronto-parallel planes), or obliquely (i.e., with one of their diagonals in such a plane). The stimuli were, therefore, just the outlines of Shapiro's square stimuli (Shapiro, 1960). Broderick and Laszlo were particularly concerned about the rotations of the drawings relative to the models that they observed in their earlier Australian study (Broderick & Laszlo, 1987). The Australian sample was drawn from a culture with compulsory education, in which literacy is widespread and children are encouraged to draw and copy. The Swazi culture differs from the Australian in all these respects. Such differences do not, however, predict differences in copying of *simple rectilinear* figures such as squares. Indeed, it could be argued that this task requires such fundamental skills that cultural influence upon its performance is unlikely to be significant. The responses of Swazi schoolchildren of all ages were found to differ from those of Australian schoolchildren by consistently containing larger proportions of rotations of obliquely presented figures. The experimental sample also included a group of rural Swazi adults with rather limited education and a group of urban Swazi with at least ten years of schooling. The rural group showed considerable rotation of the obliquely presented square whereas the urban group showed no such effect. Broderick and Laszlo interpreted their results as showing that the facility of planning and executing movements needed for the drawing of obliquely placed squares is not acquired equally by all subjects because its acquisition depends greatly on opportunities available. School is clearly a chief source of such opportunities. (For a more general discussion of the importance of schooling see Serpell, 1993, and the chapter by Serpell and Hatano, this volume).

Broderick and Laszlo's interpretation can be questioned, however, in view of the well-documented difficulties (Biesheuvel, 1952a, 1952b; Deregowski, 1977; Jahoda 1976, 1978; Ord, 1971) that subjects from certain cultural groups have with the construction of flat square patterns in the oblique orientation using small wooden tiles. Cross-cultural differences in performance on the Kohs test and its derivatives have been investigated by several workers concerned largely with this very problem of the rotation of the reproduced patterns and, in particular, with establishing whether rotations are a consequence of subjects regarding pattern orientation as of no significance (perhaps because objects do not generally change their nature on being rotated—a shoe does not decline in its "shoeness" when turned upside down), or whether they are brought about by some specific vector of cultural or ecological origin. The relevant investigations (summarized in Deregowski, 1980a) showed that there is a systematic tendency to rotate Kohs-type patterns and that this tendency is affected by two vectors. One vector is the orientation of the model pattern: oblique settings evoke systematic rotations, upright settings do not. The other is the nature of the pattern to be reproduced: patterns symmetrical about the subjects' median plane resist rotation, while skew symmetrical patterns foster it. Other patterns form intermediate categories.

Broderick and Laszlo's (1989) study can be considered in the context of these observations. The consonance between the two sets of data relating to the difficulties associated with obliquity suggests that the difficulties experienced are not connected with the task of drawing but rather that they are perceptual difficulties associated with reproducing obliques. This is due to the fact that obliques imply perceptual depth, a major tenet of the "carpentered world" theory of visual illusions (Segall, Campbell, & Herskovits, 1966), and of Gregory's (1968) explanation of the Müller-Lyer effect. It is supported by Cormack and Cormack's (1974) observation that when the "vertical" line of the "horizontal–vertical" illusion is drawn at an oblique angle, the illusory effect is increased. This relationship between obliquity of line and implication of depth was already noted by Wundt (1898) a century ago. It would seem that an oblique presents the pictorially unsophisticated subject with a depth cue which is immediately apparent. The cross-cultural prevalence of the Müller-Lyer illusion supports this, for although there are cross-cultural differences in the magnitude of this illusion, there is a universal tendency to experience this illusion.

When the presentation of an element imbued with a depth cue is followed by a request to draw it *on a plane*, difficulties inevitably arise. The subject might choose to ignore the depth cue and to reproduce the plane pattern by a plane pattern, a solution adopted by sophisticated subjects from disparate cultures. The less sophisticated cannot suppress the implicit depth cue which the obliques convey, because the demands of the task oblige them to reconcile the palpable flatness of the paper with the perceived recession of the line. They resolve the perceptual conflict by compromising between the two demands. This does not suggest that the less pictorially sophisticated are less prone to the cue of pictorial depth inherent in obliquity, on the contrary.

An inevitable corollary of such an interpretation pertains to discrimination among obliques. If planar obliques are perceived essentially as lines in recession from the observer, then the differences among such obliques will be seen as less than their angles of intersection would suggest and pairs of obliques symmetrical about the observer's median plane are bound to be mutually confused. Evidence in support of the latter hypothesis is provided by Serpell's (1971) investigation of discrimination learning by Zambian children who had the expected difficulties of discriminating between two 45° obliques at a level of intensity not encountered with American children of the corresponding age group (but inevitably of greater exposure to schooling). When the differences in schooling between the two samples were allowed for, the discrepancy in the difficulty was notably reduced. Serpell pointed out that this suggested that schooling had a particularly strong influence on this perceptual skill; both Bartel's (1958) investigation of the drawing of a box by illiterate European peasants (see Deregowski, 1986; Parker & Deregowski, 1990) and Broderick and Laszlo's (1989) Swazi studies comparing rural and urban adults sustain this view. There remains a difficulty of a plausible hypothesis for what precisely is provided by schooling as far as this particular skill is concerned. The occasionally made suggestion that learning to discriminate among letter shapes leads to superior performance on a drawing task cannot be convincingly invoked, nor does the notion of improvement of drawing skills seem useful, if only because the effect is not only in drawings but also in pattern reproduction.

Visual Illusions

The study of visual illusions is one of the enduring themes in cross-cultural psychology and Rivers' (1901, 1905) studies of illusions are among the earliest systematic cross-cultural investigations of perceptual processes. Rivers' observations are still worthy of note, as is a set of studies of the same phenomena conducted about half a century later by Segall, Campbell, and Herskovits, (1966). The findings of the latter, as well as those of numerous other studies inspired by these pioneers, are to be found in several publications, most notably Segall, Dasen, Berry, and Poortinga (1990), and will not be examined further here.

Cultural Artifacts as Perceptual Indices

Cultural artifacts, that is, manufactured objects such as sculptures, tools, and weapons, and including pictorial representations, are an alternative source of evidence for cross-cultural studies of perception. This source has not found much favor with psychologists, although anthropologists have speculated on both the cultural and the perceptual significance of artifacts. Thus Boas (1927) and Levi-Strauss (1963) commented on the "split-representations" characteristic of West-Canadian art, and Leach (1954) maintained that the traditional design found on Trobriand shields is a result of a complex perceptual transformation. Such speculations, summarized by Deregowski (1984), do not embrace empirical investigations and therefore cannot be thought of as central to cross-cultural studies of perception. An empirical element has, however, an excellent pedigree in Thouless' (1933, 1972) studies of cultural differences in shape constancy with special reference to traditional Indian art. This tradition continues in the studies of "inverse perspective"; this is a device whereby parallel edges (say, of a box) are drawn so that they diverge with increasing pictorial depth instead of converging, as is traditional in Western art. The presence of this feature in certain schools of art has led to speculation as to its significance and origin. Thus, for example, Uspenskii (1976) speculated that inverse perspective, which is one of the stylistic characteristics of Byzantine art, is a consequence of art's hieratic function. However, there is empirical evidence provided by Bartel (1958) and ten Doesschate (1964) that unquestionably shows that Western convergent perspective (where all receding parallel lines converge to a single point) is not always experienced by observers and suggests that divergent perspective may, under certain conditions, represent observers' experience more adequately than convergent perspective does. Later work by Deregowski and Parker (1994) confirmed that this is indeed so. They found that when subjects are required to adjust elements of a three-dimensional array so that it appears to them to be a cube, the adjustments made differ systematically with the placement of the array. When the array is placed in front of the subject, the adjustments are indeed what the Western convergent perspective would lead one to expect. When, however, the array is laterally displaced, the adjustments obtained are those expected from the considerations of the Byzantine divergent perspective. These findings suggest that the convergent perspective and the Byzantine perspective are equally legitimate perceptually and that, therefore, "extra-perceptual" explanations, such as those suggested by Uspenskii (1976), do not need to be invoked. They do not, however, reveal why some artistic schools choose to use convergent perspective and others to use divergent perspective. Two important conclusions can be drawn from these observations. Firstly, it is unjustified to claim that convergent perspective is inevitably right. Secondly, the study shows how cross-cultural comparisons of radically different artifacts may, on close examination, provide evidence of the same perceptual mechanism being used differently by distinct cultural groups.

Another study (Dziurawiec & Deregowski, 1992), which empirically demonstrates the sound perceptual basis of an unusual stylistic device, concerns traditional Aboriginal depictions of certain animals. Aborginal depictions of the crocodile, for example, are typically distorted: the trunk of the beast is depicted as being seen from above while the head and the tail are depicted as being seen from the side. This kind of distortion is not unique to Aboriginal art. Conceptually identical distortions are found in Ancient Egyptian art, Mediaeval Spanish art, and Modern art (Parker & Deregowski, 1990). Dziurawiec has demonstrated that they also occur in the drawings of young children and are due to the fact that the subjects prefer to draw the most characteristic outline of the models. When outlines of various distinct parts of the model are non-coplanar, they are portrayed as coplanar, resulting in a distortion of the originals.

It seems likely that there may be other aspects of exotic arts that have implications for the cross-cultural study of perception and this is an area that may repay further study.

Color Perception

In the first edition of the *Handbook,* Deregowski (1980a) noted that cross-cultural studies of color tend to fall into two domains, one deriving from a physiological tradition and the other focusing on color perception as a phenomenon that may shed light on psychological processes, notably language. He also noted that the work of Berlin and Kay (1969) suggests that, in fact, these two aspects are not as disparate as was once thought. Pickford (1972) provides further commentary on some of the older racial and cultural comparisons of color discrimination.

For the cross-cultural investigator, the main questions of interest are what differences in color perception exist among cultures and whether these are due to variations in the underlying sensory mechanisms or to such factors as linguistic or environmental heterogeneities. If differences in color discrimination are found, might these be due to differences in the pre-receptoral and receptoral organs among societies or are there deeper, psychological differences relating to language? At the perceptual level, there are questions about the naming and identification of colors, as well as about the emotional and affective properties of colors.

Although only a small amount of significant work on color perception has appeared since the publication of the first edition of the *Handbook*, some of this work has potentially important implications. Most of this work has been in the specifically perceptual, rather than the physiological, tradition. Some work on the affective properties of color is dealt with in the section on aesthetics that follows. The other main strand has been concerned with color naming.

With regard to color naming, the classic schema of basic color terms was published by Berlin and Kay (1969) and subsequently updated by them (Berlin & Kay, 1991; Kay, Berlin, & Merrifield, 1991). It is important to distinguish a person's color discriminatory ability, as measured by such tests as the Farnsworth-Munsell 100-Hue test (Farnsworth, 1943; see also scoring details in Kinnear, 1970 and scoring norms in Verriest, 1963), from their color naming ability, which can be limited by their language (the Whorfian hypothesis, that language determines thinking and perception—see M. W. Eysenck & Keane, 1990 and Hardin & Banaji, 1993 for more details). For example, it is well-known that Inuits have many more names for various shades of snow, and that some Africans have many more names for various shades of sand than people living in temperate parts of the world. Does this mean, however, that Inuits and Africans have better color discrimination? There is no evidence that this is so.

MacLaury (1992) presented a comprehensive review of cross-cultural surveys of color categorization. He described the seven evolutionary stages proposed by Berlin and Kay in which focal colors are encoded as shown:

Stage	Color(s)
1	White and black
2	Red
3a	Green
3b	Yellow
4	Green and yellow
5	Blue
6	Brown
7	Purple, pink, orange

MacLaury's paper included a large amount of ethnographic data and an outline of a new theory of color categorization that he called *vantage theory*. He drew attention to concepts such as hue, brightness, warmth and coolness, and how individuals differ in whether they attend to the similarities or to the differences of unique hues. He also noted how members of some societies will routinely approach the world with a more analytical outlook than members of other societies. He pointed out that some languages emphasize brightness categories at an early stage of color-category evolution and then undergo refinement into hue categories. Among the peer commentaries on MacLaury's paper, Kinnear and Deregowski (1992) questioned the validity of the psychophysical procedures cited by MacLaury. The commentary by Saunders (1992) presented a lucid exploration of the universalism versus relativism dichotomy, drawing attention to the gap between the psychological and the physiological data for light perception; for example, the identification of chromatic and achromatic cells at the lateral geniculate nucleus does not provide a theory of color perception.

Simpson (1991) considered the relationship between a specific psychophysiological structure such as color perception and the supposed implications of this structure for cross-cultural translation. He contrasted the psychophysiological theories reviewed by Hardin (Hardin, 1988; Hardin, Levine, Teller, & Wilson, 1991), which suggest that the phenomenal features of color perception are explicable in terms of the underlying mechanisms of color vision, with the Berlin and Kay hypothesis that color language provides a bridgehead for cross-cultural translation. Simpson's conclusion was that the balance of evidence is on Hardin's side, namely that unique hues are physiologically rather than linguistically determined.

Michaels (1977) also found Berlin and Kay's scheme wanting, arguing that the linguistic criteria defining what is and is not a basic color term are *ad hoc* and ethnocentric, and that when these criteria are removed, an examination of the way in which different languages characterize the color spectrum shows an overwhelming uniformity.

In a further development of this basic idea, Shepard (1992) has argued that evolutionary perspectives may be useful in furthering our understanding of color perception. He suggested that certain characteristics of the perception and representation of color appear to be universal in the normal color vision of humans, namely the perceptual constancy of surface color (i.e., independence of color from the type of illumination), the three-dimensional structure of colors (i.e., the variables of hue, saturation, and lightness), the circularity of spectral colors (i.e. how violets and deep reds seem more similar to one another than, say, to green), and the universal organization of colors into categories and prototypes across many languages. Shepard proposed that these universal characteristics are specific adaptations to regularities of the terrestrial world and facilitate the discrimination and recognition of (and in humans, communication about) biologically significant objects. As an example of what he means by terrestrial regularities, he identifies three degrees of freedom of natural illumination, a light-dark variation (bright sunlight to moonlight), a yellow-blue variation arising from Rayleigh scattering from particles in the atmosphere giving rise to blueness when direct sunlight (yellow) is obscured, and a red-green variation depending on the elevation of the sun and the density of atmospheric water vapour (redness when the sun sets in a dry atmosphere). These three degrees are identical to the lightness variable and the two color variables known to underlie postreceptoral neural processing.

Finally, an interesting cross-cultural relationship between the size of the color vocabulary and naming latency was reported by Johnson and Tomiie (1985), who examined the color-naming skills in various populations of Australian, Greek, Greek/Australian, and Japanese children. They found that Japanese children responded the quickest but used the smallest number of color names.

Conclusions

Color perception is not an easy topic to explore within a culture, let alone across cultures. There are physiological and psychophysical problems to address, especially the psychophysical one as far as the collection of data is concerned. Apart from physical conditions such as suitable conditions of illumination of test materials, there are important matters relating to what questions are asked of the observers and what range of answers are available for them to use. Some of these issues are aired in the commentaries on MacLaury (1992).

Although there are also still many unresolved problems regarding color perception, color vocabulary, the evolution of language, and the underlying physiological mechanisms for processing visible radiation, there are signs of a consensus appearing that there is a strong degree of uniformity in the way color terms are used in different cultures. Moreover, this uniformity is consistent with Shepard's analysis of color perception in terms of adaptive mechanisms.

Aesthetics

The material covered in the preceding sections of this chapter reflects the traditional concern of studies in perception with *what* is perceived. It is obvious, however, that perception can have a variety of concomitants and consequences, including affective ones. These affective aspects are the subject matter of psychological aesthetics. That said, the definition and delineation of aesthetic experiences and responses is somewhat problematic (Berlyne, 1972, 1974, 1980). For the purposes of this section, the term aesthetic *experience* is used loosely to refer to the experience of pleasure/displeasure engendered by stimuli that are perceived as being beautiful/not beautiful, attractive/unattractive, and rewarding/unrewarding. Strictly, aesthetic *responses* are the behavioral concomitants of these experiences, such as acceptance/rejection and verbal expressions of preference, although in the interests of economy of exposition the term "aesthetic responses" will henceforth be used here to refer to both the behavioral and the experiential aspects. Although the quintessential aesthetic responses are those relating to works of art, such as paintings, music and literature, these do not appear to be fundamentally different from responses relating to many other artefacts, such as buildings and packages, or to natural objects and environments, such as flowers and landscapes (Berlyne, 1971, 1972). Aesthetic responses are sometimes said to involve *disinterested* pleasure/displeasure (Berlyne, 1980; Martindale, 1988). That is, the responses relate to stimuli that are pleasurable/displeasurable *in themselves*, rather than because they have pleasurable/displeasurable consequences stemming from functions or uses. This distinction is not, however, always easily or appropriately drawn. For example, work reviewed that follows suggests that aesthetic responses to landscapes may be mediated partly by motivational systems which evolved originally to maintain individuals in favorable environments.

Berlyne's survey of cross-cultural studies of aesthetics in the previous *Handbook of Cross-Cultural Psychology* (1980), which covered work up to 1976, remains the only major review of this area, although Pickford (1972, chapter 5) provides a useful review of some cross-cultural studies of *visual* aesthetics. The aims of this section are to update these reviews by examining the few studies that have since been carried out in the areas covered by them, to examine cross-cultural work on the aesthetics of musical harmony and on environmental aesthetics (areas not covered by Berlyne or Pickford), and to highlight some general guidelines for future research in cross-cultural aesthetics.

The existence of both substantial differences and substantial similarities in the aesthetic responses of different cultures is largely self-evident. With regard to cultural differences, a myriad of historical and geographical differences in styles and conventions in works of art and in other artifacts with aesthetic connotations point to substantial cultural relativism. As Berlyne (1980) noted, the ease with which works of art and other artifacts can often be attributed to particular historical periods and geographical regions attests to the powerful impact of culture on aesthetics. On the other hand, similarities are evident at various levels, of which the most fundamental is that art, music, and literature (or its oral counterparts) are universal features of human culture. At other levels, similarities are evident in common or "universal" themes. For example, visual art shows various cross-cultural similarities (Anderson, 1979), including the communication of meaning, through symbolism and iconography, and the depiction of certain kinds of subject matter, particularly those relating to the universal human concerns of reproduction, food, and social relations.

The central tasks for cross-cultural aesthetics are to identify similarities and differences in the aesthetic responses of cultures and to pinpoint the causes of these similarities and differences. The latter endeavor involves relating similarities and differences in aesthetic reponses to similarities and differences in the characteristics of the cultures themselves, taking account of such cultural variables as social and economic factors, beliefs, and values.

A further, related, task for cross-cultural aesthetics is the clarification of the implications of universals in aesthetic response. As noted in the introduction to this chapter, cultural universals, where they exist, suggest the possibility of responses linked to fundamental and universal characteristics of the human nervous system. This idea is implicit in Berlyne's (1960, 1974) theory that aesthetic responses are underpinned by the amount of general cortical arousal produced by aesthetic stimuli. Another example is the suggestion that aesthetic stimuli tap in to the propensity of the human brain (and animal brains) to classify input and that aesthetic responses stem from the reinforcing effects associated with such classification (Humphrey, 1973, 1983).

Empirical Aesthetics

As Berlyne noted, most of the literature relevant to these various cross-cultural issues in aesthetics comes from the long-standing approaches of philosophical aesthetics, art theory, and art criticism. To the empirical scientist, these approaches are insufficiently rigorous, although they may be valuable sources of ideas and hypotheses. *Empirical aesthetics*, in contrast, is distinguished by systematic prediction, controlled observation, and quantitative precision. This approach embraces both *correlational studies*, which make use of measurable natural variations in aesthetic phenomena, and *experimental aesthetics*, which involves formally-contrived experiments.

The Correlational Approach

In cross-cultural aesthetics, the correlational approach has mainly taken the form of attempts to link cultural differences in art with various other cultural and social factors. Berlyne (1980) reviewed the handful of studies of this type published up to 1976. The bulk of these focus on one or other of two relatively general features of the art produced by cultures: its "complexity" or its "quality." Complexity is normally assessed by a composite measure based on a number of featural and structural indices, such as complexity of design and the presence of enclosed figures (Barry, 1957). Quality is assessed by experts' ratings (Wolfe, 1969). The studies reviewed by Berlyne indicate correlations between these features and such sociocultural variables as social and economic complexity, the degree of social stratification, and the severity of child-rearing practices.

Since 1976, there has been little progress in clarifying the nature of the links between cultural differences in art and these other cultural and social factors. One empirical strand that has been extended is Barry's (1957) finding that the level of complexity of the artistic designs of 30 societies was positively correlated with a measure of the severity of socialization of children in those societies (a measure derived from child-training data compiled by Whiting & Child, 1953). Rohner (1975, p. 109) noted an apparently related association between the artistic complexity measure and a measure of parental acceptance–rejection of children (this latter measure has a *prima facie* link with socialization severity): relatively rejecting societies had more complex art. Further details of this association are given by Rohner and Frampton (1982). Of 15 societies for which data was available on both parental acceptance–rejection and artistic complexity, seven out of eight which were relatively rejecting of children were above the median level of artistic complexity, while five out of seven that were relatively accepting were below the median. This positive association between artistic complexity and a rejecting style of parenting was not found, however, in an intracultural study conducted in the United States by Rohner and Frampton (1982). In this case, adults whose retrospective recollections were of having had a relatively rejecting childhood preferred less complex art. The many methodological differences between this study and the earlier cross-cultural one, including the very different dependent variables (individuals' preferences for complexity in art *versus* the complexity of the artistic productions of cultures), are worthy of note.

The slow pace of progress in elucidating relationships between cultural differences in art and other cultural and social factors reflects the many problems encountered in this area. One general issue concerns the ultimate validity and usefulness of the global, and seemingly crude, measures of complexity and quality of art. A similar point can be made about the social variables that have been studied. Conceivably, further progress will depend upon the development of measures that reflect the many subtleties and nuances of cultural differences in both art and society. As Berlyne noted, these measures will have to be used in conjunction with multivariate statistical techniques appropriate to the investigation of the multidimensional and interactive systems that comprise both art and societies.

Understanding of the relationships between art and social variables is further hampered by problems in interpreting data from correlational studies. It seems reasonable to assume that any association between cultural variations in art and cultural variations in social factors is much more likely to be the result of social factors influencing art, rather than the other way around. Beyond this generalization, the precise interpretation of such an association is frequently unclear. The general nature of the problem can be illustrated by considering the previously-noted association between artistic complexity and childrearing practices. Berlyne suggested that, rather than childrearing practices directly affecting art, the association may be mediated by social complexity. Artistic complexity has been found to be associated with measures of social complexity including the degree of social stratification of a society (Fischer, 1961) and its degree of economic development (Lomax, 1968). According to Berlyne's suggestion, then, socially complex societies tend to produce complex art and also (for reasons not fully explained) to have more severe childrearing practices. Unfortunately for this suggestion, however, Rohner and Frampton (1982) found that Fischer's social stratification measure of social complexity was not significantly associated with Rohner's measure of parental acceptance–rejection nor with Whiting and Child's index of socialization severity (as used by Barry in the study cited above). Although this renders it unlikely that the association between artistic complexity and childrearing practices is mediated by social complexity, it would be premature to conclude that, therefore, it must be the case that childrearing practices directly influence artistic complexity. The association could be mediated by other, as yet unspecified, factors.

Rohner and Frampton (1982) argue that associations between art and social and cultural factors are potentially explainable in terms of either sociogenic or psychogenic models. According to a sociogenic model, the art of a culture is (in part) a symbolic representation of its social structure and social practices. Thus, complex art is seen as a symbolic reflection of complex society. A psychogenic model, in contrast, regards the art of a culture as (again, in part) a reflection of the personality and psychological states of the individuals who comprise it. In this case, complex individual psyche are seen as producing complex art. Although Rohner and Frampton seem to regard the two models as mutually exclusive, there appear to be no strong reasons for such an assumption. Indeed, it is reasonable to suppose that the complex art of socially complex societies is linked, perhaps in multifarious and interacting ways, with both their complex symbolism and with the varied and complex psychological states of the individuals comprising them.

Experimental Approaches

Berlyne (1980) cited some twenty experimental cross-cultural studies. Most of these are attempts to compare the aesthetic responses of subjects from two or more cultural groups to the same stimulus material. The samples examined include Canadian, American, Chinese, Indian, Japanese, French, Egyptian, and several African populations, although several of these are represented in only one study and often the subjects are drawn exclusively from student groups.

Just over half of the studies reviewed by Berlyne adopt an analytic approach, that is, the stimuli are actual works of art (or excerpts from them), including Western paintings, African designs, and Japanese music. The remainder of the studies use a synthetic approach, involving specially-constructed stimuli that embody some of the variables found in works of art. These stimuli included polygons and miscellaneous visual patterns, colors, and sound sequences. (For a discussion of the analytic and synthetic approaches, see Berlyne, 1974). The response variables in these studies are typically indices of preference and choice, indicated by verbal expressions (usually involving ratings or rankings on response scales such as likeability and pleasingness), selection of items, or looking or listening time.

Berlyne's general conclusion from these experimental studies was that, notwithstanding the many ways in which people from different cultures differ in their aesthetic responses, there are impressive cross-cultural similarities and communalities. The nature of the evidence and the interpretational problems it poses are particularly well highlighted by work on the collative properties of aesthetic stimuli, with which Berlyne's review was particularly concerned.

Collative Variables

Collative variables (Berlyne, 1960, 1974) include complexity, novelty, uncertainty, and incongruity. These variables appear to influence aesthetic responses in similar ways in subjects from different cultures. For example, Berlyne, Robbins, and Thompson (1974) found that the tendency for people to spend more time looking at complex patterns than at simpler ones, which has been reported in a number of studies with Western subjects, was also evident in Bagandan (Uganda) subjects (although it was somewhat weaker in the Bagandans, and was weaker in rural Bagandans than in urban ones).

Cross-cultural similarities in the relationship of aesthetic responses to collative variables are expected from Berlyne's theories (Berlyne, 1960, 1974). Berlyne assumed that collative variables are sources of arousal potential (that is, they have the ability to modify general cortical arousal) and that aesthetic responses are linked to changes in arousal. Given that arousal mechanisms are a human universal, the apparent ubiquity in the response to collative variables is predictable, as is the fact, noted by Berlyne, that art from all cultures appears to make use of collative properties.

These consistencies notwithstanding, various problems attend drawing conclusions about cross-cultural similarities in aesthetic response. By way of illustration, two studies may be considered here. One, cited by Berlyne, and which is in the analytic tradition, and not concerned specifically with collative factors, is Child and Siroto's (1965) finding that the aesthetic merit rank ordering of photographs of the ritual masks made by the African BaKwele people was similar in BaKwele men with experience of such masks and in American art experts (advanced art students and others). The other study, in the synthetic tradition, and not cited by Berlyne, is a report by Farley and Ahn (1973) that preference for polygons differing in complexity did not differ significantly in individuals from five different countries, living in the United States (U.S., Korea, China, India, and Turkey).

Similarities of the kind reported in these two studies can be seen as supporting the conclusion that some aesthetic values are common to different cultures. This conclusion is, however, beset by various interpretational difficulties. One obvious problem is that of drawing conclusions from negative evidence. Failure to find differences between cultures may simply indicate inadequate methodology. For example, the measures used may be insufficiently sensitive. Another possibility is that agreement may be increased by subjects responding to "incidental" (non-aesthetic) aspects of the stimuli. In the case of the Child and Siroto study, for example, it has been argued that because the photographs of the masks used varied in quality and the masks themselves varied in craftsmanship, agreement between the groups might have reflected a similar response to these factors, rather than, or as well as, agreement on actual aesthetic merit (Anderson, 1979, chapter 7).

A more fundamental problem is the possibility of acculturation, which bears upon both studies. The BaKwele have been in contact with Europeans since the late 1800s and may have been influenced by Western artistic standards. Similarly, in the Farley and Ahn study, all the subjects had been exposed to American culture (they were students attending an American university). Generalizing this point, it may be difficult to tell whether similarities in the aesthetic responses of people from different cultures reflect pan-cultural underlying mechanisms or a modern tendency towards the homogenization of cultures.

In the light of these interpretational problems, a study by Poortinga and Foden (1975) may be cited as relatively strong evidence of cross-cultural similarities in response to several collative variables. Comparing Black and White South African university students, Poortinga and Foden found little difference in the average preference scores (measured in terms of stimulus looking time or choice) of the two groups for each of the variables novelty, uncertainty, incongruity, and representational complexity. The whites did show a rather stronger preference for non-representational complexity, although Poortinga and Foden suggest that even this difference may have arisen as a consequence of the two groups interpreting the task somewhat differently, rather than from a real difference in response to complexity. This study is notable for the relatively large number of collative variables studied, and for the fact that the criticism that the lack of differences between the two groups could reflect methodological insensitivity is largely rebutted by the demonstration that the response measures were sensitive to cultural differences in preference for noncollative variables such as picture content. Acculturation also seems unlikely here: Poortinga and Foden point out that an absence of differences between the Black and White groups on psychological tests is the exception rather than the rule. Moreover, the two groups *were* found to differ in their performance on cognitive tests (tests of verbal and arithmetic reasoning, spatial ability, and induction).

Although it is possible, then, to make a tentative case for the absence of cultural differences in response to collative variables, the picture remains essentially the same as it was at the time of Berlyne's 1976 review. The experimental studies are few and embrace only a handful of cultures and a limited range of stimulus material. The pace of research in this area has, if anything, slackened in the last few years, a fact perhaps not unconnected with Berlyne's untimely death in 1976, which robbed the area of its most seminal figure.

One trend which has been evident in recent years is a shift in the focus of study, away from the collative variables towards other variables specific to particular kinds of stimuli. This aspect is evident in three further areas which will be dealt with here: color preferences, musical harmony, and environmental aesthetics.

Color Preferences

Berlyne (1980) reviewed only a small part of the relatively extensive cross-cultural literature on the aesthetics of color. Further studies were reviewed by Pickford (1972). Both reviewers came to the same general conclusion about color preferences: that, although there are some cross-cultural differences, there is also some quite substantial agreement between cultures. In particular, both reviewers drew attention to H. J. Eysenck's (1941) pooling of data from 16 studies of White and 10 studies of non-White subjects, which showed that the rank order of the average rankings of color preferences was very similar in the Whites and non-Whites. For example, in both groups blue was the most preferred color, followed by red and then green. The value of these findings is, however, limited by the crude White/non-White classification and the pooling of data from different non-White groups.

Of the cross-cultural studies of color preferences published since these reviews, some support the conclusion that there are cross-cultural similarities, while others show that cross-cultural differences can also appear. Grieve (1991) claimed that color preferences and associations held by a small sample of Black South Africans (preferences for Blacks and reds) corresponded with those of Westerners. Wiegersma and de-Klerck (1984) noted that Dutch people tended to designate red as the first color that comes to mind, whereas Americans apparently nominate blue. Further cultural differences are evident in the finding of D'Hondt and Vandewiele (1983) that the favorite color of Senegalese children was not one of the colors most evident in other studies. Primary school children from this culture chose brown as their favorite color, while secondary school children chose black. It is unclear whether color symbolism was a factor here.

Musical Harmony

Studies of harmony constitute one strand of cross-cultural research in the area of responses to auditory stimuli. Berlyne (1980) reviewed two studies (Bragg & Crozier, 1974; Vitz, 1966) employing tone sequences in which the tones varied in frequency, duration, and loudness. These studies were primarily concerned with the uncertainty and complexity of the tone sequences, but similar sequences may be used to study the aesthetics of music by simulating aspects of melody, rhythm, and harmony (Howell, Cross & West, 1985). Melody and rhythm have yet to be studied cross-culturally, but a small body of work has appeared on harmony.

The traditional music of different cultures may differ in notions of harmony (Sadie, 1980). For example, traditional Japanese music does not adhere to conventional Western harmony, and the classical music of northern India makes extensive use of harmonic intervals considered in the West to be highly dissonant. The cross-cultural synthetic approach to harmony has concentrated on simple dyads (two-note chords). Butler and Daston (1968) found that Japanese and American students showed strong agreement in their preference rankings of organ-generated tonal dyads corresponding to the 12 intervals of an octave. This implies that, notwithstanding the apparent differences in the harmony of Japanese and Western music, Japanese and Americans hear the consonance and dissonance of intervals in an essentially similar way. As Butler and Daston point out, however, isolated sensory experiences of the sort represented by discrete dyads may be rather distinct from sensory experiences provided by actual music, where the harmonic (vertical) construction is considerably more complex and is also linked to the horizontal construction of rhythm and melody. Furthermore, Maher (1976) suggested that Butler and Daston's procedure might have been relatively insensitive to differences. Specifically, their use of a preference measure was based on the assumption that preference is synonymous with pleasantness and that pleasantness can be equated with consonance. It is known, however, that preference can be influenced by factors other than pleasantness, including interestingness and complexity (Berlyne, 1974; Walker, 1981; see also Russell, 1994). Maher, in contrast, asked his subjects to rate harmonic intervals on a scale of restfulness–restlessness, on the assumption that consonant intervals are heard as relatively restful and dissonant ones as relatively restless. Maher compared the responses of Canadian and Indian students, finding that their ratings were not significantly correlated. At a detailed level, although there were some similarities in the responses of the two groups, there were also some marked differences. For example, both groups found the octave restful, but while the Canadians found the minor second extremely dissonant, the Indians found it to be relatively neutral. Maher's results suggest that there may be cultural differences in the perception of consonance and dissonance, although clarification of the nature and extent of these differences awaits further studies.

Environmental Aesthetics
The aesthetics of natural and human-made environments has received some empirical study in recent years (R. Kaplan & S. Kaplan, 1989; Wohlwill, 1976). A handful of cross-cultural studies has examined responses to scenic landscapes (sometimes containing human-made features). On the basis of this limited data, it appears, unsurprisingly, that cultural differences in the perceived aesthetic value of landscapes are most likely to appear when there are large differences between the cultures and between their native landscapes (Zube, 1984). For example, Sonnenfeld (1967) asked subjects from several Arctic Inuit populations, non-Inuit Arctic workers, and Americans with no direct Arctic contact to indicate their preference for

pictures of a variety of landscapes. The results indicated that the preferences of the different cultural groups were influenced by different factors. Subsistence-oriented Inuit tended to choose environments having similarities to their native areas (although also sometimes with predictable differences; for example, a population short of fuel preferred landscapes with more trees). The preferences of less subsistence-oriented Inuit and non-Inuit subjects were more likely to be influenced by nonsubsistence features and by features which differed from those in their native areas. Pronounced cultural differences in landscape preference were also reported by Zube and Pitt (1981). In this study, evaluations of the scenic quality of Connecticut River Valley landscapes by different groups of residents from that area were more similar than were the residents' evaluations to those of nonresidents. Among the non-residents, the evaluations of African Americans living in the city-center, whose environment might be expected to differ most from that of the Connecticut Valley, were the least similar to those of the residents. In similar vein, Zube and Pitt also found that groups of Virgin Islanders showed greater agreement in their evaluations of Virgin Islands coastal landscapes than these groups did with nonresident Americans and Yugoslavs.

Several other findings are consistent with the expectation that similar cultures will show relatively good agreement over landscape preferences. Shafer and Tooby (1973) found that American landscapes received very similar preference rankings from summer campers in both America and Scotland (the latter group including Scots and various other Europeans) and R. Kaplan and Herbert (1988) reported a similar finding for American landscapes rated by American and Australian students. Similarly, Zube and Mills (1976) found that perceptions of the scenic quality of the coastline of the Australian town of Lorne were highly similar in Lorne residents, visitors to the town, and American students.

Cross-cultural studies of human-made, as opposed to relatively natural, environments have been few. Nasar (1984) investigated the preferences of American and Japanese graduate students for urban street scenes. Although the Americans evaluated the scenes more positively than the Japanese, there was a moderately significant degree of agreement between the preferences of the two groups. There were also several similarities in the correlates of preference in the two groups: for both groups, preferred streets were those which were well-kept, had prominent vegetation, and contained few vehicles.

Future work in the area of preference for human-made environments might profitably explore the reactions of cultural groups whose living environments differ; for example, urban *versus* rural populations. Extrapolating from the conclusions drawn concerning preferences for landscapes, it can be predicted that the degree of agreement between the preferences of different cultural groups for human-made environments will be influenced by the similarity of the environments to the living environments of those groups.

Prospects for Cross-Cultural Aesthetics

Turning to more general issues, future experimental studies in cross-cultural aesthetics will, no doubt, reflect the changes in theoretical orientation that have recently been taking place in experimental aesthetics generally. Three recent trends of significance for cross-cultural aesthetics are: (1) the shift, noted earlier, away from the previous strong focus on collative variables towards other factors, notably prototypicality; (2) the adoption of an evolutionary perspective; and (3) the more rigorous specification of the dependent variables.

The Concept of Prototypicality

It has long been clear that collative variables are not the only general influences on aesthetic responses and there is now a growing feeling that they may not even be the most important influences (Martindale, 1988; Martindale, Moore & West, 1988). A number of recent studies in aesthetics have, therefore, focused upon other stimulus variables, particularly the so-called ecological variables, which include the meaning, value, and associative properties of a stimulus. Most of these studies have been concerned with prototypicality (or typicality). The concept of a prototype as a representation of the best example of a category has been developed notably by Rosch (1973). A positive association between prototypicality, measured by subjects' ratings of how closely a stimulus matches a category prototype, and aesthetic appeal has been reported for various types of stimuli, including furniture (Whitfield & Slatter, 1979), representational paintings (Hekkert & van Wieringen, 1990), houses (Purcell, 1984), and colors (Martindale & Moore, 1988). Moreover, prototypicality may account for more of the variance in aesthetic appeal than does novelty or complexity (Hekkert & van Wieringen, 1990; Martindale, Moore, & West, 1988; Whitfield, 1983). Hekkert and van Wieringen, working with cubist paintings, found that preference for relatively highly representational paintings was positively and linearly associated with prototypicality but was unrelated to complexity. Preference for relatively non-representational, abstract paintings was, however, associated with complexity (in a curvilinear manner) but was unrelated to prototypicality. Results of this kind are consistent with the expectation that aesthetic response to a work of art having a strong representational element will be related particularly to ecological and associative factors bearing upon the work's meaning. Aesthetic responses to less representational works may, in contrast, be more closely linked with collative variables.

Conclusions about the usefulness of the concept of prototypicality in aesthetics must, however, be tempered by some reservations. As Boselie (1991) notes, an association between prototypicality and aesthetic preference is not conclusive evidence that prototypicality is a causal determinant of preference. Indeed, the converse could be true: preferring a stimulus might lead to it being seen as prototypical.

The Evolutionary Perspective

The adoption of an evolutionary perspective on aesthetics has, so far, been most evident in work on environmental preferences (Kaplan, 1987, 1992; Orians & Heerwagen, 1992). Specifically, it has been suggested that aesthetic responses to environments may be associated with behavior that increases the individual's ability to learn about and function in the environment. Orians and Heerwagen argue that natural selection should have favored individuals who were motivated to explore and settle in favorable environments, that is, environments that provide good resources and low risks. Because the human species is presumed to have evolved in tropical African savannah, it may be predicted that savannah-type environments will be preferred over other biomes. In a direct test of this prediction, Balling and Falk (1982) found that 8-year-old American children preferred photographs of savannah over photographs of other biomes, including various kinds of forest. Older children and adults liked savannah, deciduous forest, and coniferous forest about equally. Balling and Falk interpret these results as suggesting that there is an innate disposition to prefer savannah, and that this is later modified by experience of particular environments (in this case American woodlands). This interpretation implies that a savannah preference will be evident in young children irrespective of culture, a prediction that has yet to be tested.

Evolutionary arguments for universality have also been advanced in the area of musical aesthetics. The fact that music exists in all human cultures and appears to show some pan-cultural characteristics may reflect a basis in adaptive perceptual and motivational systems (Roederer, 1984; Sloboda, 1985, chapter 7). The value of the evolutionary perspective here, and the possible extension of this perspective to art in general, are themes which remain to be explored.

Dependent Variables
The other general trend in experimental aesthetics is towards more rigorous specification of the dependent variables in aesthetics research and, relatedly, more consideration of the implications of using different measures of aesthetic response. Berlyne (1969) argued that we cannot assume that all putative measures of aesthetic preference do actually measure the same thing. More recently, evidence has been presented that even verbal judgments of preferability and likeability, which have high apparent ecological validity, may be factorially complex and not always easily interpretable (Russell, 1994; Russell & George, 1990; Russell & Gray, 1991).

Concluding Comments

The three strands of cross-cultural work presented in this chapter are largely distinct and separate from one another. If there is a general conclusion that applies to all three, it is surely that the progress made in each of the areas since their examination in the first edition of the *Handbook of Cross-Cultural Psychology* is distinctly modest. Given that, as noted in the introduction to this chapter, various other areas of cross-cultural study in perception included in the first edition of the *Handbook* have seen even less progress, the overall picture is unimpressive. In view of the potential importance of cross-cultural studies of perception, this lack of progress is disappointing. For the most part, the paucity of new contributions to the area as a whole appears to be a reflection of changing research fashions rather than of the issues involved having been satisfactorily resolved or ceasing to be of theoretical and practical interest.

Even where there has been some recent work, much of this has tended to continue the tendency for cross-cultural psychologists to engage in "safari research," where data collection is driven by the serendipitous availability of subjects from two or more cultural groups, rather than by theoretical considerations. This kind of research is particularly evident in some of the literature reviewed earlier in the sections on color perception and on aesthetics. Although it can be argued that research demonstrating psychological similarities or differences among cultural groups is never without some value, cross-cultural work is likely to be most fruitful when the cultures examined are chosen to permit the testing of specific hypotheses bearing on psychological theory.

It seems likely that any future revitalization of cross-cultural work on perception will depend upon the emergence of some new theoretical paradigms. One possible contender here may be the evolutionary perspective. As some of the work just reviewed suggests, this perspective is beginning to provide a degree of impetus for research in aesthetics and, to a lesser extent, color perception. Given the growing interest in the evolutionary perspective within psychology generally, marked by the emergence of evolutionary psychology as a named discipline (Barkow, Cosmides, & Tooby, 1992; see also chapter by Keller, volume 1, this *Handbook*), it is surely not too much to hope that this perspective might hold some more general promise for the future direction of cross-cultural studies in perception.

References

Anderson, R. L. (1979). *Art in primitive societies*. New Jersey: Prentice-Hall.

Attneave, F. (1954). Some information aspects of visual perception. *Psychological Review, 61,* 183–193.

Balling, J. D. & Falk, J. H. (1982). Development of visual preference for natural environments. *Environment and Behavior, 14,* 5–28.

Barkow, J. H., Cosmides, L., & Tooby, J. (1992). *The adapted mind*. Oxford: Oxford University Press.

Barry, H. (1957). Relationships between child training and the pictorial arts. *Journal of Abnormal and Social Psychology, 54,* 380–383.

Bartel, K. (1958). *Perspektywa malarska*. Warszawa: Panstwowe Wydawnictwo Naukowe.

Bentley, A. M. (1986). Factors influencing the identification of incomplete pictures by Zulu children. *International Journal of Psychology, 21,* 733–742.

Bentley, A. M. & Deregowski, J. B. (1987). Pictorial experience as a factor in the recognition of incomplete pictures. *Applied Cognitive Psychology, 1,* 209–16.

Berlin, B. & Kay, P. (1969). *Basic color terms, their universality and evolution*. Berkeley and Los Angeles: University of California Press.

Berlin, B. & Kay, P. (1991). *Basic color terms, their universality and evolution. 2nd Edition*. Berkeley and Los Angeles: University of California Press.

Berlyne, D. E. (1960). *Conflict, arousal and curiosity*. New York: McGraw Hill.

Berlyne, D. E. (1969). Measures of aesthetic preference. In J. Hogg (Ed.), *Psychology and the visual arts* (pp. 129–145). Harmondsworth: Penguin.

Berlyne, D. E. (1971). *Aesthetics and psychobiology*. New York: Appleton-Century-Crofts.

Berlyne, D. E. (1972). Ends and means of experimental aesthetics. *Canadian Journal of Psychology, 26,* 303–325.

Berlyne, D. E. (1974). *Studies in the new experimental aesthetics.* New York: Wiley.

Berlyne, D. E. (1980). Psychological aesthetics. In H. C. Triandis & W. J. Lonner (Eds.), *Handbook of cross-cultural psychology* (Vol. 3, pp. 323–361). Boston: Allyn and Bacon.

Berlyne, D. E., Robbins, M. C., & Thompson, R. (1974). A cross-cultural study of exploratory and verbal responses to visual patterns varying in uncertainty. In D. E. Berlyne (Ed.), *Studies in the new experimental aesthetics* (pp. 259–278). New York: Wiley.

Berry, J. W. (1971). Ecological and cultural factors in spatial perceptual development. *Canadian Journal of Behavioral Science, 3,* 324–36.

Berry, J. W., Van de Koppel, J., Sénéchal, C., Annis, R. C., Bahuchet, S., Cavalli-Sforza, L. L., & Witkin, H. A. (1986). *On the edge of the forest.* Lisse: Swets & Zeitlinger.

Biesheuvel, S. (1952a). The study of African ability. Part 1: The intellectual potentialities of Africans. *African Studies, 11,* 45–48.

Biesheuvel, S. (1952b). The study of African ability. Part 2: A survey of some research problems. *African Studies, 11,* 105–17.

Boas, F. (1927). *Primitive art.* Oslo: Institutet for Sammenlignende Kulturforskning.

Boselie, F. (1991). Against prototypicality as a central concept in aesthetics. *Empirical Studies of the Arts, 9,* 65–73.

Bragg, B. W. E. & Crozier, J. B. (1974). The development with age of verbal and exploratory responses to sound sequences varying in uncertainty level. In D. E. Berlyne (Ed.), *Studies in the new experimental aesthetics* (pp. 91–108). New York: Wiley.

Broderick, P. & Laszlo, J. I. (1987). The drawing of squares and diamonds: A perceptual-motor task analysis. *Journal of Experimental Child Psychology, 43,* 44–61.

Broderick, P. & Laszlo, J. I. (1989). The copying of upright and tilted squares by Swazi children and adults. *International Journal of Psychology, 24,* 333–350.

Butler, J. W. & Daston, P. G. (1968). Musical consonance as musical preference, a cross-cultural study. *The Journal of General Psychology, 79,* 129–142.

Child, I. L. & Siroto, L. (1965). BaKwele and American aesthetic evaluations compared. *Ethnology, 4,* 349–360.

Clegg, J. (1995). About pictures, echidnas and cats. *Rock Art Research, 12,* 11–13.

Colomb, E. H. A. & Dasen, P. R. (1986). La perception des relations spatiales dans le dessin et le développement des opérations concrètes. *International Journal of Psychology, 21,* 71–90.

Conley, B. G. (1985). *Theories of pictorial representation, Goodman's relativism and the similarity theory.* Ph.D. Thesis, University of Minnesota.

Cormack, E. O. & Cormack, R. H. (1974). Stimulus configuration and line orientation in the horizontal-vertical illusion. *Perception and Psychophysics, 16,* 208–212.

Davidson, I. & Noble, W. (1993). On the evolution of language. *Current Anthropology, 34,* 165–170.

Deregowski, J. B. (1968). Difficulties in pictorial depth perception in Africa. *British Journal of Psychology, 59,* 195–204.

Deregowski, J. B. (1976). Implicit shape constancy as a factor in pictorial perception. *British Journal of Psychology, 67,* 23–29.

Deregowski, J. B. (1977). A study of orientation errors in response to Kohs-type figures. *International Journal of Psychology, 12,* 183–91.

Deregowski, J. B. (1980a). Perception. In H. C. Triandis & W. J. Lonner (Eds.), *Handbook of cross-cultural psychology* (Vol. 3, pp. 21–115). Boston: Allyn and Bacon.

Deregowski, J. B. (1980b). *Illusions, patterns and pictures.* London: Academic Press.

Deregowski, J. B. (1980c). Some aspects of perceptual organization in the light of cross-cultural evidence. In N. Warren (Ed.), *Studies in cross-cultural psychology.* London: Academic Press.

Deregowski, J. B. (1984). *Distortion in art, the eye and the mind.* London: Routledge and Kegan Paul.

Deregowski, J. B. (1986). Kazimierz Bartel's observations of drawings of children and illiterate adults. *Psychology, 4,* 331–333.

Deregowski, J. B. (1989). Real space and represented space: cross-cultural perspectives. *Behavioral and Brain Sciences, 12,* 51–119.

Deregowski, J. B. (1990). On two distinct and quintessential kinds of pictorial representation. In K. Landwehr (Ed.), *Ecological percep-*

tion research, visual communication, and aesthetics (pp. 29–42). Berlin: Springer-Verlag.

Deregowski, J. B. (1995). Perception-depiction—perception and communication. *Rock Art Research, 12*, 3–11 & 18–22.

Deregowski, J. B. & Bentley, A. M. (1986). Perception of pictorial space by Bushmen. *International Journal of Psychology, 21*, 743–52.

Deregowski, J. B. & Bentley, A. M. (1987). Seeing the impossible and building the likely. *British Journal of Psychology, 78*, 91–97.

Deregowski, J. B. & Byth, W. (1970). Hudson's pictures in Pandora's box. *Journal of Cross-Cultural Psychology, 1*, 315–23.

Deregowski, J. B., Muldrow, E. S., & Muldrow, W. F. (1972). Pictorial recognition in a remote Ethiopian population. *Perception, 1*, 417–25.

Deregowski, J. B. & Parker, D. M. (1992). Convergent perspective and divergent perspective. *Perception, 21*, 441–447.

Deregowski, J. B. & Parker, D. M. (1994). The perception of spatial structure with oblique viewing, an explanation for Byzantine perspective? *Perception, 23*, 5–13.

D'Hondt, W. & Vandewiele, M. (1983). Colors and figures in Senegal. *Perceptual and Motor Skills, 56*, 971–978.

Duncan, H. F., Gourlay, N., & Hudson, W. (1973). *A study of pictorial perception among Bantu and white primary school children in South Africa.* Johannesburg: Witwatersrand University Press.

Dziurawiec, S. & Deregowski, J. B. (1992). 'Twisted perspective' in young children's drawings. *British Journal of Developmental Psychology, 10*, 35–49.

Eysenck, H. J. (1941). A critical and experimental study of color preferences. *American Journal of Psychology, 54*, 385–394.

Eysenck, M. W. & Keane, M. T. (1990). *Cognitive psychology: A student's handbook.* London: Lawrence Erlbaum.

Farley, F. H. & Ahn, S-H. (1973). Experimental aesthetics: Visual aesthetic preferences in five cultures. *Studies in Art Education, 15*, 44–48.

Farnsworth, D. (1943). The Farnsworth-Munsell 100 hue and dichotomous tests for color vision. *Journal of the Optical Society of America, 33*, 568–578.

Fischer, J. L. (1961). Art styles as cognitive maps. *American Anthropologist, 63*, 79–83.

Fortes, M. (1940). Children's drawings among the Tallensi. *Africa, 13*, 293–95.

Fortes, M. (1981). Tallensi children's drawings. In B. Lloyd & J. Gay (Eds.), *Universals of human thought* (pp. 46–70). Cambridge: Cambridge University Press.

Gibson, E. J. (1969). *Principles of perceptual learning and development.* New York: Appleton-Century-Crofts.

Gollin, E. S. (1965). Perceptual learning of incomplete pictures. *Perceptual and Motor Skills, 21*, 439–445.

Golomb, C. (1992). *The child's creation of pictorial world.* Berkeley: University of California Press.

Goodenough, F. L. (1926). *Measurement of intelligence by drawings.* Chicago: World Book Company.

Gregory, R. L. (1968). *Eye and brain.* London: World University Library.

Gregory, R. L. (1973). The confounded eye. In R. L. Gregory & E. H. Gombrich (Eds.), *Illusion in nature and art* (pp. 49–95). London: Duckworth.

Grieve, K. W. (1991). Traditional beliefs and color perception. *Perceptual and Motor Skills, 72*, 1319–1323.

Haeckel, E. (1866). *Generale Morphologie der Organismen.* Berlin: G. Reimer.

Halverson, J. (1987). Art for art's sake in the Palaeolithic. *Current Anthropology, 28*, 63–89.

Halverson, J. (1992). The first pictures: Perceptual foundations of Palaeolithic art. *Perception, 21*, 389–404.

Halverson, J. (1995). Information and typicality. *Rock Art Research, 12*, 14–15.

Hardin, C. L. (1988). *Color for philosophers, unweaving the rainbow.* Indianopolis/Cambridge: Hackett.

Hardin, C. L. & Banaji, M. R. (1993). The influence of language on thought. *Social Cognition, 11*, 277–308.

Hardin, C. L., Levine, J., Teller, D. Y., & Wilson, H. R. (1991). Color, unweaving the rainbow. *Philosophical Psychology, 4*, 19–81.

Harris, D. B. (1963). *Children's drawings as measures of intellectual maturity.* New York: Harcourt Brace & Jovanovich.

Hekkert, P. & van Wieringen, P. C. W. (1990). Complexity and prototypicality as determinants of the appraisal of paintings. *British Journal of Psychology, 81,* 483–495.

Howell P., Cross, I., & West, R. (1985). *Musical structure and cognition.* London: Academic Press.

Hudson, W. (1960). Pictorial depth perception in sub-cultural groups in Africa. *Journal of Social Psychology, 52,* 183–208.

Hudson, W. (1962). Pictorial perception and educational adaptation in Africa. *Psychologia Africana, 9,* 226–239.

Humphrey, N. K. (1973). The illusion of beauty. *Perception, 2,* 429–439.

Humphrey, N. K. (1983). *Consciousness regained.* Oxford: Oxford University Press.

Jahoda, G. (1976). Reproduction of Kohs-type drawings by Ghanaian children: orientation error revisited. *British Journal of Psychology, 67,* 203–11.

Jahoda, G. (1978). Cross-cultural study of factors influencing orientation errors in reproduction of Kohs-type figures. *British Journal of Psychology, 69,* 203–11.

Jahoda, G. (1991). Dessins primitifs, dessins d'enfants et la question de l'évolution. *Gradhiva, 10,* 60–70.

Johnson, E. G. & Tomiie, T. (1985). The development of color-naming in four- to seven-year old children: A cross-cultural study. *Psychologia—An International Journal of Psychology in the Orient, 28,* 216–227.

Kaplan, R. & Herbert, E. J. (1988). Familiarity and preference, a cross-cultural analysis. In J. L. Nasar. (Ed.), *Environmental aesthetics* (pp. 379–389). Cambridge: Cambridge University Press.

Kaplan, R. & Kaplan, S. (1989). *The experience of nature.* Cambridge: Cambridge University Press.

Kaplan, S. (1987). Aesthetics, affect and cognition. *Environment and Behavior, 19,* 3–32.

Kaplan, S. (1992). Environmental preference in a knowledge-seeking, knowledge-using organism. In J. H. Barkow, L. Cosmides & J. Tooby (Eds.), *The adapted mind* (pp. 581–598). Oxford: Oxford University Press.

Kay, P., Berlin, B., & Merrifield, W. R. (1991). Biocultural implications of systems of color naming. *Linguistic Anthropology, 1,* 12–25.

Kinnear, P. R. (1970). Proposals for scoring and assessing the 100-Hue test. *Vision Research, 10,* 423–433.

Kinnear, P. R. & Deregowski, J. B. (1992). Comment on MacLaury's article. *Current Anthropology, 33,* 163–164.

Leach, E. R. (1954). A Trobriand Medusa? *Man, 54,* 103–5.

Leach, M. L. (1975). The effect of training in the pictorial depth perception of Shona children. *Journal of Cross-Cultural Psychology, 6,* 457–70.

Levi-Strauss, C. (1963). *Structural anthropology.* New York: Basic Books.

Lewis-Williams, J. D. & Dowson, T. A. (1988). The signs of all times, entoptic phenomena in Upper Palaeolithic art. *Current Anthropology, 29,* 201–45.

Lomax, A. (1968). *Folk song style and culture.* Washington: American Association for the Advancement of Science.

MacLaury, R. E. (1992). From brightness to hue: An explanatory model of color-category evolution (article, commentaries and reply). *Current Anthropology, 33,* 137–186.

Maher, T. F. (1976). "Need for resolution" ratings for harmonic musical intervals. *Journal of Cross-Cultural Psychology, 7,* 259–276.

Marshack, A. (1989). Methodology in the analysis and interpretation of Upper Palaeolithic image: Theory versus contextual analysis. *Rock Art Research, 6,* 17–38.

Martindale, C. (1988). Aesthetics, psychobiology and cognition. In F. H. Farley & R. W. Neperud (Eds.), *The foundations of aesthetics, art and art education.* New York: Praeger.

Martindale, C. & Moore, K. (1988). Priming, prototypicality and preference. *Journal of Experimental Psychology, Human Perception and Performance, 14,* 661–670.

Martindale, C., Moore, K., & West, A. (1988). Relationship of preference judgments to typicality, novelty and mere exposure. *Empirical Studies of the Arts, 6,* 79–96.

Michaels, D. (1977). Linguistic relativity and color terminology. *Language and Speech, 20,* 333–343.

Mishra, R. C. (1982). Perception and comprehension of some pictorial symbols as a function of familiarity and nature of depicted object. *Perceptual and Motor Skills, 55,* 962.

Mishra, R. C. (1987). A re-examination of socio-cultural differences in the perception of pictorial symbols. *Indian Journal of Current Psychological Research, 2*, 65–73.

Mishra, R. C. (1988). Perception and comprehension of dual scene pictures. *Journal of Psychological Researchers, 33*, 121–127.

Modiano, N., Macdonaldo, L. M. P., & Villasana, S. B. (1982). Accurate perception of colored illustrations, rates of comprehension in Mexican-Indian children. *Journal of Cross-Cultural Psychology, 13*, 490–495.

Nadel, S. F. (1939). The application of intelligence tests in the anthropological field. In F. C. Bartlett, M. Ginsberg, E. J. Linkgren, & R. H. Thouless (Eds.), *The study of society, methods and problems* (pp. 184–198). London: Kegan Paul.

Nasar, J. L. (1984). Visual preferences in urban street scenes. *Journal of Cross-Cultural Psychology, 15*, 79–93.

Nicholson, J. R., Seddon, G. M., & Worsnop, J. G. (1977). Teaching understanding of pictorial spatial relationships to Nigerian secondary school students. *Journal of Cross-Cultural Psychology, 8*, 401–414.

Nurse, G. T. & Jenkins, T. (1977). Serogenetic studies on the Kwango peoples of South West Africa. *Annals of Human Biology, 4*, 465–478.

Ord, I. G. (1971). *Mental tests for pre-literates.* London: Ginn.

Orians, G. H. & Heerwagen, J. H. (1992). Evolved responses to landscapes. In J. H. Barkow, L. Cosmides & J. Tooby (Eds.), *The adapted mind* (pp. 555–579). Oxford: Oxford University Press.

Parker, D. M. & Deregowski, J. B. (1990). *Perception and artistic style.* Amsterdam: North-Holland.

Pickford, R. W. (1972). *Psychology and visual aesthetics.* London: Hutchinson.

Poortinga, Y. & Foden, B. I. M. (1975). A comparative study of curiosity in black and white South African students. *Psychologia Africana, Monograph Supplement No. 8.*

Purcell, A. T. (1984). The aesthetic experience and mundane reality. In W. R. Crozier & A. J. Chapman. (Eds.), *Cognitive processes in the perception of art* (pp. 189–210). Amsterdam: North Holland.

Reuning, H. & Wortley, W. (1973). Psychological studies of the Bushmen. *Psychologia Africana, Monograph Supplement No. 7.*

Rivers, W. H. R. (1901). Vision. In W. H. R. Rivers (Ed.), *Reports of the Cambridge anthropological expedition to Torres Straits.* Cambridge: Cambridge University Press.

Rivers, W. H. R. (1905). Observations on the senses of the Todas. *British Journal of Psychology, 1*, 321–396.

Roederer, J. G. (1984). The search for a survival value of music. *Music Perception, 1*, 350–356.

Rohner, R. P. (1975). *They love me, they love me not.* New Haven: HRAF Press.

Rohner, R. P. & Frampton, S. B. (1982). Perceived parental acceptance–rejection and artistic preference. *Journal of Cross-Cultural Psychology, 13*, 250–259.

Rosch, E. (1973). On the internal structure of perceptual and semantic categories. In T. E. Moore (Ed.), *Cognitive development and the acquisition of language* (pp. 111–114). New York: Academic Press.

Russell, P. A. (1994). Preferability, pleasingness and interestingness, relationships between evaluative judgments in empirical aesthetics. *Empirical Studies of the Arts, 12*, 141–157.

Russell, P. A. & George, D. A. (1990). Relationships between aesthetic response scales applied to paintings. *Empirical Studies of the Arts, 8*, 15–30.

Russell, P. A. & Gray, C. D. (1991). The heterogeneity of the preferability scale in aesthetic judgments of paintings. *Visual Arts Research, 17*, 76–84.

Sadie, S. (1980). *The new grove dictionary of music and musicians, Volume 9.* London: Macmillan.

Saunders, B. A. C. (1992). Comment on MacLaury's article. *Current Anthropology, 33*, 165–167.

Seddon, G. M., Eniaiyeju, P. A., & Chia, L. H. (1985). The factor structure for mental rotations of three-dimensional structures presented in diagrams. *Research in Science and Technological Education, 3*, 29–42.

Seddon, G. M., Eniaiyeju, P. A., & Jursho, I. (1984). The visualization of rotation in diagrams of three-dimensional structure. *American Educational Research Journal, 21*, 25–38.

Seddon, G. M., & Nicholson, J. R. (1985). Developmental trends in the ability of primary school children to construct models from diagrams. *Educational Psychology, 5,* 55–64.

Seddon, G. M. & Shubber, K. E. (1984). The effects of presentation mode and color in teaching the visualization of rotation in diagrams of molecular structure. *Research in Science and Technological Education, 2,* 167–176.

Seddon, G. M., Tariq, R. H., & Dos Santos Veiga, J. (1984). The transferability of two pictorial scientific tasks between different spatial dimensions. *British Journal of Educational Psychology, 54,* 276–83.

Segall, M. H., Campbell, D. T., & Herskovits, J. M. (1966). *Influence of culture on visual perception.* Indianapolis: Bobbs-Merrill.

Segall, M. H., Dasen, P. R., Berry, J. W., & Poortinga, Y. H. (1990). *Human behavior in global perspective: An introduction to cross-cultural psychology.* New York: Pergamon.

Serpell, R. (1971). Discrimination of orientation by Zambian children. *Journal of Comparative and Physiological Psychology, 75,* 312–316.

Serpell, R. (1979). How specific are perceptual skills? A cross-cultural study of pattern reproduction. *British Journal of Psychology, 70,* 365–80.

Serpell, R. (1993). *The significance of schooling.* Cambridge: Cambridge University Press.

Serpell, R. & Deregowski, J. B. (1980). The skill of pictorial perception: An interpretation of cross-cultural evidence. *International Journal of Psychology, 15,* 145–80.

Shafer, E. L. & Tooby, M. (1973). Landscape preferences, an international replication. *Journal of Leisure Research, 5,* 60–65.

Shapiro, M. B. (1960). The rotation of drawings by illiterate Africans. *Journal of Social Psychology, 52,* 17–30.

Shaw, B. (1969). *Visual symbols survey.* London: Centre for Educational Development Overseas.

Shepard, R. N. (1992). The perceptual organization of colors: An adaptation to regularities of the terrestrial world? In J. H. Barkow, L. Cosmides, & J. Tooby (Eds.), *The adapted mind.* Oxford: Oxford University Press.

Simpson, C. (1991). Color perception, cross-cultural linguistic translation and relativism. *Journal for the Theory of Social Behavior, 21,* 409–430.

Sinha, D. (1977). Some social disadvantages and development of perceptual skills. *Indian Journal of Psychology, 52,* 115–132.

Sinha, D. & Mishra R. C. (1982). Some social disadvantages and skill for perception of pictorial symbols. *Personality Study and Group Behavior, 2,* 111–121.

Sloboda, J. A. (1985). *The musical mind.* Oxford: Oxford University Press.

Sonnenfeld, J. (1967). Environmental perception and adaptation level in the Arctic. In D. Lowenthal (Ed.), *Environmental perception and behavior* (pp. 42–59). Chicago: Department of Geography Research Papers, University of Chicago.

Spitz, H. H. & Borland, M. (1971). Redundance in line drawings of familiar objects: effects of age and intelligence. *Cognitive Psychology, 2,* 196–205.

ten Doesschate, G. (1964). *Perspective, fundamentals, controversials, history.* Nieuwkoop: B. De Graff.

Thouless, R. H. (1933). A racial difference in perception. *Journal of Social Psychology, 4,* 330–39.

Thouless, R. H. (1972). Perceptual constancy or perceptual compromise. *Australian Journal of Psychology, 24,* 133–140.

Traill, A. (1985). Private letter to Dr. Christine Liddell.

Tzeng, O. C. S., Trung, N. T., & Rieber, R. W. (1990). Cross-cultural comparisons on psychosemantics of icons and graphics. *International Journal of Psychology, 25,* 77–97.

Uspenskii, B. (1976). *The semiotics of the Russian icon.* Lisse: Peter de Ridder Press.

Verriest, G. (1963). Further studies on acquired deficiency of color discrimination. *Journal of the Optical Society of America, 53,* 185–195.

Vitz, P. C. (1966). Affect as a function of stimulus variation. *Journal of Experimental Psychology, 71,* 74–79.

Walker, E. L. (1981). The quest for the inverted U. In H. I. Day (Ed.), *Advances in intrinsic motivation and aesthetics* (pp. 39–70). London: Plenum.

Whitfield, T. G. A. (1983). Predicting preferences for familiar, everyday objects, an experimental confrontation between two theories of aesthetic behavior. *Journal of Environmental Psychology, 3,* 221–237.

Whitfield, T. G. A. & Slatter, P. E. (1979). The effects of categorization and prototypicality on aesthetic choice in a furniture selection task. *British Journal of Psychology, 70,* 65–75.

Whiting, J. W. M. & Child, I. L. (1953). *Child training and personality.* New Haven: Yale University Press.

Wiegersma, S. & de-Klerck, I. (1984). The "blue phenomenon" is red in the Netherlands. *Perceptual and Motor Skills, 59,* 790.

Wohlwill, J. F. (1976). Environmental aesthetics: The environment as a source of affect. In I. Altman & J. F. Wohlwill (Eds.), *Human behavior and environment* (Vol. 1, pp. 37–86). New York: Plenum Press.

Wolfe, A. W. (1969). Social structural basis of art. *Current Anthropology, 10,* 3–44.

Wundt, W. (1898). *Die geometrisch-optischen Täuschungen.* Leipzig: B.G. Teubner.

Young, A. & Deregowski, J. B. (1981). Learning to see the impossible. *Perception, 10,* 91–105.

Zube, E. H. (1984). Themes in landscape assessment theory. *Landscape Journal, 3,* 104–109.

Zube, E. H. & Mills, L. V. (1976). Cross-cultural explorations in landscape perceptions. In E.H. Zube (Ed.), *Studies in landscape perception* (pp. 162–169). Amherst, MA: University of Massachusetts.

Zube, E. H. & Pitt, D. G. (1981). Cross-cultural perceptions of scenic and heritage landscapes. *Landscape Planning, 8,* 69–87.

5

COGNITION AND COGNITIVE DEVELOPMENT

R. C. MISHRA[1]
Banaras Hindu University
India

Contents

Introduction

This chapter discusses cultural influences on cognition and cognitive development. Cognition refers to every process by which individuals obtain and utilize knowledge. It encompasses processes such as thinking, reasoning, recognition, labelling, analysis, categorization, and planning through which people comprehend their environment and achieve successful adaptations to it.

The study of cognitive processes has been fundamental to psychologists and educationists for a long time. Learning theorists have always shown concern for the development of general principles regarding the acquisition of knowledge and skills; developmental psychologists have tried to comprehend the growth of knowledge and skills as a function of the maturation of human organisms and their ever increasing and qualitatively changing interaction with the world; psychometricians have tried to develop tools and techniques for the measurement of skills and abilities of individuals; and educationists have been concerned with the application of psychological knowledge about individuals to the process of teaching and learning.

Interest in the topic has led not only to a sizable amount of empirical work, but also to a number of models and theories of cognitive development. Although most of the theorizing has been based on data obtained from Euro-American settings, the discovery of cultural diversity as well as panhuman principles about cognition have been set as important goals of cross-cultural research on cognition (Berry & Dasen, 1974).

Theoretical Issues

The identification and description of links between culture and cognition have been made since the late 1800's. A detailed account of these efforts is available in Berry and Dasen (1974), Segall, Dasen, Berry, and Poortinga (1990), and Altarriba (1993). The historical development of the field has been traced by Jahoda and Krewer in Volume 1 of this *Handbook*. Research has been so pervasive that in the first edition of this *Handbook*, some eleven chapters were devoted, at least in part, to the discussion of cognition.

Three Main Questions

There are three major questions with which most cross-cultural studies of cognition are concerned (Berry & Dasen, 1974):

1. Are there *qualitative differences* in cognitive processes among different cultural groups, or are the processes identical, with the apparent differences attributable to the different cultural materials entering into the processes?
2. Are there *quantitative differences* in cognitive processes among different cultural groups? That is, are some groups more able, more competent, or more

intelligent in their cognitive operations than others ? Crucially important here is another question : Able for what, competent for what, and intelligent for what?

3. Are the *characteristics of development* of cognitive operations (both qualitative and quantitative) and their organization uniform in all cultural groups, or are these dissimilar across groups? If cognitive development and its organization are largely a function of the biological unfolding of capacity during maturation, then we would expect to find little cross-cultural variation in cognitive operations; but if they are largely a function of cultural impact, then we would expect to find little similarity in these operations across cultures.

These questions have interested cross-cultural psychologists over the span of the entire century, and they are equally important in the field today. Recent cross-cultural research, however, disapproves of the notion of "superiority–inferiority" on the part of different cultural groups. It shows that people in different cultural contexts develop different patterns of skills and learn different ways of perceiving the world and solving problems. There are clear indications that cultures vary not only in the salience attached to certain skills, but also in the organization of the cognitive processes that are called upon in a given context, and in the order in which particular cognitive skills are acquired (Cole, 1988, 1992; Irvine & Berry, 1988). Cross-cultural psychologists do accept the existence of performance differences, but try to understand how cognitive behavior of people in various settings is shaped by the cultural experiences available to them. Thus, rather than denying the existence of differences in cognition, they interpret them in terms of "culturally shaped experiences" without assigning any value, status, or hierarchy to cognitive behaviors or, for that matter, to individuals and groups. This has not been so in the early history of research on culture and cognition. Nor is this position held by all psychologists, some of whom do attempt a ranking of groups according to cognitive ability (e.g., Rushton, 1995).

Nature–Nurture Controversy

There are two schools of thought associated with research on cognitive development: the *nativists*, and the *empiricists*. The nativists assert that all perceptual and cognitive phenomena are inborn, that there is an inherent organization in information received from stimuli, and that perception of the world does not require any active construction by the organism. The empiricists argue that the way organisms respond to stimuli in the environment exemplifies the role of experience and learning.

Empiricist theories have taken several forms in the course of their development. The one most frequently employed in cross-cultural research on cognition is the functional approach, which emphasizes the *adaptive* aspects of organism–environment interaction. The approach has been used to explain a variety of perceptual and cognitive phenomena (Berry, 1976; Berry, van de

Koppel, Sénéchal, Annis, Bahuchet, Cavalli-Sforza, & Witkin, 1986; Mishra, Sinha, & Berry, 1996).

The essence of the nature–nurture controversy related to cognitive development is partly captured in the theory of Jean Piaget. According to this theory, a child, in the course of its development, passes through four sequential stages (sensorimotor, preoperational, concrete operational, and formal operational). Each stage is characterized by the appearance of certain cognitive structures that incorporate the previous structures. While the sequence of these stages and the qualitative changes in cognitive structures characteristic of each stage are considered invariant and universal, it is postulated that the interactive influences of physical environment (Piaget, 1974), and sociocultural transmissions (Piaget, 1972) may alter the rate of psychological development at any stage. The theory suggests that the nativist and empiricist view points are complementary to each other.

Empirical Problems

A number of empirical issues relating to cognition have emerged in the cross-cultural literature in recent years. These are related to: (a) the validity of inferences drawn from cognitive behaviors (manifested in data) about cognitive processes and their organization, (b) the validity of the linkage between cognitive behaviors and cultural variables, and (c) the validity of generalizations made from cognitive behaviors (often test scores) about the broader cognitive life of people represented in their day-to-day activities.

The use of a test with cultural groups other than the one for which it was originally designed has led to sharp controversies. The central question is whether a test score has the same meaning for all cultural groups. Related to this main issue are the issues of "culture fairness" of tests and "test transfer" to other cultures; both have received substantial attention in cross-cultural research (Irvine & Berry, 1983; 1988; Poortinga & Van der Flier, 1988). The evidence suggests that "culture fairness" of a test is only a "fiction"; it is not useful to have "test transfer" made to a different cultural setting on a wholesale basis, and it is not easy to draw inferences about cognitive processes simply on the basis of test performances (i.e., test scores).

The understanding of cognition and cognitive development in cross-cultural perspective needs to begin from the observation of what people do cognitively in the course of their day-to-day activities. The notions of "everyday cognition" (Rogoff & Lave, 1984), "practical intelligence" (Sternberg & Wagner, 1986), "indigenous cognition" (Berry, Irvine, & Hunt, 1988), and "cognitive apprenticeship" (Rogoff, 1990) used in respect of the characterization of cognitive life of individuals, are basically rooted in such observations (see Schliemann, Carraher, & Ceci's chapter in this volume).

These conceptions bring us close to the issue of understanding the local cultural meaning of "cognitive competence." The question is: What sorts of behaviors are considered as intelligent or cognitively competent in a given eco-cultural setting? Each society considers certain behaviors as highly valuable for its members, and its socialization processes tend to inculcate those valued behavioral rep-

ertoires. There is much evidence to suggest that the meaning of cognitive competence varies across cultures (Berry, 1984; Berry & Bennett, 1992; Dasen, 1984; Dasen,
Dembele, Ettien, Kabran, Kamagate, Koffi, & N'guessan, 1985; Serpell, 1989; 1993),
and that societies may have diverse sets of cognitive goals that may sharply differ
from the ones valued in Western societies (Berry, 1988). Thus, in order to make any
valid assessment of cognitive processes, we need to have a full understanding of
the ecological context in which people carry out their day-to-day activities, of the
cognitive goals that are set for individuals in their respective cultures, and of the
manner in which these are transmitted to the developing individual. The degree
to which these components are represented in an assessment procedure defines
the "ecological validity" of the test (Berry, 1980).

The pursuit of these analyses is also important for an appraisal of the progress
made by individuals on the path of cognitive development. Without knowing the
goal, how can we understand the distance one has travelled in that direction?
Reviews of cultural definitions of intelligence (Berry, 1984; Dasen, 1984; Serpell,
1989; Tapé, 1994) reveal that in some societies holistic rather than analytic problem
solving is culturally valued, and deliberation rather than haste is considered as
the proper course of action. In these societies, collective discussion rather than
individual reflection may be the preferred cognitive mode. In a society with such
a cluster of values about cognition, individuals tested with a standard Western
psychological instrument are most likely to show a low level of cognitive development with respect to "quick–analytic–individualistic" criteria. But if allowed to
display it, they may show a high level of cognitive development with respect to
"reflective–holistic–collectivistic" criteria. Hence the level of development cannot
be reliably gauged unless the cultural values of that society about cognition are
known.

The various theoretical approaches adopted to explain cognitive development
across cultures largely deal with these issues. We now turn to a discussion of these
approaches. Some representative research on each theoretical position will be
presented.

Four Conceptualizations

Historically, four distinct theoretical positions have been employed for understanding the relationship between culture and cognition (Berry, Poortinga, Segall,
& Dasen, 1992). These approaches are general intelligence, genetic epistemology,
specific abilities, and cognitive styles. Distinctions among these approaches are
made on the basis of three major issues: conceptualization of ecological and cultural contexts, patterning or organization in cognitive performances, and the links
between these two through various cognitive processors.

General Intelligence

The general intelligence approach is based on the idea of a unitary cognitive competence, called "general ability," which is evidenced by a set of positive correla-

tions among performances on a number of cognitive tasks such as verbal, spatial, numerical, and so forth. There is a belief in the existence of a general central cognitive processor that accounts for varying levels of intelligence across individuals in a population. Ecological and cultural contexts (such as economic pursuits, cultural and educational experiences) are considered to form a cluster. A large cluster represents an "enriched" environment, whereas a small cluster represents a "deprived" one. An individual who has an enriched sociocultural or experiential background is likely to have greater opportunity to develop the central processor, and hence exhibit greater intelligence. Many theories of intelligence involve the notion of "g" (Carroll, 1983; Sternberg, 1985).

In cross-cultural studies of intelligence, the existence of more specialized factors (e.g., verbal, mathematical, and conceptual reasoning) besides "g" has been demonstrated (Burg & Belmont, 1990; Vernon, 1969). The distinction between "Intelligence A" (genetic equipment), "Intelligence B" (potentiality developed through interaction with cultural environment), and "Intelligence C" (performance on a particular test) is equally important (Vernon, 1969). Because the standard tests do not provide for any direct assessment of "Intelligence B," the performance (C) does not represent the intelligence that really exists among individuals or groups. Factors such as language, item content, and motivation have been reported to contribute to an individuals' performance on tests (Sternberg, 1994). In view of these, it is extremely difficult to draw inferences about "Intelligence B" or "Intelligence A" based on data that speak only about "Intelligence C." Unless intelligence tests accommodate the activities that people perform in their day-to-day life, the tests will continue to be biased against some cultural groups. The history of intelligence measurement has been full of such biases ("C–B" discrepancy), impossible inferences ("B–A" discrepancy), and ethnocentric interpretations (some groups being viewed as competent, others as stupid). Attempts have been made to gain direct access to Intelligence A (Eysenck, 1988; P. A. Vernon, 1990) by way of measuring brain activity through evoked potential and EEG measures, but the findings are still questionable (Matarazzo, 1994).

The debate about population differences in general intelligence has been fueled recently by two volumes that claim a substantial genetic basis for intelligence (Herrnstein & Murray, 1994; Rushton, 1995). Rushton (1995) makes a crude classification of the world's people into three "races" (called by him "Mongoloid," "Caucasoid," and "Negroid") based on a few superficial characteristics (e.g., skin color, hair texture), none of which can be shown to have any links to psychological characteristics. He then makes the classic error of extending a possible genetic basis for individual differences in intelligence test scores *within a group* to a claim for a similar basis for cross-group differences in these scores. There is a highly selective use of the research literature on which to base his arguments, and there is virtually no attention paid to cultural and ethnic factors. Indeed, neither in the index nor glossary do the terms "culture" or "ethnicity" appear. Any possible cultural basis for differential cognitive development is entirely ignored, while he pursues his "idée fixe" that race explains all (see Horowitz, 1995).

The belief that intelligence has an underlying biological or genetic substrate implies the notion of "deficit," whereas the cultural viewpoint suggests the notion of "difference". McShane and Berry (1988) have examined a number of deficit and difference models of explanation for individual or group differences in test performance. Besides the genetic and physiological deficits suggested in the literature, such explanations also involve the role of individual deprivation (poverty, poor nutrition, health), cultural disorganization, and cultural disruption. It has been argued that making a negative value judgment is an inherent characteristic of deficit models, whereas in difference models, intellectual processes are viewed as essentially the same across all cultural groups, and levels of competence are considered adaptive to context.

The belief in a general cluster of cultural experiences lies at the heart of the general intelligence approach. Vernon (1969) has outlined several more differentiated sets of factors to account for variations in intelligence test performance. These include: perceptual and kinesthetic experiences, varied stimulation, demanding but democratic family climate, linguistic and conceptual stimulations (e.g., books, travel), absence of magical beliefs, tolerance of nonconformity in the family, regular and prolonged schooling, positive self concept, and broad cultural and other leisure interests. Many of these factors have been used in studies of cognitive competence and found to account for significant variation in test performance.

A distinction between "low inference" and "high inference" contextual variables has been made in an analysis of the role of "non-test" variables in intelligence test performance (Irvine, 1983). The former category includes variables, such as practice, coaching, incentives, and the nature of schooling, which tend to have a direct relationship with test scores. The latter category includes such variables as caste, socioeconomic status, ethnicity, and gender for which some mediating mechanisms have to be sought in order to explain their relationships with test performance. In industrialized countries, high inference variables tend to have more pronounced effects on test scores than low inference variables. This pattern is reversed in many Third World countries (Irvine, 1983). Such findings make it imperative to keep the two sets of variables clearly distinct in cross-cultural studies of intellectual functioning.

A more recent perspective on this debate is provided by studies of acculturation and its influence on cognitive test performance. The number of years of formal schooling (often introduced from outside the culture) has been found to be the single best predictor of intelligence test performance in many studies, and it accounts for significant variation in intelligence test scores (Ceci, 1994). Thus, an important reason for intercorrelations found among a variety of test scores may be a common "a" (acculturation) rather than a fundamental "g" factor. In order to make any valid inference about "g," it is necessary to control for acculturation experience of individuals in studies of general intelligence (Berry et al., 1992).

Genetic Epistemology

This approach largely deals with developmental processes that unfold in a chronological sequence; however, it posits coherence among performances on various cognitive tasks. The influence of "cultural context" has been studied particularly at the concrete and formal operational stages of development (Dasen & Heron, 1981; Super, 1981).

Cross-cultural studies using *concrete operational tasks* have generally focused on the development of conservation, elementary logic, and spatial thinking. Despite facing serious methodological problems, researchers have employed Piagetian stage categorization in numerous societies and cultures (Shayer, Demetriou, & Pervez, 1988). However, some studies have revealed the existence of supplementary stages in the sequence described by Piaget. Saxe (1981, 1982) studied the development of number concepts among the Oksapmin of Papua New Guinea who use a number system that employs the names of body parts. While the Oksapmin children follow the stages described by Piaget in the development of number concept, a supplementary stage appears to be linked to specific features of their number system, which poses difficulty in distinguishing between the cardinal values of two symmetrical body parts.

Cultural differences have also been noted with respect to the age at which the various stages are attained. Some evidence suggests that some people in some cultures may altogether lack concrete operational reasoning, evidenced by asymptotic developmental curves. Dasen (1982) has shown that this is a performance, rather than a competence, phenomenon, because it tends to disappear with brief training sessions given to children. Other authors have argued that cultural differences in concrete operational development may be nothing more than a performance phenomenon, or methodological artifacts (Irvine, 1983; Nyiti, 1982).

The "orthodox" Piagetian tradition has been criticized for involving the risk of assigning a fully functioning adult a "child like" status (Cole & Scribner, 1977). Dasen, Berry, and Witkin (1979) have argued that cultural differences could be interpreted just as differences, without attaching any value judgments, if an ecocultural framework is adopted. Rapid acquisition of spatial reasoning in nomadic hunting and gathering societies, and of quantitative reasoning in sedentary agricultural societies (Dasen, 1975) reveals the adaptive value of these concepts for the respective societies. Dasen (1984) has examined the cultural context of concrete operational thought. A negative relationship between spatial operational development and locally valued aptitudes among the Baoulé of Côte d'Ivoire in terms of the meaning of intelligence held by parents has been documented (Dasen, 1988; Dasen et al., 1985). Further research with samples varying in ecocultural pressures operating on children is needed. However, evidence collected so far suggests that cognitive development is neither totally culturally relative, nor completely uniform everywhere.

Cross-cultural studies using *formal operational tasks* have revealed that secondary level schooling is a necessary condition for success on these tasks (Dasen & Heron, 1981; Shea, 1985). In a study with high school and university students in Australia, and with Malay, Indian, and Chinese students in Malaysia, Keats (1985) found evidence of formal operational thinking for some subjects within all groups, but not for all subjects within any group. Considerable improvement in performance was revealed after a proportionality training session, suggesting that differences among groups were largely at the level of performance.

In studies with unschooled subjects, difficulties have been found, possibly due to stylistic differences in thinking. Research with secondary school pupils of rural and urban areas and with illiterate adults in Côte d'Ivoire (Tapé, 1994) using several Piagetian tasks of formal operations (permutation, pendulum, flexibility of rods) demonstrated a holistic approach in nonschooled subjects, which was in consonance with their everyday experience with similar problems. Tapé has derived evidence for two different styles of thinking among adolescents that correspond to two ways of assigning meaning to the natural world. One is the analytic "experimental" style, which corresponds to "formal" logic that is used to establish causal laws. Another is the "experiential" style, which works through symbolic representations, and corresponds to a "pragmatic" (action-oriented) logic that is used to search for the end results. Tapé argues that the second style corresponds to Bantu philosophy, and is produced by informal education.

These findings caution us against using culturally inappropriate situations with nonschooled subjects for the study of formal operational thinking. Saxe's (1981) work with Ponam islanders in Papua New Guinea presents a good example of developing a culturally appropriate task. The Ponam islanders use a system of child naming in which daughters are given a name according to their birth order in relation to their female siblings. The same rule is followed in naming sons, but using another series of names. Saxe developed a task of formal operational thinking using the familiar rules of name attribution to boys and girls. Subjects were asked to construct hypothetical families in accordance with the rules of name attribution. It was found that subjects were able to resolve questions pertaining to each sex at around thirteen years of age. On the other hand, questions involving both sexes (which implied a form of combinatory reasoning) were not resolved until about nineteen years of age. The findings suggested that the subjects had the ability to carry out formal operational thinking, although the indicators were relatively loose when viewed in terms of strict Piagetian criteria of formal thinking. Shea (1985) argues that this should not be taken to mean that certain societies are not capable of formal reasoning. It is likely that scientific reasoning is not particularly valued in all cultures. Therefore, it would be possible to determine the final stage of development only by understanding the cognitive value system of a society, and then assessing where individuals of that particular society have actually moved in the course of development.

There have been attempts towards the revival of Piagetian theory by integrating both structural and contextual aspects. These "neo-Piagetian theories" look for structural invariants accounting for developmental changes, with an insistence on the necessity to take situational variables into account. These are represented, in particular, in the works of Pascual-Leone (1988), Case (1985), Fischer (1980) and Demetriou, Efklides, and Platsidou (1993). All of these theories have in common a steady increase in processing capacity with age. Dasen and de Ribaupierre (1987) have examined many of these newer propositions in terms of their potential for accommodating cultural and individual differences. They find none of them to be a clear winner, and argue that cross-cultural testing of their propositions is a major task that requires immediate attention. Some recent work (Case & Okamoto, 1996) suggests that the highest forms of thought are dependent on the mastery of systems that are cultural creations, not universal human attainments.

Specific Skills

Advocates of this approach (Cole, Gay, Glick, & Sharp, 1971) have criticized alternative approaches that tried to relate cognitive performances to a general or central processor. They laid emphasis on the study of the relationship between a particular feature of the eco-cultural context (e.g., an experience or role) and a specific cognitive performance (e.g., on a classification task). Assuming that cognitive processes are universal, they held the view that ". . . cultural differences in cognition reside more in the situations to which particular cognitive processes are applied than in the existence of a process in one cultural group and its absence in another" (Cole et al., 1971, p. 233).

In essence, the approach emphasized the eco-cultural features of groups and their relationship with cognitive performance, but rejected the existence of a central processor to mediate the effect of culture on cognition (Laboratory of Comparative Human Cognition, LCHC, 1982, 1983). The approach also appeared to be unconcerned with searching out patterns in cognitive skills as well as the nature of the organization of those skills in different cultural contexts (Berry, 1983). Such a pursuit posed serious problems of generalization. As Jahoda (1980) argues, it represented ". . . endless explorations of quite specific pieces of behaviour . . . lacking in global theoretical constructs" (p. 126).

Support for this theoretical position has been claimed in many reviews of the work of other researchers dealing with congitive processes (LCHC, 1982, 1983). Studies by Cole et al. (1971) with Kpelle farmers on estimation of the quantity of rice, by Price-Williams, Gordon, and Ramirez (1969) on conservation of mass among children of Mexican potters, by Serpell (1979) on pattern reproduction among Zambian and Scottish children, and by Jahoda (1983) on the understanding of "profit" among Scottish and Zimbabwean children, provide good examples of research that tend to support the specificity of cognitive processes.

Similar evidence was reported in the study of the effect of literacy on cognitive performance among the Vai people (Scribner & Cole, 1981). A battery of tasks measuring a wide variety of cognitive functioning was given to unschooled Vai literate individuals. The findings suggested that literacy did not transform individuals' cognition in a general way. Instead, only some specific test performances (descriptive communications and grammatical judgments) were related to Vai script acquisition. It was concluded that literacy ". . . makes some difference to some skills in some contexts" (Scribner & Cole, 1981, p. 234). This limited effect of literacy was interpreted in terms of its "restricted" use among the members of the community.

Berry and Bennett (1991) replicated this study among the Cree of Northern Ontario where literacy in a syllabic script is widely used for many purposes, but is partially restricted in that it is not associated with all aspects of their cultural life. They found no evidence for a general cognitive enhancement of performance on Raven's Progressive Matrices, but there was some evidence of the effect of syllabic literacy on spatial tasks, which involved cognitive operations that are essential for the use of this script. Although there was no evidence for any general change in the ways of individuals' thinking due to literacy, the study did demonstrate positive intercorrelations among all test scores, suggesting a definite patterning in the data.

Patterning in performance has been reported in other studies also in which the effect of a particular cultural experience (e.g., weaving) on reproduction of patterns through a variety of media (e.g., pencil-paper, sand, wire, and hand positioning) has been examined (Mishra & Tripathi, 1996). Similarly cultural experiences, rather than occurring as discrete elements or situations, are found to be intertwined (Mishra & Tripathi, 1994) and intricately embedded in the learning context of individuals (Berry, 1983). The advocates of the specific skills theory have realized some difficulties with this approach. A major problem is ". . . its failure to account for generality in human behavior" (LCHC, 1983, p. 331). They feel that "skills and knowledge acquired in one setting often do appear in other settings under recognizably appropriate circumstances. In order for the distributed processing approach to work, it must provide some way to represent the fact that the individual events forming the base of the knowledge system are related to each other" (LCHC, 1983, p. 331). More recently Cole (1992) has adopted the concept of "modularity." He maintains that psychological processes are domain-specific, but considers different domains as modules that are intricately related to cultural contexts, and whose inputs are fed into a central processor that operates on them. This new formulation appears to be quite useful; however, there is need to test the new propositions in cross-cultural research. With some new data in hand, we may hope that there will be some rapprochement between the specific skills approach and those who look for some organization or patterning on both the context and performance sides of the culture–cognition relationship.

Cognitive Styles

The cognitive styles approach was first articulated by Ferguson (1956) who argued that "cultural factors prescribe what shall be learned and at what age; consequently different cultural environments lead to the development of different patterns of ability" (p. 156). The cognitive style approach looks for interrelationships (patterns) in cognitive performances, and postulates different patterns of abilities to develop in different ecocultural settings, depending on the demands placed on an individual.

Among various cognitive styles, the field dependent–field independent (FD-FI) style has received substantial attention in cross-cultural research (Witkin & Goodenough, 1981). Cross-cultural studies of FD-FI cognitive style have largely been persued in an ecocultural framework proposed by Berry (1976, 1987). Comprehensive reviews of the relevant literature are available in Berry (1981, 1991).

The main issues addressed are consistency in scores on tests tapping different domains, sex differences in FD-FI style, stability in style, and the role of ecological pressures and acculturative influences.

Studies with children of nomadic hunting–gathering, transitional, and established agricultural groups of tribal and other cultures in India (D. Sinha, 1979; 1980) have revealed that hunters and gatherers are psychologically relatively more differentiated (more FI) than agriculturalists, and that in different societies, distinct sex roles are culturally prescribed, leading to differing psychological outcomes for males and females. The roles of social structure and socialization practices attendant on them have been tested with children from monogamous, polyandrous, and polygynandrous families (D. Sinha & Bharat, 1985). Family experiences (e.g., mother and father involvement), disciplinary practices used with children and mother–father dominance, which showed some variations across family types, were not found to be strong enough to reliably influence the level of psychological differentiation of children. Hill ecology supported by certain cultural practices of the Brahmin group has been found to reinforce the process of differentiation among Nepalese children (D. Sinha & Shrestha, 1992). The effects of the experiences of schooling, urbanization, and industrialization on the cognitive style of children of Santhal tribal culture (India) have also been found in the predicted direction (G. Sinha, 1988).

An extensive test of both Witkin's theory and the ecocultural model has been attempted in Central Africa (Berry et al., 1986). Male and female children and adults of the Biaka (Pygmy hunters and gatherers), the Bangandu (mainly agriculturalist, but with some hunting and gathering), and the Gbanu (full-fledged agriculturalist) cultural groups were studied using eight tests of cognitive differentiation in visual, auditory, and tactual domains. Looking, telling, and sitting behaviors were also assessed as indicators of differentiation in the social domain. Socialization was studied through parent and neighbor interviews, child-ratings, and observation of parent-child interaction on a specially designed task. Contact-acculturation (defined as changes in cultural features of people due to contact with other cultures, such as language spoken or clothing worn) and test-acculturation (degree of ease reflected in test situations, or understanding test materials) of groups were also assessed.

Factor analysis of the cognitive test data broadly supported the existence of a FD-FI cognitive style. Evidence for differential socialization for independence in the three groups also corresponded to the general predictions of the ecocultural model. However, the predictive validity of socialization for the development of cognitive style appeared to be doubtful. On the other hand, there was clear evidence for the effect of both test-related and contact acculturation on test performance. Cultural group differences in performance were evident, particularly when the covarying effect of acculturation was partialled out.

A more recent study has been carried out in India with Birhor (nomadic hunter–gatherer group), Asur (recent settlers pursuing a mixed economy of hunting–gathering and agriculture), and Oraon (long-standing agriculturalists) tribal cultural groups in the State of Bihar (Mishra et al., 1996). In each group, variations were obtained with respect to a number of objective and subjective measures of contact and test acculturation. Socialization emphases (pressure towards compliance or assertion) of the groups were assessed through a combination of observation, interview, and testing. Story–Pictorial EFT (Sinha, 1978), Tactile EFT (Berry et al., 1986), and Block Designs were used as measures of cognitive style.

The effects of ecocultural and acculturational features of groups were in the predicted direction. The interaction between ecocultural background and acculturation revealed the latter's effect largely for the Oraon group with a nonexistent or negligible effect for Birhor and Asur groups. A "threshold hypothesis" was used to explain the culture-bound effect of acculturation: acculturation can change the psychological characteristics of groups only when it has made its way into the people's life beyond a threshold point. Although test-acculturation appeared to be an important predictor of test performance, it could not displace the effect of the long-standing ecocultural adaptation of groups as hunters or as agriculturalists. The findings revealed that parent or child-reported socialization emphases were weak predictors of children's cognitive style, while variables like parental helping and feedback could reliably predict children's cognitive style in the expected direction.

These studies indicate that the cross-cultural study of cognitive style has followed a common road in the course of research. Unpackaging of "acculturation," especially the distinction between "test" and "contact" acculturation (Berry et al., 1986; Mishra et al., 1996) is quite useful. However, there appears to be little consistent evidence within cultures for the postulated role of socialization in the development of cognitive style. A valid role for socialization can be claimed only when evidence for its importance is demonstrated across and within cultures. At present, only the former appears to be consistently present for socialization, so a new theoretical framework is warranted.

Enormous diversity exemplified in the four major theoretical approaches does not permit us to draw a conclusion with respect to the relationship between culture and cognition. By viewing these relationships through an ecocultural perspective and adopting a nonethnocentric attitude, we can conclude that cognitive processes are commonly shared by all individuals, that cognitive competencies develop in different ways according to the demands of one's ecology and culture, and that valid inferences about these competencies can be drawn only by situating assessment in the broader cultural life of individuals or groups.

Cultural Influences on Cognitive Processes

With an understanding of the issues facing cross-cultural studies of cognition, and of the theoretical positions adopted to address them, we now turn to a discussion of recent studies related to certain cognitive processes to illustrate how and to what extent they are shaped by cultural factors.

Categorization and Color Terms

Perception gives us such a diverse knowledge of the surrounding world that the division of various stimuli into categories becomes an essential cognitive activity to organize and retain them. People speaking different languages name objects in their natural environments in dissimilar ways. Such a terminological difference has often led to the assumption that people from different cultures would have differential cognitive partitioning of the environment.

For a long time, the "linguistic relativity hypothesis" (Whorf, 1956) was proposed to illustrate this relationship between culture and cognition. Studies pertaining to color codability had demonstrated that people in different societies did not have the same array of color terms to partition the color spectrum. The hypothesis was radically challenged by Berlin and Kay (1969) who argued that the "focal color" terms were similar in all languages, though the number of basic color terms in a language varied enormously. An evolutionary progression in color terms was noted; culturally "simpler" societies tended to have fewer basic color terms than culturally "complex" (e.g., large scale, industrial) societies. Thus, the partitioning of color spectrum reflected a cultural relativity that was constrained by societal complexity. Recent work has adopted both neural (Kay, Berlin, & Merrifield, 1991) and eco-cultural (Mac Laury, 1991) perspectives. A comprehensive discussion related to color naming is available in Russell, Deregowski, and Kinnear's chapter in this volume.

There has been a renewed interest in the relationship between language and thought in studies of "cognitive linguistics" (Hill & Mannheim, 1992) in which linguistic differences across different language groups are viewed as manifesting conceptual differences. Slobin's (1990, 1991) work reveals that children who speak different languages interpret pictures in different ways, suggesting that languages do have a "subjective orientation" (see chapter by Semin & Zweir in Volume 3).

Ethnobiology

More compelling evidence about culturally shaped categorization can be obtained from recent research on ethnobiology in which folk classification systems of plants and animals are examined (Berlin, 1992). The central issue has been concerned with the categorical and nomenclatural distinctions that members of traditional societies make among species of plants and animals. A commonsense approach would suggest that plants and animals, which are most important to a society in terms of its survival, are the most likely objects of discrimination and naming, whereas Berlin (1992) claims that the natural world impinges on all human beings in a common way, and that they all perceive it in highly similar ways. For example, all societies distinguish trees from vines and insects from rodents. Such *taxa* (groupings of species) are distributed across certain mutually exclusive and hierarchically organized levels (kingdom, life form, intermediate, generic, specific, and varietal).

Where do cultural influences enter into the systems of classification and nomenclature? Berlin argues that they appear at the level of *subgeneric* taxa (i.e., specifics and varietals), a major proportion of which is associated with domesticated species of plants and animals. This evidence suggests that the increased importance of animals and plants in a society's subsistence will lead to subgeneric conceptual distinctions.

Cross-cultural comparisons also suggest considerable variation in categories at the level of "life-form." The economic importance of plants and animal species has been reported to be the most significant factor determining people's categorization. Differential knowledge of categories and nomenclature often found associated with factors like gender, age, and division of labor in studies has also been taken as an important evidence of cultural influence on classification (Berlin, 1992). For example, Aguaruna Jivaro men (of the Amazon Basin) compared to women exhibited relatively more knowledge about woodpeckers due to their frequent experience with these birds in the course of hunting. On the other hand, women were more accurate than men in recognizing and naming the species of manioc, perhaps due to their sole responsibility for its cultivation.

Prototypes

The foregoing discussion indicates how cognitive anthropologists have tried to conceptualize and study the influence of culture on the organization of concepts. Cognitive psychologists tend to adopt an approach that is largely based on "prototypicality analysis." In this approach, people from different societies are asked to rate the goodness of an item as an example of a specific category term (e.g., how good "rabbit" is as an example of the category "animal"). Analyses of such prototypical judgments have provided evidence for both some culture-specific and some universal patterns in categorization systems.

Schwanenflugel and Rey (1986) compared the prototypical judgments of Spanish- and English-speaking (both monolingual) groups living in Florida for a considerable period of time. They found a substantial correlation (+ .64) for the typicality ratings of the two groups over a large number of categories; however, there was also evidence for considerable variation between them for categories like "bird" and "fruit." Cross-cultural variations in category structure tend to increase as cultures become more distinct from each other, for example, Taiwanese–Chinese and American (Lin & Schwanenflugel, 1995; Lin, Schwanenflugel, & Wisenbaker, 1990). In relatively similar cultures (e.g., German and American), on the other hand, less variation in category structure has been reported (Hasselhorn, 1990).

There may exist certain prototypes generally shared by all members of a cultural group. Schwanenflugel and Rey (1986) have pointed out that category typicality across cultures could be predicted from the similarity of the cultural prototypes for a particular domain. Thus, for "body parts," where the cultural prototypes were highly similar, the relative prototypicality of other body parts was also perceived similarly cross-culturally as compared to "birds" where the prototypes varied considerably for the two groups. These findings tend to imply that cultural familiarity is a crucial factor in determining cross-cultural variation in the structure of categories. In various studies, however, only 6 to 15 percent of the variation in prototypicality judgments has been accounted for by this factor. Blount and Schwanenflugel (1993) argue that cultural familiarity can determine the order in which children will learn category instances in a culture.

In general, these findings suggest differences in categorization and labelling of categories to be relative to the cultural features of individuals or groups. Even knowledge- or familiarity-based explanations offered for categorization differences across groups in some studies tend to be rooted in cultural features of the groups.

Sorting

Studies of categorization carried out in relatively more controlled settings have often used a sorting procedure. In earlier studies, developmental and cultural differences in using color and form as the basis for grouping stimuli were frequently outlined (see Pick, 1980). Later work using "constrained" and "free" sorting procedures has explored the dimensions (taxonomic, functional, perceptual) along which differences in categorization can be evaluated. Populations have been found to vary in the preferred dimensions of classification, the ease or difficulty of changing dimensions of categorization, and the verbalization of the dimensions used in sorting as a function of their ecocultural characteristics (Rogoff, 1981; S. Mishra, 1982).

Mishra et al. (1996) examined the sorting behavior of Birhor, Asur, and Oraon tribal groups of Bihar (India) with the expectation that differences in ecocultural characteristics of groups would encourage different patterns of sorting. Subjects were asked to make a free sorting of twenty-nine familiar and locally salient objects, which were expected to belong to six familiar categories. The findings revealed that, in general, Birhors sorted objects in fewer categories and produced fewer subcategories than Asurs and Oraons. Contact acculturation of groups did not influence the overall production of categories, or of categories conforming to the expected categories, or subcategories. All the groups sorted objects predominantly on a functional basis.

Wassmann and Dasen (1994) studied classification among six Yupno samples of Papua New Guinea whose worldview classifies everything into "hot," "cold," and "cool." Only experts (sorcerers) can manipulate these states. The task consisted of nineteen objects that could be clearly classified as either "hot" or "cold," but could also be classified according to other criteria such as color, form, function, or taxonomy. It was found that only the sorcerers used the category of "hot/cold" explicitly. The other older adults used it implicitly through function, whereas schooling induced sorting by color. Children, whether schooled or unschooled, predominantly sorted by color. Form was never used, and taxonomy very seldom, as criteria of classification of objects.

These findings tend to refute the notion that some cultural groups show less abstraction or generality in thought processes as compared to others. Differential familiarity with testing materials does not seem to be the only influence. It appears that groups can categorize objects in spite of their differential familiarity with stimuli (Dasen, 1984), and they can categorize even familiar stimuli differently in terms of their specific experiences associated with them and the cultural appropriateness of the way their skills are assessed (Wassmann, 1993). The evidence is not in favor of differences in the capacity of cultural groups to process information.

Learning and Memory

Learning and memory have great practical significance for a diverse set of activities in one's life. The role of cultural elements in memory and the strategies used in acquisition and recollection of stimuli have particularly been addressed in cross-cultural studies (see Wagner, 1981).

The effect of cultural elements on memory is primarily brought out in studies of memory of stories drawn from two cultures. Steffensen and Calker (1982) tested U.S. and Australian Aboriginal women for recall of two stories about a child getting sick. The child was treated by Western medicine in one story, and by native medicine in another. There was evidence for better recall of stories consistent with people's own cultural knowledge. Similar results have been reported by Harris, Schoen, and Lee (1986) for recall of stories by American and Brazilian subjects, and by Harris, Schoen, and Hensley (1992) for recall of stories by U.S. and Mexican cultural groups.

These findings differ from the results reported by Mandler, Scribner, Cole, and De Forest (1980). They found relatively few differences in the amount or pattern of story recall by U.S. and Liberian children and adults, and argued that story recall was a culturally universal process. The studies of story memory focus on the effect of cultural knowledge on recall of culturally discrepant stories or story-like events rather than on the organization of that knowledge in particular cultures (Harris, et al., 1992). The appearance of one's cultural contents in the recall of stories representing contents of other cultures points to a tendency towards assimilation of a discrepant knowledge, which marks one of the major processes of cognitive development. Providing familiar codes to unfamiliar objects or events is the most common form of mnemonic strategies used by people. Differences in recall of stories consistent with one's cultural knowledge indicate that people from diverse cultures have similar capacity to use such mnemonics.

Cultural factors in memory may operate in other ways, too. A cultural group that is in the habit of managing life without lamps or other sources of light at night would place a strong demand on individuals to keep things in fixed places and remember them. Mishra and Singh (1992) studied such a group from the Asur tribal culture in Bihar (India). Intentional and incidental recall of children for "locations" and "pairs" of pictures were compared. There was evidence for greater recall accuracy for the "location" than the pair of pictures, irrespective of intentional or incidental learning condition.

The role of culture in learning and memory has also been studied through an analysis of the effect of school and school environment. Different forms of schools found within or across cultures tend to have different outcomes for learning and memory (see chapter by Serpell & Hatano, this volume). A comparison of learning strategies of traditional Quranic (Wagner, 1985, 1993) and Sanskrit (Mishra, 1988) school students with those in Western-type schools reveals differences in the use of learning strategies and learning outcomes. Rote memory appears to be the dominant learning strategy of traditional school children (Wagner, 1985; Wagner & Spratt, 1987). With respect to the use of organizational strategy, Mishra (1988) found that children in Sanskrit and Western-type schools tended to organize list items according to what was most important for them. The former group's organization was based on "importance of objects," whereas the latter's was based on the "importance of events."

Studies pursued with children attending "good" and "ordinary" quality of schools also bring out interesting results. Good schools are characterized by sufficient space for students and staff, transportation, facilities for sports, games and recreational activities, library and reading room, trained teachers, and use of new teaching technology (Mishra & Gupta, 1978; D. Sinha, 1977). Ordinary schools are less well equipped with these facilities. Such school environments have a significant influence on cognitive test performances (Irvine, 1983).

Agrawal and Mishra (1983) noted that "ordinary school" children took more trials to learn a verbal task and exhibited less clustering in recall than "good school" children. Mishra (1992) found that differences in recall and clustering of "good" and "ordinary" school children were evident particularly in list learning. However, the differences were reduced when the same items were presented in the context of familiar stories.

Cross-cultural studies of learning have also focused on the activities of students and the role of teachers, both leading to different learning outcomes. Comparison of Chinese and Japanese students with American students has shown that the former not only engage in more academic activities, but their teachers also impart more information. On the other hand, American teachers tend to show greater concern with organization and discipline in the classroom (Fuligini, 1993; Hawkins, 1983; Stevenson, Lee, & Stigler, 1986).

Large class sizes, authoritarian climate, excessive homework, and expository teaching methods focused on preparing students for examinations generally characterize the learning and teaching context in many developing countries. This results in differences in activities of students and teachers, and the level of parental involvement in children's school related activities (e.g., home work). Techniques of reward and punishment, and the situations in which these are delivered, also show many cross-cultural variations. In Asian cultures, praise for good performance is rare, whereas punishment in the form of ridicule and shaming the child is quite frequent (Ho, 1981). Praise is given only for exceptional achievements or other virtues, but it is seldom given publicly (Salili, Hwang, & Choi, 1989). In such an environment reward has a high motivating effect on learning outcomes.

Researchers have often commented on Asian students being passive learners, showing heavy reliance on rote learning and employing low-level learning strategies focused on passing examinations (Murphy, 1987). Such a learning strategy combined with an emphasis on appropriate behavior and discipline has often been blamed for the lack of thinking and creativity among them (Murphy, 1987) . The phenomenon has been interpreted differently by researchers engaged in emic studies. Lin (1988) has argued that reproduction of memorized textbook materials or lecture notes of teachers could be an extension of filial piety, that is, accepting and obeying teachers or authorities, something that is deliberately taught to children during socialization. Thus, the dominant use of a rote learning strategy is to be viewed as an expression of a culturally valued scheme of learning; it does not suggest that children of traditional cultures do not or cannot acquire and employ other mnemonics to aid learning and memory if the situations so warrant.

Literacy

The consequences of literacy have been popular domains of discussion among scholars for a long time (see Serpell & Hatano's chapter in this volume). The role of literacy can be observed at cultural as well as behavioral levels. While at the cultural level, the concern is with the emergence of social institutions; at the individual level, changes in individuals' day-to-day behaviors, such as access to information and new forms of communication, are analyzed (Berry & Bennett, 1991). Scribner and Cole (1981) have distinguished between two kinds of effects of literacy at the individual level. One relates to the growth of mind as a result of the assimilation of knowledge and information that is transmitted by written texts. The other relates to the content of thought and the processes of thinking. Theoretical assertions about the effect of literacy on cognitive functioning are very strong (e.g., Goody, 1968), but empirical evidence in support of such claims is weak. Methodologically it has been difficult to isolate the effect of literacy from schooling (e.g., Das & Dash, 1990; Rogoff, 1981; Tulviste, 1989). Wide variations in the form of literacy across studies further complicate conclusions about its effect.

Effects of literacy have been largely studied with children acquiring Quranic literacy. Wagner's (1993) work with Muslim children in Morocco has demonstrated that on a variety of serial memory tasks, the Quranic students remember better than nonschooled children; however, Quranic school children perform the same as modern public school children. This is explained by the observation that rote memorization is not yet eliminated from the pedagogy of modern Islamic schools (Wagner, 1993). Scribner and Cole (1981) found that Quranic literates tended to learn lists more by "rote" than by clustering. From a strategic point of view, "rote" learning is considered to be a less effective strategy. More research on the effect of literacy on cognitive processes is needed. The available research reveals no substantial evidence for its effect on these processes.

Spatial Cognition

Spatial cognition is a process through which individuals gain knowledge of the objects and events situated in or linked with space. In spite of its acknowledged importance for human functioning, research on spatial cognition has yet not identified its key issues. An important reason seems to be the study of children's spatial understanding as an end in itself, rather than as a major component of practical problems faced by children in their day-to-day activities (Gauvain, 1993a, 1993b).

Cross-cultural research on spatial cognition has focused on the role of communicative conventions in describing space, the role of symbolic tools in representing space, and the role of cultural practices in organizing knowledge about and use of space.

All of us talk about the location of various objects or places in the environment. Description of route is the most common part of our communication. Spencer and Darvizeh (1983) compared the route descriptions of British and Iranian preschool children. The latter group gave more vivid and fuller accounts of sites along a route, but less directional information than the former. By three years of age, children were found to communicate spatial information to others in the manner of adults in their culture, suggesting that communicative competence in the spatial domain involves the acquisition of culturally patterned skills for describing space.

Cultural artifacts, such as pencil and paper or maps, may facilitate or amplify the capabilities of individuals to think about space and describe it. Uttal and Wellman (1989) have demonstrated that from maps even preschool children can acquire an integrated knowledge of several locations in a large-scale space. However, certain kinds of maps, such as those devised by some Australian Aboriginal groups (Gould, 1969; Klich, 1988), may not be available to all people; hence, they are unlikely to be understood. Vygotsky (1987) has argued that participation in the practices and conventions related to these tools is essential to develop spatial thinking. The long distances travelled by Puluwat navigators (Gladwin, 1971; Hutchins, 1983) using star paths and a traditional navigation system represent great achievements in their spatial cognitive domain through participation in such activities.

The role of cultural practices in thinking has been documented in research on everyday cognition and reasoning (Rogoff & Lave, 1984); practical intelligence (Sternberg & Wagner, 1986), cognitive apprenticeship (Rogoff, 1990), cultural practice, and development (LCHC, 1983; Saxe, 1991); and situated learning (Lave, 1988, Lave & Wenger, 1990) (see chapter by Schliemann, Carraher & Ceci, this volume). Frake (1980) analyzed the use of absolute directions (e.g., east, west, south, north) and contingent directions (e.g., left–right, forward–behind) in two different cultures. There is evidence to suggest that cultures differ in the use of directional words. In traditional navigation in southeast Asia, "south" is often used to refer to "seaward" rather than "landward," and virtually never for true south. The impact of such absolute orientation systems on spatial representation is being studied in several locations around the globe (Levinson, 1995). For example, Wassmann and Dasen (in press) found that in Bali, where such an absolute system predominates in their language and culture, but where relative terms (right/left) also exist, young children (ages 4 to 9 years) use only an absolute encoding of spatial arrays, while older children (11 to 14) and adults use an absolute encoding more often than a relative one, but are able to switch from one to the other.

All cultures use some heuristics to organize spatial information and remember the location of sites. The adaptive value of day-to-day spatial activities and practices of individuals is an important factor in the development of spatial skills. Munroe and Munroe (1971) had found a relationship between the distance Kenyan children played from their village and the development of their spatial skills. Similar results have been obtained with children of the Birjia tribal cultural group in India (Mishra, in press). In a longitudinal follow up study, Munroe, Munroe, and Brasher (1985) reported that directed distances travelled from home (e.g., while herding, running errands) appeared to be a major predictor of spatial skills among boys, but not among girls. In a study of Baoulé children in Côte d'Ivoire, Dasen et al. (1985) found that being away from home (more than 3 kms.) and the variance of the distances from home (an index of the variety of places visited by children) were correlated with spatial concept development (assessed with Piagetian tasks), but for boys only. These measures did not apply well to girls, because they were found to be within 200 meters from home in 87 percent of the observations. Cohen and Cohen (1985) found similar results in respect of spatial memory of boys, and interpreted this as an outcome of adult-defined goal-directed activity.

Poag, Cohen, and Weatherford (1983) have reported adult-controlled spatial experiences to be a hindrance to the development of spatial knowledge, whereas children's opportunity for the exploration of space under their own control has been found to promote spatial understanding. It appears that interference by others during spatial exploration is a crucial variable in the development of spatial cognition. To the extent that the exploration process remains uninterrupted (despite being directed) by adults, one can expect its positive contribution to the development of spatial thinking.

These findings suggest that prior experience in a setting, demands associated with subsistence activities of children, their day-to-day activities, and cultural practices, which encourage and support a particular kind of activity in a given cultural context, are useful in comprehending the development of spatial cognition.

Problem Solving and Reasoning

Problem solving represents a high form of cognitive activity of individuals. It requires an analysis of information and the perception of relationships among them to draw certain logical inferences. Cross-cultural studies have focused on mathematical problem solving and conditional reasoning. We shall briefly examine some of this work here, while studies related to moral reasoning are discussed by Eckensberger and Zimba in this volume.

Mathematical problems provide a good test of reasoning ability, hence, cultural differences in mathematical skills have attracted the attention of researchers. Eastern cultures (e.g., Chinese) have been claimed to be supportive of the development of numerical abilities. Stevenson, Lee, Chen, Lummis, Stigler, Fan, and Ge (1990) tested this claim, and found better performance by Chinese than American students on several mathematical achievement measures. Geary, Fan, and Bow-Thomas (1992) found that on problems of simple addition, Chinese children showed greater accuracy and speed than Americans. Chinese children showed great reliance on strategies such as direct retrieval and decomposition, whereas American children used counting as their main strategy. In terms of the development of strategies, the American children lagged three to four years behind Chinese children. Differences of instruction used by parents and teachers and time spent by children to master the basic skills of mathematics were held responsible for better performance by Chinese than American children. Parental instruction and socialization have also been reported as important factors in the development of mathematical and thinking skills in other studies (Burg & Belmont, 1990; Van de Vijver & Willemsen, 1993).

Davis and Ginsburg (1993) compared Beninese (African), American, and Korean children and found little difference in their performance on informal mathematical problems, whereas on formal problems, the Korean children excelled the other groups. These differences were accounted for by the classroom instructions and parental training that Korean children received in respect of formal mathematics. A positive effect of schooling on problem solving abilities of Beninese children was also evident. On the other hand, the mathematical skills of unschooled children and those working in the marketplace found expression only in the activities they performed in day-to-day life (e.g., counting money required for a drink). Transfer of these skills to formal mathematical situations seems to be doubtful (Carraher, 1991; Saxe, 1991; see also chapter by Schliemann, Carraher & Ceci, this volume).

Studies of *deductive and conditional reasoning* have focused on the role of linguistic factors. Politzer's (1991) work with native speakers of Chinese and Tamil (a South Indian language) in Kuala Lumpur, using problems in English or Malay language, provides no reliable evidence of differences in their reasoning. Cara and Politzer (1993) reported similar results with Native English and Chinese speakers, suggesting that conditional reasoning is not constrained by linguistic features of cultural groups.

Reasoning has also been studied by using tasks that form part of one's day-to-day experiences. Hollos and Richards (1993) adopted this approach in a study with Nigerian boys and girls. In Nigerian culture girls generally stay home and perform domestic chores, while boys spend their time outside of the home, particularly during the adolescent years. Pictures of two healthy and two ailing plants were shown to subjects along with description of their specific treatments (e.g., water, fertilizer, and insecticide). The subjects were asked to answer a set of questions (e.g., "What makes the healthy plant grow well?). The reasoning of Nigerian boys and girls corresponded to that of Western samples, except that between the ages twelve and seventeen, girls did not perform as well as boys. These differences were viewed as consistent with the differential socialization experiences of Nigerian boys and girls. The findings suggested a covariation between life-cycle experiences and performance on reasoning tasks. However, more research relating observable social experiences to reasoning processes is required.

Syllogistic reasoning is a basic cognitive operation that is known to be sensitive to cultural influences. It is concerned with logical truths that are different from empirical truths. A distinction between logical and empirical truths, and an explanation of this distinction defines the ability for syllogistic reasoning. Logical truths require comprehension and inference, whereas empirical truths are learned from one's own experiences or from the testimony of others.

Luria's (1976) work demonstrates that illiterate peasants in Uzbekistan were able to grasp the empirical truths, but they failed to appreciate the logical truths. Schooling contributes significantly to syllogistic reasoning (Scribner & Cole, 1981), suggesting that through school education, logical truths can be inculcated among children. Bickersteth and Das (1981) compared syllogistic reasoning of young children from Canada and Sierra Leone. Although children from Sierra Leone performed better than those from Canada, differences between the two cultural groups were not present as long as their education and intelligence were comparable.

In a study in India, Dash and Das (1987) found that schooled children performed better on "conjunctive" type syllogisms (e.g., A dog and a horse always move together. The horse is moving in the jungle now. What is the dog doing?), whereas unschooled children performed better on "contrary-to-experience" type syllogisms (e.g., If the horse is well fed, it cannot work well. Rama Babu's horse is well fed today. Can it work well today?). These two types of syllogism both used content that was familiar to participants in the study, whereas previous research employed unfamiliar content (e.g., Luria, 1976, referred to "white bears in Siberia" with participants from Uzbekistan). The difference in results between these two studies may thus be attributable to the familiarity dimension: unschooled children in India probably have better first-hand knowledge of horses than schooled children, and hence are able to respond correctly to the syllogism.

Taken together, these results nevertheless suggest that logical truths can be grasped even by nonschooled children with the same level of competence as by schooled children. However, children may perform poorly when empirical and logical truths interfere with logical inferences. There is still need to analyze the role of cultural practices, values, and belief systems of groups in cross-cultural studies of syllogistic reasoning in order to assess the precise role of culture in this process.

Creativity

Creativity is the most valued cognitive process that individuals can display when they attempt to solve a problem. There is no consensus on the nature of creativity or its existence as a qualitatively distinct cognitive process. Tests of creativity attempt to measure it in terms of originality, flexibility, and fluency of ideas or products.

There is very little cross-cultural work on creativity; however, some studies have sought to analyze its environmental supports (Stein, 1991). The social psychology of creativity has stressed the importance of the child's ecological context in the development of creativity (Harrington, 1990). Children's relationships with parents along with supports and stimulations received from them appear to be good predictors of creativity (Simonton, 1987).

Studies examining the role of cultural factors in creativity have focused on cultural pressures and socialization practices that operate on children. Colligan (1983) analyzed the development of musical creativity in the Samoan, Balinese, Japanese, and Omaha Indian cultures, drawing upon the anthropological evidence available in respect of fostering of musical innovativeness among them. In both the Samoan and Balinese cultures, the dancers are encouraged to recognize their individuality (as a person in Samoa, and as a member of a group in Bali); hence in these cultures, they tend to develop unique individual styles within the basic framework of their society's art. The Japanese and Omaha Indian cultures, on the other hand, have no cultural sanctions supporting innovation and originality; instead, there is great pressure on the stability of form and style. Hence, these cultures have continued to live with an unchanged form of music. Colligan (1983) argues that for creativity to occur, societies must have rules recognizing the existence of an individual style.

Mar'i and Karayanni (1982) have reviewed the research carried out on creativity in Arab cultures. In general, males were found to score higher than females on both the verbal and figural creativity measures, a difference which gradually became less with sociocultural changes taking place in Arab society. More "modern" subjects showed greater creativity than less "modern" subjects, with evidence for little sex difference in younger and more "modern" samples than in relatively older and more "traditional" samples. There was also evidence for the Arab subjects to score higher on verbal than figural measures of creativity, which was interpreted in terms of the emphasis on achieving verbal proficiency in the Islamic culture.

Creativity can be fostered by encouraging children to participate in certain playful activities. The role of "make-believe" play has been found to depend on the variety of adult roles available in the culture; this variety tends to increase with acculturation. In a study in West Africa, creativity was also found to be stimulated by the fact that toys were not given by adults but constructed by children themselves, for example, with wire (Dasen, 1988; Segall et al., 1990). To the degree to which such play activities form part of the socialization process of children in any culture, we can predict the influence of culture on creativity. There is a need to analyze creativity as it is reflected in mundane daily activities of children in various cultures.

Conclusions

The literature dealing with cognitive processes reveals substantial interest by cross-cultural psychologists in the study of these processes. There are good indicators of the progress made in this field since 1980. Commendable efforts have been made to extend the research beyond the framework provided generally by laboratory-type settings. Researchers have demonstrated sensitivity to the cultural context of subjects in developing tasks and situations for the measurement of cognitive processes. While the problems addressed in many studies have remained almost the same as those studied in earlier decades, new parameters have been adopted and new interpretations have been advanced for some of these processes with respect to their development across cultures.

In earlier decades, a tendency for "convenient research" was evident, which suggested more "fun" than real probing into cognitive processes or phenomena. This tendency is witnessed in some research on cognition even today. Thus, data collection driven by an easy availability of subjects from two or more cultural groups is not uncommon in comparative studies of cognitive processes. However, there are numerous examples of good studies in which theoretical concerns seem to be deeply rooted. It is not simply the similarities and differences of groups that are emphasized, but the concerns transcend these superficial issues by selecting samples aimed at answering questions of theoretical significance. With the availability of new data, the relationship between culture and cognition has appeared to be more complex than was generally thought in previous years. Hence, all theoretical positions have shown signs of revision in order to accommodate the newer data in their framework. The Piagetian, specific skills, and cognitive style approaches are laying emphasis on developing an "emic" perspective by analyzing the cognitive activities and underlying processes of individuals or groups as they are brought into use in day-to-day life. Unfortunately some work still attempts to interpret cognitive abilities solely in terms of a priori constructs and genetically determined superficial "racial" characteristics. On the other hand, it is heartening to see other theories emphasizing cognitive processes as "adaptive" to the ecological and cultural contexts of individuals or groups. Attempts to understand both the extent and direction of cognitive development in tune with ecocultural pressures operating on individuals present a healthy sign for the development of a nonethnocentric psychology of cognition.

At the theoretical level, the four conceptualizations dealing with the relationship between culture and cognition seem to draw closer to each other. Admission of a "central processing" mechanism and the perceived probability of "transfer" of skills from one situation to another in the specific skills approach now brings it closer to other views. Hopefully, there will be even more correspondence among them, allowing the development of a more unified approach to the study of culture–cognition relationship than we find today.

Endnote

1. The help rendered by Dr. J. Altarriba, Department of Psychology, State University of New York, Albany, New York is gratefully acknowledged.

References

Agrawal, S., & Mishra, R.C. (1983). Disadvantages of caste and schooling, and development of category organization skill. *Psychologia, 26,* 54–61.

Altarriba, J. (Ed). (1993). *Cognition and culture: A cross-cultural approach to cognitive psychology.* Amsterdam: Elsevier Science.

Berlin, B. (1992). *Ethnobiological classification: Principles of categorization of plants and animals in traditional societies.* Princeton: Princeton University Press.

Berlin, B., & Kay, P. (1969). *Basic color terms: Their universality and evolution.* Berkeley: University of California Press.

Berry, J. W. (1976). *Human ecology and cognitive style: Comparative studies in cultural and psychological adaptation.* New York: Sage/Halsted.

Berry, J. W. (1980). Ecological analyses for cross-cultural psychology. In N. Warren (Ed.), *Studies in cross-cultural psychology* (Vol. 2, pp. 157–189). New York: Academic.

Berry, J. W. (1981). Developmental issues in the comparative study of psychological differentiation. In R. H. Munroe, R. L. Munroe, & B. B. Whiting (Eds.), *Handbook of cross-cultural human development* (pp. 475–498). New York: Garland.

Berry, J. W. (1983). Textured contexts: Systems and situations in cross-cultural psychology. In S. H. Irvine & J. W. Berry (Eds.), *Human assessment and cultural factors* (pp. 117–125). New York: Plenum.

Berry, J. W. (1984). Toward a universal psychology of cognitive competence. *International Journal of Psychology, 19,* 335–361.

Berry, J. W. (1987). The comparative study of cognitive abilities. In S. H. Irvine & S. Newstead (Eds.), *Intelligence and cognition: Contemporary frames of reference* (pp. 393–420). Dordrecht: Nijhoff.

Berry, J. W. (1988). Cognitive values and cognitive competence among the bricoleurs. In J. W. Berry, S. H. Irvine, & E. B. Hunt (Eds.), *Indigenous cognition: Functioning in cultural context* (pp. 9–20). Dordrecht: Nijhoff.

Berry, J. W. (1991). Cultural variations in field dependence–independence. In S. Wapner & J. Demick (Eds.), *Field dependence–independence: Cognitive style across the life span* (pp. 289–308). Hillsdale, NJ: Erlbaum.

Berry, J. W. & Bennett, J. A. (1991). *Cree syllabic literacy: Cultural context and psychological consequences.* Tilburg: Tilburg University Press.

Berry, J. W. & Bennett, J. A. (1992). Cree conceptions of cognitive competence. *International Journal of Psychology, 27,* 1–16.

Berry, J. W. & Dasen, P. (Eds.). (1974). *Culture and cognition.* London: Methuen.

Berry, J. W., Irvine, S. H., & Hunt, E. B. (Eds.). (1988). *Indigenous cognition: Functioning in cultural context.* Dordrecht: Nijhoff.

Berry, J. W., Poortinga, Y. H., Segall, M. H., & Dasen, P. R. (1992). *Cross-cultural psychology: Research and applications.* New York: Cambridge University Press.

Berry, J. W., van de Koppel, J. M. H., Sénéchal, C., Annis, R. C., Bahuchet, S., Cavalli-Sforza, L. L., & Witkin, H. A. (1986). *On the edge of the forest: Cultural adaptation and cognitive development in Central Africa.* Lisse: Swets & Zeitlinger.

Bickersteth, P. & Das, J. P. (1981). Syllogistic reasoning among school children from Canada and Sierra Leone. *International Journal of Psychology, 16,* 1–11.

Blount, B. G. & Schwanenflugel, P. (1993). Cultural bases of folk classification systems. In J. Altarriba (Ed.), *Cognition and culture: A cross-cultural approach to cognitive psychology* (pp. 3–22). Amsterdam: Elsevier Science.

Burg, B. & Belmont, I. (1990). Mental abilities of children from different cultural backgrounds in Israel. *Journal of Cross-Cultural Psychology, 21,* 90–108.

Cara, F. & Politzer, G. (1993). A comparison of conditional reasoning in English and Chinese. In J. Altarriba (Ed.), *Cognition and culture: A cross-cultural approach to cognitive psychology* (pp. 283–298). Amsterdam: Elsevier Science.

Carraher, D. (1991). Mathematics learned in and out of schools: A selective review of studies from Brazil. In M. Harris (Ed.), *Schools, mathematics, and work* (pp. 169–201). London: Falmer.

Carroll, J. B. (1983). Studying individual differences in cognitive abilities: Implications for cross-cultural studies. In S. H. Irvine & J. W. Berry (Eds.), *Human assessment and cultural factors* (pp. 213–235). New York: Plenum.

Case, R. (1985). *Intellectual development: Birth to adulthood.* New York: Academic Press.

Case, R. & Okamoto, Y. (1996). The role of central conceptual structures in the development of children's thought. *Monographs of the Society for Research in Child Development.* serial no. 246, Vol. 61, Nos. 1–2.

Ceci, S. J. (1994). Schooling. In R.J. Sternberg (Ed.), *Encyclopedia of human intelligence*, Vol. 2, (pp. 960–964). New York: Macmillan.

Cohen, S. & Cohen, R. (1985). The role of activity in spatial cognition. In R. Cohen (Ed.), *The development of spatial cognition* (pp. 199–223). Hillsdale, NJ: Erlbaum.

Cole, M. (1988). Cross-cultural research in the socio-historic tradition. *Human Development, 31,* 137–157.

Cole, M. (1992). Context, modularity and the cultural constitution of development. In L.T. Winegar & J. Valsiner (Eds.), *Children's development within social context, Vol. 2* (pp. 5–31). Hillsdale, NJ: Lawrence Erlbaum.

Cole, M., Gay, J., Glick, J., & Sharp, D. (1971). *The cultural context of learning and thinking.* New York: Basic Books.

Cole, M. & Scribner, S. (1977). Developmental theories applied to cross-cultural cognitive research. *Annals of the New York Academy of Sciences, 285,* 366–373.

Colligan, J. (1983). Musical creativity and social rules in four cultures. *Creative Child and Adult Quarterly, 8,* 39–44.

Das, J. P. & Dash, U. N. (1990). Schooling, literacy and cognitive development: A study in rural India. In C. K. Leong & B. S. Randhawa (Eds.), *Understanding literacy and cognition: Theory, research and application* (pp. 217–244). New York: Plenum.

Dasen, P. R. (1975). Concrete operational development in three cultures. *Journal of Cross-Cultural Psychology, 6,* 156–172.

Dasen, P. R. (1982). Cross-cultural aspects of Piaget's theory: The competence/performance model. In L. L. Adler (Ed.), *Cross-cul-*

tural research at issue (pp. 163–170). New York: Academic Press.

Dasen, P. R. (1984). The cross-cultural study of intelligence: Piaget and the Baoulé. *International Journal of Psychology, 19,* 407–437.

Dasen, P. R. (1988). Développement psychologique et activités quotidiennes chez des enfants africains. [Psychological development and everyday activities among African children.] *Enfance, 41,* 3–24.

Dasen, P. R., Berry, J. W., & Witkin, H. A. (1979). The use of developmental theories cross-culturally. In L. Eckensberger, Y. H. Poortinga, & W. Lonner (Eds.), *Cross-cultural contributions to psychology* (pp. 69–82). Amsterdam: Swets & Zeitlinger.

Dasen, P. R., Dembele, B., Ettien, K., Kabran, K., Kamagate, D., Koffi, D. A., & N'guessan A. (1985). N'gloûélé, l'intelligence chez les Baoulé (N'gloûélé, intelligence among the Baoulé). *Archives de Psychologie, 53,* 293–324.

Dasen, P. R. & de Ribaupierre, A. (1987). Neo-Piagetian theories: Cross-cultural and differential perspectives. *International Journal of Psychology, 22,* 793–832.

Dasen, P. R. & Heron, A. (1981). Cross-cultural tests of Piaget's theory. In H. C. Triandis & A. Heron (Eds.), *Handbook of cross-cultural psychology* (Vol. 4, pp. 295–342). Boston: Allyn and Bacon.

Dash, U. N. & Das, J. P. (1987). Development of syllogistic reasoning in schooled and unschooled children. *Indian Psychologist, 4,* 53–63.

Davis, J. C. & Ginsburg, H. P. (1993). Similarities and differences in the formal and informal mathematical cognition of African, American and Asian Children: The role of schooling and social class. In J. Altarriba (Ed.), *Cognition and culture: A cross-cultural approach to cognitive psychology* (pp. 343–360). Amsterdam: Elsevier Science.

Demetriou, A., Efklides, A., & Platsidou, M. (1993). The architecture and dynamics of the developing mind: Experiential structuralism as a frame for unifying cognitive developmental theories. *Monographs of the Society for Research in Child Development, 58,* (Serial No. 234).

Eysenck, H. J. (1988). The biological basis of intelligence. In S. H. Irvine & J. W. Berry (Eds.), *Human abilities in cultural context* (pp. 70–104). New York: Cambridge University Press.

Ferguson, G. A. (1956). On transfer and abilities of man. *Canadian Journal of Psychology, 10,* 121–131.

Fischer, K. W. (1980). A theory of cognitive development: The control and construction of hierarchies of skills. *Psychological Review, 87,* 477–531.

Frake, C. (1980). The ethnographic study of cognitive systems. In C. Frake (Ed.), *Language and cultural descriptions* (pp. 1–17). Stanford: Stanford University Press.

Fuligini, A. J. (1993). Time-use activity involvement of adolescents in Japan, Taiwan and the United States. Paper presented at the *60th meeting of the Society for Research in Child Development,* New Orleans, Louisiana.

Gauvain, M. (1993a). The development of spatial thinking in everyday activity. *Developmental Review, 13,* 92–121.

Gauvain, M. (1993b). Spatial thinking and its development in socio-cultural context. *Annals of Child Development, 9,* 67–102.

Geary, D. C., Fan, L., & Bow-Thomas, C. (1992). Numerical cognition: Loci of ability differences comparing children from China and the United States. *Psychological Science, 3,* 180–185.

Gladwin, T. (1971). *East is a big bird.* Cambridge, MA: Harvard University Press.

Goody, J. (1968). *Literacy in traditional societies.* New York: Cambridge University Press.

Gould, R. A. (1969). *Yiwara: Foragers of the Australian desert.* New York: Scribners.

Harrington, D. M. (1990). The ecology of human creativity: A psychological perspective. In M. A. Runco & R. S. Albert (Eds.), *Theories of creativity* (pp. 143–169). Newbury Park, CA: Sage.

Harris, R. J., Schoen, L. M., & Hensley, D. L. (1992). A cross-cultural study of story memory. *Journal of Cross-Cultural Psychology, 23,* 133–147.

Harris, R. J., Schoen, L. M., & Lee, D. J. (1986). Culture-based distortion in memory of stories. In J. L. Armagost (Ed.), *Proceedings of the twentieth annual mid-American conference.* Manhattan: Kansas State University Press.

Hasselhorn, M. (1990). Typizitätsnormen zu zehn Kategorien für Kinder von der Vorschule bis zur vierten Grundschulklasse. *Sprache & Kognition, 9,* 26–43.

Hawkins, J. N. (1983). The people's Republic of China. In R. M. Thomas & T. N. Postlethwaite (Eds.), *Schooling in East Asia* (pp. 137–187). Oxford: Pergamon Press.

Herrnstein, R. J. & Murray, C. (1994). *The bell curve.* New York: The Free Press.

Hill, J. H. & Mannheim, B. (1992). Language and world view. *Annual Review of Anthropology, 21,* 381–406.

Ho, D. Y. F. (1981). Traditional patterns of socialization in Chinese society. *Acta Psychologica Taiwanica, 23,* 81–95.

Hollos, M. & Richards, F. A. (1993). Gender-associated development of formal operations in Nigerian adolescents. *Ethos, 21,* 24–52.

Horowitz, I. L. (1995). The Rushton file. In R. Jacoby & N. Glauberman (Eds.), *The bell curve debate* (pp. 170–200). New York: Random House.

Hutchins, E. (1983). Understanding Micronesian navigation. In D. Gentner & A. Stevens (Eds.), *Mental models* (pp. 191–226). Hillsdale, NJ: Erlbaum.

Irvine, S. H. (1983). Testing in Africa and America: The search for routes. In S. H. Irvine & J. W. Berry (Eds.), *Human assessment and cultural factors* (pp. 45-58). New York: Plenum.

Irvine, S. H. & Berry, J. W. (Eds.). (1983). *Human assessment and cultural factors.* New York: Plenum.

Irvine, S. H., & Berry, J. W. (Eds.). (1988). *Human abilities in cultural context.* New York: Cambridge University Press.

Jahoda, G. (1980). Theoretical and systematic approaches to cross-cultural psychology. In H. C. Triandis & W. W. Lambert (Eds.), *Handbook of cross-cultural psychology* (Vol. 1, pp. 69–141). Boston: Allyn and Bacon.

Jahoda, G. (1983). European "lag" in the development of an economic concept: A study in Zimbabwe. *British Journal of Developmental Psychology, 1,* 113–120.

Kay, P., Berlin, B., & Merrifield, W. (1991). Biocultural implications of systems of color naming. *Journal of Linguistic Anthropology, 1,* 12–25.

Keats, D. M. (1985). Strategies in formal operational thinking: Malaysia and Australia. In I. Reyes Lagunes & Y. H. Poortinga (Eds.), *From a different perspective: Studies of behavior across cultures* (pp. 306–318). Lisse: Swets & Zeitlinger.

Klich, L. Z. (1988). Aboriginal cognition and psychological nescience. In S. H. Irvine & J. W. Berry (Eds.), *Human abilities in cultural context* (pp. 427–452). New York: Cambridge University Press.

Laboratory of Comparative Human Cognition (1982). Culture and intelligence. In R. Sternberg (Ed.), *Handbook of human intelligence* (pp. 642–719). New York: Cambridge University Press.

Laboratory of Comparative Human Cognition (1983). Culture and cognitive development. In P. H. Mussen & W. Kessen (Eds.), *Handbook of child psychology* (Vol. 1, pp. 295–356). New York: Wiley.

Lave, J. (1988). *Cognition in practice*. Cambridge: Cambridge University Press.

Lave, J. & Wenger, E. (1990). *Situated learning: Legitimate peripheral participation*. Palo Alto, CA: Institute for Research on Learning.

Levinson, S. C. (1995). Frames of reference and Molyneux question: Cross-linguistic evidence. In P. Bloom, M. Peterson, L. Nadel, & M. Garrett (Eds.), *Language and space* (pp. 109–169). Cambridge, MA: MIT Press.

Lin, P. J. & Schwanenflugel, P. J. (1995). Cultural familiarity and language factors in the structure of category knowledge. *Journal of Cross-Cultural Psychology, 26,* 153–168.

Lin, P. J., Schwanenflugel, P. J., & Wisenbaker, J. M. (1990). Category typicality, cultural familiarity, and the development of category knowledge. *Developmental Psychology, 26,* 805–813.

Lin, Y. N. (1988). Family socio-economic background, parental involvement and students' academic performance by elementary school children. *Journal of Counselling, 11,* 95–141.

Luria, A. R. (1976). *Cognitive development: Its cultural and social foundations*. Cambridge, MA: Harvard University Press.

Mac Laury, R. E. (1991). Exotic color categories: Linguistic relativity to what extent? *Journal of Linguistic Anthropology, 1,* 26–51.

Mandler, J. M., Scribner, S., Cole, M., & De Forest, M. (1980). Cross-cultural invariance in story recall. *Child Development, 51,* 19–26.

Mar'i, S. & Karayanni, M. (1982). Creativity in Arab culture: Two decades of research. *Journal of Creative Behaviour, 16,* 227–238.

Matarazzo, J. D. (1994). Biological measures of intelligence. In R. J. Sternberg (Ed.), *Encyclopedia of human intelligence, Vol. 1,* (pp. 193–200). New York: Macmillan.

McShane, D. & Berry, J. W. (1988). Native North Americans: Indian and Inuit abilities. In S. H. Irvine & J. W. Berry (Eds.), *Human abilities in cultural context,* (pp. 385–426). New York: Cambridge University Press.

Mishra, A. (1992). *Role of age, school-related differences and contextual change in recall and organization.* Unpublished doctoral thesis, Banaras Hindu University.

Mishra, R. C. (1988). Learning strategies among children in the modern and traditional schools. *Indian Psychologist, 5,* 17–24.

Mishra, R. C. (in press). Perceptual differentiation in relation to children's daily life activities. *Social Science International.*

Mishra, R. C. & Gupta, V. (1978). Role of schooling and exposure in perceiving pictorial sequence. *Psychologia, 21,* 231–236.

Mishra, R. C. & Singh, T. (1992). Memories of Asur children for locations and pairs of pictures. *Psychological Studies, 37,* 38–46.

Mishra, R. C., Sinha, D., & Berry, J. W. (1996). *Ecology, acculturation and psychological adaptation: A study of Adivasi in Bihar.* New Delhi: Sage.

Mishra, R. C. & Tripathi, N. (1994). *The role of family and home experiences in the development of pattern reproduction skill in two cultural groups.* Unpublished manuscript.

Mishra, R. C. & Tripathi, N. (1996). Reproduction of patterns in relation to children's weaving experiences. In J. Pandey, D. Sinha, & D. P. S. Bhawuk (Eds.), *Asian contributions to cross-cultural psychology* (pp. 138–150). New Delhi: Sage.

Mishra, S. (1982). *Ecological disadvantage and skill for pictorial perception and classification.* Unpublished doctoral dissertation, Banaras Hindu University.

Munroe, R. L. & Munroe, R. H. (1971). Effect of

environmental experience on spatial ability in an East African society. *The Journal of Social Psychology, 83,* 15–22.

Munroe, R. L., Munroe, R. H., & Brasher, A. (1985). Precursors of spatial ability: A longitudinal study among the Logoli of Kenya. *The Journal of Social Psychology, 125,* 23–33.

Murphy, D. (1987). Offshore education: A Hong Kong perspective. *Australian University Review, 30,* 43–44.

Nyiti, R. M. (1982). The validity of "cultural differences explanations" for cross-cultural variation in the rate of Piagetian cognitive development. In D. A. Wagner & H. W. Stevenson (Eds.), *Cultural perspectives on child development* (pp. 146–165). San Francisco: W. H. Freeman.

Pascual-Leone, J. (1988). Organismic processes for neo-Piagetian theories: A dialectical causal account of cognitive development. In A. Demetriou (Ed.), *The neo-Piagetian theories of cognitive development: Toward an integration* (pp. 25–64). Amsterdam: North Holland.

Piaget, J. (1972). *The principles of genetic epistemology.* London: Routledge & Kegan Paul.

Piaget, J. (1974). Need and significance of cross-cultural studies in genetic psychology. In J. W. Berry & P. R. Dasen (Eds.), *Culture and cognition* (pp. 299–309). London: Methuen.

Pick, A. D. (1980). Cognition: Psychological perspectives. In H. C. Triandis & W. Lonner (Eds.), *Handbook of cross-cultural psychology* (Vol. 3, pp. 117–154). Boston: Allyn and Bacon.

Poag, C., Cohen, R., & Weatherford, D. L. (1983). Spatial representations of young children: The role of self versus other-directed movement and viewing. *Journal of Experimental Child Psychology, 35,* 172–179.

Politzer, G. (1991). Comparison of deductive abilities across language. *Journal of Cross-Cultural Psychology, 3,* 389–402.

Poortinga, Y. H. & Van der Flier, H. (1988). The meaning of item bias in ability tests. In S. H. Irvine & J. W. Berry (Eds.), *Human abilities in cultural context* (pp. 166–183). New York: Cambridge University Press.

Price-Williams, D., Gordon, W., & Ramirez, M. (1969). Skill and conservation. A Study of pottery-making children. *Developmental Psychology, 1,* 769.

Rogoff, B. (1981). Schooling and the development of cognitive skills. In H. C. Triandis & A. Heron (Eds.), *Handbook of cross-cultural psychology* (Vol. 4, pp. 233–294). Boston: Allyn and Bacon.

Rogoff, B. (1990). *Apprenticeship in thinking: Cognitive development in social context.* New York: Oxford University Press.

Rogoff, B. & Lave, J. (Eds.). (1984). *Everyday cognition: Its development in social context.* Cambridge, MA: Harvard University Press.

Rushton, J. P. (1995). *Race, evolution, and behavior: A life history perspective.* New Brunswick, NJ: Transaction.

Salili, F., Hwang, C. E., & Choi, N. F. (1989). Teachers' evaluative behavior: The relationship between teachers' comments and perceived ability in Hong Kong. *Journal of Cross-Cultural Psychology, 20,* 115–132.

Saxe, G. B. (1981). Body parts as numerals: A developmental analysis of numeration among remote Oksapmin village populations in Papua New Guinea. *Child Development, 52,* 306–316.

Saxe, G. B. (1982). Culture and the development of numerical cognition: Studies among the Oksapmin of Papua New Guinea. In C. J. Brainerd (Ed.), *Children's logical and mathematical cognition* (pp. 157–176). New York: Springer.

Saxe, G. B. (1991). *Cultural and cognitive development: Studies in mathematical understanding.* Hillsdale, NJ: Erlbaum.

Schwanenflugel, P. J. & Rey, M. (1986). The relationship between category typicality and concept familiarity: Evidence from Spanish- and English-speaking monolinguals. *Memory & Cognition, 14,* 150–163.

Scribner, S. & Cole, M. (1981). *The psychology of literacy.* Cambridge, MA: Harvard University Press.

Segall, M. H., Dasen, P. R., Berry, J. W., & Poortinga, Y. H. (1990). *Human behavior in global perspective: An introduction to cross-cultural psychology.* Boston: Allyn and Bacon.

Serpell, R. (1979). How specific are perceptual skills? A cross-cultural study of pattern reproduction. *British Journal of Psychology, 70,* 365–380.

Serpell, R. (1989). Dimensions endogènes de l' intelligence chez les A-chewa et autres peuples africains. In J. Retschitzky, M. Bossel-Lagos, & P.R. Dasen (Eds.), *La recherche interculturelle* (pp. 164–179). Paris: Harmattan.

Serpell, R. (1993). *The significance of schooling: Life-journeys in an African society.* Cambridge: Cambridge University Press.

Shayer, M., Demetriou, A., & Pervez, M. (1988). The structure and scaling of concrete operational thought: Three studies in four countries and only one story. *Genetic Psychology Monographs, 114,* 307–376.

Shea, J. D. (1985). Studies of cognitive development in Papua New Guinea. *International Journal of Psychology, 20,* 33–61.

Simonton, D. K. (1987). Developmental antecedents of achieved eminence. *Annals of Child Development, 5,* 131–169.

Sinha, D. (1977). Social disadvantage and development of certain perceptual skills. *Indian Journal of Psychology, 52,* 115–132.

Sinha, D. (1978). Story-Pictorial E.F.T.: A culturally appropriate test for perceptual disembedding. *Indian Journal of Psychology, 52,* 160–171.

Sinha, D. (1979). Perceptual style among nomadic and transitional agriculturalist Birhors. In L. Eckensberger, W. Lonner, & Y. H. Poortinga (Eds.), *Cross-cultural contributions to psychology* (pp. 83–93). Lisse: Swets & Zeitlinger.

Sinha, D. (1980). Sex differences in psychological differentiation among different cultural groups. *International Journal of Behavioral Development, 3,* 455–466.

Sinha, D. & Bharat, S. (1985). Three types of family structure and psychological differentiation: A study among the Jaunsar-Bawar society. *International Journal of Psychology, 20,* 693–708.

Sinha, D. & Shrestha, A. B. (1992). Eco-cultural factors in cognitive style among children from hills and plains of Nepal. *International Journal of Psychology, 27,* 49–59.

Sinha, G. (1988). Exposure to industrial and urban environments, and formal schooling as factors in psychological differentiation. *International Journal of Psychology, 23,* 707–719.

Slobin, D. (1990). The development from child speaker to native speaker. In J. W. Stigler, R. A. Shweder, & G. Herdt (Eds.), *Cultural Psychology: Essays on comparative human development* (pp. 223–256). Cambridge: Cambridge University Press.

Slobin, D. (1991). Learning to think for speaking: Native language cognition and rhetorical style. *Pragmatics, 1,* 7–26.

Spencer, C. & Darvizeh, Z. (1983). Young children's place-description, maps and route-findings: A comparison of nursery school children in Iran and Britain. *International Journal of Early Childhood, 15,* 26–31.

Steffensen, M. S., & Calker, L. (1982). Intercultural misunderstandings about health care: Recall of descriptions of illness and treatments. *Social Science and Medicine, 16,* 1949–1954.

Stein, M. (1991). On the sociohistorical context of creativity programs. *Creativity Research Journal, 4,* 294–300.

Sternberg, R. J. (1985). *Beyond I.Q.: A triarchic theory of human intelligence.* New York: Cambridge University Press.

Sternberg, R. J. (Ed.). (1994). *Encyclopedia of intelligence, Vol. 1.* New York: Macmillan.

Sternberg, R. J., & Wagner, R. K. (1986). *Practical intelligence: Nature and origins of competence in the everyday world.* Cambridge: Cambridge University Press.

Stevenson, H. W., Lee, S. Y., Chen, C., Lummis, M., Stigler, J., Fan, L., & Ge, F. (1990). Mathematical achievement of children in China and the United States. *Child Development, 61,* 1053–1066.

Stevenson, H. W., Lee, S. Y., & Stigler, J. W. (1986). Mathematics achievement of Chinese, Japanese and American children. *Science, 231,* 693–699.

Super, C. M. (1981). Cross-cultural research on infancy. In H. C. Triandis & A. Heron (Eds.), *Handbook of cross-cultural psychology* (Vol. 4, pp. 17–53). Boston: Allyn and Bacon.

Tapé, G. (1994). *L'intelligence en Afrique: Une étude du raisonnement expérimental.* Paris: L'Harmattan.

Tulviste, P. (1989). Education and the development of concepts: Interpreting results of experiments with adults with and without schooling. *Soviet Psychology, 27,* 5–21.

Uttal, D. H. & Wellman, H. M. (1989). Young children's representation of spatial information acquired from maps. *Developmental Psychology, 23*, 514–520.

Van de Vijver, F. & Willemsen, M. E. (1993). Abstract thinking. In J. Altarriba (Ed.), *Cognition and culture: A cross-cultural approach to cognitive psychology* (pp. 317–342). Amsterdam: Elsevier Science.

Vernon, P. A. (1990). The use of biological measures to estimate behavioral intelligence. *Educational Psychologist, 25*, 293–304.

Vernon, P. E. (1969). *Intelligence and cultural environment*. London: Methuen.

Vygotsky, L. S. (1987). *The collected works of L. S. Vygotsky, Vol. 1*. New York: Academic Press.

Wagner, D. A. (1981). Culture and memory development. In H. C. Triandis & A. Heron (Eds.), *Handbook of cross-cultural psychology* (Vol. 4, pp. 187–232). Boston: Allyn and Bacon.

Wagner, D. A. (1985). Islamic education: Traditional pedagogy and contemporary aspects. In T. Husen & T. N. Postlethwaite (Eds.), *International encyclopedia of education: Research and studies*, (pp. 2714–2716). New York:Pergamon.

Wagner, D. A. (1993). *Literacy, culture and development: Becoming literate in Morocco*. New York: Cambridge University Press.

Wagner, D. A. & Spratt, J. E. (1987). Cognitive consequences of contrasting pedagogies: The effects of Quranic preschooling in Morocco. *Child Development, 58*, 1207–1219.

Wassmann, J. (1993). When actions speak louder than words: The classification of food among the Yupno of Papua-New Guinea. *Newsletter of the Laboratory of Comparative Human Cognition, 15*, 30–40.

Wassmann, J. & Dasen, P. R. (1994). "Hot" and "Cold": Classification and sorting among the Yupno of Papua-New Guinea. *International Journal of Psychology, 29*, 19–38.

Wassman, J. & Dasen, P. R. (in press). Une combinaison de méthodes ethnographiques et psychologiques dans l'étude des processsus cognitifs. In B. Krewer (Ed.), *Théorie et pratique de l'interculturel*. Paris: L'Harmattan

Whorf, B. L. (1956). *Language thought and reality*. Cambridge, MA: MIT Press.

Witkin, H. A. & Goodenough, D. R. (1981). *Cognitive style: Essence and origins*. New York: International University Press.

6

EVERYDAY COGNITION

ANALÚCIA D. SCHLIEMANN
Tufts University
United States

DAVID W. CARRAHER
Universidade Federal de Pernambuco
Brazil

STEPHEN J. CECI
Cornell University
United States

Contents

Introduction

The expression "everyday cognition" may appear redundant. After all, do not all instances of thinking represent "everyday cognition"? If so, why do we not simply drop the useless adjective? To understand why, it helps to contrast "everyday cognition" with "laboratory cognition." Some social scientists preface the word "cognition" with "everyday" to register a complaint; namely, that data, results, and interpretations based upon traditional laboratory studies may not generalize or, worse yet, may not even be relevant to life beyond the laboratory. Other everyday cognition researchers would endorse some research conducted in laboratories but, nevertheless, be leery about attempts to build general theories about people's thinking, reasoning, problem solving, communicating, and symbol-using, solely or even primarily, on the basis of data collected in laboratories. Their skepticism may be likened to that of a primate specialist who is asked whether one can adequately understand chimpanzees by observing them caged in zoos.

Researchers in everyday cognition are prone to believe that "contexts" play important roles in human thinking and reasoning, although they may differ widely in what they consider to be contexts. They believe that studies of learning and thinking in context require special approaches and new methods of observing and obtaining data that take contexts into account. Their concern, however, goes beyond issues of methodology.

Studies of human reasoning in everyday situations have often revealed that individuals perform remarkably well on tasks that are formally similar to tasks on which they perform unsuccessfully in traditional investigatory settings. Such findings have prodded researchers to question traditional views of intelligence and intellectual abilities. They suggest not simply that some people may have more intelligence than they are given credit for, but also that life beyond the laboratory teems with ways of thinking, communicating, and using symbols that rarely come to light in laboratory investigations. This draws attention to another important aspect of everyday cognition research. Thinking is regarded as a truly social and cultural enterprise: thought, communication, and action are not unconstrained free productions of the individual. They must be understood in terms of the symbolic systems (for example, linguistic, mathematical, metaphorical, aesthetic, scientific, metaphysical, folklore, and religious systems) people draw upon in acting and interpreting events, including those involving the actions of others. Furthermore, to gain a broad understanding of human cognition in contexts, one often needs to analyze how social roles and relations, historical events, institutional traditions, concerns, and objectives bear upon phenomena under investigation. This, by no means, eliminates the individual from analysis, for individuals attempt to realize their personal objectives in the most socially constrained of settings; furthermore, they will interpret phenomena in accordance with their personal knowledge and background of experience. It does suggest, however, that everyday cognition cannot totally fit into the field of individual psychology. The study of human thinking requires perspectives usually associated with cultural anthropology, sociology, social psychology, and even history.

This chapter first describes the historical evolution of studies of human cognition from the laboratory to everyday contexts. This is followed by a discussion of different approaches for the analysis of context and cognition, and by a brief account of studies contrasting cognitive performance in laboratory settings to performance in everyday settings. We then focus on how everyday cognition studies became an important issue in cross-cultural psychology. Our review of studies of everyday cognition begins by considering the diverse areas researchers have studied in the last decades. Then, focusing mainly on mathematical knowledge in out-of-school, out-of-laboratory contexts, we discuss issues such as how everyday knowledge differs from school knowledge, how general can be the knowledge developed in specific everyday contexts and what are the strengths and limitations of knowledge developed in everyday settings. Finally, we consider some implications of studies of everyday cognition for cognitive and psychological theories, research methodology, and education.

Psychology: From Laboratories to Everyday Cognition

Everyday cognition can be distinguished from other topic areas not by its natural object of study, but rather by the theoretical issues with which it attempts to contend. These issues did not spring forth at once; rather, they emerged slowly as a result of developments within, and influences across, diverse scientific traditions, three of which merit special mention.

Firstly, there is the "empirical–experimental" contribution to the field of everyday cognition. Some researchers from an empirical–experimental background began to question assumptions and methods employed in research and to increasingly pay attention to how individuals draw upon their experience from outside the laboratory.

A second tradition that requires mention is the "sociohistorical" school of thought. Originally this tradition referred primarily to the work of Vygotsky, Luria, Leontiev, and other authors of the former Soviet Union. In recent years, the sociohistorical school witnessed development, reinterpretation, and extension as a result of work conducted outside this region.

Finally, everyday cognition benefited from much of the research and theoretical developments, largely Piagetian, regarding the individual's construction of logico–mathematical knowledge from early infancy to adolescence. This contribution is more difficult to discern than the former two because Piagetian research was usually conducted in situations staged by the interviewer, and Piaget's theory does not assign a major role to sociocultural factors in human development, particularly before the period of formal operations. Nonetheless, Piaget provided a wealth of empirical and theoretical findings as a major alternative to the experimentalists' accounts (see Piaget & Inhelder, 1969), and thereby made important contributions to the analyses of how knowledge develops in everyday contexts. Piaget's theory of how knowledge develops had a major impact upon everyday cognition conceptions about knowledge and thinking, even among researchers who strongly opposed some basic Piagetian assumptions and viewed the study of everyday cognition as an alternative to his analysis. Their debt to Piaget reveals itself most clearly in their tendency to conceive of knowledge as a construction by an active subject, and not a result of a transmission process nor an imposition of the object over the subject.

In the following section we provide a look at how the field developed and how it now stands, although "stands" is probably not the best term, for the field is still developing. There is not even a general consensus about what the major issues are and how they might be settled. We hope, however, that this chapter will aid in clarifying the issues and challenges to the field.

An Historical Overview

In their struggle to develop Psychology as a science, early psychologists such as Ebbinghaus adopted an experimental-laboratory paradigm. Ebbinghaus reasoned that if he used everyday memory tasks, such as recalling shopping lists and addresses, the differential familiarity with such materials could obscure the assessment of the "true" memory ability. He decided to use, in his memory studies, nonsense words rather than sentences or real words, thereby supposedly controlling an undesirable source of variation, namely, familiarity with the stimuli. Relatively meaningless, unrepresentative situations were thus valued for their contribution to experimental control.

Ebbinghaus' approach to human memory was to have a major influence on the practices and values of cognitive psychologists for several decades. Many researchers conducted thousands of studies of basic processing parameters and used highly artificial conditions and stimuli. They were in search of universal principles, not stimulus-specific findings. And they found many such principles—or so they thought. Even today many cognitive researchers, following such an approach, view the study of cognition as a "pure" science rooted in the same kind of universal principles that exist in areas such as classical physics. Their pursuit of knowledge about human cognition resulted in research on thinking and reasoning that is disembedded from the everyday contexts in which people develop. However, it would be misleading to say that Ebbinghaus advocated the study of human memory "out of context," or "in context-free" settings. A setting would have to be totally devoid of meaning and structure in order to be totally context-free. This is not the case for laboratory settings. Although a laboratory may constitute an unrepresentative or questionable context for the study of certain phenomena, it does not follow that laboratory settings are devoid of meaning.

Ebbinghaus' approach to cognition is traditionally contrasted with that of Bartlett, who departed from a mechanical view of human cognition, and in its place, proposed that cognition was a dynamic process in which one's prior beliefs, values, experience, and knowledge were used to make sense of events. He referred to this process as "effort after meaning," by which he meant that human beings attempt to make sense of what they confront in a task, deploying their beliefs and knowledge in the process. For example, Bartlett's (1932) subjects were given stories about rich and complex events and later asked to recall them. When attempting to recall such stories, subjects reconstructed the plot to make it consistent with their own beliefs and prior experience. Through findings such as these, Bartlett challenged the tradition of Ebbinghaus by asserting that the study of cognition should reflect and take into account the individual's social experience.

By the late 1960s, the so-called "cognitive revolution" was just getting underway in psychology, and Bartlett was rediscovered. A new generation of cognitivists departed from the mechanical view of Ebbinghaus in favor of an approach similar to Bartlett's. This shift is reflected in the reintroduction of concepts such as "schema" and the use of new concepts such as "scripts" and "semantic representations" to explain the manner in which one's past knowledge and beliefs influence present cognition. The term *schema*, used in a non-Kantian sense, refers to a body of facts about a concept that organizes information in an orderly representation (e.g., one has a schema for baseball, wild animals, and so on). A related term, *script*, refers to temporally-ordered information about a habitual event (e.g., what normally happens in a given setting or situation such as dining at a restaurant, visiting a doctor's office, or attending an exercise class). Scripts presumably lead us to expect which events occur and their temporal order—first, second, and so on. When stories are presented that violate their script, subjects commonly reorder the sequence of events to fit the script. Scripts can be changed, but for this to happen, there usually must occur repeated violations of a pre-existing script.

By invoking concepts like schema and script, cognitivists were stepping outside of Ebbinghaus' tradition; they were promulgating a view that embedded cognition in a larger framework including not only a set of encoding, storage, and retrieval processes, but also an individual's knowledge and feelings about what was being processed.

Bartlett's approach has enjoyed increasing recognition by cognitive researchers in great part due to the influence of Ulric Neisser (1967, 1976, 1982). Neisser (1976) enjoined cognitive psychologists to study the types of cognition that occur in everyday contexts and urged psychologists not to build laboratory models of memory processes that had no real-world analogs. He did not argue against laboratory studies of cognition, but only against those laboratory studies that have no real world analog. In making this entreaty, he lamented psychology's "thundering silence" on questions of interest and importance in our everyday lives (Neisser, 1982).

When researchers ventured outside of the laboratory and examined cognition in everyday contexts, they made discoveries that were difficult to reconcile with the principles they constructed exclusively on the basis of laboratory studies. In their search for universal cognitive mechanisms, laboratory researchers have misconstrued *Homo Sapiens'* ability to adapt to the environment, to respond differentially to different contexts. This insight led Bronfenbrenner (1979) to decry the search for context–invariant mechanisms as illusory:

One can question whether establishing transcontextual validity is the ultimate goal of science. . . . Given the ecologically interactive character of behavior and development in humans, processes that are invariant across contexts are likely to be few in number and fairly close to the physiological level. What behavioral scientists should be seeking, therefore, are not primarily these universals but rather the laws of invariance at the next higher level—principles that describe how processes are mediated by the general properties of settings and of more remote aspects of the ecological environment (p. 128).

The field of everyday cognition shares and extends Bartlett's and Neisser's focus on meaningful situations and Bronfenbrenner's concerns about the ecological environment. But this is only part of the story. Everyday cognition must also be understood in terms of the Soviet sociohistorical tradition from which it drew inspiration. It was largely through the work of Cole and his associates that the sociohistorical tradition came to be influential, first in cross-cultural analyses, and later in the study of cognition and cognitive development. Cole (1988) summarizes the central thesis of the sociohistorical tradition established by Leontiev (1981), Luria (1976), and Vygotsky (1978) as follows:

The structure and development of human psychological processes are determined by humanity's historically-developing, culturally mediated, practical activity (pp. 137–38).

For those familiar with the Soviet tradition, this sentence conveys an underlying wealth of new ideas—"new" from the point of view of the European–American empirical traditions of cognitive psychology. These ideas now constitute the core of many recent approaches for the study of human knowledge in everyday contexts.

Cognition in the Laboratory versus Cognition in Everyday Contexts

One of the major challenges to a theory of cognition, everyday variety or not, consists in the handling of context. Although most social scientists would agree that human behavior and cognition depend heavily on contexts, they are likely to entertain widely different understandings of their nature and role.

Investigators in cognitive psychology have often discussed "context" in terms of a polarity corresponding roughly to the subject–object distinction in epistemology. The "object" side of the polarity stresses contexts as referring to the environment external to the individual (Bronfenbrenner, 1979). Physical and social settings are frequently discussed as examples of environmental contexts. The "subject" pole refers to the psychological framework persons carry within them. Each individual, it is argued, perceives and understands phenomena by means of structured representations; that is, phenomena are assimilated into a preexisting mental framework, or else a new mental framework is created or altered to accommodate what is being experienced.

Although the mental–environmental polarity might seem to provide a straightforward framework for discussing contexts, it may oversimplify some issues that require more careful consideration. To understand this, it may help to consider some examples.

A psychologist steeped in classic Gestalt tradition might cite, as an example of the importance of context, how the perception of a stimulus acquires characteristics related to a pattern of neighboring stimuli. For example, a written symbol might be interpreted either as "13" or as the letter "B" depending upon whether it is encountered in the midst of letters or digits. One is tempted to summarize this finding with a statement such as "the interpretation of the stimulus depends upon the context in which it appears." Such a conclusion seems reasonable. And for those who believe that individual stimuli exert a direct, characteristic influence on behavior, the finding may be unsettling. Specifically, the finding that a particular stimulus, S_1, may elicit any of several responses undermines one's confidence in a traditional S-R theory.

It is now widely recognized that external stimuli rarely act as radical empiricists had supposed. In perception and sensation, the contrast and juxtaposition of stimuli play an important role. Color perception, for instance, is not the direct result of the frequency of reflected light; the very same color stimulus (with hue, saturation, and brightness kept constant) will be perceived as having one color or another depending on the properties of the surrounding color patches. It would be convenient if we could handle such cases by redefining what the stimulus is. Perhaps the "real" stimulus, one might argue, is not the single patch of color but rather the whole collection of color patches or, as some thought, the Gestalt. Perhaps the "real" stimulus is not the individual written mark but rather the whole sentence, or even the whole text, of which the individual bits of notation are parts.

Unfortunately, the problem goes far deeper than this. Perception is not the result of the epistemological object acting directly upon the subject. Nor is it reducible to the action of the subject projecting subjective representations onto the object. Perception, and more generally, cognition, is the result of interactions between the subject and the object. This bears important implications for the discussion of context and its role in everyday cognition. If human cognition is best understood as involving interaction, the interplay between characteristics of individuals and of situations in which they participate, then we must be skeptical towards attempts to regard contexts as reducible to characteristics of the object (environmental context) or characteristics of the subject (mental context).

Consider the following cases. A social psychologist asked to describe contexts might focus on implicit social norms that members of a group use to guide and interpret social interaction. Another might draw attention to the role of the prior history of events, peculiar to a certain group, as a background for predicting the outcome of a power struggle between competing members. A reading researcher might consider how background knowledge regarding a text is drawn upon in order to interpret the meaning of sentences. An investigator of mathematical reasoning may look at the role the job responsibilities and concerns of a worker play in how mathematical computations are carried out and looked upon by the worker. So diverse are the uses of the term "context."

It is important to note that "context" is not an explanatory construct. Context invariably refers to complex relations between characteristics of the subject and those of the setting in which one acts. Analyzing such processes requires viewing the subject and the object, the mental and the physical, and other such polarities less rigidly than we usually do. In this spirit Lave proposes the dissolution of boundaries between the individual and the contexts where cognition takes place. Lave's (1988) analysis is an example of such a view applied to the study of everyday cognition. Criticizing approaches that conceive of contexts as environmental aspects determining behavior or as the environment of social interaction, Lave proposes a dialectical analysis that focuses on settings that are conceived as "a *relation* between acting persons and the arenas in relation with which they act" (p. 150). In keeping with Lave's views, situated learning theorists consider that cognitive activities take place in specific contexts that, far from being incidental, are essential to what is learned and thought.

Despite theoretical differences regarding conceptions about the meaning of context, empirical studies are rather consistent in pointing out how much the performance in cognitive tasks of different types is related to the contexts. The importance of one's previous experiences and of the contexts in which cognition takes place was recognized even by Piaget (1972) himself, who had earlier proposed a theory of cognitive development based on the generality and universality of mental structures. In his 1972 paper, although maintaining the belief that formal operations are logically independent of the reality content to which they are applied, Piaget admitted that "it is best to test the young person in a field which is relevant to his career and interests" (p. 1). He conceded that despite limited formal education, carpentry, locksmith, and mechanics might well display formal reasoning in tasks related to their field of experience while failing in the school-oriented formal operations tasks he analyzed in his studies.

Glick (1981) provides an example of how cultural contexts are intimately related to the display of cognitive abilities. The example consists of previously unpublished findings from an earlier set of studies (Cole, Gay, Glick, & Sharp, 1971) in which the researchers had constructed a list of objects that could be categorized as foods, clothes, tools, and eating utensils. Five instances of objects in each one of these categories were presented to members of the Kpelle tribe of Liberia who were asked to "put the ones together that go together." In contrast to schooled Western subjects, Kpelle subjects did not use overarching categories (tools, foods, etc.), but tended to employ functional categories. A subject might state, for instance, that "the knife and the orange go together *because the knife cuts the orange.*" This answer was initially thought by the researchers as being inferior to an answer organized around equivalence relations (oranges and potatoes are both food). Faced with the interviewer's frustration at repeatedly receiving "low level, functional" answers, a subject volunteered the observation that his answers reflected how a "wise person" would classify the objects. When the interviewer impatiently asked how a "stupid" person would classify the objects, he received a surprising answer: a stupid person would group the objects according to general classes (tools, foods, and so forth)! Clearly, the Kpelle subjects could classify familiar items according to Western standards of intelligence. But it made more sense to the Kpelle to put together those objects that function together in natural settings.

As stressed by Cole (1988):

> . . . *cultural differences in cognition reside more in the contexts within which cognitive processes manifest themselves than in the existence of a particular process (such as logical memory or theoretical responses to syllogisms) in one culture and its absence in another (Cole, 1988, p. 147).*

More importantly, such findings raise doubts about the validity of studies in the field of culture and cognition undertaken by foreigners to the culture. One of the problems with studying contexts is that they are not objective features of physical reality but rather sociohistorical creations peculiar to the group at hand.

"Context" has been given a certain degree of attention in developmental psychology, albeit without the sociocultural and historical dimensions. As an example, children who fail in the traditional Piagetian conservation, class inclusion, or perspective-taking tasks demonstrate logical reasoning in similar tasks when the same questions are phrased in more natural and meaningful ways (see, among others, Donaldson, 1978; Light, Buckingham, & Robbins, 1979; McGarrigle & Donaldson, 1974).

As shown by Ceci and Bronfenbrenner (1985) in their analysis of children's memory-monitoring strategies in a laboratory environment and at home, even microlevel cognitive strategies, such as the temporal calibration of one's psychological clock, are affected by the context in which the task to be performed is set. Children were significantly more likely to engage in a sophisticated form of calibration in their homes than in a laboratory setting.

Children's multicausal reasoning also varies greatly depending on the motivational context of the task: Ceci and Bronfenbrenner (see Ceci, 1990, 1993) gave children a "distance-estimation" task referring either to a butterfly chase (i.e., predicting where on a computer screen a graphic butterfly would migrate) or to displacements of a geometrical shape. Children were much more efficient in considering all the variables determining the butterfly's displacements than they were in determining the displacements of a geometrical shape on the screen, despite the fact that identical variables were involved in both tasks.

Concerning linguistic abilities, Labov (1970) shows that African-American students, who appeared extremely limited in verbal ability while in traditional interview settings, engaged in rich non-standard English dialogue when the interviewer broke norms of interviewing and took on a playfully irreverent role.

Syllogistic reasoning also seems to be strongly affected by the context in which presentation of premises takes place. Dias and Harris (1988) found that young children who failed to draw counterfactual conclusions from verbally stated premises succeeded in solving the same type of syllogistic problems when they were presented in a make-believe context.

The comparison of subjects' performance on IQ tests to their performance on tasks related to their everyday experience also shows the relevance of contexts. In their characterization of academic versus nonacademic intelligence, Ceci and Liker (1986) found that the levels of reasoning complexity displayed by expert and nonexpert racetrack handicappers, when they dealt with variables that were relevant for successful handicapping, were not related to their performance on IQ tests. Their study demonstrated that the levels of reasoning displayed in contexts that are a part of one's everyday experience cannot be predicted by how one copes with the academic tasks included in IQ tests.

Studies of context and cognition such as the ones just reported called into question the adequacy of analyses relying purely on laboratory data. They also provided a starting point for clarifying the role of contexts and emphasized the need for studies of cognition in everyday settings in order to develop a complete understanding of what is knowledge and how knowledge develops.

Cross-Cultural Psychology and Everyday Cognition

Until recently, cross-cultural psychology downplayed the importance of contextual aspects in cognitive achievement and explored issues related to cognition and cognitive development through standardized tests or interview results. Earlier approaches to cross-cultural psychology focused on systematic comparisons between individuals from different countries, usually industrialized developed countries, in comparison to developing countries. But as *emic* and ecocultural approaches to cross-cultural psychology such as Berry's (1976) began to appear, variables that are intimately linked to everyday activities became the object of cross-cultural studies (see also Berry, Irvine, & Hunt, 1988). Recently, we have seen the development of a large number of studies (see Dasen & Bossel-Lagos, 1989) focusing on everyday cognition within the same culture. As a result, traditional conceptions about cross-cultural psychology are changing and, as already pointed out by Segall, Dasen, Berry, and Poortinga (1990), research in everyday cognition contrasting the knowledge of ordinary people with school, expert, or scientific knowledge is essentially regarded as part of cross-cultural psychology.

An influential landmark in the shift from the use of standardized interviews and tests towards the analysis of cognition in everyday contexts was the investigations conducted by Cole and his associates. Their studies of cognitive development among the Kpelle in Africa (Gay & Cole, 1967; Cole et al., 1971) represent a systematic effort to identify practical activities that could serve as models for cognitive tasks or as opportunities for a more appropriate assessment of cognitive skills. Their work opened up a new way of analyzing cognition across cultures and inspired new theoretical and methodological ways for looking at knowledge development in everyday contexts.

Nowadays, across cultures or within the same culture, studies of everyday cognition are found in different areas, under different denominations, such as indigenous cognition (Berry, 1993), ethnomathematics (D'Ambrosio, 1985), practical intelligence (Sternberg & Wagner, 1986), situated cognition (Brown, Collins, & Duguid, 1989), cognition in context (Laboratory of Comparative Human Cognition, 1983), socially shared cognition (Resnick, Levine, & Teasley, 1991), or everyday cognition (Rogoff & Lave, 1984). Inspired by different questions and theoretical approaches, everyday cognition has become a field of study in itself. Subjects as varied as navigation skills, tailoring, weaving, shopping, betting in horse racing, weight watching, work in a dairy plant, carpentry, house building, cooking, lottery betting, fishing, market selling, and so on have been investigated. The questions dealt with have included: What kind of understanding develops in everyday activities? How is the knowledge developed through everyday working activities different from the knowledge acquired in schools through formal explicit instruction? How does everyday knowledge interact with and is influenced by school experience? What are the limits in the development of knowledge in everyday settings in the absence of school instruction? How specific is the knowledge acquired in everyday activities? How is it related to performance on psychological tests? How do studies of everyday cognition help clarify issues related to intelligence, learning, or transfer? How do culture, cultural tools, cultural symbolic systems, and social interactions relate to knowledge development?

In the following sections we will describe empirical studies of everyday cognition that helped provide answers to some of these questions.

A General Overview of Studies of Everyday Cognition

Faced with the task of reviewing the increasingly large number of studies of everyday cognition, with occasional exceptions, we will describe in detail studies that look at everyday activities performed by individuals with little or no school experience. Several edited volumes on everyday cognition among schooled subjects are now available that will complement and expand this review (see, for instance, Chaiklin & Lave, 1993; and Voss, Perkins, & Segal, 1991, as well as some of the chapters in Detterman & Sternberg, 1993; Rogoff & Lave, 1984; and Sternberg & Wagner, 1986). We chose first to provide an overview of the scope of everyday cognition studies, and then, by focusing mainly on studies of arithmetical knowledge developed in everyday working activities, we address in more depth some of the psychological and educational questions that everyday cognition research has helped to answer.

Memory, Motor Skills, Logical Reasoning, and Video Games in Everyday Contexts

Before psychologists began to look at cognition in everyday contexts, anthropologists were observing how people cope with challenges in real-life contexts. Recent examples of anthropological studies, specially relevant for the description of reasoning characteristics in everyday settings, are Hutchins' (1980) analysis of inferences in everyday discourse among the Trobriand Islanders and Hutchins' (1983) description of Micronesian navigation skills. Such studies are particularly relevant in pointing out the use of logical reasoning among unschooled people in the everyday activities of traditional societies. They also question conclusions reached by previous analyses based on superficial knowledge of the cultures under examination.

As already pointed out by Hatano (1990), although starting from a different methodological tradition and theoretical framework, studies of conceptual development and change share with everyday cognition studies the conclusion that, independently of school instruction, children develop a fairly rich body of knowledge about scientific topics through their everyday experiences in the world. Examples of such an approach are analyses by Carey (1985), Gelman (1979), Hughes (1986), Inagaki (1990), Inagaki and Hatano (1987), Resnick (1986), and Vosniadou (1991), as well as Piaget's analysis of children's logico-mathematical and scientific concepts. Also, studies of cognitive development in sociocultural context, such as Rogoff (1990), clearly focus on children's everyday activities as a source of development.

Memory is one of the areas to give early recognition to the importance of everyday contexts. A set of papers selected and commented on by Neisser (1982) provide an overview of remembering and forgetting in real-world types of situations. His own work on everyday memory includes the analysis of the testimony produced by John Dean, a defendant in the American Watergate scandal in 1974 (Neisser, 1981), of children's recollections of the Challenger space shuttle disaster in 1987, and of adults' recollections of their earliest childhood experiences (Usher & Neisser, 1993).

Memory among nonliterate people has been the focus of studies in different cultures. Of special interest for analysis of how memory processes relate to everyday experiences are the studies by Cole et al. (1971) and by Dube (1982). Cole et al. demonstrated that, contrary to what happened in free recall tasks, Liberian Kpelle subjects used categorization and benefited from it in tasks where items to be memorized were inserted in a story, whereby the sequence of events provided reason for categorization. Dube showed that recall of events presented in the context of an orally narrated story was higher among the nonliterate Botswana in South Africa than among American high school students, a fact that may be explained by the higher frequency of oral story telling activities among Botswana adolescents and adults.

Motor skills in everyday settings were studied by Bril (1986) and by Bril and Roux (1993). Bril described how girls in a Mali village, from as early as three years of age, were asked by their mothers to accomplish goal-oriented tasks such as bruising, crushing, and pounding condiments or cereals. Despite the absence of explicit teaching regarding the actions to be performed, Mali children, by age five, showed temporal and coordination patterns for pounding cereals similar to those of the adult. Bril and Roux documented the way in which workers in India planned and acted during the process of chipping and shaping stone beads. Data from their observations in natural environments and from experiments performed in a workshop with different materials and bead forms suggested that, to achieve their goals of obtaining regular shapes from the available raw material, workers relied not only on their motor skills but also on a planning process involving perception and use of environmental cues which together contributed to the optimization of their actions.

Logical categorization has been the focus of many cross-cultural analyses (Cole et al. 1971; Luria, 1976; Okonji, 1971). More recently, through a careful combination of anthropological and psychological approaches, Wassmann (1993), and Wassmann and Dasen (1994), looked at categorization in the everyday activities of the Yupno of Papua New Guinea. Wassmann showed that different Yupno categorization systems for food depend on the everyday context where classification takes place. Working with the same population, Wassmann and Dasen found that the categories "hot," "cool," and "cold" described everything in the Yupno world, and although known by most members of the population, could only be manipulated by sorcerers. As a consequence, only sorcerers explicitly used the categories in sorting tasks.

Another set of studies explored everyday syllogistic reasoning, a subject examined by Luria (1976) in relation to educational experience, by Hutchins (1979) in the context of everyday discourse, by Scribner (1977) with illiterate Kpelle farmers in Liberia, and by Dias (1987) with Brazilian bricklayers and engineers. An important distinction proposed by Scribner is that between theoretical versus empirical bias in people's approaches to syllogistic problems. The general conclusion of studies in this area seems to be that the theoretical approach to syllogistic problems is typical of schooled subjects, while unschooled subjects, although able to reason syllogistically in everyday situations (see Hutchins, 1979), most often tend to adopt the empirical approach, refusing to reason about unknown facts or to reach conclusions contrary to the facts.

An analysis of responses to Wason's (1966) four-card problems showed the role the content of premises played in deductive reasoning. As found by Johnson-Laird, Legrenzi, and Legrenzi (1972), when the problem refers to symbols that are not connected to everyday activities, subjects thought to be highly intelligent fail in the task. When, however, the content of the problem refers to a real-life context, most subjects find the correct answer.

Different perspectives were adopted in the characterization of everyday or informal reasoning, as opposed to formal logical reasoning (see, among others, the work of Cheng & Holyoak, 1985; Johnson-Laird, 1982; Perkins, 1986; and Voss & Post, 1988). For those interested in the area, the edited volume by Voss, Perkins, and Segal (1991) provides a good overview of studies on informal reasoning and argumentation in everyday and in school settings.

Recently Greenfield (1994) proposed that children's video game activities offered a good opportunity to look at everyday cognition in a context where the child interacts with a particular type of cultural artifact. An increasingly large number of studies analyzed the cognitive consequences of the everyday experience with video games. Their results showed that, for instance, dynamic representation of space (Greenfield, Brannon, & Lohr, 1994; Okagaki & Frensch, 1994; Subrahmanyam & Greenfield, 1994), use of the iconic code of computer graphics (Greenfield, Camaioni, Ercolani, Weiss, Lauber, & Perucchini, 1994), and attentional skills (Greenfield, deWinstanley, Kilpatrick, & Kaye, 1994) benefited from video game experience.

These studies provided support for the ideas that knowledge develops in everyday settings, and that cognitive performance is closely associated to the everyday meaning of the tasks. But the content areas dealt with are too diverse to allow for deeper analysis of the characteristics of everyday knowledge. Let us now turn to the studies of everyday mathematics, an area that inspired so many studies that, we believe, it can offer more detailed insights into the nature of everyday cognition.

Everyday Mathematics: Measurement and Geometry

Mathematics is the most frequently studied area of everyday cognition. In her study of Liberian tailors, Lave chose to look at arithmetic for reasons that explain why mathematical knowledge became a popular subject of analysis. Besides being a part of people's everyday activities in all cultures, arithmetic problem solving is part of a formal system with well determined notations and properties and, as such, allows for relatively precise analysis of problem solving strategies and inferences about cognitive processes taking place during solution (Reed & Lave, 1979). Since then many studies have focused on the widespread use of mathematics in everyday settings and on the development of mathematical concepts independently from school instruction (see reviews by D. W. Carraher, 1991, and by Nunes, 1992). Three main areas of mathematics have been the focus of studies: measurement, geometry, and arithmetic.

Measurement is one of the most frequently encountered mathematical activities in everyday settings, even among groups with very little access to school instruction. Gay and Cole (1967) found that Kpelle rice farmers, who apparently did not deal with any other kind of mathematical concepts, used a system for estimating volume that allowed them to perform more accurately than American students in volume estimation tasks.

Saxe and Moylan (1982) described a system used by the Oksapmin of Papua New Guinea for measuring the depths of string bags widely used in their culture. Oksapmin people measure the size of a particular bag according to how far its top reaches on one's arm (wrist, forearm, inner elbow, biceps, or shoulder) when one's hand touches the bottom of the bag. Because people's arms vary in length, measurement units vary across individuals. Further, Saxe and Moylan reported that unschooled adults performed better than school children but still had difficulties in judging whether the same sizes would be found in measurements performed by children and adults.

In a survey study by Saraswathi (1989), illiterate, semi-literate and literate adults in India were asked to describe linear dimensions of objects, distances, or events.

Their answers showed frequent use of British (Imperial) units and minimal use of metric units. Certain dimensions (heights, depths, distances, short lengths, and area) were more prone to elicit answers involving standardized units of measurement, while others (medium lengths, girth or perimeter, diameter, incline, and rainfall) were more often described according to body measures or nonspecific descriptions, or were not measured at all. The majority of the interviewed subjects knew how to use any of the measuring systems to describe objects or distances, but chose one or the other, depending on their previous exposure and experiences with the specific situations under discussion. Saraswathi (1988) also provided a description of how the same population plans, measures, and reckons with time. Along with the use of clocks, hours, and minutes, subjects use movements of the sun, the moon, or stars for reckoning time. They also employ time-measuring devices based on shadows or on a finely calibrated water container.

Following the introduction of the metric system in Nepal, Ueno and Saito (1994) documented the invention of artifacts and rules for measuring and for conversion between the old measuring systems and the metric system enforced by the government. One of the artifacts created by vendors as a result of the socioeconomic reorganization of market activities was the fusion of old and new units in one new system. This new system allowed the use of traditional computation strategies, because it maintains the binary structure of the old system where each unit represented the double of another unit. Another artifact created by social agreement consisted of the use of approximate conversion rates. Use of either approach allows computation of prices through ingenious computation strategies that preserve proportional relations between prices and measured units.

The above data on everyday measurement provide good descriptions of the widespread use of measuring devices in everyday activities. The relevance of measurement in everyday life, the powerful mathematical systems that are embedded in measuring tools and activities, and their relevance for education point to a very fruitful area for future analysis of everyday cognition. Let us now see what is offered by studies on everyday geometry.

Zaslavsky (1973) provided an overview of the use of geometrical concepts in the design of African geometrical patterns. Gerdes (1986; 1988a, b), who uses the ethnomathematics approach proposed by D'Ambrosio (1985), described the mathematics created and used in cultures and communities that are thought to be mathematically illiterate, because they have no access to the procedures and representations of mathematics as it is taught in schools. He found use of geometrical concepts and patterns among fishermen, house builders, and basket weavers in Mozambique. Harris (1987, 1988) provides examples of geometrical reasoning among women doing needlework or working with textiles at home and in factories.

Millroy (1992) analyzed the geometrical concepts embedded in the everyday work of a group of South African carpenters. Her results showed that carpenters made extensive use of geometrical concepts such as congruence, symmetry, and straight and parallel lines in their everyday work. She also found frequent use of spatial visualization, logical argumentation related to mathematical proof, and revision of decontextualized problem questions in terms of contextualized problems involving carpentry tools and carpentry situations.

Traditional agricultural activities constitute a rich setting for studying everyday mathematics, especially regarding different ways for computing area. Abreu and D. W. Carraher (1989), Acioly (1994), and Grando (1988) documented a system of measures and formulas used by unschooled farmers in Northeastern and Southern Brazil to calculate the areas of plots of land. Such a system was not taught in schools. Despite certain limitations, due to the approximate nature of their calculations, the system allowed farmers to obtain meaningful and adequate answers for their needs. Acioly focused on Brazilian sugar cane workers' procedures and ideas about the distortions introduced into their results of area computations. She found that when asked to compute the area of uncommon quadrilateral and triangular plots with side measures being given orally by the examiner and without drawings showing the relationship of the sides, workers used their non-precise everyday procedures. The choice of measures included in the computations was closely related to the workers' social niche and to the financial consequences of the calculations: sugar cane cutters, paid according to the area of land cleared, consistently chose elements that overestimated the area of the plots; supervisors and administrators, in charge of paying workers according to the amount of land cleared, chose procedures that underestimated the final result. When asked to compute the area and to compare the surfaces of plots represented in drawings with the same perimeter but different shapes (and consequently, different areas), the subjects employed new computational strategies, apparently to correct distortions resulting from the irregular shapes of the plots shown in the drawings. This transition to a different strategy demonstrates an awareness of the distortions resulting from the choice of elements included in their computations. Moreover, their answers revealed that such distortions were compensated for or minimized by other social mechanisms. Acioly's study is not only a good example of how problem solving activity is closely related to sociocultural settings, but it also provides insights into people's awareness about the consequences of their choices when they solve problems in everyday settings.

As a whole, studies on everyday geometry attest to the worldwide presence of geometrical patterns in people's lives, and the development of everyday procedures for geometrical computations in close relationship to the sociocultural environments where they are developed and used.

Everyday Arithmetic: Some Leading Questions

Besides measurement and geometry, arithmetic has been the most widely analyzed area of knowledge in everyday cognition studies. The available results on the development and uses of arithmetic in everyday settings help clarify general issues related to cognition, cognitive development, and education. Some of the questions concern the characteristics, the scope, and the limitations of everyday knowledge, as opposed to knowledge developed as a result of school instruction, and the problems posed by the specificity of everyday knowledge. In this section we will address the following general themes: (1) cognition at work versus cognition in schools, (2) the problem of transfer of knowledge developed in everyday settings, and (3) the strengths and limitations of mathematical knowledge developed in everyday activities.

Cognition at Work versus Cognition in Schools

The contrast between cognition in school and cognition at work is as important as the contrast between cognition in the laboratory and cognition in everyday contexts. The first most visible difference between the two settings concerns the way teaching and learning takes place (see also Serpell & Hatano, this volume, for a description of the characteristics of formal education as opposed to apprenticeship). Although the characteristics of everyday learning may differ from group to group and may evolve as a result of changes in society, certain features seem typical of the informal teaching–learning process in most cultures and settings.

In their description of the informal teaching of weaving among the Zinacantecos in Southern Mexico, Greenfield and Childs (1977) and Childs and Greenfield (1980) emphasized the scaffolded, nearly error-free process where help was provided according to the learner's needs. In a follow-up study Greenfield (1993) contrasted present-day informal teaching modes in Zinacantan to those encountered twenty years ago. She found that independent trial and error learning, more adequate to the development of innovation that is currently valued in the community, is replacing the errorless scaffolded activity which was adequate for the transmission of the traditional patterns that previously were the only ones produced.

How social and cultural values shape the characteristics of informal modes of transmission of "know-how" was the focus of Chamoux's (1981, 1986) work. She studied the transmission of "know-how" among the Nahuas in Mexico for such everyday activities as weaving, stitching, cooking, or agriculture. General "know-how," which is accessible to all through observation, was contrasted with specific knowledge, which is acquired through apprenticeship with a master. The transmission of "know-how" was found to be based mainly on observation in real-life situations with no time constraints and infrequent verbal instructions. She also found that social rules determine who is allowed to use a certain type of "know-how" or to develop some type of specific knowledge.

The role parents play in relation to the development of children's mathematical knowledge in everyday activities was examined by Guberman (1993, 1995) in Brazilian shantytown communities. He found that when parents sent their children to make purchases at local stands (a common activity in the observed communities), the arithmetic complexity of responsibilities assigned to children was related to their age and level of arithmetic skills. Adults seemed to play an important role, not through explicit mathematical instruction, but by facilitating and supporting connections between the child's competence and the everyday activities involving computing prices and change.

A systematic account of the main characteristics attributed to school teaching, as opposed to informal teaching, is found in Greenfield and Lave (1982). Teaching in schools is characteristically set apart from everyday life contexts and is the responsibility of teachers who must cover, with a high degree of systematization, a certain number of contents explicitly determined in the curriculum. Instruction in schools is mainly verbal, with presentation of general principles that should be learned for their own sake, not for their relevance in achieving social practical goals. In contrast, learning outside of schools usually takes the form of apprenticeship embedded in daily life activities. The learner develops knowledge and skill through participation in socially relevant activities. More skilled participants may help, but there is no systematic curriculum to be followed and little verbal explanation. Instead, demonstration, observation, and imitation are thought to be ways of learning. More recently, summarizing the results of various studies, Resnick (1987) contrasted learning in and out of school, proposing that school learning focuses on individual cognition, pure thought activities, symbol manipulation, and general principles, while out of school learning is characterized by shared cognition, tool manipulation, contextualized reasoning, and situation-specific competencies.

What are the cognitive consequences of learning in schools as opposed to learning in everyday contexts? As also argued by Serpell and Hatano (this volume), both schools and the workplace provide children and adults with opportunities to develop knowledge. The question of how knowledge differs across these two cultural contexts was the focus of the studies on arithmetic problem solving, to be reviewed next. The relatively large amount of data gathered during the last decades by various authors, across countries and working sets, may provide insights about cognitive processes and their relation to the sociocultural contexts where problem solving takes place.

In her first study of mathematical knowledge at work, Lave (1977; see also Reed & Lave, 1979) looked at Liberian tailors' arithmetical problem solving on the job and on a school-like test. Her results showed that everyday experience in the tailor shop provided opportunities for arithmetic learning that focused on manipulation of quantities. Despite their limitations, methods learned in the shop ensured that no big mistakes with serious practical consequences would occur. By contrast, school experience provided the subjects with systems of representation and rules that allowed the solution of more complex arithmetic problems through manipulation of symbols. Although more powerful, school methods were more likely to result in big mistakes.

The differences between arithmetical problem solving in school-like tasks and in everyday situations was further analyzed by Lave, Murtaugh, and de la Rocha (1984; see also Lave, 1988, and Murtaugh, 1985). They conducted extensive interviews and observations on arithmetic problem solving by schooled adults in California. The everyday activity they chose to observe was grocery shopping in a supermarket. A wide discrepancy between the number of correct answers was found when the data from the two settings were compared: while on an arithmetic school-like test, subjects gave, on an average, 59 percent correct answers, in the grocery store, 98 percent of the arithmetical problems that emerged, and were accepted by them, were correctly solved. Lave et al. concluded that the high success rate in real-life problems was due to the powerful monitoring of a dialectical process between the setting and the activity that creates and brings problems and solutions together. De la Rocha's (1985; see also Lave, 1988) study of a weight watcher's problem solving in the kitchen exemplifies this process. In one example, to solve the problem of taking 2/3 of 3/4 cup of cottage cheese, a subject started by spreading out a cup of cheese in a circle on a counter; she then divided it into four parts, removed one of the parts and took two of the remaining three. The contrast between this approach and the school-prescribed solution to the problem "What is the answer to 2/3 times 3/4?" shows the difference between the everyday and the school approach, despite the mathematical equivalence of the two problems.

Through a thoughtful combination of ethnographic observation and simulated tasks, Scribner (1984, 1986) investigated practical reasoning among dairy workers. Two main tasks involving use of mathematics to accomplish practical goals were studied. Experienced workers' procedures were compared to those of the less experienced and students. For both tasks, an overwhelming tendency to use flexible and effort-saving strategies was found among workers. This was in sharp contrast to students' approach; students mostly chose to apply the same algorithmic procedure to solve all the problems, even when simpler and effortless solutions were possible. This search for effort-saving strategies, together with a focus on meaning, was also found by Khan (1993) in the work of carpet weavers in Kashmir when they interpreted instructions for reproducing weaving patterns. On the basis of her analysis of dairy workers' strategies, Scribner (1986) characterized practical thinking as activities that are instrumental to mental or manual accomplishments, in contrast to mental tasks performed as an end in themselves, as happens most often in schools.

In a series of studies developed by Carraher, Carraher, Schliemann, and their students, some characteristics of everyday mathematical knowledge at work, as opposed to mathematical knowledge in schools, were analyzed (see Nunes, Schliemann, & Carraher, 1993, for an account of some studies). In their first analysis of street mathematics, T. N. Carraher, Carraher, and Schliemann (1982, 1985) showed that if arithmetic problems had to be solved at work by young street vendors, answers were usually correct, while in school-like situations correct answers were rare. In a follow-up study, T. N. Carraher, Carraher, and Schliemann (1987) found that differences in performance across situations could be explained by the use of different procedures. At work, or in work-like situations, oral procedures were the preferred strategy and led, in most cases, to correct answers. Written procedures were chosen in the same proportion for solving computation exercises but the results were usually wrong. The contrast in an individual's problem solutions made it clear that the quality and effectiveness of mathematical reasoning depended upon the nature of the representations employed. Street vendors appear to develop the basic logical abilities needed for solving arithmetic problems in their work settings; their difficulties with school arithmetic seem to be related to the mastery of particular symbolic systems adopted by schools. Because of its emphasis on the fixed steps to manipulate numbers in the solution of any problem, school algorithms set meaning aside. In contrast, arithmetic oral strategies developed at work preserve meaning throughout solution, thus avoiding nonsense errors.

In India, Menon and Kaur (1994) compared problem-solving abilities of schooled non-vendors to unschooled and schooled vendors on computation problems, school-type word problems, and vending-type word problems. Significantly better results were found for vending type problems in both groups of vendors, while non-vendors showed no difference across contexts. In all problem types, non-vendors used oral strategies less frequently than did the vendors, and showed a higher number of errors classified as absurd errors (i. e., results that are impossible to be obtained if one considers the meaning of the problem being solved). Both groups of vendors showed less absurd errors in vending-type problems where oral solution strategies were preferred.

In Brazil, Schliemann (1985) analyzed professional carpenters' and students' approaches to a problem related to the practice of carpentry. The group of students was composed of adolescents from poor backgrounds who attended a three-year course of instruction in carpentry and who had at least four years of school instruction in mathematics. The problem consisted of determining the amount of wood needed to build a piece of furniture. Results showed that carpentry apprentices, who had received formal school instruction on computation of volume of fictitious pieces, but had no work experience in calculating volume, tended to approach the problem by computing the total volume of wood needed. In most cases, they did so by first adding up the lengths, the widths, and thicknesses of all the furniture parts. They would then multiply the three values, obtaining a result that grossly overestimated the amount of wood needed, although generally they did not seem to be aware that an error had been committed. Experienced carpenters, in contrast, started by determining the number of standard pieces of wood they would need to buy in order to cut from it the parts for the intended piece of furniture. To determine the total volume of wood needed, carpenters would then compute the volume of each of the standard pieces of wood, adding up at the end the measures thus obtained.

The contrast between nonsense results in school contexts versus meaningful correct results in work contexts was also documented by Grando (1988; see also Nunes et al., 1993). Analyzing how farmers and students in Southern Brazil solved mathematical problems relevant to farming, she found that farmers' incorrect answers fell within a sensible range while students' wrong answers tended to be either too small or too large to be possible.

The previously mentioned studies consistently show that the rule-bound solutions traditionally taught in schools seem to provide subjects with procedures that are not always understood and become useless in generating appropriate solutions to problems out of school contexts. In contrast, the strategies developed by individuals as tools to solve problems out of school are characterized by their flexibility and by constant monitoring of the meaning of the situation, the problem questions, and the quantities involved. As summarized by Nunes (1993), the two most important differences between the two types of mathematics are that, (1) while outside of schools mathematics is used as a tool to achieve some other goals, in schools mathematics is an aim in itself, and (2) the situations where mathematics is used out of schools give meaning to computations, while mathematics, as it is traditionally taught in schools, becomes mainly a process of manipulation of numbers.

However, everyday mathematics has been thought to develop as a way to deal with specific everyday situations, while knowledge developed in school settings is supposed to aim at general principles that could be applied to any situation (Scribner & Cole, 1973). Would this focus on the specific aspects of the situations in everyday mathematics prevent transfer? Is everyday mathematical knowledge sufficiently general to be applied to other situations that are not the ones where it is usually practiced? Questions such as these have been raised and it can been argued that the specificity of everyday knowledge would set limits to its generality and prevent its transfer. The set of studies we will describe next addresses the question of transfer of arithmetic knowledge developed in specific everyday settings.

Transfer of Everyday Mathematical Knowledge

Given the traditional characterization of everyday knowledge as specific, and school knowledge as general, discussions about transfer became a central issue to the area of everyday cognition. Greenfield and Lave (1982) addressed the issue through a systematic comparison between formal and informal knowledge on the basis of the available data, Lave's (1977) analysis of arithmetic problem-solving skills of Liberian tailors, and data on weaving skills and the development of pattern representations among the Zinacantecos in Southern Mexico (Childs & Greenfield, 1980; Greenfield & Childs, 1977). They concluded that:

> . . . each of the diverse educational forms we investigated can lead to generalization from existing problem solving skills to problem situations that are related in definable ways. The limited nature of generalization skills is characteristic of all of the educational forms discussed here, including schooling (Greenfield & Lave, 1982, p. 207).

Since Greenfield and Lave's paper, a number of studies of everyday cognition have dealt with the problem of transfer of knowledge developed in specific everyday activities. Lave (1988) criticized laboratory studies of transfer and the conception of transfer as a "process of taking a *given* item and applying it somewhere else." The proposal—that knowledge is always context specific (see Laboratory of Comparative Human Cognition, 1983), situated (Brown, Collins, & Duguid, 1989), and not an individual's ability or a general way to approach problems—became so influential that many would argue that there is no point in studying transfer of knowledge at all. But it is our view that people are constantly using previous knowledge in order to address new problems. As such, the analysis of how knowledge developed in one cultural setting is used in other settings is basic for a proper evaluation and understanding of the characteristics of everyday knowledge, and to clarify issues such as how knowledge develops as an individual participates in different cultural settings and experiences.

Schliemann (1988), and Schliemann and Acioly (1989) analyzed whether lottery bookies with different schooling levels recognize that the same rules they use at work to determine the number of permutations for a set of digits would apply to sets of letters and sets of colors. They found success on the transfer tasks to be significantly correlated to levels of schooling. Although illiterate subjects could sometimes recognize that the same rule would apply to different sets, they often failed to show transfer, as the following interview excerpt from Schliemann & Acioly, 1989, p. 206 illustrates:

> *Examiner:* I want you to find out in how many different ways you can arrange the letters in the word CASA (show word written on paper) without leaving any letter out and without putting in any other letter.
>
> *Subject:* This one is even harder because I can't read.
>
> *E:* But you don't have to read. I want you to tell me about how many different ways you can change the position of these letters.
>
> *S:* This one I cannot do.
>
> *E:* What if you try to do it as in the Animal Game?
>
> *S:* This is very hard because reading is more difficult than working with numbers. I know how to do a few calculations but I don't know how to read.
>
> *E:* What if you make believe that "C" is a number like "1," the "A" a number like "2," the "S" is number "3," and this "A" is number "2." Couldn't you do it?
>
> *S:* No, because one thing is different from the other.

Schliemann (1988) found that, despite the contribution of school experience, recognition of the similarity between the transfer tasks and the everyday tasks involving permutations used was more frequent among lottery bookies than among students who were asked to consider the same transfer tasks and their school experience on permutations.

Failure to transfer procedures related to permutations among unschooled lottery bookies could be due to the way they dealt with permutations at work. Their everyday activity did not require working out the permutations but only the knowledge of possible arrangements for a given set of numbers. Because tables listing the number of arrangements for each possible set are available, they only had to memorize the correct answers, without understanding the structure of the task. In other words, they did not have to develop conceptual knowledge about permutations and could simply rely on procedural knowledge. As Hatano (1982) suggested, exclusive reliance on procedural knowledge could prevent transfer from occurring. Analysis of transfer from everyday tasks, that are performed with the understanding of the mathematical relations involved, could provide different results concerning transfer of abilities used in everyday settings by unschooled people. Proportionality seems to be an area that would allow a better analysis of the issue.

Schliemann and Nunes (1990) analyzed transfer of strategies for solving proportionality problems among the participants of a community of fishermen in Northeastern Brazil. In that community, fishermen's everyday experience required them to repeatedly compute the price of a certain number of items to be sold, given the price of one item. Their understanding of proportional relations, however, appeared to go beyond this repetitive procedure. They were able to invert their procedures and compute the price of one item, given the price of more than one, and therefore show flexibility, one of the characteristics of conceptual knowledge (Hatano, 1982). Regardless of their levels of schooling, fishermen were able to transfer their procedures in order to solve proportionality problems relating quantity of processed to unprocessed seafood, a relationship they referred to in their activities but for which no computing problems were ever solved.

Working with cooks, Schliemann and Magalhães (1990; see also Schliemann & Carraher, 1992) provided another analysis of transfer of strategies for solving proportionality problems. Female cooks newly enrolled in an adult literacy class, or enrolled one year before they participated in the study, were asked to solve a series of missing value proportionality problems. The problems were devised in two contexts that were part of the subjects' everyday experience (a sales transaction context and a cooking context), and in one unknown context (that of a pharmaceutical mixture of ingredients). The cooks were randomly assigned to three groups, each group receiving problems in the following different orders:

Group 1: recipe, price, recipe, and pharmaceutical mixture problems
Group 2: price, recipe, pharmaceutical mixture, and recipe problems
Group 3: pharmaceutical mixture, price, pharmaceutical mixture, and recipe problems

Performance on the first problem context varied considerably: while price problems were nearly always precisely solved by Group 2, the recipe problems (the first set given to Group 1) were only occasionally answered precisely, as was the case for the initial mixture problems first given to Group 3. When recipe problems were first approached by subjects in Group 1 roughly half of the answers were reasonable estimates and justifications provided for them tended to be informal, such as "I think that's enough" or "That's how I do it." For pharmaceutical mixture problems, about one-half of the answers were outright wrong and appeared to be obtained by guessing or by performing a meaningless operation upon the given quantities. Results for second round recipe problems and pharmaceutical mixture problems, after subjects had solved price problems, were strikingly different from those for the first presentation. For recipe problems (Group 1) the percentage of correct responses jumped from 18 percent to 61 percent. The increase was not so pronounced for pharmaceutical mixture problems (from 8 percent to 27 percent) when they were presented after money problems but before recipe problems (Group 2). However, after solving money problems, followed by recipe problems (Group 3), the improvement for pharmaceutical mixture problems was quite remarkable (62 percent correct answers). Recipe and pharmaceutical mixture problems tended to be solved with slightly better success among subjects who had enrolled in the literacy course one year before the interviews than among those who had just started school. This finding suggests that although general conceptual knowledge can be developed in specific everyday activities, transfer is most likely to occur among subjects who have had some school experience, especially when transfer tasks go beyond one's previous direct experience.

Saxe (1982, 1985, 1991) studied the cognitive consequences of using a traditional numeration system based on body parts among the Oksapmin people of Papua New Guinea. His analyses focus on how the introduction of schooling and Western currency for economic transactions affected people's practices involving number and arithmetic operations. Saxe's results show that experienced adult store owners are able to use the traditional counting system in order to solve new arithmetical problems. With increasing school instruction on the decimal system, children restructure their previous traditional counting system and then develop new and more sophisticated ways to accomplish enumeration goals, as was the case for the experienced store owners. Brenner (1985) also found the use of everyday and school strategies among Vai students in Liberia. The performance was better with the combined use of the two approaches rather than the exclusive use of either one. Such results point to the important role played by mutual transfer and interactions between everyday experience and school instruction in the development of new mathematical knowledge and strategies.

Saxe (1988a, b, 1991) systematically examined the interplay between school mathematics and street mathematics among Brazilian candy sellers. He found no correlation between schooling and accuracy in the solution of currency arithmetic and ratio comparison tasks. However, school seemed to play an important role in the understanding of written number notation, in the use of written arithmetic procedures, and in providing new ways to look at mathematical relations such as considering unit retail prices and profits per unit of candies, despite their practice of buying and selling candies by boxes or a few at a time. The influence of street selling experience on mathematics problem solving in school was clear in the use of street mathematics procedures to solve school problems, and in the greater accuracy of the solutions of sellers when compared to that of non-sellers (all of whom were schooled).

Use of everyday mathematics procedures to solve school problems, however, does not seem to be the rule. As already discussed, when problems are given in school-like settings, children (T. N. Carraher, Carraher, & Schliemann, 1985, 1987) as well as adults (Lave, 1977), usually choose to use school-prescribed algorithms. Consequently, as found by Oloko (1994) in Nigeria, full-time school children show better performance in tasks within time-limit constraints than do street sellers who also attend school. Failure to use everyday mathematics in school settings was also documented by Abreu (1995) who argued that the higher status attributed to school mathematics seemed to prevent children from using their everyday mathematical knowledge in the classroom.

Beach (1992) analyzed transfer not only as continuities between activities but as transformation and construction of new knowledge. He compared the transformations that take place in people's arithmetic practice when they move from school to work or from work to school. Subjects were Nepalese high school students who started working as shopkeeper apprentices and unschooled shopkeepers who enrolled in an adult education class. After one month of experience in their respective new environments, students continued to exclusively use school written procedures for calculations in the shop, with a slight increase in the combination of written and non-written strategies. On the other hand, shopkeepers showed a sharp decrease in the use of non-written strategies, a slight increase in the use of written numbers, and a major development of strategies combining written and non-written procedures. With practice, students' use of a linear organization of mathematical operations and of column algorithms decreased in favor of the use of nonlinear organization and non-written strategies such as decomposition, iteration, and estimation. Among shopkeepers, there was a clear decrease of a nonlinear organization in favor of the linear organization, together with a decline in the exclusive use of non-written strategies and a sharp increase in the use of combination methods.

As a whole, the previous review provides a more optimistic view concerning transfer than did earlier laboratory studies. Guberman and Greenfield (1991) concluded, in agreement with Hiebert and Lefevre (1986), that conceptual knowledge, as opposed to rule-bound procedural knowledge, will support transfer across situations. The studies described seem to support the conclusion that everyday activities do promote the development of conceptual knowledge rather than only procedural knowledge for specific problems. As such, knowledge acquired in specific everyday activities does transfer to other activities, but this is more likely to occur for those subjects who also benefited from school instruction. Moreover, some understanding of the target situation is needed in order to recognize that previously learned strategies would fit the new problem at hand.

But how far can one develop mathematical knowledge without formal school instruction? What are the strengths and the limitations of mathematical knowledge developed without the benefit of school instruction? And what role is left for schools to play if people seem to learn mathematics out of schools? These are the questions we will deal with next.

The Strengths and Limitations of Everyday Mathematics

As shown in the previous sections, analyses of the general characteristics of mathematical knowledge in everyday settings consistently point to meaning as the most important and relevant aspect in everyday problem solving. Moreover, everyday knowledge seems to be general enough to allow people to address new problems with strategies they develop in specific everyday situations. However, questions may be raised concerning the scope of everyday mathematics, especially if one considers the wider variety of mathematical situations that could be dealt with in schools as compared to what people naturally encounter in everyday settings. In this section, we will provide an overview of the different mathematical concepts, procedures, and understandings developed in everyday situations. The specific questions in focus are: How far can one develop mathematical knowledge outside of schools? Do everyday situations provide opportunities for people to understand the different aspects and principles involved in the mathematical concepts and operations they learn outside of schools? Taking into account the strengths and the limitations of everyday knowledge, the section will close with a discussion on the relation between human experience and the development of scientific and mathematical knowledge.

T. N. Carraher et al.'s (1985, 1987) analysis of street sellers' and school children's oral strategies for solving arithmetic problems across contexts shows that two main aspects of mathematical knowledge that are traditionally thought to be learned in schools appear to develop as a result of activities in everyday settings. These are an understanding of the decimal system and proportional relations.

When orally solving addition and subtraction problems, children and adults used decomposition strategies that revealed a clear understanding of the properties of the number system as shown in the following transcript where a child subtracts 57 from 252:

> *Take fifty-two, that's two hundred, and five to take away, that's one hundred and ninety five. [The child decomposed 252 into 200 and 52; 57 was decomposed into 52 and 5; removing both 52, there remained another 5 to take away from 200.] (from Nunes et al., 1993, p. 41).*

Understanding and use of the properties of the decimal system, among illiterate people or among people with little school experience in the solution of arithmetic problems, was also documented in Mozambique by Draisma (1993) and in Brazil by T. N. Carraher (1985) and by Schliemann, Santos, and Canuto (1993).

Solution to proportionality problems and understanding of proportional relations independent of school instruction appears mainly when problems requiring multiplication are orally solved in order to determine the price of items people buy or sell. One example is the following answer given by a coconut seller when computing the price of 10 coconuts at the unit price of 35 cruzeiros:

> *Three are one hundred and five, with three more, two hundred and ten (pause). There are still four. It is (pause) three hundred and fifteen (pause), it seems it is three hundred and fifty (from T. N. Carraher et al., 1985, p. 23).*

This solution, although based on repeated additions, shows an understanding that the two variables, number of coconuts and cost, are proportionally related (see Schliemann & Carraher, 1992, for a detailed analysis of the characteristics of everyday understanding of proportionality).

T. N. Carraher (1986) also documented the understanding of proportionality in the everyday activities of construction foremen who have to deal with the relationship between different scales of measurement in the blueprints and the actual size of construction. She gave her subjects tasks that consisted of determining the real size of a wall shown in a blueprint from the information about the real size of other walls in the same blueprint. Foremen preferred to solve this problem first by finding a relation between the blueprint and the real size of the wall (for which information was given) and then transferring this relation to the second wall. This procedure reveals understanding of ratios and proportions and the development, at work, of mathematical procedures that are not taught in schools.

Use of proportional reasoning and understanding of mathematical principles are also described by McMurchy-Pilkington (1995) who analyzed the work of New Zealand's Maori women. While engaged in planning and preparing traditional meals for large groups of tourists, Maori women, who are often thought of as underachievers in mathematics, solved simple and multiple proportion problems using strategies that are usually not taught in schools.

Besides measurement, geometry, addition, subtraction, and proportional reasoning, everyday mathematics can also encompass other areas, such as permutations and probability which were described by Schliemann and Acioly (1989) among lottery bookies in Brazil. Subjects were observed while they solved problems at work, and later, were given transfer tasks related to the ones appearing in their job. Together with understanding and efficiency in oral solutions of arithmetic operations, bookies displayed, as a result of their everyday practice in the game, an understanding of permutations and of probability.

Studies of everyday mathematics show that the same cultural and social environments that foster the construction of knowledge may also constrain and limit the kind of knowledge children and adults will come to develop and understand. For instance, failure to recognize the commutative law for multiplication among nonschooled subjects was documented by Petitto and Ginsburg (1982) in a study of Dioula tailors and cloth merchants. For addition and subtraction problems, their subjects could easily and correctly use associativity and commutativity. For multiplication problems, however, they could solve a problem involving 100×6 by adding 100 six times, but they did not accept that the same result would apply for the computation of 6×100. Schliemann, Araujo, Cassundé, Macedo, and Nicéas (1994) found that young street sellers with restricted school experience compute the price of many items, given the price of one item, by repeatedly adding the number referring to price as many times as the number denoting the amount of items to be sold. Their solutions preserved throughout the necessary computations clear reference to physical quantities, a typical feature of computation procedures in real life situations where number is rarely conceived without referents. It seemed inappropriate for them to consider such operations on physical quantities as commutative, that is, to add the number of items as many times as the price of each one to find the total price. When compared to school children who received instruction on multiplication, it was only at a later age that street sellers accepted to employ commutativity for solving multiplication problems.

Everyday procedures described above to compute the price of many items from the price of a few fall into what Vergnaud (1988) describes as the scalar approach for missing value proportionality problems. In the scalar solution, each variable remains independent of the other, and parallel transformations that maintain the proportional relationship are carried out on both of them. In the functional approach, also discussed by Vergnaud, the focus is on the ratio between the starting values of the two variables, which is then applied to the final pair in order to find the missing value. Exclusive use of the scalar approach seems to set limits to street sellers' problem solving ability when problems are presented in such a way that the relation between price and number of items (the functional relation) is easier to work out than the relation between the starting and the ending quantities (the scalar relation) (cf. Schliemann & Carraher, 1992). While school children most often focus on the functional relation, street sellers continue to use the scalar strategy, even when this requires cumbersome computations.

Data on negative numbers by T. N. Carraher (1990) also show the constraints imposed by everyday mathematical solutions to mathematical problems. She found that, from their everyday experience with money, schooled and unschooled subjects were able to solve problems involving the addition of directed numbers by marking the negative numbers as losses or debts. When asked to use the written notation for signs, however, they experienced difficulties related to the interference of their everyday methods, which did not correspond to the procedural steps in the school approach.

The limitations of knowledge developed in everyday settings, as opposed to school knowledge, are also found in other areas of expertise. For instance, Luz, Khoury, and Schliemann (1994) contrasted the understanding about radiation developed by radiotherapy technicians with no formal school training in this area with that of physicists with post-graduate education in the nuclear field. Although schooling apparently promoted problem solving and the acquisition of scientific terminology about ionizing radiation and radiotherapy, it did not necessarily lead to more productive intuitions about how radiation works. The technicians studied were prone to introduce misleading parallels to the situations at hand by drawing on what they knew about other physical processes. Experience is not always a trustworthy guide. This may be especially true in learning about phenomena, such as radiation, the expansion of the universe, and quantum physics, for which intuitions grounded in experience may require extensive adjustment, adaptation, or even containment.

The relation between lived experience and the development of scientific knowledge is a subtle one. If mathematical ideas acquire meaning by virtue of their ties to everyday situations, then how can we reasonably hope that students will come to understand concepts such as infinity, groups, rings, and so forth, that would seem to bear only a tenuous relation to daily experience? Must mathematical knowledge be directly tied to daily experience at every turn? Frege (1953) showed that J. S. Mill's belief that mathematical knowledge ultimately rested on our perception of physical objects was doomed even for the simple case of integer addition. The situation can only be bleaker for higher order concepts. An upshot of this is that psychological theories need to make allowance for conceptual objects and relations that are not directly translatable into physical objects and actions.

Abandoning physicalism opens the way for studying the relations between concepts that otherwise would have little in common. Consider, for example the concepts of measurement and division. To an experienced mathematician these concepts are intimately intertwined: a dividend is like a measured magnitude, a divisor is like a unit of measure, a quotient corresponds to how many times the unit of measure fits into the target measure, and the remainder corresponds to the quantity that is "left over" (D. W. Carraher, 1995). To elementary school pupils, division and measurement may appear to be different, perhaps even unrelated concepts and operations. How do disparate elements of knowledge become integrated into more general, abstract wholes?

We suspect that for people to understand such concepts as embodying similar relations they will draw upon what they know about comparing magnitudes and determining how many times one magnitude is "contained" in another. This is neither the direct result of experience nor a matter of subjects projecting their ideas directly onto the object. However, once the work of integration has been achieved, it may well appear that the individual's "daily experience" with dividing provided a meaningful basis for understanding measurement, just as his or her experience in measuring might appear to play a role in understanding more clearly the nature of division.

Because the development of mathematical knowledge takes considerable time, we may arrive at different conclusions about the role of daily experience in the emergence of mathematical knowledge depending upon the time framework adopted. If we focus on the time period when children are taught to "do" division and measurement, the knowledge acquired in one set of situations may appear isolated from and irrelevant to the knowledge acquired in another set of situations. One thus leans towards a strict "situated cognition" type of analysis. If, on the other hand, one scans a much wider period of time, knowledge acquired in one type of situation may ultimately make substantial contributions in other domains.

This analysis argues that we should be highly skeptical of attempts to classify concepts as concrete or abstract, as if these were fixed properties inherent in the concepts themselves. So-called concrete knowledge acquired in everyday, familiar situations may ultimately play a fundamental role in the development of "abstract" knowledge. Furthermore, as Cassirer (1923) convincingly showed, general concepts are powerful not by their detachment from particular instances and situations but, on the contrary, due to their usefulness in explaining and illuminating a wide range of particular phenomena. The abstract is thus inextricably bound to the concrete.

A similar analysis could be initiated regarding the development of knowledge in societies over large periods of time. It is well known that everyday activities such as farming, commerce, and astronomy played a fundamental role in the slow emergence of mathematics as a field of scientific inquiry (Kline, 1962). But just as a college student's knowledge of mathematics cannot be reduced to the sum of former everyday experiences that made such intellectual achievements possible, the field of mathematics cannot be reduced to the circumstances that gave rise to its emergence. Once knowledge assumes higher forms, it tends to behave in ways relatively autonomous from its origins. This is true for the individual learner; it is also true for the scientific community as a whole, which receives, as a legacy from former generations, the symbolic tools for formulating and thinking about problems thenceforth. Scientific and mathematical reasoning is always indebted to its origins in human activity without becoming enslaved to it.

Conclusions

The findings of everyday cognition studies call for new theoretical approaches concerning the nature of knowledge, cognition, intelligence, and cognitive development. Methods and techniques are not isolated from theoretical, educational, and social concerns, and psychological research methods are changing as a result of everyday cognition findings. Qualitative methods, ethnographic methods, open-ended interviews, along with previously accepted methods, are now part of the psychological tradition. Also, traditional boundaries between anthropology, sociology, psychology, and history must be overlooked in the search for answers to questions, such as how symbol systems that are part of one's cultural legacy become appropriated and adapted to group and individual needs.

The relevance of contexts in the development and use of cognitive functions has led researchers to replace conceptions of cognition as an individual's ability or an individual's general way to approach intellectual problems by notions such as "situated cognition" (Brown, Collins, & Duguid, 1989), "shared cognition" (Resnick et al., 1991), or "distributed cognition" (Hutchins, 1993). Cognitive development and learning have been described in terms of the creation of communities of practice through legitimate peripheral participation (Lave & Wenger, 1991), apprenticeship through guided participation (Rogoff, 1990), and social construction of responses (Perret-Clermont, Perret, & Bell, 1991). Such approaches share the belief that cognition and learning are part of the social context where cognition takes place and cannot be viewed in isolation.

Many new theoretical proposals are emerging (see review on cultural psychology and social constructionism by Miller, Volume 1, this *Handbook*). Irvine and Berry (1988), drawing on Ferguson's (1956) analysis, used the idea of law of cultural differentiation to explain cross-cultural differences in intellectual tasks, as opposed to positive correlations across tasks within the same group. Their view (see also Berry, 1972, 1987) is that "abilities develop in response to ecological demands that themselves are modified by skill acquisition" (Irvine & Berry, 1988, p. 4). Ceci (1990, 1993) provided an analysis that showed that the notion of a general, singular, inherited intelligence should be replaced by a contextual model of intelligence where the potential for intellectual achievement develops as a result of one's experience in specific contexts. Rogoff (1990) and Saxe (1991) designed models for cognitive development that preserve the notion of individual cognitive development and one's prior understandings, but attempt to reconcile it with sociocultural analysis. Building on the "Soviet" sociohistorical tradition, Wertsch (1991) proposed that individuals create their environments and themselves through the actions they undertake. Bringing into discussion the principles of the sociohistorical psychology proposed by Leontiev (1981), Luria (1976), and Vygotsky (1978), together with empirical results attesting the context-specific character of cognition, Cole (1988) reinterprets results of cross-cultural research, emphasizing the importance of social, historical, political, and economical changes for the organization and development of human activity and modes of cognitive functioning, but questioning whether traditional societies would fail to develop more abstract and general thinking processes.

Everyday cognition research shows that individuals who perform poorly on laboratory tasks, IQ tests, or school assignments may use, in their everyday, out-of-school activities, intellectual skills thought to be lacking. This suggests that failure in school need not imply an inherent inability to understand. In the case of mathematical knowledge, subjects are occasionally well versed in some of the mathematical properties they seem not to comprehend in school. These properties and relations are, of course, embodied very differently in and out of school. Mastery of mathematical concepts in school goes hand in hand with the appropriation of specialized symbolic systems that have their own peculiar structure, conventions, and logic. Mathematical symbolic vehicles such as algebraic notation are lean condensations of an enormous amount of thinking (Rothstein, 1995), and hence do not automatically bestow on their users the range of meanings they may represent for the professional mathematician. The present analysis shifts emphasis away from the issue of general psychological structures and stages of development to the question of meaning. What sorts of activity are likely to promote meaningful appropriation of such symbolic systems?

Some have concluded from this that educators should bring to the classroom activities similar to those from out-of-school contexts or that apprenticeship training should replace teaching. Engaging in everyday activities such as buying and selling, sharing, betting, and so on, even if simulated, may help students establish links between their experience and intuitions already acquired and topics to be learned in school. However, we believe it would be a fundamental mistake to suggest to educators that schools should attempt to imitate or reproduce out-of-school activities in classrooms (see Schliemann, 1995). First, through discussion one can establish rich links to out of school activities without actually reenacting them in the classroom. In so doing, the activities become objects of reflection and public discourse in fundamentally new ways. But in addition to this, we must recognize that children require a range of activities that will enrich and complement the activities they participate in outside of school. Schools may provide access to a variety of symbolic systems and representations essential for establishing links between concepts and situations that would otherwise remain unrelated. To achieve this, educational agents need to create situations where symbolic representations act as tools for achieving goals of a very special nature. The goals of classroom activities are different from and probably no less complex than goals in other, out-of-school settings. Strangely, cognitive psychology's traditional emphasis on abilities of individuals has provided researchers with disappointingly few insights into the nature and use of goals in classrooms and how they differ from goals in out-of-school situations.

It is difficult to imagine what the field of everyday cognition will look like a generation or two from now. But if one compares the theories of thinking, communicating, problem solving, and symbolic representation from the first half of this century with those that have emerged in the last five decades, one is struck by how much has changed. Not only has the scope of research and research methodology greatly widened, but fundamental premises about what thinking is and how it should be investigated have undergone major revision as well. Researchers increasingly view thinking and reasoning as eminently social phenomena that emerge in cultural contexts as people engage in activities and social practices and take on social and individual identities. Motivation itself, once strongly associated with physiological states, drive reduction, and the pursuit of individual wants, has taken on a social character. Goals of individuals are now commonly discussed in the context of group and institutional values, norms, traditions, and practices rather than as aims capriciously set by the individual. Symbols are not merely the result of the individual's creative imagination but also an integral part of a group's cultural heritage. Meaning becomes increasingly important as a topic of scientific investigation. If present trends are any indication, we expect to see a closer alliance between researchers in cognitive psychology and those in anthropology, sociology, and history. Also, as epistemology gradually moves closer to semiotics and aesthetics, we expect to see more research probing into how human activity and thought not only serve to make the object intelligible to the subject, but also how they might allow people to individually and collectively achieve goals, including those of an expressive nature, where issues such as prestige, play, social identity and perspectives, trust, ethics, and beauty play fundamental roles. Such developments resonate with Quine's (1953) expectations that the 20th century would witness a decline in logical positivism as logic and meaning take on an increasingly pragmatic nature. Reductionism and the rigid dichotomy between analytic and synthetic issues have by and large been abandoned by researchers. But it is still too early to know whether we will be successful in developing a theoretical framework and philosophy to lend coherence to the many aims and influences in the field of Everyday Cognition.

References

Abreu, G. de (1995). Understanding how children experience the relationship between home and school mathematics. *Mind, Culture and Activity, 2,* 119–142.

Abreu, G. de & Carraher, D. W. (1989). The mathematics of Brazilian sugar cane farmers. In C.

Keitel, P. Damerow, A. Bishop, & P. Gerdes (Eds.), *Mathematics, education and society,* (pp. 68–70). Paris: Science and Technology Education Document Series, UNESCO, No. 35.

Acioly, N. (1994). *La juste mesure: Une étude des compétences mathématiques des travailleurs de la canne à sucre du Nordeste du Brésil dans le domaine de la mesure.* Unpublished doctoral dissertation. Paris, France: Université René Descartes, Paris V.

Bartlett, F. (1932). *Remembering.* Cambridge: Cambridge University Press.

Beach, K. (1992). *The role of leading and non-leading activities in transforming arithmetic between school and work.* Paper presented at the 1992 Annual Meeting of the American Educational Research Association, San Francisco, CA.

Berry, J. W. (1972). Radical cultural relativism, and the concept of intelligence. In L. J. Cronbach & P. J. D. Drenth (Eds.), *Mental tests and cultural adaptation* (pp. 77–88). The Hague: Mouton.

Berry, J. W. (1976). *Human ecology and cognitive style: Comparative studies in cultural and psychological adaptation.* New York: Sage/Halsted/Wiley.

Berry, J. W. (1987). The comparative study of cognitive abilities. In S. H. Irvine & S. E. Newstead (Eds.), *Intelligence and cognition: Contemporary frames of reference* (pp. 393–420). Dordrecht: Nijhoff.

Berry, J. W. (1993). Indigenous cognition: A conceptual analysis and an empirical example. In J. Wassmann & P. R. Dasen (Eds.), *Alltagwissen. Les savoirs quotidiens. Everyday cognition.* Freiburg: Universitätsverlag Freiburg.

Berry, J. W., Irvine, S. H. & Hunt, E. B. (Eds.). (1988). *Indigenous Cognition.* Dordrecht: Nijhoff.

Brenner, M. E. (1985). The practice of arithmetic in Liberian schools. *Anthropology and Education Quarterly, 16,* 177–186.

Bril, B. (1986). The acquisition of an everyday technical motor skill: The pounding of cereals in Mali (Africa). In M. G. Wade & H. T. A. Whiting (Eds.), *Themes in motor development* (pp. 315–326). Dordrecht: Nijhoff.

Bril, B. & Roux, V. (1993). Compétences impliquées dans l'action: Le cas de la taille des perles en pierre dure (Khambat, Inde). *Raisons Pratiques, 4,* 267-286.

Bronfenbrenner, U. (1979). *The ecology of human development.* Cambridge, MA: Harvard University Press.

Brown, J. S., Collins, A., & Duguid, P. (1989). Situated cognition and the culture of learning. *Educational Researcher, 18,* 32–42.

Carey, S. (1985). *Conceptual change in childhood.* Cambridge, MA: MIT Press.

Carraher, D. W. (1991). Mathematics in and out of school: A selective review of studies from Brazil. In M. Harris (Ed.), *Schools, mathematics and work* (pp. 169–201). London: The Falmer Press.

Carraher, D. W. (1995, April). *Building upon students' understanding of ratio and proportion.* Paper presented at the Annual Meeting of the American Educational Research Association, San Francisco, CA.

Carraher, T. N. (1985). The decimal system: Understanding and notation. In L. Streefland (Ed.), *Proceedings of the Ninth International Conference for the Psychology of Mathematics Education* (Vol. 1, pp. 288–303). Noordwijkerhout, The Netherlands.

Carraher, T. N. (1986). From drawings to buildings: Working with mathematical scales. *International Journal of Behavioural Development, 9,* 527–544.

Carraher, T. N. (1990). Negative numbers without the minus sign. *Proceedings of the Fourteenth International Conference for the Psychology of Mathematics Education* (Vol. 3, pp. 223–230). Oaxtepec, Mexico.

Carraher, T. N., Carraher, D. W., & Schliemann, A. D. (1982). Na vida, dez; na escola, zero: Os contextos culturais da educação matemática. *Cadernos de Pesquisa, 42,* 79–86.

Carraher, T. N., Carraher, D. W., & Schliemann, A. D. (1985). Mathematics in the streets and in schools. *British Journal of Developmental Psychology, 3,* 21–29.

Carraher, T. N., Carraher, D. W., & Schliemann, A. D. (1987). Written and oral mathematics. *Journal for Research in Mathematics Education, 18,* 83–97.

Cassirer, E. (1923). *Substance and Function.* New York: Douglas Publications.

Ceci, S. J. (1990). *On Intelligence... more or less: A bio-ecological treatise on intellectual development.* Englewood Cliffs, NJ: Prentice Hall Century Psychology Series.

Ceci, S. J. (1993). Some contextual trends in cognitive development. *Developmental Review, 13,* 403–435.

Ceci, S. J., & Bronfenbrenner, U. (1985). Don't forget to take the cupcakes out of the oven: Strategic time-monitoring, prospective memory and context. *Child Development, 56,* 175–190.

Ceci, S. J. & Liker, J. (1986). Academic and non-academic intelligence: An experimental separation. In R. Sternberg & R. Wagner (Eds.), *Practical Intelligence: Nature and origins of competence in the everyday world* (pp. 119–142). New York: Cambridge University Press.

Chaiklin, S. & Lave, J. (1993). *Understanding practice: Perspectives on activity and context.* New York: Cambridge University Press.

Chamoux, M. N. (1981). Les savoir-faire techniques et leur appropriation: Le cas des Nahuas du Mexique. *L'Homme, 21,* 71–94.

Chamoux, M. N. (1986). Apprendre autrement: Aspects des pédagogies dites informelles chez les indiens du Mexique. In P. Rossel (Ed.), *Demain l'artisanat?* (pp. 211–335). Paris: Presses Universitaires de France.

Cheng, P. W. & Holyoak, K. J. (1985). Pragmatic Reasoning schemas. *Cognitive Psychology, 17,* 391–416.

Childs, C. & Greenfield, P. M. (1980). Informal modes of learning and teaching: The case of Zinacanteco weaving. In N. Warren (Ed.), *Studies in cross-cultural psychology* (Vol. 2, pp. 269–316). New York: Academic Press.

Cole, M. (1988). Cross-cultural research in sociohistorical tradition. *Human Development, 31,* 137–157.

Cole, M., Gay, J., Glick, J. A., & Sharp, D. W. (1971). *The cultural context of learning and thinking.* New York: Basic Books.

D'Ambrosio, U. (1985). Ethnomathematics and its place in the history and pedagogy of mathematics. *For the Learning of Mathematics. 5,* 44–48.

Dasen, P. R. & Bossel-Lagos, M. (1989). L'étude interculturelle des savoirs quotidiens: Revue de la littérature. In J. Retschitzky, M. Bossel-Lagos, & P. R. Dasen (Eds.), *La recherche interculturelle* (pp. 98–114). Paris: L'Harmattan.

De la Rocha, O. (1985). The reorganization of arithmetic practices in the kitchen. *Anthropology and Education Quarterly, 16,* 193–198.

Detterman, D. K. & Sternberg, R. J. (1993). *Transfer on trial: Intelligence, cognition, and instruction.* Norwood, NJ: Ablex Publishing Co.

Dias, M. G. (1987). Da lógica do analfabeto à lógica do universitário: Há progresso? *Arquivos Brasileiros de Psicologia, 39,* 29–40.

Dias, M. G. & Harris, P. L. (1988). The effect of make-believe play on deductive reasoning. *British Journal of Developmental Psychology, 6,* 207–221.

Donaldson, M. (1978). *Children's minds.* Glasgow, UK: Fontana/Collins.

Draisma, J. (1993). *How to handle the theorem 8 + 5 = 13 in (teacher) education?* Paper presented at the Second International Conference "Political Dimensions of Mathematics Education". Broederstroom, South Africa, April 2–5.

Dube, E. F. (1982). Literacy, cultural familiarity, and "intelligence" as determinants of story recall. In U. Neisser (Ed.), *Memory observed: Remembering in natural contexts* (pp. 274–292). San Francisco: W. H. Freeman & Co.

Ferguson, G. A. (1956). On transfer and the abilities of man. *Canadian Journal of Psychology, 10,* 121–131.

Frege, G. (1953). *The foundations of arithmetic.* Oxford: Blackwell.

Gay, J. & Cole, M. (1967). *The new mathematics and an old culture.* New York: Holt, Rinehart & Winston.

Gelman, R. (1979). Preschool thought. *American Psychologist, 44,* 134–141.

Gerdes, P. (1986). How to recognize hidden geometrical thinking: A contribution to the development of anthropological mathematics. *For the Learning of Mathematics, 6,* 10–17.

Gerdes, P. (1988a). A widespread decorative motive and the Pythagorean theorem. *For the Learning of Mathematics, 8,* 35–39.

Gerdes, P. (1988b). On culture, geometrical thinking and mathematics education. *Educational Studies in Mathematics, 19,* 137–162.

Glick, J. (1981). Functional and structural aspects

of rationality. In I. Sigel, D. Brodzinsky, & R. Golinkoff (Eds.), *New directions in Piagetian theory and practice* (pp. 219–228). Hillsdale, NJ: Lawrence Erlbaum Ass.

Grando, N. (1988). *A matemática na agricultura e na escola.* Unpublished masters thesis, Universidade Federal de Pernambuco, Recife, Brazil.

Greenfield, P. M. (1993). *Historical change and cognitive change: A two-decade follow-up study in Zinacantan, a mayan community of Southern Mexico.* Paper presented at the Sylvia Scribner Memorial Symposium: Culture, Activity, and Development, Society for Research in Child Development, New Orleans.

Greenfield, P. M. (1994). Video games as cultural artifacts. *Journal of Applied Developmental Psychology, 15,* 3–12.

Greenfield, P. M. & Childs, C. (1977). Weaving skill, color terms and pattern representation: Cultural inferences and cognitive development among the Zinacantecos of Southern Mexico. *Interamerican Journal of Psychology, 2,* 23–48.

Greenfield, P. M., Brannon, C., & Lohr, D. (1994). Two-dimensional representation of movement through three-dimensional space: The role of video game expertise. *Journal of Applied Developmental Psychology, 15,* 87–104.

Greenfield, P. M., Camaioni, L., Ercolani, P., Weiss, L., Lauber, B. A., & Perucchini, P. (1994). Cognitive socialization by computer games in two cultures: Inductive discovery or mastery of an iconic code? *Journal of Applied Developmental Psychology, 15,* 59–86.

Greenfield, P. M., deWinstanley, P., Kilpatrick, H., & Kaye, D. (1994). Action video games and informal education: Effects on strategies for dividing visual attention. *Journal of Applied Developmental Psychology, 15,* 105–123.

Greenfield, P. M., & Lave, J. (1982). Cognitive aspects of informal education. In D. Wagner & H. Stevenson (Eds.), *Cultural perspectives on child development* (pp. 181–207). San Francisco: Freeman.

Guberman, S. (1993, July). *Changing activities and skills: Links between the commercial transactions and arithmetic achievements of some Brazilian children.* Paper presented at the Twelfth Biennial Meetings of the International Society for the Study of Behavioural Development. Recife, Brazil.

Guberman, S. (1995). *The development of everyday mathematics in Brazilian children with limited formal education.* Unpublished manuscript, University of Colorado at Boulder.

Guberman, S. R. & Greenfield, P. M. (1991). Learning and transfer in everyday cognition. *Cognitive Development, 6,* 233–260.

Harris, M. (1987). An example of traditional women's work as a mathematics resource. *For the Learning of Mathematics, 7,* 26–28.

Harris, M. (1988). Common threads-Mathematics and textiles. *Mathematics in School, 17,* 24–28.

Hatano, G. (1982). Cognitive consequences of practice on culture specific skills. *Quarterly Newsletter of the Laboratory of Comparative Human Cognition, 4,* 15–18.

Hatano, G. (1990). The nature of everyday science: A brief introduction. *British Journal of Developmental Psychology, 8,* 245–250.

Hiebert, J. & Lefevre, P. (1986). Conceptual and procedural knowledge in mathematics: An introductory analysis. In J. Hiebert (Ed.), *Conceptual and procedural knowledge: The case of mathematics* (pp. 1–27). Hillsdale, NJ: Erlbaum.

Hughes, M. (1986). *Children and number.* Oxford: Blackwell.

Hutchins, E. (1979). Reasoning in Trobriand discourse. *The Quarterly Newsletter of the Laboratory of Comparative Human Cognition, 1,* 13–17.

Hutchins, E. (1980). *Culture and inference.* Cambridge, MA: Harvard University Press.

Hutchins, E. (1983). Understanding Micronesian navigation. In D. Gentner & A. Stevens (Eds.), *Mental models* (pp. 191–225). Hillsdale, NJ: Erlbaum.

Hutchins, E. (1993). Learning to navigate. In S. Chaiklin & J. Lave (Eds.), *Understanding practice: Perspectives on activity and context* (pp. 35–63). New York: Cambridge University Press.

Inagaki, K. & Hatano, G. (1987). Young children's spontaneous personification as analogy. *Child Development, 58,* 1013–1020.

Inagaki, K. (1990). Young children's use of knowledge in everyday biology. *British Journal of Developmental Psychology, 8,* 281–288.

Irvine, S. H. & Berry, J. W. (Eds.). (1988). *Human*

abilities in cultural context. Cambridge: Cambridge University Press.

Johnson-Laird, P. N. (1982). Thinking as a skill. *Quarterly Journal of Experimental Psychology, 34A*, 1–29.

Johnson-Laird, P. N., Legrenzi, P., & Legrenzi, M. (1972). Reasoning and a sense of reality. *British Journal of Psychology, 63*, 395–400.

Khan, F. A. (1993). Cognitive organization and work activity: A study of carpet weavers in Kashmir. *The Quarterly Newsletter of the Laboratory of Comparative Human Cognition, 15*, 48–52.

Kline, M. (1962). *Mathematics: A cultural approach.* Reading, MA: Addison-Wesley.

Laboratory of Comparative Human Cognition. (1983). Culture and cognitive development. In P. H. Mussen (Ed.), *Handbook of child psychology: Vol. 1. History, theory and methods* (pp. 295–356). New York: Wiley.

Labov, W. (1970). The logic of non-standard English. In F. Williams (Ed.), *Language and poverty* (pp. 153–189). Chicago: Markham Press.

Lave, J. (1977). Cognitive consequences of traditional apprenticeship training in Africa. *Anthropology and Educational Quarterly, 7*, 177–180.

Lave, J. (1988). *Cognition in practice: Mind, mathematics, and culture in everyday life.* Cambridge: Cambridge University Press.

Lave, J. & Wenger, E. (1991). *Situated learning: Legitimate peripheral participation.* New York: Cambridge University Press.

Lave, J., Murtaugh, M., & De la Rocha, O. (1984). The dialectic of arithmetic in grocery shopping. In B. Rogoff & J. Lave (Eds.), *Everyday cognition: Its development in social context* (pp. 67–94). Cambridge, MA: Harvard University Press.

Leontiev, A. N. (1981). *Problems of the development of the mind.* Moscow: Progress Publishers.

Light, P., Buckingham, N., & Robbins, A. (1979). The conservation task as an interactional setting. *British Journal of Educational Psychology, 49*, 304–310.

Luria, A. R. (1976). *Cognitive development: Its cultural and social foundations.* Cambridge, MA: Harvard University Press.

Luz, L. P., Khoury, H., & Schliemann, A. D. (1994).

Understanding radiation: Knowledge development about physical concepts at work and in school. Paper presented at the Fourteenth Biennial Meetings of the International Society for the Study of Behavioural Development. Amsterdam.

McGarrigle, J. & Donaldson, M. (1974). Conservation accidents. *Cognition, 3*, 341–350.

McMurchy-Pilkington, C. (1995). *Maori women engaging in mathematical activities in Marae kitchens.* Master's Dissertation. University of Auckland, Auckland, New Zealand.

Menon, S. & Kaur, B. (1994, Dec.). *Children's computational skills across situations.* Paper presented at the Annual Conference of the National Academy of Psychology, Allahabad, India.

Millroy, W. L. (1992). An ethnographic study of the mathematical ideas of a group of carpenters. *Journal for Research in Mathematics Education* (Monograph no. 5). Reston, VA: The National Council of Teachers of Mathematics.

Murtaugh, M. (1985). The practice of arithmetic by American grocery shoppers. *Anthropology and Education Quarterly, 16*, 186–192

Neisser, U. (1967). *Cognitive psychology.* New York: Appleton-Century-Crofts.

Neisser, U. (1976). *Cognition and reality. Principles and implications of cognitive psychology.* New York: W. H. Freeman & Co.

Neisser, U. (1981). John Dean's memory: A case study. *Cognition, 9*, 1–22.

Neisser, U. (Ed.). (1982). *Memory observed. Remembering in natural contexts.* San Francisco: W. H. Freeman & Co.

Nunes, T. (1992). Ethnomathematics and everyday cognition. In D. Grouws (Ed.), *Handbook of research in mathematics education* (pp. 557–574). New York: MacMillan.

Nunes, T. (1993). The socio-cultural context of mathematical thinking: Research findings and educational implications. In A. Bishop, K. Hart, S. German, & T. Nunes (Eds.), *Significant influences on children's learning of mathematics.* Paris, Science and Technology Education Document Series, UNESCO, No. 47.

Nunes, T., Schliemann, A. D., & Carraher, D. W. (1993). *Street mathematics and school mathematics.* New York: Cambridge University Press.

Okagaki, L. & Frensch, P. A. (1994). Effects of video

game playing on measures of spatial performance: Gender effects in late adolescence. *Journal of Applied Developmental Psychology, 15*, 33–58.

Okonji, O. M. (1971). The effects of familiarity on classification. *Journal of Cross-Cultural Psychology, 2*, 39–49.

Oloko, B. A. (1994). Children's street work in urban Nigeria: Dilemma of modernizing tradition. In P. M. Greenfield & R. R. Cocking (Eds.), *Cross-cultural roots of minority child development* (pp. 197–224). Hillsdale, NJ: Erlbaum.

Perkins, D. N. (1986). *Knowledge as design*. Hillsdale, NJ: Erlbaum.

Perret-Clermont, A.-N., Perret, J.-F., & Bell, N. (1991). The social construction of meaning and cognitive activity in elementary school children. In L. Resnick, J. Levine, & S. Teasley (Eds.), *Perspectives on socially shared cognition* (pp. 41–62). Washington, DC: American Psychological Association.

Petitto, A. & Ginsburg, H. (1982). Mental arithmetic in Africa and America: Strategies, principles and explanations. *International Journal of Psychology, 17*, 81–102.

Piaget, J. (1972). Intellectual evolution from adolescence to adulthood. *Human Development, 15*, 1–12.

Piaget, J. & Inhelder, B. (1969). The gaps in empiricism. In A. Koestler & J. R. Smythies (Eds.), *Beyond reductionism: New perspectives in the life sciences* (pp. 118–165). Boston: Beacon Press.

Quine, W. V. O. (1953). Two dogmas of empiricism. In W. V. O. Quine (Ed.), *From a logical point of view* (pp. 20–46). Cambridge, MA: Harvard University Press.

Reed, H. J. & Lave, J. (1979). Arithmetic as a tool for investigating relations between culture and cognition. *American Anthropologist, 6*, 568–582

Resnick, L. (1986). The development of mathematical intuition. In M. Perlmutter (Ed.), *Minnesota symposium on child psychology*, (Vol. 19). Hillsdale, NJ: Erlbaum.

Resnick, L. (1987). Learning in school and out. *Educational Researcher*, Dec. 1987, 13–20.

Resnick, L., Levine, J., & Teasley, S. (Eds.). (1991). *Perspectives on socially shared cognition*. Washington, DC.: American Psychological Association.

Rogoff, B. & Lave, J. (Eds.). (1984). *Everyday cognition: Its development in social context*. Cambridge, MA: Harvard University Press.

Rogoff, B. (1990). *Apprenticeship in thinking. Cognitive development in social context*. New York: Oxford University Press.

Rothstein, E. (1995). *Emblems of mind: The inner life of music and mathematics*. New York: Times Books.

Saraswathi, L. S. (1988). Practices in identifying (reckoning), measuring and planning for utilization of time in rural Tamil-Nadu (India): Implications for adult education programs. *Journal of Education and Social Change, II(3)*, 125–140.

Saraswathi, L. S. (1989). Practices in linear measurements in rural Tamil-Nadu: Implications for adult education programs. *Journal of Education and Social Change, III(1)*, 29–46.

Saxe, G. B. (1982). Developing forms of arithmetic operations among the Oksapmin of Papua New Guinea. *Developmental Psychology, 18*, 583–594.

Saxe, G. B. (1985). The effects of schooling on arithmetical understandings: Studies with Oksapmin children in Papua New Guinea. *Journal of Educational Psychology, 77(5)*, 503–513.

Saxe, G. B. (1988a). Candy selling and math learning. *Educational Researcher, 17*, 14–21.

Saxe, G. B. (1988b). The mathematics of child street vendors. *Child Development, 59*, 1415–1425.

Saxe, G. B. (1991). *Culture and cognitive development: Studies in mathematical understanding*. Hillsdale, NJ: Lawrence Erlbaum.

Saxe, G. B. & Moylan, T. (1982). The development of measurement operations among the Oksapmin of Papua New Guinea. *Child Development, 53*, 1242–1248.

Schliemann, A. D. (1985). Mathematics among carpenters and carpenters apprentices: Implications for school teaching. In P. Damerow, M. Dunckley, B. Nebres & B. Werry (Eds.), *Mathematics for all*, Paris, Science and Technology Education Document Series, UNESCO, No. 20.

Schliemann, A. D. (1988). Understanding permutations: Development, school learning, and work experience. *The Quarterly Newsletter of the Laboratory of Comparative Human Cognition, 10,* 3–7.

Schliemann, A. D. (1995). Some concerns about bringing everyday mathematics to mathematics education. In L. Meira & D. Carraher (Eds.), *Proceedings of the XIX International Conference for the Psychology of Mathematics Education* (Vol. 1, pp. 45–60). Recife, Brazil.

Schliemann, A. D. & Acioly, N. M. (1989). Mathematical knowledge developed at work: The contribution of practice versus the contribution of schooling. *Cognition and Instruction, 6,* 185–221.

Schliemann, A. D., Araujo, C., Cassundé, M. A., Macedo, S., & Nicéas, L. (1994). School children versus street sellers' use of the commutative law for solving multiplication problems. *Proceedings of the Eighteenth International Conference for the Psychology of Mathematics Education* (Vol. 4, pp. 209–216). Lisbon, Portugal.

Schliemann, A. D. & Carraher, D. W. (1992). Proportional reasoning in and out of school. In P. Light & G. Butterworth (Eds.), *Context and cognition: Ways of learning and knowing* (pp. 47–73). New York: Harvester Wheatsheaf.

Schliemann, A. D. & Magalhães, V. P. (1990). Proportional reasoning: From shops, to kitchens, laboratories, and, hopefully, schools. *Proceedings of the Fourteenth International Conference for the Psychology of Mathematics Education* (Vol. 3, pp. 67–73). Oaxtepec, Mexico.

Schliemann, A. D. & Nunes, T. (1990). A situated schema of proportionality. *British Journal of Developmental Psychology, 8,* 259–268.

Schliemann, A. D., Santos, C. M., & Canuto, S. F. (1993). Constructing written algorithms: A case study. *Journal of Mathematical Behavior, 12,* 155–172.

Scribner, S. (1977). Modes of thinking and ways of speaking. In P. Wason & P. Johnson-Laird (Eds.), *Thinking: Readings in cognitive science* (pp. 483–500). New York: Cambridge University Press.

Scribner, S. (1984). Studying working intelligence. In B. Rogoff & J. Lave (Eds.), *Everyday cognition: Its development in social context*

(pp. 9–40). Cambridge, MA: Harvard University Press.

Scribner, S. (1986). Thinking in action: Some characteristics of practical thought. In R. Sternberg & R. Wagner (Eds.), *Practical intelligence. Nature and origins of competence in the everyday world* (pp. 13–30). New York: Cambridge University Press.

Scribner, S. & Cole, M. (1973). Cognitive consequences of formal and informal education. *Science, 182,* 553–559.

Segall, M. H., Dasen, P. R., Berry, J. W., & Poortinga, Y. H. (1990). *Human behavior in global perspective.* New York: Pergamon Press.

Sternberg, R. & Wagner, R. (Eds.). (1986). *Practical intelligence. Nature and origins of competence in the everyday world.* New York: Cambridge University Press

Subrahmanyam, K. & Greenfield, P. M. (1994). Effect of video game practice on spatial skills in girls and boys. *Journal of Applied Developmental Psychology, 15,* 13–32.

Ueno, N. & Saito, S. (1994, June). *Historical transformations of mathematics as problem solving in a Nepali bazaar.* Paper presented at the Thirteenth Biennial Meetings of the ISSBD, Amsterdam.

Usher, J. & Neisser, U. (1993). Childhood amnesia and the beginnings of memory for four early life events. *Journal of Experimental Psychology: General, 122,* 155–165.

Vergnaud, G. (1988). Multiplicative structures. In J. Hiebert & M. Behr (Eds.), *Number concepts and operations in the middle grades* (Vol. 2). LEA/NCTM.

Vosniadou, S. (1991). Children's naive models and the processing of expository text. In M. Carretero, M. Pope, R.-J. Simons, & J. I. Pozo (Eds.), *Learning & instruction: European research in an international context* (Vol. 3, pp. 325–336). Oxford: Pergamon Press.

Voss, J., Perkins, D., & Segal, J. (1991). *Informal reasoning and education.* Hillsdale, NJ: Erlbaum.

Voss, J. F. & Post, T. A. (1988). On the solving of ill-structured problems. In M. T. H. Chi, R. Glaser, & M. Farr (Eds.), *The nature of expertise.* Hillsdale, NJ: Erlbaum.

Vygotsky, L. S. (1978). *Mind in society.* Cambridge, MA: Harvard University Press.

Wason, P. (1966). Reasoning. In B. Foss (Ed.), *New horizons in psychology* (pp. 135–151). Harmonsworth: Penguin.

Wassmann, J. (1993). When actions speak louder than words: The classification of food among the Yupno of Papua New Guinea. *Quarterly Newsletter of the Laboratory of Comparative Human Cognition, 15,* 30–40.

Wassmann, J. & Dasen, P. R. (1994). "Hot" and "Cold": Classification and sorting among the Yupno of Papua New Guinea. *International Journal of Psychology, 29,* 19–38.

Wertsch, J. (1991). *Voices of the mind: A sociocultural approach to mediated action.* Cambridge, MA: Harvard University Press.

Zaslavsky, C. (1973). *Africa counts.* Boston: Prindle and Schmidt, Inc.

7

LANGUAGE ACQUISITION AND BILINGUALISM

AJIT K. MOHANTY
Utkal University
India

CHRISTIANE PERREGAUX
University of Geneva
Switzerland

Contents

Introduction

In the previous *Handbook* (Triandis & Heron, 1981), two chapters were devoted to the questions of language acquisition and processing, and to bilingualism. Because the two themes are interrelated and somewhat overlapping, in this volume they are discussed in a single chapter divided into two parts. The first part incorporates some new developments in thinking about language acquisition, particularly as a result of the impact of a growing number of cross-linguistic studies. In the second section, we show how studies of bilingualism have led to new understandings in bilinguals' acquisition and processing of language(s) and the links between bilingualism, cognition and education.

Research on language development in a cross-cultural perspective has increasingly turned away from the simple validation of linguistic models, mostly based directly or indirectly on Chomsky's ideas, toward the notion of language as a cultural phenomenon and as a socially embedded communication system. While an increasing number of cross-linguistic studies show a preoccupation with the formal structure of language and its rules, studies of individual differences in language development and the role of cultural parameters in such development point to the emergence of a distinct cross-cultural approach. The chapter by Bowerman (1981) in the earlier edition of the *Handbook* has discussed the major directions, and theoretical and methodological issues in the field. Here, our emphasis is on looking at the cultural and cross-linguistic bases of the acquisition of communicative competence in a social context.

The second part of the chapter is about bilingualism. Over the years, views on the nature of bilingualism and its implications for the individual and society have undergone several changes. In the previous edition of the *Handbook*, Segalowitz (1981) has shown how the approaches in this area had changed since the early studies. More recent sociolinguistic, ethnolinguistic, and psycholinguistic work on bilingualism has given rise to new conceptualizations of the knowledge of multiple languages. The debate is no longer confined to the comparison between monolingual and bilingual performances; rather the study of the social context, which determines the necessity to speak in one language or another as an effective strategy to facilitate communication and to achieve social objectives through such communication, has become quite important. Bilingualism is now taken as a composite system of pluralistic competences and not merely as a sum of two or more language abilities. The later studies of bilingualism, including some recent ones from non-Western societies, have effectively exposed the myth of bilingual handicap in respect to cognitive and social functions and have generated interest in bilingual educational policies for minority and majority groups in most countries. However, these policies have diverse objectives, and it has not been possible to comprehensively cover needs of the majority and the minority groups within a single theoretical framework.

Language Acquisition and Processing

While active interest in the psychology of language can be traced back to the pre-Wundtian days, modern psycholinguistic research derived its early impetus from Chomsky's (1957, 1965) theory of grammar. However, as this dominant theory of language has undergone several changes (Chomsky, 1957, 1965, 1986), psycholinguists wedded to the idea of testing linguistic theories have found themselves chasing a theory that has either been too powerful or too evasive. Further, accumulation of language acquisition and processing data from increasingly diverse sources, particularly from non-English languages, made it evident that some of the earlier findings and assumptions about linguistic processes had to be discarded in the face of contradictory evidence from different languages.

Cross-Linguistic and Cross-Cultural Studies

Slobin (1985a) dealt with the necessity and methodological aspects of cross-linguistic studies of acquisition. The different formal structures and grammatical devices in languages of the world create different types of problems for the child's acquisition of language and thus influence the course of development. For example, English is a language with a relatively fixed word order which, therefore, serves as a device for marking grammatical relationships. But, in many other languages, word orders are variable, requiring different devices (such as word endings) to mark grammatical relationships. With accumulation of cross-linguistic data, it has become clear that the ways in which children deal with the problems of word order and grammatical relationship in their languages vary from one language to another (Aksu-Koc & Slobin, 1985).

In his introduction to the third volume of *The Cross-linguistic Study of Language Acquisition*, Slobin (1992) has shown a steady growth of a cross-linguistic database during recent years. These volumes reported acquisition data from twenty-eight languages belonging to fourteen major language families. A computerized data bank system, the Child Language Data Exchange System (CHILDES) has been developed (MacWhinney & Snow, 1985) to collect cross-linguistic data and child language transcripts, which can be available through the system for reference and analysis by the researchers. The system has stored profiles and language transcripts of a large number of normal and special children from many languages. It is a very useful database for cross-linguistic researchers, and has improved the scope for language acquisition research across different languages in recent years.

A distinction, however, must be made between cross-cultural and cross-linguistic studies of language acquisition. Because language is a distinctly cultural phenomenon, the latter can be considered a subset of the former. In cross-linguistic studies, the focus is usually on the form and nature of language without much consideration of the cultural context of its use. As such, these studies fall short of the requirements of cross-cultural psycholinguistic research, which must view language use and acquisition as phenomena embedded in interpersonal contexts structured by a given culture. Slobin (1992) himself admits that barring a few studies, the research on acquisition of different languages "has been far more cross-*linguistic* than cross-*cultural*" since "the children studied . . . lived in the common international world of professional families in urban and semi-urban settings" (p. 6). Cross-linguistic studies have been quite productive for language acquisition research, but a cross-cultural perspective in such studies would definitely be more insightful.

Theoretical Trends in Language Acquisition Research

As the literature on child language acquisition has continued to grow with a distinctly cross-linguistic perspective in recent years, a number of facts have emerged about the process of acquisition. Slobin (1992) and Perera (1994) have discussed the major findings, theoretical concepts, and emerging trends in child language research. Comprehensive summaries of the developments in the field are also given in Aitchison (1989), Goodluck (1991), and Berko-Gleason and Bernstein Ratner (1993). Despite an enormous database, language acquisition is considered quite a complex process about which a lot more remains to be known.

In recent research on child language, there has been a shift of emphasis that is of interest to cross-cultural psychology. While the early research on language acquisition, even before Chomsky, was clearly biased towards discovering the universals of acquisition rather than the particulars (Slobin, 1985a), recent studies are looking for differences as well as similarities across languages. Slobin (1985a) has discussed the null hypothesis and the hypothesis of specific language effects as methodological and conceptual approaches in cross-linguistic research "to reveal both developmental universals and language specific developmental patterns" (p. 5). After the great initial success of Chomsky's theory, it has now been shown that the child's approximation of adult grammar is not as dramatic as Chomsky predicted; it seems to be a slow and gradual process (Maratsos, 1978). Sometimes children seem to produce utterances that show complete disregard for, or a total lack of awareness of, universal constraints. Knowledge of universal constraints also appears to be gradually acquired, if at all. One collection of papers (Weissenborn, Goodluck, & Roeper, 1992) addressed the issue of continuity or discontinuity in the availability of Chomsky's Universal Grammar; that is, whether children already have the principles of Universal Grammar or whether they acquire the notion of this Grammar later in their development. The authors supported a continuity position, arguing that when the grammar of the child appears to violate the constraints, such structures may be possible in other languages if not in the target language.

It is interesting to note that, under the sweeping influence of Chomsky's theory, the empiricist approach to language learning had been relegated to a position of relative insignificance. However, Braine (1994) has advocated the application of empiricism in studying learning mechanisms in language acquisition in order to explain the ontogenesis of cognitive primitives assumed under the nativistic position.

Cognitive Development and Language Acquisition

A different way of approaching a child's ability to deal with linguistic input has been to assume a close relationship between the general intellectual or cognitive development and language acquisition. According to this view, a certain level of conceptual development is to be presupposed for the development of specific linguistic skills (Sinclair-de-Zwart, 1969). However, although indices of language and cognitive development are normally correlated, there are many cases in which the conceptual level does not quite predict the linguistic development, suggesting that the correlation between the two may only be incidental (see, e.g., Curtis, 1981, 1982). The suggestion that linguistic and cognitive development are mutually interdependent is uninteresting from the acquisition point of view; some even consider it "tautological" (Fodor, Bever, & Garrett, 1974). The Piagetian framework of relating the conceptual and semantic basis of language use to the development of structural knowledge in language acquisition has continued to provide theoretical insights (e.g., Schlesinger, 1982, 1988). Some psycholinguists view language acquisition as dependent on certain cognitive prerequisites or strategies necessary to predispose the language-acquiring child to process the linguistic input in a certain way. Slobin (1973, 1985b) stated a number of operating principles that enable the child to expect some regularities in analyzing linguistic input. In his analysis of cross-linguistic studies of language acquisition, Slobin (1985b, 1992) has suggested some modifications to these principles to account for a number of similarities and differences in the patterns of acquisition across several languages.

While it is possible for the operating principles to conflict with one another, which some (e.g. Bowerman, 1985) see as a potential problem, the relative salience of each operating principle in a given language may determine the priorities for the language user. In their competition model of sentence processing, some authors (Bates & MacWhinney, 1987; MacWhinney, 1987; MacWhinney & Bates, 1989) suggested that the information value of given linguistic forms or their cue validity in a given language depends on their frequency and consistency of occurrence in the language and, when the cues are in conflict, the relative cue validity determines the weight assigned to them by the language user. Cross-linguistic studies of sentence processing (MacWhinney & Bates, 1989) in a number of languages (e.g., Dutch, English, Hebrew, French, Hindi, Hungarian) and, more recently, in Chinese (Li, Bates, Liu, & MacWhinney, 1992) lend considerable support to the competition model. In their opinion, with post facto determination of cue validity, almost any difference in cross-linguistic processing can be explained. In any case, the concept of operating principles seems to provide a promising view of language acquisition and processing. With the availability of more cross-linguistic data and information on language acquisition in diverse settings, the model can be expected to be developed further.

Maternal and Environmental Input

Some attempts have been made, in recent years, to account for language development by examining the relationship of child language with maternal input or the child directed speech of the mother, the caregiver, and other adults. Certain features of the mother's speech tend to occur in the child's speech, giving rise to the view that the child may be learning *motherese*. But simple statistical correlation for groups of mother–child pairs does not really explain much about the manner in which language (or, even, motherese) is acquired. Some studies (e.g., Dellacorte, Benedict, & Klein, 1983; Hampson & Nelson, 1993) have shown that early maternal speech is related to the styles of language acquisition, whereas others (Hampson, 1988; Scarborough & Wyckoff, 1986) found no effects of the child directed speech. Findings on the motherese hypothesis have not been consistent (e.g., Newport, Gleitman, & Gleitman, 1977; Furrow, Nelson, & Benedict, 1979). Gleitman, Newport, and Gleitman (1984) do not find the hypothesis to hold promise. However, Hampson and Nelson (1993) suggested that the negative studies on the motherese hypothesis may have been looking for the effects of maternal speech too late in the children's language development. Thus, it is not yet possible to reach a definite conclusion with respect to the role played by the child-directed speech of the mother and other adults in language acquisition.

If cross-cultural studies have established that all children in the world learn to speak in a social context, they also show quite clearly that interactions are not the same in all cultures. Many differences exist in terms of specific linguistic properties, such as voice intensity, utterance quality, rate of articulation, and so on (Sabatier, 1986). Studies show that children's early speech sounds are shaped in contact with specific language(s) and are gradually modeled after it (Mehler, 1990; Moreau & Richelle, 1981). Children who develop in a plurilingual environment rapidly discriminate between the specific sounds of the languages they hear (Eilers, Gavin, & Oller, 1982; Hamers & Blanc, 1983).

What is, of course, more important than a straightforward reflection of adult speech in the child is the manner in which adults are able to support the child by various socialization devices employed through different forms of language use and verbal routines. Considerable evidence suggests that individual differences in language acquisition within a given culture (and a language) can be attributed to the social processes involved in the verbal interactions with children that vary from culture to culture. Examination of the role of cultural factors in shaping the course of language development and in language socialization of the child seems to be an interesting possibility, particularly for cross-cultural psychology.

Language Socialization and Individual Differences in Child Language

It is evident from an analysis of the child language literature that despite some emphasis on the universals of acquisition, there is a great deal of intra-cultural and inter-cultural variation in the processes and styles of language development. It has come to be widely accepted that children show individual variations in the pattern of their early speech acquisition (Goldfield & Snow, 1993; Nelson, 1981a). The dimensions on which such variations occur have been variously characterized. For example, the referential and expressive styles (Nelson, 1973) differ in the composition of the early vocabulary: referential children show a predominance of common nouns, while expressive children show a preference for personal–social words, proper names, action words, and routine social phrases. Nelson (1981a; Furrow & Nelson, 1984) suggested that a number of environmental and cultural variables affect the nature of individual differences in language acquisition. Hampson (1988) has shown that referential style is related to a higher proportion of adult contact in the child's experience and a lower proportion of peer contact. The stylistic variation in language development in terms of the referential-expressive distinction has received wide empirical support (e.g., Dellacorte, Benedict, & Klein, 1983; Furrow & Nelson, 1984; Hampson & Nelson, 1993; Olsen-Fulero, 1982). However, doubts have been raised about the basis of the referential–expressive classification which has been viewed as being used inconsistently (Lieven, Pine & Barnes, 1992).

Nelson, Hampson, and Shaw (1993) have suggested some conceptual categories for analysis of nouns in the early lexicon. On the whole, the analyses of individual differences in early language development have been quite productive, going beyond the theoretical assumptions of the early acquisition literature, and looking at the external social variables influencing the process of acquisition. It has become evident that the view of an autonomous child acquiring language with little concern for the sociocultural contexts and nature of language input is slightly overstated. The family and the sociocultural environment exercise communicatively significant influences on the child's language. Thus, the manner in which a child is socialized to communicate in culturally appropriate and meaningful ways is important for explaining language acquisition.

Language Socialization

As we have noted, in the literature on language acquisition, much has been said about the processes by which children acquire the formal aspects of language, its structure and the rules of grammar in their abstract form usually independent of the content. Only recently have researchers in child language turned to an analysis of the mechanisms of language socialization, defined as the process of "socialization through language and socialization to use language" (Ochs, 1986, p. 2). Language learning involves learning meanings in context by organizing and relating the contexts of sociocultural interaction, in which language use is embedded (Nelson, 1981b), and a child has to integrate "the code knowledge with sociocultural knowledge" (Ochs & Schieffelin, 1984, p. 307) in order to use language in a culturally appropriate manner.

Children develop competence in their sociocultural functions and communication through participation in social interactions (Gardner, 1984; Ochs, 1986; Vygotsky, 1978). Such interactions provide the contexts for language, which not only act as a transmitter of sociocultural knowledge, but also as a powerful medium of socialization. The use of language and the speech acts are structured by adults to provide the necessary "scaffolding" (Bruner, 1975, 1978) for the development of children's competence in language use and also for the acquisition of cultural competence. Stern (1985) argued for the essential role of the mother in bringing "the infant's behaviour to her framework of created meanings" (p. 134). Peters (1983) discussed many techniques, such as marked stress, chunking, repetition, substitution, expansion, and so forth, that caregivers use to facilitate children's language acquisition. It seems that while all cultures use language in social interactional contexts as a tool for, and as a process of socialization, they vary in the specific strategies. "Social interactions in a given culture have predictable patterns of interactional routines or sequences of exchanges in which one speaker's utterance, accompanied by appropriate nonverbal behaviour, calls forth one of a limited set of responses by one or more other participants" (Peters & Boggs, 1986, p. 81). Through participation in such routines, a child learns the appropriate social roles, and the affective and cognitive aspects of the social use of language. Further, because such routines usually involve set patterns of linguistic form and structure, they provide practice for refinement of specific structures to help language development in general. A number of acts or events in social discourse—such as turn taking, prompting, announcing, and so on—are used by the mothers, other caregivers, and adults to support the child in the process of language socialization.

Cultural Devices in Language Socialization

Recent studies in a number of cultures have documented various cultural devices in the process of language socialization. Bakeman, Adamson, Konner, and Barr (1990) studied the nature of interaction between Kung infants (in the Kalahari) and their caregivers with respect to object exploration. It was found that, although these children showed developmental changes in their object involvement and manipulation, beginning at about four months of age, their object manipulation and play episodes were generally ignored by the caregivers and other adults; the infant–adult verbal interactions were more focused on social relations. Comparing the styles of verbal interactions of French and West African mothers in Paris with their children in object play situations, Rabain-Jamin (1994a) also noted that the African mothers were less responsive to the child's object-related verbal initiatives. However, they were more responsive to the social initiatives by their children. It seems that the African mothers put greater emphasis on defining and constructing the social relations for children and placing them in the network and hierarchy of relationships in their society.

Mothers' conversational behavior can be characterized as either intended to control children's action or to encourage conversational participation (McDonald & Pien, 1982; Rabain-Jamin, 1994b; Rabain-Jamin & Sabeau-Jouannet, 1994). Watson-Gegeo and Gegeo (1986) studied the role of calling out and repetition routines in the language socialization of the Kwara'ae children in Malaita (Solomon Islands). They found that children learned the appropriate social behaviors associated with adults' calling out routines and used them in their peer group play activities. The Kwara'ae caregivers organized the discourse situation for their infants by telling them what to say and asking them to repeat ('uri -[say] like this'). Use of similar prompts by the adults, to provide children with models of socially appropriate language use and with necessary practice for such use and for acquisition of role and status appropriate speech forms through participation in socially structured discourses in adult interactions, have also been demonstrated in studies with Samoan (Platt, 1986), Bosotho (Demuth, 1986), and Anglo-American children (Anderson, 1986). In all cultures, different speech acts such as teasing, shaming, and assertion are used in socially structured interactional contexts, exposure to which forms an important aspect of language socialization. Some studies (e.g., Eisenberg, 1986; Miller, 1986; Schieffelin, 1986) have analyzed the processes involved in these verbal routines in language socialization of children in different cultures.

Cross-Cultural Interpretations of Verbal Interactions

A notable feature of these studies on language socialization across cultures is the shifting of emphasis from dyadic mother–child interactions typical of Euro-American cultures to the polyadic interactions characteristic of African and some other non-Western societies (Ochs & Schieffelin, 1984; Rabain-Jamin, 1994a). Rabain-Jamin (1994a) speaks of "the importance of mediation of direct mother–infant relationships through real or fictitious reference to a third person" (p. 158) for Wolof immigrant mothers in France. In most non-Western societies, embedding of child's social interactions with the caregiver(s) in the context of polyadic verbal exchanges is the norm rather than the exception. Therefore, in cross-cultural studies, it is necessary to reexamine the social influences on language acquisition and socialization often attributed in Western studies primarily to the mother. In her study of language development in India, Singh (1994) showed the significant role of the grandmothers and other adults in Indian joint families in shaping children's linguistic behavior.

Thus, the growing literature on language socialization shows that, although specific modes and strategies may vary, in all cultures verbal exchanges involving the child, the mother, and other adults have a crucial role in language acquisition and socialization. Besides orienting the children towards different cultural priorities such as people- or object-centered communication, status hierarchy, and so forth, and providing exposure, practice, and purposive instruction in culturally appropriate verbal routines (and the linguistic forms and structures that usually go with them), these exchanges are value oriented and have affective significance for their social and communicative development.

The literature on individual differences in language development has also shown that the child's functional priorities and stylistic preferences are influenced by the nature of her interaction with the mother and other adults—for example, by mothers' intrusiveness (Nelson, 1973) and conversational intent (Olsen-Fulero, 1982). However, because the nature of language socialization practices through structured social interactions is governed by complex cultural parameters, studies in diverse cultures and careful interpretations of cross-cultural similarities and differences are required. In interpreting alien cultural phenomena, it is difficult not to slip into categories and frameworks conditioned by a researcher's own culture, often overlooking alternative possibilities and meanings. For example, a number of studies have noted that compared to Western mothers, African mothers tend to engage in less verbal and more physical and postural interactions with their infants (e.g., Richman et al., 1988) and their communication is more interpersonal than referential (Bakeman et al., 1990; Rabain, 1979; Rabain-Jamin, 1994a).

These findings have usually been interpreted as showing that, for African mothers, the child's object manipulations are less significant than social relations, and as showing that in African cultures, words are endowed "with the educational function of planning, as an organizer of ongoing activity. . . . They place value on the definition and construction of social activity" (Rabain-Jamin, 1994a, p. 156). However, to the extent that socialization is a purposive activity, it is possible that language socialization practices have evolved in different cultures to set priorities and emphases in areas most needed to facilitate a functional development of the child. Therefore, in some cultures, where scope for less restrained object manipulations is available to the child at some point in development, it would perhaps be more functional for the verbal exchanges to be structured and focused around social interaction areas. Rabain-Jamin (1994a) showed that for young African children there are fewer restrictions on direct manipulation of objects. In view of this, it can be argued that it would be much more educative for the verbal interactions to emphasize social and interpersonal relations. This is an alternate possibility worth examining.

In summing up, it can be said that language acquisition research, despite the dominant impact of linguistic theories, is beginning to view language more as a sociocultural phenomenon. As a result, the formal properties of language as a symbol system (the form and structure of language) have gradually received less attention compared to the social and communicative aspects of language use. Thus, sociolinguistic and anthropological approaches to the study of language have influenced the current trends in cross-cultural research on language development. Linguistic theories have had a more direct influence on first language (L1) acquisition research, whereas their influence on second language (L2) acquisition studies has been somewhat secondary. There are certain parallels between L1 and L2 acquisition and some researchers have proposed "an integrated pedagogy" for L1 and L2 (e.g., Roulet, 1980, 1995). Nevertheless, perhaps due to a dominant monolingual bias, the model of first language development has provided the point of reference for analysis of the process of second language acquisition. The language learning strategies, the errors and the order of acquisition in second language development have been viewed as providing some insights regarding the extent to which the processes of L1 and L2 acquisition are similar. Such comparisons are clearly motivated by a view of bilingualism as a deviant phenomenon which ignores the fact that in most parts of the modern world, particulary in multilingual non-Western societies, bilingualism is the norm and monolinguism a deviation.

In multilingual societies, bilingualism does not simply involve acquiring two or more formal systems of language; it also means growing up in and acquiring two or more cultures. This means that the question of bilingualism is related to the question of cultural relations in plural societies (see chapters by Gudykunst & Bond and Berry & Sam in Volume 3 of this *Handbook*). With large-scale population migrations for economic and political reasons, most Western countries are now forced to reexamine their dominant and exclusive monolingual, monocultural, and assimilationist perspectives. This, in turn, has also made it necessary to take a fresh look at the issues linked with bilingualism and bilingual education, some of which are examined in the following sections.

Bilingualism

The growing number of studies in the field of bilingualism has gradually led to the emergence of a new view of communicative competence in multiple languages. There are two reasons for this development. The first pertains to the migrations of communities speaking foreign languages in several countries and to the questions about the integration of these immigrants and their families into the host culture. The second results from reflection on the role and function of different languages (own country and colonial languages) in many countries that had been subjected to European colonization. In both cases, we are faced with the questions of hierarchization of languages, their social roles, the necessity for planning the language of instruction and the effects of bilingualism on the individual and the society. The popular (Western) view of bilingualism as an exception is changing and now we find that bilingual people (in the social and contextual definitions) constitute the majority in the world. When we speak of languages in contact, we also speak of people in contact making bilingualism or multilingualism an intercultural phenomenon.

Concept and Definition

Due to the multifaceted nature of the phenomenon and the diversity of contexts, the term "bilingualism" has been variously used (e.g., Bowerman, 1985; Mohanty, 1994). These divergent but complementary ways of defining the concept make cross-cultural comparisons rather difficult, more so because of the considerable fuzziness of the boundaries between languages, codes, varieties and dialects, and so forth across different cultures. Further, with the changing emphasis from formal to functional aspects of language, bilingualism has come to be seen more as a communicative skill instead of knowledge of the formal rules.

Skutnabb-Kangas (1984) has identified four types of definitions of bilingualism using different criteria. Definitions by origin view bilingualism as a developmental phenomenon; definitions by competence are based on linguistic competence in two or more languages; functional definitions emphasize the functions that the use of languages serves for the individual or the community; and some social psychological definitions stress the speaker's attitude toward or identification with two or more languages. However, one can identify in the literature a set of core criteria in defining the concept, making some generalizations across studies in different contexts and cultures possible. In its core meaning, bilingualism can be defined as the ability of persons or communities to meet (in their normal functioning) the communicative demands of the self or the society in two or more languages in interaction with the speakers of any or all of these languages. Besides being simple and general, this definition leaves open questions relating to the level of bilingual competence and identification with the language(s) and their culture(s). By emphasizing the functional communicative skills in a normal interactional situation, the definition leaves scope for the possible changes in a bilingual's level of functioning across different shifts in the context of language use. For example, a Hindi–English bilingual in India may not be able to function adequately in his second language (English) when he visits England for higher studies. Further, different contexts of acquisition of bilingual skills or L2 learning can be accommodated within the scope of the definition. For cross-cultural comparison purposes, it would, however, be essential to elaborate the specific characteristics of the bilingual persons or communities and the conditions under which they function.

Bilingual persons or communities have been characterized using a number of descriptive or classificatory labels (Mohanty, 1994). Three of those are: social psychological or sociolinguistic classifications based on the social contexts or pattern of language use (e.g., individual and societal bilingualism and diglossia); classifications based on relative levels of skills in language use (e.g., dominant and balanced bilingualism); and classifications based on the context of development of bilingual skills and the outcome of such development (e.g., additive and subtractive bilingualism, compound and coordinated bilingualism).

Assessment of Bilingualism

A number of authors (e.g., Baker, 1993; Cummins, 1984; Skutnabb-Kangas, 1984) have discussed various assessment issues in the area of bilingualism. In cross-cultural research on bilingualism, a major assessment problem of relevance is the monolingual bias in measurement of bilingual proficiency. Such measures can be designed with reference to the monolingual norm or can be specifically designed for the bilingual population. The former, as Skutnabb-Kangas (1984) noted, is guided by the purpose of comparing the bilingual person either with the native speaker of the target language assumed to be monolingual, or with the norm of proficiency in the target language that a monolingual speaker might expect to have of a foreign language. This has resulted in the use of two types of tests: one that attempts to determine what a bilingual has in common with a monolingual, and the other that seeks to assess the language proficiency characteristic of a bilingual (as different from a monolingual). Often, the tests to assess bilingual linguistic proficiency in both languages assume that a bilingual speaker is two native speakers in one, seeking to test each of the two languages of the bilingual with reference to the monolingual proficiency as a norm. Application of such tests have often resulted in negative findings with bilingual populations.

The Bilingual Holistic View and the Question of Assessment

Since the pioneering work of Lambert (1975), many studies on bilingualism have assessed linguistic balance or dominance of bilinguals as a methodological requirement. The balance measures are usually comparisons of speed and efficiency in dealing with the stimuli presented in two languages in a variety of tasks (word association, picture naming, sentence translation, etc.). Such tests of balance are often based on the untenable assumption that balanced bilingualism implies equal and native-like proficiency in each language. The concept of bilingual balance is related to what Grosjean (1982) called "the monolingual (or fractional) view of bilingualism as opposed to the bilingual (or holistic) view." "The bilingual" as Grosjean (1982) pointed out, "is NOT the sum of two complete or incomplete monolinguals; rather he or she has a unique and specific linguistic configuration" (p. 471). The monolingual view is typical of the dominant monolingual societies of the West, whereas the pluralistic multilingual societies can be characterized as projecting a true bilingual view, in which a bilingual's space of communicative interactions is finely differentiated into several domains with one or other of his languages as the specific preferred language (Dodson, 1985). This, of course, implies that bilingual balance or dominance is not uniform across different domains or contexts of communication. Lüdi and Py (1986), for example, discussed different levels of the social representations of bilingualism with respect to the basic competence of the bilinguals, the interactions between monolingual and bilingual groups, and the role of the "bilingual competence" formed in a migration context.

With respect to assessment issues, as has been pointed out, the monomodel of bilingualism leads to the use of monolingual native speakers' (hypothetical) competence as the yardstick for assessing bilingual competence. In the holistic or multilingual view (Grosjean, 1982), on the other hand, bilingualism is taken as a composite system of bilingual competence and not as a sum of two or more competences. This latter definition is characterized as a "container view" that has resulted in the deficit approach of identifying some bilinguals as double semilinguals, where they are taken to have deficient levels of proficiency in their languages. Unfortunately, this assumption forms the basis of justifying school failure, particularly in societies that receive a large number of migrant children (Oksaar, 1989; Perregaux, 1994). In the holistic approach, a true (ideal) state of bilingual balance is a misnomer (except in a limited and methodologically operational sense) because a bilingual is viewed as a competent user of bilingual language and not of any one language independent of the other. This makes the phenomena of borrowing, code switching and code-mixing in multilingual contexts interesting in their own right, and not just because they are perceived as problems arising out of the possible interferences or failure of any one of the language systems. In fact, mutual influences of languages, or the so-called interferences between languages, is not necessarily a negative phenomenon (Othenin-Girard, 1995). It can be viewed as an effective strategy to facilitate communication and to illustrate the cultural density of the experiences in each language (Pujol, 1990; Py, 1991).

Thus, in the conceptualization and assessment of bilingualism cross-culturally, it is necessary to differentiate between the monolingual and the multilingual perspectives. Further, in view of the underlying continuity between these two perspectives across cultures, it is often essential to describe in detail the sociolinguistic and cultural context of bilingualism to facilitate meaningful comparison of studies in different cultural contexts.

Development of Bilingualism

Some questions are commonly asked about the development of bilingualism: How is bilingual acquisition similar to or different from the acquisition of a first language? Is there an optimal age or a critical period for the development of proficiency in a second language? Is the second language better learned during early childhood, in an informal learning environment or, later in life, through formal instruction? Some of these questions have been addressed by researchers working in different linguistic contexts.

A major distinction has been made between simultaneous and successive bilingualism (McLaughlin, 1978). The former refers to the acquisition of two or more languages during early childhood. Such bilingualism is usually spontaneous and natural, developing like the first language, without any formal or deliberate instruction and with similar processes and motivation for language acquisition. Romaine (1989) has discussed six different types of early childhood bilingualism of the simultaneous type. Her categories depend upon the languages of the parents, the community, the dominance relationship between them, and the strategy that parents follow in their verbal interaction with the child. She has also reviewed several case studies of each type to conclude that the outcome in each case depends on several individual factors including the nature of exposure to the different languages, parents' consistency in language use, attitude towards languages and bilingualism, and so on. Sequential bilingualism develops later in life, more often by deliberate and formal learning of a second language. McLaughlin (1984b, 1985) believes that all cases of bilingualism developed after the age of three are of the successive type.

The earliest reported case study of simultaneous acquisition of bilingualism in a one-parent, one-language situation is by Ronjat (1913). However, Leopold's (1939–1949) study of his German-English bilingual daughter remains, until now, the most detailed and elaborate account of simultaneous bilingual development. Leopold noticed a clear differentiation between the two languages of his daughter at the age of three years, when she consistently used different languages depending on who she was talking to, and started translating from one language to the other. In the study of his two German–English bilingual sons, Saunders (1988) refered to three stages in becoming a bilingual. In the first stage, usually lasting up to two years, the two languages are undifferentiated, most likely functioning with a single lexical system. During the second stage, vocabulary becomes progressively separated with only occasional code mixing. The child also functionally differentiates between the two languages showing understanding of which language is to be spoken, with whom and in what situation. Maximal differentiation between the language systems occurs during the third stage of bilingual development. In respect of the developmental sequence and the processes of development involved in the acquisition of the languages, there does not seem to be any difference between bilingual and monolingual children (Romaine, 1989). However, cross-linguistic studies of bilingual development in different languages are needed to establish the generality of these findings. Further, as Baker (1993) pointed out, there might be a single language system underlying a bilingual's first and second languages, which are likely to be "fused and integrated inside the linguistic-cognitive system of the bilingual" (p. 71).

It is generally believed that younger children can learn a second language more easily, and better, compared to adults and older children. And, because simultaneous acquisition of bilingualism is an early age phenomenon, it is also believed that the level of bilingual proficiency achieved in such acquisition is better than that in successive acquisition. There is, however, no definite evidence on either of these issues. Singleton (1989) suggested that there may not be any age-related differences between simultaneous and successive acquisitions in respect to the processes of language learning, developmental sequence, and level of language proficiency attained. On the other hand, young children may have an advantage over adults in acquiring the phonological and syntactic systems of a new language.

Cognitive and Social Consequences of Bilingualism

A common view of the bilingual person, supported by some early empirical findings, was that of a person shattered and somewhat disabled by divided loyalties and distributed mental abilities. Later studies, however, have dispelled the myth of the bilingual handicap. The following review of the cognitive and social consequences of bilingualism shows the emergence of a positive perspective in bilingualism research.

Bilingualism and Cognitive Functions

Poor scholastic performance of bilinguals, often belonging to the minority and immigrant groups, was a dominant concern in the early Western literature. In view of the supposed relationship of intelligence and creativity with school achievement, these variables were also the most favored ones in early studies with quite atypical samples of school children (like the Spanish+English bilinguals in the United States and Welsh+English bilinguals in Wales), who generally had difficulty in adjustment and school performance. Most of these studies found negative consequences of bilingualism when bilingual children were compared with monolingual ones. Bilingual students were often selected on the basis of having immigrant parents or a foreign surname or having a foreign language spoken at home; the samples were usually uncontrolled for socioeconomic status differences. The level of bilingualism and skill in the second language were not assessed and, as a result, the tests, particularly the verbal tests often administered in the second language of the bilinguals, were biased against them. As Lambert (1977) pointed out, failure to control for the level of skill in the language of testing, the sociocultural and economic differences, and test bias would account for the negative findings in most of the early studies.

In these studies, conducted prior to 1960, bilingualism was viewed as a disease, a mental burden and, in schools, immigrant children were punished for speaking their home language and made to feel ashamed of their language and culture (Cummins, 1984).

However, the trend of negative findings was reversed with a carefully controlled study by Peal and Lambert (1962) described in the previous edition of the *Handbook* (Segalowitz, 1981). After this pioneering work, many studies in different cultural contexts using a variety of tasks and approaches have shown a positive relationship between bilingualism and general intellectual and cognitive functioning (Segalowitz, 1981). Thus, the positive cognitive consequences of bilingualism have been shown to be fairly general across languages and cultures. Besides the methodological sophistication, the later studies also indicate a de-emphasis on intelligence as a unitary measure. In a cross-cultural perspective, the problems with respect to psychological measures such as IQ and the universality of approach to psychological tests are discussed by Dasen (1993), who contended that in psychology and even in cross-cultural psychology, it has been difficult to break away from the absolutism and Western bias in psychological testing. It is, therefore, refreshing that researchers in bilingualism have turned away from global IQ measures in favor of using a variety of measures of cognitive development, particularly information processing and theory-driven measures of specific mental skills such as metalinguistic ability.

Following the pioneering studies on the relationship between bilingualism and cognitive development and metalinguistic skills, new data have come to light on this question in quite different contexts (Bialystok, 1990; Hamers & Blanc, 1983; Harris, 1992; Perregaux, 1994). In the studies by Mohanty and his associates (Babu & Mohanty, 1982; Mohanty, 1982a, b, 1990; Mohanty & Babu, 1983; Patnaik & Mohanty, 1984) among the Kond in India, the bilinguals have been shown to perform better than the monolinguals on a number of cognitive and metalinguistic tasks. These studies are unique in that the bilingual and monolingual samples were drawn from the same culture controlled for age, sex, and socioeconomic status. Further, in these studies, bilingualism of the children was not a result of schooling; they grew up as simultaneous bilinguals learning to use Kui, the group's language, in their homes, and Oriya, the language of the province and of the contact group, through their outside interactions in the villages. A comparison of unschooled bilingual and monolingual Kond children (Mohanty & Das, 1987) has also shown positive performance of the bilinguals. Another Indian study (Southworth, 1980) with a sample of 1,300 children including native speakers of Malayalam and other languages (Tamil, Konkani etc.) showed that the classroom performance of bilinguals was better than monolinguals across all school grades (first through ninth) and all five levels of socioeconomic status. Thus, the post-1960 studies on the effects of bilingualism on intelligence, information processing and other cognitive skills, metalinguistic awareness, creativity and cognitive flexibility, and classroom achievement strongly support the claim of bilinguals' superiority over their monolingual counterparts. Given the significant methodological improvements in these studies conducted in a wide range of linguistic and cultural contexts, the positive findings can be taken to be quite robust. Systematic cross-cultural and cross-linguistic studies with in-depth analysis of the sociolinguistic conditions of bilingualism can throw further light on the specific mechanisms that make bilingualism a positive factor in the cognitive development of children and on the contextual factors that mediate the relationship.

Lambert (1975) has distinguished between the additive and subtractive forms of bilingualism (depending upon whether progressive acquisition of L2 tends to enrich or to replace L1) and has opined that ethnic minority children in most of the early studies may have been subtractive type bilinguals with low proficiency in their languages. Cummins (1976, 1979, 1981a, b, 1984, 1987) has further argued that positive influences of bilingualism can be obtained only with a certain minimum threshold level of bilingual proficiency. He proposed two thresholds; a "lower threshold . . . sufficient to avoid any negative effect"; and a higher threshold "necessary to lead to accelerated cognitive growth" (1981a, pp. 38–39). The threshold hypothesis seeks to explain the discrepant findings about the role of bilingualism in different sociolinguistic settings.

Bilingualism and Metalinguistic Awareness

The question, "How does bilingual proficiency affect the thought process of the individual?" can be addressed within the framework of the concept of linguistic relativity (Whorf, 1956; Fishman, 1960; see Segalowitz, 1981), suggesting that the lexical items and linguistic structures of two different languages influence the thought processes of bilinguals by enriching their cognitive system and making it easier for them to encode their experience in diverse ways. However, the Whorfian concept of linguistic relativity seems to imply a linguistic deficit position that some languages and codes may not be as good as others in promoting cognitive development. Such controversial implications and lack of sufficient empirical support may have resulted in limiting the scope of the Whorfian framework in the literature on bilingualism and cognition.

Another theoretical framework follows from Vygotsky's (1962, 1985) view that the capacity to express the same thought or experience in different languages enables a bilingual child to "see his language as one particular system among many, to view its phenomena under more general categories and this leads to awareness of his linguistic operations" (1962, p. 110). Leopold (1939–1949), in a longitudinal study of his bilingual daughter, observed that bilingualism accelerates the separation of sound and meaning, or name and object, because of parallel exposure to two linguistic terms to refer to the same object (for other studies, see Segalowitz, 1981). A number of empirical and theoretical studies (Bialystok, 1990, 1992; Cummins, 1978; Galambos & Hakuta, 1988; Perregaux, 1994; Ricciardelli, 1992; Titone, 1994) have found positive relationships between bilingualism and different metalinguistic abilities. In a study of language differentiation by a bilingual infant, Vihman (1985) has shown that "the ability to attend to language qua language" (p. 314) emerged fairly early in the form of talking about his own language [e.g., I said "good night" (to) my mother.] just before age two, and in the form of correction of others' speech (e.g., It isn't "in the room," it's "in the kitchen.") by the age of two years and two months. In the case of her bilingual subject, Vihman (1985) also reported explicit metalinguistic reference to language, such as reporting or requesting translations in either language and quoting his own speech acts, by the age of two years and one month. Thus, it can be said that in the case of bilingual children, there is an early development of awareness of language and the rules for its use or a sensitivity to language (McLaughlin, 1984a). Mohanty (1994) has shown that bilingual children were not only more proficient in detecting structural ambiguity in sentences, they also had greater sensitivity to intonational cues, successfully utilizing these cues to perceive the intonation-appropriate meaning of sentences.

By her awareness of the rules of different languages and strategies for resolution of possible conflicts between them in a variety of sociolinguistic contexts, the bilingual child seems to develop special reflective skills that generalize to other metacognitive processes as well. These processes help the child exercise greater control over cognitive functions and make them more effective, improving the level of performance in a variety of intellectual and scholastic tasks (Gombert, 1990; Mohanty, 1994). In view of the superior metalinguistic skills and linguistic sensitivity of bilinguals, they can be hypothesized to be better language learners. Studies by Thomas (1988), Bild and Swain (1989) and Cenoz and Valencia (1994) provide some supportive evidence. Comparing monolingual and bilingual children in their literacy development, Perregaux (1994) found that the bilingual had a greater facility in deletion of phonemic units of non-words, a metalinguistic skill known to have a positive relationship with literacy acquisition (Rieben & Perfetti, 1991a & b). In all other segmentation tasks (words, syllables, or phonemic segmentation), bilingual immigrant children showed the same performance as monolinguals from the same socioeconomic level.

Despite the empirical support for the metalinguistic and metacognitive hypothesis in understanding the relationship between bilingualism and intellectual performance, it would be too simplistic to assume that the relationship is independent of the cultural context of bilingualism. At a very broad level, the ethos of bilingualism as a sociocultural phenomenon is quite different in monolingual and multilingual nations. For example, discussing the sociolinguistic aspects of Indian multilingualism, Mohanty (1994) has argued that in India bilingualism is a strategy toward maintenance of languages and linguistic diversity and not a point in transition toward language shift. The social norm influences the individual in favor of many languages and not one, making bilingualism a positive force in his or her life. Thus, when other factors are controlled, social psychological and cognitive consequences of bilingualism can be expected to be positive in pluralistic and multilingual cultures.

Social Implications of Bilingualism

Sharing of languages also involves sharing of cultures. Thus, from a social psychological perspective, bilingualism is an interesting phenomenon because it involves changes in the individual's attitudes and identities with respect to languages and cultures, and in the nature of intergroup relations in a culture and language contact situation. An understanding of the social psychological processes in bilingualism is necessary to explain why some situations of language contact lead to additive and stable bilingualism at the individual or group levels, whereas others lead to transitional or subtractive bilingualism.

The outcome of intergroup contact and interaction in terms of group identity and maintenance of cultural and linguistic distinctiveness can be examined through a number of social psychological models and theories. In the ethnolinguistic vitality model of intergroup relations and language maintenance, Giles and his associates (Giles, Bourhis, & Taylor, 1977) have identified a set of three group vitality factors to predict the outcome in a language contact situation: social support factors including sociopolitical and economic power of the ethnolinguistic group and the status of the ethnic language; demographic factors including the size, concentration, and pattern of distribution of the group in a geographical area; and the factors of institutional support that a language and its speakers receive from various sociopolitical institutions, such as education, media, government, and organized language movements. In addition to the objective factors of ethnolinguistic vitality, Bourhis, Giles, and Rosenthal (1981) have suggested the concept of perceived or subjective vitality that has been shown to explain intergroup relations and language attitudes in a variety of linguistic settings (e.g., Bourhis & Sachdev, 1984; Giles & Johnson, 1981; Giles, Rosenthal & Young, 1985; Ryan, Hewstone, & Giles, 1984). Recently, the vitality model has also been used in Israel (Kraemer & Olshtain, 1989), and in the Spanish-Basque (Azurmendi & Espi, 1994; Cenoz & Valencia, 1993) and the Spanish-Galician (Romay-Martinez & Garcia-Mira, 1994) contact situations in Spain to analyze the nature of the contact process. Giles and Byrne (1982) have extended the vitality model to specifically explain second language acquisition in language contact situations.

Clément's (1980) model of communicative competence in a second language postulates two levels of social motivational processes—primary and secondary. The primary motivational process is determined by the antagonistic interplay of an individual's affective dispositions toward the other culture ("integrativeness") and the fear of assimilation, that is, the fear that learning and using the second language might lead to the loss of the first language. These two tendencies interact subtractively (Labrie & Clément, 1986) to determine the net primary motivational tendency. This, in turn, leads to the secondary motivation of establishing contact with the second language and for the development of communicative competence in that language. The model assumes that the contact with a second language group is a matter of choice, which may not be the case in many sociolinguistic contexts including the multilingual ones.

Berry's model of cultural relations in plural societies (1980, 1984, 1990) describes the psychological processes of acculturation in situations of contact between different cultural groups both at the community and individual levels. The model is based on an analysis of the acculturation attitudes defined as "the ways in which an individual (or a group) of culture B wishes to relate to culture A" (Berry, 1990, p. 244). The acculturation attitude of an individual or a group involves choices along two dimensions: the first relating to the maintenance of one's own identity, culture, language and way of life; and the second relating to establishing and maintaining a relationship with the other group. The attitudes on each dimension can be represented on a continuum of responses which, for sake of conceptual clarity, can be dichotomously represented as "yes" responses, yielding four outcomes described as assimilation, integration, separation and marginalization (see chapter by Berry & Sam, Volume 3, this *Handbook*).

The sociolinguistic outcomes of language contact can be viewed within the framework of Berry's model. An integrative relationship in a language contact situation can be considered as one leading to stable bilingualism and language maintenance. Transitional bilingualism leading to language shift is the result of assimilative type of orientation. In the case of voluntary assimilation, the pressure towards the language shift is from within the group. Imposed by the dominant group, assimilation is accompanied by pressure to give up one's own language and culture and to make a quick transition to the majority language, making bilingualism not only transitional but also stressful. When the minority linguistic group in a contact situation is separation-oriented, strong linguistic nationalism and divergence with negative attitudes towards learning and using the language of the other contact group can be expected. However, when the majority or the dominant group also wishes to let the nondominant group maintain its distinctiveness and keeps it separated, the minority language tends to become isolated, enclavic, and nonfunctional. The marginalization outcome in Berry's model can be seen as what has sometimes (and controversially) been called double semilingualism (Cummins, 1979; Skutnabb-Kangas, 1975, 1984).

In view of its wide cross-cultural applications, Berry's model appears to be quite promising for analysis of the nature of bilingualism and language maintenance attitudes in language contact situations in different cultures. Commenting on the study by Ward and Hewstone (1985) on the relationship between different linguistic communities in Malaysia and Singapore, Triandis (1985) has suggested possible applications of the model to an ethnolinguistic analysis of multilingual and multicultural societies. In his studies on bilingualism and integration in the Kond tribal–nontribal contact situation in India, Mohanty (1991, 1994) has used Berry's model to analyze the intergroup relations in a language contact situation.

These studies show that when the two linguistic groups in contact are bilinguals, the intercultural attitude of both the groups is integration oriented, whereas the relationship between the Kond tribals and non-tribals in a monolingual contact situation tends to be segregation oriented. In addition to demonstrating the cross-cultural application of Berry's acculturation model in a sociolinguistic context, these findings are of interest because they show that, in a language contact situation, bilingualism at the individual level has positive attitudinal effects promoting social integration.

An implication of Berry's analysis of the culture contact process is that, as minority languages and cultures become more potent due to factors positively affecting the cultural identification (such as enhancement of ethnolinguistic vitality), assimilative trends may change in the direction of integration. A study in the Basque–Spanish contact situation in Spain (Azurmendi & Espi, 1994) showed that positive changes in the objective and subjective ethnolinguistic vitality indices led to the development of a Basque–Spanish bicultural identity replacing a polarized Basque identity. Identity and integration are important issues in migration situations. Camilleri and colleagues (1990) have analyzed the multicultural identity strategies of young immigrants and have demonstrated that questions of identity are linked with the status of language—how the mother tongue is accepted or treated in the host country and in the educational systems. The positive or negative identity of the migrant children, it seems, depends on the answer to this question. Thus, in situations of language and culture contact, stable bilingualism and positive social relationships between the contact groups are interdependent (see chapter by Camilleri and Malewska-Peyre in this volume).

Finally, the question of generalizability of the bilingualism studies to trilinguals and polyglots is of interest. There are a few studies of trilingual children or of bilinguals in the process of acquiring proficiency in a third language (e.g., see Cenoz & Valencia, 1994; Helot, 1988; Hoffman, 1985; Titone, 1994). Generally, these studies confirm the expectation that findings in respect of bilingual development and its cognitive and social implications are also applicable to trilinguals.

Bilingualism and Education: Intercultural Perspectives

Some Issues in Bilingual Education

There is no comprehensive typology for all existing and possible models of bilingual education and for the relationship between the two or more languages in the context of such educational programs. Mackey (1970, 1976) counted nearly one hundred types of bilingual education. Some authors (e.g., Hamers & Blanc, 1983; Baker, 1993) have provided a useful description of various categories, and have explored the factors influencing the nature of bilingual education in practice in different cultural contexts. The term " bilingual education" is a traditional Anglo-Saxon term. Until recently, French researchers, except a few (e.g., Dabène, 1991; Lüdi & Py, 1986), were more concerned with questions of second and foreign language acquisition rather than bilingual education in a wider sense. The questions regarding the education of children of linguistic or ethnic minorities has been studied in the wider "intercultural" domain (Abdallah-Pretceille, 1986). In recent years, there has been an increasing interest in bilingual education, and in many countries, schools are faced with a need for policy decisions on this issue.

The necessity for educational consideration of bilingualism has arisen for several reasons. Decolonization after World War II has left the emerging young states with a problem of choosing official language(s) from among many tongues. The chief question was to build a new state with one language; linguistic diversity seemed to be a danger for national unity in the same manner as the regional languages were a danger for nation states after the French revolution in Europe. The issues and approaches were also quite similar in many Asian countries, including India and in several African countries. The question of national unity, the unrecognized status of the country's language(s) in the international scene, the lack of writing systems and, sometimes, the competition between different cultural/linguistic groups for imposition of their language resulted in continuation of one or another European language as the official and elitist language. In fact, all of these countries are multilingual and are now looking for ways to promote their own languages vis-a-vis English or French (Pakir, 1993).

In Western countries, population migrations from around the world for political and economic reasons have had important implications for educational policies with respect to the new immigrants speaking different language(s). In several Western cities, classrooms include a large number of children who do not speak the dominant language. Further, a common phenomenon in all parts of the world is the emergence of minority groups struggling for recognition of their language and their own identity. In the American continent, the Amerindian and Inuit populations require simultaneous teaching of their languages along with English, French, Spanish, or Portuguese; in Europe, where languages of culturolinguistic minorities have been oppressed for a long time by the state centralism, schools are forced to incorporate several minority languages in their teaching program (Siguan & Mackey, 1986; Skutnabb-Kangas & Cummins, 1988; Vermès & Boutet, 1987, 1988). In Asia, too, minority language issues have surfaced in the form of political movements and separatism in almost all multilingual countries. Thus, the question of bilingual education has social and political ramifications. For example, in the countries of the European Community, there are proposals for bilingual or multilingual communication to promote better understanding (Coste & Hébrard, 1991; Tschoumy, 1994). Further, the question of ensuring equality of opportunity to all children for learning the regional, national, and international link languages necessary for school and social success cannot be ignored.

Thus, the question of the links between bilingualism and education are not neutral questions. The emotional charge of the debate surrounding this issue has often had nothing to do with school questions as such; often it relates to the social status of the languages and their socioeconomic and political significance. Some authors see this purely as a political question whereas others (Cummins, 1984;

Skutnabb-Kangas & Cummins, 1988) view the question as fundamental to the education of linguistic minorities.

The complexity of the questions about language is another factor in the difficulty in promoting bilingual education. What language(s) must be taught? How many languages is it possible to teach at school? How can schools maintain the mother tongue of the linguistic minorities and simultaneously teach the dominant and international link languages that are necessary? Can bilingual education be promoted for all children as an alternative to compensatory language instruction for minority children only? Obviously, there are many complex but quite vital questions. The dearth of actual bilingual education programs in a variety of sociolinguistic situations adds to this complexity. Language(s) of instruction and school failure are interrelated issues, because in most countries, there is a large number of people, particulary children, whose mother tongue is not the language of the school; they must learn to read and to write in a second language that is more prestigious than their own, resulting in gradual displacement of their mother tongue despite an apparently sympathetic school curriculum.

Types of Bilingual Education Programs

In an exhaustive analysis, Baker (1993) described two categories of education for bilingualism and biliteracy. The first one, which she calls the weak form, does not have a pluralistic goal. The mother tongue of the minority language pupils is denied and the system leads to monolingualism or a limited bilingualism. She identified several subcategories of weak programs: (a) submersion situations leading to linguistic assimilation, (b) segregationist programs where the minority linguistic pupils are taught only in their mother tongue without any links with the dominant language, (c) transitional bilingual programs in which teaching starts with the mother tongue and is gradually replaced by the dominant language; the objective is monolingualism in the dominant language without any enrichment of the mother tongue which is used as scaffolding for learning the dominant language, (d) traditional mainstream (monolingual) programs with foreign language teaching for a limited enrichment and a limited bilingualism, and, (e) separatist programs in which the minority group may have opted for preserving the minority language with autonomy and little contact with the dominant language, which results in limited bilingualism. The objectives of the second, or the strong, category are to maintain and to develop bilingualism and biliteracy. Baker included four types of bilingual education programs in this category: (a) the immersion programs (early immersion, delayed immersion, and late immersion) for the pupils of a dominant language with the school contents taught in the second language which becomes the medium of communication in the school, (b) the mainstream bilingual programs in which two majority languages are taught, (c) the maintenance or heritage language programs in the minority and majority languages with emphasis on mother tongue for pluralism, and language maintenance and development of bilingualism, and, (d) the two-way/dual language programs in which the minority and majority languages are used as languages for teaching, with the objectives of bilingual development and pluralism.

In the contemporary framework of existing bilingual programs, Baker's classification appears to be quite exhaustive. However, these programs do not cover the possibility of a bilingual education through which all children, regardless of their majority or minority group status, are given equal opportunity to maintain and develop their own language while learning the other languages. This calls for a great cultural and linguistic sensitivity and acceptance of diversity. We need a system of education for all children which is multicultural in the true sense of the term. This is a significant issue in the growing inter-cultural context throughout the world, with classrooms comprising pupils from several different mother tongues, cultures, and subcultures and calls for a different perspective to education (see also Brislin & Horvath in Volume 3 of this *Handbook*).

Bilingual Policy in Education across Cultures

In terms of the multicultural perspective previously suggested, there are three types of bilingual educational programs: dominant-language-oriented programs, minority-language-oriented programs, and integration oriented programs promoting multilingualism and multiculturalism. We shall briefly discuss each type with examples of their application drawn from different cultures and countries.

First, a number of countries have launched bilingual programs in the schools to develop broader linguistic skills in the major official language(s), sometimes including an external dominant and international language. The languages covered in these programs are usually the languages of the power groups and elites, including a high-prestige international language; the minority, minor and less powerful languages seldom find a place in this system of education. The linguistic competence with which children come to school is mostly ignored. As a result, while such programs constitute mother tongue education for some, or immersion-type programs in a language of prestige (and also a language with strong support in the homes), for a large number of children these do not provide any support for their mother tongue.

Many countries, in addition to teaching the language of the former colonial power, have programs for maintenance of the other national language(s), following UNESCO recommendations. Singapore, for example, is a multilingual and multicultural country; most (77%) are Chinese, while others are Malays, Indians, and "others," including Eurasians, Europeans, and Arabs. The four official languages do not represent all the mother tongues of the resident people. However, for the last two decades, bilingual schooling has been a reality in this country. The official policy has extended the mother tongue notion from Chinese to Malay and Tamil languages for the main ethnic groups. In addition, English is used in the program as a language of international communication with a particularly high status (Pakir, 1993).

In many countries, the questions of the links between local language(s) and "colonial" language are still debated. In India, despite the official three language policy, English has continued as an elitist language adversely affecting the fate of the mother tongues. In the erstwhile French colonies, too, the issues with respect to French and local mother tongue languages are quite similar. In Western and developed countries, although second languages are taught in schools, the approaches and outcomes are, by and large, monolingual.

In Luxembourg, a mainstream bilingual education program exists with the objective of developing trilingual competence in all pupils (whose mother tongue is Luxemburger) by the end of their schooling. Disciplines are taught in Luxemburger, French, and German (the three languages of the country) throughout the school curriculum. Here, too, the mother tongues are not given equal opportunities; the Luxemburger children and those of other minor mother tongues are somewhat discriminated against. Some other regions of Europe have bilingual programs for language maintenance and identity and, in some cases, political status. In Italy, in the Val d'Aoste region bordering France and Switzerland, people were French speakers. However, with the dominant status of Italian, there was a gradual language shift in favor of Italian. In face of this reality, the Valdotian school system decided to organize a bilingual program from preschool onward to promote bilingualism for all children.

In Spain, the end of the Franco period permitted some Spanish regions to teach the regional languages spoken in the families and/or essential for the identity of the community (Catalan, Galician, and Basque languages, for example). All children in these areas are now taught in both the regional and national languages. Under the changed circumstances, the possible problems of speakers of Spanish, now reduced to a lower status, and other languages have to be carefully examined in view of the possibility that these bilingual programs might become dominant monolingual ones in a different form.

Finally, there are the European school programs mostly for the children of the functionaries of the European Community. These schools, in Belgium, Italy, Germany, Holland, and England, promote mainstream bilingual education and offer eight different language sections for children who begin their curriculum in their native tongue and also receive second language instruction in English, French, or German. These European school programs seem to be very successful in achieving pluralistic objectives. However, the programs are still viewed as elitist in nature and the extent to which the outcomes are generalizable remains to be seen in situations where languages, their status and the attitudes towards the languages of instruction are different.

Bilingual Educational Policy for Minority Groups

With increasing economic and political migration to Western countries, and school failures of many children of the migrant communities, some special programs have been developed to accommodate mother tongues of these children in their schools. The objectives of these programs are not to promote a real bilingual education but to facilitate transition from the mother tongue to the dominant language, which eventually becomes the only language in the curriculum. In terms of Baker's (1993) categories, such programs are transitional ones. For example, the Swedish program of teaching Finnish immigrant children in their mother tongue for some time before using Swedish as the medium of instruction is transitional (Skutnabb-Kangas, 1985). The approach in these programs is one of compensatory education. Initial positive outcomes have led to an extension of such programs to other minority groups in Sweden as well as in some other European countries. In some of the minority language programs, public schools collaborate with the minority communities to obtain teachers from within the community to teach children of their community for a few hours a week, but seldom during the school time. The Canadian heritage language programs are of this type. Even with these programs of minority language instruction, it has not been possible to achieve their limited objectives for several reasons. Given the linguistic diversity in the countries of origin of the immigrants, it has not been possible to accommodate the mother tongues of all children; as a result, some of the immigrant children are left with a burden of an additional language of their home country that is not their mother tongue. In Switzerland, for example, all Spanish migrant children are taught Castilian, whereas a large number of the children have other mother tongues such as Galician and Catalan.

These programs seem to have heterogeneous objectives and philosophies, perhaps modified from time to time with inputs from sociolinguistic and psycholinguistic research and from changing policies. In the process, the programs have sometimes changed their character from being heritage to transitional programs, with some having a maintenance orientation. Under certain conditions, minority language programs are used as segregation programs (see Skutnabb-Kangas, 1985 for examples). A general observation about all these programs is that they seldom modify the hierarchical relationship and the status differential between the dominant language and the mother tongues of the minority children, and the programs do not lead to any real recognition of the minority languages. The situation is better when sometimes, to break the hierarchical relationship between the languages and the ethos of school monolingualism, foreign (minority community) and national teachers work together for some hours a week with equal status (Berthelier, 1986). The linguistic complexity of the migration and multilingual situations throughout the world have made the traditional approaches based on the simplistic notions of minority and majority languages quite inadequate. New multilingual and multicultural perspectives and radical attitudinal changes are needed, at all levels, with respect to the sociocultural and economic significance of different languages in a society. It has become imperative to devise ways of breaking the dominant monolingual bias of the educational systems and to recognize what some authors believe to be the basic linguistic human right of a child.

Integration Oriented Programs: Bilingual Policy for All

National programs of education are always meant for all children but, in reality, only some of them have the luck to become bilingual or multilingual under ideal conditions. However, a multicultural perspective is not as impossible to realize as it may seem because it does not contradict, but complements, some of the steps already taken in some multilingual contexts. Following the Bullock Report (1975) about the state of language teaching in England, several new propositions have emerged with respect to the teaching of English and its relationship to home languages. Some of these pedagogical proposals have sought to modify the orientations and attitudes toward language teaching. These approaches call for an interactive view of the relationship between the different mother tongues of children and other languages in order to develop a holistic perspective in which the home and the school languages are seen not as antagonistic but complementary to each other, forming different aspects of the child's total linguistic and communicative competence. In his proposals known as "awareness of language," Hawkins (1984) suggested specific steps toward developing consciousness and sensitivity to linguistic diversity in order to create a positive set of attitudes towards languages and their speakers. In multilingual cities and countries, from the preschool on, it is important to organize activities for the acknowledgment of all languages present in the classroom and for the familiarization with other languages. Some classrooms such as the ones in France (Caporale, 1990; Dabène, 1991; Moore, 1993) and in Switzerland (Perregaux, 1994; Perregaux, 1995; Perregaux & Magnin Hottelier, 1995; De Pietro, 1995) now promote this approach which also comes with multicultural education.

Bilingual education policies can be viewed from two directions: top-down—from the perspective of official policies—and bottom-up—from the language learners' perspective. Clearly, both of these points of view are essential for the development of a positive and realistic bilingual education policy.

Conclusions

The present review, like the ones by Bowerman (1981) and Segalowitz (1981) in the earlier edition of the *Handbook,* has shown that our understanding of the processes of language acquisition and bilingualism has benefited immensely from cross-cultural studies, although a lot more remains to be done. The discussions in the preceding sections have underscored the complexity of the psycholinguistic and social processes underlying the acquisition of language(s) and bilingualism and their social, psychological, and educational implications.

By and large, language acquisition research continues to be guided by the dominant impact of Chomsky's theory and approaches, despite their changing nature and in face of increasing opposition to Chomskian views. As the emphasis has gradually shifted away from syntax (the form and structure) to semantic and pragmatic aspects of language, researchers have shown a growing interest in studying the cultural context of language use. While the language acquisition studies of the 1960s and 1970s were focused on the observation of limited samples of children to infer general patterns in acquisition, later studies have sought to examine individual variations within languages as well as cross-linguistic and cross-cultural variations in the process of acquisition. As cross-linguistic data continue to accumulate, existing theoretical positions and assumptions about the processes involved in the development of language have come to be questioned and modified. At the same time, language-specific and universal patterns of development have also been identified. Slobin's (1973, 1985b, 1992) operating principles to account for cross-linguistic similarities and differences in language acquisition and the analyses of sentence processing in a number of languages using the competition model are good examples of the use of the cross-linguistic database for theoretical and conceptual developments in the field. However, cross-linguistic studies are limited by their emphasis on the form and structure of language and a relative lack of focus on the sociocultural context of language use.

Concerns regarding the analysis of the sociocultural dimensions of language development are reflected in attempts to examine the role of maternal input in language acquisition. The work on the "motherese hypothesis" has been quite productive, though somewhat controversial. Findings about the role of mother's speech in children's language development are not very consistent. As has been noted by Hampson and Nelson (1993), the effects of maternal speech may be noticeable early in a child's development rather than later. As such, although the initial enthusiasm with the motherese hypothesis has waned, a continuing interest, in a cross-cultural perspective, in the nature and processes of mother's impact as well as those of grandparents and other adults on individual differences in language development can be expected.

Recent studies on language socialization have also emphasized the role of the primary caretaker and other family members in the development of social competence in communication. These studies have shown that learning to communicate involves much more than the acquisition of the rules and formal structure of language; a child also has to learn the socially appropriate use of language, including the use of language to delineate different role relations and status, and to communicate affect and values. While the initial cross-cultural studies of language socialization have been primarily anthropological in orientation, future studies can be expected to be more psychological in nature, looking into the processes of language socialization and the role of the significant socializing agents in this process. From a cross-cultural point of view also, future studies on language socialization could focus on different cultural parameters and devices in transmitting the social norms of language use within a cultural context. For example, Mohanty (1994) has shown how children growing up in multilingual contexts develop awareness of different languages in their environment and the rules for the socially appropriate use of multiple languages. Quite clearly, the tasks of language socialization in multilingual societies are characteristically different from those in dominant monolingual ones. The hierarchical differentiation of varieties of language use and the complex relationships between different languages in multilingual societies make learning to communicate a much more complex process than simply learning the rules of a language and its use. The processes of language acquisition will be observed in complex sociolinguistic contexts of different non-Western settings in future cross-cultural research. The impetus for this seems to have been generated through the current cross-linguistic studies and studies on social influences on language development. As a result, one can expect to find increasing emphasis on sociocultural variables in developmental psycholinguistic research. Further, it has already been realized that the development of communicative competence hardly takes place in a pure monolingual environment for a majority of the world's children. As such, the monolingual bias in acquisition research seems unjustified and, as attempts are made to understand language acquisition in multilingual settings, some of our generalizations regarding language development (based primarily on data from dominant monolingual Western environments) will come to be questioned. The debate over the nature and role of the mother tongue and its relationship with other languages (e.g., Skutnabb-Kangas, 1984; Skutnabb-Kangas & Cummins, 1988) exemplifies the changing sociocultural perspectives on language development.

For most children in the modern world, language development usually involves simultaneous or successive acquisition of multiple languages or, at least, acquisition of one language in the context of many others in the milieu. This has made bilingualism or multilingualism a phenomenon of greater significance and challenge. In the previous edition of the *Handbook*, Segalowitz (1981) examined the field of bilingualism research to deal with the questions of social conditions responsible for bilingual development, and the cognitive and social consequences of bilingualism for the individual. The present review shows that research in the field of bilingualism has become much more broad-based, going beyond the earlier North American and European work. There is now sound evidence from a variety of cultural settings supporting the positive role of bilingualism in cognitive development, which can be attributed to the metalinguistic and metacognitive advantage of bilinguals and to the social context of bilingualism particularly in multilingual countries. As new findings from a number of different societies accumulate, bilingualism has come to be viewed as a positive social force promoting adaptive cultural relations, pluralism, and better integration. These findings have emphasized a fundamental distinction between the dominant monolingual countries and the multilingual ones in terms of the very nature of bilingualism and its consequences. Cross-cultural comparisons of social and psychological aspects of bilingualism in monolingual and multilingual contexts will further our understanding of the effects of bilingualism on the individual and society.

Finally, as the language scenario throughout the world changes with large scale migrations and language contact, the question of the role of mother tongues, minor, and minority languages in educational curricula has become quite important. Education can no longer follow a traditional monolingual framework; it has become increasingly necessary to provide bilingual education programs to accommodate the need for development of communicative and academic competence in minority mother tongues, regional and national languages, and international link languages. To cater to this growing need, bilingual education in various forms and with different rationales has been developed and tried in a large number of countries. The present review has sought to provide a conceptual analysis of bilingual education programs in a cross-cultural perspective. The increasing complexity of the sociolinguistic structure of different cultures, the changing awareness of the linguistic rights of minority groups, and the gradual acceptance of multiculturalism as national policy in different parts of the world have posed new challenges to our understanding of the processes of development and use of language(s) and their social, psychological, and educational implications. Cross-cultural analysis can help meet this challenge.

References

Abdallah-Pretceille, M. (1986). *Vers une pédagogie interculturelle*. Paris: Institut National de Recherche Pédagogique.

Aitchison, J. (1989). *The articulate mammal*. London: Unwin Hyman.

Aksu-Koc, A. A. & Slobin, D. I. (1985). The acquisition of Turkish. In D. I. Slobin (Ed.), *The crosslinguistic study of language acquisition* (pp. 839–876). Hillsdale, NJ: Erlbaum.

Anderson, E. S. (1986). The acquisition of register variation by Anglo-American children. In B. B. Schieffelin & E. Ochs (Eds.), *Language socialization across cultures* (pp.153–164). Cambridge: Cambridge University Press.

Azurmendi, M. J. & Espi, M. J. (1994). Ethnolinguistic vitality and ethnosocial identity. Paper presented at the XII International Congress of Cross-Cultural Psychology, Pamplona, Spain.

Babu, N. & Mohanty, A. K. (1982). Detection of syntactic ambiguity by unilingual and bilingual tribal children. *Indian Psychologist, 1*, 25-30.

Bakeman, R., Adamson, L. B., Konner, M., & Barr, R. G. (1990). Kung infancy: The social context of object exploration. *Child Development, 61*, 794–801.

Baker, C. (1993). *Foundations of bilingual education and bilingualism*. Clevedon: Multilingual Matters.

Bates, E. & MacWhinney, B. (1987). Competition, variation and language learning. In B. MacWhinney (Ed.), *Mechanisms of language acquisition* (pp. 157–195). Hillsdale, NJ: Lawrence Erlbaum.

Berko-Gleason, J. & Bernstein Ratner, N. (Eds.). (1993). *Psycholinguistics*. New York: Harcourt Brace.

Berry, J. W. (1980). Acculturation as varieties of adaptation. In A. Padilla (Ed.), *Acculturation: Theory, models and some new findings* (pp. 9–25). Washington: American Association for the Advancement of Science.

Berry, J. W. (1984). Cultural relations in plural societies: Alternatives to segregation and their sociopsychological implications. In N. Miller & M. Brewer (Eds.), *Groups in contact* (pp. 11–27). New York: Academic Press.

Berry, J. W. (1990). Psychology of acculturation: Understanding individuals moving between cultures. In R. W. Brislin (Ed.), *Applied cross-cultural psychology*, (pp. 232–253). London: Sage.

Berthelier, R. (1986). L'échec des enfants migrants: un problème de langue. In ANPASE (Ed.), *Enfances et cultures, problématique de la différence et pratiques de l'interculturel* (pp. 154–183). Toulouse: Privat.

Bialystok, E. (1990). *Communication strategies*. Oxford: Blackwell.

Bialystock, E. (1992). Selective attention in cognitive processing: The bilingual edge. In R. J. Harris (Ed.), *Cognitive processing in bilinguals* (pp. 501–514). Amsterdam: Elsevier.

Bild, E. R. & Swain, M. (1989). Minority language students in a French immersion program: Their French proficiency. *Journal of Multilingual and Multicultural Development, 10*, 255–274.

Bourhis, R. Y., Giles, H., & Rosenthal, D. (1981). Notes on the construction of a 'Subjective Vitality Questionnaire' for the development of ethnic groups. *Journal of Multilingual and Multicultural Development, 2*, 145–155.

Bourhis, R. Y. & Sachdev, I. (1984). Subjective vitality perception and language attitudes in

Hamilton. *Journal of Language and Social Psychology, 3,* 97–126.

Bowerman, M. (1981). Language development. In H. C. Triandis & A. Heron (Eds.), *Handbook of cross-cultural psychology* (Vol. 4, pp. 93–187), Boston: Allyn and Bacon.

Bowerman, M. (1985). What shapes children's grammar? In D. I. Slobin (Ed.), *The crosslinguistic study of language acquisition* (pp. 1257–1319), Vol. 2. Hillsdale, NJ: Erlbaum.

Braine, M. D. S. (1994). Is nativism sufficient? *Journal of Child Language, 21,* 9–31.

Bruner, J. (1975). The ontogenesis of speech acts. *Journal of Child Language 4,* 1–19.

Bruner, J. (1978). The role of dialogue in language acquisition. In A. Sinclair, R. J. Jarvella & W. J. M. Levelt (Eds.), *The child's conception of language* (pp. 241–246). New York: Springer-Verlag.

Bullock Report. (1975). *A language for life: Report of the Committee of inquiry appointed by the Secretary of State for education and science under the chairmanship of Sir Alan Bullock.* London.

Camilleri C. (1990). *Stratégies identitaires.* Paris: PUF.

Caporale, D. (1990). "L'éveil aux langages": une voie nouvelle pour l'apprentissage précoce des langues. *Lidil, 2,* 128–141.

Cenoz, J. & Valencia, J. F. (1993). Ethnolinguistic vitality, social networks and motivation in second language acquisition: Some data from the Basque country. *Language, Culture and Curriculum, 6,* 1–15.

Cenoz, J. & Valencia, J. F. (1994). Additive trilingualism: Evidence from the Basque country. *Applied Psycholinguistics, 15,* 197–209.

Chomsky, N. (1957). *Syntactic structures.* The Hague: Mouton.

Chomsky, N. (1965). *Aspects of the theory of syntax.* Cambridge, MA: MIT Press.

Chomsky, N. (1986). *Knowledge of language: Its nature, origin and use.* New York: Praeger.

Clément, R. (1980). Ethnicity, contact and communicative competence in a second language. In H. Giles, W. P. Robinson, & P. Smith (Eds.), *Language: Social psychological perspectives* (pp.147–154). Oxford: Pergamon Press.

Coste, D. & Hébrard, J. (1991). *Vers le plurilinguisme.* Paris: Hachette.

Cummins, J. (1976). The influence of bilingualism on cognitive growth: A synthesis of research findings and explanatory hypothesis. *Working Papers on Bilingualism, 9,* 1–43.

Cummins, J. (1978). Bilingualism and development of metalinguistic awareness. *Journal of Cross-Cultural Psychology, 9,* 131–149.

Cummins, J. (1979). Linguistic interdependence and the educational development of bilingual children. *Review of Educational Research, 49,* 222–251.

Cummins, J. (1981a). The role of primary language development in promoting educational success for language minority students. In California State Department of Education, *Schooling and language minority students: A theoretical framework.* Los Angeles: Evaluation, Dissemination and Assessment Centre.

Cummins, J. (1981b). *Bilingualism and minority language children.* Toronto: Ontario Institute for Studies in Education.

Cummins, J. (1984). *Bilingualism and special education: Issues in assessment and pedagogy.* Clevedon: Multilingual Matters.

Cummins, J. (1987). L'éducation bilingue: théorie et mise en oeuvre. In Centre pour la recherche et l'immigration dans l'enseignement (Ed.), *L'éducation multiculturelle* (pp. 323–353). Paris: Organisation de Coopération et de Développement Economiques.

Curtis, S. (1981). Dissociation between language and cognition: Cases and implications. *Journal of Autism and Developmental Disorders, 11,* 15–30.

Curtis, S. (1982). Developmental dissociation of language and cognition. In L. K. Obler & L. Menn (Eds.), *Exceptional language and linguistics* (pp. 286–312). New York: Academic Press.

Dabène, L. (1991). Enseignement précoce d'une langue ou Eveil aux langages. In M. Garabédian (Ed.), *Enseignements/Apprentissages précoces des langues* (pp. 57–65). Paris: Hachette.

Dasen, P. (1993). L'ethnocentrisme de la psychologie. In M. Rey (Ed.), *Psychologie clinique et interrogations culturelles* (pp. 155–174). Paris: L'Harmattan.

Dellacorte, M., Benedict, H., & Klein, D. (1983). The relationship of pragmatic dimensions of mother's speech to the referential expressive distinction. *Journal of Child Language, 10,* 35–43.

Demuth, K. (1986). Prompting routines in the language socialization of Bosotho children. In B. B. Schieffelin & E. Ochs (Eds.), *Language socialization across cultures* (pp. 51–79). Cambridge: Cambridge University Press, .

De Pietro, J.-F. (1995). Vivre et apprendre les langues autrement à l'école. *Babylonia, 2,* 32–37.

Dodson, C. J. (1985). Second language acquisition and bilingual development: A theoretical framework. *Journal of Multilingual and Multiculturel Development, 65,* 325–346.

Eilers, R. E., Gavin, W. J., & Oller, D. K. (1982). Cross-linguistic perception in infancy: Early effects on linguistic experience. *Journal of Child Language, 9,* 289–302.

Eisenberg, A. R. (1986). Teasing: verbal play in two Mexican houses. In B.B. Schieffelin & E. Ochs (Eds.), *Language socialization across cultures* (pp. 182–198). Cambridge: Cambridge University Press, .

Fishman, J. (1960). A systematization of the Whorfian hypothesis. *Behavioural Science, 5,* 323–339.

Fodor, J. A., Bever, T. G., & Garrett, M. F. (1974). *The psychology of language.* New York: McGraw Hill.

Furrow, D. & Nelson, K. (1984). Environmental correlates of individual differences in language acquisition. *Journal of Child Language, 11,* 523–534.

Furrow, D., Nelson, K., & Benedict, H. (1979). Mother's speech to children and syntactic development: Some simple relationships. *Journal of Child Language, 6,* 423–442.

Galambos, S. J. & Hakuta, K. (1988). Subject-specific and task-specific characteristics of metalinguistic awareness in bilingual children. *Applied Psycholinguistics, 9,* 141–162.

Gardner, H. (1984). The development of competence in culturally defined domains: A preliminary framework. In R. A. Shweder & R. A. LeVine (Eds.), *Culture theory: essays on mind, self, and emotion* (pp. 257–275). Cambridge: Cambridge University Press.

Giles, H., Bourhis, R. Y., & Taylor, D. M. (1977). Towards a theory of language in ethnic group relations. In H. Giles (Ed.), *Language, ethnicity and Intergroup Relations* (pp. 307–348). London: Academic Press.

Giles, H. & Byrne, J. L. (1982). An intergroup approach to second language acquisition. *Journal of Multilingual and Multicultural Development, 3,* 17–40.

Giles, H. & Johnson, P. (1981). The role of language in ethnic group relations. In J. C. Turner & H. Giles (Eds.), *Intergroup Behaviour* (pp. 199–243). Oxford: Pergamon.

Giles, H., Rosenthal, D., & Young, L. (1985). Perceived ethnolinguistic vitality: The Anglo-and Greek-Australia setting. *Journal of Multilingual and Multicultural Development, 6,* 253–269.

Gleitman, L., Newport, E., & Gleitman, H. (1984). The current status of the motherese hypothesis. *Journal of Child Language, 11,* 43–79.

Goldfield, B. & Snow, C. E. (1993). Individual differences in language acquisition. In J. Berko Gleason (Eds.), *The development of language* (3rd ed.). New York: Macmillan.

Gombert, J.-E. (1990). *Le développement métalinguistique.* Paris: PUF.

Goodluck, H. (1991). *Language acquisition.* Oxford: Blackwell.

Grosjean, F. (1982). *Life with two languages. An introduction to bilingualism.* Cambridge: Harvard University Press.

Hamers, J.-F. & Blanc, M. (1983). *Bilingualité et Bilinguisme.* Bruxelles: Mardaga.

Hampson, J. (1988). Individual differences in style of language acquisition in relation to social networks. In S. Salzinger, J. Antrobus, & M. Hammer (Eds.), *Social networks of children, adolescents and college students* (pp. 37–58). Hillsdale, NJ: Erlbaum.

Hampson, J. & Nelson, K. (1993). The relation of maternal language to variation in rate and style of language acquisition. *Journal of Child Language, 20,* 313–342.

Harris, R. J. (Ed.). (1992). *Cognitive processing in bilinguals.* Amsterdam: North-Holland.

Hawkins, W. (1984). *Awareness of language.* Cambridge: Cambridge University Press.

Helot, C. (1988). Bringing up children in English, French and Irish: Two case studies. *Language, Culture and Curriculum, 1,* 281–287.

Hoffman, C. (1985). Language acquisition in two

trilingual children. *Journal of Multilingual and Multicultural Development, 6,* 479–495.

Kraemer, R. & Olshtain, E. (1989). Perceived ethnolinguistic vitality and language attitudes: The Israeli setting. *Journal of Multilingual and Multicultural Development, 9,* 255–269.

Labrie, N. & Clement, R. (1986). Ethnolinguistic vitality, self-confidence and second language proficiency: An investigation. *Journal of Multilingual and Multicultural Development, 7,* 269–282.

Lambert, W. E. (1975). Culture and language as factors in learning and education. In A. Wolfgang (Ed.), *Education and immigrant students.* Toronto: Ontario Institute of Studies in Education.

Lambert, W. E. (1977). The effect of bilingualism on the individual: Cognitive and sociocultural consequences. In P. A. Hornby (Ed.), *Bilingualism: Psychological, social and educational implications* (pp. 15–27). New York: Academic Press.

Leopold, W. (1939–1949). *Speech development of a bilingual child* (Vols. 1–4). Evanston, IL: Northwestern University Press.

Li, P., Bates, E., Liu, H., & MacWhinney, B. (1992). Cues as functional constraints on sentence processing in Chinese. In H. C. Chen & O. J. L. Tzeng (Eds.), *Language processing in Chinese* (pp. 207–234). New York: Elsevier.

Lieven, E. V. M., Pine, J. M. & Barnes, H. D. (1992). Individual differences in early vocabulary development: Redefining the referential expressive distinction. *Journal of Child Language, 19,* 287–310.

Lüdi, G. & Py, B. (1986). *Etre bilingue.* Berne: Lang.

Mackey, W. F. (1970). A typology of bilingual education. *Foreign Language Annals, 3:4,* 596–608.

Mackey, W. F. (1976). *Bilinguisme et contact des langues.* Paris: Klincksieck.

MacWhinney, B. (1987). The competition model. In B. MacWhinney (Ed.), *Mechanisms of language acquisition* (pp. 249–308). Hillsdale, NJ: Erlbaum.

MacWhinney, B. & Bates, E. (1989). *The cross-linguistic study of sentence processing.* Cambridge: Cambridge University Press.

MacWhinney, B. & Snow, C. (1985). The child language data exchange system. *Journal of Child Language, 12,* 271–296.

Maratsos, M. (1978). New models in linguistics and language acquisition. In M. Halle, J. Bresnan, & G.A. Miller (Eds.), *Linguistic theory and psychological reality.* Cambridge, MA: Cambridge University Press.

McDonald, L. & Pien, D. (1982). Mother conversational behaviour as a function of interactional intent. *Journal of Child Language, 9,* 337–358.

McLaughlin, B. (1978). *Second language acquisition in childhood.* Hillsdale, NJ: Erlbaum.

McLaughlin, B. (1984a). Early bilingualism: Methodological and theoretical issues. In M. Paradis & Y. Lebrun (Eds.), *Early bilingualism and child development,* (pp. 19–45). Lisse, Holland: Swets & Zeitlinger.

McLaughlin, B. (1984b). *Second language acquisition in childhood. Volume 1: Preschool children.* Hillsdale, NJ: Erlbaum.

McLaughlin, B. (1985). *Second language acquisition in childhood. Volume 2: School Age Children.* Hillsdale, NJ: Erlbaum.

Mehler, J. (1990). *Naître humain.* Paris: O. Jacob.

Miller, P. (1986). Teasing as language socialization and verbal play in working-class community. In B. B. Schieffelin & E. Ochs (Eds.), *Language socialization across cultures* (pp. 199–212). Cambridge: Cambridge University Press .

Mohanty, A. K. (1982a). Cognitive and linguistic development of tribal children from unilingual and bilingual environment. In R. Rath, H. S. Asthana, D. Sinha & J. B. P. Sinha (Eds.), *Diversity and unity in cross-cultural psychology* (pp.78–87). Lisse: Swets & Zeitlinger.

Mohanty, A. K. (1982b). Bilingualism among Kond tribals in Orissa (India): Consequences, issues and implications. *Indian Psychologist, 1,* 33–44.

Mohanty, A. K. (1990). Psychological consequences of mother tongue maintenace and multilingualism in India. *Psychology and Developing Societies, 2,* 31–51.

Mohanty, A. K. (1991). Social psychological aspects of languages in contact in multilingual societies. In G. Misra (Ed.), *Applied social psychology in India* (pp. 61–83). New Delhi: Sage.

Mohanty, A. K. (1994). Bilingualism in a multilingual society: Implications for cultural integration and education. Keynote Address in the International Congress of Applied Psychology, Madrid, Spain.

Mohanty, A. K. & Babu, N. (1983). Bilingualism and metalinguistic ability among Kond tribals in Orissa, India. *The Journal of Social Psychology, 121,* 15–22.

Mohanty, A. K. & Das, S. P. (1987). Cognitive and metalinguistic ability of unschooled bilingual and unilingual tribal children. *Psychological Studies, 32,* 5–8.

Moore, D. (1993). Entre langues étrangères et langues d'origine: transformer la diversité en atout d'apprentissage. *Etudes de Linguistique Appliquée, 89,* 97–106.

Moreau, M.-L. & Richelle, M. (1981). *L'acquisition du langage.* Bruxelles. Mardaga.

Nelson, K. (1973). Structure and strategy in learning to talk. *Monograph of the Society for Research in Child Development, 38,* (1–2, Serial No. 149).

Nelson, K. (1981a). Individual differences in language development: Implications for development and language. *Developmental Psychology, 17,* 170–187.

Nelson, K. (1981b). Social cognition in a script framework. In J. Flavell & L. Ross (Eds.), *Social cognitive development* (pp. 97–118). Cambridge: Cambridge University Press.

Nelson, K., Hampson, J., & Shaw, L. K. (1993). Nouns in early lexicons: Evidence, explanations and implications. *Journal of Child Language, 20,* 61–84.

Newport, E. L., Gleitman, H., & Gleitman, L. R. (1977). Mother, I'd rather do it myself: The contribution of selected child listener variables. In C. E. Snow & C. A. Ferguson (Eds.), *Talking to children: language input and acquisition* (pp. 109–150). Cambridge: Cambridge University Press.

Ochs, E. (1986). Introduction. In B. B. Schieffelin & E. Ochs (Eds.), *Language socialization across cultures* (pp. 1–13). Cambridge: Cambridge University Press.

Ochs, E. & Schieffelin, B. B. (1984). Language acquisition and socialization: Three developmental stories. In R. A. Shweder & R. A. LeVine (Eds.), *Culture theory: Essays on mind, self, and emotion* (pp. 276–320). Cambridge: Cambridge University Press.

Oksaar, E. (1989). Minoriesierung der Muttersprache in der Schule. In B. Py & R. Jeanneret (Eds.), *Minorisation linguistique et interaction* (pp. 137–150). Université de Neuchâtel: Faculté des lettres.

Olsen-Fulero, L. (1982). Style and stability in mother conversational behaviour: A study of individual differences. *Journal of Child Language, 9,* 543–564.

Othenin-Girard, C. (1995). Bilinguisme et acquisition du langage chez l'enfant de travailleur migrant. In E. Poglia, A.-N. Perret-Clermont, A. Gretler & P. Dasen (Eds.), *Pluralité culturelle et éducation en Suisse* (pp. 221–231). Berne: Lang.

Pakir, A. (1993). Issues in second language curriculum development: Singapore, Malaysia, Brunei. *Annual Review of Applied Linguistics, 13,* 3–23.

Patnaik, K. & Mohanty, A. K. (1984). Relationship between metalinguistic and cognitive development of bilingual and unilingual tribal children. *Psycholingua,14,* 63–70.

Peal, E. & Lambert, W. E. (1962). The relationship of bilingualism to intelligence. *Psychological Monographs, 76,* 1–23.

Perera, K. (1994). Child language research: Building on the past, looking to the future. *Journal of Child Language, 21,*1–7.

Perregaux, C. (1994). *Les enfants à deux voix- Des effets du bilinguisme sur l'apprentissage de la lecture.* Berne: Lang.

Perregaux, C. (1995). L'école, espace plurilingue. *Lidil, 11,* 125–139.

Perregaux, C. & Magnin Hottelier, S. (1995). Quand l'école accueille Pierre, Pedro, Peter et Cie. *Babylonia, 2 ,* 51–56.

Peters, A. M. (1983). *The units of language acquisition.* Cambridge: Cambridge University Press.

Peters, A. M. & Boggs, S. T. (1986). Interactional routines as cultural influences upon language acquisition. In B. B. Schieffelin & E. Ochs (Eds.), *Language socialisation across cultures* (pp. 80–96). Cambridge: Cambridge University Press.

Platt, M. (1986). Social norms nad lexical acquisition in a study of deictic verbs in Samoan child language. In B. B. Schieffelin & E. Ochs (Eds.), *Language socialization across cultures* (pp. 127–152). Cambridge: Cambridge University Press.

Pujol, M. (1990). *Manifestations du comportement bilingue chez des enfants migrants: analyse d'activités langagières orales et écrites.* Thèse de doctorat: Université de Genève.

Py, B. (1991). Bilinguisme, exolinguisme et acquisition: rôle de L1 dans l'acquisition de L2. In *Network on code-switching and language contact.* (pp.115–138) Strasbourg: European Science Foundation.

Rabain, J. (1979). *L'enfant du lignage. Du sevrage à la classe d'âge chez les Wolof du Sénégal.* Paris: Payot.

Rabain-Jamin, J. (1994a). Language socialization of the child in African families living in France. In P. M. Greenfield & R. R. Cocking (Eds.), *Cross-cultural roots of minority child development* (pp. 147–166). Hillsdale, NJ: Erlbaum.

Rabain-Jamin, J. (1994b). Using language to socialze infants and toddlers: France and Senegal. Paper presented at *Interdependence and independence as cultural scripts for development,* XIIIth Biennial Meeting of the International Society for the Study of Behavioural Development (ISSBD), Amsterdam.

Rabain-Jamin, J. & Sabeau-Jouannet, E. (1994). Genèse des marques de la personne en francais et en wolof: les premiers dialogues mère-enfant. *La Linguistique, 30,* .

Ricciardelli, L. A. (1992). Bilingualism and cognitive development in relation to threshold theory. *Journal of Psycholinguistic Research, 21,* 301–316.

Richman, A. L., LeVine, R. A., Staples New, R., Howrigan, G. A., Welles-Nyström, B. & LeVine,S. E. (1988). Maternal behavior to infants in five cultures. In R. A. LeVine, P. M. Miller, & M. Maxwell West (Eds.), *Parental behavior in diverse societies* (pp. 81–98). San Francisco: Jossey-Bass.

Rieben, L. & Perfetti, C. (1991a). *L'apprenti lecteur.* Neuchâtel-Paris: Delachaux & Niestlé.

Rieben, L. & Perfetti, C. (1991b). *Learning to read.* Hillsdale, NJ: Erlbaum.

Romaine, S. (1989). *Bilingualism.* Oxford: Blackwell.

Romay-Martinez, J. & Garcia-Mira, R. (1994). Language power and ethnic identity. Paper presented in the XII International Congress of Cross-Cultural Psychology, Pamplona, Spain.

Ronjat, J. (1913). *Le développement du langage observé chez un enfant bilingue.* Paris: Champion.

Roulet, E. (1980). *Langue maternelle et langues secondes, vers une pédagogie intégrée.* Paris: Hatier-CREDIF.

Roulet, E. (1995). Peut-on intégrer l'enseignement-apprentissage décalé de plusieurs langues? *Babylonia, 2,* 22–26.

Ryan, E. B., Hewstone, M., & Giles, H. (1984). Language and intergroup attitudes. In J. R. Eiser (Ed.), *Attitudinal judgement.* New York: Springer-Verlag.

Sabatier, C. (1986). La mère et son bébé: variations culturelles. Analyse critique de la littérature. *International Journal of Psychology, 47,* 177–181.

Saunders, G. (1988). *Bilingual children: From birth to teens.* Clevedon: Multilingual Matters.

Scarborough, H. & Wyckoff, J. (1986). Mother, I'd rather do it myself: Some further non effects of 'motherese.' *Journal of Child Language, 13,* 431–437.

Schieffelin, B. B. (1986). Teasing and shaming in Kaluli children's interactions.In B.B. Schieffelin & E. Ochs (Eds.), *Language socialization across cultures* (pp. 165–181). Cambridge: Cambridge University Press.

Schlesinger, I. M. (1982). *Steps to language: Toward a theory of language acquisition.* Hillsdale, NJ: Erlbaum.

Schlesinger, I. M. (1988). The origin of relational categories. In Y. Levy, I. M. Schlesinger & M. D. S. Braine (Eds.), *Categories and processes in language acquisition* (pp. 121–178). Hillsdale, NJ: Erlbaum.

Segalowitz, N. S. (1981). Issues in the cross-cultural study of bilingual development. In H. C. Triandis & A. Heron (Eds.), *Handbook of cross-cultural psychology,* (Vol.4, pp. 55–92). Boston: Allyn and Bacon.

Siguan, M. & Mackey, W. F. (1986). *Education et bilinguisme.* UNESCO. Neuchâtel-Paris: Delachaux & Niestlé.

Sinclair-de-Zwart, H. (1969). Developmental

psycholinguistics. In D. Elkind & J. Flavell (Eds.), *Studies in cognitive development* (pp. 315–336). Oxford: Oxford University Press.

Singh, A. (1994). Role of grand parents in language development of the Indian child. Paper presented at the 23rd International Congress of Applied Psychology. Madrid, Spain.

Singleton, D. (1989). *Language acquisition: The age factor.* Clevedon: Multilingual Matters.

Skutnabb-Kangas, T. (1975). Bilingualism, semilingualism and school achievement. Paper presented at the Fourth International Congress of Applied Linguistics, Stuttgart.

Skutnabb-Kangas, T. (1984). *Bilingualism or not: The education of minorities.* Clevedon: Multilingual Matters.

Skutnabb-Kangas, T. (1985). Resource power and autonomy through discourse in conflict: A Finnish migrant school strike in Sweden. Unpublished report, Roskilde University.

Skutnabb-Kangas, T. & Cummins, J. (Eds.). (1988). *Minority education from shame to struggle.* Clevedon: Multilingual Matters.

Slobin, D. I. (1973). Cognitive prerequisites for the development of grammar. In C. A. Ferguson & D. I. Slobin (Eds.), *Studies of child language development* (pp. 175–211). New York: Holt, Rinehart & Winston.

Slobin, D. I. (1985a). Introduction: Why study acquisition crosslinguistically? In D. I. Slobin (Ed.), *The crosslinguistic study of language acquisition,* Vol.1 (pp. 3–24). Hillsdale, NJ: Erlbaum.

Slobin, D. I. (1985b). Crosslinguistic evidence for the language-making capacity. In D. I. Slobin (Ed.), *The crosslinguistic study of language acquisition, Vol. 2* (pp. 1157–1250). Hillsdale, NJ: Erlbaum.

Slobin, D. I. (1992). Introduction. In D. I. Slobin (Ed.), *The crosslinguistic study of language acquisition. Vol. 3* (pp. 1–13). Hillsdale, NJ: Erlbaum.

Southworth, F. C. (1980). Functional aspects of bilingualism. *International Journal of Dravidian Linguistics, 9,* 74–108.

Stern, D. N. (1985). *The interpersonal world of infancy.* New York: Basic.

Thomas, J. (1988). The role played by meta-linguistic awareness in second and third language learning. *Journal of Multilingual and Multicultural Development, 9,* 235–247.

Titone, R. (1994). Bilingual education and the development of metalinguistic abilities: A research project. *International Journal of Psycholinguistics, 10,* 5-14.

Triandis, H. C. (1985). Commentary. *Journal of Multilingual and Multicultural Development, 6,* 313–323.

Triandis, H. C. & Heron, A. (1981) (Eds). *Handbook of cross-cultural psychology, Vol. 4.* Boston: Allyn and Bacon.

Tschoumy, J.-A. (Ed.). (1994). *Parler européen.* Neuchâtel: Institut romand de recherche et de documentation pédagogique.

Vermès, G. & Boutet, J. (Eds.). (1987). *France, pays multilingue, tomes 1 & 2.* Paris: L'Harmattan.

Vermès, G. & Boutet, J. (Eds.). (1988). *Vingt-cinq communautés linguistiques en France, tome 1 & 2.* Paris: L'Harmattan.

Vihman, M. M. (1985). Language differentiation by the bilingual infant. *Journal of Child Language, 12,* 297–324.

Vygotsky, L. S. (1962). *Thought and language.* Cambridge: MIT Press.

Vygotsky, L. S. (1978). *Mind in society.* Cambridge: Harvard University Press.

Vygotsky, L. S. (1985). *Pensée et langage.* Paris: Editions sociales.

Ward, C. & Hewstone, M. (1985). Ethnicity, language and intergroup relations in Malaysia and Singapore: A social psychological analysis. *Journal of Multilingual and Multicultural Development, 6,* 271–296.

Watson-Gegeo, K. A., & Gegeo, D. W. (1986). Calling out and repeating routines in Kwar'ae children's language socialization. In B. B. Schieffelin & E. Ochs (Eds.), *Language socialization across cultures* (pp. 17–50). Cambridge: Cambridge University Press.

Weissenborn, J. Goodluck, H., & Roeper, T. (Eds.). (1992). *Theoretical issues in language acquisition: Continuity and change in development.* Hillsdale, HJ: Erlbaum.

Whorf, B. L. (1956). *Language, thought and reality.* Cambridge, MA: MIT Press.

8

CULTURE AND EMOTION

BATJA MESQUITA[1] *and* **NICO H. FRIJDA**
University of Amsterdam
The Netherlands

KLAUS R. SCHERER
University of Geneva
Switzerland

Contents

Theoretical and Methodological Issues

Introduction

Interest in the relations between culture and emotion began in cultural anthropology. From the outset, anthropologists and ethnologists were struck by the cultural particularities in emotion manifestations, in issues of emotional concern, and in emotion lexicons. These diversities engendered theories regarding the cultural relativity of emotion and the powerful influence of cultural factors on human behavior. They also led to a dominant focus on finding evidence to support these convictions. The emphasis given to particularities of different cultures has been tied to the dominant anthropological methodology of extensive field studies in particular cultures. Direct observation and interviews with members of the culture were the main methods used (see Lutz & White, 1986, for a review). These studies have not provided a solid basis for actual comparison across cultures, nor were they meant to do so.

The anthropological approach is in contrast to the psychobiological approach that aimed its investigations at the possible existence of emotion universals. One of the first to systematically investigate this concept was Charles Darwin. In the process of collecting data for his pioneering volume, *The Expression of the Emotions in Man and Animals* (1872/1965), he sent questionnaires to correspondents all over the world to inquire into the patterns of emotional expression in their respective cultures. This research produced evidence for phylogenetic and ontogenetic continuity of major expressive behavior patterns. After a period of neglect, the writings of Tomkins (1962, 1963) inspired a renaissance of interest in emotion research. During this renaissance, Darwin's ideas were followed up by studies on the cross-cultural similarity of human facial expressions (Eibl-Eibesfeldt, 1973, 1974; Ekman, 1972,1973; Izard, 1971). Similarity in facial expressions of emotions was taken as evidence for the universality of a number of fundamental emotions, often referred to as basic emotions.

These two seemingly incompatible approaches inevitably led to vigorous controversies (Ekman, 1994a; Mead, 1975; Russell, 1994) in which one side advocated cultural origin and specificity, and the other cross-cultural universality of emotion. On the whole, the debate has not contributed to appreciable progress in cross-cultural emotion research. The reasons are multiple. The conflicting positions appeared fixed, not allowing for fruitful discussion. In addition, the positions were taken on the basis of limited evidence, often disregarding data that were not in agreement with the adopted perspective. Most notably, the psychobiological approach has focused on similarities in emotional phenomena, whereas proponents of culture-specificity concentrated on differences. Finally, lack of research progress in the domain was due to what we consider an unprofitable view of the nature of emotions.

In this chapter we portray a balanced view of cultural variations in emotions. To this end, we will discuss the evidence for both cultural universality and relativity in emotions. Our discussion will provide a general synthesis of the patterns of the available research findings (for more exhaustive literature reviews see Lutz & White, 1986; Mesquita & Frijda, 1992; Thoits, 1989). We will base our review of the current state of the cross-cultural psychology of emotions on a model of emotions that allows for a finer comparison of emotions across cultures: a componential approach to emotions (see section on componential models).

Basic Emotions

Basic Emotion Theory

Until recently, most cross-cultural research on emotions was designed to test the hypothesis of basic emotions. Basic emotions were supposed to be a part of the human potential and, therefore, universal. The idea of basic emotions is not restricted to the contemporary psychology of emotions; it has held appeal throughout history (e.g., Descartes, 1647; Spinoza, 1677) and across cultures (e.g., Chari, 1990). Central to this concept of emotions is the notion that different emotions form independent and integral wholes in which various components (e.g., experience, facial expression, physiological response) are closely and invariably linked together. Each basic emotion, moreover, is presumably characterized by an unanalyzable quality of experience (Izard, 1977; Johnson-Laird & Oatley, 1989).

One of the arguments in favor of basic emotions is that most languages possess limited sets of central emotion-labeling words, referring to a small number of commonly occurring emotions. Anger, fear, sadness, and joy are examples of such words in English. Most major languages have words that more or less clearly correspond to them (Russell, 1991). A second argument is based on research on the cross-cultural recognition of facial expressions and of antecedent events. The claim has been that basic emotions are marked by distinct and unique facial expressions, as well as by specific types of elicitors (see below for a more extensive discussion of literature).

The theory of basic emotions includes the hypothesis that all emotions derive from the limited set of basic emotions. Non-basic emotions are either seen as lower level specifications of higher order basic emotions in a hierarchical model of semantic categorization (Agnoli, Kirson, Wu, & Shaver, 1989; Boucher, 1979; Oatley & Johnson-Laird, 1987), or as blends of such basic emotions (Arnold, 1960, Plutchik, 1980). As an illustration, take the example of jealousy. A hierarchical model of emotions would cast jealousy as sadness (the basic emotion involved) specified by the antecedent of threat to a relationship. Alternatively, jealousy would be interpreted as a blend of anger, fear, and sadness.

Implications for Cross-Cultural Research on Emotions

The search for basic emotions has been influential in shaping contemporary cross-cultural psychology of emotions. It has influenced the questions research focused on. The assumptions of the theory of basic emotions were accepted without question for many years (e.g., Izard, 1980). Although these assumptions were often not explicitly stated by researchers, they have colored much of the research efforts, and they have often resulted in a biased perspective on the role of culture in emotions.

The theory of basic emotions has influenced cross-cultural emotion research in various ways. First, cross-cultural studies of emotion have limited the focus of research efforts to the question of whether emotions are cross-culturally similar or different. The possibility that emotions can simultaneously be similar in some respects, and different in others, has been largely overlooked. Thus, for example, some research questioned whether or not anger occurs in all cultures, rather than raising the question of the extent to which emotions in the class of anger are cross-culturally similar. Likewise, universal recognition of a particular facial expression as depicting anger does not rule out the possibility that the counterparts of anger in other cultures may be different on some response modalities or antecedents (see following discussion).

Second, the basic emotions approach has focused interest in cross-cultural research on the potential for certain emotions, rather than on their practice in the sense of prevalence or significance (see section on methodological issues). For example, studies on the facial expression of emotions have shown that people from different cultures recognize facial expressions in similar ways. The ability to show facial expression was then inferred from the ability to recognize. However, hardly any information has been obtained on the ecology, the actual occurrence, or the frequency of occurrence of these facial expressions. The basic emotions approach has fostered an interest in universal emotional potential, rather than emotional practice.[2] Obviously, both approaches are valid. The study of universal emotion potential looks at the capacities and constraints of emotion, whereas the study of actual emotional practice in concrete cultural settings focuses on the forces that mold emotional life. Thus, a broader view of emotions and emotional life is needed if we are to understand the cross-cultural variations.

Finally, the focus on the search for basic emotions has furthered a conceptualization of emotions as states rather than processes. When considering emotions as states, the interest is restricted to the phenomenology of those states and to stable emotion features. This perspective on emotions does not take into consideration that emotions generally unfold as a result of external conditions, which may change as the emotion develops, and thus, affect the nature of the emotion process. Among the most prevalent emotion elicitors are social interactions that, by their nature, develop over time. The display of emotions, including some involuntary traces of emotional states, may affect the course of social interactions. Further, emotions may also develop because, for example, the appraisal changes in focus. Social interactions and the "natural" development of emotional appraisals may be subject to cultural differences. None of these cultural differences in the course of emotions have received much attention from the cross-cultural psychology inspired by the notion of basic emotions. Attention to cultural variations in the development of emotions over time, and to the factors that contribute to such development, has thus been lacking.

In sum, for some time the notion of basic emotions has dominated cross-cultural research on emotions. As a consequence, (1) universality and culture-specificity of emotions have been treated as mutually exclusive, (2) the potential for emotional responses has been emphasized in cross-cultural research at the expense of attention to emotional practice, and (3) cross-cultural differences in process characteristics of emotions, as well as in the embeddedness of emotion in social interaction, have been neglected in psychological research.

Recently, the area of culture and emotion has started to move beyond the issue of basic emotions. Both the concepts and the methods used in cross-cultural research of emotions have opened up to more complex questions rather than the limiting dichotomous view of whether or not the same emotions exist across cultures. In the next sections, we will discuss alternatives to the notion of basic emotions, indicating how they may affect the perspectives on universality and cultural specificity of emotion.

Componential Models of Emotions

Many investigators no longer consider emotions as unitary, elementary entities but, instead, view emotions as multi-componential phenomena (Frijda, 1986; Lang, 1977; Lazarus, 1991; Ortony & Turner, 1990; Scherer, 1984). Rather than assuming homogeneous emotional states, these authors underline the central importance of emotion processes consisting of concurrent changes in several different components. The emotion process is defined as a complex of changes in different subsystems of the organism's functioning. In an emotion, these subsystems (the components) are differentially elicited, and thus to some extent change independently of each other.

The emotion process, according to the componential views, generally includes the following components: a) antecedent event, b) emotional experience, c) appraisal, d) physiological change, e) change in action readiness, f) behavior, g) change in cognitive functioning and beliefs, and h) regulatory processes. Most emotion instances involve all of these components. Various components have certain independence; each has its particular determinants, in addition to the occurrence of an emotionally charged event. They also tend to influence one another; physiological change, for instance, is influenced by the vigor of the action one is ready for, or that one actually executes. The central idea in the componential approach is that different emotion components do not automatically follow from each other.

The implication for cross-cultural reseach is that each of these components may vary more or less independently from culture to culture. Therefore, if one is to establish cultural variations in emotions, each of the emotion components needs to be addressed individually. Or, to quote Shweder (1993): "To ask whether people are alike or different in their emotional functioning . . . is really to ask several more specific questions" (p. 425). Therefore, universality has to be established for components of emotion rather than for the emotion as a whole.

This is not to say that the different emotion components are completely independent of each other, or that all patterns of emotion components are equally likely to occur. One can argue that some emotional themes have universal significance in people's lives, because they reflect major contingencies of organism–environment interaction (Averill, 1994; Ekman, 1994b; Lazarus, 1991, 1994). For example, across cultures, people encounter obstacles to the satisfaction of needs or the achievement of goals, and they face danger and personal loss. Equally universal are the major interaction patterns, approach or contact-enhancement, avoidance or flight, and antagonistic interaction or fight. It is plausible to assume that major appraisal outcomes and major interaction patterns, while not invariably linked together, maintain a non-arbitrary coherence. Thus, frustration in a very general sense is universal, and across cultures, it is often followed by antagonistic interaction, or a tendency thereof. At this very general level, certain patterns of appraisal and action readiness are, thus, more likely to be found than others.

Further, at a more concrete level, it has been proposed that there are universal patterns of appraisals and corresponding patterns of expression, autonomic arousal, behavioral tendencies, and feeling states. Scherer (1984, 1994) has used the term *modal emotions* to refer to these universal patterns. We will adopt this term, despite its inadvertent statistical connotation of being most frequent (whether the universal patterns referred to are also the most frequent in various cultures is, of course, an empirical question). An example of a modal emotion would be the combination of personal loss (as appraised) resulting in crying, withdrawal, and loss of interest in one's surroundings, with specific autonomic and facial responses. Likewise, in most cultures, harm inflicted by others will give rise to a desire to retribute this harm, by threats of aggression, and by facial expressions that we recognize as "angry." The existence of such modal emotions could account for the evidence for universal emotion patterns. It is important to highlight the central difference between the notions of modal emotions and of basic or fundamental emotions: the former does not assume a definite number of homogeneous, integral categories or mechanisms that justify an a priori definition of basic or fundamental emotions. Instead, the concept of modal emotions advocates the empirical study of the frequency with which certain patterns of appraisal, accompanied by typical changes in different components of emotion, occur.

The notion of a componential emotion analysis is useful for the purposes of this review of culture and emotion because it does not presuppose the existence of a limited number of universal, biologically defined emotions. Also, it encourages the empirical study of the impact of nature and culture on different components of the emotion process. On the other hand, it does acknowledge the presence of bunching, of fuzzy modal patterns with characteristic appraisal and response profiles and associated verbal labels, and thus, encourages the comparison of these modal patterns across cultures.

Methodological Issues in the Comparison of Emotions across Cultures

Emotion Words in Cross-Cultural Studies

In the cross-cultural study of emotions, the traditional point of departure has been the occurrence and meaning of emotion words. The questions addressed have been:

Do the major emotion concepts occur cross-culturally? For example, is the concept of "anger" general, or does it not exist in some cultures? If these concepts occur universally, to what extent do they refer to the same sets of phenomena? Do various "equivalents" or translations of "anger" mean the same; do they refer to the same experiences and behaviors?

There are equivalents for most of the emotion labels commonly considered to belong to the "basic" category in almost all of the major languages of the world. Russell (1991) concluded that "there is great similarity in emotion categories across different cultures and languages" (p. 444). Consistently, in most cross-cultural comparative studies of emotion experiences (Frijda, Markam, Sato & Wiers, 1995; Mauro, Sato & Tucker, 1992; Mesquita, in preparation; Scherer, Wallbott, Matsumoto & Kudoh, 1988, Scherer & Wallbott, 1994), researchers were in fact able to translate the English terms for the emotions under study into various languages. Subsequent research has further suggested that some of the emotion categories, which have lexical equivalents in all languages, are also among the most frequently used in many, if not all, cultures (Mesquita, in preparation; Van Goozen & Frijda, 1993). At a general level of meaning, these emotion categories are cross-culturally similar in that they refer to major forms of subject–environment contingencies or appraisal, and to major forms of subject–environment interaction or action readiness.

However, at the same time, it can be easily shown that there are also considerable differences in connotations, and occasionally in core meanings, of these terms. In other words, lexical equivalents in different languages are not necessarily linguistic equivalents. The term *lexical equivalents* refers to words used as each others' translation, as opposed to linguistic equivalents referring to words that are similar in meaning. Based on elaborate semantic analyses of emotion words from very different languages, Wierzbicka (1992) concluded that, "in fact there are no emotion terms which can be matched neatly across language and culture boundaries, there are no universal emotion concepts lexicalised in all languages of the world" (p. 287). Some careful studies have shown important differences even between the semantic fields of such closely related languages as German and Swiss German (Dünker, 1979).

Methods have been developed that yield insight into the correspondences and differences in the meaning of emotion terms; differences in quality and degree can now be compared systematically. Wierzbicka (1986; 1992; 1994) presented analyses that make use of a set of semantic primitives, presumably occurring universally, to describe the meaning of emotion terms across languages. The multicomponential approach to emotions opens the same possibility to empirical research. It compares emotion words by having subjects from different cultural groups describe the patterns of components of emotion incidents, for example, incidents of anger (e.g., Frijda et al., 1995; Mauro et al., 1992; Scherer & Walbott, 1994). Both Wierzbicka's analyses and the componential approach have found that, in addition to a shared core pattern of components, differences exist with regard to all components (Frijda et al, 1995; Mesquita, in preparation; Scherer & Wallbott, 1994).

Not only may the meaning of lexically equivalent words differ to some extent, but emotion taxonomies of given languages contain emotion words that, in other languages, are not matched by even remotely similar emotion concepts (e.g., Gerber, 1985). Also, taxonomies may differ drastically, and the emotion domain can occasionally be subdivided in such a way that the major categories mentioned earlier do not appear (e.g., Levy, 1973, 1984).

In the discussion of emotion words, however, it is important to keep in mind that the activity of labeling is independent of the emotion process and of the emotional experience as a whole. It is, to some degree, an arbitrary decision as to which aspects of the emotion process are selected and labeled by a word in a language; it depends on the communicative intentions of the language users and on the social focus of emotion talk (Abu-Lughod & Lutz, 1990). It is often possible to understand emotion words from other languages, even if one's own language lacks a counterpart (e.g., Oatley, 1991). The reason is that the emotion words can be analyzed in terms of components that are familiar across cultures.

It is important to note that the absence of a specific emotion label in one or more languages does not establish the absence of a corresponding, frequently occurring pattern of appraisal results with respective componential response patterning. There is no evidence that the emotion lexicon is a better indication of occurrence and distribution of emotions in a given culture than other forms of emotion talk such as idioms and descriptions of valenced attributes of people and objects (Besnier, 1995; Briggs, 1995).

Reference Points

All cross-cultural research needs reference points, that is, bases or standards to which comparisons can be made. What is it exactly that is compared in cross-cultural emotion research? If the emotion words in different languages do not mean quite the same thing, then what can be the basis of comparison?

In line with the componential view of emotions, we think that the basis of comparison is formed by the individual emotion components. One can compare the occurrence and precise nature of various components, such as subjective experience, appraisals, action tendencies, expressions, and other modes of behavior. Alternatively, one can compare combinations of various components, such as the antecedents giving rise to particular response modes, the meanings attached to particular modes of response, the patterns of responses, and so forth.

Emotion words can be a fruitful starting point for cross-cultural comparisons of emotion, provided that their elements of meaning which are used as points of reference are explicitly stated. Such correspondence with regard to particular components of the emotion words to be compared renders comparison in other regards meaningful. It is meaningful to compare anger (English) and, for instance, *song* in the Ifaluk language (Lutz, 1982, 1985, 1987, 1988), because they both refer to emotions involving appraisal of harm from an animate agent; or to quote Wierzbicka (1994), both emotions involve the appraisal that "this person did something bad" (p. 138). They can then be found to differ in the kind of action they bring about. Anger leads to the tendency to return the other person's harm. *Song,* on the other hand, produces action that aims to alter the behavior of the offending person; such action may include aggressive behaviors, but it may also consist of such things as refusing to eat and attempted suicide. It is equally meaningful to compare shame (English) and *a'ar* (Arabic), because they both refer to norm transgression as experienced, and to some form of submissive action tendency. At the same time, one can assert or examine the considerable differences in structure and meaning of the two emotions in each set, differences that may be decisive for the roles of the emotions in the experience of the individual and in the social interaction (cf. Abu-Lughod, 1986; Goffman, 1982; Peristiany, 1965; Scheff, 1988)

This does not deny the fact that serious problems of comparison and interpretation may arise when using emotion words. How does one determine whether differences in the phenomena associated with particular emotion words are due to semantic differences or to psychological differences? For instance, when finding that different phenomena are connected to shame (English) and *lek* (its lexical equivalent in Balinese; Geertz, 1973), we do not know whether this is because the word meanings differ or because the psychological structures of emotion components in comparable contexts differ.

For this reason, it may often be preferable to inquire into similarities and differences in regard to particular components of the emotion process, and in the relations that may exist between these components. The components as such are then used as the standards of comparison. Examples of the use of such alternative points of reference are studies that investigate the association of specific facial expressions with particular antecedent events or stories (Ekman & Friesen, 1978; Haidt & Keltner, 1995). Another promising approach is one focusing on particular appraisal components. For instance, a study by Kitayama, Markus, Matsumoto, and Norasakkunkuit (in press) compared the antecedent events generated by Japanese and American subjects, when asked to describe an event that had enhanced or decreased self-esteem. The appraisal of "changed self-esteem" was used as a standard of comparison in this example. A final productive approach has been to cross-culturally compare the emotional responses to various types of antecedent events, such as "offense by an intimate other" (Mesquita, in preparation). Such alternative standards of comparison render the results of comparative emotion research transparent, and are, in fact, no more difficult to apply than emotion words.

Potential for Emotions versus Emotional Practice
We have consistently distinguished between the potential for certain types of psychological functions or behaviors, and their actual occurrence or practice in social settings. Potentials depend on the existing psychobiological structures and innately determined neurophysiological connections. They also depend on learning and socialization patterns that make certain cognitive representations available or provide behavioral models. Practice is determined by complex sets of forces in concrete cultural settings—including values, norms, habits, ecological presses, and opportunities—to make certain types of psychological processes and behaviors

more likely to occur (or more accessible).[3] It is likely, therefore, that emotional practice does not exhaust the potential provided by available emotion mechanisms. Given the cultural differences in the forces that push practice into certain directions, one can assume that while the psychobiological potential is more or less universal, emotional practice may vary widely across cultures.

As previously mentioned, cross-cultural emotion research has predominantly focused on the potential for certain emotions, while ignoring the practice of these emotions in different cultures. It has tried to find an answer to the question of whether particular emotions or patterns of emotional responses occur cross-culturally. Neither the frequency with which these emotions or emotional patterns occur in different cultures, nor their significance or focality to the culture, has drawn much attention. Most likely, the use of emotion words as standards of comparison has contributed to this neglect of the practice of emotions. The emotional phenomena compared were often those related to English emotion words and their lexical equivalents in other languages. To what extent these phenomena in other cultures share the frequency and significance they have in English-speaking culture has not been subjected to much study. In psychology, research addressing the relative significance of emotional phenomena in different cultures is scarce.

In contrast, many ethnographers have centered their work around cultural practices of emotion. They have concentrated on describing the prevalence with which certain emotional responses occur in a given culture in general, or else in particular cultural contexts (Abu-Lughod, 1986, Briggs, 1970; Levy, 1973; Lutz, 1988; Miller, 1993; Rosaldo, 1980). They have also described the combinations of emotional responses one is most likely to encounter in a given culture as well as those that are strikingly absent (to a Western researcher). And finally, they have focused on the specific contexts in which emotions or particular emotional responses are most likely to occur. Their descriptions have convincingly demonstrated that there are cultural differences in the ecology of emotions. Take, for example, the Utku Inuit culture, where anger is nearly absent. Judged by the ethnographer's account (Briggs, 1970), the only exceptions were anger towards a person who was being ostracized, and thus was no longer considered a part of the community, or anger towards dogs (aggression was apparently vented on dogs). Another example can be seen in the emotion of *hasham* of the 'Awlad Ali Bedouins, an instance of the category of shame that was seemingly omnipresent, and toward which many social rules and behaviors were geared. People reported this emotion upon damage to their honor, and the loss of autonomy. Even the slightest threat to autonomy was seen as such damage. The 'Awlad Ali were constantly engaged in attempts to avoid violations of their autonomy (Abu-Lughod, 1986). Hasham is thus an emotion that dominated the lives of the 'Awlad Ali. More examples of differences in ecology can be found in the sections addressing the individual components of emotions. At this point, it is worth noting that the ecology of emotions is a subject worth studying in and of itself. Emotion ecologies are thus among those dimensions that can be compared in cross-cultural research on emotion. Emotion ecologies also seem to have some relevance at the level of the individual's emotions (see section on the meaning of culture).

Level of Description

The last issue in the context of cross-cultural comparison of emotion is the level of description of emotional phenomena. As will become clear in the remainder of this chapter, emotional phenomena have been described at various levels of abstraction. Generally speaking, cultural differences in emotional phenomena tend to become more numerous and larger, as the level of description gets more concrete. So, for example, "thin ice" has been described as a major source of fear for the Utku Inuit, who live in an environment where the quality of ice is of vital importance (Briggs, 1970). At this level of concreteness, one could speak of a culture-specific antecedent of fear. However, described in a more general way, as an instance of physical danger, the antecedent evidently looses its specificity. This example illustrates how the very same phenomena may be considered either cross-culturally similar or cross-culturally different, depending on the level of abstraction chosen for description. Ample illustrations will be given in the discussion of the literature that follows.

The Meaning of Culture to Emotion Research

The term "culture" (as in "cross-cultural studies") is generally used in a rather loose manner. A definition of culture is rarely given in comparative research on emotions. Because of this ambiguity, not much attention has been given to the comparability of the samples (see Van de Vijver & Leung, this *Handbook*). Culture has too often been associated with national boundaries, resulting in too little attention to the emotional differences within nations (or between "subcultures"). In fact, it would be useful to study subcultural differences within any one culture, in order to evaluate the importance of cross-cultural differences relative to intra-cultural differences.

Related to the ambiguity of the notion of "culture" is a general vagueness on what aspects of culture determine the cross-cultural differences in emotions. To face this issue in a systematic fashion would require a grid specifying the relevant dimensions along which cultures vary. The work on value dimensions, such as individualism–collectivism (Kagitcibasi, Volume 3 of this *Handbook*; Triandis, 1994; Triandis, Bontempo, Villareal, Asai, & Lucca, 1988), power distance, masculinity–femininity and uncertainty avoidance (Hofstede, 1980) represents a promising beginning. But the dimensions need elaboration. Schwartz and colleagues have established a finer grid of cultural dimensions constituted of different value domains (Schwartz, 1992, 1994, 1995; Smith & Schwartz, Volume 3 of this *Handbook*). Examples of value domains are power, hedonism, achievement, and tradition. This work has shown that relations between various value domains are similar across cultures; there is thus reason to speak of a universal grid. It seems that cultures vary on their value priorities but very little on the way they represent the order of different values.

Cultural differences in value priorities have rarely been related to variations in emotions (but see Matsumoto, 1989), and equally scarce have been the attempts to theoretically clarify the relations between value priorities and emotions (a rudimentary explanation of the kind can be found in Triandis, 1994). More generally, research on the way in which cultural traits impact upon the emotional life of the individuals is scarce and scattered. Anthropological and historical work has discussed different "emotionologies." An emotionology is a culture's lore about emotions (Hochschild, 1979, 1983; Lutz, 1987; Stearns & Stearns, 1985). Supposedly included in these emotionologies are rules about how to feel (so-called feeling rules) and about how to display one's emotions (so-called display rules). These rules have been assumed to govern an individual's emotions, that is, they re-model initial emotional impulses following cultural ideals. This widely propagated idea thus implies that the cultural modeling of emotions is mostly a secondary impulse. It is likely that such influence on emotions exists. However, the concept of emotionology has failed to explain how feeling rules and display rules are formed. Furthermore, emotionologies are unlikely to be the only determinants of cultural variation in emotions.

The influence of culture on emotions can be more direct. Convergent models have been proposed that describe the direct effect of culturally significant themes on the emotions of individuals from that culture.[4] It should be clear from the outset that the empirical evidence for these models is still very sketchy. For a better understanding of cultural variations in emotions, the effort to relate cultural events to individual emotions needs to be pursued.

One recent research direction suggests that cultures have "core cultural ideas" (Markus & Kitayama, 1994a, p. 341–343), that is, culturally defined and promulgated issues of concern. Cultures vary with respect to the ideas they make salient. Obedience and tradition appear to be salient in some cultures, whereas autonomy and originality are salient in others. It is possible that what is called core cultural ideas or concerns in this research tradition can be assimilated to what is referred to as high priority values in the value literature.[5] Thus, while the precise ideas that are salient vary from culture to culture, every culture does seem to have certain concerns that are focal. According to Markus & Kitayama (1994a), preoccupation with the concerns can be seen at all levels of the culture: the collective reality (ecological, economic, and sociopolitical factors), socio-psychological processes (customs, norms, institutions), and the individual reality (recurrent episodes in the local worlds of individuals). All institutions and practices within a culture gear the individual to these core ideas. Culture thus emphasizes focal concerns in all possible ways. Core cultural ideas are likely to be highly salient to the individual, because one is constantly exposed to them. Furthermore, constant cultural emphasis on a concern renders "cultural expertise" on that concern likely.

Individuals of a culture are likely to adopt these highly salient core cultural ideas as concerns. Culturally focal concerns will be so accessible to the individual that they are likely to come to mind when appraising an event. These concerns will be, what has been called, "chronically accessible" (cf. Higgins, 1989). That means that many events will be evaluated in terms of the concerns inspired by core cultural ideas. Anthropological evidence also suggests this to be the case (e.g., Abu-Lughod, 1986; Rosaldo, 1980).

Furthermore, cultural expertise on the concern and situations affecting it will give the individual a sense of certainty when appraising the event. There is some evidence suggesting that individuals feel more certain about the meaning of events related to focal concerns, as opposed to events that are less focal; clear norms exist on how to interpret the former and how to respond to them (Mesquita & Frijda, 1992; Mesquita, in preparation). Clarity about the meaning of the event, in turn, appears to make the events related to focal concerns, as well as the subsequent emotional responses more obvious to the individual (Frijda & Mesquita, 1994; Mesquita, in preparation). Obviousness refers to a sense on the part of an individual that the emotional reaction to the event is imposed by the event rather than caused by subjective assessment or behavioral preferences. Obviousness of particular components of emotions is likely to exclude their being reconsidered and put into question, because alternative interpretations of the situation or alternative reactions are inconceivable. High accessibility of a concern will lead to a more frequent use of that concern in appraising events, and obviousness of the concern will lead to less reconsideration of its use. It can be maintained, therefore, that both high accessibility and obviousness themselves contribute to the cultural focality of the concern. And so do all the cultural manifestations of the concern, because they increase the visibility, and thus the salience, of the concern.

Not only do the concerns derived from core cultural ideas become highly accessible, but also the related emotional responses themselves may become habitual or even scripted. Therefore, emotional tendencies that are in line with the core cultural ideas may be formed. These emotional inclinations of the individual will conform to cultural practices (Abu-Lughod, 1986; Briggs, 1970; Kitayama & Markus, 1994; Shweder & Much, 1987). Kitayama, Markus, Matsumoto, and Norasakkunkuit (in press) have provided a good example of such a case. Japanese and American university students were asked to list events that had either "decreased or increased their self-esteem." Two hundred esteem-decreasing and 200 esteem-increasing events were randomly selected for a questionnaire with the restriction to hold constant the number of Japanese and American events in each of these categories. Different groups of American and Japanese university students were asked to judge the extent to which each of the events would affect their self-esteem. Both American and Japanese students deemed the American emotion antecedents to be more self enhancing, and the Japanese emotion antecedents more self diminishing, suggesting differences in the ecology of events. Moreover, Japanese students, on the whole, reported more loss of self-esteem than American students for the negative emotional events and less gain in self-esteem for the positive emotional events. The results thus suggest that the cultural differences in the types of events conform to cultural differences in the sensitivity to emotional events.

Various ethnographies have shown how major emotional themes in specific cultures dominate both the social life and the emotional experiences of individuals from that culture. Examples are Abu-Lughod's ethnography (1986) on Egyptian Bedouins that concentrated on *hasham* (translated as shame), and Rosaldo's ethnography (1980) on the Phillipine Ilongot focusing on the emotion of *liget* (translated as anger). *Hasham* and *liget* are focal emotions in the respective cultures for which they were described; they were talked about frequently; constant attention was drawn to situations relevant to those emotions; and the organization of social life was geared to steering those emotions in socially acceptable directions, either by avoiding them or by giving them shape in a socially acceptable manner. The cultural emphasis placed on these emotions is incomparable to the one placed on the emotions of shame and anger in English-speaking cultures. Ethnographies appear to support the supposed effects of focality on an individual's emotions, and so does some scattered evidence in other research.

In sum, to understand a cultural perspective, we must consider that cultural variations in emotion are relative to the cultural orientations from which they derive. Furthermore, the focal concerns of the culture must be taken into account and must be related to the conditions under which emotions emerge, as well as to the emotional responses themselves.

Cultural Variation in the Components of the Emotion Process

Antecedents of Emotion

Straightforward as it may seem, defining antecedent events of emotions is difficult. More often than not, the interpretation of what happens constitutes the eliciting event, rather than what actually happens. What makes an insulting remark an elicitor of anger is not the sounds uttered by the other person, but rather the meaning conveyed by these sounds and the interpretation of the utterance as obstructive and intended to hurt or humiliate. Cross-cultural research on emotion has been only marginally successful in finding a meaningful way to describe antecedent events. Different studies have described events at different levels of abstraction (see the example of "thin ice" used earlier). Conclusions about cultural variations in emotion antecedents have differed accordingly, with descriptions of highly abstract events yielding the most similarities across cultures, and concrete descriptions yielding the most differences.

Cross-cultural variations in antecedent events have been studied in different ways. The most frequent research question has been whether similar events cross-culturally give rise to the same emotional responses and, if so, to what degree. There has also been some research on the frequency with which particular events actually take place, as well as on the relative significance of these events in the emotional lives of people from different cultures. Next, we will discuss some instructive evidence in this regard.

Similarities in Antecedent Events
Research suggesting similarities in antecedent events, which elicit certain emotions, has been reported by Boucher and Brandt (1981; Brandt & Boucher, 1985). The research employed a recognition task. Subjects from different cultures (Ameri-

can and Malaysian in the first study and American, Korean, and Samoan in the second) described situations in which one person caused another to feel anger, disgust, fear, joy, sadness, or surprise. In the first study, a separate group of American subjects was asked to identify which of the situations mentioned by the Malaysian and American subjects had led to which of these six emotions; in the second study, subjects of all three cultures were asked to identify antecedent events of American, Korean, and Samoan origin. In both studies, 65 percent or more of the emotion antecedents were recognized. Subjects did not recognize the antecedents from their own culture any better than the antecedents from the other culture(s). The studies strongly suggest that the same events elicit similar emotions regardless of culture. Unfortunately, no information was given regarding the types of events that, in all cultures, were most readily recognized as emotion antecedents.

Evidence for similarity in antecedent events also comes from large-scale questionnaire studies among European, American, and Japanese college students (Scherer, Summerfield & Wallbott, 1983; Scherer et al., 1988; Scherer, Wallbott & Summerfield, 1986). In these studies, subjects were asked to describe a situation or event that had caused them to feel an emotion of sadness, anger, fear, or happiness. The subjects came from five Western European countries in Scherer et al. (1983), seven Western European countries and Israel in Scherer et al. (1986), and Europe, the United States, and Japan in Scherer et al. (1988). The situations mentioned by the subjects were grouped into general categories. No culture-specific categories were needed to describe the event antecedents. In all cultures, the most important event categories were: good and bad news, continuation of or problems with relationships (e.g., pleasure from contact with friends, feeling rejected, fear of quarrels), temporary meetings (e.g., meeting one's friend for dinner), separation (e.g., journey), permanent separation, birth and death, pleasure (e.g., sex, music), interaction with strangers, and success and failure in achievement situations. The categories that were needed to describe the antecedent events for each particular emotion were, to a large extent, also similar across cultures. Thus, there is evidence that particular emotions are cross-culturally elicited by similar antecedents.

These findings carry the implication that a large number of event types bear emotional meaning to many or most human beings, regardless of their cultural origin. The studies suggest a high degree of commonality in human emotional sensitivities or in basic human concerns.

Differences in Antecedent Events
There is also some evidence for cultural differences in emotion-eliciting events because (1) the same situations are interpreted differently across cultures, and therefore, lead to different emotions, (2) the living conditions in different cultures vary, resulting in the occurrence of culture-specific events, or (3) events derive their significance from certain culture-specific beliefs.

Various cultures interpret the condition of "being alone" differently. Among the Utku Inuit, the circumstance of being alone, or being left alone, always represents serious social isolation and leads to sadness or, more precisely, loneliness (Briggs, 1970). Tahitians take a different perspective: Being alone is perceived as an opportunity for spirits to bother a person, causing uncanny feelings and sometimes also fear (Levy, 1973). The Pintupi Aboriginals of Australia consider it unusual that one could be happy sitting alone, because it means not being among kin and not showing or being shown affection. Sitting alone is an indication that the relationships between the individual and those considered as kin are not running smoothly, which prevents one from experiencing happiness (Myers, 1979). In some Western cultures, being alone may be welcomed as an occasion of privacy, leading to feelings of contentment or happiness, or alternatively not leading to any particular feelings at all.

Cultural differences in antecedent events can also be related to different social or physical conditions. Racism is an example of a social condition from which some groups of people will suffer more than others. In a study among Dutch, Surinamese, and Turkish people in the Netherlands, we found that 10 percent of the Surinamese and Turkish but none of the Dutch respondents reported discrimination as an anger antecedent (Mesquita, in preparation). In this case, differences in the nature of anger antecedents are clearly due to a different exposure of the dominant group as opposed to the minorities of the country. Differences in the types of events eliciting specific emotions have also been found as a result of specific physical living conditions. The Utku emotions *kappia* and *iqhi*, for example, are reported as "both alike [to] apply to fear of dangerous animals, evil spirits, natural hazards such as thin ice or a rough sea, angry people, and an angry God" (Briggs, 1970, p. 344). Physical conditions account for part of the variation in the antecedent events of emotions in the category of fear.

Some of the antecedents of *kappia* and *iqhi* are created by the specific spiritual beliefs, which constitute a distinct source of differences in emotion-eliciting events, in addition to differences due to different interpretations and differences due to different physical and social circumstances. Other examples abound where such spiritual beliefs constitute the antecedents of emotion: the concern with black magic in Surinam (Wooding, 1981), the constant fear of God among 17th century white Americans, and the firm belief of Jehovah's Witnesses to be saved from the world's decline.

Whether one finds similarities or differences depends, to some degree, on the level of description. On the one hand, it is conceivable that similarities yielded by questionnaire studies would be less pervasive if the event categories were chosen at a more concrete level. Many culture-specific emotion antecedents, on the other hand, would be non-specific at a slightly more general level of description (see above). To the extent that universal meanings (e.g., risky conditions) explain as much of the variation in emotional responses as do the concrete antecedent events (e.g., thin ice and evil spirits), we consider the cultural differences in antecedents to be trivial.

Not all differences in antedent events are trivial, though. Some antecedent events represent culture-specific meanings. This means that the emotional responses to antecedent events cannot be understood unless the culture-specific meaning of the events is taken into account. It is impossible, for instance, to understand the emotional responses to "black magic," when black magic is reduced to the universal antecedent category of "harm by another person." We suggest that a level of description be selected that accounts for the variation in emotional responses to a particular antecedent event; that is, the level of description should leave out details that are irrelevant to the consequent emotional reactions, but should include those aspects of meaning that account for subsequent emotional reactions. The research practice, thus far, has been that antecedent events are described without justifying the degree of concreteness chosen.

The distinction of potential versus practice may be thought to apply to antecedent events as well. Even those events that potentially elicit emotions across cultures do so more readily in some cultures than in others. In one of our own studies, we found that "harm inflicted by another person" elicited anger and/or sadness in Dutch and Surinamese respondents, but that these emotions were elicited to different degrees; the Dutch reported more sadness, whereas the Surinamese reported more anger (Mesquita, in preparation). Another example comes from Haidt, Koller, and Dias (1993), who found that social transgressions and unconventional food and sex practices were more readily appraised as immoral by Brazilians than by Americans, and less appraised in terms of morality by highly educated than by less educated subjects in both cultures. The authors assume that the appraisal of something as immoral is likely to elicit a response of disgust. Therefore, social transgressions, unconventional food and sex more readily elicited a reaction of disgust in the Brazilian and less educated samples than in the American and higher educated samples.

In sum, cultural differences and similarities in the nature of antecedent events have been found. Some of the differences appear to be irrelevant to the nature of emotions; this is the case when the emotional response to concrete events can be understood by reducing those events to their universally shared meanings. It is not always possible to understand the emotional responses to an event without maintaining some of its culture-specificity. In the latter case, the nature of antecedent events differs across cultures in a non-trivial way. Most of the cultural differences that occur are differences with respect to the frequency with which certain events elicit particular emotional responses.

Subjective Experience

Subjective emotional experience is, in some theories, that which cannot be further reduced or analyzed in terms of components, and which can only be designated by the corresponding emotion words. Usually, in these theories, one assumes the existence of a small set of qualia, identified with "basic emotions" (see section on basic emotions).

This hypothesis is obviously unprofitable for cross-cultural research, because it prejudices the issue of cross-cultural generality, and runs into the problem just discussed, where the lexical equivalents of basic emotion terms (to the extent that they exist in a particular language) are not linguistically identical.

Emotional experiences, including those falling into one of the "basic" classes, can be profitably analyzed in terms of components. Emotional experiences may consist of the awareness of one's: a) appraisals, b) state of action readiness, c) physiological upset, or d) further cognitive components, notably, cognitive connotations and implications, and (e) evaluation of one's emotions.

There is one qualitative dimension that can be considered as an unanalyzable element of experience, and that is hedonic experience, or the experiences of pleasure and pain. Their basic status is attested by introspective analysis (Wundt, 1902), dimensional analyses of emotion words, similarities of facial expressions, and emotional experiences. Factor analyses of such data have yielded hedonic tone (together with emotional activation) as the major factor, a finding confirmed by the results of cross-cultural research (Russell, 1983).

Different emotional experiences, then, correspond to varied patterns of values on the components, including a core feeling component that can be described as the hedonic tone. For the cross-cultural study of subjective emotional experience, one would need a comparative study of the building blocks of these experiences (that is, of the separate components and the values these can take).

In principle, it is possible to find experiences that lack certain components, even core hedonic feeling, and that still qualify as emotional experiences because of their antecedents. There may be culturally determined phenomena of this kind. For instance, Tahitians are said to become just tired in response to threatening events or losses (Levy, 1973; 1984); whether that fatigue should be called a variant of sadness presents the same kind of problem (and no other kind of problem) as that confronting a Western psychiatrist who has to understand a patient's loss of interest in life following personal loss.

The labeling of emotional experience largely follows the patterns of the components as described in the remainder of this section. However, emotional experience is not described adequately as a pattern of such components at a specific moment. In line with the process view of emotions, emotional experiences include awareness of the temporal development of the emotions, and of their likely implications with regard to their social context. Emotional experiences include reflections of the fit between one's emotion and social norms or expectations, of expected social reactions to one's emotion, and of the implications of one's emotion for further social interactions. Presumably, it makes a considerable difference for the emotional experience whether one feels one's emotion to be in line with or counter to social norms, or whether one feels it has social consequences or is a private affair. Experiences of "shame," for example, or of the emotional response to events involving honor, can be expected to differ considerably in England and in Mediterranean countries for that reason (cf. Abu-Lughod, 1986; Blok, 1980; Scheff, 1988). Another aspect presumably influencing the quality of emotional experiences is the obviousness of emotion-related appraisals. We have shown that the meaning of both concern-relevant situations and consequent emotional responses become better defined, and consequently, the experience of the emotion becomes more obvious, as the concern becomes more culturally focal (see section on the meaning of culture).

It follows then that subjective experiences of the same emotion can be considerably different in different cultures, depending on which components of the emotion dominate in the experience. Two emotions of anger may be experienced in totally different manners, according to whether the response is felt as socially approved, obvious, enhancing social standing and leading to overt rejection of the offensive agent, or whether it is hardly felt at all because of the awareness that it will isolate one from other people and damage self esteem. There is no contradiction in arguing that what dynamically is the "same" emotion can be experienced in quite different fashions in different cultures. This explains why the subjective similarities between particular emotions, as assessed by free grouping methods (e.g., Lutz, 1982), may drastically differ form one culture to another, while the emotions (the component patterns) may still be regarded as the same, or at least as closely related.

Appraisal

Appraisal processes are presumably nonconscious and automatic. They can be conceived of as a series of automatic evaluations with respect to a set of appraisal dimensions (Scherer, 1984). The major dimensions discussed in the literature are attention to changing conditions (novelty/familiarity); a sense of pleasure or distaste (unpleasantness/pleasantness); a sense of uncertainty (or certainty); perception of an obstacle; a sense of being in control or being out of control (controllability); attribution of agency (human or nonhuman agent, agency by oneself or someone else); a sense of changed self-esteem (enhanced or decreased); a sense of the likely praise, censure, or ridicule of one's group (enhanced or decreased status); and an ultimate judgment of the value or fitness of what has happened (norm (in)compatibility) (Ellsworth, 1994; Frijda, 1986; Lazarus, 1991; Ortony, Clore & Collins, 1988; Roseman, 1984; Scherer, 1988, Smith & Ellsworth, 1985). Different patterns of appraisal are assumed to correspond to different emotions, and empirical evidence supports this assumption (e.g., Frijda, Kuipers, & Terschure, 1989; Smith & Ellsworth, 1985)

In spite of widely divergent disciplinary and historical traditions, there is a high degree of convergence with respect to the nature of the appraisal dimensions postulated by different theories (see Lazarus & Smith, 1988; Manstead & Tetlock, 1989; Reisenzein & Hofmann, 1990; 1993; Roseman, Spindel, & Jose, 1990; Scherer, 1988). In addition to this convergence, several recent empirical studies have provided support for the notion that a limited number of appraisal or evaluation dimensions are sufficient to explain the elicitation and differentiation of emotional states.

The notion of appraisal is closely linked to motivational concepts like that of concern, goal or need. The notion of concern will be used here to refer to goals, motives, values, and expectations about oneself or others, and about the world in which one lives. Examples of concerns are: concern for physical well-being and safety, self-esteem, the status of one's group, and for closeness of loved ones. What is labeled "concerns" also includes values and norms that are shared in a culture, inasmuch as they are held by the individual: religious observance, honor of one's country, people, or tribe; intellectual freedom; and so forth. An event may be relevant to more than one concern simultaneously. For instance, a failure may be harmfully relevant for one's material pursuit, self-worth, and for the prestige of one's family. The appraisal outcomes will be accordingly complex.

Both the appraisal dimensions and the concerns against which the event's impact are checked may vary cross-culturally. As in antecedent events, however, differences emerge more often in degrees, and are only rarely a matter of absence in one culture and presence in another.

Appraisal Dimensions

Research seems to show that people in different cultures evaluate events along similar appraisal dimensions, but that the frequency with which certain appraisal dimensions are used in the emotional assesssment of events is subject to variation. Analogous to our discussion of the antecedent events, we will consider to what extent and in what respects emotional appraisal varies across cultures, rather than concentrate on whether or not emotional appraisal differs cross-culturally.

Several recent studies have provided evidence that the appraisal dimensions used by people are similar across cultures (Frijda et al., 1995; Matsumoto, Kudoh, Scherer & Wallbott, 1988; Mauro, Sato, & Tucker, 1992; Wallbott & Scherer, 1988). Some of these studies have compared emotion words from disparate languages with respect to the outcomes on various appraisal dimensions. In most studies, subjects were presented with a particular emotion word and asked to report a situation or event that had caused them to experience that emotion. Emotion words used in different languages were each others' translations. Subsequently, subjects were asked to rate the emotion-eliciting event just reported with respect to various appraisal dimensions. Various studies have yielded two findings that suggest cross-cultural similarity. The first is that lexically equivalent emotion words have largely similar appraisal patterns (Frijda et al, 1995; Roseman, Dhawan, Rettek, Naidu & Thapa, 1995). For example, Frijda et al. (1995) found a similar core of appraisal for anger words in Japanese, Indonesian, and Dutch, "consisting of the experience of something unpleasant and that has obstructed one's reaching one's goals, which event was felt to be unfair but inevitable, and for which someone else is to blame" (p. 139). Other studies have found similar appraisal patterns for anger words in English (e.g., Ellsworth & Smith, 1988; Roseman, 1991). The agreement in appraisal patterns for various emotions is not surprising, because emotion words are translated on the basis of, in part at least, such agreement. The second finding is less self-evident: A common set of appraisal dimensions accounts, to a considerable extent, for the differentiation between emotion words in all languages of study. There is some evidence for cross-cultural similarity in the relative significance of various appraisal dimensions accounting for most of the variation (Frijda et al., 1995; Mauro et al., 1992; Scherer, in press). Thus, the same appraisal dimensions provide a satisfactory descriptive framework for emotions in different languages.

Some evidence for cross-cultural convergence in the appraisal of particular types of situations has also been found. Mesquita (in preparation) asked Dutch, Surinamese, and Turkish people living in the Netherlands to rate a list of appraisal questions for six situation types. Examples of some of the situation types were "receiving compliments or admiration," "success," "offense by a non-intimate other," and "offense by an intimate other." The appraisals in the three cultures were, to a large extent, similar. For example, all three groups appraised the situation of offense by a non-intimate other as "unpleasant, unexpected, another person's responsibility, avoidable, and harmful for self-esteem." More research is required to decide whether similarity in the appraisals of such types of situations can be more generally found across cultures.

Cross-cultural research on appraisal has been less than systematic, which renders it difficult to draw firm conclusions on the cross-cultural similarity. It is unclear to what extent the appraisal dimensions thus far included in research are exhaustive for the different ways in which emotional events are evaluated. Appraisal dimensions have mainly been generated on the basis of intuition. It may be that there are additional, and possibly culture-specific, dimensions of appraisal that have as yet been overlooked (see Ellsworth, 1994, for a similar argument). For instance, none of the appraisal theories has proposed a dimension of divine agency, magical sources, or fate. There is no reason why these would not be added to the repertoire of agency dimensions that do occur in Western, secular emotion theories (such as other responsible, self responsible, nobody responsible).

Cultural differences in appraisals can be understood as differences in the practice, or propensity, to use certain appraisal dimensions. Matsumoto et al. (1988) found cultural differences with respect to the number of subjects who were unwilling to attribute the responsibility for joy, fear, anger, disgust, shame, and guilt antecedents to either themselves or other people. For all emotions, significantly more Japanese than American subjects responded "not applicable," when asked about responsibility for the emotional event (percentages were not provided). Consistently, Scherer et al. (1988) found that, compared to the American and European groups, Japanese subjects reported relatively fewer instances of injustice as anger antecedents (21 percent of the American and European anger antecedents, but only 4 percent of the Japanese). These findings correspond with those of Mauro et al. (1992) who reported, among others, that the use of the appraisal dimension of responsibility differed cross-culturally, such that students from the United States made more use of the responsibility dimension than students from Japan.

Ethnographies, pointing to the conspicuous presence or absence of a particular type of emotion in a given cultural group, also suggest culture-specific appraisal propensities. For instance, Solomon (1978) linked the low incidence of anger among the Utku to a reluctance to blame another person for a negative event. He argued that ". . . . anger violates the Utku 'rational' worldview, and includes judgements and structures which are unjustifiable. . . . Anger adds blame to frustration and annoyance. It includes a quasi-moral 'ought'-type claim. . . . The Utku, much more than any of us, are used to extreme hardship and discomfort. Their philosophy therefore, is that such things must be tolerated, not flailed against. . . . Aggression only makes things more unpleasant and does no good, so the rational attitude under the circumstances is simple resignation and acceptance" (p. 193/ 194). Such an interpretation of difference in anger occurrence is, of course, distinct from interpretations assuming that anger was actually evoked by acts from actors appraised as blameworthy, but the expression of which was subsequently suppressed.[6]

In sum, various appraisal dimensions appear to be cross-culturally useful in the description of emotional events and cross-culturally relevant to the distinction between different emotion categories. There is no evidence for the existence of culture-specific appraisal dimensions, although this does not rule out that such dimensions may exist. The currently available evidence suggests that the appraisal potential is largely similar across cultures. As holds true for the antecedents, cultural differences tend to emerge with respect to the prevalence of specific appraisal categories. Propensities to use certain appraisal dimensions rather than others appear to differ cross-culturally.

Concerns and Values

Although there is little research that systematically compares concerns in different cultures, it seems evident that universalities in the human condition bring along some similarity in concerns. The loss of attachment figures, the esteem received from other people, one's own well-being and that of intimate other people, all must be among such universal concerns. Even concerns that appear to be cross-culturally different at one level of description, often lose their culture-specificity when described at a slightly more general level. For example, the concern for honor may be specific to Mediterranean cultures, among others, but the cultural differences are likely to dissolve if the same concern is described as a concern for personal integrity or social status. It is questionable, however, that the generalization of honor to a concern of a higher level of abstraction (such as social or moral status) does justice to those aspects of the concern that account for the emotional reactions provoked by concern-relevant events. Further, it is certainly questionable that one can have a full-blown understanding of honor-related emotions, such as shame and pride, without reference to honor. Honor has to do with a person's moral caliber and that of the other people. In addition, honor depends on external validation: one's moral caliber is not reflected as honor unless other people are (made) aware of it. With that said, one has to realize that honor has many emotion-relevant meanings, not included in concepts like morality and social status. There appear to be clear sex differences (cf. Abu-Lughod, 1986; Blok, 1981, Pitt-Rivers, 1965). Men's honor consists of being in control of their own family and of outperforming or impressing other men. Women's honor consists of confirming their husbands' and fathers' guidance by modesty and faithfulness. Likewise, shameful events have been reported to elicit different reactions: men try to restore their honor by showing off, by aggression, or by retaliation; women will react to (potentially) shameful events by extraordinary submissive behavior and avoidance (see e.g., Abu-Lughod, 1986). It is interesting to note that the emotional phenomena are better understood when a culture-specific description of the concern (such as honor) is adopted than when the concern is aggregated to a universal concern. There is thus evidence for culture-specific concerns. Analogous to the antecedent events, it is difficult to arrive at a level of description of concerns that leaves out irrelevant details, but maintains information relevant to the understanding of subsequent emotional reactions.

Cultural differences are also found in the focality of concerns (see section on the meaning of culture). Value priorities are likely to determine which concerns are focal. It seems quite plausible that events that have an impact on the family or social group have greater importance in collectivistic as compared to individualistic cultures, as found in some recent research (Markus & Kitayama, 1991; 1994b; Mesquita, in preparation). Conversely, self-esteem and achievement might be more central concerns in individualistic cultures. Cultural focality of concerns makes for a qualitative difference in appraisal, in addition to a difference in accessibility (see earlier discussion).

In sum, it is plausible that there are some universal human concerns, despite some differences in the concerns that are available or most accessible. The precise nature of concerns as well as the focality of concerns may differ across cultures. Cultural focality of a concern seems to further appraisal of events in terms of that concern.

Physiological Reactions

Another question addressed in cross-cultural research on emotions is related to the cross-cultural variations in the physiological responses accompanying particular emotions. The hypothesis underlying much of this research is that different emotions are universally accompanied by specific and unique patterns of physiological responses.

Measurement of Physiological Responses

To study cross-cultural variations in the physiological responses accompanying certain emotions, one has to actually measure physiological responses. This approach has been far from popular; in fact, few studies along this line exist. One study measured physiological responses in young Minangkabau men living in West Sumatra under conditions thought to be relevant to certain "basic emotions," and compared the results with those obtained in previous studies with American students (Levenson, Ekman, Heider, & Friesen, 1992). The study made use of the Directed Facial Action task, in which subjects are asked to voluntarily move their face muscles according to the directions given to them (e.g., raise, lower, or tighten certain parts of the face, such as eyebrow, cheek, lip). The directions led to various facial expressions prototypical for some basic emotions; for instance, subjects were asked to pull their lips down and make several other movements for a disgust face. The physiological measures taken were heart rate, finger temperature, skin conductance, finger pulse transmission time, finger pulse amplitude, respiratory period, and respiratory depth. The results were complicated, but led the authors to claim that the data lend support to cross-culturally consistent physiological differentiation between the basic emotions. There is reason to challenge this claim, though. Penetrating critique has been aimed at the kind of study reported (see Cacioppo, Klein, Berntson & Hatfield, 1993; Zajonc & Macintosh, 1992). The most important reason for this critique is the lack of consistency of results across studies. The overwhelming evidence from experimental research done in Western cultures, so far, indicates the absence of unique patterns of physiological responses differentiating between different emotions (Stemmler, 1989). The failure to find unique patterns of physiology may be due to the relatively low intensities of emotions evoked in the laboratory.

The focus of a study like the preceding one is on the potential for certain patterns of physiological responses. Provided that this potential is cross-culturally similar, independent cultural differences may still occur with respect to the practice or propensity to certain (patterns of) physiological responses, due to different degrees in which certain responses are tolerated or valued. For example, crying among the Bedouins in the Egyptian desert (Abu-Lughod, 1986) is considered a sign of weakness, whereas in other cultures, like the Turkish, under many circumstances, it is considered a perfectly acceptable social response. Differences in the prevalence of certain physiological responses may also follow from different appraisal or action readiness propensities. For instance, Harburg et al. (1973) reported that socioculturally deprived African-Americans in Detroit responded to frustrations with sharper increases in blood pressure than European Americans. In all likelihood, there were parallel sociocultural differences in the emotional meaning of the frustrations, such as perceived control. A similar relationship between action readiness propensities and culture-specific physiological patterns is conceivable; for example, the inclination to aggressive responses may be related to the tensing of muscles, and increased heartbeat. Research addressing the issue does not exist.

Self-Reports of Physiological Responses

A second type of approach to the question of cross-cultural similarity in physiological patterns has been to ask the subjects to report the physiological symptoms that had accompanied a particular emotional experience. Thus, respondents reported an instance of a particular emotion, for example, anger, and were then asked to describe the physiological reactions that had accompanied the emotion. A recent and comprehensive study in this vein compared the physiological responses in thirty-seven countries reported to accompany seven emotions: joy, fear, anger, sadness, disgust, shame, and guilt (Scherer & Wallbott, 1994). Distinct patterns of physiological responses were similarly reported across cultures. For example, joy was on the average characterized by feeling warm and a faster heart beat, and sadness by tense muscles, lump in the throat, and crying/sobbing. A considerably larger part of the variation in reported physiological responses was explained by the type of emotion than was accounted for by either country or the interaction of country and type of emotions. Still, there was some variation due to country (and since country is not necessarily the best operationalization of culture, the effect of culture may even be larger than suggested by the authors). The patterns of variation were not reported.

This consistency contrasts with the usually weak or negative findings with actual measurement of evoked physiological response patterns in various emotions (Stemmler, 1989). The explanation is an open question. A possible interpretation is that cross-culturally stable physiological reactions in intense emotion instances have given rise to stereotyped expectations concerning the changes that occur with these emotions (Rimé, Philippot & Cisamolo, 1990). The stereotyped expectations may not necessarily correspond to the changes that actually occur.

Some cultural differences in the propensities to report certain physiological changes have been found. A comparison between the physiological changes reported by subjects from Southern and Northern European regions yielded, for instance, that "the reputedly 'hot-blooded' southerners reported significantly more blood pressure changes (in joy, sadness, and anger), whereas the cold northerners reported significantly more stomach sensations (for joy and fear) and muscle symptoms (for anger)" (Rimé & Giovannini, 1986, p. 90/91). Other examples of such differences are available in the literature (e.g., Scherer et al., 1988), explanations for which are rare, and largely speculative.

Action Readiness

Emotions involve changes in action readiness: an increase or decrease in the general state of activation, or the emergence of particular action tendencies. Forms of activation include hyper- and hypo-activation (or exuberance and apathy, respectively), tenseness, and inhibition. Various forms of action readiness are best described in terms of their relational meaning; that is, as relational aims. In fact, forms of action readiness in emotion are forms of readiness for major interaction patterns. Major examples of action tendencies are approach, withdrawal and avoidance, rejection, help-seeking, hostility, breaking contact, dominance, and submission (Davitz, 1969; Frijda, 1986). Different emotions tend to involve different kinds of action readiness, or tend to be defined by them. For instance, the impulse to protect oneself from a danger is a state usually called "fear" in English. Changes in action readiness do not always lead to changes in actual behavior. They may only be felt impulses or lack of impulse, and thus be part of emotional experience. The behaviors, that manifest a given form of action readiness, usually are highly variable; impulse to stop being bothered by an offender may result in one of the many physical and non-physical forms of hostile behavior, or merely in breaking off contact.

Attention to changes in action readiness are of recent origin in cross-cultural research. There are a few studies cross-culturally comparing the action readiness patterns reported for different emotions (see discussion that follows). Subjects in these studies were asked to recall an instance of an emotional experience, indicated by an emotion word, and then to answer questions about changes in action readiness.

Similarities in Action Readiness

In the extensive cross-national study cited earlier (Scherer & Wallbott, 1994), subjects were asked about seven major emotions. Included in the questionnaire were questions asking whether their emotional experience had led them to move toward, move away from, or move against (aggress) the object of emotion. Considerable cross-cultural similarity was found in the action readiness patterns for the emotions studied. As would have been expected, joy caused more approach behaviors than the other emotions studied, anger elicited more aggression, and withdrawal was most common in sadness, disgust, shame, and guilt. Emotion accounted for most of the variation in action readiness responses. Some variation was accounted for by country, and by the interaction between country and emotion, however.

When described at a high level of abstraction, considerable cross-cultural generality in action readiness modes appears. Frijda and his colleagues studied action readiness changes associated with nineteen lexically equivalent words in Japanese, Indonesian, and Dutch (Frijda et al., 1995). The questions in their action readiness questionnaire were more numerous, and at a more concrete level of description, than those of Scherer and Wallbott (1994). The former included such questions as: "Did you feel like avoiding or fleeing? Did you feel the tendency to break contact with another person or did you feel finished with that other person? Did you have the tendency to keep or push something away?" Again, considerable similarity was found for the major lexical equivalents. Furthermore, separate factor analyses for the three cultural groups indicated five rather similar factors: moving away, moving towards, moving against, helplessness, and submission. Note that the first three factors correspond to the action readiness questions used in the Scherer and Wallbott (1994) study. These factors may be seen as representing the core of the relational meaning of the action readiness modes.

Incidentally, a major aspect of emotional action readiness is its character of impulse, involving a shift of behavioral control and a tendency to override other concerns of the moment. This feature can be considered as more or less defining the scientific category of emotion. So far, there is no evidence that this control precedence (Frijda, 1986) is not universal. This implies that, even when the concept of "emotion" may not be present in all languages (cf. Russell, 1991; Van Brakel, 1994), the phenomenon of emotion is still likely to be present in the cultures concerned.

Differences in Action Readiness

Differences in action readiness have been found as well. First, in the study just described (Frijda et al., 1995), the contribution to explained variance by the factors differed drastically from one culture to the other. "Moving away," for instance, was twice as important for the Dutch than for the other two groups, while the reverse held for "moving towards." Individual items also differed sharply, in the factors they loaded on, in the average values across the emotions included in the study, and in their value for discriminating one emotion term from another. For instance, "wish to depend on someone else" and "apathy" scored much higher for the Japanese than for the other two groups. The Japanese also more often reported feelings of helplessness and urges to protect themselves as aspects of the various emotional experiences. These results converge with studies using quite different methodologies, which suggest that depending on intimate others as well as acceptance by others (harmonizing with the environment) are important and valued components of emotional life in Japan (Lebra, 1976, 1983; Markus & Kitayama, 1994b).

Important differences were also found for individual emotion categories. For instance, impulse toward hostile behavior was more important for anger (or in the moving against factor) for the Dutch group, and "boiling inwardly" for the other two.

Changes in action readiness in response to different types of situations were examined in a study comparing Dutch, Surinamese, and Turkish people living in the Netherlands (see section on appraisal). Significant group differences emerged. For example, the latter two groups reported that, in situations in which they had themselves behaved immorally towards an intimate other, they did not dare to look the other person in the face, and that they had the desire not to be noticed or seen; while in similar situations, the Dutch reported no such tendencies. The disparities were again best described as differences in degree. In situations in which the subject had been offended by an intimate other, subjects in all three groups reported "boiling inwardly," and feeling an inclination to physical as well as verbal aggression, but the Dutch group reported these action readiness modes to a lesser degree than the other two groups.

Emotional Expression

Cross-cultural study of emotional behavior has mainly focused on facial expression. This research is interesting and important; yet, in our view, its importance has been overrated. There is no good reason why facial expression should be treated the way it often is, as the major criterion of the occurrence of a particular emotion in a given culture, or as an indication for the universality of a given emotion (see e.g., Ekman, 1994a; Levenson et al., 1992). The presumption in adopting facial expressions as the decisive criterion of emotions is that the facial expressions are discrete and typical for basic emotions. However, this argument has little empirical basis. We consider facial expression as just one component, though an important one, because it is an elementary channel through which action readiness becomes manifest. The issues of major interest for cross-cultural psychology are those of the evidence for universality and innateness of facial expressions, and for cultural specificities and learning.

Cultural Similarities in Expression
Research on the possible universality of facial expressions has mainly made use of one paradigm: presenting the subjects with still photographs showing face and shoulders, each face with a different (usually posed) expression. In most studies, the photographs shown were selected out of much larger collections, on the grounds

of likely or proven unambiguity (Izard, 1994; Russell, 1994). Subjects were asked to identify the facial expressions. Various methods have been used: (a) checking one out of a small set (6–10) of emotion words (the "standard method"), (b) rating each expression on a small set of emotion scales, (c) having subjects produce their own label for each expression, and (d) matching the expressions with a small set of brief stories describing an emotional event (the "Dashiell method").

There is overwhelming evidence for universality of a set of facial expresssions of emotion. The evidence is mostly indirect, as it comes from cross-cultural correspondence in the recognition or labeling of facial expressions. The number of universal facial expression patterns is at least six; that is the number of emotions that has been discriminated. The number of universally discriminable expressions should be larger since it is likely to include laughter, crying, pouting, and the nonfacial expression of foot-stamping (Eibl-Eibesfeldt, 1974). The universal patterns of expression are presumably innate, either as patterns or with regard to the components, such as frowning and eye-widening, that may be seen as their building blocks (Scherer, 1992; Smith, 1989).

Although subjects from nearly all cultures investigated reliably distinguished posed expressions, supposedly corresponding to anger, sadness, disgust, fear, happiness, and surprise, from one another, the degree to which they did so is appreciably higher in subjects from literate than illiterate cultures (Russell, 1994). With the standard method (see above), the average percentage agreement in labeling was about 70 percent for subjects from literate groups, and approximately 40 percent for subjects from illiterate groups. In both cases, however, the percent "correct" recognitions (that is, correspondence with the emotion label meant by the experimenters) was far above chance (Ekman, 1994a; Russell, 1994). Compared to the standard method, free labeling techniques yield appreciably lower percentages "correct" identifications, but usually still way above chance level.

The universal facial expressions provide strong support for the hypothesis that certain central emotion mechanisms (modes of action readiness, or of interpersonal messages relevant to certain interpersonal contingencies) are indeed universal. The expressions that were universally recognized must have some common core of emotional meaning. These core meanings are roughly reflected by the English words happiness, sadness, fear, anger, disgust, surprise, and, perhaps, contempt. Evidence for universality of facial expressions of emotion would indicate the existence of a universal potential for emotion communication. Research endeavors have largely been based on the assumption that basic emotions are marked by distinct and unique facial expressions, and the research outcomes have been treated in the context of the putative universality of six to ten basic emotions (Ekman & Friesen, 1975; Ekman, Friesen, & Ellsworth, 1982; Izard, 1971). As discussed in the introduction, that linkage is not necessarily correct.

The conclusion that universality in the recognition of facial expressions demonstrates the existence of universal basic emotions is, therefore, not warranted. Rather than understanding facial expressions in terms of basic emotions, we view them as first manifestations of different types of action readiness, that is, types of interpersonal messages relevant to person–environment interactions (for an elaborate discussion see Frijda & Tcherkassof, in press; Russell, 1994).

Cultural Differences in Expression

Universality of the patterns notwithstanding, there are significant group differences in the percentages of agreement in assigning specific labels to particular expressions. The percentage of agreement is rarely perfect in any cultural group. Recognition rates range from 98 percent (for "happiness" in an American sample) to 49 percent (for the equivalent of "fear" in an "African" group) for literate subjects, and from 99 percent (for "happiness" in a pidgin Fore sample) to 19 percent (for "surprise" in an isolated Fore sample) (figures taken from Russell, 1994).

Apart from cultural differences in task familiarity, at least two explanations for the established cross-cultural differences in expression are conceivable. First, the meaning of certain expressions might be distinctly different in different cultures, due to differential learning. So far, there has been no evidence in support of this explanation. Second, cultural differences in recognition rates may be due to differences in word meanings, or in the precise emotional connotations of stories used in the Dashiell method. Even when a given word (say, *marah* in Indonesian) is considered the best translation of a given English word (in this case, "anger"), its connotations may be (and in fact are) distinctly different. It is possible that the degrees to which lexical equivalents in different languages correspond to certain types of facial expressions differ.

Evidence for culture-specific facial expressions exists, but is limited. One of these is tongue protrusion as a sign of shame in the Indian Orissa culture (Menon & Shweder, 1994). This type of facial expression is presumably culturally learned.

The previous discussion pertains to potential for facial expressions of emotion. It has little or nothing to do with the practice of facial expressions in daily interaction, nor with their frequency, their prominence or typicality, or even their precise nature. Little is known about cross-cultural differences in the ecology of facial expressions.

The universality finding does not imply that given emotions as categorized by the language, invariably produce the same facial expression. Fear, for instance, may be manifest in frowning as described by Ekman and Friesen (1978), but it may also be expressed by widely opened eyes and lifted eyebrows (in which case it is close to the one defined as surprise by Ekman and Friesen, hence the confusion in some illiterate cultures). Likewise, different expressions of anger can be distinguished (Klineberg, 1938). Cultural differences in the recognition or production of facial expressions may result from culturally different tendencies to use one type of expression rather than another.

Ekman and Friesen (1969) have coined the important notion of *display rules* to explain such differences in the ecology of facial expressions. Cultures may differentially suppress, attenuate, and/or enhance facial expressivity or particular expressions in particular social contexts. Although direct observational evidence for the operation of such rules is sparse (but see Ekman, 1982), prescriptions are widely found in informal, anthropological (Briggs, 1970; Lutz, 1987), and etiquette literature (e.g., Elias, 1969). In addition, empirical studies exist on how such rules are learned (e.g., Saarni, 1979, 1984).

"Display rules" may not be the most appropriate general term to refer to the source of cultural variations in expressive behavior, because the issue of importance may not be the expression per se, but rules of conduct and respect in certain interactions. For the Japanese, facial expressions of displeasure seem to be replaced by the expression corresponding to polite intercourse (the smile), rather than suppressed in face-to-face contact (Lebra, 1976). Display rules may also affect emotions more profoundly, influencing them beyond expression per se. Smiling in Japanese people, for example, may help them to focus on the interaction, and thus, draw their attention away from the source of discontent. In that sense, the term display rules is not very well chosen (see Zajonc & McIntosh, 1992, for a similar critique).

Finally, particular facial expressions may have appreciably different meanings in different cultures, notwithstanding the fact that their basic emotional message is similar. A smile may be an expression of pleasure or friendliness everywhere, but showing friendliness may be insolence in one culture, a reason for distrust in another, and a requirement in social interaction in a third. In other words, cross-cultural correspondence with regard to facial expression at one level in no way rules out the possibility of wide differences in the role and meaning of such process at another level.

Cognitive Consequences

There is ample evidence that emotional states may have consequences for cognitive processing.[7] People who experience positive affect differ from those who experience negative affect regarding memory access, strategies of problem solving and categorization, and regarding the evaluative judgments they make of other people and of their lives in general (Bower, 1981; Clore, Schwarz & Conway, 1994; Schwarz & Clore, 1988). Different negative emotions may shape cognitive processing in different ways. For instance, anger has been found to lead to more personal attribution of negative events and circumstances, as compared to both sadness and neutral conditions; whereas sadness leads to a tendency to understand negative circumstances as more due to impersonal forces (Keltner, Ellsworth & Edwards, 1993). Also, emotional states may lead to belief changes,[8] which may either last briefly or permanently. They result from generalizing the emotional appraisal of the eliciting event to a class of events or actors (Frijda, Mesquita, Sonnemans & Van Goozen, 1991). For example, a failed love affair may lead to loss of faith in relationships in general, and an unpleasant incident involving a member of a particular group may lead to, or support, group prejudice. It is not hard to imagine that there would be cultural differences in the cognitive processes accompanying emotions, even though research in this area is scarce.

Cultural differences in emotions may result in differences in emotion-related cognitive processes; for example, differences in the frequency of positive emotions may lead to a different use of heuristics, or to a difference in the tendency to give positive evaluations, and so forth. Recent studies have pointed to cultural differences in the degree to which people strive for and experience positive emotions. Kitayama, Markus, and Kurokawa (referred to by Markus & Kitayama, 1994b) asked American and Japanese students living in the United States to report on the frequency with which they experienced certain emotions in daily life. "The Americans reported an overwhelmingly greater frequency of experiencing positive than negative self-relevant feelings, but there was virtually no such effect among the Japanese" (p. 108). It is an empirical question whether the different ratios of positive self-feelings, in Americans, result in corresponding differences in the use of cognitive strategies found to accompany positive affect. Also, Akiyama (1992), working with a large sample of elderly Japanese people, did not find the inverse correlation between positive and negative affect characteristic of the comparable American samples. In the Japanese sample, there was virtually no correlation between positive and negative emotions. Moreover, the Japanese levels of both positive and negative affect were considerably lower than those of Americans. The impression these studies give is that there are differences in the frequency of positive affect, and possibly also in the intensity of both positive and negative affect. The cognitive strategies that are dominant in cultures as different as the American and the Japanese can be predicted to diverge on the basis of differences in the emotional practice in these cultures. Provided that the nature of the respective cognitive consequences of positive and negative affect do not differ cross-culturally, the dominant cognitive strategies will differ between Americans and Japanese people. Compared to the latter, the former will be found to more readily adopt strategies associated with positive affect or with intense feelings.

Also, cultural differences in emotions may be reinforced or amplified by the cognitive changes to which they give rise. As reported, anger in Americans gave rise to a stronger tendency to attribute negative events to human agency, whereas sadness tended to lead to attribution of the same events to impersonal factors. It may be argued that the appraisal of blame (something negative attributed to human agency) is a central condition to the emergence of anger. Hence, anger may be expected to have cognitive consequences that, in turn, facilitate the emergence of more anger. Significant cultural differences in the tendency to react with anger may be due to this self-reinforcing mechanism. Evidence of the cognitive consequences of other emotions than the ones mentioned does not exist; speculation about cultural differences in these cognitive consequences thus seems pointless.

There also may exist differences in some general parameters of the cognitive consequences of emotions across cultures. Some evidence suggests that the degree to which people form belief changes, as a result of their emotions, differs for people from different cultures. For instance, when asked to recall how they had reacted when harmed by another person, Turkish and Surinamese respondents in a study by Mesquita (in preparation) reported that their confidence in and respect for the other person had changed, and they did so to a significantly higher degree than the Dutch respondents. They also reported that it had tended to change their confidence in other people generally, whereas the Dutch subjects reported not to have undergone that change. In principle, the consequences of such belief changes can be pervasive, because they may serve as a frame of interpretation for subsequent events, and thus, influence the emotional appraisals of later events.

Conclusion

As has become painfully obvious in this chapter, the study of emotion in cultural context suffers from flagrant neglect by the research community at large, and from methodological insufficiency. Another pressing issue is the uncertain status of the concept of "culture." The large majority of psychological studies reported in this chapter has simply compared different countries, or more exactly, often a specific group of the population (mostly students) in one of the major urban centers. Anthropologists, on the other hand, have tended to study rural populations in remote areas of the world. Not surprisingly, the data are hardly comparable. As pointed out before, major subcultural differences, such as urban–rural, age or cohort differences, social class differences, and exposure to media have not been taken into consideration.

Universal Aspects of Emotion

The main conclusion from the the available evidence is that emotions exist in all cultures, regardless of the presence or absence of the corresponding linguistic notions (cf. Russell, 1991). Cross-culturally, events considered relevant to major concerns are seen to elicit emotional responses, including facial expressions, physiological changes, hedonic experiences, and important shifts in the control of behavior pertinent to interactions with the environment.

Also, particular combinations of emotional appraisal and impulse appear to exist in most, if not all, cultures. In most cultures, individuals are emotionally sensitive to contingencies such as loss of intimates, thwarting of strivings by others, arriving at goals after difficulties, danger of rejection by the group or by valued group members; across cultures the response to such contingencies include loss of interest in the outer world and crying, hostile tendencies, enhanced activity and seeking contact with others, and submissive or hostile behavior.

Cross-Cultural Differences in Emotion

There is evidence of consistent cultural differences as well as similarities in each component of emotions. The first rule seems to be that cross-cultural similarities in emotional phenomena are more likely to be found when these phenomena are described at a rather high level of abstraction. An emphasis on the concrete features of emotional phenomena, on the other hand, appears to enhance the likelihood of finding cultural differences. The second rule concerns the emphasis on potential as opposed to practice. Research focusing on emotional potential is more likely to document cultural similarities, while research emphasizing the practice of certain emotional phenomena is bound to yield differences. Cultures may differ significantly in the frequency and focality of various appraisal features or behavior tendency response types, and other aspects of the role of the corresponding emotional phenomena and linguistic emotion categories in the culture. Thus, people from different cultures appear to be similar in their emotion potential, especially when this potential is described at a higher level of meaning. Yet, despite the similarities in basic elements of emotional life, concrete emotional realities in different cultures may vary widely.

Cultures may differ with respect to the ways meaning gets expressed, filled in, and elaborated. The kinds of events that correspond to certain appraisal contingencies may vary greatly, and the same types of events may engender drastically different appraisals. Both the presence and the specific nature of the behavior corresponding to various tendencies can be drastically different from one culture to the other. Similarity in repertoire thus does not seem to preclude differences in the actual emotional lives of people in different cultures. Also, all the contingencies that engender emotions are not easily grouped under the contingencies that make a claim to universality.

While the presently available evidence of cultural differences in the potential for emotional phenomena is at best to be called modest, hardly any systematic information is available on emotion ecology, the way and the degree to which emotion potential is transformed into emotion practice in various cultures.

The Influence of Culture on Emotion

Very little is known, too, on the ways cultures influence the emotional lives of their members. Almost no systematic information exists on cultural differences in the social manifestations and social consequences of emotions, and the reciprocal influences upon the emotions themselves. There is growing consensus that cultures may shape the emotional lives of their members at different levels (Markus & Kitayama, 1994a; Mesquita, in preparation; Shweder, 1993). For these reasons, it should be acknowledged simultaneously that certain socially and individually important emotional response types are universal or near-universal, and that the experience, phenomenology, and social role of these response types may be different in essential regards. Even where universal patterns of appraisal and response exist, these universal cores may be submerged in the culturally determined contexts of experience, meaning, and social interaction. However, data have to be collected that pinpoint the place of universal mechanisms in the patterns, and that include the interactional significance of emotions in particular cultures.

Methodology

These conclusions are reached, in part, through the paradigm shift in the cross-cultural psychology of emotion. The research methodology has changed accordingly. Studies have begun to focus on different components of emotions simultaneously. It is no longer assumed that cross-cultural similarities found in one emotion component, such as facial expressions or overall appraisal patterns, imply similarity in other facets of emotion. Whether cross-cultural similarities in one component exist along with either differences or similarities in other components has become an empirical question. When "the same" emotion is studied in different cultures—that is, when the emotion labels used can be considered each other's translation with respect to certain major components—similarities and differences in the emotional phenomena associated with these labels are investigated for each component of the emotion process separately. For this reason, there has been a tendency to move away from emotion words as the basis of comparison.

The move away from emotion words has led to new methodological developments that can be expected to expand in the near future. In particular, additional recent studies of emotion have focused on the cross-cultural comparison of emotional responses to phenomena known to be relevant to all cultures of comparison (e.g., Haidt & Keltner, 1995; Mesquita, in preparation). Although the phenomena concentrated on may not be the most prevalent ones overall, this approach provides a better guarantee than the previous ones that the phenomena under study have at least some relevance to all cultural groups included for comparison.

Another novel strategy in the psychological cross-cultural studies on emotions has been to examine the most salient emotional phenomena in each culture, regardless of whether the salient phenomena in different cultures overlap. An example was provided by Markus and Kitayama's (1991) study of Japanese emotion words. Rather than selecting those words that were the closest translations of English emotion words, they chose to study words that were salient in the Japanese culture. Analogously, one may focus on the most frequent emotion antecedent in different cultures, regardless of the overlap between the cultures of comparison. This strategy offers the advantage that information can be obtained about the most important emotional phenomena in different cultures. The disadvantage of such a strategy clearly is that the most prevalent emotional phenomena in different cultures may not overlap. This type of research would, therefore, focus on different emotions for each culture, rendering comparison at the level of individual emotions more difficult.

A More Comprehensive Perspective on Cultural Variation in Emotions

Although our discussion has certainly given an impression of the range of cultural variations in emotions, it probably does not give a full account of the differences that do, in fact, exist. Such a full account can, in our view, only be obtained when the process character of emotions receives the attention it deserves. Emotion as process, as hinted at earlier, has several aspects. First, the different components of emotions are not independent. Differences found to occur in one component probably tend to bring along differences in the other components. For instance, a cultural tendency to blame other people for unpleasant events may well be found to co-occur with a propensity to aggressive behavior (see e.g., Cohen & Nisbett, 1994).

Second, emotions are multilayered processes, because the emotional response to an event is in itself a significant event to be appraised emotionally (Ellsworth, 1994; Fischer, 1991). Thus, the initial appraisal of the event may be modified by a secondary appraisal, focusing on the emotional response elicited by the event. Cultural differences in the development of the emotion process may thus be due to differences in secondary appraisal. There is evidence that cultures vary in their beliefs about which emotions are most significant or revealing, which emotions are good or bad, and which emotions are appropriate to particular social roles or social settings (Briggs, 1970; Ellsworth, 1994; Gerber, 1985; Markus & Kitayama, 1994a; White, 1990, 1994). These cultural differences in the meaning attached to emotions (or certain emotional responses) themselves may bring about cultural variations in secondary appraisals, and may thus produce differences in the course of emotions.

Third, emotions as such, or the behaviors following from the emotions, may affect the environment, thus changing the situation by which the emotions were elicited in the first place. Emotions, in other words, represent transactions with the environment (Lazarus, 1991). An appraisal of the situation as changed may override or modify the original appraisal. Thus, situational changes brought about by the emotional response feed back into the emotion process. Many emotions emerge in social interactions, which may change, not only as an effect of instrumental action, but also because other people understand and act upon the signal value or meaning of emotion or emotional behavior (Frijda & Mesquita, 1991; 1994). On the grounds that both signal value and meaning of emotions and emotional behaviors appear to be variable across cultures, cultural differences in the course of emotion may be expected, and this holds the more empathically if emotional interactions, rather than only the emotional phenomena within one individual, are studied.

Finally, the process character of emotions appears rather clearly in that emotions have cognitive consequences, such as belief changes. Various cognitive consequences may well cause cultural differences in emotional inclinations to be amplified. As we saw in the section on cognitive consequences, strategies of cognitive processing appear to vary with moods, and even with emotional states, for the duration of such states. Anger, for example, leads people to understand their environment in terms of agency; the appraisal of human agency is likely to be facilitated by a bias towards the perception of agency. Cultural differences in the tendency for anger may thus reinforce themselves. Whereas cultures with a high incidence of anger will tend to perceive agency, and thus, be likely to develop more anger, cultures with a low incidence of anger will not perceive the world in terms of agency, and therefore, be less inclined to anger. More permanent belief changes will also feed back into the emotions. Belief changes will lead to certain emotional sensitivities. Thus, cultural differences in the tendencies to develop (certain types of) belief changes are likely to lead to cultural variations in the sensitivities for (particular types of) events. All this, quite obviously, is subject matter for future research endeavors.

In all, there is ample reason to assume that cultural differences in emotions will be more pronounced (a) when the different components of emotion are studied in their temporal and functional relation, (b) when attention is focused on the way the meaning and social effects of emotions feed back into the emotion process, and (c) when the focus of research will be shifted from individual emotions to emotion ecologies, and factors that influence cultural differences in emotion ecologies. The field has only begun to address these issues empirically.

Endnotes

1. The present work was supported by the Maison des Sciences de l'Homme, Paris. The first author was supported by the Netherlands Organization for Scientific Research (NWO) and by the Royal Netherlands Academy of Arts and Sciences. Her work on this chapter was, furthermore, facilitated by the hospitality of the Institute for Social Research, University of Michigan, and the support of Phoebe Ellsworth, Diane Holmberg, Laura Kubzansky, Hazel Markus, and Twila Tardif. The authors also wish to thank Dr. Kao for his literature suggestions, and Matti Chiva, Heiner Ellgring, Tony Manstead, Ype Poortinga, Pio Ricci-Bitti, Bernard Rimé, and Michael Zajonc for their comments on earlier versions of this chapter.

2. A analogous distinction between maximal and typical performance has been made by Lonner & Berry (1986, p. 105).

3. The distinction between availability and accessibility of concepts is borrowed from the social cognition paradigm (see e.g., Wyer & Srull, 1981, 1986).

4. We combine closely related models as described in Markus & Kitayama (1994) and in Frijda & Mesquita (1994), Markus & Kitayama speak of "core cultural ideas," and Frijda & Mesquita use the term "focal concerns." There is enough overlap between those concepts to use them interchangeably, which we will do in the following.

5. To our knowledge, the value literature does not elaborate on the way values are materialized in, or even derived from, cultural practice; nor does it make clear how value priorities shape other psychological practices such as emotions. It may well be that the two literatures end up converging.

6. Self-esteem has often been treated as a dimension of appraisal. We think it is more accurate to represent it as a concern.

7. See e.g., Clore, Schwarz, & Conway (1994) for various theoretical explanations of the emergence of emotion- and mood-specific cognitive processing.

8. There is not much clarity about the mechanisms that may underly the formation of belief changes, but see Frijda et al. (1991).

References

Abu-Lughod, L. (1986). *Veiled sentiments.* Berkeley: University of California Press.

Abu-Lughod, L. & Lutz, C. A. (1990). Introduction: Emotion, discourse, and the politics of everyday life. In C. A. Lutz & L. Abu-Lughod (Eds.), *Language and the politics of emotion* (pp. 1–23). Cambridge: Cambridge University Press.

Agnoli, A., Kirson, D., Wu, S., & Shaver, P. R. (1989). *Hierachical analysis of the emotion lexi-con in English, Italian, and Chinese.* Paper presented at the International Society for research of emotion, Paris.

Akiyama, H. (1992, June). *Measurement of depressive symptoms in cross-cultural research.* Paper presented at the International Conference on Emotion and Culture, University of Oregon, Eugene.

Arnold, M. B. (1960). *Emotion and personality, Vols. 1 and 2.* New York: Columbia University Press.

Averill, J. R. (1994). It's a small world, but a large stage. In P. Ekman & R. J. Davidson (Eds.), *The nature of emotion: Fundamental questions* (pp.143–145). Oxford: Oxford University Press.

Besnier, N. (1995). The politics of emotion in Nukulaelae gossip. In J.A. Russell, A. S. R. Manstead, J. C. Wellenkamp, & J. M Fernandez-Dols (Eds.), *Everyday conceptions of emotion: An introduction to the psychology, anthropology and linguistics of emotion* (pp.221–240). Dordrecht, the Netherlands: Kluwer.

Blok, A. (1980, June). Eer en de fysieke persoon [Honor and the physical person]. *Tijdschrift voor Sociale Geschiedenis*, pp. 211–230.

Blok, A. (1981). Rams and billy-goats: A key to Mediterranean code of honor. *Man, 16,* 427–440.

Boucher, J. D. (1979). Culture and emotion. In A. J. Marsella, R. G. Tharp, & T. V. Ciborowksi (Eds.), *Perspectives on cross-cultural psychology* (pp. 159–178). San Diego, CA: Academic Press.

Boucher, J. D. & Brandt, M. E. (1981). Judgement of emotion: American and Malay antecedents. *Journal of Cross-Cultural Psychology, 12,* 272–283.

Bower, G. H. (1981). Mood and memory. *American Psychologist, 36,* 129–148.

Brand, M. E. & Boucher, J. D. (1985). Judgments of emotions from the antecedent situations in three cultures. In I. R. Lagunes & Y. H. Poortinga (Eds.), *From a different perspective: Studies of behavior across cultures* (pp.348–362). Lisse, The Netherlands: Swets & Zeitlinger.

Briggs, J. L. (1970). *Never in anger: Portrait of an Eskimo family.* Cambridge, MA: Harvard University Press.

Briggs, J. L. (1995). The study of Inuit emotions. Lessons from a personal retrospective. In J. A. Russell, A. S. R Manstead, J. C. Wellenkamp, & J. M Fernandez-Dols (Eds.), *Everyday conceptions of emotion. An introduction to the psychology, anthropology and linguistics of emotion* (pp. 203–220). Dordrecht: Kluwer.

Cacioppo, J. T., Klein, D. J., Berntson, G. G., & Hatfield, E. (1993). The physiology of emotion. In M. Lewis & J. M. Haviland (Eds.), *Handbook of emotions* (pp. 119–142). New York: The Guilford Press.

Chari, V. K. (1990). *Sanskrit criticism.* Honolulu: University of Hawaii Press.

Clore, G. L., Schwarz, N., & Conway, M. (1994). Affective causes and consequences of social information processing. In R. S. Wyer & T. K. Srull (Eds.), *Handbook of social cognition* (Vol. 1, pp. 323–417). Hillsdale, NJ: Lawrence Erlbaum Associates.

Cohen, D. & Nisbett, R. E. (1994). Self-protection and the culture of honor: Explaining southern violence. *Personality and Social Psychology Bulletin, 20,* 551–567.

Darwin, C. (1872). *The expression of emotions in man and animals.* London: John Murray [1965, Chicago: University of Chicago Press].

Davitz, J. R. (1969). *The language of emotion.* San Diego, CA: Academic Press.

Descartes, R. (1647). *Les passions de l'âme.* Amsterdam: Elsevier. (Paris: Vrin, 1970).

Dünker, J. (1979). *Mimischer Affektausdruck und sprachliche Kodierung* (Facial emotion expression and verbal coding of affect). Dreieich, Switzerland: Stritzinger.

Eibl-Eibesfeldt, I. (1973). The expressive behavior of the deaf-and-blind-born. In M. von Cranach & I. Vine (Eds.), *Social communication and movement* (pp. 163–194). New York: Academic Press.

Eibl-Eibesfeldt, I. (1974). Similarities and differences between cultures in expressive movements. In R.A. Hinde (Ed.), *Nonverbal communication* (pp. 20–33). Cambridge: Cambridge University Press.

Ekman, P. (1972). Universals and cultural differences in facial expressions of emotions. *Nebraska symposium on motivation,* Vol. 19. (pp. 207–283). Lincoln: University of Nebraska Press.

Ekman, P. (Ed.). (1982). *Emotion in the human face, 2nd ed.* New York: Cambridge University Press.

Ekman, P. (1973). Cross-cultural studies of facial expressions. In P. Ekman (Ed.), *Darwin and facial expression* (pp. 169–222). New York: Academic Press.

Ekman, P. (1994a). Strong evidence for universals in facial expression: A reply to Russell's mistaken critique. *Psychological Bulletin, 115,* 268–287.

Ekman, P. (1994b). Antecedent events and emotion metaphors. In P. Ekman & R. J. Davidson (Eds.), *The nature of emotion: Fundamental questions* (pp. 147–149). Oxford: Oxford University Press.

Ekman, P. & Friesen, W. V. (1969). The repertoire of nonverbal behavior: Categories, origins, usage, and coding. *Semiotica, 1,* 49–98.

Ekman, P. & Friesen W. V. (1975). *Unmasking the face.* Englewood Cliffs, NJ: Prentice-Hall.

Ekman, P. & Friesen, W. V. (1978). *The facial action coding system.* Palo Alto, CA: Consulting Psychologists Press.

Ekman, P., Friesen, W. V., & Ellsworth, P. (1982). What are the similarities and differences in facial behavior across cultures? In P. Ekman (Ed.), *Emotion in the human face* (pp.128–146). Cambridge: Cambridge University Press.

Elias, N. (1969). *The civilizing process.* New York: Urizen Books.

Ellsworth, P. (1994). Sense, culture and sensibility. In S. Kitayama & M. R. Markus (Eds.), *Emotion and culture: Empirical studies of mutual influence* (pp.23–50).Washington, DC: American Psychological Association.

Ellsworth, P. C. & Smith, C. A. (1988). From appraisal to emotion: Differences among unpleasant feelings. *Motivation and Emotion, 12,* 271–302.

Fischer, A. H. (1991). *Emotion scripts: A study of the social and cognitive facets of emotions.* Leiden, The Netherlands: DSWO-Press.

Frijda, N. H. (1986). *The emotions.* Cambridge: Cambridge University Press.

Frijda, N. H., Kuipers, P., & Terschure, E. (1989). Relations between emotion, appraisal, and emotional action readiness. *Journal of Personality and Social Psychology, 57,* 212–228.

Frijda, N. H., Markam, S., Sato, K., & Wiers, R. (1995). Emotions and emotion words. In J. A. Russell, A. S. R. Manstead, J. C. Wellenkamp, & J. M. Fernandez-Dols (Eds.), *Everyday conceptions of emotion. An introduction to the psychology, anthropology and linguistics of emotion* (pp.121–143). Dordrecht: Kluwer.

Frijda, N. H. & Mesquita, B. (1991, July).*The various effects of emotion communication.* Paper pre-sented at the 1991 meeting of the International Society for Research of Emotion, Saarbrücken.

Frijda, N. H. & Mesquita, B. (1994). The social roles and functions of emotions. In S. Kitayama & H. Markus (Eds.),*Emotion and culture: Empirical studies of mutual influence* (pp. 51–88). Washington, DC: American Psychological Association.

Frijda, N. H., Mesquita, B., Sonnemans, J., & Van Goozen, S. (1991).The duration of affective phenomena or emotions, sentiments and passions. In K. T. Strongman (Ed.), *International review of studies on emotion* (Vol. 1, pp. 187–225). Chichester, England: John Wiley and Sons.

Frijda, N. H. & Tcherkassof, A. (in press). Facial expression and modes of action readiness. In J. Russell & J. M. Dols (Eds.), *New directions in facial expression.* Cambridge: Cambridge University Press.

Geertz, C. (1973). Person, time and conduct in Bali. In Geertz, C. (Ed.), *The interpretation of cultures* (pp. 360–411). New York: Basic Books.

Gerber, E. R. (1985). Rage and obligation: Samoan emotion in conflict. In G. M. White & J. Kirkpatrick (Eds.), *Person, self and experience: Exploring Pacific ethnopsychologies* (pp. 121–167). Berkeley: University of California Press.

Goffman, E. (1982). On face-work. In E. Goffman (Ed.), *Interaction ritual* (Chap. 1: pp. 5–45). Garden City, NY: Doubleday-Anchor.

Haidt, J. & Keltner, D. (1995, June). *Emotion and culture: New methods, new faces.* Paper presented at the American Psychological Society, New York.

Haidt, J., Koller, S. H., & Dias, M. G. (1993). Affect, culture and morality, or is it wrong to eat your dog? *Journal of Personality and Social Psychology, 65,* 613–628.

Harburg, E., Erfurt, J. C., Hauenstein, L. S., Chape, C., Schull, W. J., & Schork, M. A. (1973). Socio-ecological stress, suppressed hostility, skin-color and Black–White male blood pressure: Detroit. *Psychosomatic Medicine, 35,* 276–296.

Higgins, E. T. (1989). Knowledge accessibility and activation: Subjectivity and suffering from unconscious sources. In J. S. Uleman & J. A.

Bargh (Eds.), *Unintended thought* (pp. 75–123). New York: Guilford.

Hochschild, A. R. (1979). Emotion work, feeling rules, and social structure. *American Journal of Sociology, 85,* 551–575.

Hochschild, A. R. (1983). *The managed heart.* Berkeley: University of California Press.

Hofstede, G. (1980). *Culture's consequences: International differences in work-related values.* Beverly Hills, CA: Sage.

Izard, C. E. (1971). *The face of emotion.* New York: Appleton-Century-Crofts.

Izard, C. E. (1977). *Human emotions.* New York: Plenum Press.

Izard, C. E. (1980). Cross-cultural perspectives on emotion and emotion communication. In H.C. Triandis & W. Lonner (Eds.), *Handbook of cross-cultural psychology, Vol. 3* (pp. 185–221). Boston: Allyn and Bacon.

Izard, C. E. (1994). Innate and universal facial expressions: Evidence from development and cross-cultural research. *Psychological Bulletin, 115,* 288–299

Johnson-Laird, P. N. & Oatley, K. (1989). The language of emotions: An analysis of a semantic field. *Cognition and Emotion, 3,* 81–123.

Keltner, D., Ellsworth, P. C., & Edwards, K. (1993). Beyond simple pessimism: Effects of sadness and anger on social perception. *Journal of Personality and Social Psychology, 64,* 740–752.

Kitayama, S. & Markus, M. R. (Eds.). (1994). *Emotion and culture: Empirical studies of mutual influence.* Washington, DC: American Psychological Association.

Kitayama, S. H., Markus, H. R., Matsumoto, H., & Norasakkunkuit, V. (in press). Individual and collective processes of self-esteem management: Self-enhancement in the United States and self-depreciation in Japan. *Journal of Personality and Social Psychology.*

Klineberg, O. (1938). Emotional expression in Chinese literature. *Journal of Abnormal and Social Psychology, 33,* 517–520.

Lang, P. J. (1977). Physiological assessment of anxiety and fear. In J. D. Cone & R. P. Hawkins (Eds.), *Behavioral assessment: New directions in clinical psychology* (pp. 178–195). New York: Brunner/Mazel.

Lazarus, R. (1991). *Emotion and adaptation.* New York: Oxford University Press.

Lazarus, R. (1994). Universal antecedents of the emotions. In P. Ekman & R. J. Davidson (Eds.), *The nature of emotion: Fundamental questions* (pp. 146–149). Oxford: Oxford University Press.

Lazarus, R. S. & Smith, C. A. (1988). Knowledge and appraisal in the cognition–emotion relationship. *Cognition and Emotion, 2,* 281–300.

Lebra, T. S. (1976). *Japanese patterns of behavior.* Honolulu: University of Hawaii Press.

Lebra, T.S. (1983). Shame and guilt: A psychocultural view of the Japanese self. *Ethos, 11,* 192–209.

Levenson, R. W., Ekman, P., Heider, K., & Friesen, W. V. (1992). Emotion and autonomic nervous system activity in the Minangkabau of West Sumatra. *Journal of Personality and Social Psychology, 62,* 972–988.

Levy, R. I. (1973). *Tahitians: Mind and experience in the Society Islands.* Chicago: University of Chicago Press.

Levy, R. I. (1984). Emotion, knowing, and culture. In R. A. Schweder & R. A. LeVine (Eds.), *Culture theory: Issues on mind, self, and emotion* (pp. 214–237). Cambridge: Cambridge University Press.

Lonner, W. J. & Berry, J. W. (1986). Sampling and surveying. In W. J. Lonner & J. W. Berry (Eds.), *Field methods in cross-cultural research* (pp. 85–110). Beverly Hills: Sage.

Lutz, C. (1982). The domain of emotion words on Ifaluk. *American Ethnologist, 9,* 113–128.

Lutz, C. (1985). Ethnopsychology compared to what? Explaining behavior and consciousness among the Ifaluk. In G. M. White & J. Kirkpatrick (Eds.), *Person, self, and experience: Exploring Pacific ethnopsychologies* (pp. 35–79). Berkeley: University of California Press.

Lutz, C. (1987). Goals, events and understanding in Ifaluk emotion theory. In N. Quinn & D. Holland (Eds.), *Cultural models in language and thought* (pp. 290–312). Cambridge: Cambridge University Press.

Lutz, C. (1988). *Unnatural emotions: Everyday sentiments on a Micronesian atoll and their challenge to western theory.* Chicago: University of Chicago Press.

Lutz, C. & White, G. M. L. (1986). The anthropology of emotions. *Annual Review of Anthropology, 15,* 405–36.

Manstead, A. S. R. & Tetlock, P. E. (1989). Cognitive appraisals and emotional experience: Further evidence. *Cognition and Emotion, 3,* 225–240.

Markus, H. R. & Kitayama, S. (1991). Culture and the self: Implications for cognition, emotion, and motivation. *Psychological Review, 98,* 224–253.

Markus, H. R. & Kitayama, S. (1994a). The cultural shaping of emotion: A conceptual framework. In S. Kitayama & M. R. Markus (Eds.), *Emotion and culture. Empirical studies of mutual influence* (pp. 339–351). Washington, DC: American Psychological Association.

Markus, H. R. & Kitayama, S. (1994b). The cultural construction of self and emotion: Implications for social behavior. In S. Kitayama & M. R. Markus (Eds.), *Emotion and culture: Empirical studies of mutual influence* (pp. 89–130). Washington, DC: American Psychological Association.

Matsumoto, D. (1989). Cultural influences on the perception of emotion. *Journal of Cross-Cultural Psychology, 20,* 92–105.

Matsumoto, D., Kudoh, T., Scherer, K., & Wallbott, H. (1988). Antecedents of and reactions to emotions in the United States and Japan. *Journal of Cross-Cultural Psychology, 19,* 267–286.

Mauro, R., Sato, K. & Tucker, J. (1992). The role of appraisal in human emotions: A cross-cultural study. *Journal of Personality and Social Psychology, 62,* 301–317.

Mead, M. (1975). Review of Darwin and facial expression. *Journal of Communication, 25,* 209–213.

Menon, U. & Shweder, R. A. (1994). Kali's tongue: Cultural psychology and the power of shame in Orissa, India. In S. Kitayama & H. Markus (Eds), *Emotion and culture* (p. 241–284). Washington, DC: American Psychological Association.

Mesquita, B. (in preparation). *Cultural variations in emotions. A comparative study of Dutch, Surinamese and Turkish people in the Netherlands.* New York: Oxford University Press.

Mesquita, B. & Frijda, N. H. (1992). Cultural variations in emotion: A review. *Psychological Bulletin, 112,* 179–204.

Miller, W. I. (1993). *Humiliation. And other essays on honor, social discomfort, and violence.* Ithaca, NY: Cornell University Press.

Myers, F. (1979). Emotions and the self. *Ethos, 7,* 343–70.

Oatley, K. (1991). Living together. A review of Unnatural emotions: Everyday sentiments on a Micronesian atoll and their challenge to western theory. *Cognition and Emotion, 5,* 65–79.

Oatley, K. & Johnson-Laird, P. N. (1987). Towards a cognitive theory of emotions. *Cognition and Emotion, 1,* 29–50.

Ortony, A. & Turner, T. (1990). What's basic about basic emotions? *Psychological Review, 97,* 315–331.

Ortony, A., Clore, G., & Collins, A. (1988). *The cognitive structure of emotions.* Cambridge: Cambridge University Press.

Peristiany, J. G. (1965). *Honor and shame: The values of Mediterranean society.* London: Weidenfeld and Nicholson.

Pitt-Rivers, J. (1965). Honor and social status. In J. G. Peristiany (Ed.), *Honor and shame: The values of Mediterranean society* (pp. 18–77). London: Weidenfeld and Nicholson.

Plutchik, R. (1980). *Emotion: A psychoevolutionary synthesis.* New York: Harper & Row.

Reisenzein, R. & Hofmann, T. (1990). An investigation of dimensions of cognitive appraisal in emotion using a repertory grid technique. *Motivation and Emotion, 9,* 19–38.

Reisenzein, R. & Hofmann, T. (1993). Discriminating emotions from appraisal-relevant situational information: Baseline data for structural models of cognitive appraisals. *Cognition and Emotion, 7,* 271–294.

Rimé, B. & Giovannini, D. (1986). The physiological patterns of reported emotional states. In K. R. Scherer, H. G. Wallbott, & A. B. Summerfield (Eds.), *Experiencing emotion. A cross-cultural study* (pp. 84–97). Cambridge: Cambridge University Press.

Rimé, B., Philippot, P., & Cisamolo, D. (1990). Social schemata of peripheral changes in emotion. *Journal of Personality and Social Psychology, 59,* 38–49.

Rosaldo, M. Z. (1980). *Knowledge and passion: Ilongot notions of self and social life.* Cambridge: Cambridge University Press.

Roseman, I. J. (1984). Cognitive determinants of emotion: A structural theory. In P. Shaver (Ed.), *Review of personality and social psychology* (Vol. 5, pp. 11–36). Beverly Hills, CA: Sage.

Roseman, I. J. (1991). Appraisal determinants of discrete emotions. *Cognition and Emotion, 5,* 161–200.

Roseman, I. J., Dhawan, N., Rettek, S. I., Naidu, R. K., & Thapa, K. (1995). Cultural differences and cross-cultural similarities in appraisals and emotional responses. *Journal of Cross-Cultural Psychology, 26,* 23–48.

Roseman, I. J., Spindel, M. S., & Jose, P. E. (1990). Appraisals of emotion-eliciting events: Testing a theory of discrete emotions. *Journal of Personality and Social Psychology, 59,* 899–915.

Russell, J.A. (1983). Pancultural aspects of human conceptual organization of emotions. *Journal of Personality and Social Psychology, 45,* 1281–1288.

Russell, J. (1991). Culture and the categorisation of emotions. *Psychological Bulletin, 110,* 426–450.

Russell, J. (1994). Is there universal recognition of emotion from facial expression? A review of cross-cultural studies. *Psychological Bulletin, 115,* 102–141.

Saarni, C. (1979). Children's understanding of display rules for expressive behavior. *Developmental Psychology, 15,* 424–429.

Saarni, C. (1984). An observational study of children's attempts to monitor their expressive behavior. *Child Development, 55,* 1504–1513.

Scheff, T. J. (1988). Shame and conformity: The deference-emotion system. *American Sociological Review, 53,* 395–406.

Scherer, K. R. (1984). Emotion as a multicomponent process: A model and some cross-cultural data. In P. Shaver (Ed.), *Review of personality and social psychology, 5* (pp. 37–63). Beverly Hills, CA: Sage.

Scherer, K. R. (1988). Criteria for emotion-antecedent appraisal: A review. In V. Hamilton, G. H. Bower & N. H. Frijda (Eds.), *Cognitive perspectives on emotion and motivation* (pp. 89–126).

Dordrecht: Kluwer.

Scherer, K. R. (1992). What does facial expression express? In K.T. Strongman (Ed.), *International review of studies of emotion, Vol. 2* (pp. 139–165). New York: Wiley.

Scherer, K. R. (1994). Toward a concept of "modal emotions." In P. Ekman & R. J. Davidson (Eds.), *The nature of emotion: Fundamental questions* (pp. 25–31). Oxford: Oxford University Press.

Scherer, K. R. (in press). Patterns of emotion-antecedent appraisal across cultures. *Cognition and Emotion.*

Scherer, K. R., Summerfield, A. B., & Wallbott, H. G. (1983). Cross-national research on antecedents and components of emotion: A progress report. *Social Science Information, 22,* 355–385.

Scherer, K. R. & Wallbott, H. G. (1994). Evidence for universality and cultural variation of differential emotional response patterning. *Journal of Personality and Social Psychology, 66,* 310–328.

Scherer, K. R., Wallbott, H. G., Matsumoto, D., & Kudoh, T. (1988). Emotional experience in cultural context: A comparison between Europe, Japan, and the United States. In K. R. Scherer (Ed.), *Facets of emotions* (pp. 5–30). Hillsdale, NJ: Lawrence Erlbaum.

Scherer, K. R., Wallbott, H. G., & Summerfield, A. B. (Eds.) (1986). *Experiencing emotion: A cross-cultural study.* Cambridge: Cambridge University Press.

Schwartz, S. H. (1992). Universals in the content and structure of values: Theoretical advances and empirical tests in 20 countries. *Advances in Experimental Social Psychology, 25,* 1–65.

Schwartz, S. H. (1994). Are there universal aspects in the structure and content of human values? *Journal of Social Issues, 50,* 19–45.

Schwartz, S. H. (1995). Identifying culture-specifics in the content and structure of values. *Journal of Cross-Cultural Psychology, 26,* 92–116.

Schwarz, N. & Clore, G. L. (1988). How do I feel about it? Informative functions of affective states. In K. Fiedler & J. Forgas (Eds.), *Affect, cognition and social behavior* (pp. 44–62). Toronto: Hogrefe.

Shweder, R. A. (1993). The cultural psychology of the emotions. In M. Lewis & J. Haviland

(Eds.), *Handbook of emotions* (pp. 417–433). New York: Guilford.

Shweder, R. A. & Much, N. C. (1987). Determinations of meaning: Discourse and moral socialization. In W. Kurtjus & J. Gewirtz (Eds.), *Social interaction and socio-moral development* (pp. 197–244). New York: Wiley.

Smith, C. A. (1989). Dimensions of appraisal and physiological response to emotion. *Journal of Personality and Social Psychology, 56,* 339–353.

Smith, C. A. & Ellsworth, P. C. (1985). Patterns of cognitive appraisal in emotion. *Journal of Personality and Social Psychology, 48,* 813–838.

Solomon, R. S. (1978). Emotions and anthropology: The logic of emotional world views. *Inquiry, 21,* 181–199.

Spinoza, B. (1677). *Ethica.* Amsterdam: Rieuwertsz.

Stearns, P. N. & Stearns, C. Z. (1985). Emotionology: Clarifying the history of emotions and emotional standards. *American Historical review, 90,* 813–836.

Stemmler, D. G. (1989). The autonomic differentiation of emotions revisited: Convergent and discriminant validation. *Psychophysiology, 26,* 617–632.

Thoits, P. A. (1989). The sociology of emotions. *Annual Review of Sociology, 15,* 317–342.

Tomkins, S.S. (1962). *Affect, imagery and consciousness, Vol. 1. The positive affects.* New York: Springer.

Tomkins, S. S. (1963). *Affect, imagery and consciousness, Vol. 2. The negative affects.* New York: Springer.

Triandis, H. C. (1994). Cultural syndromes and emotion. In S. Kitayama & H. Markus (Eds.), *Emotion and culture. Empirical studies of mutual influence* (pp. 285–306). Washington, DC: American Psychological Association.

Triandis, H. C., Bontempo, R., Villareal, M. J., Asai, M., & Lucca, N. (1988). Individualism and collectivism: Cross-cultural perspectives on self-ingroup relationships. *Journal of Personality and Social Psychology, 54,* 323–338.

Van Brakel, J. (1994). Emotions: A cross-cultural perspective on forms of life. In *Social Perspectives on Emotion, Vol. 2,* (pp. 179–237). Greenwich, CN: Jai Press.

Van Goozen, S. & Frijda, N. H. (1993). Emotion words used in six European countries. *European Journal of Social Psychology, 23,* 89–95.

Wallbott, H. G. & Scherer, K. R. (1988). How universal and specific is emotional experience? Evidence from 27 countries. In Scherer, K. R. (Ed.), *Facets of emotions* (pp. 31–56). Hillsdale NJ: Lawrence Erlbaum.

White, G. M. (1990). Moral discourse and the rhetoric of emotions. In C. A. Lutz & L. Abu-Lughod (Eds.), *Language and the politics of emotions* (pp. 46–48). Cambridge: Cambridge University Press.

White, G. M. (1994). Affecting culture: Emotion and morality in everyday life. In S. Kitayama & H. Markus (Eds.), *Emotion and culture* (pp. 219–239). Washington, DC: American Psychological Association.

Wierzbicka, A. (1986). Human emotions: Universal or culture-specific? *American Anthropologist, 88,* 584–594.

Wierzbicka, A. (1992). Talking about emotions: Semantics, culture, and cognition. *Cognition and Emotion, 6,* 285–319.

Wierzbicka, A. (1994). Emotion, language, and cultural scripts. In S. Kitayama & H. Markus (Eds.), *Emotion and culture* (pp. 133–196). Washington, DC: American Psychological Association.

Wooding, C. (1981). Een Afrosurinaamse casestudy [An Afro-Surinamese case study]. *Maandblad voor Geestelijke Volksgezondheid, 36,* 668–681.

Wundt, W. (1902). *Grundzüge der physiologischen Psychologie, Vol. 3.* Leipzig: Engelmann, 5th. Ausgabe.

Wyer, R. S. & Srull, T. K. (1981). Category accessibility: Some theoretical and empirical issues concerning the processing of social stimulus information. In E. T. Higgins, C. P. Herman, & M. P. Zanna (Eds.), *Social cognition: The Ontario Symposium.* Hillsdale, NJ: Erlbaum.

Wyer, R. S. & Srull, T. K. (1986). Human cognition in its social context. *Psychological Review, 93,* 322–359.

Zajonc, R. B. & McIntosh, D. N. (1992). Emotion research: Some promising questions and some questionable promises. *Psychological Science, 3,* 70–74.

9

THE DEVELOPMENT
OF MORAL JUDGMENT

LUTZ H. ECKENSBERGER[1]
University of the Saarland
Germany

RODERICK F. ZIMBA
University of Namibia
Namibia

Contents

Introduction

This chapter deals with the development of normative standards for the ethical evaluation of individual actions and social interactions. According to Geertz (1973), rules as normative regulators for human interactions are central to definitions of culture. Hence, this topic forms the core of cross-cultural psychology and is necessary for the understanding of human beings, and of culture in general.

Because the issue of morality was not represented in the first edition of the *Handbook*, literature produced before 1980 will also be discussed. The focus will be on cognitive developmental theories. Among these, Kohlberg's theory and research will serve as a pivot. But first, early cross-cultural research triggered by Piaget's *Moral Judgment of the Child* (1932/1965) will be outlined. Then, investigations aimed at testing Kohlberg's thesis about the universality of moral judgment will be examined, followed by a short summary of Kohlberg-related research. Some views will be presented bearing on the claim that Kohlberg's theory is too global or undifferentiated, and that the relation of the moral domain to other (social) normative frameworks or rule systems (such as conventions and personal concerns) is essential. Finally, the chapter will close with some critical remarks and suggestions for future research.

There are a number of comprehensive reviews of moral development from a cross-cultural perspective (Eckensberger, 1993, 1994a; Edwards, 1981, 1986; Gielen, 1991a, b; Moon 1986; Snarey, 1985; Snarey & Keljo, 1991; Vine, 1986), while others refer to specific regions (Brazil: Biaggio, 1993; Germany: Eckensberger, 1983; Japan: Naito, 1994; Java: Setiono, 1994). In addition, surveys on the understanding of other rule systems (conventions and personal concerns) were also useful in preparing this chapter (Shweder, Mahapatra, & Miller, 1987; Turiel, Killen, & Helwig, 1987).

Research is only possible, in general, by making explicit the theoretical assumptions that drive research and justify the methods. This is particularly true for cross-cultural research (Eckensberger & Burgard, 1983). Thus, all sections will begin by outlining the assumptions that are more or less *hidden* in the theories. These include brief descriptions of the model of man to which the author adheres; basic ideas about developmental processes, mechanisms, as well as incitement conditions for development; and, most important, views on the universalism/relativism distinction (cf. the etic/emic distinction, Berry, 1989) and the conceptualization of the relation between content and structure of moral judgment.

The Influence of Piaget's *Moral Judgment of the Child*

Because the bulk of cross-cultural research in the tradition of Piaget's theory of development of moral judgment was conducted in the 50s and 60s, it might be considered outdated. This would be wrong for two reasons: First, the model of man he introduced to psychology strongly influenced later work (e.g., by Kohlberg,

Rest, and Turiel). Second, many of the early problems endure in present-day cross-cultural work; in a way, they are simply rediscovered.

Piaget's Theory and Its Basic Assumptions

Piaget's general ideas about development are based on the assumption of an *organismic model of development* (Reese & Overton, 1970). He starts with the notion that humans actively construct or reconstruct the meaning of the world. The locus of the developmental dynamic is primarily within the individual, who develops by actively creating interpretation schemes about social as well as nonsocial aspects of the world.

Piaget (1932/1965) defined morality in general as a set of rules, and viewed the morals of the person as respect for these rules. Broadly speaking, he reconstructed the development of moral judgment as a movement from heteronomous to autonomous reasoning, that is, from a reasoning oriented towards external rules to that governed by inner standards. He thus organized, in a developmental order, two types of morality already distinguished by Kant (1785/1959). Piaget assumed that interpretation schemes are constructed holistically (as structured wholes) and their development (transformation) follows a developmental logic. Thus, transformation of the sequence of different interpretation schemes was taken to be necessarily qualitative, and therefore, stage-like. Significantly, on the empirical level, Piaget (1932/1965) explicitly refused the stage concept for the development of moral judgment.

In the Piagetian model, the developed structure maintains a dynamic equilibrium with its (cultural) context, and this equilibrium strives for an optimum. Thus, at least theoretically, development has a terminal state, the highest stage. Although criticized in modern developmental psychology (Klahr, 1982), the mutually complementing processes of assimilation (of experiences to the cognitive schemes) and accommodation (of cognitive schemes to cultural conditions) underlie most assumptions about how development is triggered and carried on.

Piaget has often been accused of conceptualizing development as a process taking place inside an isolated individual, and that in his theory affect is of no significance. But for Piaget, in the domain of moral development, it is above all the interaction with peers, more precisely an interaction among equals, and the feelings accompanied by experiences of injustice, which trigger moral development.

Piaget distinguished several dimensions that all follow the developmental trend from heteronomy to autonomy. Yet, in cross-cultural research only three of these dimensions have been examined: First is the understanding of rules of games. Here, the heteronomous understanding refers to an origin of rules in authorities, which goes hand in hand with the conviction that rules cannot be changed, whereas the autonomous orientation implies that rules can be changed by consensus. Second is the decrease in immanent justice. Here, the heteronomous orientation is represented by the idea that any punishment for a rule transgression follows intrinsically from the act itself (is immanent to the very act), whereas the autonomous orientation does not see this connection. This dimension is clearly related to cognitive development because the pre-operational child interprets the world as anthropomorphic. And third is the change from objective to subjective responsibility. Here, the heteronomous orientation means that the wrongness of an act is defined by its objective outcome (e.g., the amount of damage it produces), whereas the autonomous orientation refers to the bad or good intentions of the act.

The organismic model of development implies a universalistic orientation, in which the generalizability of a concept or developmental stage sequence is tested. Although this orientation is particularly found in early Piagetian cognitive developmental cross-cultural studies, and certainly holds true for Kohlberg and his followers, Piaget himself took a different (in fact a quite contemporary) stance in the domain of moral development. He distinguished traditional and modern societies in which the same behaviors may have different meanings (Piaget, 1947). Havighurst and Neugarten (1955) elaborated on this point and argued that a traditional society "will make children more, rather than less, rigid in their moral theory as they grow older and will exercise more, rather than less, moral constraints on them. If this society will have a worldview which includes a supernatural power that watches over men and rewards and punishes their actions, then belief in immanent justice will probably be as strong in older children as in young ones, or even stronger" (p. 144). The same would be true for rules of games that are related to these powers. This idea has been (re)introduced much later under the label "unearthly belief-mediated" moral events (Turiel et al., 1987, see below).

The question of the universality or relativity of moral judgments, and of social rule systems in general, is closely related to the theoretical and empirical distinction of structure and content in all domains of thought (i.e., in social as well as nonsocial domains). Organismic theories assert that only the underlying structures are universal, not the concrete content of behavioral prescriptions or rules. But for Piaget, structure and content are not independent, but are closely interrelated in the moral domain, since "form (equality, mutual respect) acts upon the content (the formation of the concept of goodness)" (Piaget, 1932/1965).

Piaget analyzed the moral judgment and practice of rules of games of 3- to 12-year-old boys (a domain he considered at least analogous to morality in concrete actions). He also discussed with children a variety of specific stories that systematically varied one or more of the moral dimensions mentioned above (objective vs. subjective responsibility, immanent justice vs. naturalistic concept of justice, lie vs. truth, etc.). Although these stories were not empirically collected from children's daily lives, they were adapted to their context, and therefore, were not "hypothetical" in the narrow sense of the word.

Cross-Cultural Evidence on Piaget's Theory

Samples employed to test Piaget's theory are far from representative of the cultures of the world. In addition to research in the United States and the Western world (Switzerland, United Kingdom, Germany, Belgium), studies are known from eight cultural groups (twelve Native American cultures in the United States, Congo, Taiwan, Ghana, Israel, Lebanon, Nigeria, and Turkey).

Usually, all three dimensions of Piaget's theory, as mentioned, were not analyzed in the same study. Further, researchers contextualized the methods instead of applying them unchanged. Their comparability is based upon their "structural equivalence," hence, the assumed common framework, indispensable for any kind of comparison, can be named a "structural universal" (Eckensberger & Burgard, 1983).

There is not much information on the reliability of Piagetian tasks on moral judgment. In an early investigation, Havighurst and Neugarten (1955) claimed that their results "over the whole group were stable enough to generalize out of the average of the group" (p. 148). Maqsud (1977a) noted an interrater reliability of r = .97 in Nigeria.

Understanding of Rules

A number of findings are available in various areas. Havighurst and Neugarten (1955) examined the understanding of rules of 6- to 18-year-old children from seven Native American cultures (Navajo, Papago, Sioux, Zuni, Zia, and two groups of Hopi). For only two of these could an increase in the conviction that rules are changeable be shown. For some of the groups the trend was not clear, and for two (especially the Navajo) it was even reversed. Particularly with reference to the traditional games, older children were more often convinced that these games must not be changed because of respect for the ancestors. Hoffman (1970) considered this a falsification of Piaget's theory. However, this is a severe misunderstanding, because Hoffman confounded the underlying structural theory and the overt operationalization in specific contexts, a mistake noted several times in the domain of cross-cultural studies of cognitive Piagetian tasks (see Davids, 1983). As mentioned, Piaget (1947) even expected such inverse trends in cultures he called "traditional." Thus, he was aware of the problem that the developmental trends he found in his Swiss samples were due to the conditions under which these structures occurred. In present-day terms one could argue that in "modern" societies, rules of common children's games in fact represent social conventions (only the consensus about rule changes itself is morally based), but in "traditional" societies, games possess their own moral quality, associated with some relation to the ancestors. The prior discussion not only indicates how difficult it is to separate possible universal, structural trends from their contextualistic contents, but also foreshadows a topic to be elaborated on later, namely how troublesome but crucial it is to separate (conceptually and methodically) moral judgment systems from conventional and transcendental (religious) belief systems.

Immanent Justice

This domain has been analyzed somewhat more systematically than the rules of games. The most prominent starting point again is Havighurst and Neugarten's study (1955) which asked Native Americans about their concept of immanent justice by employing a variation of a story invented by Piaget: Two boys are discovered stealing a melon. One is caught and the other (Paul) escapes. Paul, thereafter, cuts his foot with an axe when chopping wood. Three questions are to be answered: (a) Why do you think Paul's foot was cut? (b) If Paul had not stolen the melon, would he have cut his foot? (c) Did the axe know that Paul stole the melon? The first two questions showed a decrease in immanent justice responses with increasing age. The third one, however, revealed some deviation, especially in one cultural group. Because these results do not relate to experiences of acculturation, the authors interpreted them in terms of the specific ontology of this group, including supernatural beliefs possessing moral power. Jahoda (1958) raised the objection that Havighurst and Neugarten's data are an artifact because the authors interpreted the answers based on religion as indicating a conception of immanent justice. He demonstrated with a Ghanaian sample that his critique can be supported empirically, provided these categories are controlled for, and argued for a universal decrease in the conception of immanent justice. Loves (1957) and Najarian-Svajian (1966), however, weakened Jahoda's position by showing in Congo and Lebanon that content (especially religious content) can hardly be separated from structure (see also Lickona's 1976 data on religious fundamentalists in the United States). Again, these early studies highlight the difficulties in contextualizing or decontextualizing moral judgments, and in separating different rule systems (religion, morality).

Objective versus Subjective Responsibility

Edwards (1981) quoted several studies from industrialized nations (Belgium, Switzerland, United Kingdom, United States) that replicated Piaget's findings of a decrease in the importance of objective action consequences versus action intentions. There is limited research from non-Western cultures. Maqsud (1977a, b) studied Yoruba and Islamic Hausa children in Nigeria as well as Pakistani Punjabi children, and detected the same trend, but delayed in age, as did Kugelmass and Breznitz (1967) with 11- to 18-year-olds living in cities and in a Kibbutz (Israel). Finally, Edwards refers to an (unpublished) study by Kohlberg, described in more detail by Lickona (1976), in which responses of children (aged 6 to 18 years) from non-industrialized groups (Atayal of Taiwan and twelve Native American cultures) to a version of a classical Piaget task (damage of a large number of cups when a child tried to help versus damage of a small number of cups when the child broke a rule) were analyzed. In one case, a deviation from the classical trend in Piaget's original data was observed: there was first a decrease and then an increase of reference to the consequences of an action. But also these data do not necessarily contradict Piaget's theory. First, it is also known that in some Western societies older age groups consider again the consequences of an action (Walster, 1966). Second, the delayed occurrence of the trend in Maqsud's data is interpreted by him with reference to the strong rule systems of the Islamic context of some of the children investigated.

Stage Consistency

In early cross-cultural studies evidence can be found that moral judgments vary in different domains. For example, Havighurst and Neugarten (1955) discovered that Native American children's conception of the changeability of rules in different games (games of the Whites and Native American games) diverged considerably, and in Nigeria, Moslem children's orientation towards authority seemed to be independent of their conceptions of objective versus subjective responsibility (Maqsud, 1977a). Note that these results do not contradict Piaget's basic theoretical assumptions. Rather, they call for a systematization, that is, an attempt to assess empirically and explain theoretically the consistencies in the inconsistencies (Burgard, 1989; Eckensberger, 1989).

Kohlberg's Theory of the Development of Moral Judgment

Basic Assumptions of Kohlberg's Theory

Kohlberg's theory has been modified several times over the last thirty years. While the stage descriptions were altered very little, central theoretical positions have undergone remarkable changes (Kohlberg, 1976; Kohlberg, LeVine, & Hewer, 1983; Kohlberg, 1986).

Kohlberg explicitly followed Piaget's approach and subscribed to the organismic model of man (Reese & Overton, 1970). He also assumed that the course of development is stage-like, and consequently, employed assimilation and accommodation as explanatory concepts for development. In one of his later writings (Kohlberg, 1986), he also referred to the concept of reflective abstraction, introduced by Piaget for cognitive development. But in respect to the stage assumptions, he was in a way more Piagetian than Piaget himself. First, in the course of time, his stage concept grew more and more strict. Therefore, a very important criterion for the validity of theory and method consists in the internal consistency of the stages (Colby, Kohlberg, Gibbs, & Lieberman, 1983). Second, for Kohlberg (e.g. 1976; 1986), developmental progress always takes place in a nonreversible sequence, that is, no stages should be skipped and regressions to former stages are theoretically excluded.

Although rarely discussed, Kohlberg (1958) had already in his doctoral dissertation distinguished morality from cultural rules that today one would call conventions. In his early writings, he also considered the role of affect in moral judgments (Kohlberg, 1969). Later, he definitely excluded affects like sympathy and love from the moral domain (Kohlberg et al., 1983).

However, beyond these general similarities with Piaget, there exist differences in details. Instead of the two Piagetian stages, Kohlberg distinguished six stages organized on three levels with two stages each (see Figure 9–1), and he also determined transitional stages between the six main stages. Compared to Piaget, Kohlberg extended the age range of his subjects and narrowed the scope of methods. He studied subjects from age ten through old age and used only a limited number of hypothetical moral dilemmas and standardized questions. These dilemmas in fact have a different structure (cf. Eckensberger & Reinshagen, 1980): they sometimes represent conflicts between laws/rules and moral issues (stealing a drug for one's wife, who suffers from cancer; playing the role of a judge, who has to weigh moral intentions against legal rules), and they sometimes represent conflicts between moral issues and personal relations or authority (breaking a promise given to a son or sister). Especially in a cross-cultural perspective, it is essential to realize that Kohlberg intentionally tried to decontextualize his dilemmas (i.e., they were only meant to prototypically represent a central moral conflict, which by no means was supposed to actually exist in a society or culture). He, thereby, followed a strict notion from Kant (1785/1959), who claimed that any ethic should be kept clean of empirical elements. Beyond this, his scoring procedures became more and more standardized over the years. During the last thirty years, the criteria for linking a particular judgment to a moral stage were modified. At present, there exists a comprehensive manual containing criterion judgments for the stages of all nine dilemmas (Colby & Kohlberg, 1987a,b).

Over the years, not only the definitions of structure (form) and content changed, but also the assumptions about their interrelationship. When talking about "holding content constant" so as to examine structure (Kohlberg, 1978, p. 55), structure and content are viewed as relatively independent from one another. In the final versions of the theory (Kohlberg, 1986), structure is on the one hand defined by justice operations (equality, equity, reciprocity, and reversibility), and on the other, by the subject's social–moral perspective (egocentric perspective, the perspective of the other, the group, the social system, and general principles). Contents are values (e.g., life, property, truth, affection, law) and ethical positions are so-called elements (e.g., taking into account the consequences of one's actions for concrete others or a group, maintenance of the character, respect for oneself, serving the social harmony, dignity, and autonomy). Content also refers to the normative orientation at each stage. Additionally, Kohlberg distinguishes hard and soft stages, of which the first are cognitive (structural), and the latter form (functional) stages of ego development.

The previously mentioned criterion judgment (as the unit of analysis in the manual) is, therefore, a combination of content (values and elements) and structure (the social perspective taken at each stage). By means of these criterion judgments, one can calculate "stage scores." The justice operations outlined earlier, which are important in the theory, did not explicitly enter the scoring procedure. From this emphasis on the social perspective as a criterion for structure, it follows that, above all, role-taking opportunities and participation in decision processes are global incitement conditions that trigger the development of moral judgment.

Kohlberg et al. (1983, p. 66f), again differing from Piaget, explicitly elaborated a set (of nine) meta-ethical assumptions that underlie his theory, which all have relevance for cross-cultural research and theorizing. The most important, however, is the assumption of moral universality. Usually, universality is discussed with reference to the structure of stages, but Kohlberg et al. (1983, p. 75) stated that moral content (norms and elements) is also universal, although not assumed to be defined exhaustively. In the culture-relativistic research atmosphere of the 60s and

70s, this claim obviously stirred numerous protests (the most prominent was probably the one by Simpson, 1974). In the postmodern atmosphere of the late 80s, the universality claim again came under attack (Shweder et al., 1987).

At this point, two possible misunderstandings should be mentioned that are sometimes connected to the universalistic position. First, one may equate the postulate of universal structural sequences with the claim that, because they are universal, they are biologically or naturally determined. But one has to remember that Kohlberg, like Piaget, by assuming a developmental logic in the nature–nurture discussion, follows a third position. Universal stages of moral judgment are explained logically and not biologically (Vogel & Eckensberger, 1988). Second, the thesis of universal, nonreversible stage sequences does not imply that the highest forms of moral categories will be empirically found in every culture; that would rather depend upon a culture's specific incitement conditions. But this does not mean that a given culture, in which individuals do not attain higher stages of moral judgment, is less moral than another in which individuals show higher stages. Instead, the stages found in a culture are local adaptations in the sense that they are obviously sufficient and adequate for the solution of relevant conflicts. Therefore, the universalistic assumptions made in organismic theories do not contradict culture-relativistic positions.

A final modification of Kohlberg's theory interestingly closes the circle to Piaget again. Beginning with stage 5, Kohlberg (1973) first contrasted two orientations within each stage, the A- and B-substages, of which the earlier was considered a rather immature, and the latter a more mature form of a stage. Later, he identified these orientations as substages or types, which represent a heteronomous (A) and an autonomous (B) orientation. First (Kohlberg, 1976), these substages were defined by the elements a person referred to. Substage A consisted of egoistic and group consequences, and substage B represented ideal and harmony serving consequences, and fairness orientation. Later (Kohlberg et al., 1983), only substage B was defined by some Kantian and Piagetian criteria, and if these did not apply, an argument was considered as representing substage A. Developmentally, it is assumed (and demonstrated empirically) that, throughout main stage development, one can stay either at substage A or B, but if a change of substages occurs, it is always from A to B. To the present authors, the status of these substages is rather unclear. Although some researchers (Tappan et al., 1987) seem to conceive these substages as a further refinement of the theory, Gielen (1991a) rightly stated that Kohlberg's moral types (A and B) "do not exhibit the same logical tightness and inner consistency that his moral stages do since the types intermingle structure and content to a considerable degree" (p. 34). Also the present authors interpret the formulation of these substages rather as an indication of unresolved problems in Kohlberg's theory (particularly the definition of structure). Eckensberger (1986) has demonstrated that the substages in the manual are highly correlated with main stages (B substages increase and A substages decrease continuously with main stages), and has pointed to the fact that the substage B criteria are barely discernible from criteria that define principled (postconventional) stages. Hence, both the main stages as well as the substages represent an increasing trend towards autonomy (see also Tappan et al., 1987). Moreover, the incitement conditions for sub-stage B development are difficult to discriminate from the ones hypothesized for conventional and postconventional development (institutions and societies emphasizing democracy, equality, cooperation, and mutual relationships; see Gielen, 1991a).

Figure 9–1 shows basic aspects of Kohlberg's theory. Because it aims at the integration of many aspects of the theory, it deviates from the diagrams published by Kohlberg, and it therefore may go beyond his intentions. It depicts the labels of the six main stages and the three levels, structural features of each stage (socio-moral perspective), specific deficiencies (D) that cannot be handled at a stage n and are then solved at stage n + 1, specific incitement (I) conditions leading to the emergence of stage n + 1 (by reflective abstraction, see above), and reference to stage content. A and B substages are not represented.

Sample of Cultures

Snarey (1985) pointed out that the sample of cultures in which development of moral judgment has been studied was not representative of the variability of world cultures. Even so, the number and range of the cultures studied are considerable. Seven longitudinal studies were carried out outside the United States and Canada (Bahamas, India, Indonesia, Iceland, Israel, Taiwan, and Turkey). Additionally, cross-sectional studies from twenty-one locations have been reported (Alaska, Brazil, Germany, Guatemala, Honduras, Hong Kong, India, Iran, Japan, Java, Kenya, Mexico, New Guinea, New Zealand, Nigeria, Pakistan, Poland, Puerto Rico, Thailand, Yucatan, and Zambia). Developmental psychology in general would be better off if all its theories had undergone such an extensive cross-cultural test.

Validity and Reliability of Methods

Method of Inquiry and Hypothetical Dilemmas
It is often argued that the situations used in the dilemmas cannot be applied cross-culturally because they are hypothetical, and thus, do not take into account specific cultural contexts. However, one may argue that this very decontextualization makes possible a comparison of ethical thinking, because it represents the moral structure rather purely, and secures the structural equivalence of responses (Eckensberger & Burgard, 1983) by not confounding it with local cultural knowledge. Yet, this argument presupposes a very precise and explicit concept of structure, and one can doubt that the social–moral perspective taken at each stage in the manual is sufficient (Eckensberger, 1986; Eckensberger & Reinshagen, 1980; Guindon, 1978). Additionally, when reformulating moral dilemmas out of a cultural context, one has to deal with more than cognitive moral structures. Of concern also are the relation of moral judgments to other cognitive domains (beyond the domains of personal concerns and conventions), especially religious beliefs

FIGURE 9–1 Summary table of Kohlberg's theory of the development of moral judgment: Stage structures, developmental conditions, and related contents.

STAGE/LEVEL	STRUCTURE	DEFICIENCY/INCITEMENT	CONTENT
POSTCONVENTIONAL			
(6) Universal ethical principles	**MORAL POINT OF VIEW** Ideal role taking "veil of ignorance"	D: Restriction to situations I: ?	Following self-chosen ethical principles
	Reflect. Abstract.		
(5) Social contract or utility and individual rights	**PRIOR TO SOCIETY PERSPECTIVE** Consideration of moral and legal points of view, difficult to integrate them. Mechanisms of agreement, contract.	D: Restriction to concrete systems I: Experience of different roles of real responsibility; opportunity of self-realization	Equality, equity, reciprocity as values; maximization of individual rights; rules and values are relative to the group; some nonrelative values (life, liberty) must be upheld in any society, regardless of majority opinion.
	Reflect. Abstract.		
CONVENTIONAL			
(4) Social system and conscience	**SYSTEM PERSPECTIVE** Takes the point of view of the system that defines roles and rules.	D: Restriction to shared good motives, no competence to deal with laws I: Experience of responsibility in role contexts	Laws have to be upheld except in extreme cases where they conflict with other fixed social duties; fulfilling the actual duties to which you have agreed
	Reflect. Abstract.		
(3) Mutual interpersonal expectations, relationships, and interpersonal conformity	**CONCRETE RELATIONS** Aware of shared feelings, agreements and expectations that take primacy over individual interests.	D: No coordination of interests of different subjects I: Participation in decisions	Living up to what is expected by people close to you or what people generally expect from people in your role as son, brother, friend; it means keeping mutual relationships, trust, loyalty, respect
	Reflect. Abstract.		
PRECONVENTIONAL			
(2) Individualism, instrumental purpose, and exchange	**CONCRETE OTHERS** Aware that everybody has his/her own interest to pursue (conflict), so rights are relative.	D: Endless circle of retaliation I: Role taking opportunities	Right is what's fair, what's an equal exchange, a deal, an agreement; following rules when it is someone's immediate interest and needs, and letting others do the same.
(1) Heteronomous morality	**EGOCENTRISM** Doesn't relate two points of view. Actions = physical. Confusion of authority's perspective with one's own.		To avoid breaking rules backed by punishment, obedience for its own sake, avoiding physical damage to persons and property; following concrete rules

(Jahoda, 1958; Vasudev, 1986); prudence and factual knowledge (Eckensberger & Gähde, 1993; Zimba, 1995); and even more important, affective processes of coping and defense (cf. Eckensberger, 1993; Villenave-Cremer & Eckensberger, 1985), and anxiety (Biaggio, 1993).

Social psychological influences, such as a person's language and status, may also affect cross-cultural data assessment. In the Kohlbergian tradition, cultural adaptation simply meant translating the dilemmas and interviews. Sometimes singular elements (e.g., the hero's name) were modified, rarely the whole story. When adaptations were used, their effect was hardly tested (Snarey, 1985). White, Bushnell, and Regnemer (1978) claimed that their culture-typical dilemmas did not yield results different from Kohlberg. Contradictory findings were reported by Maqsud (1977a),[2] who detected a difference in the discussion of a "suggestive stage 4" with Moslem children in Nigeria solely brought about by changing the names in the Heinz dilemma (using names of Moslem leaders). A minimal claim for cultural adaptation of dilemmas could therefore be that, (a) they contain a real moral conflict for the individual, (b) all the facts mentioned in the dilemma are familiar to the subject, and (c) no situational (social and language) factors mask the individual's moral stage. Of the cross-cultural studies reported, it is usually not known whether they meet these criteria.

Method of Data Analysis, Manual and Criterion Judgments

Although there are good reasons for keeping dilemmas hypothetical, one encounters two main difficulties when it comes to the manual as a transculturally valid framework for the responses: content (values) and structure (stages) of moral judgments are empirically interrelated (Eckensberger, 1986), and the criterion judgments are solely derived from an American subsample, so that any possible cultural variation in content is excluded from research. Therefore, a rigid adherence to the manual's examples (Colby & Kohlberg, 1987b) does not seem justified. As will be pointed out later, exactly the material that is not scoreable by means of the manual ("guess scores") seems to be the most interesting in present-day research.

Reliability

Of the 40 or so implicitly or explicitly cross-cultural studies on Kohlberg's stages summarized by Snarey (1985), fifteen did not report reliability scores. Only two early researchers showed a retest-correlation of approximately r = .50. In recent studies, correlations of more than r = .80 have been reported, six of them higher than r = .90. Interrater reliabilities on data analyzed with Colby and Kohlberg's (1987b) manual vary between r = .77 and r = .98, with a modal value of around r = .90. For an appraisal of the increase in the reliability of the moral judgment interviews in cross-cultural studies, however, two critical remarks are in order. First, it went hand in hand with an increase in the "difficulty" of the stages: some material that was scored on higher stages earlier is now scored on lower stages (Eckensberger, 1986). Second, the manual's increasing standardization does not automatically improve the material's comparability, which is rather a question of validity.

The Universality of Stages of Moral Judgment in a Cross- in a Cross-Cultural Perspective

Homogeneity of the Stages

Most cross-cultural Kohlbergian research provides very little information about the homogeneity of stages. Lei (1994) recently published the most accurate study on the structured wholeness of stages in cross-cultural research for Chinese data. He followed Colby and Kohlberg's (1987b) analysis of American data and also utilized three checks of consistency: (1) proportion of reasoning scored at each of the five stages, (2) number of meaningful stages used, and (3) factor analysis based upon the intercorrelation of stage scores on each of the six issues across dilemmas, which should show a g-factor.[3] Lei's results demonstrated a high stage consistency, although slightly lower than in the U.S. samples. Moreover, there are some hints (Snarey, 1985) that in cross-cultural studies, the range of the stages decreases with increasing age, an observation that Kohlberg published in 1973 for his longitudinal data. Quite generally, it seems that inconsistencies are more frequently reported by researchers outside Kohlberg's group (Burgard, 1989; Eckensberger, 1989; Teo, Becker & Edelstein, 1995).

Transcultural Invariance of the Stages

Roughly 85 percent of the cross-sectional studies revealed a positive correlation between stage and age. Only 15 percent showed trends of shifting back to lower stages, especially in adulthood. Such trends were explained through presumed cohort effects which, in a sequential analysis (White, 1986) with data from the Bahamas, were supported empirically. Additionally, Niemczynski, Czyzoswska, Pourkos and Mirski (1988), in interpreting similar trends in their Polish data, noted that, in general, the adult stages were not yet fully understood.

But strictly speaking, only by an ipsative analysis of longitudinal data, can the transcultural invariance of stage development be examined. Snarey (1985) contended that longitudinal studies, using Kohlberg's moral judgment interview, did not show any regressions for test–retest intervals of less than two years. For longer time intervals, some regressions appeared but did not exceed the protocols' unreliability, and can, therefore, be regarded as measurement errors not weakening the developmental stage invariance hypothesis. There is also no indication that stages can be skipped. The trend of these findings has been strongly supported by Lei (1994). However, these results are at least partly due to the fact that, in general, higher stages are more difficult to attain in later studies than in earlier manuals (see endnote 3). Hence, to restrict the analysis to material based upon the last manual decreases the chance to falsify the theory.

Transcultural Existence of All Stages

The investigation of whether all Kohlberg stages exist cross-culturally, especially if stage 5 prevails only in Western middle-class subjects (Simpson, 1974), yielded the result that stages 2 to 4 can be seen as universal, but this was not necessarily the case for stages 1 and 5. Stage 1 was hardly encountered in the U.S., Bahamas,

Turkey, and Tibet. Surprisingly, stage 5 was also not detected in Kohlberg's latest longitudinal United States data (Colby et al., 1983), but occurred in Kibbutzim, in Israel (Snarey, 1983; Bar-Yam, Kohlberg, & Naame, 1980), Germany (Eckensberger, 1986), India (middle and upper class, Vasudev, 1983), Poland (Niemczynski et al., 1988), and China (Lei, 1994). Further, transition between stage 4 and 5 (that is, between conventional and post-conventional level) was often found in the Taiwanese protocols (Lei, 1994). On the other hand, studies of cultures in a number of developing countries revealed rather weak evidence for principle-oriented reasoning on stage 5 (summary tables can be found in Snarey, 1985; Snarey & Keljo, 1991).

A and B Substages

Three studies from non-Western cultures reanalyzed data and aimed at testing the existence of a developmental trend in the A/B moral types (heteronomous/autonomous). Logan, Snarey, and Schrader (1984) reanalyzed longitudinal data from Snarey's (1983) Kibbutz study, Tappan et al. (1987) reanalyzed Nisan and Kohlberg's longitudinal study with Turkish males (Nisan, 1987), and Lei (1983) reported data from his Taiwanese longitudinal study. In the Kibbutz and Taiwanese samples, as in an American sample, a clear correlation between B substages and main stages was found; only the Turkish sample remained primarily on substage A. All of the longitudinal data in these investigations basically support the hypothesis that changes of types primarily occur from A to B (with only 6 to 9 percent exhibiting the reverse trend). There were no gender differences in substage distributions. However, none of the studies resolved the basic problems concerning the status of the substages in relation to main stages just discussed.

Gender Differences

Gilligan (1982) criticized Kohlberg's justice-oriented theory and method for having a sex bias favoring boys/men over girls/women. She introduced a "morality of responsibility and care," assumed to be gender-related, representing "a different voice" of women. A careful analysis of the literature (cf. Walker, 1984), however, did not uncover evidence of gender relatedness, although the two moral orientations (justice versus responsibility and care) actually seem to represent different aspects of morality (see Puka, 1986; Walker, deVries & Trevethan, 1987). Snarey's (1985) review of cross-cultural studies also did not support the assumption of a gender bias in Kohlberg's theory. Of seventeen investigations in which both sexes were examined, only three revealed gender differences. Strictly speaking, they were only noticeable in one English study (Simpson & Graham, 1971). Moreover, in the single case, it is difficult to assess whether it is a sex bias of the theory and/or method, or whether valid differences can be explained contextually, such as different gender-specific role coercions and stimulating conditions in a culture. A study by Bar-Yam et al. (1980) in Israel showed that, similar to Maqsud's (1977b) findings, Moslem girls attained lower stage values than boys or girls of a Jewish or Christian background. Although Vasudev and Hummel (1987) were not able to detect gender differences in an Indian sample, a study by Sengupta,

Saraswathi, and Konantambigi (1994) in India not only tested gender differences in the justice orientations, but also reanalyzed data by means of an adapted version of Lyons' (1982) scoring manual for the care and responsibility orientation. First, the hypothesis that the care mode is more salient in India than in Western cultures was not confirmed. The authors argued that in India, socialization practices limit or mold moral thinking in prescribed ways associated with justice reasoning. Second, there were no gender differences in justice reasoning, but females scored higher in care, and males in a combination of justice and care. Hence, Gilligan's hypothesis has been partly supported. Additionally, an interaction between the moral orientation and the dilemma type was detected; that is, personal dilemmas elicited more combinations of care and justice, and impersonal dilemmas more justice orientations. The authors also discussed the relation between decontextualized (Kohlberg's) and contextualized (Gilligan's) dilemmas by showing that the moral issue in question determines the moral orientation used to resolve it, a point highly relevant for cross-cultural research. Note that even within the Kohlbergian justice orientation, inconsistencies in scores are in fact consistent with reference to "personal dilemmas" (e.g., Joe and his father) and "transpersonal dilemmas" (e.g., mercy killing), as empirically demonstrated by Burgard (1989), Eckensberger (1989), and Teo et al. (1995).

Here the question arises whether individuals in some cultures scored at a "lower moral level" (in terms of the theory) because of the lack of incitement conditions relevant for the development of moral judgment, or whether in other cultures, there exist other moral principles than the justice principle, which forms the basis of Kohlberg's theory.

Is There a Western Bias in Kohlberg's Theory?

This question was already touched upon in the context of the discussion of the transcultural existence of all stages. There the answer was ambiguous: On the one hand, postconventional stages are not restricted to Western cultures; on the other hand, in a number of developing countries stage 5 reasoning was absent. To deal with this question more systematically, one may distinguish two approaches. First, this question is dealt with inductively from bottom up and second, it is handled deductively from top down. In the first case, it is analyzed whether there exists material in the moral judgment interviews, that cannot be matched to the manual, although it clearly represents moral arguments. In the second case, the moral code of a culture is discussed on a meta-ethical level and compared with Kohlberg's meta-ethical assumptions, specifically the justice principle.

What about the completeness of the standard manual for the moral judgment interview? As pointed out by Snarey (1985), in trying to answer this question, one indeed discovers some interesting shortcomings of Kohlberg's theory, which altogether seem to indicate that the justice principle as a core of the theory seems to be deficient. In his 1985 review, Snarey listed many different examples of unscoreable material and later (Snarey & Keljo, 1991) tried to put these into a theoretical perspective. Much of the data resembles Kohlberg's stage 3 (which emphasizes connectedness, feelings, etc.). Setiono's (1994) for instance linked the Javanese concepts of *rukun* (oneness with a group) and *hormat* (respect for older people) to Kohlberg's stage 3, and claimed that Javanese people showed a local adaptation, meaning that they had already reached an optimal moral development at stage 3. Also Lei and Cheng (1984) pointed out that some of their interviews were difficult to analyze, because their subjects referred to different types of "collective conflict-solving strategies" not mentioned by Kohlberg. Tietjen and Walker (1984) were faced with similar problems in Papua New Guinea. Snarey (1983) reported answers of Kibbutzniks referring to a concept of "collective happiness."

Top down arguments were elaborated by Gielen and Chirico-Kelly (1993), Ma (1988), Vasudev (1986), and Huebner and Garrod (1991). Ma (1988) complemented Kohlberg's higher stages (4, 5, 6) with Chinese versions based upon the Confucian principle of *jen* (love, benevolence, human-heartedness, man-to-manness, sympathy, perfect virtue). Gielen and Chirico-Kelly (1993), as well as Vasudev (1986), mentioned reasoning pertaining to the principle of respect for all life as a moral principle, which leads to the principle of nonviolence *(ahimsa)* in Hinduism. Especially the value of animal life and the embeddedness of humans into the cosmos are viewed very differently from Kohlberg (Eckensberger & Kern, 1986). Answers respecting animal life cannot be analyzed adequately with Kohlberg's scoring manual even in a Western context, because they mostly do not refer to justice but to suffering and feelings. They therefore are scored at stage 3, although they often contain system- or principle-oriented reasoning and should indicate higher stages. The surprisingly low moral stages of monks in Ladakh (Gielen & Chirico-Kelly, 1993) can therefore probably be traced back to this culturally limited aspect of Kohlberg's theory. Huebner and Garrod (1991) pointed out that in some Hindu and Buddhist cultures, morality is embedded in conceptions about the nature of human existence itself. There, especially the law of *karma* (i.e., the adding up of good *[dharma]* and bad *[adharma]* actions that may also have been committed in earlier lives) is crucial as it leads, according to the authors, to types of moral reasoning totally different from the ones defined in Kohlberg's stage theory and manual.

Ma (1988) and Edwards (1986) also raised questions about the strict definition of Kohlberg's stage 4 in terms of law and institutions. From her investigations of face-to-face societies, Edwards concluded that the social perspective of an informal understanding of roles should be sufficient for a scoring at stage 4. Kenyan leaders in communal groups did not use formal concepts such as law, but rather exhibited an understanding of social roles and positions in a social system. Nisan (Nisan & Kohlberg, 1982) also proposed guess scores for a transitional stage between stage 3 and 4 for subjects' reasonings based upon either family tradition or relatedness of the actors.

Although most doubts concerning the manual's (and of course the theory's) comprehensiveness refer to an underestimation of higher stages, recently also the formulation of lower stages was also considered inadequate or at least incomplete by Keller, Eckensberger, and von Rosen (1989). The authors compared interview data from Iceland and Germany and found, in following Kohlberg's manual, structurally clear stage 2 judgments, but these already contained content references to interpersonal relations. Therefore, the adequacy of the instrumentalistic formulation of stage 2 in Kohlberg's theory and manual was questioned. Keller, Schuster, and Edelstein (1993) recently elaborated on this aspect for lower stages.

Two consequences may be drawn from these data and discussions. First, Vasudev (1986) and Huebner and Garrod (1991) showed that a separation of morality from religion, as in the West, is not feasible in every culture; this problem was already touched upon by Jahoda (1958) in the context of studies on immanent justice. Second, not only do the highest principled stages (5 and 6) appear to be too narrowly defined by the justice principle, but the concept of "relatedness" seems to enter all stages in some cultures; this principle probably comes close to the ethical principle of benevolence, accepted by Kohlberg in one of his latest writings (Kohlberg, Boyd, & LeVine, 1986).

From this perspective, Snarey and Keljo's (1991) application of Tönnies' (1887/1957) distinction between *Gesellschaft* (society) and *Gemeinschaft* (community) to the cross-cultural observations is very plausible, especially the distinction between *Gemeinschaft* and "new Gemeinschaft," the latter relating to a "*Gemeinschaft* of a higher order," which is a "telos of social evolution" (Snarey & Keljo, 1991, p. 400). While some authors (e.g., Edwards, 1986) proposed either to change the definition of stage 4 (into a stage of community role understanding) or to regard these materials as transitions between 3 and 4 (Nisan & Kohlberg, 1982), Snarey and Keljo (1991) argued that the unscoreable data suggested an understanding of a particular morality which, similar to Gilligan's (1982) claim for a morality of responsibility and care, and Ma's principle of *jen*, was based upon the principle of connectedness. These arguments also suit the findings of Keller et al. (1989) in that they represent even lower stages within an ethic of connectedness. Thus, although Gilligan's claim of a gender bias in the justice orientation mostly did not materialize cross-culturally, the caring perspective (based upon the principle of benevolence) remains relevant in cross-cultural contexts.[4]

Eisenberg's (1986) theory of prosocial reasoning is also relevant here. Because her theory is rather eclectic and her method different from Kohlberg's (she uses ratings for scoring on criteria only loosely related to his theory), the results of her research cannot easily be compared with those of Piaget and Kohlberg. Although Eisenberg is unsure about the universality of prosocial reasoning, she assumes at least some similarity in the development of prosocial reasoning across cultures, while expecting marked cross-cultural differences on the basis of her socialization theory and the content (value) orientation of the developmental levels. She was not as much interested in the generalization of her levels, as in the cultural and subcultural influences upon prosocial moral reasoning. Given the assumptions on the role of content learning, it should be realized that Eisenberg has no structural theory. Hence, she cannot easily utilize structure as a framework for comparison. Rather, one would expect her to first look for culture-specific situations of helping behavior, and then turn to the underlying reasoning. But due to the use of standard dilemmas, her data-gathering follows the cognitive developmental tradition.

There are four cross-cultural studies on Eisenberg's theory, two of which deal with Western cultures in the broadest sense (Germany: Eisenberg, Boehnke, Schuhler, & Silbereisen, 1985; Israel: Fuchs, Eisenberg, Hertz-Lazarowitz, & Sharabany, 1986), and the others with non-Western cultures (Japan: Sakagami & Namiki, 1982; Papua New Guinea: Tietjen, 1985). Rater reliability was, according to Eisenberg (1986), satisfactorily high. In one study, the dilemmas were adapted to the culture, that is, contextualized. Consistent with the theoretical orientation, three of the studies started with hypotheses about the impact of socialization experiences upon the level attainment of prosocial reasoning, and only one (Sakagami & Namiki, 1982) aimed at testing a possible level of universality. Although the method used in the Japanese study differed from that of Eisenberg (the authors used preference scaling of items), the emerging factor structure suggests at least some transcultural invariance of Eisenberg's categories (levels). The other three studies underline the connection between a *Gemeinschafts*-orientation and prosocial ethics of care and responsibility, as proposed by Snarey and Keljo (1991).

Incitement Conditions for the Development of Moral Judgment

Global Characteristics Differentiating Cultures
As already mentioned, the delay of developmental trends or the absence of higher (principled) stages in some cultures, are not only interpreted as a possible bias in Kohlberg's theory, but reference is usually made to the traditionality of these cultures, implying that they lack certain incitement conditions. In fact, Snarey (1985), in relating the range of stages in cross-cultural studies to the cultures' global characteristics, concluded that the most important source of variance is not the dichotomy "Western versus non-Western cultures," rather it is the "cultural complexity" or "folk versus urban societies," a characteristic resembling Piaget's distinction between traditional and modern cultures. But this variable has to be broken down considerably before it gains a psychological meaning.

Global Intracultural Incitement Conditions
There exists clear evidence that stage development correlates with socioeconomic status (Snarey, 1985), religiosity (Bar-Yam et al., 1980; Maqsud, 1977a), urbanization (Turiel, Edwards, & Kohlberg, 1978), and modernization (Edwards, 1978, 1982; Harkness, Edwards & Super, 1981; Maqsud, 1977a). But the psychological meaning of these sources of variance are usually difficult to interpret. On the one hand, some of these data can be plausibly interpreted with the previously mentioned stimulating conditions (role-taking opportunity and participation in decisions); on the other hand, one has to remember, that they are frequently confounded with other conditions such as education and/or IQ (Lei, 1994, p. 79). Some researchers have tried to explain the development of a system perspective (stage 4) by specific participation and experiences in social systems. In a number of studies this perspective was seldom attained in small tribal societies (Kenya: Edwards, 1975; rural

areas in Turkey: Turiel et al., 1978; Bahamas: White, 1975, 1977; White et al., 1978; British Honduras: Gorsuch & Barnes, 1973). Edwards (1975) and Harkness et al. (1981), therefore, tested the hypothesis whether tribal leaders in ethnic groups (Kikuyu, Luhia, Kipsigi, and Israeli) reached these stages comparably more often than African students (Edwards, 1982) and generated relatively un-equivocal results: formal education seems to be the most important condition for stage 4.

Childrearing as a Specific Incitement Condition that Varies within and across Cultures

In many studies, childrearing is used as a post hoc explanation, but it has rarely been investigated directly. Data on childrearing and moral development stem from Parikh (1980) and Saraswathi and Sundaresan (1980) in India, and O'Connor (1980) in three European cities. Saraswathi and Sundaresan (1980), following Hoffman (1970), examined the influence of educational styles (power assertion, induction, and love withdrawal) on moral development. The correlation patterns followed the expectations formulated on the basis of American data: Power assertion corre-lated negatively, and induction positively with stage values of moral judgment, although reaching significance only for upper-middle-class girls. Note that these authors doubted the general applicability of the childrearing styles in India. Parikh (1980) subsumed participation (encouraging children to participate in group discussions) under induction and also measured the parents' moral judg-ment. These data showed a positive correlation between the stages of moral judgments of mothers and their children. Moreover, the parents' moral judg-ment indicated an interesting connection with encouraging behavior: encour-aging parents argued at least on the conventional level, but not vice versa, and parents' encouraging behavior corresponded with higher moral judgments of the children. Additionally, a positive influence of induction was shown, but only for mothers and not for fathers. O'Connor (1980) investigated students' moral judgment in Essex (England), St. Andrews (Scotland), and Montpellier (France) by means of a short interview, scoring the results only on the three levels (pre-conventional, conventional, post-conventional). Employing a ques-tionnaire, he examined educational styles such as permissiveness, moralizing education (emphasis on right or wrong behavior), achievement-oriented so-cialization, and eventually a "left" educational ideology with strong support of political activities. Generally, in all three samples, "left educational ideol-ogy" strongly correlated positively with post-conventional and negatively with conventional judgments.

Rest's Contribution: Defining Issues Test

Paper and pencil tests have become increasingly attractive for an empirical defini-tion of moral judgments in cross-cultural research, because of their easy applica-bility (Moon, 1986). These include Rest's (1979, 1986) Defining Issues Test (DIT) and variations thereof (Lind, 1980), as well as Gibbs et al.'s (1984) questionnaire, although it follows a slightly different logic.

Rest's understanding of morality differs from Kohlberg's; the same is true for his theoretical assumptions about the nature of stages and his method. He defines morality primarily in terms of the function it serves for cooperation between different individuals' expectations. However, he also distinguishes six universal stages which resemble Kohlberg's and formulated similar antecedent conditions. But Rest does not conceive structure and content as independent from one another (Rest, 1979, p. 45). The DIT consists of dilemma stories in which the subject has to choose from preformulated arguments. A person's moral judgment is defined in two ways: by the percentage of principle-oriented stage preferences (5A, 5B, 6), expressed by a percent score (p-score); and by a d-score, formed by a weighted judgment of the single stage ratings and considered to be a objective indicator of moral judgment. The technique does not measure the same aspects of moral judgment as Kohlberg's Moral Judgment Interview. Correlations between the two methods vary cross-culturally, from r = .40 to r = .70 (Moon, 1986). The DIT's retest correlations also vary greatly, between r = .32 (Hong Kong) and r = .99 (Australia). Rest himself considered the statements in the test to be a mixture of content and structure, and this obviously increased the problem of item comparability. Because items with a fixed content are used, in principle, the validity of each item has to be tested anew for each culture. However, it is important to realize that any result in cross-cultural research confirming a hypothesis derived from central assumptions of the theory could also be interpreted as an indicator of the test's cross-cultural construct validity.

The DIT has been used in Western (e.g., United States, Germany, Ireland, Finland, the Netherlands and Austria) and non-Western cultures/nations (Arab countries, Brazil, Greece, Hong Kong, India, Israel, Japan, Java, Mexico, the Philippines, Taiwan, South Africa, South America, and South Korea). Gielen and colleagues have been particularly active in this field. Regrettably, only few studies from the former socialist countries are available; an exception is Lind's (1986) research employing the Moral Judgment Test with students in former Yugoslavia and Poland. Gibbs' questionnaire was adapted and applied in Brazil (Biaggio, 1993).

Summaries of this research are given by Moon (1986) and Gielen (1991b). On the whole, the present authors consider the results generated from cross-cultural studies as an indicator of a weak construct validity of the DIT for cross-cultural usage for many reasons. First, positive correlations of p- or d-scores with age are difficult to interpret because in most investigations age and formal education were confounded. Second, correlations between d-scores and age are, generally, rather low (between r = .15 and r = .35), and attained significance merely because of large samples. Any differential correlation between d- and p-scores with age (as demonstrated in the study of Gielen, Cruickshank, Johnston, Swanzey & Avellani, 1986) is a theoretically challenging finding. Future research is needed to help to clarify the relationship between principled reasoning (p-scores) and cultural contexts (more prominent in d-scores). Third, Gielen, Miao, and Avellani (1990) assumed that the differences in stages and p-scores can be traced back to rather global cultural characteristics instead of different stimulating conditions within the cultures. They argue that the complexity of a culture, degree of industrialization, and existence of supportive, less coercive educational institutions lead to a higher p-score (cf. Snarey, 1985). Fourth, the most global intra-cultural incitement conditions (SES and sociodemographic characteristics of the family) were not detected as antecedent conditions for morality as measured by the DIT, nor did the participation in secondary institutions explain much of the variance in DIT scores. Fifth, the search for specific intracultural incitement conditions (child rearing) of p- or d-scores has been even less successful, although Gielen and his colleagues conducted several studies aimed at answering this question (cf. Gielen, 1991b). Finally, with respect to Gilligan's thesis of gender differences, statistically significant differences on DIT scores between the stage scores of females and males are very rare. The few reported differences do not support Gilligan's thesis of gender differences in morality of the "justice type," on which Rest's test is also based, and some are even contradictory (Moon, 1986).

Despite the problems of validity and reliability, this instrument possesses one specific attraction for cross-cultural psychology. It has often been argued that the principle-oriented stages in Kohlberg's theory represent a specific Western bias. But this may be true only if the arguments justifying a decision in a dilemma have to be formulated actively. It is possible, however, that a preference test is more sensitive to the existence of higher-stage arguments, particularly (via the p-scores) of principled thinking. And it may be worthwhile to note that the thesis of a Western bias in Rest's theory has not been supported by the p-scores. In the Far East, they were found to be even higher than in the United States (Gielen et al., 1990).

Turiel's Constructivist/Interactionist Theory

In detailed presentations, Turiel (1983) and his colleagues (Turiel et al., 1987; Turiel, Hildebrandt, & Wainryb, 1991) have discussed major shortcomings of Kohlberg's theory of moral development. They argued that moral development unfolds as a series of progressive differentiations among different domains of social knowledge, mainly proposing that "with age, children come to distinguish convention from morality, subordinating the former to the latter" (Turiel et al., 1991), whereas Kohlberg treats all social issues as belonging to the moral domain. Turiel et al. contended that subject–object interactions are so variegated that they bring about different conceptions of social knowledge (Turiel & Davidson, 1986). Relatively early in their lives, children come to distinguish among prototypical concepts of morality, convention, personal preference, prudence, and religious prescription (see Turiel et al., 1987; Turiel et al., 1991; Nucci, 1985; Smetana, 1982).

Turiel's Theory and its Basic Assumptions

Turiel's (1983) cognitive developmental and epistemological positions are in consonance with those of developmental constructivists such as Piaget and his followers. He too adopted an organismic position (Reese & Overton, 1970) when discussing the process of social cognitive development. He held that processes of self-construction and co-construction incite development. Originally, properties inherent in social events were thought to determine their assignment to particular domains of social knowledge. In addition to justifications of others' welfare, justice, fairness, obligation, custom, social coordination, personal choice and religious command, the criteria of rule/custom alterability, generalizability, impersonality and social consensus are applied to assess domain membership of social transgressions (Turiel, 1983; Turiel et al., 1987). Over forty studies (reviewed by Helwig, Tisak, & Turiel, 1990; Turiel et al., 1991) support the finding that moral concepts are structured by justice, fairness, rights, others' welfare, and objective obligation. Examples of these are stealing, murder, harm to others, unfair discrimination on racial, gender and any other grounds, and the violation of human rights. Hence, in the moral domain, intrinsic and inherent (i.e., context-independent) characteristics of the wrongness and rightness of prototypical moral events determine their content. Social conventional and personal events, however, both tend to be context-dependent. Concepts of a conventional nature are structured by matters of social organization, authority, custom, and social coordination, (i.e., by consensual agreement and alterability of social sanctions). Examples are customs, such as forms of address, dress, and table manners, (i.e., beliefs and rules pertaining to social organization and coordination). Personal choice has been found to structure personal concepts, (e.g., friendship choice).

At the structural level, social knowledge is organized vertically and horizontally. The heterogeneous object–subject interactions determine and set cognitive structural boundaries among various domains in the horizontal dimension. In the vertical dimension, cognitive structural transformations (development) take place within each domain (Turiel & Davidson, 1986). Turiel's most prominent contribution in terms of stages is in the development of social conventions. He proposed seven stages of the development of understanding conventions, which alternate between a "positive understanding" of conventions at stages 1, 3, 5 and 7, and a "negative evaluation" of the respective structures at stages 2, 4, and 6. Materials needed for the developmental processes (and for the distinction of different rule systems) are direct social experience and personal interaction. The heterogeneity of sources of experience and interaction is emphasized to highlight that internalization or socialization do not primarily promote social cognitive development (Turiel, 1983; Turiel et al., 1987).

Recently, it has become necessary to include the understanding of non-prototypical social issues, because "issues cannot be classified wholly independently of how they are construed by individuals and that how individuals reason about issues is not independent of features of the issues" (Turiel et al., 1991, p. 4). Their understanding is based on a variety of orientations that reflect ambiguities, consistencies, inconsistencies, agreements, and disagreements regarding conceptions of reality, situational features and consequences of particular actions, as well as different views of normality and the natural order (Turiel et al., 1991). For example, based on alternative perspectives regarding when human life begins, abortion may be judged by some people to be always wrong, and by others, to be wrong only after a particular period during pregnancy. Moreover, some people may consider reasoning about abortion to be a personal matter, others may locate it in the moral domain (Smetana, 1982). From a cross-cultural perspective, it would be interesting to know whether non-prototypical events are understood in a heterogeneous or global manner in non-Western cultures. Empirical evidence on orientations used to reason about these events in various cultures would be theoretically illuminating.

The universalism/relativism of the interactionist theory has been elaborately treated (Turiel, 1978, 1983; Turiel et al., 1987; Turiel et al., 1991). In summary, by using the formal criteria, (i.e., justifications, mechanisms and processes of development), distinctions amongst domains of social knowledge can be demonstrated universally in the cross-cultural context. In addition, social knowledge development that is premised on self-construction and co-construction should also yield cross-cultural similarities. The implication is that in all cultures, moral issues presented in the form of justice, fairness, others' welfare, and harm would be understood as universally binding, whereas social convention breaches would not. A sphere of personal preference, in which issues are assessed by criteria other than moral and conventional ones, would also exist in all cultures.

Cross-Cultural Evidence

The main focus of Turiel's theory is the onset of horizontal distinctions of social domains, rather than on their (vertical) development. The methods of data gathering and analysis differ from those of Piaget and Kohlberg. Mostly, prototypical events are offered to subjects, and criterion judgments and justification categories are applied that represent the discriminating features of the domains. These criteria, different from those of Kohlberg, allow for the attribution of an event to one of the domains.

Following Kohlberg et al.'s (1983) challenge that Turiel's position was based on insufficient cross-cultural data, studies were conducted in a number of countries (Helwig et al., 1990), including India (Shweder et al., 1987), Israel (Nisan, 1987), Indonesia (Carey & Ford, 1983), Korea (Song, Smetana, & Kim, 1987), The Virgin Islands (Nucci, Turiel, & Encarnacion-Gawrych, 1983), Nigeria (Hollos, Leis, & Turiel, 1986) and Zambia (Zimba, 1987). Except for findings from India, and partially from Israel, data from other countries, in general, support Turiel's domain specificity claim. However, there still remain matters requiring critical discussion and clarification.

Nisan (1987, 1988) contributed to this discussion by maintaining that distinctions among moral, conventional, and personal issues are patterned by normative and rationalistic orientations, especially in the case of moral issues. In the normative orientation, the criterion for the evaluation of a given behavior is the social norm attached to it, different from the rationalistic orientation where criteria are human welfare and law (Nisan, 1988). In the latter, intrinsic and inherent characteristics of moral issues may form a sufficient basis to judge them right or wrong irrespective of context. This may not be the case in the former orientation, where judgments would have to take into account contextual considerations. Nisan's point seems to be that distinguishing between moral and other issues solely on the basis of the rationalistic orientation does not take into account moral issues that may only arise when a normative orientation is employed. This is an important point from a cross-cultural perspective, because in many cultures, what constitutes harm and interpersonal responsibility is often understood from a localized normative orientation point of view (Zimba, 1994; Miller & Bersoff, 1992, p. 551). Turiel and his colleagues may not totally disagree with this, because they acknowledge the role of culturally-defined factual or informational content, including assumptions about the natural and supernatural order, although they have doubts about the explanatory power of the concept of culture as a basis of social–cognitive development. And they call for an examination of "social experiences in the context of the different functions and aims of social relationships, institutional practices, societal goals, and varying social contexts within cultures" (Turiel et al., 1987, p. 142). Nisan's (1988) normative orientation seems to provide at least a first answer to the question about how culture contributes to social development that is not global.

Another contribution to this discussion stems from Shweder and colleagues (Shweder et al., 1987). They have made many conceptual clarifications, of which only three are discussed here. The first is akin to Nisan's (1987, 1988) argument that because conventions can be imbued with moral significance by linking them to moral principles of harm, justice, and natural law, they would not, in many cultures of the world, be distinguished from prototypical moral issues. For instance, if violating a dress code is perceived to cause harm to others, the convention of form of dress assumes a moral character. Shweder et al., therefore, question the existence of universal developmental processes that lead children to differentiate moral from conventional obligations.

Shweder et al.'s (1987) second criticism concerns the rather exclusive manner in which the moral object, sometimes also called "moral patient," was conceptualized in the original version of the interactionist theory, because it contained only sentient human beings. The new category of "unearthly-belief mediated moral events" (Turiel et al., 1987) subsumed the idea of also protecting ancestors and souls of dead relatives from harm, as already argued by Piaget (1947) and Havighurst and Neugarten (1955). Indeed, many societies have in their moral codes the link between conscious life and life after death. Moral obligations between the living and the dead are also perceived to exist.

A study by Zimba (1994) may clarify this point. The Chewa and Tumbuka of Zambia distinguish sexually "hot" individuals (teenagers and adults of child-bearing age) from sexually "cold" ones (infants, seriously sick persons, neophytes in the rites of passage, and adults who have ended their sexual involvement). They also believe that engaging in *chigololo*, that is, premarital sex of the "hot" individuals, causes illness (the outbreak of *vumba*—a type of influenza) among the "cold" moral patients. *Chigololo* pollutes sexually "hot" individuals and makes them transmit the pollution to sexually "cold" individuals through fire, touch, salt, and air.

The harm "cold" individuals may suffer due to the sexual misconduct of "hot" individuals is "real" harm as far as the Chewa and the Tumbuka are concerned. Consequently, they interpret (different from American university students) pre-marital sex as a moral issue.

The causal chain of the harm that the Chewa and the Tumbuka perceive is not believed in on a universal level. However, the way of protection from harm of moral patients, however these may be conceived in a specific context, can take different forms, conceptualization and characteristics. Actions that do not protect moral patients from any form of harm are wrong on moral grounds. As a matter of principle, whether it is localized or universalized, whether it is allowed or not allowed, harm is harm.

Shweder et al.'s (1987) third criticism is that Turiel et al. (1987) underplay the significance of tacit and explicit communication and other forms of socialization in the development of social knowledge. Shweder et. al. extensively relied on Edwards (1985, 1987) work, who analyzed childrearing episodes of Luo-speaking Oyugis community members from the South Nyanza district of Kenya, and of U.S. university students (New York). These episodes were categorized into moral categories (justice, harm and welfare, work ethic) and conventional clusters (Edwards, 1987, pp. 126-127).

Edwards found that in the Kenyan case, (a) moral and conventional rules were learned in the same kinds of social encounters involving accusations, sanctions, commands and responsible suggestions; (b) children showed "as strong a commitment to rules delineating social roles and proper social behavior as to rules concerning justice, aggression and care of others" (Edwards, 1987, p. 139); and (c) the learning of all rule systems did not depend mainly on the victim's response, but rather on explicit communication by "moral guardians" of various value norms. Moreover, a difference was uncovered between the childrearing styles in Kenya and New York (the nursery school teachers in the latter case de-emphasized sanctions and, instead, stressed the rationale or underlying purpose for upholding particular norms). From these findings she concluded that distinctions between moral and conventional events were not clearly made, and that "it is the culture, not the child, that decides which normative and regulatory rules and standards are most important, necessary for social life, and obligatory" (Edwards, 1987, p. 148).

Shweder's Social Communication Theory

Based upon these criticisms, Shweder et al. (1987) recently articulated the social communication theory as an alternative to both Kohlberg's theory of moral development and Turiel's theory of social knowledge development. Although a cognitivist, Shweder diverges from Turiel's constructivist position. He holds that the organismic view of man is incomplete, because it overemphasizes the rational orientation at the expense of the nonrational one. According to him, the development of social knowledge is not based mainly on self-construction, but on "other-dependent learning." Social cognitive development (e.g., moral development) is not assumed to be stage-like, but involves "frame switching" that draws on socialization as tacit communication (Shweder & Much, 1987). Shweder proposed that the concept of moral obligation is a universal of childhood, not preceded by the idea that obligations derive their authority from consensually-based conventions. He, in fact, questioned the existence of universal developmental processes that lead the child to differentiate moral from conventional obligations. Rather, morality is acquired by children through communications of cultural judgments and ideology. Specifically, moral evaluations and judgments are transmitted to children by "local guardians of the moral order, (e.g., parents)" (Shweder et al., 1987). How this process takes place has not been explained, and no systematic developmental framework of how concepts emerge has been developed. Because of this, it is difficult, according to the theory, to distinguish between mature and less mature moral judgments.

Using social practices as the main source of moral content, social communication theory attempts to explicate premises and principles applied in arriving at moral judgments. Underlying these premises and principles are various cultural conceptions of persons, society, morality, and nature, and the relations between these (Shweder et al., 1987, p. 4). The developmental structure of the theory has not been provided.

Shweder (1986; Shweder et al., 1987) proposed distinct rationality within the moral domain:

a. There exists more than one rationally defensible moral code.
b. In any moral code with rational appeal, some concepts are mandatory. Without these, the code loses its rational appeal. Other concepts are discretionary, i.e., permit replacement by alternative concepts whose substitution into the code would not diminish its rational appeal.
c. Every rationally defensible moral code is built up of both mandatory and discretionary concepts. The three mandatory features are the idea of natural law, the principle of harm, and the principle of justice. The six discretionary features are a conception of natural law premised on natural rights; a conception of natural law premised on voluntarism, individualism, and a prior-to-society perspective; a particular idea of what or who a person is; a particular conception of where to draw the boundaries around the territories of the self; a conception of justice in which similarities are emphasized and differences overlooked; and a rejection of the idea of divine authority (Shweder et al., 1987, pp. 18–19).

Consequently, Shweder and colleagues found plausible the existence of context-independent and context-dependent moral obligations. They criticized Kohlberg and Turiel for universalizing one moral code based on a discretionary feature of "rights" to the exclusion of other moral codes premised on "duties" and "goals." They contended that, in a duty-based moral code, the moral quality of duties associated with particular role relationships is given more prominence than the moral quality of individuals per se. Moreover, "attention is focused on the moral quality of individual acts per se, on the degree of conformity of each act to a code for proper conduct. It is the code that takes precedence . . . while the individual per se and his various interior states, . . . intentions, or motives are of little interest or concern. The purity of the motive is less important than the quality of the act" (Shweder et al., 1987, pp. 20–21). For this reason, Kohlberg and Turiel are blamed for expecting moral agents from the "duty-based" orientation to make moral judgments on the basis of a "rights-based" orientation.

Shweder et al. also criticized Kohlberg's and Turiel's conception of the individual abstracted from society and his or her attributes and personality. Kohlberg and Turiel consider this notion of the abstract individual to be central, because it allows moral patients to start from the same level with the same intrinsic value. Shweder et al. maintained that universalizing this position misses the point that not all societies perceive the intrinsic value of the abstract individual in the same way. For this reason, what may appear to be some form of injustice and unfairness, from the "abstract individual" point of view, may not be perceived as such from the perspective of the duty-based moral code.

Shweder (Shweder et al., 1987) compared a number of "behavioral cases," representing a range of family life and social practices (like eating beef regularly, the marriage of a widow, playing cards as woman or cooking rice as men, bearing children as brother and sister, kissing in public, beating one's wife) in two cultures (Bhubaneswar, India, and Hyde Park, U.S.A.). The task was to assess the perceived seriousness of the potential transgression event in each case. He wanted to determine, primarily, the extent to which the social order is perceived as moral or conventional, and if there exists, at all, a distinction between morality and conventions in the two cultures. For a distinction of morality and conventions, he used similar criteria as Turiel (amongst others, universality, inalterability for morality, change by consensus for conventions). He found that the Indian sample (Brahmans and Untouchables) did not think that most of the cases could be changed; in the United States, only small children had this conviction, but with increasing age interpreted these cases as being conventions. Shweder considered this finding as supporting his theory.

Conclusion and Outlook

The focus of the chapter has been on moral judgment (not on morally relevant behavior), using Kohlberg's theory as a pivot. Because the chapter represents already a highly condensed summary of cross-cultural research and discourse on moral judgment, to summarize this would be neither possible nor useful. Instead, a general evaluation and critique of this field will be presented.

Two main themes appeared frequently throughout this chapter. First, questions centered around the dichotomy "universalism" versus "relativism," which is related to the dichotomy "abstract moral reasoning " versus "contextualized argumentation" and, of course, to the dichotomy "structure" versus "content" of moral judgments. The second question centered around the (vertical) dimension of the development of moral judgments and the (horizontal) distinction between different normative (social) rule systems.

Huebner and Garrod (1991) distinguish three levels of a discourse on morality. The empirical level (what is considered to be morally good or bad), the level of normative standards (what ought to be good), and metaethical beliefs (the nature of human existence itself). Although these three levels are intrinsically interrelated, they will serve as a framework for the following discussion.

Are moral judgments universal or context bound normative orientations of humans? In applying the levels of discourse proposed by Huebner and Garrod (1991) it is evident that a caveat is in order. Kohlberg himself proposed that important distinctions should be made between: (a) the universal empirical existence of stages in all cultures, (b) the operation of universality, which means that a particular set of actions apply to all human beings, and (c) the operation of universalizability, which implies that all actors should act in a specific way in similar situations (Kohlberg et al., 1983, p. 46).

On the empirical level, there is much material that supports the claim of universal developmental trends, as articulated in organismic theories. From a quantitative point of view, stages 2 to 4 seem to exist transculturally, but from a qualitative point of view doubts are articulated. Some of them stay within Kohlberg's scheme, only calling for modification, like Edwards' (1986) reformulation of stage 4. Others are more substantial in that it is argued that Kohlberg's theory is at best incomplete, or at worst misleading and wrong.

Whether these doubts are formulated on the basis of empirical material, (i.e., not scoreable in the manual) or whether they are derived from non-Western ethics, some of them aim at the level of normative standards and others at the level of ethical beliefs, because they claim that the justice principle which serves as the core of Kohlberg's understanding of human beings and ethics is too narrowly defined and (Western) biased. As reviewed in this chapter, a variety of culture-specific perspectives and principles has been proposed to compensate for these deficiencies. These include: the Confucian principle of *giri-ninjo* (obligation), which seems to be close to the Indian ethic of duty (Miller, 1994; Shweder et al., 1987); the Javanese principles of *hormat* (respect for older people) and *rukun* (harmonious social relations); the principles of collective happiness, filial piety, collective utility, communal interconnectedness and harmony; the Chinese principle of *jen*; and the Indian principle of respect for all life based upon the notion of *ahimsa* (nonviolence).

Once it is realized that this discourse is on the level of normative standards and ethical beliefs, the status of these proposals, within themselves, becomes vague. First, it is sometimes unclear whether these concepts can be understood within Kohlberg's scheme and belong to a specific stage (which would not damage or falsify the theory) or whether they in fact represent ethical principles in their own right. Setiono (1994), for instance, claims that the Javanese concepts of *rukun* and *hormat* resemble Kohlberg's stage 3, but at the same time they are called moral principles by Setiono. Second, the relationship of some of these principles to Western ethics (the justice ethic and the ethic of responsibility and care) remains nebulous. This is especially important, because Kohlberg himself tried to integrate both of these perspectives when defining the "co-ordination between justice and benevolence" as the structure of stage 6 in one of his last writings (Kohlberg et al., 1986). It remains unclear, however, whether both the Confucian principle of *giri-ninjo* as well as the *karma*-based Indian ethic of duty can be understood as a specific type of a justice ethic (cf. Shweder, 1991). The Chinese principle of *jen*, the Javanese principles of *hormat* and *rukun*, the principles of collective happiness, filial piety, collective utility, communal interconnectedness and harmony all seem to represent principles close to Gilligan's (1982) concept of care and responsibility. Altogether these represent moral matters encompassing the communitarian voice (*Gemeinschaft*; Snarey & Keljo, 1991). Miller's (1994) work indicates, however, that Gilligan's concept of caring may itself vary cross-culturally. Caring in Gilligan's sense is based upon Western cultural views of the self and thus culturally bound. Americans (and perhaps others from Western cultures) conceptualize caring in highly voluntaristic terms whereas Indians (and perhaps others from non-Western cultures) conceptualize it as based on perceived intrinsic duties. Miller (1994) argues for an "individually-oriented" interpersonal moral code in the United States in contrast to a "duty based" interpersonal moral code in India, which gives less weight to individual discretion and choice in interpersonal responsibilities. All these examples primarily aim at the level of normative standards, while others refer to meta-ethical principles, (i.e., to the nature of human existence itself), because they understand humans as a part of nature. This is true for the Indian respect for life principle based upon the notion of *ahimsa*, and for Ma's formulation of the *jen*-principle.

These questions cannot be answered on the level of empirical cross-cultural research alone; they require instead a new cross-cultural research strategy, which deviates from the classical imposed etic emic derived etic strategy proposed by Berry (1989). This new strategy would start with an explication of the (hidden) models of man in different cultures existing on the level of meta-ethical beliefs, then explicating the normative standards on the level of the cultural beliefs by a process Eckensberger (1994b) has called "consensual validation" of concepts, and which can then be transformed into collected empirical data. It is important to note, however, that this procedure does not necessarily invalidate the central idea of a genetic epistemology, the crucial notion of the development of moral judgment itself. As outlined by Greenfield (1976) and others for the domain of cognitive development, it might be a promising approach to first look for different moral principles in various cultures, and then reconstruct them by the very logic of Kohlberg's stage theory. On the other hand, it is evident that the developmental processes (assumptions about proximate causes of development), as assumed in organismic theory, are under attack from those whose theories rely on content learning (Shweder, Edwards).

Interestingly, this discourse would be fruitful from both the Western and non-Western perspectives. It would become evident, for instance, that Ma's principle of *jen* clearly represents a naturalistic fallacy from the point of view of Western philosophy, because normative consequences are derived from empirical facts; what is in accord with nature is (therefore) good.

Also, Shweder's conceptualization of the moral patient under the duty-based moral code would certainly benefit from such a discussion. Within this code one may conclude that harming some moral patients may be permitted, simply because they occupy particular social stations and social roles. According to this moral code, harm endured by a particular category of persons may be perceived to be less serious than the same harm endured by another category of persons occupying an ascribed higher status. That is, with the conceptualization of discriminating concepts comes the exclusion of some moral patients from being eligible for protection from harm. However, on the very basis of the mandatory concept of harm, this would be morally wrong. This issue leads to the question of how the mandatory moral concepts in Shweder's theory are interrelated: how can beating up one's wife be interpreted as a moral event since it is considered as universalizable by a subject, although it definitely produces harm? This example also demonstrates that most definitions of ethics or morality, as well as their distinction from conventions, are based upon the operation of universalizabilty which refers to the agency (that all actors should act in a specific way in a similar situation), but not to the operation of universality, which refers to the moral patients (that a set of actions applies to all human beings). These authors suggest that any moral code should, in the final analysis, enhance and ensure the well-being of all moral patients.

Additionally, Shweder cannot distinguish between the opinion of unchangeability of an event on heteronomous and autonomous grounds. Shweder's concept of a morality of duty may well be based upon external constraints or rule following. This is demonstrated in his main empirical study (Shweder et al., 1987) when he renounced asking his subjects for reasons or justifications of their opinions, which is, however, the basic requirement of Kohlberg's approach.

However, such a discussion would also benefit Kohlberg's theory. The A-substage (heteronomous) and B-substage (autonomous) distinction, for instance, and its relation to mainstage development is still an open question, which casts serious doubts on whether Kohlberg's choice of structure (justice operations and social perspective) was the only and most fruitful one. The first author, for instance, has proposed to use the complexity of the actions perceived in a dilemma as a criterion for the structure of moral arguments. The justification of this choice to define the structure of moral arguments was simple. It was initially based upon the fact that the human action (which implies a choice and therefore a subjective decision) is the only way to define and conceptualize morality, which makes the conceptualization of responsibility possible (Eckensberger, 1986; Eckensberger & Reinshagen, 1980). Second, it was based upon the assumption that the human action is intrinsically a universal framework. All humans have goals, choose means, and produce effects and results by acting. He applied the structure of human action and its elements (goals, means, results, and consequences) first to Kohlberg's and then to his own data (Eckensberger, 1986), resulting in a finer-grained stage theory (eleven stages summarized into four levels). A crucial assumption is that the stages are first developed within an "interpersonal social space," where concrete individuals (agencies) interact, and then repeated in a "transpersonal social space," where roles and institutions are being reconstructed. In both "spheres of social interpretation" a development from heteronomy to autonomy has been defined. Thus, both "developmental paths" implied in Kohlberg's theory are somehow reversed in their importance. Since even in the "interpersonal sphere" the highest stage is equilibrated and comprised of mutual respect and autonomy (including justice and benevolence), many problems defined in face-to-face societies, as well as the difficulty of handling a system perspective in cross-cultural research, could be dealt with. Further, the phenomenon that different dilemmas trigger different stages (antithetical to the consistency assumption) is not a problem, and is even expected (Burgard, 1989; Eckensberger, 1989).

On the empirical level much criticism pertains to the dilemmas' hypothetical quality. It has been demanded that specific content be adapted to specific cultural contexts. As previously outlined, however, this criticism is not particularly convincing. Yet the criticism is not unjustified because it points to the problem of using dilemmas and a scoring procedure preformulated in one culture and applied (more or less in a cookbook fashion) in another one. Eckensberger and Reinshagen (1980) therefore proposed a slightly different method that used only the "core of a dilemma" (in the case of the Heinz story where a young man wants to get a drug from a druggist, who refuses to give it to him); the interviewee was then given the chance to ask further questions about the issue, and in return, to be asked about the reasons for his curiosity about the issue. This method has been applied several times by the first author (Eckensberger 1986; Eckensberger, Sieloff, Kasper, Schirk, & Nieder, 1992); it allows the interviewee to refer to as much culture-specific material and justifications as he/she wants. Of course, these answers are then scored by means of the action structures referred to above, a procedure which does not need a scoring manual like the one Kohlberg and his group developed (which by necessity is content loaded and therefore culture bound).[5]

This leads to the second central question of cross-cultural research on moral judgment. Do moral judgments emerge from personal concerns and conventions (vertical dimension) or are personal concerns, conventions, and morality, distinct rule systems, differentiated early in life? A number of authors claim, on empirical as well as on analytical grounds, that Kohlberg confounds the domains of morality, conventions (Turiel, 1983), and (premoral) personal concerns (Nucci, 1985; Smetana, 1982) with the developmental sequence of preconventional, conventional, and postconventional thinking. It is questionable, however, whether this criticism is as plausible as it initially appears.

First, on the empirical level, matters are more complicated. Shweder and his colleagues, for instance, doubt his claim of a domain specificity of the normative rule system. Instead, his Indian data suggest that the moral domain appears to be the only one available for making social reasoning judgments

(Shweder et al., 1987); he also relied on Edwards' (1987) data in developing his argument.

These authors doubt, however, that there was clear evidence in Edwards' (1987) study, because neither the Kenyan nor the American analyses lead to this deduction. Her assertion implies that because the Oyugis' learning environment merged morality and other social domains, the Oyugis children did not (and were not given the opportunity to) distinguish between moral and conventional domains. Because this was not assessed, there are no grounds for such conclusions. The fact that children are equally committed to moral and conventional rules, and that they learn in the same kinds of social encounters, does not necessarily mean that they do not make distinctions between them. Obviously, had adequate judgment criteria been applied, it could have shown that they do indeed locate them in the same or different domain of knowledge. What emerges for cross-cultural psychology is the need to verify propositions not only by applying comparable paradigms but also by using comparable methods (Turiel et al., 1987, p. 208).

Beyond this, the empirical cross-cultural study of Zimba (1987) presents a different picture. Although some of the conventions, through social meaning, were understood in "moral ways," others were clearly distinguished from prototypical moral events. This suggests that the distinctions among prototypical domains of social knowledge are, in fact, made cross-culturally, but not as unequivocally as normally demonstrated in the West.

Studies by Bersoff and Miller (1993) and Miller and Luthar (1989) support this position. These studies showed that in India, contrary to the data presented by Shweder et al. (1987), distinctions among social domains are made. Yet, situational and accountability appraisal parameters determine the nature of these distinctions.

Another crucial issue concerns within-domain vertical (developmental) studies. There is a lack of longitudinal studies to verify, cross-culturally, the interactionist theory's claim that stage-like and vertical development takes place within each domain of social knowledge. Turiel's (1983) work on the conventional domain, and Smetana's (1982) work on the personal, has apparently not been followed up anywhere else in the world. Furthermore, the present authors are unaware of longitudinal studies using the interactionist theory's narrowed concept of morality. How this kind of morality develops vertically in a non-Kohlbergian sense has yet to be articulated.

These results clearly call for more analytical work leading to empirical studies in this field. From a theoretical perspective, for example, it is indisputable that Kohlberg's scenarios (dilemmas) belong primarily to the moral domain, and not to conventions, for they deal with promise keeping, life, and death.[6] Although in the moral domain reference is also made to personal (egocentric) and conventional (group) perspectives, this does not mean that these are therefore personal concerns or conventions. There is no question, however, that Kohlberg's interviews should be supplemented by some criterion judgments, such as those of Turiel and others.

Endnotes

1. The authors would like to thank the German Academic Exchange Service and the German Research Foundation for enabling them to meet in Germany and Namibia to prepare this chapter. They would also like to thank Lou Iozzi and Joan Miller for comments on the content of the chapter. Jane Gross, Baljit Kaur, and Bernd Puschner improved the style of various versions of the chapter. Franka Berrang and Johannes Gross proofread the text and checked the references.

2. Snarey (1985) correctly argues that studies carried out before the existence of the standard scoring manual (1978) are difficult to compare with later investigations. Hence, in his review he primarily focuses on the later ones. When we refer to studies from before 1978, we do not use them for the definition of stage scores, but only for the determination of the relations of stages to other conditions.

3. Kohlberg's as well as Lei's data should be interpreted cautiously, though. First, the increase of stage difficulty in the 1978 manual (Eckensberger, 1986) also implies a reduction in variation of stage scores. Second, neither Cronbach's Alpha nor the g-factor are adequate tests for consistency of scores across the dilemmas. Both by definition remove from the calculations the mean differences of intercorreleted variables.

4. Here an interesting cross-reference to the individualism/collectivism discussion in cross-cultural psychology would be possible. This would, however, also call for a discussion of the relationship between individualism and autonomy, which is clearly beyond the scope of this chapter. See chapter by Kagitçibasi, Volume 3, of this *Handbook*, for a comprehensive overview of individualism/collectivism.

5. At a different place Shweder (1991) gives an interesting example of a Heinz-interview that follows the Kohlbergian tradition. Interestingly, this interview was scored by Kohlberg himself on stage 3/4, which in the view of the first author is a heteronomous structure (cf. Eckensberger, 1986).

6. Two dilemmas involve the decision of a judge, and may be justifiably attributed to the tension between morality and law; but law is also to be differentiated from conventions.

References

Bar-Yam, M., Kohlberg, L., & Naame, A. (1980). Moral reasoning of students in different cultural, social and educational settings. *American Journal of Education, 88,* 345–362.

Berry, J. W. (1989). Imposed etics emics derived etics: The operationalization of a compelling idea. *International Journal of Psychology, 24,* 721–735.

Berry, J. W., Poortinga, Y. H., Segall, M. H., & Dasen, P. R. (1992). *Cross-cultural psychology: Research and applications.* Cambridge: Cambridge University Press.

Bersoff, D. M. & Miller, J. G. (1993). Culture, context, and the development of moral accountability judgments. *Developmental Psychology, 29,* 664–676.

Biaggio, A. (1993). Moral judgment, anxiety, and aggression. Presidential address delivered at the Interamerican Congress of Psychology. Santiago, Chile (unpublished).

Burgard, P. (1989, July). Consistencies in inconsistencies in moral judgments: Microanalysis of stage variations within moral dilemmas. Poster presented at the poster session "Moral Development" at the tenth biennial meeting of the ISSBD, Jyväskylä, Finland.

Carey, N. & Ford, M. (1983). Domains of social and self-regulation: An Indonesian study. Paper presented at the meeting of the American Psychological Association, Los Angeles.

Colby, A. & Kohlberg, L. (1987a). *The measurement of moral judgment. Vol. I: Theoretical foundations and research validation.* Cambridge: Cambridge University Press.

Colby, A. & Kohlberg, L. (1987b). *The measurement of moral judgment, Vol. II: Standard issue scoring manual.* Cambridge: Cambridge University Press.

Colby, A., Kohlberg, L., Gibbs, J., & Lieberman, M. (1983). A longitudinal study of moral judgment. *Monographs of the Society for Research in Child Development, 48* (1–2, Serial No. 200).

Davids, M. F. (1983). Some implications of regional psychologies for a Piagetian approach to the development of cognition. In J. B. Deregowski, S. Dziurawiec, & R. C. Annis (Eds.), *Expiscations in cross-cultural psychology* (pp. 129–143). Lisse: Swets & Zeitlinger.

Eckensberger, L. H. (1983). Research on moral development. *The German Journal of Psychology, 7,* 195–244.

Eckensberger, L. H. (1986). Handlung, Konflikt und Reflexion: Zur Dialektik von Struktur und Inhalt im moralischen Urteil. In W. Edelstein & G. Nunner-Winkler (Eds.), *Zur Bestimmung der Moral: Philosophische und sozialwissenschaftliche Beiträge zur Moralforschung* (pp. 409–442). Frankfurt/M., Germany: Suhrkamp.

Eckensberger, L. H. (1989). Consistencies in inconsistencies in moral judgments: Stage variations between dilemmas. Poster presented at the poster session "Moral Development" at the tenth biennial meeting of the ISSBD, Jyväskylä, Finland.

Eckensberger, L. H. (1993). Moralische Urteile als handlungsleitende normative Regelsysteme im Spiegel der kulturvergleichenden Psychologie. In A. Thomas (Ed.), *Einführung in die kulturvergleichende Psychologie* (pp. 259–295). Göttingen, Germany: Hogrefe.

Eckensberger, L. H. (1994a). Moral development and its measurement across cultures. In W. J. Lonner & R. Malpass (Eds.), *Psychology and culture* (pp. 71–78). Boston: Allyn and Bacon.

Eckensberger, L. H. (1994b). On the social psychology of cross-cultural research. In A.-M. Bouvy, F. J. R. van de Vijver, P. Boski & P. Schmitz (Eds.), *Journeys into cross-cultural psychology* (pp. 31–40). Lisse: Swets & Zeitlinger.

Eckensberger, L. H. & Burgard, P. (1983). The cross-cultural assessment of normative concepts: Some considerations on the affinity between methodological approaches and preferred theories. In S. H. Irvine & J. W. Berry (Eds.), *Human assessment and cultural factors* (pp. 459–480). New York: Plenum Press.

Eckensberger, L. H. & Gähde, U. (Eds.). (1993). *Ethische Norm und empirische Hypothese.* Frankfurt/M., Germany: Suhrkamp.

Eckensberger, L. H. & Kern, E. (1986). *Öko-ethisches Denken: Ein Versuch, aus philosophischen Begründungen Kategorien für eine entwicklungspsychologische Studie zu gewinnen.* (Arbeiten der Fachrichtung Psychologie No. 104). Saarbrücken, Germany: Universität des Saarlandes.

Eckensberger, L. H. & Reinshagen, H. (1980). Kohlbergs Stufentheorie der Entwicklung des Moralischen Urteils: Ein Versuch ihrer Reinterpretation im Bezugsrahmen handlungstheoretischer Konzepte. In L. H. Eckensberger & R. K. Silbereisen (Eds.), *Entwicklung sozialer Kognitionen: Modelle, Theorien, Methoden, Anwendung* (pp. 65–131). Stuttgart, Germany: Klett-Cotta.

Eckensberger, L. H., Sieloff, U., Kaper, E., Schirk, S., & Nieder, A. (1992). Psychologische Analyse eines Ökonomie-Ökologie-Konflikts in einer saarländischen Region: Kohlekraftwerk Bexbach. In K. Pawlik & K. H. Stapf (Eds.), *Umwelt und Verhalten* (pp. 145–168). Bern: Huber.

Edwards, C. P. (1975). Societal complexity and moral development: A Kenyan study. *Ethos, 3,* 505–527.

Edwards, C. P. (1978). Social experience and moral judgement in Kenyan young adults. *The Journal of Genetic Psychology, 133,* 19–29.

Edwards, C. P. (1981). The comparative study of the development of moral judgment and reasoning. In R. H. Munroe, R. I. Munroe, & B. B. Whiting (Eds.), *Handbook of cross-cultural human development* (pp. 501–528). New York: Garland STPM Press.

Edwards, C. P. (1982). Moral development in comparative cultural perspective. In D. A. Wagner & H. W. Stevenson (Eds.), *Cultural perspectives on child development* (pp. 248–279). San Francisco: W. H. Freeman.

Edwards, C. P. (1985). Another style of competence: The caregiving child. In A. D. Vogel & G. F. Melson (Eds.), *The origins of nurturance* (pp. 95–121). New York: Erlbaum.

Edwards, C. P. (1986). Cross-cultural research on Kohlberg's stages: The basis for consensus. In S. Modgil & C. Modgil (Eds.), *Lawrence Kohlberg: Consensus and controversy* (pp. 419–430). London: The Falmer Press.

Edwards, C. P. (1987). Culture and the construction of moral values: A comparative ethnography of moral encounters in two cultural settings. In J. Kagan & S. Lamb (Eds.), *The emergence of morality in young children* (pp. 123–154). Chicago: University of Chicago Press.

Eisenberg, N. (1986). *Altruistic emotion, cognition and behavior.* Hillsdale, NJ: Erlbaum.

Eisenberg, N., Boehnke, K., Schuhler, P., & Silbereisen, R. K. (1985). The development of prosocial behavior and cognitions in German children. *Journal of Cross-Cultural Psychology, 16,* 69–82.

Fuchs, I., Eisenberg, N., Hertz-Lazarowitz, R., & Sharabany, R. (1986). Kibbutz, Israeli city, and American children's reasoning about prosocial moral conflicts. *Merill-Palmer-Quarterly, 32,* 37–50.

Geertz, C. (1973). *The interpretation of cultures: Selected essays.* New York: Basic Books.

Gibbs, J. C., Arnold, K. D., Morgan, R. L., Schwarz, E. S., Gavaghan, M. P., & Tappan, M. B. (1984). Construction and validation of a multiple-choice measure of moral reasoning. *Child Development, 55,* 527–536.

Gielen, U. P. (1991a). Kohlberg's moral development theory. In L. Kuhmerker (with U. Gielen & R. L. Hayes) (Eds.), *The Kohlberg legacy for the helping professions* (pp. 18–38). Birmingham, AL: R.E.P.

Gielen, U. P. (1991b). Research on moral reasoning. In L. Kuhmerker (with U. Gielen & R. L. Hayes) (Eds.), *The Kohlberg legacy for the helping professions* (pp. 39–60). Birmingham, AL: R.E.P.

Gielen, U. P., & Chirico-Kelly, D. (1993). Traditional Buddhist Ladakh and the ethos of peace. *International Journal of Group Tensions, 23,* 5–23.

Gielen, U. P., Cruickshank, H., Johnston, A., Swanzey, B., & Avellani, J. (1986). The development of moral reasoning in Belize,

Trinidad-Tobago, and the USA. *Behavior Science Research, 20,* 178–207.

Gielen, U. P., Miao, E., & Avellani, J. (1990). Perceived parental behavior and the development of moral reasoning in students from Taiwan. In Chinese Culture University, Proceedings of CCU-ICP International Conference, Moral Values and Moral Reasoning in Chinese Societies (pp. 464–506). Chinese Culture University, Taipei, Taiwan.

Gilligan, C. (1982). *In a different voice: Psychological theory and women's development.* Cambridge, MA: Harvard University Press.

Gorsuch, R. L. & Barnes, M. L. (1973). Stages of ethical reasoning and moral norms of Carib youths. *Journal of Cross-Cultural Psychology, 4,* 283–301.

Greenfield, P. M. (1976). Cross-cultural research and Piagetian theory: A paradox and progress. In K. Riegel & J. A. Meacham (Eds.), *The developing individual in a changing world* (Vol. 1, pp. 322–333). Paris: Mouton.

Guindon, A. (1978). Moral development: Form, content and self. A critique of Kohlberg's sequence. *University of Ottawa Quarterly, 48,* 232–263.

Harkness, S., Edwards, C. P., & Super, C. M. (1981). Social roles and moral reasoning: A case study in a rural African community. *Developmental Psychology, 17,* 595–603.

Havighurst, R. J. & Neugarten, B. L. (1955). *American Indian and White children: A sociological investigation.* Chicago: University Press.

Helwig, C. C., Tisak, M. S., & Turiel, E. (1990). Children's social reasoning in context: Reply to Gabennesch. *Child Development, 61,* 2068–2078.

Hoffman, M. L. (1970). Moral development. In P. H. Mussen (Ed.), *Carmichael's manual of child psychology* (Vol. 2., pp. 261–359). New York: Wiley.

Hollos, M., Leis, P. E., & Turiel, E. (1986). Social reasoning in Ijo children and adolescents in Nigerian communities. *Journal of Cross-Cultural Psychology, 17,* 352–374.

Huebner, A. & Garrod, A. (1991). Moral reasoning in a karmic world. *Human Development, 34,* 341–352.

Jahoda, G. (1958). Immanent justice among West

African children. *The Journal of Social Psychology, 47,* 241–248.

Kant, I. (1959). *Foundations of the metaphysics of morals.* (L. W. Beck, Trans.). New York: The Liberal Arts Press. (Original work published 1785).

Keller, M., Eckensberger, L. H., & von Rosen, K. (1989). A critical note on the conception of preconventional morality: The case of stage 2 in Kohlberg's theory. *International Journal of Behavioral Development, 12,* 57–69.

Keller, M., Schuster, P., & Edelstein, W. (1993). Universelle und differentielle Aspekte in der Entwicklung sozio-moralischen Denkens: Ergebnisse einer Untersuchung mit isländischen und chinesischen Kindern. *Forum für interdisziplinäre Forschung, 11,* 89–104.

Klahr, D. (1982). Nonmonotone assessment of monotone development: An information processing analysis. In S. Strauss (Ed.), *U-shaped behavioral growth.* New York: Academic Press.

Kohlberg, L. (1958). *The development of modes of moral thinking and choice in the years 10 to 16.* Unpublished doctoral dissertation, University of Chicago.

Kohlberg, L. (1969). Stage and sequence: The cognitive-developmental approach to socialization. In D. Goslin (Ed.), *Handbook of socialization theory and research* (pp. 347–480). Chicago: Rand McNally.

Kohlberg, L. (1973). Continuities in childhood and adult moral development revisited. In P. Baltes & K. W. Schaie (Eds.), *Life-span developmental psychology: Personality and socialization* (pp. 180–204). New York: Academic Press.

Kohlberg, L. (1976). Moral stages and moralization: The cognitive–developmental approach. In T. E. Lickona (Ed.), *Moral development and behavior: Theory, research, and social issues* (pp. 31–55). New York: Holt, Rinehart, and Winston.

Kohlberg, L. (1978, September). The meaning and measurement of moral development. Invited address at the Convention of the American Psychological Association, Toronto, Canada.

Kohlberg, L. (1986). A current statement on some theoretical issues. In S. Modgil & C. Modgil (Eds.), *Lawrence Kohlberg: Consensus and controversy* (pp. 485–546). London, Philadelphia: The Falmer Press.

Kohlberg, L., Boyd, D., & LeVine, C. (1986). Die Wiederkehr der sechsten Stufe: Gerechtigkeit, Wohlwollen und der Standpunkt der Moral. In W. Edelstein & G. Nunner-Winkler (Eds.), *Zur Bestimmung der Moral: Philosophische und sozialwissenschaftliche Beiträge zur Moralforschung* (pp. 205–240). Frankfurt/M., Germany: Suhrkamp.

Kohlberg, L., LeVine, C., & Hewer, A. (1983). *Moral stages: The current formulation of Kohlberg's theory and a response to critics.* Basel: Karger.

Kugelmass, S. & Breznitz, S. (1967). The development of intentionality in moral judgment in city and Kibbutz adolescents. *The Journal of Genetic Psychology, 111,* 103–111.

Lei, T. (1983). Toward a little but special light on the universality of moral judgment development: A study of moral stage and moral type in a Taiwanese sample. Unpublished qualifying paper, Harvard Graduate School of Education.

Lei, T. (1994). Being or becoming moral in a Chinese culture: Unique or universal? *Cross-Cultural Research, 28,* 58–91.

Lei, T. & Cheng, S. W. (1984). An empirical study of Kohlberg's theory and scoring system of moral judgment in Chinese society. Unpublished manuscript, Harvard University, Cambridge, MA.

Lickona, T. E. (1976). Research on Piaget's theory of moral development. In T. E. Lickona (Ed.), *Moral development and behavior: Theory, research, and social issues* (pp. 219–240). New York: Holt, Rinehart, & Winston.

Lind, G. (1980). *Moralisches-Urteil-Test (m-u-t). Hinweise zum Einsatz und zur Interpretation eines Forschungsinstruments.* (Arbeitsunterlage 68). Forschungsprojekt Hochschulsozialisation, Universität Konstanz.

Lind, G. (1986). Cultural differences in moral judgment competence? A study of West and East European university students. *Behavior Science Research, 20,* 208–225.

Logan, R., Snarey, J., & Schrader, D. (1984). Heteronomous and autonomous moral types among Israeli kibbutz adolescents: A cross-cultural, longitudinal study. Unpublished manuscript, Harvard University, Cambridge, MA: Center for Moral Development and Education.

Loves, H. (1957). Ancestral beliefs and Christian catecheses. Enquiry in 55 classes in Kwango, Belgian Congo. *Lumen Vitae, 12,* 157–180.

Lyons, N. P. (1982). *Conceptions of self and morality and modes of moral choice: Identifying justice and care in judgments of actual moral dilemmas.* Unpublished doctoral dissertation, Harvard University, Cambridge, MA.

Ma, H. K. (1988). The Chinese perspectives on moral judgment development. *International Journal of Psychology, 23,* 201–227.

Maqsud, M. (1977a). The influence of social heterogeneity and sentimental credibility on moral judgments of Nigerian Muslim adolescents. *Journal of Cross-Cultural Psychology, 8,* 113–122.

Maqsud, M. (1977b). Moral reasoning of Nigerian and Pakistani Muslim adolescents. *Journal of Moral Education, 7,* 40–49.

Miller, J. G. (1994). Cultural diversity in the morality of caring: Individually-oriented versus duty-based interpersonal moral codes. *Cross-Cultural Research, 28,* 3–39.

Miller, J. G. & Bersoff, D. M. (1992). Culture and moral judgment: How are conflicts between justice and interpersonal responsibilities resolved? *Journal of Personality and Social Psychology, 62,* 541–554.

Miller, J. G. & Luthar, S. (1989). Issues of interpersonal responsibility and accountability: A comparison of Indians' and Americans' moral judgments. *Social Cognition, 3,* 237–261.

Moon, Y. L. (1986). A review of cross-cultural studies on moral judgment development using the Defining Issues Test. *Behavior Science Research, 20,* 147–177.

Naito, T. (1994). A survey of research on moral development in Japan. *Cross-Cultural Research, 28,* 40–57.

Najarian-Svajian, P. H. (1966). The idea of immanent justice among Lebanese children and adults. *The Journal of Genetic Psychology, 109,* 57–66.

Niemczynski, A., Czyzoswska, D., Pourkos, M., & Mirski, A. (1988). The Cracow study with Kohlberg's moral judgement interview: Data pertaining to the assumption of cross-cultural validity. *Polish Psychological Bulletin, 19,* 43–53.

Nisan, M. (1987). Moral norms and social conventions: A cross-cultural comparison. *Developmental Psychology, 23,* 719–725.

Nisan, M. (1988). A story of a pot, or a cross-cultural comparison of basic moral evaluations: A response to the critique by Turiel, Nucci, and Smetana (1988). *Developmental Psychology, 24,* 144–146.

Nisan, M. & Kohlberg, L. (1982). Universality and variation in moral judgment: A longitudinal and cross-sectional study in Turkey. *Child Development, 53,* 865–876.

Nucci, L. P. (1985). Children's conceptions of morality, societal convention, and religious prescription. In C. G. Harding (Ed.), *Moral dilemmas: Philosophical and psychological issues in the development of moral reasoning* (pp. 137–174). Chicago, IL: Precedent Publishing.

Nucci, L. P., Turiel, E., & Encarnacion-Gawrych, G. (1983). Children's social interactions and social concepts. Analysis of morality and convention in the Virgin Islands. *Journal of Cross-Cultural Psychology, 14,* 469–487.

O'Connor, R. E. (1980). Parental sources and political consequences of levels of moral reasoning among European university students. In R. W. Wilson & G. J. Schochet (Eds.), *Moral development and politics* (pp. 237–255). New York: Praeger.

Parikh, B. (1980). Development of moral judgement and its relation to family environmental factors in Indian and American families. *Child Development, 51,* 1030–1039.

Piaget, J. (1965). *The moral judgment of the child.* (M. Gabain, Trans.). New York: Free Press. (Original work published 1932).

Piaget, J. (1947). *The moral development of the adolescent in two types of society, primitive and modern.* Lecture given at the UNESCO Seminar on Education for International Understanding. Unesco, Paris.

Puka, B. (1986). Vom Nutzen und Nachteil der Stufe 6. In W. Edelstein & G. Nunner-Winkler (Eds.), *Zur Bestimmung der Moral* (pp. 241–290). Berlin: Suhrkamp.

Reese, H. W. & Overton, W. F. (1970). Models of development and theories of development. In L. R. Goulet & P. B. Baltes (Eds.), *Life-span developmental psychology* (pp. 115–145). New York: Academic Press.

Rest, J. (1979). *Development in judging moral issues.* Minneapolis, MN: University of Minnesota Press.

Rest, J. (1986). *Manual for the Defining Issues Test: An objective test of moral judgment development* (3rd ed.). Minneapolis, MN: University of Minneapolis, Center for the Study of Ethical Development.

Sakagami, M. & Namiki, H. (1982). Structure of prosocial moral judgment. *Studies in Sociology, Psychology, and Education, 22,* 51–57.

Saraswathi, T. S. & Sundaresan, J. (1980). Perceived maternal disciplinary practices and their relation to development of moral judgment. *International Journal of Behavioral Development, 3,* 91–109.

Sengupta, J., Saraswathi, T. S., & Konantambigi, R. (1994). *Gender differences in moral orientations: How different is the voice?* Unpublished manuscript, M.S. University of Baroda, India.

Setiono, K. (1994, July). *Morality from the viewpoint of Javanese tradition.* Paper presented at the Symposium "Eco-Ethical Thinking From A Cross-Cultural Perspective," Kirkel, Germany.

Shweder, R. A. (1986). Divergent rationalities. In D. W. Fiske & R. A. Shweder (Eds.), *Metatheory in social science: Pluralism and subjectivities* (pp. 163–196). Chicago, IL: University of Chicago Press.

Shweder, R. A. (1991). Commentary. *Human Development, 34,* 353–362.

Shweder, R. A., Mahapatra, M., & Miller, J. G. (1987). Culture and moral development. In J. Kagan & S. Lamb (Eds.), *The emergence of morality in young children* (pp. 1–83). Chicago, IL: University of Chicago Press.

Shweder, R. A. & Much, N. C. (1987). Determinations of meanings: Discourse and moral socialization. In W. M. Kurtines & J. L. Gewirtz (Eds.), *Moral development through social interaction* (pp. 197–244). New York: Wiley.

Simpson, A. L. (1974). Moral development research. A case study of scientific cultural bias. *Human Development, 17,* 81–106.

Simpson, A. L. & Graham, D. (1971). *The development of moral judgement, emotion and behaviour in British adolescents.* Unpublished manuscript, University of Durham, England.

Smetana, J. G. (1982). *Concepts of self and morality: Women's reasoning about abortion.* New York: Praeger.

Snarey, J. (1983). *The social and moral development of Kibbutz founders and Sabras: A cross-sectional and longitudinal cross-cultural study* (Doctoral dissertation, Harvard University, 1982). Dissertation Abstracts International, 43(10), 3416b.

Snarey, J. (1985). Cross-cultural universality of socio-moral development: A critical review of Kohlbergian research. *Psychological Bulletin, 97,* 202–232.

Snarey, J. & Keljo, K. (1991). In a Gemeinschaft voice: The cross-cultural expansion of moral development theory. In W. M. Kurtines & J. L. Gewirtz (Eds.), *Handbook of moral behavior and development: Vol. I: Theory* (pp. 395–424). Hillsdale, NJ: Erlbaum.

Song, M. J., Smetana, J. G., & Kim, S. Y. (1987). Korean childrens' conceptions of moral and conventional transgressions. *Developmental Psychology, 23,* 577–582.

Tappan, M., Kohlberg, L., Schrader, D., Higgins, A., Armon, C., & Lei, T. (1987). Heteronomy and autonomy in moral development: Two types of moral judgments. In A. Colby & L. Kohlberg (Eds.), *The measurement of moral judgment, Vol. I: Theoretical foundations and research validation* (pp. 315–380). Cambridge: Cambridge University Press.

Teo, T., Becker, G., & Edelstein, W. (1995). *Variability in structured wholeness: Context factors in L. Kohlberg's data on the development of moral judgment.* Manuscript submitted for publication.

Tietjen, A. M. (1985). *Prosocial reasoning among children and adults in a Papua New Guinea society.* Unpublished manuscript.

Tietjen, A. & Walker, L. (1984). *Moral reasoning and leadership among men in a Papua New Guinea village.* Unpublished manuscript. University of British Columbia, Vancouver, Canada.

Tönnies, F. (1957). *Community and society* (C. P.

Loomis, Trans.). New York, Harper & Row. (Original work published 1887).

Turiel, E. (1978). The development of concepts of social structure: Social convention. In J. Glick & A. Clarke-Steward (Eds.), *The development of social understanding* (pp. 25–107). New York: Garden Press.

Turiel, E. (1983). *The development of social knowledge. Morality and convention.* Cambridge: Cambridge University Press.

Turiel, E. & Davidson, P. (1986). Heterogeneity, inconsistency, and asynchrony in the development of cognitive structures. In J. Levin (Ed.), *Stage and structure: Reopening the debate* (pp. 106–143). Norwood, NJ: Ablex.

Turiel, E., Edwards, C. P., & Kohlberg, L. (1978). Moral development in Turkish children, adolescents and young adults. *Journal of Cross-Cultural Psychology, 9,* 75–86.

Turiel, E., Hildebrandt, C., & Wainryb, C. (1991). Judging social issues. *Monographs of the Society for Research. Child Development, 56,* 1–103.

Turiel, E., Killen, M., & Helwig, C. C. (1987). Morality: Its structure, functions, and vagaries. In J. Kagan & S. Lamb (Eds.), *The emergence of morality in young children* (pp. 155–243). Chicago: University of Chicago Press.

Vasudev, J. (1983). *A study of moral reasoning at different life stages in India.* Unpublished manuscript, University of Pittsburgh, PA.

Vasudev, J. (1986). Kohlbergs Universalitäts postulat aus indischer Sicht. In W. Edelstein & G. Nunner-Winkler (Eds.), *Zur Bestimmung der Moral* (pp. 145–177). Frankfurt/M., Germany: Suhrkamp.

Vasudev, J. & Hummel, R. (1987). Moral stage sequence and principled reasoning in an Indian sample. *Human Development, 30,* 105–118.

Villenave-Cremer, S. & Eckensberger, L. H. (1985). The role of affective processes in moral judgment performance. In M. W. Berkowitz & F. Oser (Eds.), *Moral Education: Theory and application* (pp. 175–196). Hillsdale, NJ: Erlbaum.

Vine, I. (1986). Moral maturity in socio-cultural perspective: Are Kohlberg's stages universal? In S. Modgil & C. Modgil (Eds.), *Lawrence Kohlberg: Consensus and controversy* (pp. 431–450). London: The Falmer Press.

Vogel, C. & Eckensberger, L. H. (1988). Arten und Kulturen–Der vergleichende Ansatz. In K. Immelmann, K. R. Scherer, C. Vogel, & P. Schmook (Eds.), *Psychobiologie–Grundlagen des Verhaltens* (pp. 563–606). Stuttgart, Germany: Gustav Fischer Verlag.

Walker, L. J. (1984). Sex differences in the development of moral reasoning: A critical review. *Child Development, 55,* 677–691.

Walker, L. J., de Vries, B., & Trevethan, S. D. (1987). Moral stages and moral orientations in real-life and hypothetical dilemmas. *Child Development, 58,* 842–858.

Walster, E. (1966). Assignment of responsibility for an accident. *Journal of Personality and Social Psychology, 3,* 73–79.

White, C. B. (1975). Moral development in Bahamian school children: A cross-cultural examination of Kohlberg's stages of moral reasoning. *Developmental Psychology, 11,* 535–536.

White, C. B. (1977). *Moral reasoning in Bahamian and United States elders: Cross-national comparison of Kohlberg's theory of moral development.* Unpublished manuscript, University of Texas Health Science Center, Dallas.

White, C. B. (1986). Moral reasoning in Bahamian and United States adults and children: A cross-cultural examination of Kohlberg's stages. *Behavior Science Research, 20,* 47–71.

White, C. B., Bushnell, N., & Regnemer, J. L. (1978). Moral development in Bahamian school children: A 3-year examination of Kohlberg's stages of moral development. *Developmental Psychology, 14,* 58–65.

Zimba, R. F. (1987). *A study on forms of social knowledge in Zambia.* Unpublished doctoral dissertation, Purdue University.

Zimba, R. F. (1994). The understanding of morality, convention, and personal preference in an African setting: Findings from Zambia. *Journal of Cross-Cultural Psychology, 25,* 369–393.

Zimba, R. F. (1995). Secondary school students' risks that may promote HIV infection and the spread of AIDS: A Namibian study. *School Psychology International, 16,* 67–78.

10

EDUCATION, SCHOOLING, AND LITERACY

ROBERT SERPELL
University of Maryland, Baltimore County
United States

GIYOO HATANO
Keio University
Japan

Contents

Becoming Human: Socialization and Enculturation in the Course of Development

Human development involves the appropriation of various types of cultural resources that collectively define the essence of humanness. This chapter focuses on the intersection among studies of learning, education, literacy, culture, and human development, all of which contribute to our understanding of what it means to become human. Only through culture can humans interpret their own nature, even though many of their distinctive characteristics are biologically based. The human species, more than any other, acquires behavioral characteristics through learning. Moreover, our species is unique in its purposeful organization of opportunities for learning to socialize or enculturate the young in particular ways that vary dramatically from one social group to another. Education has emerged from this species-specific tendency as a conceptualization of how to manage planfully the process of human development to conform with the economic goals and cultural values of a society.

Individual literacy can be construed in a variety of ways (Levine, 1982; Wagner, 1993b). In its most restricted sense, it is the capacity to extract meaning from a particular script (e.g., Gibson & Levin, 1975). More ambitious advocates portray it as a complex system of knowledge, skills, beliefs, and attitudes that pervade an individual's activities across a wide range of domains (e.g., Illich, 1991). Education in the contemporary world is often construed as a cumulative progression with two broad phases: the foundational acquisition of basic literacy skills that are subsequently deployed by the individual, and the acquisition of cultural knowledge and understanding on a higher plane. From this two-tier perspective, the designation of a person as relatively literate or illiterate has two alternative types of meaning. It may refer to whether one has completed the foundational phase, or it may indicate the degree to which one has progressed on the higher plane. In order to mark this distinction, policy analysts often refer to the foundational phase as basic education, and to its outcome as basic, or functional, literacy (Levine, 1982).

Schooling is likewise organized in many contemporary societies in tiers, with a primary, or elementary, program of instruction designed to afford opportunities for the foundational acquisition of basic literacy skills, followed by a secondary or high school program designed to build on that foundation while introducing students to various domains of cultural knowledge, such as the natural sciences, artistic and philosophical literature, history, and social or civic studies.

Superimposed in most modern societies on this two-tier conceptualization of literacy, education, and schooling, and ultimately serving to legitimize it, is a set of assumptions regarding the appropriate stages of human development for enrolling students in the successive phases of schooling designed to afford an education that results in the cumulative acquisition of literacy. Primary schooling is prescribed for children between the initial mastery of linguistic communication and the onset of puberty, whereas secondary education is reserved for the period of adolescence, and tertiary education for young adults. Preschool education is principally designed to prepare children for primary schooling, and is reserved for young children below the age prescribed for initial enrollment in primary schools.

This congruence of developmental stages with types of educational provision has come to appear natural. Indeed, it informs a "paradigmatic" conception of the relationship between basic education in schools and parenting that is often advanced by contemporary educators. The paradigm supposes that a population of primary caregivers agrees on the need to organize some parts of their children's socialization on a collective basis, building on and extending developmental processes initiated at home. Yet, the history of this paradigm is quite short, and there are many exceptions to it in the contemporary world.

Much of the cross-cultural psychological research on education, schooling, and literacy in the 1960s and 70s tended to build on Western theoretical accounts of cognition that had been formulated without explicit reference to culture. It tended to ask how various dimensions of cognition are impacted by culture, conceived as an exogenous variable. In this chapter, we accord culture a more primary significance. Cultural systems of activity and meaning constitute the organizing framework for our conceptualization of culture–cognition relationships (cf. Serpell, 1993c). Due to limitations of space, we shall only touch lightly on the consequences for development of perception, cognition, language, identity, and moral reasoning arising from the particular patterns of literacy and education that we discuss. These are examined in more detail in other chapters of this volume (Deregowski, & Russell, Kinnear; Mishra; Mohanty & Perregaux; Camilleri & Malewska-Peyre; Eckensberger & Zimba). As Miller (this *Handbook,* Volume 1) has noted, different audiences approach the same topic with varying intellectual interests. The primary concerns addressed by this chapter are those of child development and educational psychology.

In the next section, we argue that the potential of literacy for social progress should not be reduced to the sum of its impacts on individuals, either as a form of direct cognitive empowerment or as a way of opening avenues for social mobility. Its influence is better construed in terms of socially distributed cognition and bicultural mediation. In the third section, we turn our attention to theoretical conceptions of the processes of education and pedagogy, which have come to be construed by many people in contemporary societies as a specialized domain wherein schoolteachers have unique professional expertise. We note that schooling is just one of many forms of enculturation, one that has some distinctive, but not always essential or even optimal characteristics as a context for individuals to appropriate the cultural resources of literacy. Social practices in the domain of childrearing and education reflect and are interpreted by cultural models, some of which are implicit and others explicit.

The fourth section discusses philosophical premises and social histories of formal systems of education. In it, we compare and contrast some enduring thematic preoccupations of three different literate cultural traditions that inform the design of educational practices in various school systems around the world. Our analysis seeks to highlight the cultural relativity of the institutional forms of Western education that have become widely influential in many parts of the contemporary world. Our selection of particular cultural traditions for description and discussion was partly informed by the limited range of cultures in which each of us has long-term, first-hand, participatory experience: Western Europe and the United States, Japan, and sub-Saharan Africa. Related issues and concerns have been discussed with reference to the long literate tradition of India by Naik (1975), Kumar (1991), and others (cf. Sinha, Volume 1 of this *Handbook*); and with reference to the political and cultural interactions in Latin American societies by Ferreiro (1994), Hornberger (1994), and others.

In the fifth section on cross-cultural contact and diffusion, we examine various ways in which these and other cultural systems of meaning interact to determine the actual forms and consequences of education in the contemporary world: deliberate import and adaptation, hegemonic imposition, and modernization and indigenization. The apparent alignment in the contemporary world between religious fundamentalism, male domination, and cultural conservatism opens the advocacy of respect for the authenticity of indigenous cultural practices to the charge of reactionary resistance to social progress. Conversely, the alignment between secularization, industrialization, and Western cultural forms that have found their way into Third World countries, as a result of various admixtures of political domination, and religious and economic intrusion, places the advocacy of schooling as an instrument of social progress at risk for the charge of disguised Western hegemony.

In the final section, we propose the outline of an integrative scheme that draws together the themes of the earlier sections. We draw attention to two pedagogical features that seem to be distinctive relative to other socialization practices in the pattern of Institutionalized Public Basic Schooling that has begun to emerge in many contemporary societies as a quasi-universal, institutional paradigm: advance preparation, and authorized competence. We conclude our review with a recommendation that educational theorists and planners examine critically the origins of the pedagogical practices currently institutionalized in their schools, because they may become the focus of secondary patterns of student motivation and assessment, with limited relevance to more fundamental dimensions of human development. In particular, the Western paradigm, often misleadingly termed "modern," may benefit from incorporating a feature more prominent in some, non-Western, "traditional" paradigms, by explicitly situating the agenda of cultivating cognitive competence within a framework of moral accountability. We also advocate the adoption of a new educational theme for the increasingly interdependent world in which we live: sensitizing students to multiple strands of their cultural heritage and to ways of mediating between them.

Literacy and Cognition

Does literacy transform the nature of communication, and hence the cognitive capabilities of individuals? Two widely entertained answers to this question represent literacy as a torch or as a hinge. Each of these metaphors contains a grain of truth but also oversimplifies. In their place, we advance a third (more process-oriented) conception of literacy as a resource for socially distributed cognition.

Literacy as a Torch: Classic Views

Political and economic plans in the "modern world" tend to treat literacy as a basic human need, which must be met through the provision of a standardized system of formal education. Moreover, those who miss the opportunity to acquire this package are stigmatized as developmentally incomplete (Serpell, 1993a). Their supposed deprivation is treated as a form of deviance that constitutes a societal problem (Cook-Gumperz, 1986). Education for literacy, according to this ideology, is an essential, liberating process that opens the way for its participants to move from ignorance to enlightenment, empowering them with a unique repertoire of cognitive resources to understand the world in ways that are inaccessible to non-literate minds. In short, literacy provides them with a torch that will illuminate the world for them.

According to this view, there exist fundamental differences in cognitive capabilities between "literates" and "non-literates" (including non-literate adults and pre-literate children who are members of literate societies). This has been described as the "great divide" perspective. Among the exponents of this "great divide" perspective, specification of how becoming literate transforms the student's intellect has been the subject of a good deal of research spanning the disciplines of linguistics, history, anthropology, psychology, and education (Goody & Watt, 1963; Greenfield, 1972; Havelock, 1976; Olson, 1977). According to Goody (1968, p. 44):

> . . . *writing establishes a different kind of relation between the word and its referent, a relationship that is more general and more abstract, and less closely connected with the particularities of person, place and time than obtains in oral communication.*

Goody (1977) focuses on the intrinsic potentialities of written text for organizing ideas into tables and lists, which in turn, "not only permits the reclassification of information by those who can write, and legitimizes such reformulations for those who can read, but it also changes the nature of the representations of the world (cognitive processes) for those who cannot do so" (p. 109–110). Thus, a technical feature of literacy is thought to lead to a higher-order, cultural awareness of the possibilities of logic, history and science.

Mastery of the cognitive forms and procedures distinctive to a written culture is held to be intrinsically empowering, and by the same token also domesticating, committing the student to conformity with a powerful but nonetheless limited mode of thought (Olson, 1977).

These hypotheses about the significance of literacy are deeply rooted in the rational, progressivist philosophical convictions of the European Enlightenment that we discuss in the next section. One influential formulation that resonates with the belief in the transcendental power of literacy was advanced by Bruner (1966) and elaborated by Cole and Bruner (1971) and Cole and Griffin (1980): Literacy can be regarded as a culturally mediated "cognitive amplifying tool." Rogoff (1981), on the other hand, in her chapter for the first edition of this *Handbook,* noted that many researchers in this field have attributed to formal schooling the promotion, over and above literacy per se, of a particular pattern of competencies that are especially wide in their range of applicability, by focusing students' attention on formal, abstract principles, and encouraging them to search for general rules to order large bodies of new information.

Literacy as a Torch: Moderate Views

The classic views of literacy as a torch have been the target of extensive criticism (e.g., Street, 1984), mainly for two reasons. First, they inevitably underestimate the general cognitive competence of non-literate people, who may have rich and highly developed skills of orality. Second, they involve a reductionist strain that tends to highlight technological features of writing as more cardinal than the social practices with which they are associated. To meet these criticisms, proponents of the Enlightenment conceptualization of literacy have reformulated their position, claiming a more moderate significance of literacy acquisition for intellectual development.

In his more recent formulations, Olson (1991, 1994) acknowledges some additional reasons for rejecting this hypothesis of an intrinsic cognitive potential inherent in written language. A number of linguists (e.g., Biber, 1986) have concluded that most of the lexical, syntactic, and discursive differences once attributed to the oral and written modes of language are, in fact, due to differences on other dimensions, for example, whether productions are pre-edited or interactive. Oral language is different from written language, but how much the modality matters needs more careful examination. Furthermore, the acquisition of literacy skills, separated from schooling and used in restricted situations, does not produce general cognitive effects. Scribner and Cole (1981), for instance, studying three different forms of literacy (in the Arabic, Roman and Vai scripts) among the Vai people of Liberia, concluded that the effects of learning to read and write are rather specific and that the uses to which these skills are put depend on the wider social context in which they are acquired. Eisenstein (1979) has also traced how many social and economic changes flowing from the invention of printing in the 15th century joined with the standardization of particular textual conventions to revolutionize the character of literate communication in Europe.

One moderate view suggests that literacy can serve as a torch empowering individuals, but in more specific ways, depending on what people do with their literacy (Griffin & Cole, 1987). In technologically advanced societies, many practices, including administration, religion, and science, require their participants to use the written language, so that the acquisition of literacy enables an individual to enter one of these practices. Participation then inevitably enhances the development of the body of knowledge and cognitive skills that are used in the role.

Another moderate view claims that written language, in whatever practice it is used, elaborates some specific ways of communication and/or thought, and may even facilitate modes of thinking in general (Olson, 1991). The writing system produces an oral metalanguage that enables speakers to refer to metalinguisitic entities, such as letters, words, sentences, and paragraphs. Such devices make "linguistically expressed propositions into objects of thought" (Olson & Astington, 1990, p. 705). Moreover, speech act verbs (e.g., assert) and mental state verbs (e.g., assume), also included in metalanguage, are elaborated only in literate cultures. They enable people to make finer distinctions among similar sentences or propositions, and thus to carry on more precise discussions about truth and falsity. Although these authors acknowledge that children in literate cultures may become competent in the oral use of metalanguage irrespective of their learning to read and write, this formulation implies that the acquisition of literacy necessarily facilitates capabilities for talking about talk and thought.

Literacy as a Hinge

What kind of amplifying tool is literacy? It seems evident that the invention of writing was a necessary precursor to certain other cultural inventions, such as the accumulation of information in libraries and experimental science based on detailed records and mathematical computation, without which modern education could not have taken on its present form. But this is not to say that the cognitive strategies required for scholarship and science are directly imparted to the individual by the acquisition of literacy. Indeed, for the vast majority of elementary school students around the world, the prospects of literacy are far removed from the rhetoric of the curriculum planners.

A somewhat less euphoric, and more politically loaded alternative to the enlightenment view has been advanced in recent years by a group of social scientists disappointed by the failure of education to deliver the promised enfranchisement of "equal opportunity." According to this formulation, when literacy empowers an actor, it functions like a hinge rather than a torch. Those who achieve political freedom or economic advancement by virtue of their literate education do so by opening doors that are closed to their non-literate contemporaries. Literacy is a necessary condition for those doors to open, but not a sufficient one. It can have positive consequences only when it allows learners to gain access to culturally enriching practices.

In addition, the literate person must negotiate access, which involves knowing "how to make friends and influence people." Not all of the necessary competence is imparted through literacy, so that, in the extreme case, an educated member of an oppressed minority group may find herself staring through a "glass ceiling" at goals for which she is theoretically qualified, and which are nevertheless unattainable. Building on this perspective, Ogbu (1990) explains how some members of oppressed, involuntary minority cultural groups respond by developing an oppositional social identity, rejecting as alien the values of the mainstream, literate culture.

Although this hinge metaphor captures some aspects of the reality, it misses other significant characteristics of literacy. It underestimates the potential of literate cognition for *bootstrapping*, for the imaginative adaptation of technological resources to new ends (Serpell, 1994b). It is true that entrenched political and economic interests tend to constrain the opportunities for advancement of oppressed social groups. But the interface between individual cognitive development and cultural change includes a quality of open-endedness:

> *The possibility of psychological empowerment **through** cultural commitment arises from the fact that society values most highly those of its members who innovate. And the need for society to tolerate non-conformity in its young arises from the fact that the most effective method for recruiting a new member is to assign them responsibility for participation (Serpell, 1993b, p. 366).*

Literacy as a Resource for Socially Distributed Cognition

A third conception of literacy blends some of the insights of the two metaphors of torch and hinge that we have already critically examined. Literacy can be construed as a cultural resource at the disposal of the participants in various socially organized activities. Its technological characteristics are both constraining and empowering (Gardner, 1991). The cognitive possibilities are mediated by co-constructive processes that imply the acknowledgment of author–audience interdependencies (Serpell, 1990).

The sharing of responsibility for cognitive work in everyday activities has been termed "socially distributed cognition" (Hutchins, 1991) and "co-construction" (Valsiner, 1991). Reder (1987) likewise has offered an account of "literacy as a collaborative practice" in three different cultural minority communities in the United States—an Eskimo fishing village, a community of Hmong immigrants from Laos, and a partially migrant, partially settled Hispanic community—arguing that the particularities of each sociocultural setting serve to specify optimal local criteria for literate practices and programs of literacy instruction. Reder describes how three different layers of competence (technological, functional, and social) contribute to the utilization of literacy for the attainment of practical goals, and argues that they need not all be represented in any one individual participant. Rather, different members of a social group may display different and complementary modes of engagement within a collective literacy event.

In a Third World setting, Wagner (1993a) presents a vignette of a typical literacy transaction in contemporary Morocco that illustrates the reciprocal interdependency of the participants. A gas station attendant prepares a receipt for sale of gas by applying a rubber stamp to a blank sheet of paper, and hands it to the driver to fill in the date, the amount of gas, and the price paid. In this "joint literacy act," the attendant, "who cannot read or write," is nevertheless the custodian of the symbol of bureaucratic power, the rubber stamp, which serves as "the official guarantor of official literacy in Morocco" (Wagner, 1993a, p. 15). In Wagner's terms, various individuals serve as "mediators" of the cultural resource of literacy in different ways.

Baynham (1993) has pointed out that the role of a literacy mediator in collaborative literacy events is analogous to that of an interpreter in bilingual settings. By switching between linguistic codes, or between the spoken and written modes of representation, the specialized technical knowledge of the intermediary is put to work at the service of others, who are thus enabled to pursue their own agenda. The "joint accomplishment" (p. 301) of literacy events, thus, involves negotiation of shared meanings (cf. Serpell, 1994a).

Theoretical Conceptions of the Processes of Education and Pedagogy

A Variety of Cultural Arrangements for Learning

Although lay people often assume that children acquire the cognitive skills needed by their society primarily, if not exclusively, through school instruction, schools are merely one of several possible institutional arrangements for structuring learning opportunities, and important areas of cognitive skill are often acquired in other contexts. These contexts, too, are structured culturally but are very different from the standard modern school, in the sense that there is no specified time and place for teaching–learning, no fixed curriculum, nor professional teacher. Teaching may not be intended, learning may not be monitored consciously, and what has been acquired may not be evaluated explicitly.

Learning outside school usually takes the form of participating in culturally organized practices, which are interesting and/or significant to learners (Goodnow, Miller, & Kessel, 1995). Repeated participation enhances the cognitive skills needed to perform well in these practices, even when learners do not aim at improving their skills. This analysis applies to everyday activities, such as those related to production, ritual, and so forth (cf. Schliemann, Carraher & Ceci, this volume.)

Situated Learning in the Workplace
Mastering effective skills for production requires extensive experience usually provided through apprenticeship in the workplace. As Lave and Wenger (1991) have pointed out, this also applies to many other culturally valued practices. Novices or newcomers are often able to participate with little or no pretraining, because the practices have various built-in physical and social supports. Participating in practice results in learning to perform more and more effectively. Novices are initially assigned to relatively simple and peripheral parts of the practice, and come to fulfill gradually more difficult and central parts as they gain better skills and the understanding of the total practice. For example, Lave (1988) reported that apprentice tailors in Liberia are given jobs such as fixing buttons,

which are simple and repairable but constitute authentic and essential parts of trouser-making.

Similar processes of gaining expertise through apprenticeship are observed in a variety of craftwork practices ranging from blacksmithing to Artificial Intelligence programming (Chaiklin & Lave, 1993). To generalize, the collaboration between the master and apprentices is directed primarily toward producing valuable goods, though both of them may take it as an opportunity for apprentices to improve their skills. When the master can manage to maintain a balance between the goals of increasing productivity and learning, and when apprentices are committed to the collaborative practice, this arrangement for learning can be effective and enjoyable. Indeed, the intrinsic motivation of "centripetal participation" in such contexts may obviate the need for explicit didactic methods such as praise for good performance (Lave & Wenger, 1991).

Informal Learning at Home and in the Neighborhood

Skills for many everyday activities can easily be learned through observation and very few trials and errors. However, parents, older siblings, and more knowledgeable friends sometimes take responsibility for teaching complex skills to young children in an apprenticeship-like way (Rogoff, 1990). In some cases, this may be necessitated because home is a workplace, too. For example, weaving skills are transmitted within families in Mexico (Greenfield, 1984) and Brazil (Saxe, 1991). More often, however, informal learning at home, especially in industrialized countries, is geared to facilitating the development of academic and other culturally valued skills related to nutrition, hygiene, entertainment, and so forth (Baker et al., 1994). In such contexts, the parents or other more knowledgeable persons, while assuming responsibility for harder parts of the joint work and monitoring the entire process, focus their concern on the child's learning more than on their joint performance. The adult may allow the child to try steps beyond his capability and even tolerate his failure, if this is likely to induce useful experience for the learner. In this sense, teaching is separated from performance and is foregrounded as the focus of joint activity.

Out-of-School Learning for Literacy

Given that schools are not the only place for learning skills, are they the only place for acquiring academic skills? The answer is certainly no. Even literacy, numeracy or scientific understanding can be acquired by learning in nonschool settings. Because everyday mathematics and science are discussed elsewhere (Schliemann et al., this volume), our discussion of this topic will focus on literacy skills.

Acquiring Literacy without Schooling

Unlike the ability for spoken language, skills for written language are not universal for the human species. They are a historical product, transmission of which requires learning in culturally arranged settings. The history of literacy makes it clear that some individuals can acquire the relevant skills without the institution of schooling. However, in societies where literacy has been adopted as a universal goal of basic education, the further question arises whether a substantial portion of the population can acquire literacy outside school.

Three studies have shown that the skills involved in literacy can be acquired without schooling. The Vai writing system consists of about 200 characters, each representing a syllable. About twenty percent of adult males in the Vai society were literate in this script in Scribner and Cole's (1981) study. They found that Vai literacy was acquired in an exceedingly short period of time, and always outside of school. It was usual for Vai people to learn how to read and write in an informal, face-to-face lesson provided by a friend on request. Likewise in Japanese, literacy skills for kana syllabaries, about 70 characters, each representing a mora (a rhythmic unit that often constitutes a syllable in the language), can be learned rapidly, easily and usually without systematic teaching. Its complete acquisition prior to schooling is not unusual, when parents are willing to give some help (Hatano, 1986; Tobin, Wu & Davidson, 1989). In a third case study, Cree children and adults reported learning to read and write in a syllabic script, sometimes in a matter of a few days (Berry & Bennett, 1991). These reports suggest that learning informally (e.g., from friends) was easier than learning the script in school.

The importance of schooling for literacy acquisition may depend on how appealing and how easy it is to participate in major literacy practices. Because the ease of participation depends heavily on the nature of orthography (the type of scripts and how they represent the spoken words), it may be significant that the Vai and the Cree, and the children's version of Japanese literacies are based on syllabaries. We have not seen reports of widespread literacy acquisition without schooling in cultures with an alphabetic script. However, the acquisition of literacy is often prepared through culturally organized activities, as we will discuss next.

Cultural Preparation for Literacy Acquisition

The cultural arrangements that enhance the ease with which children master alphabetic scripts before they are enrolled in school have become the focus of a growing research literature on "emergent literacy" (Sulzby & Teale, 1991). One illuminating study examined the influence of young children's culturally structured play activity on the acquisition of English literacy. A number of previous studies (e.g., Bradley & Bryant, 1983) have shown that children's phonological awareness, more specifically, their ability to judge whether or not words rhyme (like "cat" and "hat") is a prerequisite of learning to read English words. Children high in phonological awareness in preschool years tend to be good readers in lower grades, and the training to improve phonological awareness facilitates learning to read. Maclean, Bryant, and Bradley (1987) went one step further by analyzing culturally organized activity for the development of phonological awareness. They examined the relation between the acquisition of nursery rhymes, which often include alliterations as well as rhymes, and the development of phonological awareness. They found that the more nursery rhymes children knew, the better developed their phonological awareness tended to be several months later. This relation remained significant even when children's intelligence and parental education were controlled. The British culture prepares children for learning to read by providing them with opportunities to learn nursery rhymes, which enhances the development of phonological awareness, an important basis for the acquisition of English literacy.

A similar analysis has been advanced by Hatano (1986), showing how the Japanese play activity of cap verses, in which a child has to say a word beginning with the last syllable, or *mora*, of the word another child said, requires young children to segment words into *morae*, and thus impacts the rate of acquisition of literacy.

Cultural Models and Beliefs about Teaching–Learning

Children and newcomers in every community receive assistance in acquiring needed competencies for appropriating the culture, because enculturation is essential for the human species to survive. This universal practice creates the context for cultural models of teaching-learning (Quinn & Holland, 1987) or folkpsychology–folkpedagogy (Olson & Bruner, 1996). Such models include both conceptual components, (e.g., what the process of development is like) and procedural components, (e.g., what is the best way to teach certain skills). While explicit formal theories consisting of verbalizable principles may make a contribution, much of the content of such popular, cultural models tends to remain implicit (cf. Super & Harkness, this volume). Among the explanatory conceptions widely invoked by cultural models of education are the metaphors of production, growth, and travel (Kleibard, 1975); and the metaphors of enlightenment, a staircase, amplifying tools, and struggle (Serpell, 1993a). An interesting question that deserves further investigation is whether folktheories of education are more or less universal across cultures and times. Horton (1982) has argued convincingly that in the background of different cultures' folktheories, there lies a common core of primary components, grounded in universal aspects of human behavior and experience. On the other hand, many salient components of folktheories in the foreground vary from culture to culture, because the range of skills that have to be acquired and the arrangement of settings for acquisition differ across cultures.

For instance, among the Chewa, an agricultural community of eastern Zambia, the people's notion of *nzelu* (broadly corresponding to intelligence) includes the *-tumikila* dimension, a form of responsibility indexed by aptitude for being sent (*-tuma*) (Serpell, 1993a). In this and many other African societies, sending a person on an errand is a very pervasive practice, beginning with asking a toddler to fetch you something you cannot reach without standing up, and extending to commissioning a friend to make a purchase for you while away on a journey out of the neighborhood. To be "sent" on such an errand is an opportunity for a child to enhance, as well as demonstrate, competence. The appearance of strictness that many traditional African parents project to Western eyes arises in part from the frequency with which such assignments are given to children at an early age.

Another example is the conception of teaching traditional Noh music in Japan described by Zeami, a great composer and performer in the 14th century. Although it was apparently an individual idea, it certainly reflected the folktheory of his time, and also has influenced Japanese folktheories for generations. He emphasized a student's active and repeated attempts to imitate the master's performance, without being given any verbal explanation. At the same time, however, he indicated that emulation is not the end state of mastery. The student should be able to do what his master does (or did) without any consciousness of imitation (Ikuta, 1987). Zeami's perspective still prevails both in theory and practice in many culturally arranged settings for learning in Japan, especially of artistic skills, such as the Suzuki method of teaching violin and other instruments of Western music, as well as in various genres of Japanese traditional music (see Umemoto, 1985).

Legitimation of a Theory of Teaching–Learning in the Public Discussion of Schooling

A variety of culturally arranged settings for acquiring skills exists even in a relatively small and homogeneous community. Similarly, there exist many different folktheories of teaching and learning, some of which may remain implicit. However, once educating the younger generation becomes a policy issue (e.g., when a public system of schooling is established), an official, explicit and detailed theory of teaching–learning comes into greater demand. Making theories of teaching–learning explicit often serves to legitimize the current or a proposed system of schooling by explaining why certain goals are important and how effective specific methods are. Moreover, such claims may be further supported with empirical data, such as the correlates of scores on achievement tests (cf. Zigler & Finn-Stevenson, 1992).

Serpell (1993a) has distinguished three visionary rationales, or agendas for schooling: the promotion of economic progress, the transmission of culture from one generation to the next, and the cultivation of children's intellectual and moral development. In theory, education, institutionalized in schools of various sorts, might aspire to address all three agendas together in a harmoniously coordinated manner. In practice, however, educational programs have consistently fallen short of such an ideal synthesis. In many contemporary societies in the Third World, and in disadvantaged minority communities, the economic and cultural agendas of schooling often come into conflict.

The pedagogic agenda of schooling, cultivation of children's intellectual and moral development, presupposes a certain degree of social consensus on what constitutes appropriate ways of preparing children for later life. Responsibility for the care and upbringing of the child is generally entrusted first to his or her mother and then gradually extended to a widening circle of people who make up the family and the community. These caregivers share both a physical environment and a cultural system of meanings, practices, and institutions. When institutionalized schooling is added as a component of this ecocultural niche constituted by caregivers, the relationship between its cultural characteristics and those of other socialization practices in the children's family and community environment becomes an issue of considerable complexity (cf. Super & Harkness, this volume).

In much of the contemporary discourse of international planning for education, it is assumed that schooling would build on and extend the process of enculturation that families begin with the child at home. However, the paradigm of schooling as a natural extension of parental socialization was "a rather late and incidental arrival among the various defining characteristics of formal education. Schools as institutions arose initially as mechanisms for transmitting specialized bodies of knowledge to learners of various ages" (Serpell, 1993a, p. 2). We turn now to an examination of those mechanisms and their cultural origins.

Philosophical Premises and Social Histories of Formal Systems of Education

In this section, we compare and contrast some of the major philosophical preoccupations and patterns of institutional practice that have emerged within the social histories of schooling in three different sociocultural traditions: the Western tradition of Europe and the United States; the Sino-Japanese tradition linking China with Japan, and the Islamic tradition. We will examine the pattern of schooling in each society from the perspective of multiple, voluntary decisions taken purposively within certain material and ideological constraints.

In each of these three traditions certain distinctive themes can be identified in the pattern of discourse about child development and in the design of educational practices. In Western culture, central themes have been individual self-expression, cognitive detachment, and technical expertise; in the Sino-Japanese tradition, moral perfectibility and emulation; and in the Islamic tradition, the definitive authority of sacred text. These enduring preoccupations have been taken up and elaborated in a variety of ways over the centuries.

The Educational Tradition of Western Europe

The history of Western education is portrayed in a vast body of literature, to which it will only be possible to make brief allusions here. Following the standardization of alphabetic scripts in the first millennium BC, the Greek and Roman civilizations emerged during the "classical" period extending from the fifth century B.C. to the first century A.D., and were imposed through imperial expansion on the indigenous peoples of a substantial region centered around the Mediterranean Sea. Despite military conquest during the period from about 500 to 800 A.D. by invaders originating from non-literate cultures to the northeast, the writings of this period were preserved in what was to become the literate core of "Western culture" over the succeeding centuries.

This relatively localized cultural tradition gradually gave rise to a particular form of school-based education that is currently construed by many international agencies as an essential part of "modernity." Some of the most notable historical processes through which this took place were:

1. The evolution of Western archival scholarship from the first great libraries of Alexandria and Pergamon, through the Byzantine and Islamic libraries and the early Christian monasteries, to the establishment of university libraries in medieval Europe and the invention of the printing press.
2. The transformation of formal educational institutions in Europe from the medieval monasteries through the universities of the Renaissance to the public schools of the 18th century.
3. The philosophical articulation of education as a means of enlightenment, closely tied to the emergence of the ideology of Western science in the 17th and 18th centuries.
4. The deployment of teaching as a vehicle for religious proselytization, democratization of knowledge and cultural imperialism. (cf. Serpell, 1993a, p. 77)

Two fundamental cultural premises of this tradition are as follows. First, cognition, in post-renaissance Western thought, has been persistently conceived as private, transcendental, absolute, and independent of will. Second, humans are conceived as developing not only physically, but also spiritually; children are not merely weak, but incomplete as human beings.

In addition, several, more particular cultural themes emerged in the social organization of educational practices. In the period known as the Enlightenment, Western scholars became increasingly fascinated with explicit methodology, an intellectual disposition that has exercised an enduring influence on modern science, and epitomized by Berlin (1956) as a belief in "the certainty of method." In addition to this philosophical preoccupation, the institutional form of Western schooling reflects the cumulative influence of other more pragmatic considerations. As the clientele of formal schooling expanded, teachers began to organize instruction on a group basis, which generated first a need for some form of gradation of the curriculum into a sequence of steps, each of which builds on skills and knowledge imparted at the preceding step. According to Aries (1962), this gradation was for several centuries used solely as a method of matching instruction to the level of prior learning of the student, without regard to biological age. Later, however, requirements of residential accommodation gave rise to a set of concerns about the relative maturity of students that set in motion a gradual historical trend toward the grouping of students in developmentally homogeneous classes. Eventually, during the 20th century, the gradation of the curriculum into a sequence of steps, each of which must be mastered before the student may embark on the next, has become a crucial tenet of modern educational orthodoxy. Two historical factors appear to have been critical in generating this pedagogical pattern:

the formalization of didactic process, and the stepwise matching of instruction with age (Serpell, 1993a, ch. 3).

This particular form of social organization adopted in Western societies for education has given rise to some unplanned, yet far-reaching, conceptual consequences:

1. Stigmatization of the unschooled as developmentally incomplete persons, an ideological formulation that served to legitimize proselytization, both among the poor in Europe, and among non-Christian peoples abroad;

2. Problematization of non-modal rates of mastery of curriculum elements, justifying concepts of educational subnormality, mild mental retardation, specific learning disabilities, and so on;

3. Infusion of the instructional process with social connotations of condescension, an attitude that came to problematize adult education and to generate some enduring socio-emotional problems for special education, remedial education, and so forth; and

4. A widespread societal preoccupation with the rate of educational progress, equated with rate of completion of the curriculum, that motivates public pressure in many Western societies for early enrollment, preschooling, compensatory early intervention, and so on.

The Sino-Japanese Educational Tradition

The two cultural themes we have identified as characterizing the educational tradition of Chinese culture are moral perfectibility and emulation, both of which are connected to Confucianism. Confucian thought was formed and elaborated by incorporating folktheories of human nature; at the same time, it made the folktheories more explicit and sustainable. In this sense, Confucian principles and other philosophical themes inform the distinctive character of Chinese education's emphasis on moral maturity, and mode of organizing the process of teaching–learning.

The Confucian view of man as "an integral part of an orderly universe with an innate moral sense to maintain harmony" (Dien, 1982, p. 331) implies not only that education should enhance the development of some specific moral values, such as filial piety and diligence, but also that moral maturity should be taken as the supreme goal of education. In fact, even in post-revolutionary China, moral education is widely viewed as the national priority (Lin, 1988). Moreover, as Lee and Zhen asserted (1991, p. 364), "traditional Chinese moral concepts are more enduring in their impact on contemporary socialization than those introduced in recent decades." It appears implausible to suppose that the idea of moral perfectibility has remained unaffected by several decades of Communist regimen, but it is conceivable that educators have sought to reinterpret it harmoniously with the new political context rather than discarding it.

As to the second characteristic (emulation), Munro (1975, p. 335) described the Confucian heritage that informs the use of "models" as comprising three principles: (a) both children and adults learn primarily through the imitation of models; (b) the most effective way to inculcate any regular conduct is to introduce a model for students to imitate; and (c) a legitimate goal for a person to seek is to be a model. Although Munro's evaluation of Chinese education was generally positive, he believed the extensive use of models tended to "impede creativity in the technical sphere" (p. 347), because the emulator "learns to accept without question the antecedently established norms manifest in the model" (p. 348).

Similarly, Paine (1990, p. 50) described a "virtuoso" paradigm of teaching in China, in which the role of the teacher is "demonstrating, and the obligation of students to follow the teacher's model. The focus of teaching is on performance, the goal to produce a virtuoso performance." Like Munro, she interpreted this as knowledge transmission from teacher to students through modeling, the teacher serving as a role model.

Paine cited the following weaknesses of the virtuoso model: (a) its orientation is conservative, its practice to reproduce; (b) learning tends to be passive; (c) it underemphasizes the possibilities for interaction; (d) it does not take into account individual differences; and (e) it prescribes a fixed role for teacher and text. She wondered if these characteristics are insufficiently problematic from the perspective of the larger society to generate a felt need to change the belief in teaching as masterful performance, which is grounded in Confucian norms of orthodoxy. However, she also acknowledged virtues in this approach: the emphasis on emulation "allows for carefully supervised innovation" (p. 75), and "the metaphor of teaching as virtuoso performance incorporates both a recognition of the importance of knowledge and an acknowledgement of the role of the personal, humanistic qualities of aesthetics, affection, and commitment" (p. 76).

Chinese philosophical and social thoughts constitute a very important component of the Japanese intellectual tradition, though this fact is sometimes concealed by more recent European and American influences. Among others, direct and indirect influences of Confucianism cannot be ignored even in the recent and current educational practices. When a new government was established through the Meiji Restoration in 1868, the core of moral education that it proposed was based on Confucianism. Whereas the Meiji government well recognized the value of importing Western science and technology, in order to enrich and strengthen the nation state by promoting economic growth, it also emphasized the preservation of Confucian moral codes coupled with Imperial ideologies. The government distributed the Imperial Rescript on Education in 1890, in order to reinforce the moral codes, which dominated the whole of Japanese formal education until Japan's defeat in the Second World War (Yamazumi, 1980), and is still widely regarded as a valid and respectable guide by people belonging to older generations.

Probably as a result, Japanese educators, like their Chinese colleagues observed by Paine (1990), have to confront a serious problem of how to enhance students' active exploration and creativity. Furthermore, the emphasis on modeling and being modeled naturally leads to educating children in a fairly large group, rather than as an individual or in a small group, consistent with the observations by Tobin, Wu, and Davidson (1989).

Confucianism may have been interpreted a little differently in Japan than in China. Its original version seems to have evolved as wisdom in people's life and thus includes considerable elements of rational, practical, and even innovative thought. When it was imported, only those moral codes favored by the government were emphasized, ignoring these aspects. As a result, the imported version in Japan has been more conservative and somewhat irrational. Indeed, education of Confucian moral codes reinforced authoritarianism and militarism in the pre-World War II Japanese society. The Japanese version also seems to have produced belief-in-effort (Hatano, 1982), not just diligence. Many Japanese educators take the position that effort makes a difference everywhere: in other words, if one exerts enough effort, one will necessarily succeed. This theme serves as the inspiration driving large numbers of students to prepare for entrance exams to prestigious universities, expending great time and effort over many years.

It is tempting to attribute, at least in part, the superior performance on mathematics and science achievement tests by Chinese and Japanese students to the cultural tradition we have described, shared by both teachers and parents (Holloway, Kashiwagi, Hess & Azuma, 1986), in which the themes of perfectibility, emulation, and diligence are effectively woven into a coherent system of instruction (Stigler & Perry, 1990). Impressive evidence has accumulated that even the less talented students in these societies reliably solve some of the easier problems, producing a considerably higher class average than that in the United States (Stevenson, Lee, & Stigler, 1986; Stevenson & Stigler, 1992). The same cultural influence may have operated to produce quite a number of good orchestral players of Western music from East Asia. On the other hand, this educational tradition may have incurred a cost: enhancing students' spontaneity and creativity has been a serious challenge for both Chinese and Japanese educators (Hatano, 1990; Inagaki, 1986).

Islamic Education

The range of Islamic educational practices is quite broad, and includes more than twenty nations with widely differing linguistic, social and historical characteristics (e.g., Senegal, Egypt, Iran, Bangladesh, and Indonesia). A core belief of the Islamic religion is that children should be instructed in the teachings of the Prophet, Muhammad, as these are represented in the text of the Qur'an.

Two fundamental cultural premises stand out in the tradition of Islamic education. First, the Word of God is known but difficult to understand. The Qur'an is believed to be a set of revelations made to the Prophet by God. The Prophet and his companions then interpreted the verses in a set of commentaries, the Hadith, a corpus of interpretations that is continually expanding. Second, teaching involves the interpretation of authoritative texts, to provide guidance for the patterning of everyday routine activities and for the solution of real-world problems. The texts themselves are regarded as definitive and immutable. Another salient feature of the Islamic educational tradition presumably arose partly as a response to the pragmatic need to ensure the precise retention of immutable, definitive text: the Word of God is celebrated through recitation. The word Qur'an means "recitation," and its contents are regarded as literally the word of God. Religious belief thus provides a powerful rationale for a conspicuous emphasis on memorization.

The preoccupation of Islamic education with the definitive authority of sacred text gives rise to a quite different set of attitudes towards instruction and pedagogy than the Enlightenment fascination with explicit methodology, which has preoccupied Western educators. Qur'anic schooling in most parts of the world focuses on grapheme–phoneme correspondence and postpones to a higher level of education, attained by only a few, the process of interpreting the semantic content of texts. This sharp disjunction which appears paradoxical from a contemporary, Western pedagogical perspective may in fact be necessitated by the high degree of stratification that characterizes language use in most Islamic communities. In Bangladesh, Indonesia, Liberia, and Senegal, for instance, the languages of everyday discourse for students and teachers do not include *any* variety of Arabic, and belong to structurally completely distinct language families (e.g., Bengali, Bahasa, Vai, Wolof). Yet, as Santerre (1973) described among the Fulbe people of northern Cameroon, where Islam is the dominant religion, Qur'anic elementary schooling is conducted entirely in Arabic, a language never used in everyday discourse, with the result that students learn to read or memorize texts without any comprehension. In Morocco, the Berber-speaking population have access to public education only in the medium of Arabic or French (Wagner, 1993a). Moroccan Arabs, on the other hand, use a spoken variety of Arabic that is quite remote from the "classical" Arabic of the Qur'an, in which they and the Berbers receive their education at school. Even in Egypt, there has long existed a distinct stratification of linguistic usage within Arabic, more sharply defined than the various registers acknowledged in many European languages.

Thus, because in many parts of the Arab world the language in which students talk about social and scientific ideas is extremely different from the language in which the Qur'anic texts are written, an abstract connection needs to be forged by the teacher and the student from the content of those texts with other dimensions of the school curriculum, let alone with everyday cognition. Even in Arabic-speaking Egypt, the challenge posed by this phenomenon was explicitly recognized by the scholar and educational policy maker, Tahor Hussein, in 1938 with the aphorism: "Others read in order to learn, whereas we learn in order to [be able to] read" (Ibrahim, 1994, p. 3). The sample of Arabic culture represented in written texts is mainly esoteric both in vocabulary and in grammatical form. Thus, although the script has a fairly regular relationship with the sounds of the language, in order to make sense of most texts, an Arab must become versed in a specialized set of cultural practices and understand their associated system of meanings.

In Santerre's (1973) view, the curriculum of elementary Qur'anic schooling was designed to socialize the students into submissive acceptance of traditional authority, with texts serving a primarily ritual function. Intellectual enrichment only became a significant goal in the more advanced, "complementary" phase, where a small elite of male students were engaged in self-paced, tutorial study of law and literature. In its original form, the Qur'anic tradition aspired to educate the whole person, including physical, professional, social, religious, and intellectual development. But, in the face of competition with the expanded official schooling provided by the state, its focus had narrowed in northern Cameroon in the 1960s to only the latter two dimensions. Indeed, Santerre (1971) concluded that it had begun to degenerate into obsolescence.

Nevertheless, from a comparative analysis of the two parallel systems introduced by external forces into a society without its own indigenous formal educational tradition, Santerre (1971) noted certain advantages of Qur'anic schooling over the new Cameroonian state's modern, French-style official schools. Unlike the institutional separateness of Western schooling, located in a specialized building, Qur'anic schooling was organized as a group of students gathered around a master in his family home. The curriculum was fixed in content, but highly flexible in age of enrollment and progression rate. The Qur'anic teachers *(mallum)* were not only more mature and stable, but also socially better integrated into the local community they served than the teachers in official schools. By virtue of their own indigenous socialization, their status as representatives of the dominant religion, and their extensive connections with the local ruling class, they commanded a higher level of public prestige and were in a position to perform more authentically the role of interpreter of society to the younger generation. Although they did not discriminate among potential students by wealth, their financial support came directly from the local community.

This integrative approach to the patterning of pedagogy may have enabled Islam to settle more comfortably than Christianity into the fabric of the indigenous cultures in West Africa (Derive, 1994). Despite his criticism of its fundamentally conservative orientation, Santerre (1975) suggests that the Qur'anic educational tradition may be a valuable source of ideas for "the emergence of a truly African pedagogy" (p. 337). Specifically, by comparison with Western-style schools in Africa, Qur'anic schooling has a stronger tradition of individualized instruction, of focusing on the development of the whole person, and of flexible scheduling.

More controversially, Santerre (1975) also suggested the Qur'anic emphasis on oral memory may be a source of strength both in connecting with indigenous African cultural traditions, and in preparation for the trend toward audiovisual information dissemination in the latest phase of global technology. It may be that the disjunction between textual recitation and comprehension in Islamic literacy perplexes observers from a Western perspective, mainly because of the tendency to think of basic literacy as a foundational tier for the subsequent cumulative acquisition of cultural knowledge and understanding, a modularized viewpoint that we critiqued earlier. According to Street's (1984) ethnographic study conducted in a rural community in pre-revolutionary Iran, literate adults displayed not only a knowledge of the actual texts memorized, but also an understanding of how elements of the Hadith could be mobilized as interpretive resources for argumentation about practical matters in the present world. It is unclear to what degree this intellectually empowering set of consequences depended on the particular religious and linguistic conditions of pre-revolutionary Iranian society.

Wagner (1993a) presented a synthesis of his studies with Ezzaki and Spratt spanning more than a decade on the nature of literate and educational practices in Morocco. He argued that Western educators have tended to underestimate the potential of Qur'anic preschooling for cultivating valuable foundational skills that can be built on by modern Western forms of pedagogy in the mainstream school systems of African countries such as Morocco. In his view, the exercise in rote memorization afforded by Qur'anic preschooling constitutes an effective introduction to basic decoding skills that can feed into the more meaning-oriented early reading curriculum of both Arabic and French-medium elementary schooling. While Wagner's interpretation focuses on component cognitive processes, our cultural analysis leads us to place greater emphasis on the significance of the activity of prayer recitation within the indigenous meaning-system. Without such a coherent system to give purposive focus to behavior, mere recitation appears to us unlikely to be an effective way of cultivating a new skill. Thus, the success of Qur'anic preschooling in Morocco may depend critically on the sociocultural meaning of prayer.

None of the themes whose significance has been discussed above for one of the three cultural traditions is exclusive to a single culture, but each has taken on a unique constellation of meanings from the ways in which it was elaborated in the indigenous language of the culture and reflected in its institutional practices. Although each of these themes can be recognized in another culture, it is often portrayed as a danger of excess. For instance, the Confucian themes of perfectibility and emulation are sometimes construed as presumptuous or authoritarian in contemporary Western educational circles. Yet excellence in the performance of an instructional presentation remains an important criterion for the assignment of superlatives to teaching. Likewise, the Islamic theme of textual authority, which once was an important theme of Christian education, is now often criticized in Western educational circles, and by Third World advocates of "modernization," as excessively literal or dogmatic. Conversely, the emphasis of contemporary Western schooling on cognitive detachment and technical expertise is sometimes criticized by Islamic and Chinese educators as liable to underplay the importance of cultivating moral responsibility. And the Western emphasis on self-expression is criticized by some Japanese educators as according insufficient attention to group loyalty (Spence, 1985; Tobin, Wu & Davidson, 1989). Needless to say, there are always some conflicts within the educational community of each culture (e.g., Horio, 1988), and thus, the modal educational practice may be criticized even more severely by critics within the culture.

Cross-Cultural Contact and Diffusion

Given the contrasts we have just analyzed, it might appear self-evident that different systems of schooling and literacy are radically incompatible. Yet, in the contemporary world, few, if any, societies are fully insulated against external cultural influence. (See chapter by Berry & Sam, Volume 3 of this *Handbook,* for a discussion of the consequences of culture contact). In this section, we discuss several different types of contact between the educational systems of different cultures. We argue that, regardless of the intentions informing them, these experiments in cross-cultural contact always tend, in practice, to pose cognitive challenges for the individual student that call for processes of bicultural mediation.

Deliberate Import and Adaptation

Theoretically, this type of contact is an ideal set of circumstances, because selection and tuning might be expected to ensure that imported tools, ideas, and institutions would be compatible with the existing indigenous culture, thus minimizing difficulties of individual adaptation. However, even well-meaning, conscientious planners are unlikely to envisage all of the ramifications of their initiatives, and hence, to protect the enterprise against unanticipated, dysfunctional consequences.

Let us consider the case of the decision (noted previously) by the rulers of Japan in the period of the Meiji restoration to borrow from Western industrialized societies certain aspects of their system of public schooling. The Ministry of Education of the Meiji Government invited a German Herbartian scholar, Hausknecht, to teach at the University of Tokyo in 1887. The Herbartian movement, based on the writings of the long deceased philosopher Herbart (1776–1841), advocated a series of instructional steps to be followed by the teacher for any given topic and a historically ordered sequence of topics spread over several years of the curriculum. However, rather than building a new system of education based on the theory, or providing a resource to help educators develop better methods of teaching, the main goal of Japan's planners was to standardize teaching methods, and lend them some of the authority that flows from scientific discipline by relying on selected parts of a famous scholar's work (Inagaki, 1972).

When the Meiji Government was established in 1869, the Ministry of Education gave priority to the training of primary school teachers as part of a program of expansion of primary schooling. Teachers needed training in teaching a fairly large group of students at a time, though not a few of them had had experience before the restoration of teaching basic literacy and numeracy to a small group of children.

The Japanese bureaucracy pursued a highly centralized system in education (Horio, 1988), as it did in other areas of government. By 1885 the Ministry had already acquired the control of content by distributing a series of orders and ordinances as well as the Emperor's Rescript on Education. The standardization of teaching methods would further strengthen the bureaucracy's central control of education, by reducing the freedom, initiative, and inventiveness of teachers.

Around the same time, the Herbartian movement was successfully exported to the United States, although it was eclipsed by other educational philosophies within a few decades (Dunkel, 1970). As Inagaki (1986, p. 79) pointed out, whereas in the United States the Herbartian theory of curriculum and material construction was adopted and developed, in Japan, "where the government regulated curriculum and materials, the concept of formal steps, specifying the teacher's instructional procedures, was the element adopted."

This case study of Herbartianism illustrates the general phenomenon that theory is modified and adapted to the new cultural milieu when it is imported (cf. Serpell, 1995). The considerations that led to the adoption of Herbartian methods in Japanese schools in the Meiji era included, in addition to pragmatic requirements, factors which bore no intrinsic connection with the theoretical issues addressed by these methods. Yet such diverse factors are often packaged in the course of human history and come to acquire an appearance of intrinsic connectedness.

Hegemonic Imposition

A quite different, and historically more recurrent, type of encounter between different cultural traditions arises when one politically powerful group seeks to impose its cultural forms on another less powerful group. The sociological contexts of such encounters include overt political conquest, economic penetration, and religious proselytization. All three factors have played a part in the evolution of contemporary public schooling in post-colonial African states, which Mazrui (1986) described as struggling to integrate a triple cultural heritage: from its own indigenous traditions, from the West and from Islam (cf. Erny, 1981; Santerre & Mercier-Tremblay, 1982). As Nsamenang (1992, p. 97) observed, "the scars of slavery, the stigma of colonial bondage, and the coercive suppression of West Africa's cultural patterns and religious practices" by European and Arabic missionaries have all conspired to provoke an enduring complex of cultural inferiority and resentment.

The indigenous traditions of education in Africa tend to be expressed diffusely in the pattern of everyday social practices rather than in separate and specialized institutions (Erny, 1972; Fortes, 1938). The main opportunities for learning about moral values and technical skills occur in the context of activities that are not deliberately pedagogical, along the lines of apprenticeship discussed earlier. The traditional wisdom encoded in African proverbs and sayings identifies many principles of optimal childrearing without prescribing any exercises for their application. Against this background, the formal institutions of Qur'anic and Christian missionary schools, along with their conspicuous technology of script, are easily misconstrued as introducing education into a cultural vacuum. For the propagators of exogenous forms of schooling, this misconception derived further credibility from their belief that they were bringing the definitive religious truth to a culturally deprived society. The nature of that deprivation was characterized as an amalgam of technological and social factors, with moral and intellectual consequences.

The foundations of the educational model exported from the West to many societies around the world in the 19th and 20th centuries were laid within the

Zeitgeist of the Enlightenment philosophy just described. Confident in the technical validity of this rationale, many European missionaries in Africa regarded schooling as an effective instrument for deliberately inducing a process of cultural change. Not only were they committed to a particular religious interpretation of social and moral behavior, but they were also deeply attached to the principles of contemporary Western civil life, including commerce and administration. As a result, they generally saw little or no conflict between their evangelizing objectives and the imperialistic expansion of their governments' sphere of influence (Snelson, 1974; Tignor, 1976).

Whereas their preoccupation with recitation of the definitive Qur'anic text ensured that Islamic schools taught children to read only in the foreign language of Arabic, Christian missionaries offered schooling as a way of enabling Africans to understand the word of God, and incidentally to acquire the skills of literacy. In pursuit of this objective, some of them translated the Bible into local languages, and in the process established the first orthography for many of the African languages. Yet the choice of linguistic medium of instruction has been an enduring policy problem for public education in Africa. Colonial governments throughout the continent institutionalized the European language of the metropolitan power as the medium of public administration. Even after independence, political and economic pressures have combined to enhance the value for modern Africans of becoming literate in the language of the former colonial power relative to their indigenous languages. For many political analysts, this paradoxical phenomenon appears indicative of neocolonial hegemony (e.g., Kashoki, 1990).

In recent decades, several indigenous governments in Africa have advanced a rationale for retaining the language of a former colonial power as the sole or principal medium of schooling and literacy, challenging the earlier consensus view upheld by UNESCO that children should be first introduced to the foundational skills of literacy in their home language. The rationale has several strands, including the pragmatic, economic, and administrative convenience of using a single language; the pedagogical value of early familiarization with the medium of higher education and international communication; and the cognitive malleability of young children's linguistic competence (Serpell, 1978).

Of special significance for the field of cross-cultural psychology is the claim sometimes made for the last of these arguments that it is grounded in systematic, empirical research on bilingual "immersion" programs. Yet, subsequent analyses of such programs have found that their outcomes depend critically on the sociopolitical environment in which they are situated (cf. Mohanty & Perregaux, this volume). To the extent that the language of basic schooling is regarded as alien to, or oppressive of, the language and culture of everyday discourse, students are liable to find themselves confronted with difficult choices between loyalty to the moral and aesthetic standards of indigenous culture and the economic advantages of mastery of exogenous linguistic and cultural forms.

Essentially similar considerations apply also to curriculum content and the organization of instruction. As Mukene (1988) and others have noted, the entire design of public schooling in Africa tends to bear very little relevance to the demands of economically productive adult life in rural settings, where the vast majority of school-leavers will spend their lives. For most parents, teachers, and students in rural African schools, the primary definition of educational success remains extractive, luring students up and out of their community of origin along a staircase of progress toward increasingly alien cultural goals (Serpell, 1993a).

In contrast, a recurrent theme in the autobiographical and semi-autobiographical writings of African intellectuals about their childhood is an exhilarating sense of liberation through the acquisition of literacy (e.g., Akinasso, 1991; Ngugi, 1964). A famous case in point is the life of the Senegalese writer and politician, Leopold Senghor (Vaillant, 1990). His initial formal education under French colonial rule in Senegal socialized Senghor so fully into the mainstream of French culture that he was able to qualify for appointment as Minister of Education in Paris. Yet, later in his career, Senghor displayed strong cultural and political independence.

Unfortunately, sociopolitical and economic constraints dictate that such revolutionary life trajectories are accessible to only a tiny elite in Africa. Nevertheless, the World Bank and other international funding agencies argue that even a basic primary schooling brings significant benefits to the community in the form of enhanced productivity (Colclough, 1980) and/or knowledge about health care and nutrition (Court & Kinyanjui, 1985). However, the evidence supporting these contentions is quite tenuous. The few studies of actual competence in tasks demanding literacy among African school-leavers with less than a full primary course of education suggest that although they may find some opportunities to use their basic literacy skills in everyday life, very few such opportunities exist in rural communities for the written language of the state (Eisemon, 1988; Serpell, 1993a; Wagner, 1993a).

The offer of access to literacy in the context of a hegemonically imposed form of education requires most students to negotiate a sharp discontinuity between the culture of their home and that of the school (cf. Mutome, 1982). Those who succeed in making this transition achieve what has been termed *bicultural mediation,* a topic we address below.

Modernization and Indigenization

The dominant motive for exporting educational practices in the twentieth century has been modernization theory, advanced as a universalistic principle to justify the transplantation of many Western cultural inventions. Inspired by the Enlightenment philosophical belief in the possibility of designing effective methods and areas of human endeavor, Western social scientists have liberally applied their theories to the explanation of "problems" confronting societies whose political leaders aspired to promote their economic and social "development" along the lines pioneered by the Western industrialized nations (e.g., Inkeles & Smith, 1974; McClelland, 1961). These rationalizations, however, have been discredited in recent years by the international economic ascendancy of countries such as Japan and Korea that have achieved a rapid rate of industrialization, while publicly endorsing a collectivist form of motivation quite alien to Weber's famous "Protestant ethic" (cf. Hui & Luk Chapter, Volume 3, this *Handbook*).

Indeed, reversing the Western hegemonistic argument of earlier decades, Stevenson and Stigler (1992) argued from a cross-cultural comparison of outcomes that the pedagogical methods of Japanese public schooling deserve special consideration as sources of inspiration for the reform of American education. As Hatano (1990) has pointed out, however, this analysis ignores the culturally embedded nature of pedagogical methods, and overestimates the feasibility of transplanting them from one culture to another.

A more plausible form of educational application for comparative cultural analysis is the design of curricula that are responsive to identifiable features of the indigenous culture. Tharp and his colleagues (1984) described an elaborate program of this type developed over several years in the public schools of Hawaii. And Allen and Boykin (1992) outlined the case for a prescriptive pedagogy inspired by experimental studies of distinctive cultural strengths among the African-American population. Paradoxically, in countries formerly colonized by Western European powers, where one might expect to find less institutional bias in favor of the old model, attempts to indigenize the pattern of schooling have tended to remain relatively superficial, concentrating on the content of the social science components of the curriculum. In Africa, many intellectuals have written eloquently of the inadequacies of their contemporary systems of public schooling for the cultivation of children's development along dimensions of indigenous value (Mbele, 1993; Mukene, 1988; Nsamenang, 1992), but reports of coherent alternative programs implemented in practice are rare (Bamgbose, 1976; Champion, 1979; Fafunwa, 1975).

Despite the obvious limitations of the Western model of schooling described above, it has become part of an enduring orthodoxy within the international development agencies that individualism makes a key contribution to modernity, and that Western style of education is uniquely well adapted to its cultivation. Other components of the package that schooling is held to deliver in the context of Third World countries' "development programs" are the acquisition of basic literacy and numeracy, which are construed as prerequisites for full citizenship. Schooling is thus construed as an instrument of progressive social change, designed to prepare the next generation for effective and responsible participation in a growing economy with changing patterns of production and social organization (e.g., Forje, 1993). Many national governments endorse this ideological view (Jomtien, 1990), and invest substantial proportions of their revenue in the expansion of public education.

In addition to imparting technical skills and knowledge necessary for specialized occupations in an industrialized society, formal schooling based on the Western model can be credited in many Third World societies with having increased social mobility for disadvantaged sections of the population, including oppressed minority groups (Naik, 1975), women (Kagitçibasi, 1986), and persons with sensory and motor impairments (ILO, 1986). By contrast, the degree to which the religious embeddedness of Qur'anic schooling has placed women at a disadvantage with respect to educational opportunity in the Islamic world is a point of contention. Writing from the perspective of an indigenous feminist scholar committed to a modernization agenda in Turkey, Kagitcibasi (1995) contends that "religious education does not just impart specific memory skills. It inculcates a religious world view which is antithetical to a scientific worldview" (p. 211).

Bray, Clarke, and Stephens (1986) survey a number of attempts to "modernize" Islamic education in Africa, often involving some form of integration with Western-style schooling. But they note that, in northern Nigeria where they conducted field research, strong opposition has been mobilized against these attempts based on ideological, economic, and political factors. On the other hand, Otayek (1993) argues that the confluences of a crisis of credibility for Western-style education, revival of Islamic religion, and expansion of economic aid from Arabic nations seems to be generating a renaissance of Islamic education in sub-Saharan Africa.

The social and economic successes claimed for schooling based on the Western model in Third World societies need to be set alongside some disturbing anomalies. Serpell's (1993a) longitudinal study of how schooling impacted on the everyday lives and careers of young people born in a rural community of Zambia, a nation with a relatively strong educational profile by U.N. standards, found many who were disillusioned and few who were adequately skilled to enter technical occupations in a relatively stagnant labor market. In many African countries, the basic curriculum remains essentially alien in both form and content from the indigenous culture of students' homes, where a more socially responsible conception of intelligence (such as the Chewa concept of *nzelu* described earlier) is often favored over the cognitive detachment and technical expertise prioritized at school.

Even in the United States, numerous researchers have questioned whether the form of schooling currently standardized in the cultural mainstream is adequately responsive to the pattern of cognitive competencies and dispositions fostered in the homes of cultural minority groups (Boykin, 1986; Gallimore & Goldenberg, 1993; Laosa, 1984; Tharp, 1989; Thompson, Mixon, & Serpell, 1996). As Myers (1992) pointed out, it seems more productive to shift the focus of educational attention toward the reciprocal question of how well the schools are prepared to receive and accommodate the minority group children than to continue to problematize their unpreparedness for the demands of school.

Towards an Integrative Framework

The patterns of schooling emerging from particular cultural traditions have interacted through a variety of processes of contact and diffusion, giving rise to tensions, compromises, and syncretic forms. With increasing international communication among educational planners toward the end of the twentieth century, a tendency has emerged for many societies to converge on a single, standardized model. For instance, the assumption of a sequence of tiers is widely shared. Furthermore, most nations now plan for boys and girls to study together in a special-ized institutional setting between the ages of about seven and twelve, and during that basic phase of their education to be taught the elements of literacy and numeracy as well as being introduced to the natural and social sciences. We shall refer to this model as the Institutionalized Public Basic Schooling (IPBS) model. There have been many attempts to design innovative alternatives even at the ba-sic level. Nevertheless, the model we describe tends to dominate elementary edu-cation of most, if not all, countries of the contemporary world.

Institutionalized Public Basic Schooling: An Emergent Paradigm

In search of integrative themes, we first focus on two distinctive characteristics of this model relative to the full range of culturally structured settings devised by human societies for child development: (1) systematic preparation in advance as against giving minimal help at the time when needed, and (2) institutionally au-thorized competence as against competence needed for practical problem-solving.

Advance Preparation as against On-The-Spot Assistance

IPBS is usually expected to provide children with opportunities to acquire basic literacy and other foundational skills. The competence to be produced by it may not have any immediate practical value, but is important, at least in the public eye, as a foundation for learning something significant in future, especially for a variety of occupational training programs. Thus it is maintained primarily for advance preparation.

By contrast, in the context of apprenticeships, engaging in socially significant practices precedes the development of skills needed to perform well in them (Lave & Wenger, 1991; Scribner & Cole, 1981). However, the need for the master to play a dual role may get burdensome as the target skill becomes more complicated and demanding, and/or failure by the apprentice to perform the skill aptly leads to serious danger or damage (Schank, 1993/94). Thus, a training school has to be established to enhance the development of the skill in advance, as has been the case in several industrialized countries for driving a motorcar. The activities of a training school are exclusively for the exercise of learners' skills and are located outside of the situation where the skills are actually used. However, unlike IPBS, they are designed to help interested learners' acquisition of specific skills that are useful in production and other socially meaningful activities. Moreover, a training school pro-vides situations representing, or highly similar to, the actual situations.

Learning activities in IPBS, however, are directed toward preparation for the future in general, not preparation for specific skills to be used as soon as they are ready. IPBS is conducted by teachers, who are regarded as specialists and are in charge of choosing contents and methods of teaching. They are often motivated to make teaching efficient, and rely on didactic methods that require students, as "recipients" of teaching, to manipulate symbols instead of handling real objects in meaningful contexts.

In those societies where almost all students are expected eventually to master a variety of complex skills and advanced knowledge (in the context of further schooling or occupational training), IPBS serves a significant advance preparatory function by providing an opportunity to acquire literacy skills and other foundational abilities essential for later learning. However, motivating students to learn is often problematic, because they do not easily appreciate the significance of IPBS as "preparation for preparation for practices." Moreover, it is difficult to induce skills that are useful and can be readily used outside of school, because of the rather restricted learning contexts offered in IPBS. Thus IPBS tends to make students less active and, in a sense, less competent than out-of-school youths (Greenfield & Lave, 1982; Resnick, 1988).

Authorized Competence as against Practical Competence

In apprenticeship or other forms of learning at the workplace, learners increase their practical competence, often as an unintended by-product of successful collaborative activities. Likewise, learners go to a training school in order to acquire immediately useful skills for solving problems. When schooling is optional, parents send their children to a school to develop foundational abilities that they believe will be useful in future. In these forms of education, there is no discrepancy or conflict between instruction and learning in the goals or contents of education.

In contrast, IPBS tends to rely on the premise that the skills and knowledge taught by it are valuable in and of themselves, irrespective of their utility outside school. The value of the competence that IPBS aims to provide to its students thus derives its legitimacy from the philosophy of the institution: it is institutionally authorized and is based on the school system's own self-defined agenda. This may have some positive consequences. IPBS may cultivate foundational abilities of literacy and numeracy in some students, whose parents do not see any practical value of these abilities. It may also enable students to go beyond practical concerns, and to pursue, for example, deep understanding of a phenomenon, humanistic and critical attitudes toward the world, intellectual autonomy, and so on.

However, such a happy resolution of the discrepancy or conflict has been rare. The practical competence that learners want to acquire and the authorized competence professional educators aim at, may not be easily integrated. The principle of authorized competence tends to produce tension between the teaching and learning sides that often results in lay people's negative attitudes toward IPBS. This may lead to parental unwillingness to send children to IPBS, blaming educators and withdrawing financial support from them, or even physically demolishing school buildings and facilities.

This is likely to be the case when one of the agendas of schooling (e.g., promoting the nation's economic growth) receives excessive emphasis at the expense of others, and/or when an exogenous system of schooling is imported and imposed. These conditions have often co-occurred in recent history for non-Western societies into which the Western school system has been transplanted and Western science and technology assigned a central place in education. Outright refusal by parents to accept IPBS was reported in the early Meiji era in Japan (Yorita & Yamanaka, 1993), in the early phase of colonial administration in Africa (King, 1975; Schoffeleers & Linden, 1972), and among the indigenous peoples of North America (Rogoff, 1981). In the contemporary world, such resistance is often more muted, but remains a significant challenge for national and international programs aimed at the universalization of basic schooling, especially in the face of widespread decline in the viability of school-leaving certificates for entry into the labor market.

The Cultural Specificity of Extrinsic Features

Our cross-cultural analysis in the preceding sections illustrates how complex are the origins of many characteristics of IPBS. Along with the distinctive features we have identified, the model has accumulated over the course of history a great deal of baggage that is at best extrinsic to the principal goals of basic education, and may often serve to obstruct those goals. Students in IPBS are congregated in a class facing a single teacher; lessons are strictly scheduled into planned periods of time; authoritative texts are memorized; the performance of individual students is competitively ranked; a highly conformist pattern of discipline is imposed. Some of these features may reflect culturally specific, philosophical preoccupations, while others arose from purely pragmatic considerations that may not apply to the present, local context.

Although, as we have emphasized, there exists a variety of forms of educational practice, IPBS is by definition accorded a special, privileged status: it is taken as the only institution for developing abilities in general, authorized by the nation state. As a result, the ranking of students according to their achievement within the school system is often extrapolated to their status in the wider society. What students learn changes when this ranking function of schooling becomes salient. Instead of developing foundational abilities of socially significant problem solving, students attempt to maximize their scores on tests by which their achievement is assessed. Indeed, they often develop strategies for answering questions without comprehension (Cole & Griffin, 1983). Thus IPBS has generated a new kind of motivation for learning: to seek being evaluated as competent rather than competence itself.

Two complementary implications flow from this analysis, one for the assessment of students' learning, the other for the design of educational policy. The degree to which a student's performance on a given school task coincides with the stated target is only evidence of learning in a narrow sense. In order to assess the wider significance of the performance, the particular task must be situated not only with reference to the school curriculum, but also with reference to broader social goals. Because there are many different ways of teaching literacy (or mathematics, science, etc.), there must be many ways of learning it. A culturally sensitive method of assessment for cognitive development must go beyond conformity with preestablished norms (Garcia & Pearson, 1991; cf. Mishra, this volume).

For policy development the implication is that the premises underlying existing educational practices deserve careful scrutiny. Some premises may be outdated or even ideologically alien for the concerns that are most central to the current phase of educational planning. Tharp and Gallimore (1988), for instance, argue convincingly that elementary school teaching can be more effectively organized around multiple, small-group activity centers than by relying exclusively on lecturing to the whole class. And Gardner (1991) has reviewed numerous examples of innovative approaches to IPBS, involving apprenticeship-like arrangements, museums, and other out-of-class, flexibly scheduled activities. Analyzing educational outcomes in terms of scores on standardized tests focuses attention on the relatively few goals that are amenable to such objective measurement at the expense of other more subtle goals, which in contexts of rapid sociocultural change tends to bias decision-making in favor of conservatism.

Our analysis also suggests that the sociocultural goals of education deserve a more prominent place on the agenda of reform than they currently tend to receive. The preeminent emphasis on cognitive, technological skills in IPBS arises from a very particular, historically situated set of circumstances including industrialization and cultural imperialism, and is ill-suited to the primary needs of many of the world's contemporary local communities. Moreover, the best safeguard of public accountability for education is to base it on fully negotiated goals. Such goals are liable to reach beyond the scope of what is currently dominant in the professional subculture of education.

Preparing Students for Life in a Multicultural World

Very few contemporary societies are insulated against the intrusion of foreign cultures, and increasing numbers of students find themselves commuting between two or more different cultural worlds in their family home, their neighborhood, and their school. Education, thus, confronts a new set of responsibilities at the interface between different value systems, languages, and practices. The tradition of teaching foreign languages is already well established as a part of many national educational curricula, especially at secondary and higher levels of schooling. Yet, it is often seen as a relatively peripheral addition to basic education. Indeed, many people in the United States tend to regard bilingualism as an anomaly, despite growing evidence of the cognitive empowerment that it can confer (Diaz, 1985; Mohanty & Perregaux, this volume), and despite the fact that it is a normal condition for a vast proportion of the world's population. Indigenous citizens of the Third World countries and minority culture-bearers in the industrialized countries are often charged with teaching a basic IPBS curriculum that is linguistically and culturally different from their own primary socialization. Under these circumstances, they often seem reluctant to deploy the indigenous part of their cognitive repertoire in respect of their pedagogical activities (Hornberger, 1988; Serpell, 1993a). Yet, it can be argued that such bicultural "teachers have a special responsibility as 'intercultural brokers,' who will either bridge or widen the cultural gaps that occur in classroom life" (Serpell & Boykin, 1994, p. 402).

The social status of teachers is constrained by economic and political factors that often militate against innovation. Yet, a focus on ways of dealing with cultural diversity may be responsive to felt needs in the profession. Although research on individual biculturation is scarce, studies of language use by multilingual individuals in multilingual societies have revealed several forms of psychological integration (Gumperz, 1982). Expanding this type of analysis to other aspects of cross-cultural psychology could be an extremely valuable contribution to education, for it is almost certain that the citizens of the next generation will live in a world in which diverse cultures interact with ever greater intensity.

Acknowledgments

The authors wish to acknowledge constructive suggestions for the improvement of earlier drafts from the following: David Olson, Tadahiko Inagaki, Tom Weisner, and an anonymous reader from India. We are also grateful for their assistance with the bibliography to Gustave Callewaert, Hiro Inokuchi, Walter Meyer, Francois Rochat, Theressa Rose, and Vicki Goddard-Truit.

References

Akinasso, F. N. (1991). Literacy and individual consciousness. In E. M. Jennings, & A. C. Purves (Eds.), *Literate systems and individual lives: Perspectives on literacy and schooling* (pp. 73–94). Albany, NY: SUNY Press

Allen, B. A. & Boykin, A. W. (1992). African-American children and the educational process: Alleviating cultural discontinuity through prescriptive pedagogy. *School Psychology Review, 21*, 586–596.

Aries, P. (1962). *Centuries of childhood* (R. Baldick, Trans). London: Cape.

Baker, L., Sonnenschein, S., Serpell, R., Fernandez, S., & Scher, D. (1994). *Contexts of emergent literacy: Everyday home experiences of urban prekindergarten children* (Reading Research Report No. 24). Athens, GA: NRRC. Universities of Georgia and Maryland, College Park.

Bamgbose, A. (Ed.). (1976). *Mother tongue education: The West African experience*. London: Hodder & Stoughton.

Baynham, M. (1993). Code-switching and mode-switching: Community interpreters and mediators of literacy. In B. Street (Ed.), *Cross-cultural approaches to literacy* (pp. 294–314). Cambridge: Cambridge University Press.

Berlin, I. (1956). Introduction. In I. Berlin (Ed.), *The age of enlightenment*. New York: Mentor.

Berry, J. W. & Bennett, J. A. (1991). *Cree syllabic literacy: Cultural context and psychological consequences*. (Tilburg University Monographs in Cross-Cultural Psychology). Tilburg: Tilburg University Press.

Biber, D. (1986). Spoken and written textual dimensions in English: Resolving the contradictory findings. *Language, 62*, 384–414.

Boykin, A. W. (1986). The triple quandary and the schooling of Afro-American children. In U. Neisser (Ed.), *The school achievement of minority children* (pp. 57–92). Hillsdale, NJ: Erlbaum.

Bray, M., Clarke, P. B. & Stephens, D. (1986). *Education and society in Africa*. London: Arnold.

Bradley, L. & Bryant, P. E. (1983) Categorising sounds and learning to read—a causal connection. *Nature, 301*, 419–421.

Bruner, J. S. (1966). An overview. In J. S. Bruner, R. R. Olver & P. M. Greenfield (Eds.), *Studies in cognitive growth* (pp. 319–326). New York: Wiley.

Chaiklin, S. and Lave, J. (1993). *Understanding practice: Perspectives on activity and context*. Cambridge: Cambridge University Press.

Champion, J. (1979). Les langues maternelles dans l'enseignement en Afrique. In *Langage et pédagogie en France et en Afrique.* Paris: Editions Anthropos.

Colclough, C. (1980). *World Bank Staff Working Paper 339.* Washington, DC: World Books.

Cole, M. & Bruner, J. S. (1971). Cultural differences and inferences about psychological processes. *American Psychologist, 26,* 867–876.

Cole, M. & Griffin, P. (1980). Cultural amplifiers reconsidered. In D. R. Olson (Ed.), *The social foundations of language and thought* (pp. 343–364). New York: Norton.

Cole, M. & Griffin, P. (1983). A socio-historical approach to remediation. *Quarterly Newsletter of the Laboratory of Comparative Human Cognition, 5,* 69–74.

Cook-Gumperz, J. (1986). Literacy and schooling: An unchanging equation? In J. Cook-Gumperz (Ed.), *The social construction of literacy* (pp. 16–44). Cambridge: Cambridge University Press.

Court, D. & Kinyanjui, K. (1985). *Education and development in sub-Saharan Africa: The operation and impact of education systems.* (Working Paper 421). Nairobi, Kenya: Institute for Development Studies.

Derive, J. (1994, September). La pratique lettrée dans les sociétés de culture orale, un exemple négro-africain. Paper presented at the European Science Foundation's Workshop on Contexts of Literacy. Nice, France.

Diaz, R. M. (1985). The intellectual power of bilingualism. *Quarterly Newsletter of the Laboratory of Comparative Human Cognition, 7,* 16–22.

Dien, D. F. (1982). A Chinese perspective on Kohlberg's theory of moral development. *Developmental Review, 2,* 331–341.

Dunkel, H. B. (1970). *Herbart and Herbartianism: An educational ghost story.* Chicago: University of Chicago Press.

Eisemon, T. O. (1988). *Benefiting from basic education, school quality and functional literacy in Kenya.* Oxford: Pergamon.

Eisenstein, E. L. (1979). *The printing press as an agent of change: Communications and cultural transformations in early-modern Europe.* Cambridge: Cambridge University Press.

Erny, P. (1972). L'*enfant et son milieu en Afrique noire.* Paris: Payot.

Erny, P. (1981). *Ecoles d'église en Afrique noire.* Immensee.

Fafunwa, A. B. (1975). Education in the mother-tongue: A Nigerian experiment—The six-year (Yoruba medium) Primary Education Project at the University of Ife, Nigeria. *West African Journal of Education, 19,* 213–227.

Ferreiro, E. (1994). Problems and pseudo-problems in literacy development. Focus on Latin America. In L. Verhoeven (Ed.), *Functional literacy: Theoretical issues and educational implications* (pp. 223–235). Amsterdam: Benjamin.

Forje, J. W. (1993). Technological education, the child, and national development in Africa. *Journal of Psychology in Africa, 1,* 64–80.

Fortes, M. (1938). Social and psychological aspects of education in Taleland. *Africa, 11,* 1–64 (Supplement).

Gallimore, R. & Goldenberg, C. (1993). Activity settings of early literacy: Home and school factors in children's emergent literacy. In E. A. Forman, N. Minick, & C. A. Stone. (Eds.), *Contexts for learning: Sociocultural dynamics in children's development* (pp. 315–335). Oxford: Oxford University Press.

Garcia, A. E. & Pearson, P. D. (1991). The role of assessment in a diverse society. In Hiebert, E. (Ed.), *Literacy for a diverse society* (pp. 253–278). New York: Teachers College Press.

Gardner, H. (1991). *The unschooled mind: How children think and how schools should teach.* New York: Basic Books.

Gibson, E. J. & Levin, H. (1975). *The psychology of reading.* Cambridge, MA: MIT Press.

Goodnow, J., Miller, P. & Kessel, W. (1995). *Cultural practices as contexts for human development.* San Francisco: Jossey-Bass.

Goody, J. (1968). Restricted literacy in Northern Ghana. In J. Goody (Ed.), *Literacy in traditional societies* (pp. 199–264). Cambridge: Cambridge University Press.

Goody, J. (1977). *The domestication of the savage mind.* Cambridge: Cambridge University Press.

Goody, J. & Watt, I. (1963). The consequences of literacy. *Comparative Studies in Society and History, 5,* 304–326.

Greenfield, P. M. (1972). Oral and written language: The consequences for cognitive development in Africa, the United States, and England. *Language and Speech, 15,* 169-178.

Greenfield, P. M. & Lave, J. (1982). Cognitive aspects of informal education. In D. Wagner & H. Stevenson (Eds.), *Cultural perspectives on child development* (pp. 181–207). San Francisco: Freeman.

Greenfield, P. M. (1984). A theory of the teacher in the learning activities of everyday life. In B. Rogoff & J. Lave (Eds.), *Everyday cognition: Its development in social context* (pp. 117–138). Cambridge, MA: Harvard University Press.

Griffin, P. & Cole, M. (1987). New technologies, basic skills, and the underside of education: What's to be done? In J. Langer (Ed.), *Language, literacy, and culture: Issues of society and schooling* (pp. 199–231). Norwood, NJ: Ablex.

Gumperz, J. J. (1982). *Discourse strategies.* Cambridge: Cambridge University Press.

Hatano, G. (1982). Should parents be teachers too?: A Japanese view. *Dokkyo University Bulletin of Liberal Arts,17,* 54–72.

Hatano, G. (1986). How do Japanese children learn to read? Orthographic and eco-cultural variables. In B. Foorman and A. Siegel (Eds.), *Acquisition of reading skills: Cultural constraints and cognitive universals* (pp. 81–114). Hillsdale, NJ: Erlbaum.

Hatano, G. (1990). Toward the cultural psychology of mathematical cognition: Commentary. In Stevenson, H. W. & Lee, S. *Contexts of achievement. Monographs of the Society for Research in Child Development, 55* (1–2) (Serial No. 221), 108–115.

Havelock, E. A. (1976). *Origins of Western literacy.* Toronto: Ontario Institute for Studies in Education.

Holloway, S., Kashiwagi, K. Hess, R.D., & Azuma, H. (1986). Causal attributions by Japanese and American mothers and children about performance in mathematics. *International Journal of Psychology, 21,* 269–286.

Horio, T. (1988). *Educational thought and ideology in modern Japan: State authority and intellectual freedom* (S. Platzer, Ed. & Trans). Tokyo: University of Tokyo Press.

Hornberger, N. (1988). Language planning orientations and bilingual education in Peru. *Language Problems and Language Planning, 12,* 14–29.

Hornberger, N. H. (1994). Continua of biliteracy: Quechua literacy and empowerment in Peru. In L. Verhoeven (Ed.), *Functional literacy: Theoretical issues and educational implications* (pp. 237–256). Amsterdam: Benjamin.

Horton, R. (1982). Tradition and modernity revisited. In M. Hollis & S. Lukes (Eds.), *Rationality and relativism* (pp. 201–260). Oxford: Blackwell.

Hutchins, E. (1991). The social organization of distributed cognition. In L. B. Resnick, J. M. Levine, & S. D. Teasley (Eds.), *Perspectives on socially shared cognition* (pp. 283–307). Washington, DC: American Psychological Association.

Ibrahim, A. H. (1994, September). L'alphabétisation dans un contexte diglossique Arabe. Paper presented at the European Science Foundation's Workshop on Contexts of Literacy. Nice, France.

Ikuta, K. (1987). *Knowing through performing ('waza').* Tokyo: University of Tokyo Press. [in Japanese].

Illich, I. (1991). A plea for research on lay literacy. In D. R. Olson, & N. Torrance. (Eds.), *Literacy and orality* (pp. 28–46). Cambridge: Cambridge University Press.

ILO. (1986). *Employment of disabled persons: Manual on selective placement.* Geneva: ILO.

Inagaki, T. (1972). *Education in contemporary Japan.* Tokyo: Hyoron-sha. [in Japanese].

Inagaki, T. (1986). School education: Its history and contemporary status. In H. W. Stevenson, H. Azuma & K. Hakuta (Eds.), *Child development and education in Japan* (pp. 75–92). New York: Freeman.

Inkeles, A. & Smith, D. H. (1974). *Becoming modern: Individual change in six developing countries.* London: Heinemann.

Jomtien. (1990). *World declaration on education for all.* New York: UNICEF (inter-agency commission for the world conference on education for all).

Kagitçibasi, C. (1986). Status of women in Turkey: Cross-cultural perspectives. *International Journal of Middle Eastern Studies, 18,* 485–499.

Kagitçibasi, C. (1995). *Family and human development across cultures: A view from the other side.* Hillsdale, NJ: Erlbaum.

Kashoki, M. E. (1990). *The factor of language in Zambia.* Lusaka: Kenneth Kaunda Foundation.

Kleibard, H. W. (1975). Metaphorical roots of curriculum design. In W. Pinar (Ed.), *Curriculum theorising: The reconceptualists* (pp. 84–85). Berkeley, CA: McCutchan.

King, K. J. (1975). Nationalism, education and imperialism in the Southern Sudan (1920–70). In G. N. Brown & M. Hiskett (Eds.), *Conflict and harmony in education in tropical Africa* (pp. 296–318). London: Allen & Unwin.

Kumar, K. (1991). *Political agenda of education: A study of colonialist and nationalist ideas.* New Delhi: Sage.

Laosa, L. (1984). Social policies toward children of diverse ethnic, racial, and language groups in the United States. In H. W. Stevenson & A. E. Siegel (Eds.), *Child development research and social policy* (pp. 1–109). Chicago: University of Chicago Press.

Lave, J. (1988). *Cognition in practice: Mind, mathematics and culture in everyday life.* Cambridge: Cambridge University Press.

Lave, J. & Wenger, E. (1991). *Participation in practices.* Cambridge: Cambridge University Press.

Lee, L. C. & Zhen, G. (1991). Political socialization and parental values in the People's Republic of China. *International Journal of Behavioural Development, 14,* 337–373.

Levine, K. (1982). Functional literacy: Fond illusions and false economies. *Harvard Educational Review, 52,* 249–266.

Lin, C. D. (1988). Moral development in a changing world: A Chinese perspective. *School Psychology International, 9,* 13–19.

Maclean, M., Bryant, P., & Bradley, L. (1987). Rhymes, nursery rhymes, and reading in early childhood. *Merrill-Palmer Quarterly, 33,* 255–281.

Mazrui, A. A. (1986). *The Africans.* New York: Praeger.

Mbele, C. R. (1993). L'enfant et la communauté humaine. *Journal of Psychology in Africa, 1* (5), 1–10.

McClelland, D. (1961). *The achieving society.* Princeton: Van Nostrand.

Mukene, P. (1988). *L'Ouverture entre l'école et le milieu en Afrique noire: Pour une gestion pertinente des connaissances.* Fribourg: Editions Universitaires.

Munro, D. J. (1975). The Chinese view of modeling. *Human Development, 18,* 333–352.

Mutome, E. H. (1982). Conflit linguistique entre milieux familial et scolaire. In R. Santerre, & C. Mercier-Trembley (Eds.), *La quete du savoir* (pp. 716–735). Montréal: Presses de l'Université de Montréal.

Myers, R. G. (1992). *The twelve who survive: Strengthening programmes of early childhood development in the Third World.* London: Routledge and Kegan Paul.

Naik, J. P. (1975). *Elementary education in India: A promise to keep.* Bombay: Allied Publishers.

Ngugi, W. T. (1964). *Weep not child.* London: Heinemann.

Nsamenang, A. B. (1992). *Human development in cultural context: A Third World perspective.* Newbury Park, CA: Sage.

Ogbu, J. (1990). Cultural models, identity and literacy. In J. W. Stigler, R. A. Shweder & G. Herdt (Eds.), *Cultural psychology: essays on comparative human development* (pp. 520–541). New York: Cambridge University Press.

Olson, D. R. (1977). The languages of instruction: The literate bias of schooling. In R. C. Anderson, R. J. Spiro & W. E. Montague (Eds.), *Schooling and the acquisition of knowledge* (pp. 65–89). Hillsdale, NJ: Erlbaum.

Olson, D. R. (1991). Literacy as metalinguistic activity. In Olson, D. R. & Torrance, N. (Eds.), *Literacy and orality* (pp. 251–270). Cambridge: Cambridge University Press.

Olson, D. R. (1994). *The world on paper.* Cambridge: Cambridge University Press.

Olson, D. R. & Astington, J. W. (1990). Talking about text: How literacy contributes to thought. *Journal of Pragmatics, 14,* 705–721.

Olson, D. R. & Bruner, J. S. (1996). Folk psychology and folk pedagogy. In D. R. Olson & N. Torrance (Eds.), *Handbook of education and human development: New models of learning, teaching and schooling* (pp. 9–27). Oxford: Blackwell.

Otayek, R. (1993). Introduction. In R. Otayek (Ed.),

Le radicalisme islamique au sud du Sahara: Da'awa, arabisation et critique de l'Occident (pp. 7–18). Paris: Karthala.

Paine, L. W. (1990). The teacher as a virtuoso: A Chinese model for teaching. *Teachers College Record, 92,* 49–81.

Quinn, N. & Holland, D. (1987). Culture and cognition. In D. Holland & N. Quinn (Eds.), *Cultural models in language and thought* (pp. 3–40). Cambridge: Cambridge University Press.

Reder, S. M. (1987). Comparative aspects of functional literacy development: Three ethnic American communities. In D. A. Wagner (Ed.), *The future of literacy in a changing world* (pp. 250–270). New York: Pergamon.

Resnick, L. B. (1988). Learning in school and out. *Educational Researcher, 16,* 13–20.

Rogoff, B. (1981). Schooling and the development of cognitive skills. In H. C. Triandis & A. Heron (Eds.), *Handbook of cross-cultural psychology* (Vol. 4, pp. 233–294). Boston: Allyn and Bacon.

Rogoff, B. (1990). *Apprenticeship in thinking: Cognitive development in social context.* New York: Oxford University Press.

Santerre, R. (1971). Aspects conflictuels de deux systèmes d'enseignement au Nord-Cameroun. *Revue Canadienne des Etudes Africaines, 2,* 157–169.

Santerre, R. (1973). *Pedagogie musulmane d'Afrique noire: L'école coranique peule du Cameroun.* Montréal: Presses de l'Université de Montréal.

Santerre, R. (1975). La pédagogie coranique. *Recherche, Pédagogie et Culture, 20,* 12–17.

Santerre, R. & Mercier-Tremblay, C. (Eds.). (1982). *La quête du savoir; Essais pour une anthropologie de l'éducation camerounaise.* Montréal: Presses de l'Université de Montréal.

Saxe, G. B. (1991). *Culture and cognitive development: Studies in mathematical understanding.* Hillsdale, NJ: Erlbaum.

Schank, R. C. (1993/94). Goal-based scenarios: A radical look at education. *Journal of Learning Sciences, 3,* 429–453.

Schoffeleers, M. & Linden, I. (1972). The resistance of the Nyau societies to the Roman Catholic missions in colonial Malawi. In T. O. Ranger & I. N. Kimambo (Eds.), *The historical study of African religion* (pp. 252–273). Berkeley: University of California Press.

Scribner, S. & Cole, M. (1981). *The psychology of literacy.* Cambridge, MA: Harvard University Press.

Serpell, R. (1978). Some developments in Zambia since 1971. In S. I. Ohannessian and M. E. Kashoki (Eds.), *Language in Zambia* (pp. 424–447). London: International African Institute.

Serpell, R. (1990). Audience, culture and psychological explanation: A reformulation of the emic-etic problem in cultural psychology. *Quarterly Newsletter of the Laboratory of Comparative Human Cognition, 12,* 99–132.

Serpell, R. (1993a). *The significance of schooling: Life-journeys in an African society.* Cambridge: Cambridge University Press.

Serpell, R. (1993b). Interface between socio-cultural and psychological aspects of cognition: A commentary. In E. Forman, N. Minick & A. Stone (Eds.), *Contexts for learning: Sociocultural dynamics in children's development* (pp. 357–368). Oxford: Oxford University Press.

Serpell, R. (1993c). Interaction of context with development: Theoretical constructs for the design of early childhood intervention programs. In L. Eldering & P. Leseman (Eds.), *Early intervention and culture* (pp. 23–43). Paris: UNESCO.

Serpell, R. (1994a). Negotiating a fusion of horizons: A process view of cultural validation in developmental psychology, *Mind Culture and Activity, 1,* 43–68.

Serpell, R. (1994b, September). Beyond the mirage of enlightenment through literacy: curricular ideologies versus contextualized practices. In U. Frith, G. Lüdi, M. Egli, & C.-A. Zuber (Eds.), *Proceedings of the workshop on contexts of literacy, Vol. III: Network on written language and literacy* (pp. 17–45). Strasbourg: European Science Foundation.

Serpell, R. (1995). Situated theory as a bridge between experimental research and political analysis. In L. Martin, K. Nelson & E. Tobach (Eds.), *Cultural psychology and activity theory: Essays in honor of Sylvia Scribner* (pp. 21–42). New York: Cambridge University Press.

Serpell, R. & Boykin, A. W. (1994). Cultural dimensions of cognition: A multiplex, dynamic system of constraints and possibilities. In R. J. Sternberg (Ed.), *Handbook of Perception and Cognition, Vol. 12: Thinking and Problem-solving* (pp. 369–408). San Diego, CA: Academic Press.

Snelson, P. D. (1974). *Education development in Northern Rhodesia 1883–1945*. Lusaka: NEDCOZ.

Spence, J. (1985). Achievement American style: The rewards and costs of individualism. *American Psychologist, 40*,1285–1295.

Stevenson, H. W., Lee, S. Y., Stigler, J. W. (1986). Mathematics achievement of Chinese, Japanese, and American children. *Science, 231*, 693–699.

Stevenson, H. & Stigler, J. W. (1992). *The learning gap*. New York: Summit Books.

Stigler, J. W. & Perry, M. (1990). Mathematics learning in Japanese, Chinese, and American classrooms. In J. W. Stigler, R. A. Shweder, & G. Herdt (Eds.), *Cultural psychology: Essays on comparative human development* (pp. 328–353). New York: Cambridge University Press.

Street, B. (1984). *Literacy in theory and practice*. Cambridge: Cambridge University Press.

Sulzby, E. & Teale, W. (1991). Emergent literacy. In R. Barr, M. L. Kamil, P. Mosenthal, & P. D. Pearson (Eds.), *Handbook of reading research, Vol. II* (pp. 727–758). New York: Longman.

Tharp, R. (1989). Psychocultural variables and constants: Effects on teaching and learning in schools. *American Psychologist, 44*, 349–359.

Tharp, R. & Gallimore, R. (1988). *Rousing minds to life: Teaching, learning, and schooling in social context*. New York: Cambridge University Press.

Tharp, R. G., Jordan, C., Speidel, G. E., Av, K. H.-P., Klein, T. W., Calkins, R. P., Sloat, K. C. M., & Gallimore, R. (1984). Product and process in applied developmental research education and the children of a minority. In M. E. Lamb, A. L. Brown, & B. Rogoff (Eds.), *Advances in developmental psychology, Vol. 3* (pp. 9–141). Hillsdale, NJ: Erlbaum.

Thompson, R., Mixon, G., & Serpell, R. (1996).

Engaging minority students in reading: Focus on the urban learner. In L. Baker, P. Afflerbach, & D. Reinking (Eds.), *Developing engaged readers in school and home communities* (pp. 43–63). Hillsdale, NJ: Erlbaum.

Tignor, R. L. (1976). *The colonial transformation of Kenya*. Princeton, NJ: Princeton University Press.

Tobin, J. J., Wu, D. Y. H., & Davidson, D. H. (1989). *Preschool in three cultures: Japan, China, and the United States*. New Haven, CT: Yale University Press.

Umemoto, T. (1985). Teaching and learning methods in Japanese traditional music. In T. Umemoto, A. Nakahara, & U. Mabuchi (Eds.), *Apsaras* (pp. 177–190). Tokyo: Ongakunotomo-sha, 1985. [in Japanese].

Vaillant, J. G. (1990). *Black, French and African: A life of Leopold Sedan Senghor*. Cambridge, MA: Harvard University Press.

Valsiner, J. (1991). Introduction: Social co-construction of psychological development from a comparative-cultural perspective. In J. Valsiner (Ed.), *Child development within culturally structured environments, Vol. 3: Comparative-cultural and constructionist perspectives* (pp. 1–22). Norwood, NJ: Ablex.

Wagner, D. A. (1993a). *Literacy, culture, and development: Becoming literate in Morocco*. Cambridge: Cambridge University Press.

Wagner, D. A. (1993b). *Literacy: Developing the future*. UNESCO Yearbook of Education, Vol. 43. Paris.

Yamazumi, M. (1980). *The imperial rescript on education*. Tokyo: Asahi-Shinbunn-sha. [in Japanese].

Yorita, M. & Yamanaka, Y. (Eds.). (1993). *History of education in Japan*. Kyoto: Minerva-shobo. [in Japanese].

Zigler, E. & Finn-Stevenson, M. (1992). Applied developmental psychology. In M. H. Bornstein & M. E. Lamb (Eds.). *Developmental psychology: An advanced textbook* (pp. 677–729). Hillside, NJ: Erlbaum.

11

CHILDREN IN PARTICULARLY DIFFICULT CIRCUMSTANCES

LEWIS APTEKAR
San Jose State University
United States

DANIEL STÖCKLIN
University of Fribourg
Switzerland

Contents

Introduction

The children whom UNICEF (1986) refers to as "in particularly difficult circum stances" are those whose suffering entails the highest risk to mental health. They include children traumatized by war, or natural and technological disasters, and those living and working without parents (street children). Other children face especially difficult circumstances, either from extreme poverty, severe malnutrition, forced prostitution, labor exploitation, or excessive family violence. But we dwell on those cited by UNICEF, not only because they face such drastic circumstances, but also because of the role culture plays in forming their psychological reactions.

"Children in particularly difficult circumstances" can be a culturally misleading category. It is defined mainly by outsiders who view the children as passive targets of violence or abuse. But the cultural context may shape responses to extreme stress. The children's victimization cannot be measured in absolute terms. It is more than the degree to which they have been abused, neglected, or tortured. The significance the child attaches to the trauma, which in large part is mediated by cultural factors, also determines how the child responds. Children's resilience and vulnerability cannot be explained merely by individual differences in temperament. The literature on the psychology of children in particularly difficult circumstances has described diverse and often contradictory reactions to trauma, ranging from extreme and enduring psychopathology to improved mental health. This is largely because culture influences children's responses to trauma. The child's inner resources and the social context interact with each other (Kostelny & Garbarino, 1994; ICCB, 1995).

Events, experienced in one society as traumatic, may not be problematic in another. In certain parts of Kenya and Nigeria, for instance, children are force fed by their parents. This is accomplished by holding their nostrils shut and, as the children open their mouths gasping for air, pouring gruel down their throats. Loving parents are capable of such behavior because they see childrearing as a continual medical emergency (LeVine, 1980; LeVine & LeVine, 1981).

The question of why and how cultural factors impact a child's response to extreme trauma requires sustained investigation; research tools and paradigmatic choices influence results. Readers interested in pursuing cross-cultural research, and in knowing how programs have been evaluated in a cross-cultural context might want to consult MacPherson (1987) and Blanc (1994) for extreme poverty; Cassidy (1987) for severe malnutrition; Naversen (1989), and Bruce (1991) for child prostitution; Moorhead (1990a; 1990b), Myers (1991), and Weiner (1991) for labor exploitation; and Levinson (1989), Gelles & Cornell (1983), and Briere (1992) for excessive family violence.

Issues of cultural relativism cannot be divorced from the general study of child abuse. Abused children are victims of behaviors which inflict great harm, and intense pain or suffering. These behaviors raise questions about basic moral values, and possibly universal, or at least widespread, standards of human conduct toward children. Are there some childrearing practices that are universally reprehensible?

One concept of ideal childhood sees the child as innocent, in need of and deserving constant attention. To incorporate this concept of children across cultures, notably when asserting allegiance to the United Nations (U.N.) Convention on the Rights of the Child, poses problems, because the "best interests of the child" are defined almost entirely by adults, who may ignore the ties between the conception of rights, cultural values, and socioeconomic situations. In the first section we deal with the relativity of child abuse.

In the second section we define post-traumatic stress disorder (PTSD), particularly in assessing children's reactions to the extreme stress of war and disasters, and focus on three ways in which culture interacts with childrens' reactions to extreme stress. First, we discuss how culture mediates the possible range of child responses from post-traumatic stress disorder to a relatively benign reaction, and finally to actually improved mental health. Second, we focus on street children and show how they use culture to cope. Street children are not passively exposed to cultural factors. Rather, they actively use their knowledge of the sociocultural environment to turn dismal circumstances into opportunities. They are capable of coping precisely because they are active and skilled in using cultural factors to their advantage. Third, in discussing the violence against street children, we show the effects of cultural stigmatization. In the third section, we focus on research issues and discuss potential methodological problems stemming from personal biases, which can be quite poignant when working with children in particularly difficult circumstances. We also illustrate research problems associated with the cross-cultural nature of the work, and with specific logistical difficulties of studying these children.

Ultimately, there is the question of applicability. What value is research in helping children in need? Are there cultural factors that constrain or facilitate the transfer of research into policy and practice? For example, because we consider street children as social actors, and not as passive recipients of abuse or neglect, new views of programmatic and policy applications emerge.

Child Abuse or Cultural Differences?

The United Nations Convention on the Rights of the Child has incorporated into international law the inalienable rights of all children (Queloz, 1988; Vittachi, 1986). In the process, a difficult set of questions has emerged. Principle 6 states that, "The child for the full and harmonious development of his personality, needs love and understanding. He shall, wherever possible, grow up in the care and under the responsibility of his parents, and in any case in an atmosphere of affection and of moral and material security. . . . Society and the public authorities shall have the duty to extend particular care to children without a family and to those without adequate means of support" (Ennew & Milne, 1989, p. 45). And, Principle 10 states that, "The child shall be protected from practices which may foster racial, religious and any other forms of discrimination. He shall be brought up in a spirit of understanding, tolerance, friendship among peoples, peace and universal brotherhood. . . ." (Ennew & Milne, 1989, p. 77). These are lofty and important principles, but their cross-cultural application is quite complicated.

On the most fundamental level, the definition of childhood must be quantified in order to address any of the individual principles. For example, at what age should children be given adult responsibilities? There are many instances of what appears to be unusually harsh forms of training for early independence in the developing world. Many ten-year-old street children are quite capable of earning a living, and taking care of their basic needs, yet they are not given the privileges and responsibilities of adults (Aptekar, 1994b).

There are also problems in applying the principles of children's rights in developed countries. The United States, for example, is out of compliance with international law, because it adjudicates "children," that is, individuals under the age of 18, as adults (Cohen & Davidson, 1990). This can lead to minors spending a good portion of their lives in jail. To many cultures of the developing world, this might appear as unusually harsh treatment for children.

Another question, posed by the cross-cultural application of the Convention, concerns the point at which a child is considered to be human (i.e., the point at which life begins). In some societies, infants are not considered human until their first cry (see Segall, Ember & Ember, Volume 3, this *Handbook*). Letting them die before this time is not considered infanticide (Wagatsuma, 1981). In China, the state has condoned killing infants in times of famine. The reason given to parents is that the well-being of the state (which cannot afford too many children during famine) is more important than the parents' personal well-being (Potter & Potter, 1987; Wu, 1981). Although these examples are abhorrent to many North Americans and Europeans, it is perhaps appropriate to point out that many people view abortion as murder, even though it has legal sanction in some cultures.

In fact, stringent compliance with the Convention can result in blaming parents for child abuse, instead of addressing the causes that bring parents to make what is often a rational, but abhorrent choice. It might, for example, be difficult to understand why some poor mothers in Brazil let some of their children starve to death. But when one considers, as these mothers do, that this practice increases the possibility of survival for the majority of family members, the decision becomes more difficult to condemn (Scheper-Hughes, 1987). Many other examples, where behaviors can be considered abusive from an "outsider's" perspective have been reported (Bonnet, 1993; Breiner, 1990; Hausfater & Hardy, 1984; Hausweld, 1987; Johansson, 1984; Korbin, 1981a, 1981b; Langer, 1983; Langness, 1981; Oliver & Reardon, 1982; Olson, 1981; Poffenberger, 1981; Ritchie & Ritchie, 1981; Rushwan, 1984). Even seemingly panhuman terms, such as "maternal protection," "critical periods," "attachment" and "bonding," have been described as ethnocentric pseudo-biological descriptions by Scheper-Hughes and Stein (1987) and de Vries (1987b).

Cultural factors must also be accounted for in describing an abusive person. In a worldwide study of malnutrition, Cassidy (1987) found that where parents could not afford to give all their children full care, many parents concentrated their resources only on a few. One interpretation sees the behavior as a way of adapting to shortage of resources, and judges the mother's behavior as abusive because of the immediate consequences to the child. A longer term view can see her behavior as less abusive by taking into account the desire to maintain the survival of the lineage even at the expense of a particular child. Of course, neither view is acceptable, but the parent's behavior illustrates different cultural values, and shows that decisions although abhorrent cannot be described solely as abusive.

Until recently the profile of a child abuser in the developed world was considerably different from that in the developing world (Korbin, 1987). In the first instance, child abusers were associated with mental disorders and abuse involved deliberate attempts to hurt the child. (See Kempe & Kempe [1983] for a description of the battered child syndrome in developed countries, and Wolfner & Gelles [1993], for a profile of battering parents in the developed world.) In developing countries, this type of child abuser was not found. Recently, however, there has been evidence from New Guinea (Townsend, 1985), Zambia (Mumba, 1981), and Nigeria (Okeahialam, 1984) to suggest that child abuse, comparable to the battered child syndrome, is beginning to emerge in less developed countries.

Rohner and Rohner (1980) have pointed out that worldwide, cultural factors are more important than personal factors in determining child abuse and neglect. Abuse and neglect are more likely in cultures (1) that resist family planning and thus have an abundance of unwanted children, (2) where there are no caretakers besides the children's parents, (3) where there is lack of the fathers' involvement in childrearing, and (4) where families are not connected to their community. This is not to say that two-parent families engaged in community affairs, who have one wanted child and extra caretakers to care for the child will not abuse their children. It does point out the cultural specificity of this profile, and places the relative degree to which this form of abuse occurs in context.

In view of such difficulties in applying the United Nations Convention on the Rights of the Child, a cross-cultural schema is needed to help develop hypotheses about childrearing practices that would include child abuse definitions across cultures. This is no easy task, in large part because these differences are deeply embedded in a culture's moral framework, which includes harsh judgments against parents who allegedly abuse their children.

So far we have considered how cultural variations in individual care given to children can be interpreted as abusive. However, in some situations child abuse stems from state pressures or political conflicts. In these cases abuse comes under state authority, and its justification comes mainly from the abusers. The abuse described earlier may involve culturally adaptive practices, for instance, in Cassidy's example about malnutrition, but how can abuse be justified when the aim is maintenance of privileged positions of state power?

Invoking the "superior interests of the state" often leads to the most painful dilemmas regarding childrearing. During the "Dirty War" in Argentina, children were tortured in front of their parents in order to motivate the parents to offer information to the state (Suarez-Orozco, 1987). Some children of these suspected dissidents were taken away from their parents by the state and placed in families who supported the regime (Hilton, 1990). Years later, the grandmothers of the surviving "foster" children pressured the new government to have their grandchildren returned. Should the state separate these children from the only people they had known as caretakers, even though the children were not with their biological parents (Lykes and Liem, 1990)? A similar situation of forced "fostering" occurred in Switzerland up to 1950 with Gipsy children.

During the recent war between Iraq and Iran, Iranian children willingly marched to the head of the front lines in order to trip the mines that were planted there. Their actions saved a large number of adults who would fight the infidels. The children's behavior was condoned by the state and the children were given the status of religious martyrs (Boothby, 1986). Would it, however, be an exaggeration to conclude that there can be total agreement between cultural groups on whether this behavior was abusive? Or, is this behavior reprehensible no matter what the circumstances?

The importance of the State in defining childhood is also evident in the case of China's one-child policy. Children born to families that exceeded the permitted birth quotas were "out-of-plan," and amounted to nearly 40 percent of the annual births (Stöcklin, 1992). Yet, by virtue of the state's policy, they should not officially exist (Bianco & Hua, 1989). Hidden by parents who feared sanctions, many remained unregistered and deprived of social services (Li & Ballweg, 1994). Children in orphanages and begging on the streets are mostly girls. Research is being conducted to determine the extent to which unregistered children entered a life of marginality and abuse (Stöcklin, 1993). Thus, in China, child abuse is based in institutional pressures (population control) defining what is a good child (planned) and a bad child (unplanned). Hence, the U.N. Convention on children's rights may not only be facing the problems of cultural variations or political domination, but also the adverse combinations of cultural and structural elements. While a child's birth may be positively desired by Chinese parents, it is simultaneously defined by the State in stigmatizing terms (Thireau, 1989). As a result of the one-child policy, the gender distribution of children has been modified; female infanticide and differential abortion have both increased (Aird, 1990; Hull, 1990).

Post-Traumatic Stress Disorder: Children's Reactions to Extreme Stress

Certain psychopathological reactions to extreme stress have been classified as post-traumatic stress disorder (PTSD). Imagine Franisse, a six-year-old Mozambiquan boy. Before being kidnapped by a soldier, he was made to light the match that set his family's hut ablaze. When his mother and father ran out of the house, he was forced to watch as the soldiers cut their heads off. Franisse had the typical PTSD reactions, which included recurrent and intrusive dreams and daytime thoughts of what had happened, intense discomfort when experiencing anything similar again, and avoidance of stimuli which brought up any memory of those incidents. His mind, in short, was captured by memory, overwhelmingly expressed at certain moments, completely underground at other times (Richman, Kanji, & Zinkin, 1988).

In case of a single severe trauma, a child like Franisse must learn to readjust to the fact that the world is no longer benign, or predictable. Yet, the most damaging factor to children's mental health is not a single horrible event, but multiple stressors (Cohn, Holzer, Koch & Severin, 1980; Klingman, Sagi, & Raviv, 1993; Randal & Boustany, 1990; Ressler, Tortoricci, & Marcelino, 1993; Straker & Moosa, 1988; Terr, 1991; Toner, 1994; Zahava, 1988). Take the example of a 14-year-old black South African boy. In six weeks he experienced the murder of an important adult mentor, the bombing and total destruction of his home, a violent police raid of his neighborhood, exile from his community, and arrest and assault by police (Straker, 1991). In this situation he not only learned, like Franisse, that happiness is unreliable but he was also faced with the more difficult problem of losing a sense of justice, becoming simultaneously pessimistic about the future and yearning for an overly romanticized fictionalized past. Over repeated severe trauma, the person gives up hope, cannot live in the present, and becomes captive to obtrusive thoughts about the past and the future, neither of which bring resolution or peace.

The fourth edition of the Diagnostic Statistical Manual (DSM-4) of the American Psychiatric Association (1994) is the definitive classification of mental disorders in the developed world. The International Statistical Classification of Diseases and Related Health Problems (ICD) is a World Health Organization publication (1992) and serves as the definitive source for the developing world. The two reference works are compatible with one another. In either source, there is little information to distinguish different psychological reactions to single and multiple trauma. This itself is a cultural bias, because multiple traumatic events are considerably more likely to occur in the developing world, where war and disaster are common. Of the 127 wars, including civil conflicts from the end of the Second World War to 1989, all but two occurred in the developing world. Over 21 million people, a large percentage of whom were children, were killed (MacPherson, 1987). During the 1980s, a million and a half children were killed as a result of armed conflicts, almost all in the developing world (UNICEF, 1990b). Likewise, although extreme environmental events occur in all parts of the world, 95 percent of human loss from environmental disasters occur in the developing world (Aptekar, 1994a; Kent, 1987; Seitz & Davis, 1984; Shah, 1983).

Children's reactions to extreme trauma(s) are age related, and can generally be categorized into two age groups: (1) early childhood (roughly between 4 and 8 years of age), (2) childhood and early adolescence (approximately between 9 and 14 years of age) (Aptekar & Boore, 1990). Children's reactions also demonstrate many cognitive changes. They become pessimistic about the future. They repeatedly tell the story of what has happened to them without any apparent sign of emotion. They develop "omens," which are irrational thoughts devised to provide some logic to the illogical trauma they have experienced. These characteristics have been shown to occur in several cultures (see Table 11–1).

Like adults, older children with PTSD also experience intrusive thoughts of the trauma, rumination over the occurrence of another stressor, phobic avoidance of events that remind the child of the trauma, and psychic numbness. When 450 Ugandan children, two-thirds of whom had experienced the death of a parent or close relative, were asked to write essays about the time they spent under the Amin regime, they wrote with very little emotion, as if everyday life was as common as it had been before the war (Dodge & Raundalen, 1987). The same finding comes from children in Mozambique, where as many as three-quarters of the children had witnessed murder, physical torture, and rape, and more than half had been tortured themselves (de Maistre & de Maistre, 1992; McCallin, 1992b).

Older children with PTSD manifest an increased amount of symptoms unique to their developmental level, such as psychosomatic conversions, sleep disturbances (including terrifying dreams seemingly unrelated to the event), and an increase in aggression, delinquency, and alcohol and drug abuse. These findings come from cross-national and cross-disaster studies, and include single as well as repeated traumas (see Table 11–2).

TABLE 11–1   Studies finding PTSD in early childhood

Author	Type of trauma	Place of study
Punamaki (1982)	war	Palestine
Eth & Pynoos (1985a; 1985b)	war and community violence	cross-cultural
Chikane (1986)	community violence	South Africa
Raphael (1986)	natural disaster	Australia
Chimienti, Nasr & Khalief (1989)	war	Lebanon
Lima, Pai, Lozano & Santacruz (1990)	natural disaster	Colombia
Yule & Williams (1990)	ship disaster	United Kingdom
Bat-Zion & Levy-Shiff (1993)	war	Israel and Palestine
Magwaza, Killian, Peterson & Pillay (1993)	community violence	South Africa

TABLE 11–2   Studies finding PTSD in childhood and early adolescence

Author	Type of trauma	Effects	Place of study
Punamaki (1982)	war	increased delinquency	Palestine
Grinberg & Grinberg (1984)	war refugees	increased delinquency	Central America
Hussain (1984)	war	psychosomatization	Vietnam
Frederick (1985)	natural & techno-nologic disasters	sleep disturbance & increased delinquency	USA
McHan (1985)	war	increased delinquency	Lebanon
Galante & Foa (1986)	earthquake	increased delinquency	Italy
Handford et al. (1986)	technologic disaster	sleep disturbance	USA
Rayhida, Shaya & Armenian (1986)	war	cognitive pessimism	Lebanon
Mollica, Wyshak & Lavelle (1987)	war refugees	increased violence	South-Eastern Asia
Mahjoub, Leyes, Yzerbyt & de Giacomo (1989)	war	psychosomatization	Palestine
Martin-Boro (1989)	war	psycho-social deterioration	El Salvador
Ronstrom (1989)	war	sleep disturbance	Central America
Baker (1991)	war	psychosomatization	Palestine
de Maistre & de Maistre (1992)	war	psychic numbness	Mozambique
Garbarino, Kostelny & Dubrow (1992)	war refugees	increased delinquency	cross-cultural
McCallin (1992a; 1992b)	war refugees	psychosomatization	South-Eastern Asia
Cicchetti & Lynch (1993)	community violence	increased delinquency	USA
Liddell, Kemp & Moema (1993)	community violence	increased delinquency	South Africa
Masalha (1993)	war	increased aggression	Palestine
Richters & Martinez (1993)	community violence	increased delinquency	USA
Simpson (1993)	community violence	increased delinquency	South Africa

Culture as a Mediating Variable: Non-Pathological Reactions to Extreme Trauma

Contrary to the above findings, there is considerable evidence to suggest that many children do not develop PTSD (see Table 11–3).

There are several potential explanations for these conflicting results, for example, issues of assessment. It is difficult to ascertain the differences between PTSD and non-pathological reactions to extreme trauma, because the symptoms are similar but differ in duration and intensity (Wilkenson & Vera, 1985; Wortman, 1983;

TABLE 11–3   Studies not finding PTSD following trauma

Author	Type of trauma	Effects	Place of study
Mc Whirter, Young & Majury (1983)	war	adjustment to continual violence	Ireland
Rosenblatt (1983)	war	higher moral standard	Ireland
Williams & Westermeyer (1983)	war refugees	resilience	South-Eastern Asia
Boothby (1986)	war	resilience	Ireland
Coles (1986)	community violence	improved mental health	USA
Lorenc & Brantwaite (1986)	war	no increased violence	Northern Ireland
Dodge & Raundalen (1987)	war	improved mental health	Uganda
Gibson (1987; 1989)	community violence	participation reduced stress	South Africa
Punamaki (1988; 1989)	war	active coping reduced stress	Palestine
Cairns & Wilson (1989)	war	effective use of denial	Ireland
Baker (1990; 1991)	war	increased self-esteem	Palestine
Dawes (1990)	community violence	no increased violence	South Africa
Rouhana (1989)	war	improved mental health	Palestine
Garbarino, Kostelny & Dubrow (1991a; 1991b; 1992)	war/community violence	enhanced sense of morality	cross-cultural
Cairns & Toner (1993)	war	coped well with stress	Ireland
Dawes, Tredoux & Feinstein (1993)	community violence	less than 10% had PTSD	South Africa
Cohn & Goodwin-Gil (1993)	war	active better than passive	cross-cultural

Wortman & Silver, 1989). Also, the symptoms of healthy stress have different cultural manifestations. For example, the degree to which denial, the use of which is helpful to some children facing overwhelming events, is tolerated varies widely among cultures (Arroyo & Eth, 1985; Cairns & Wilson, 1989; Harbison, 1983; Horowitz, 1993; Pynoos & Eth, 1984, 1985).

Further, it is difficult to differentiate between the causes and the effects of trauma. In Uganda, researchers were not able to determine if the violence from the Amin era caused parents to be unsupportive of their children (because parents only had the energy to care for themselves), or if the children's post-traumatic responses to the Amin terror stressed their parents to such a degree that parental effectiveness was reduced (Dodge, 1990; Dyregrov & Raundalen, 1987). Punamaki (1989) faced the same dilemma in her study on the West Bank.

Several personality variables that are confounded with cultural factors could account for the lack of PTSD. Temperament, assumed to be predominantly biological, was found to be a significant moderator to children's response to war and other extreme trauma (Elbedour, Ten Besel, & Bastien, 1993; Wertleib, Weigel, Springer, & Feldstein, 1990). Temperament has different effects on parents in various cultures. In most developed countries, difficult-to-care-for children are more likely to be abused (Finklehor, 1985; Muller, Caldwell, & Hunter, 1993), but among the Masaai (de Vries, 1987a) and among the poor of northeastern Brazil (Scheper-Hughes, 1987), the more demanding child is more likely to be attended to, while the less demanding child is deemed more self-sufficient and is left alone.

Different levels of pre-traumatic functioning might also contribute to the discrepant findings. Resilient children are better able than non-resilient children to understand, make sense of, and respond without psychopathology to stressful situations (Anthony & Cohler, 1987; Garmezy, 1983, 1986; Losel & Bliesener, 1990; Losel, Bliesener & Korferl, 1990; Rutter, 1986; Weisaeth & Eitinger, 1993; Werner, 1990; Williams & Westermeyer, 1983; Yuder, 1992). Yet, resilient behaviors, which are considered stoic or self-indulgent in one culture, have different meanings in another. Examples might include the degree to which a child withholds or expresses emotion, and which emotions can or cannot be expressed. In one culture these behaviors might imply insight, while in another, they could indicate self-indulgence. In one culture, a reaction might imply independence and initiative, and in another culture, it might suggest disrespect and brashness.

Another pre-traumatic personality factor is a person's belief system. One cross-cultural study compared children of different ideological commitments who were victimized by violence in the inner city of Chicago, in the West Bank, and in Israel. The study found that among the African-Americans in Chicago, it was the militant Black Muslims who coped best with stress. Similarly, the militant Hamas on the West Bank and the extreme Zionists in Israel suffered least from stress related to armed conflict (Garbarino, Kostelny, & Dubrow, 1991b). Ideological commitment plays an important role in determining individual response to trauma. However, strong ideological commitment can also prevent compromise (Cutting, 1988; Punamaki, 1988). Protestant and Catholic children in Northern Ireland, who were ready for peace, were prevented from it when their parents did not permit a more reasoned view of the opposition (Conroy, 1987; Hosin & Cairns, 1984).

The degree to which they have overcome stress in the past also contributes to whether or not children in particularly difficult circumstances will develop PTSD to current trauma. Continual stress on Israeli children living in civil war helped them prepare for future stress (Breznitz, 1983). As the conflict in Lebanon wore on, children (and their mothers) were more affected by the long lines, shortages of food and water, difficulty of getting clothes, and finding medical and social services than they were by the war itself (Bryce, Walker, & Peterson, 1989). After a few years of the trouble in Northern Ireland, children became more upset by fights in their families than they did by the fighting in the streets (McWhirter, Young, & Majury, 1983). Other studies also point to the importance of habituation (Klingman, 1992; McWhirter & Trew, 1982; Punamaki, 1982).

The most researched explanation for the lack of PTSD among traumatized children concerns the ability of parents to support their children. One cross-cultural study of children in war found that "most children can cope with horrible experiences and high levels of stress if they have a secure relationship with parents, or effective substitutes, and if these adults themselves can continue to function as sources of support and encouragement (Garbarino, Kostelny, & Dubrow, 1991a, p. xxi)." Similar findings come from many other studies (see Table 11–4). Reviews which include cross-cultural information on the value of a positive parental or adult attachment in mediating the effects of extreme stress can be found in Garmezy and Rutter (1985), Hobfoll et al. (1991), Ressler, Boothby and Steinbock (1988), and Saylor (1993).

In contrast, two studies of children in war (Dubrow & Garbarino, 1989; Punamaki, 1989), a study of children who witnessed the murder of one or both of their parents (Malmquist, 1986), and an in-depth longitudinal study of kidnapped children (Terr, 1990), suggest that even strong parental support cannot erase the horror of severe trauma.

Similar to the ameliorative effects of parental presence are studies showing that community support reduces the number of psychopathological reactions. These studies suggest that cultural factors, such as common ideological values, and shared in-group attitudes and out-group hostilities, help relieve stress. The data come from a wide variety of studies on various stressors and nations (see Table 11–5). However, cases of negative consequences of community support have also been reported. In the Israel–Lebanon war of 1982 community support actually reduced the family's ability to cope (Hobfoll & London, 1986). The authors attributed this to the tightly-knit networks within the community which helped to pass along vague information, and increased hearsay that added to anxiety. Reviews on the effects of community support in war can be found in Eisenbruch (1988), Garbarino, Kostelny and Dubrow (1991b), and Saylor (1993).

Cross-culturally, a common theme that runs through the data on children who escape PTSD when faced with severe trauma is that action is more rewarding than inaction, particularly when action is associated with a "cause." Under these circumstances, participation in even horrendous events can reduce children's feel-

TABLE 11–4   The ameliorative effect of family

Author	Stressor	Country
Boman & Edwards (1984)	refugees	Indochina
Lystad (1984)	disasters	developed world
Benedek (1985)	disasters	developed world
Bryce (1986)	war	Lebanon
Kinzie, Sack, Angell, Manson & Rath (1986)	refugees	Cambodian in USA
Sack, Angell, Kinzie & Rath (1986)	refugees	Cambodian in USA
Tsoi, Yu, & Lieh-Mak (1986)	refugees	Vietnamese in Hong Kong
Allodi (1989)	refugees	Latin America
Mahjoub, Leyes, Yzerbyt & de Giacomo (1989)	war	Palestine
McCallin & Fozzard (1990)	war refugees	Mozambique
McFarlane (1990)	natural disaster	Australia
Garbarino, Kostelny & Dubrow (1991a; 1992)	war refugees & community violence	cross-cultural
Ajudukovic & Ajudukovic (1993)	refugees	Croatia
Zeidner, Klingman & Itzkovitz (1993)	war	Israel

ings of helplessness and give them a sense of power and purpose. Examples come from Palestinian children who participated in the Intifada, black South African children who opposed apartheid, children who fought in the "troubles" of Northern Ireland, and children in Central America and Africa who were ideologically committed to changing their political situations (Garbarino, Kostelny & Dubrow, 1991a). Some African-American children living in violent political circumstances adjusted by developing a high standard of moral reasoning, in large part, by seeing what was inappropriate and taking action against it (Coles, 1986). For similar reasons the mental health of street children who left abusive or neglectful homes also improved (Aptekar, 1988c; Swart, 1990b). These studies suggest that it is not just the type or degree of violence a child experiences that determines his or her psychological response. Specific cultural details mediate even the horrendous events children in particularly difficult circumstances face.

TABLE 11–5   The ameliorative effect of community support

Author	Stressor	Country
Oliver-Smith (1977)	avalanche	Peru
Gleser, Green & Winget (1981)	flood	USA
Milgram (1982)	war	Israel
Breznitz (1983)	war	Israel
Golec (1983)	disaster	USA
Kaffman & Elizur (1983)	war	Israel
Raviv & Klingman (1983)	war	Israel
Shisana & Celentano (1987)	war	Namibia
Ayalon & Van Tasel (1987)	war	Israel
Protacio-Marcelino (1989)	civil confllict	Phillipines
Soloman (1989)	disaster	USA

Using Culture as a Coping Strategy: The Example of Street Children

UNICEF (1990a) estimated that in 1980 there were 369 million poor children under age fifteen in the cities of the developing world. Almost all of these children worked and most of them gave what they earned to their parents (Boyden, 1991; Cervini & Burger, 1991; Ennew, 1986; Myers, 1991). Working children living with and contributing to their families (children on the streets) and street children who do not live with adults and who support themselves (children of the street) are often not differentiated. This is because statistics are compiled by visual observations (both groups wear less than tailored clothes and are not perfectly clean) rather than by in-depth study of factors that could lead to determining living conditions. The result is highly inflated estimates of the number of reported street children. For many years, UNICEF held that there were 100 million street children in the world (UNICEF 1985). Estimates for Latin America alone reached between 40 and 50 million street children (Holinsteiner & Tacon, 1983; Ortiz & Poertner, 1992). These numbers would mean that more than 45 percent of all Latin America's children are street children (Ennew, 1986)! Interested readers should see Alves (1991), Lucchini (1993), and Yopo (1989), for more accurate and less dramatizing information about the prevalence of street children.

The public is alarmed by the inflated numbers of street children, and concerned by several hypotheses that have been advanced to explain street children's origins (Baizerman, 1988; Boyden, 1990). One hypothesis relates to urban poverty, which allegedly leads to a breakdown of families and moral values. A second hypothesis concerns aberrant families who abandon, abuse, or neglect their children. A third hypothesis is associated with adverse effects of modernization, including the breakdown of family values (Agnelli, 1986; de Galan, 1981; Kilbride & Kilbride, 1990; Mishra, 1989; Munoz & Pachon, 1980; Rizzini & Rizzini, 1991; Subrahmanyam & Sondhi, 1990; Suda, 1993).

The majority of research defines street children according to only two dimensions: the time spent in the street, and the absence of contact with responsible adults (Vanistendael, 1987). Yet, the child's subjective experience is essential to understand what it means to be a street child. It is only possible to appreciate street children's survival strategies by examining the social relations among street children and between them and society (Lucchini, 1993; Visano, 1990). When the child's perspective is taken into account, the children emerge as social actors, who develop a specific "microculture" that emerges from balancing what they need to survive and the widespread cultural values often impinging upon them. Grasping the street child's subjective sense of being in the street is quite important to understand him or her, and to improve social work with them (Lucchini, 1993, 1996; Williams,1993).

Using children's subjective experiences also breaks down the monolithic cultural view that presents street children mainly as victims or as delinquents ready for re-education (Combier, 1994; Pirenne, 1989; Poloni, 1994). The objective perspective has fallen into the trap of ethnocentric assumptions. Descriptive works relying on patient and detailed analysis of children's accounts can help to understand current prejudices (see Table 11–6). Several common assumptions have become erroneously accepted, for example, that there was little difference between street and poor working children, that the street children had inferior mental health than their poor counterparts who stay at home, and that most street children have been abandoned.

Rather than being abandoned, street children almost always leave home in an intentional manner, initially staying away for a night or two, then step by step, spending more time away from home. Gradually the amount of time they spend with other children increases. Yet, contrary to common belief, they rarely break family ties completely. As many as 90 percent of street children maintain contact with their families, and most of them contribute to family income.

Many studies illustrate the positive characteristics of street children. Even though there is some empirical evidence to suggest that the children succumb to abuse and neglect, other work has documented psychologically resilient coping strategies. In fact, the mental health of street children (particularly street boys) is better understood when their situation is seen as enabling early independence, empowerment, and familial responsibility. Similar views of the street children's mental health have been found in many places (see Table 11–6).

The claim that street children have inadequate mental health is difficult to support by research, while the claim that they have adequate mental health is difficult for the populace to accept. (A similar situation exists for these children's families who are seen quite negatively by the public, but who according to empirical studies function considerably better than the popular perceptions). Negative

TABLE 11–6   Studies of street children contradicting popular assumptions

Author	Results	Country
Tacon (1982)	less than 10% abandoned	Latin America
Boyden (1986)	only 3% abandoned	Peru
Scharf, Powell & Thomas (1986)	leaving home improved mental health	South Africa
Espinola, Glauser, Ortiz, Ortiz de Carrizosa (1987; 1990)	better mental health than thought	Paraguay
Aptekar (1988a, 1988b; 1988c)	gradual move to the streets, do not break family ties, better mental health than poor counterparts	Colombia
Felsman (1989)	only 3% abandoned, do not break family ties, better mental health than poor counterparts	Colombia
Hickson & Gaydon (1989)	act of going to the streets improved mental health	South Africa
Lusk, Peralta & Vest (1989)	do not break family ties	Mexico
Valverde & Lusk (1989)	do not break family ties	Costa Rica
Connolly (1990)	gradual move to the street, living better in the streets than at home	Colombia, Guatemala
Ojanuga (1990)	contribute earning to their families	Nigeria
Swart (1990a; 1990b)	as wide a range of personality as found in broad population, eat better and have less abuse on streets, going to the streets improves mental health	South Africa
Tyler, Tyler, Echeverry & Zea (1991)	high degree of autonomy and empowerment	Colombia
Jansen, Richter & Griesel (1992)	less drug abuse	South Africa
Lusk (1992)	better mental health than thought	Brazil
Oliveira, Baizerman & Pellet (1992)	many positive coping strategies	Brazil
Rosa, de Sousa & Ebrahim (1992)	contribute 90% of earning to family	Brazil
Veale (1992)	no evidence of deviance	Ethiopia
Wright, Kaminsky & Wittig (1993)	less malnutrition among street children	Honduras
Lucchini (1993)	high degree of autonomy, gradual move to the street	Brazil
Campos et al. (1994)	do not break family ties	Brazil
Donald & Swart-Kruger (1994)	children's health is not easily reducible to vulnerability or resilience	South Africa
Lucchini (1996)	maintain family connections	Uruguay

and largely inaccurate portrayals of mental health are seen in relation to the children's alleged drug addiction (Chadwick, 1991; Esterle, 1991; Medina-Mora, 1987; Ortiz, 1988), the amount of violence between and toward street children, the extent of their involvement in sex, and the prevalence of HIV among them (Peerun, 1994; Raffaelli et al., 1993). Most of these pejorative claims do not come from empirical research; in fact, empirical findings are considerably more positive. (For a detailed analysis of these discrepancies see Ennew [1994] and Glauser [1990].) There are at least two reasons for these discrepancies. One is connected to the cultural factors that define appropriate behavior for children, and the other to the public perception of street children, which is, in large part, dependent upon the way they are portrayed in the press.

Culture as a Stigmatizing Factor: Violence against Street Children

Families who produce street children are likely to be composed of three generations of women, often living together in the same house (Aptekar, 1988a, 1988b). Only seven percent of the street children, in a Jamaican study, had two-parent families (Brown, 1987), and 85 percent of the "parking boys" of Nairobi were brought up by a single parent in a female-headed family (Wainaina, 1981). Swart (1990b) reported that more than a third of South African street children had no information of their biological fathers.

It is not surprising that the male children in impoverished families are encouraged to begin working and contributing to family income at an early age. In short, young boys often fulfill the roles of adult men. Because street children are perceived as uncontrollable, and because they come from families with no male authority, public functionaries (who themselves often come from two-parent families with unequal gender rights and strong reliance on male authority) tend to treat street children with disdain and hostility.

Violence toward street children is also related to class and cultural differences. The elite and the masses in Latin America, for example, have different family traditions. Among the elite Latin American homes, fathers are present and powerful. Boys learn to respect their authority. In contrast, among the poor in Latin America, it is common to have women at the center of the families. Boys are raised not so much to respect authority as for an early independence from home. Much of the negative attitude toward street children in Latin America comes from the ethnocentric perception that street children are not beholden to proper adult authority (Aptekar, 1992).

Almost every study of street children, despite cultural variation, concludes that the children's greatest fear is not of going hungry or of missing the security of their family, but of police brutality (see Table 11–7). Street children have reason to fear hostility. For example, between 1987 and 1990 alone there were 1,397 violent deaths of Brazilian street children (Swart, 1990a). In fact, the total number of street children killed in Brazil has exceeded the casualties in the civil war in Lebanon (Leite & Esteves, 1991).

TABLE 11–7   Studies documenting hostility toward street children

Author	Country
Patel (1983; 1990)	India
Pereira (1985)	Brazil
McLaghlan (1986)	South Africa
Randall (1988)	London
AIDSWATCH (1989a)	Colombia
AIDSWATCH (1989b)	Brazil
Aptekar (1988b; 1994b)	Latin America, cross-cultural
Dimenstein (1990)	Brazil
Swart (1990b)	South Africa
Leite & Esteves (1991)	Brazil
Verma & Dhingra (1993)	India

One approach to understanding violence toward street children is to look at the societies that have street children, but have not reacted with such hostility toward them. This approach would investigate cross-cultural differences in attitudes toward street children. There appears, for example, to be less violence toward street children in Ethiopia and Sudan (than in any place in Latin America), where children feel that the current regime has treated them with kindness (Lalor, et al., 1992). Another approach that could be used to understand the violence toward street children is to look for cross-cultural constants. In Latin America, it has been suggested that the police are hired to get rid of street children by local shopkeepers, who perceive the children's presence to be a threat for their business (AIDSWATCH, 1989b; Dimenstein, 1990). In Kenya, semi-private policemen were hired by local business people to "take care" of the street children problem (Aptekar, Cathey, Ciano & Guardino, in press). And, in South Africa, the commercial sector advocated that street children be removed from the streets (Swart, 1990b).

It would also be worthwhile to examine cross-culturally why street children are described as being delinquent, worthy, or pitiful, but not as having PTSD. Not only would this lead to understanding the cultural values inherent in the definition of PTSD, but it might also lead to understanding why these children receive such hostility.

Whatever the method taken to research violence toward street children, it is clear that their inaccurate profile, the inaccurate perception of their relationship to the much larger group of working children, the pejorative descriptions of their families, and the children's alleged psychopathology are all influenced by cultural factors and ethnocentric or egocentric moral values. While the level of hostility varies among cultures, the primary source of hostility (the police and the petite bourgeoisie) appears to be constant across cultures (Aptekar, 1994b). Cross-cultural comparisons could help explain and hopefully reduce the degree of violence the children face.

Research Issues in Cross-Cultural Perspective

Garbarino (1993) articulated risks for observers of children involved in war. The first is to be overly objective. One could avoid emotion and be purely descriptive. He rejected this when he stood under the tree that soldiers in the Pol Pot regime used to bash in the heads of the enemy's children. The second risk is to respond with too much emotion and fail to grasp the complexity of the intellectual issues. One might fail to elucidate the multiplicity of reactions to different degrees of trauma.

These two potential risks are sometimes enhanced by the public and by the international organizations that serve children. The public wants to hear worse-case scenarios or unusual cases of ingenuity rather than typical situations. Reporters, eager to find readers, follow the public's lead. Thus the press is more likely to publish feature articles than objective news. International organizations seeking funding use their publications to make a case for financial allocations. They rely on showing the youngest, the most drug dependent, the most violent, and the most traumatized. Even though these groups are motivated by high ideals and perform excellent services, they can contribute to the existing biases against the children (Felsman, 1989; Ennew, 1994; Tyler, Tyler, Echeverry, & Zea, 1991).

Most research on children in particularly difficult circumstances holds a conception of childhood which is overly idealistic and ethnocentric. The ideal child (who is also seen as typical) is conceived as carefree, playful, and innocent. (In contrast to the adult who is worried, serious, and duplicitous). Few children in the developing world, because their lives are far from carefree, could be included in the idealized category of childhood. Does this mean that they are children in particularly difficult circumstances? This contributes to the widely differing demographic data about the numbers of children in particularly difficult circumstances.

There are several additional problems related to doing research with children in particularly difficult circumstances. First, there are larger cross-cultural methodological problems, such as defining the independent variable without cultural bias, the use of culturally free data collection instruments, and the difficulty of equating language, cognitive, and perceptual stimuli across cultures (Mileti, 1987; Segall, 1983). There is also the fact that almost all of the data come from the United States and other developed countries. Of the 297 references from a U.S. National Institute of Mental Health bibliography on natural disasters and mental health only thirteen deal with less developed countries (Ahearn & Cohen, 1984). Further, in many cases, agency personnel producing agency "research" documents do not have research training or experience. Invalid information is often passed along as "scientific fact" (Wagner, 1986).

The more the children are studied in their natural habitat, the more difficult it will be to have the type of control to which empirical research aspires (Saraswathi & Dutta, 1988). Collecting data is difficult in times of war and natural disasters because the infrastructure (schools, hospitals, child care institutions, etc.) is disrupted or destroyed. Some researchers like to use archival data, but in many developing countries, there is almost no preexisting archival database.

A variety of other practical problems also exist. It is rare, for example, for children in particularly difficult circumstances to have birth certificates. In Brazil alone, there are 12 million children without birth certificates (Lusk, 1992). Given the possibility of malnutrition, and therefore delayed physical growth, it is difficult to know a child's age. In addition, it is also difficult to equate developmental periods across cultures and circumstances (Krener & Sabin, 1985; Miller, Onotera & Denard, 1983). Age determination problems are made more difficult because children in particularly difficult circumstances usually live on some form of relief from the international community. Knowing their survival can depend upon understanding the bureaucratic rules of the relief agency, it is not uncommon for a child to claim that he is seven years of age in order to get benefits meant for young children, and say that he is twelve or thirteen for another set of favorable circumstances (Aptekar, 1988b).

Whenever psychological tests are used, it is not only important to know the cultural biases of tests and testing, but also the children's age. Further, the tests have to be as independent of reading skills as possible. In the developing world, 20 million of the 100 million primary school age children do not attend school, and an additional 30 million drop out by the fourth grade (UNICEF, 1990a). The statistics are more extreme for children in particularly difficult circumstances. Supporting test data with ethnographic information is imperative, but this too is problematic. The timing of ethnographic data collection is extremely important for the study of children victimized by severe trauma. Reactions to stress are cyclical; they appear, disappear, and resurface. Without multiple time samplings it is possible to miss them. The onset of PTSD symptoms can also be delayed for years (Horowitz, 1990; 1993).

In most situations with children in particularly difficult circumstances, it is difficult to do anything but ex post-facto research. The most common method of getting pre-disaster or pre-war information from children is to interview them after the disaster and ask for their recollections. Although children's stories are valuable interpretations of their experiences, they do not necessarily reflect the actual events.

Sampling problems also abound in research on street children. For example, the majority of street children are studied in the programs that are serving them, which means that in many ways the children studied are the failures, the ones who could not make it on the street (Connolly, 1990; Ennew, 1994). Collecting ethnographic data on street children is difficult. Although it may appear that the children are free to talk and spend time with the researcher, the fact is they are busy working, and working for these children means survival. It is difficult to get their sustained attention unless they are paid (Dallape, 1987), and because employees have a tendency to pass pleasing information onto their bosses, the reports may be flawed.

Data for street children has to be collected during the day as well as the night. In Rio de Janeiro, for example, during the day the vast majority of children on the streets are boys, who work by shining shoes, washing cars, small scale vending, and so forth. At night, the percentage of girls and older children increases considerably (Lusk, 1992). The children found at night have different family situations, and the two groups of children function differently. Street children have developed an extraordinary capacity to tell stories. Lying about their ages, family background, reasons for being on the streets, and their current circumstances are common tricks and are easily given in their well-rehearsed scripts (Felsman, 1989; Leite & Esteves, 1991; Verma & Dhingra, 1993).

Collecting data from other categories of children in particularly difficult circumstances can be dangerous. In addition to the obvious problems of disease and violence, the children may be in unsafe and hard-to-access situations. It may be legally difficult to contact them due to child protection regulations, or other access difficulties typical of sensitive topics (Herzberger, 1993). In several political conflicts, it has been necessary for researchers to declare their positions before being allowed to enter the areas where the children were (Punamaki, 1989; Richter, 1991). The researcher can be faced with conflicting values having to pledge allegiance to and collect data from the side they consider to be the enemy.

There is no easy solution. However, by combining several methods, such as psychological tests and other sources of psychological assessment, including mental status interviews and open-ended questionnaires, ethnographic observations by multiple observers and in different situations and times, and by the use of secondary sources, it is possible to generate empirical information about the children with reasonable assurance. It would be helpful to clearly present to the reader the logic explaining the methods of data collection and what techniques were adopted to overcome methodological problems.

Conclusion

We began by discussing cultural relativism, showing that it was difficult to clearly define the difference between certain acceptable cultural practices and abuse. This made it problematic to apply cross-culturally the U.N. Convention on the Rights of the Child. Several of its provisions were especially difficult to implement outside of Western cultural contexts. Culturally variable assumptions about the time at which an embryo or a newborn becomes a child or when childhood ends render any universal provisions for state intervention, such as allowing the state to take away a child from abusive parents, a problematic question. The situation gets further complicated when the abuser is the state itself.

One indication of the problems associated with studying children in particularly difficult circumstances is the conflicting results of the many studies examined in this chapter. Some work pointed to the inevitable and enduring nature of PTSD for children who experienced extreme stress, while other studies suggested resilience and recovery. These discrepancies emerged from a variety of methodological issues as well as variations of culture.

In the second part of this chapter, we discussed the psychological reactions to extreme stress (PTSD), and pointed out that culture acts as a mediator to children's perceptions and reactions to difficult circumstances. Children are not just passive recipients of extreme stress. In the case of street children, there usually was no major traumatic event (beyond poverty) that reduced them to be victims. The violence endured by street children came less from the hard conditions of the street than from the societal reactions to them. Cultural factors related to culturally specific definitions of childhood caused street children to be labelled, excluded, and treated with hostility. Culture itself became the difficult circumstance. Its combination with state pressures gives rise to additional adverse effects: in China, contradicting policies (birth control and economic reforms) created a category of unwanted children and exacerbated cultural traits leading to discrimination against girls.

In the third part, we evidenced how cross-cultural researchers studying children in particularly difficult circumstances walk a delicate line. The closer they are to the children, the closer they place themselves in full view of the underbelly of human nature, where they must weigh at an intimate level the amount of cultural relativism that can be endured. Yet, cultural relativity can end in blind relativism, and annihilate any step toward comprehensive understanding of suffering and a corresponding definition of universally reprehensible conduct toward children. Coming to terms with the apparent dichotomy between cultural relativism and universalism is one central problem (and task) of cross-cultural researchers working with children in particularly difficult circumstances. This is no easy task, as it is both difficult to accept universalism without being considered culturally imperialistic, and difficult to accept relativism without being considered culturally naive.

There are several contributions made by cross-cultural researchers toward the well-being of street children. They have shown, for example, that street children are social actors, not merely victims (Lucchini, 1993, Invernizzi & Lucchini, 1996). Understanding the children's experiences and placing their view of life in the context of helping them has improved policy and programmatic efforts (Aptekar, 1994b; Aussems, 1991).

By pointing out the importance of cultural variables in understanding resistance to stress, cross-cultural researchers have shown that resilience is more than a fixed attribute of an individual (Rutter, 1990). Similar perspectives concerning vulnerability would also be valuable. The study of children in war has led to understanding that protective mechanisms are built up, not in the absence of stress, but like immunizations, in repeated and increased doses. This implies that children in highly stressful environments learn to cope. If so, what are the cultural factors which accelerate this phenomenon?

Cross-cultural researchers can also be helpful by showing how culture acts detrimentally in certain situations. For example, resiliency and coping are not always positive attributes. In certain cultural conditions, for instance, children fighting for extremist positions, resilience has led to more violence, because children having strong beliefs and strong cultural supports for their beliefs become more efficacious in their fighting. This, in turn, increases their self reliance, sense of positive identity, and a stronger will to achieve, all of which contribute to resilience and more destruction.

Cross-cultural studies can point out that just because nuclear families with at least one supportive parent–child relationship have been associated in the developed world with positive mental health in children, it does not mean that nuclear families are the only possible supportive context for children in all cultural circumstances. The World Health Organization (1987) has estimated that 80 million children are living without any family. Most of these children though poor, live adequately. Cross-cultural study of children in particularly difficult circumstances will increase our understanding of different family structures, thus helping children left without parents or biological family. We know, for example, very little about families of peers, where children parent each other, even though such "families" abound because of extreme stress. One group of more than 10,000 Sudanese children have lived without adult parenting for several years, moving from the Sudan, to Ethiopia, and to Kenya, yet they have not been studied to see how they cope and what they might teach us about other children living without parental support.

There are many societies where sibling relationships are more important than parent–child relationships for learning skills and psychological support (Weisner, 1989). More work in the area of family diversity can teach us not only how children in particularly difficulty circumstances find "familial" support, but also how other children without supportive families could manage. It might also contribute to reducing the violence street children receive.

The adoption of the 1989 Convention on the Rights of the Child by the United Nations transformed the concept of childhood from an age in need of protection to a time that gives children inalienable rights to protection. This has, in effect, reduced the "legal" cross-cultural differences between children of various cultures. Does this increase children's problems by establishing a cross-cultural imperative based on standards found in the developed world, or does it ensure adequate care for children in all cultures? Are children all over the world entitled, independent of tradition, ethnicity, or culture, to health care, education, and culture outlined in the Convention? The answer should come from cross-cultural researchers.

One of the most promising opportunities for cross-cultural researchers is to carefully examine the term "children in particularly difficult circumstances." By bringing in all that is diverse among cultural variations of children's suffering, cross-cultural studies can contribute to defining what is universal about children's rights and, therefore, help to link the rights of children mentioned in the Convention to the reality of children's lives in diverse cultural situations.

References

Agnelli, S. (1986). *Street children: A growing urban tragedy.* London: Weidenfeld and Nicholson.

Ahearn, F. & Cohen, R. (1984). *Disasters and mental health: An annotated bibliography.* Rockville, MD: National Institute of Mental Health, Center for Mental Health Studies in Emergencies, U.S. Department of Health.

AIDSWATCH. (1989a). *Colombia: Crusading effects bring signs of progress. 1,* 1.

AIDSWATCH. (1989b). *Death squads kill one child every two days in Brazil. 7,*1.

Aird, J. S. (1990). *Slaughter of the innocents: Coercive birth control in China.* Washington, DC: American Enterprise Institute Press.

Ajudukovic, M. & Ajudukovic, D. (1993). Psychological well-being of refugee children. *Child Abuse and Neglect, 17,* 843–854.

Allodi, F. (1989). The children of victims of political persecution and torture: A psychological study of a Latin American refugee community. *International Journal of Mental Health, 18,* 3–15.

Alves, A. (1991). Meninos de rua e meninos da rua: Estrutura e dinâmica familiar [Children on the street and children of the street: Family structure and dynamics]. In A. Fausto & R. Cervini (Eds.), *O trabalho e a rua: Crianças e adolescentes no Brasil urbano dos anos 80* (pp. 117–132). [Work and the street: Children and adolescents in urban Brazil during the 80s]. Sao Paulo: Cortez.

American Psychiatric Association 4th edition. (1994). *Diagnostic and statistical manual of mental disorders.* Washington, DC: American Psychiatric Association.

Anthony, E. & Cohler, B. (Eds.). (1987). *The invulnerable child.* New York: Guilford Press.

Aptekar, L. (1988a). The street children of Colombia: How families define the nature of childhood. *International Journal of Sociology of the Family, 18,* 283–296.

Aptekar, L. (1988b). *Street children of Cali.* Durham, NC: Duke University Press.

Aptekar, L. (1988c). Colombian street children: Their mental health and how they can be served. *International Journal of Mental Health, 17,* 81–104.

Aptekar, L. (1992). Are Colombian street children neglected? The contributions of ethnographic and ethnohistorical approaches to the study of children. *Anthropology and Education Quarterly, 22,* 326–349.

Aptekar, L. (1994a). *Environmental disasters in global perspective.* New York: G.K. Hall/ Macmillan.

Aptekar, L. (1994b). Street children in the developing world: A review of their condition. *Cross-Cultural Research, 28,* 195–224.

Aptekar, L. & Boore, J. (1990). The emotional effects of disaster on children: A review of the literature. *International Journal of Mental Health, 19,* 77–90.

Aptekar, L., Cathey, P.J., Ciano, L., & Guardino (in press). Street children in Nairobi, Kenya, *African Insights.*

Arroyo, W. & Eth, S. (1985). Children traumatized by Central American warfare. In S. Eth & R. Pynoos (Eds.). *Post-traumatic stress disorder in children* (pp. 101–120). Washington, DC: American Psychiatric Press.

Aussems, A. (1991). *Enfants marginalisés au Brésil. Propositions pour la formation des agents-intervenants* [Marginalized children in Brazil: Propositions for intervention]. Louvain, Belgique: Catholic University of Louvain.

Ayalon, O. & Van Tasel, E. (1987). Living in dangerous environments. In M. Brassard, R. Germain, & S. Hart (Eds.), *Psychological maltreatment of children and youth* (pp. 171–182). New York: Pergamon Press.

Baizerman, M. (1988). Street kids: Notes for designing a program for youth of and on the streets. *Child Care Worker, 6,* 13–15.

Baker, A. (1990). The psychological impact of the intifada on Palestinian children in the occupied West Bank and Gaza. *American Journal of Orthopsychiatry, 60,* 496–505.

Baker, A. (1991). Psychological response of Palestinian children to environmental stress associated with military occupation. *Journal of Refugee Studies, 4,* 237–247.

Bat-Zion, N. & Levy-Shiff, R. (1993). Children in war: Stress and coping reactions under the threat of Scud missile attacks and the effect of proximity. In L. Leavitt, & N. Fox (Eds.), *The psychological effects of war and violence on children.* (pp. 143–161). Hillsdale, NJ: Erlbaum.

Benedek, E. (1985). Children and disaster: Emerging issues. *Psychiatric Annals, 15,* 168–172.

Bianco, L. & Hua, C. H. (1989). La population chinoise face à la règle de l'enfant unique. *Actes de la Recherche en Sciences Sociales, 78,* 31–40.

Blanc, C. (1994). *Urban children in distress. Global predicaments and innovative strategies.* NY: UNICEF.

Boman, B. & Edwards, M. (1984). The Indochinese refugee: An overview. *Australian and New Zealand Journal of Psychiatry, 18,* 40–52.

Bonnet, C. (1993). Adoption at birth: Prevention against abandonment or neofanticide. *Child Abuse and Neglect, 17,* 501–513.

Boothby, N. (1986). Children and War, *Cultural Survival Quarterly, 10,* 28–30.

Boyden, J. (1986). *Children in development: Policy and programming for especially disadvantaged children in Lima, Peru.* Oxford, England: United Nations Children's Fund.

Boyden, J. (1990). A comparative perspective on the globalization of childhood. In A. James & A. Prout (Eds.), *Constructing and reconstructing childhood: Contemporary issues in the sociological study of childhood* (pp. 184–215). London: The Falmer Press.

Boyden, J. (1991). *Children of the cities.* New Jersey: Zed Books.

Breiner, S. (1990). *Slaughter of the innocents: Child abuse through the ages and today.* New York: Plenum Press.

Breznitz, S. (Ed.). (1983). *The denial of stress.* New York: International Universities Press.

Briere, J. N. (1992). *Child abuse trauma: Theory and treatment of the lasting effects.* London: Sage Publications.

Brown, C. (1987, November). *Street children in Jamaica.* Paper presented at the Conference on Street Children, University of the West Indies, Kingston, Jamaica.

Bruce, F. (1991). *The sexual exploitation of children: Field responses.* Geneva: ICCB.

Bryce, J. (1986). *Cries of children in Lebanon: As voiced by their mothers.* Beirut: UNICEF.

Bryce, J., Walker, N., & Peterson, C. (1989). Precipitating symptoms of depression among women in Beirut: The importance of daily life. *International Journal of Mental Health, 18,* 57–70.

Cairns, E. & Toner, I. (1993). Children and political violence in Northern Ireland: From riots to reconciliation. In L. Leavitt, L., & N. Fox, *The psychological effects of war and violence on children* (pp. 215–229). Hillsdale, NJ: Erlbaum.

Cairns, E. & Wilson, R. (1989) Mental health aspects of political violence in Northern Ireland. *International Journal of Mental Health, 18,* 38–56.

Campos, R., Raffaelli, M., Ude, W., Greco, M., Ruff, A., Rolf., J., Antunes, C., Halsey, N., Greco, D., & Street Youth Study Group. (1994). Social networks and daily activities of street youth in Belo Horizonte, Brazil. *Child Development, 65,* 319–330.

Cassidy, C. (1987). World-view conflict and toddler malnutrition: Change against dilemmas. In N. Scheper-Hughes (Ed.), *Child survivor* (pp. 293–324). Dordrecht, Holland: Reidel.

Cervini, R. & Burger, F. (1991). O menino trabalhador no Brasil dos anos 80s [Child workers in urban Brazil in the 80s]. In A. Fausto & R. Cervini (Eds.), *O trabalho e a rua: Criancas e adolescentes no Brasil urbano dos anos 80* (pp. 17–46). Sao Paulo: Cortez.

Chadwick, O. (1991). Does solvent abuse cause brain damage. In R. Ives (Ed.), *Soluble problems: Taking solvents, sniffing by young people* (pp. 23–30). London: National Children Bureau.

Chikane, F. (1986). Children in turmoil: The effects of unrest on township children. In S. Burman & P. Reynolds (Eds.), *Growing up in a divided society* (pp. 333–344). Johannesburg: Raven Press.

Chimienti, G., Nasr, J., & Khalief, I. (1989). Children's reactions to war-related stress. *Social Psychiatry and Psychiatric Epidemiology, 24,* 282–287.

Cicchetti, D. & Lynch, M. (1993). Toward an ecological/transactional model of community violence and child maltreatment: Consequences for children's development. *Psychiatry, 56,* 96–118.

Cohen, C. P. & Davidson, H. (Eds). (1990). *Children's rights in America: U. N. Convention on the Rights of the Child compared with United States law.* Washington, DC: American Bar Association.

Cohn, I. & Goodwin-Gill, G. (1993). *Child soldiers.* Geneva: Henry Dunant Institute.

Cohn, I., Holzer, K., Koch, L., & Severin, B. (1980). Children and torture. *Danish Medical Bulletin, 27,* 238–239.

Coles, R. (1986). *The political life of children.* Boston: Houghton Mifflin Co.

Combier, A. (1994). *Les enfants de la rue en Mauritanie* [Street children in Mauritania]. Paris: L'Harmattan.

Connolly, M. (1990). Adrift in the City: A comparative study of street children in Bogota, Colombia and Guatemala City. In N. Boxhill (Ed.), *Homeless children: The watchers and the waiters* (pp. 129–149). New York: Haworth Press.

Conroy, J. (1987). *Belfast diary.* Boston: Beacon Press.

Cutting, P. (1988). *Children of the siege.* London: Heinemann.

Dallape, F. (1987). *An experience with street children.* Nairobi, Kenya: Man Graphics.

Dawes, A. (1990). The effects of political violence on children: A consideration of South African and related studies. *International Journal of Psychology, 25,* 13–31.

Dawes, A., Tredoux, C., & Feinstein, A. (1993). Political violence in South Africa: Some effects on children of the violent destruction of their community. *International Journal of Mental Health, 18,* 16–43.

de Galan, G. (1981). *Se acaba la familia* [The end of the family]. Bogota: Editorial Pluma.

de Maistre, M. C. & de Maistre, G. (1992). *Interdit d'enfance* [Deprivation in childhood]. Paris: Albin Michel.

de Vries, M. W. (1987a). Cry babies, culture, and catastrophe: Infant temperament among the Masaai. In N. Scheper-Hughes (Ed.), *Child survival* (pp. 165–186). Dordrecht, Holland: Reidel.

de Vries, M. W. (1987b). Alternatives to mother-infant attachment in the neonatal period. In C. Super (Ed.), *The role of culture in develop-*

mental disorder (pp. 111–126). San Diego, CA: Academic Press.

Dimenstein, G. (1990). *A guerra dos meninos: Assassinatos de menores no Brasil* [The war of the children: Assassinations of minors in Brazil]. Sao Paulo: Brasilense.

Dodge, C. (1990). Health implications of war in Uganda and Sudan. *Social Science and Medicine, 31,* 691–698.

Dodge, C. & Raundalen, M. (Eds.). (1987). *War, violence, and children in Uganda.* Bergen: Norwegian University Press.

Donald, D. & Swart-Kruger, J. (1994). The South African street child: Developmental implications. *South African Journal of Psychology 24,* 169–174.

Dubrow, N. & Garbarino, J. (1989). Living in the war zone: Mothers and young children in a public housing development. *Child Welfare, 68,* 3–20.

Dyregrov, A. & Raundalen, M. (1987). Children and the stresses of war: A review of the literature. In C. Dodge & M. Raundalen, *War, violence, and children in Uganda* (pp 109–132). Bergen: Norwegian University Press.

Eisenbruch, M. (1988). The mental health of refugee children and their cultural development. *International Migration Review, 22,* 282–300.

Elbedour, S., Ten Besel, R., & Bastien, D. T. (1993). Ecological integrated model of children of war: Individual and social psychology. *Child Abuse and Neglect, 17,* 805–819.

Ennew, J. (1986). Children of the streets. *New Internationalist, 164,* 10–11.

Ennew, J. (1994). Parentless friends: A cross-cultural examination of networks among street children and street youth. In F. Nestman, & K. Hurrelmann (Eds.), *Social networks and social support in childhood and adolescence* (pp. 409–426). London: de Gruyter.

Ennew, J. & Milne, B. (1989). *The next generation: The lives of third world children.* London: Zed Books.

Espinola, B., Glauser, B., Ortiz, R., & Ortiz de Carrizosas S. (1987). *Dans les rues* [In the streets]. Bogota: UNICEF.

Espinola, B., Glauser, B., Ortiz, R., & Ortiz de Carrizosas S. (1990). *En la calle: Menores trabajadores de la calle en Asuncion, Paraguay* [In the street: Child workers in the streets of

Asuncion, Paraguay]. Asuncion, Paraguay: Imprenta El Grafico.

Esterle, E. (1991). Toxicomanes: raisons et réseaux [Drug addiction: Reasons and networks]. *Psychotropes, 8*, 15–21.

Eth, S. & Pynoos, R. (Eds). (1985a). *Post-traumatic stress disorder in children.* Washington, DC: American Psychiatric Press.

Eth, S. & Pynoos, R. (1985b). Interaction of trauma and grief in children. In S. Eth & R. Pynoos (Eds.), *Post-traumatic stress disorder in children* (pp. 171–186). Washington, DC: American Psychiatric Press.

Felsman, K. (1989). Risk and resiliency in childhood: The lives of street children. In. T. Dugan & R. Coles, *The child in our times: Studies in the development of resiliency* (pp. 56–80). New York: Bruner/Mazel.

Finklehor, D. (1985). Sexual abuse and physical abuse: Some critical differences. In. E. Newberger & R. Bourne (Eds.), *Unhappy families. Clinical and research perspectives on family violence* (pp. 21–30). Littleton, MA: PSG Publishing.

Frederick, C. (1985). Children traumatized by catastrophic situations. In S. Eth & R. Pynoos (Eds.), *Post-traumatic stress disorder in children* (pp. 73–99). Washington, DC: American Psychiatric Press.

Galante, R. & Foa, D. (1986). An epidemiological study of psychic trauma and treatment effectiveness for children after a natural disaster. *Journal of the American Academy of Child Psychiatry, 25*, 357–363.

Garbarino, J. (1993). Challenges we face in understanding children and war: A personal essay. *Child Abuse and Neglect, 17*, 787–793.

Garbarino, J., Kostelny, K., & Dubrow, N. (1991a). *No place to be a child: Growing up in a war zone.* Lexington, MA: Lexington Books.

Garbarino, J., Kostelny, K., & Dubrow, N. (1991b). What children can tell us about living in danger. *American Psychologist, 46*, 376–383.

Garbarino, J., Kostelny, K., & Dubrow, N. (1992). Developmental consequences of living in dangerous and unstable environments: The situation of refugee children. In M. McCallin (Ed.), *The psychological well-being of refugee children: Research, practice, and policy issues* (pp.

1–23). Geneva: International Catholic Child Bureau.

Garmezy, N. (1983). *Stress, coping and development in children.* New York: McGraw-Hill.

Garmezy, N. (1986). Children under severe stress: Critique and commentary. *Journal of the American Academy of Child Psychiatry, 25*, 384–392.

Garmezy, N. & Rutter, M. (1985). Acute reactions to stress. In M. Rutter and L. Herzov (Eds.), *Child and adolescent psychiatry, modern approaches* (2nd ed.) (pp. 152–176). Oxford: Blackwell Press.

Gelles, R. & Cornell, C. (Eds.). (1983). *International perspective on family violence.* Toronto: Lexington Books.

Gibson, K. (1987). Civil conflict, stress and children. *Psychology in Society, 8*, 4–26.

Gibson, K. (1989). Children in political violence. *Social Science and Medicine, 28*, 659–667.

Glauser, B. (1990). Street children: Deconstructing a construct. In A. James & A.Prout (Eds.), *Constructing and reconstructing childhood: Contemporary issues in the sociological study of childhood* (pp. 138–156). London: The Falmer Press.

Gleser, G., Green, B., & Winget, C. (1981). *Prolonged psychosocial effects of disaster: A Study of Buffalo Creek.* New York: Academic Press.

Golec, J. (1983). A contextual approach to the social psychological study of disaster recovery. *International Journal of Mass Emergency and Disasters, 1*, 255–276.

Grinberg, L. & Grinberg, R. (1984). A psychoanalytic study of migration: Its normal and pathological aspects. *Journal of American Psychoanalytical Association, 32*, 13–38.

Handford, H., Dicerkson, S., Mattison, R., Humphrey, F., Bagnato, S., Bixler, E., & Joyce Kales, J. (1986). Child and Parent Reaction to the Three Mile Island nuclear accident. *Journal of the American Academy of Child Psychiatry, 25*, 346–356.

Harbison, J. (Ed.). (1983). *Children of the troubles: Children in Northern Ireland.* Belfast: Stranmillis College Learning Resources Unit.

Hausfater, G. & Blaffer, S. (Eds.). (1984). *Infanticide: Comparative and evolutionary perspectives.* New York: Aldine Publishing Co.

Hausweld, L. (1987). Child neglect on the Navajo reservation. In N. Scheper-Hughes (Ed.), *Child survival* (pp. 145–164). Dordrecht, Holland: Reidel.

Herzberger, L. (1993). The cyclical pattern of child abuse. A study of research methodology. In M. Renzetti, M. Less (Eds.), *Researching sensitive topics* (pp. 33–51). London: Sage Publications.

Hickson, J. & Gaydon, V. (1989). "Twilight Children": The street children in Johannesburg. *Journal of Multicultural Counseling and Development, 17,* 85–95.

Hilton, I. (1990). 'Disappeared' children in Argentina. In C. Moorhead (Ed.), *Betrayal: Child exploitation in today's world* (pp. 143–160). New York: Doubleday.

Hobfoll, S. & London, P. (1986). The relationship of self-concept and social support to emotional stress among women during war. *Journal of Social and Clinical Psychology, 4,* 189–203.

Hobfoll, S., Spielberger, C., Breznitz, S., Figley, C., Folkman, S., Leper-Green, B., Meichembaum, D., Milgram, N., Sandler, I., Sarason, I., & van der Kolk, B. (1991). War related stress: Addressing the stress of war and other traumatic events. *American Psychologist, 46,* 848–855.

Holinsteiner M. & Tacon, P. (1983). Urban migration in developing countries: Consequences for families and children. In D. A. Wagner (Ed.), *New Directions for Child Development* (pp. 5–25). San Francisco: Jossey-Bass.

Horowitz, M. (1990). Post-traumatic stress disorders: Psychosocial aspects of the diagnosis. *International Journal of Mental Health, 19,* 21–36.

Horowitz, M. (1993). Stress-response syndromes: A review of post-traumatic stress and adjustment disorders. In J. Wilson & B. Raphael (Eds.), *International handbook of traumatic stress syndromes* (pp. 49–60). New York: Plenum Press.

Hosin, A. & Cairns, E. (1984). The impact of conflict on children's ideas about their country. *The Journal of Psychology, 118,* 161–168.

Hull, T. (1990). Recent trends in sex ratios at birth in China. *Population and Development Review. 16,* 63–83.

Hussain, M. (1984). Race related illness in Vietnamese refugees. *International Journal of Social Psychiatry, 142,* 153–156.

ICCB. (1995). *Surviving violence: A recovery programme for children and families.* Geneva: International Catholic Child Bureau.

Invernizzi, A. & Lucchini, R. (1996). L'image de "l'enfant de la rue" et ses contradictions: Quelque pistes pour déconstruire ce concept. [The image of the street child and its contradictions: Some avenues for deconstructing this concept]. In R. Lucchini (Ed.), *Sociologie de la survie. L'enfant dans la rue,* [Sociology of survival: The child in the street] (pp. 221–285). Paris: PUF.

Jansen, I., Richter, R., & Griesel, R. (1992). Glue sniffing: A comparison study of sniffers and non-sniffers. *Journal of Adolescence, 15,* 29–37.

Johansson, S. R. (1984). Deferred infanticide: Excess female mortality during childhood. In G. Hausfater & S. Blaffer (Eds.), *Infanticide, comparative and evolutionary perspectives* (pp. 463–488). New York: Aldine.

Kaffman, M. & Elizur, E. (1983). Bereavement responses of Kibbutz and non-Kibbutz children following the death of the father. *Journal of Child Psychology and Psychiatry, 24,* 435–42.

Kempe, R. & Kempe, H. (1983). *Child abuse.* Oxford: Oxford University Press.

Kent, R. (1987). *Anatomy of disaster relief: The international network in action.* London: Printer Publishers.

Kilbride, P. & Kilbride, J. (1990). *Changing family life in East Africa: Women and children at risk.* University Park: Pennsylvania State University Press.

Kinzie, J., Sack, W., Angell, R., Manson, S., & Rath, B. (1986). The psychiatric effects of massive trauma on Cambodian children: I. The children. *Journal of the American Academy of Child Psychiatry, 25,* 370–376.

Klingman, A. (1992). Stress reactions of Israeli youth during the Gulf War: A quantitative study. *Professional Psychology: Research and Practice, 23,* 521–527.

Klingman, A., Sagi, A., & Raviv, A. (1993). The effect of war on Israeli children. In L. Leavitt & N. Fox (Eds.), *The psychological effects of war and violence on children* (pp. 75–93). Hillsdale, NJ: Erlbaum.

Korbin, J. (Ed.). (1981a). *Child abuse and neglect.* Berkeley: University of California Press.

Korbin, J. (1981b). 'Very few cases': Child abuse and neglect in the People's Republic of China. In J. Korbin (Ed.), *Child abuse and neglect* (pp. 166–185). Berkeley: University of California Press.

Korbin, J. (1987). Child sexual abuse: Implications from the cross-cultural record. In N. Scheper-Hughes (Ed.), *Child Survival* (pp. 247–265). Dordrecht, Holland: Reidel.

Kosteny, K. & Garbarino, J. (1994). Coping with the consequences of living in danger: The case of Palestinian children and youth. In I. J. Toner (Ed.), *International Journal of Behavioral Development, 17, 4,* 595–611.

Krener, P. & Sabin, C. (1985). Indochinese immigrant children: The problems in psychiatric diagnosis. *Journal of American Academy of Child Psychiatry, 24,* 453–458.

Lalor, K., Taylor, M., Veale, A., Ali-Hussein, A., & Bushra, M. (1992, October). Victimization amongst street children in Sudan and Ethiopia: A preliminary analysis. *Proceedings of UNICRI Conference* (pp. 1–8). Rome: UNICEF.

Langer, W. (1983). Infanticide: A historical survey. *History of Childhood Quarterly, 1,* 353–365.

Langness, L. (1981). Child abuse and cultural values: The case of New Guinea. In J. Korbin (Ed.),*Child abuse and neglect* (pp. 13–34). Berkeley: University of California Press.

Leite, L. & Esteves, M. (1991). Escola Tia Ciata—a school for street children in Rio de Janeiro. *Environment and Urbanization, 3,* 130–139.

Levinson, D. (1989). *Family violence in cross-cultural perspective.* Newbury Park, CA: Sage Publications.

LeVine, R. (1980). A cross-cultural perspective on parenting. In M. Fantini & R. Cardenas (Eds.), *Parenting in a multicultural society* (pp. 17–27). New York: Longman.

LeVine, R. & LeVine, S. (1981). Child abuse and neglect in Sub-Saharan Africa. In J. Korbin (Ed.). *Child abuse and neglect* (pp. 35–55). Berkeley: University of California Press.

Li, L. & Ballweg, J. (1994). Deviant fertility in China: A theoretical approach. *Deviant Behavior, 15,* 193–210.

Liddell, C., Kemp, J., & Moema, M. (1993). The Young Lions: South African children and youth in political struggle. In L. Leavitt, & N. Fox (Eds.), *The psychological effects of war and violence on children* (pp. 199–214). Hillsdale, NJ: Erlbaum.

Lima, B., Pai, S., Lozano, J., & Santacruz, H. (1990). The stability of emotional symptoms among disaster victims in a developing country. *Journal of Traumatic Stress, 3,* 497–505.

Lorenc, L. & Brantwaite, A. (1986). Evaluations of political violence by English and Northern Ireland schoolchildren. *British Journal of Social Psychology, 25,* 349–352.

Lösel, F. & Bliesener, T. (1990). Resilience in adolescence: A study of the generalizability of protective factors. In K. Hurrelmann & F. Losel (Eds.), *Health hazards in adolescents* (pp. 299–320). New York: Walter de Gruyter.

Lösel, F., Bliesener, T., & Korferl, P. (1990). Psychische Gesundheit trotz Risikobelastung in der Kindheit: Untersuchungen zur "Invulnerabilität" [Mental health in spite of high risk in childhood: Studies in "invulnerability"]. In I. Seiffge-Krenge (Ed.), *Jahrbuch der Medizinischen Psychologie, Vol. 4* (pp. 103–123). Berlin: Springer.

Lucchini, R. (1993). *Enfant de la rue: Identité, sociabilité, drogue* [Street child: Identity, sociability, drugs]. Geneva: Librairie Droz.

Lucchini, R. (1996). *Sociologie de la survie. L'enfant dans la rue.* [Sociology of survival: The child in the street]. Paris: PUF.

Lusk, M. (1992). Street children of Rio de Janeiro. *International Social Work, 35,* 293-305.

Lusk, M., Peralta, F., & Vest, G. (1989). Street children of Juarez: A field study. *International Social Work, 32,* 243–245.

Lykes, M. B. & Liem, R. (1990). Human rights and mental health in the United States: Lessons learned from Latin America. *Journal of Social Issues, 46,* 151–165.

Lystad, M. (1984). Children's responses to disaster: Family implications. *International Journal of Family Psychiatry, 5,* 41–60.

MacPherson, S. (1987). *Five hundred million children:*

Poverty and child welfare in the Third World. New York: St. Martin's Press.

Magwaza, A. W., Killian, B. J., Peterson, I., & Pillay, Y. (1993). The effects of chronic violence on preschool children living in South African townships. *Child Abuse and Neglect, 17,* 795–803.

Mahjoub, A., Leyes, J., Yzerbyt, V., & di Giacomo, J. (1989). War stress and coping modes: Representations of self-identity and time perspective among Palestinian children. *International Journal of Mental Health, 18,* 44–62.

Malmquist, C. (1986). Children who witness parental murder: Posttraumatic aspects. *Journal of the American Academy of Child Psychiatry, 25,* 320–325.

Martin-Boro, I. (1989). Political violence and war as causes of psychosocial trauma in El Salvador. *International Journal of Mental Health, 18,* 3–20.

Masalha, S. (1993). The effect of prewar conditions on the psychological reactions of Palestinian children to the Gulf War. In L. Leavitt, & N. Fox (Eds.), *The psychological effects of war and violence on children* (pp. 131–142). Hillsdale, NJ: Erlbaum.

Medina-Mora, E. (1987). Aspectos epidemiologicos del uso de la sustancias inhalantes en la Republica Mexicana [Epidemiological aspects of the use of inhalants in Mexico]. *Salud Mental, 10,* 11–19.

Mileti, D. (1987). Sociological methods and disaster research. In. R. Dynes, B. de Marchi, & C.Pelanda (Eds.), *Sociology of disasters: Contributions of sociology to disaster research* (pp. 57–69). Milano, Italy: Franco Ageli.

Milgram, N. (1982). War related stress in Israeli children and youth. In C. Spielberger, I. Sarason, I. & N. Milgram (Eds.), *Stress and Anxiety, Vol. 8* (pp. 656–76). Washington, DC: Hemisphere Press.

Miller, V., Onotera, R., & Denard, A. (1983). Denver Developmental Screening Test: Cultural variations in Southeast Asian refugee children. *Journal of Pediatrics, 104,* 481–482.

Mishra, S. (1989). Rehabilitation of street children. *Social Welfare, 36,* 17–19, 34–35.

Mollica, R., Wyshak, G., & Lavelle, J. (1987). The psychosocial impact of war trauma and torture on Southeast Asian refugees. *American Journal of Psychiatry, 144,* 1567–1572.

Moorhead, C. (1990a). Children and work: Italy and Kenya. In C. Moorhead (Ed), *Betrayal: Child exploitation in today's world* (pp. 30–52). New York: Doubleday.

Moorhead, C. (1990b). *Betrayal: Child exploitation in today's world,* New York: Doubleday.

Muller, R., Caldwell, R., & Hunter, J. (1993). Child provocativeness and gender as factors contributing to the blaming of victims of physical child abuse. *Child Abuse and Neglect, 17,* 249–260.

Mumba, F. (1981). Adoption in Zambia. *Child Abuse and Neglect, 5,* 197–9.

Munoz, C. & Pachon, X. (1980). *Gamines: Testimonios* [Gamines: Testimonies]. Bogota: Carlos Valencia Editores.

Myers, W. (Ed.). (1991). *Protecting working children.* London: UNICEF.

McCallin, M. (1992a). The impact of current and traumatic stressors on the psychological well-being of refugee communities. In M. McCallin (Ed.), *The psychological well-being of refugee children: Research, practice, and policy issues* (pp. 68–89). Geneva: International Catholic Child Bureau.

McCallin, M. (Ed.). (1992b). *The psychological well-being of refugee children: Research, practice and policy issues.* Geneva: International Catholic Child Bureau.

McCallin, M. & Fozzard, S. (1990). *The impact of traumatic events on the psychological well-being of Mozambican refugee women and children.* Geneva: International Catholic Child Bureau.

McFarlane, A. C. (1990). An Australian disaster: The 1983 bushfires. *International Journal of Mental Health, 19,* 36–47.

McHan, E. (1985). Imitation of aggression by Lebanese children. *The Journal of Social Psychology, 125,* 613–617.

McLaghlan, F. (1986). Street children in prison. In N. Pines (Ed.), *Street Children Perspectives* (Paper No. 40, pp. 3–6). Johannesburg: Institute for the Study of Man in Africa.

McWhirter, L. & Trew, K. (1982). Children in Northern Ireland: A lost generation? In E. Anthony (Ed.), *Children in turmoil: Tomorrow's parents* (pp.69–84). New York: Wiley.

McWhirter, L., Young, V., & Majury, J. (1983). Belfast children's awareness of violent death. *British Journal of Social Psychology, 22,* 81–92.

Naversen, O. (1989). *The sexual exploitation of children in developing countries.* Stockholm: Radda Barnen.

Ojanuga, D. (1990). Kaduma beggar children: A study of child abuse and neglect in northern Nigeria. *Child Welfare, 69,* 371–380.

Okeahialam, T. (1984). Child abuse in Nigeria. *Child Abuse and Neglect, 8,* 69–73.

Oliveira, W., Baizerman, M., & Pellet, L. (1992). Street children in Brazil and their helpers: Comparative views on aspirations and the future. *International Social Work, 35,* 163–176.

Oliver, J. & Reardon, G. (1982). *Tropical Cyclone Isaac: Cyclonic impact in the context of the society and economy of the Kingdom of Tonga.* Townsville, Queensland, Australia: Center for Disaster Studies, James Cook University.

Oliver-Smith, A. (1977). Disaster rehabilitation and social change in Yungay, Peru. *Human Organization, 36,* 5–13.

Olson, E. (1981). Socioeconomic and psychocultural contexts of child abuse and neglect in Turkey. In J. Korbin (Ed.), *Child abuse and neglect* (pp. 96–119). Berkeley: University of California Press.

Ortiz, A. (1988). Estudio de seguimiento de usuarios y no usuarios de sustancias inhalantes en poblacion abierta: Comparacion de sus rendimientos cognitivos [A study of users and non-users of inhalants among the general population: Comparison of cognitive impairment]. *Psiquiatria, 2,* 165–178.

Ortiz, S. & Poertner, J. (1992). Latin American street children: Problem, programs and critique. *International Social Work, 35,* 405–413.

Patel, A. (1983). *An overview of street children in India.* New York: Covenant House.

Patel, S. (1990). Street children, hotel boys and children of pavement dwellers and construction workers in Bombay—how they meet their daily needs. *Environment and Urbanization, 2,* 9–26.

Peerun, B. (1994). *Les enfants de la rue* [Children of the streets]. Paris: Institut International de Formation et de Lutte Contre Les Drogues.

Pereira, P. (1985). *Retratro do Brasil: A situaçâo da infancia Brasileira [Profile of Brazil: The situation of Brazilian children].* Sao Paulo: Editora Politica.

Pirenne, J. (1989). *Mes fils de la rue à Addis Ababa.* [My sons of the streets in Addis Ababa]. Paris: Fayard, Les Enfants du Fleuve.

Poffenberger, T. (1981). Child rearing and social structure in rural India: Cross-cultural definition of children abuse and neglect. In J. Korbin (Ed.), *Child abuse and neglect* (pp. 71–95). Berkeley: University of California Press.

Poloni, A. (1994). Les microcultures de la rue: marginalité ou intégration? [The microcultures of the street: Marginality or Integration?]. In Y. Marguerat, & D. Poitou, (Eds.), *A l'écoute des enfants de la rue en Afrique noire.* Paris. Fayard, Les Enfants du Fleuve.

Potter, S. & Potter, H. (1987). Birth planning in rural China: A cultural account. In N. Scheper-Hughes (Ed.), *Child survival* (pp. 33–58). Dordrecht, Holland: Reidel.

Protacio-Marcelino, E. (1989). Children of political detainees in the Philippines. Sources of stress and coping patterns. *Mental Health, 18,* 71–86.

Punamaki, R. (1982). Childhood in the shadow of war: A psychological study on attitudes and emotional life of Israeli and Palestinian children. *Current Research on Peace and Violence, 5,* 26–41.

Punamaki, R. (1988). Historical-political and individualistic determinants of coping modes and fears among Palestinian children. *International Journal of Psychology, 23,* 721–739.

Punamaki, R. (1989). Factors affecting the mental health of Palestinian children exposed to political violence. *International Journal of Mental Health, 18,* 63–79.

Pynoos, R. & Eth, S. (1984). Child as criminal witness to homicide. *Journal of Social Issues, 40,* 87–108.

Pynoos, R. & Eth, S. (1985). Children traumatized by witnessing acts of personal violence: Homicide, rape, or suicide behavior. In S. Eth, & R. Pynoos, *Post-traumatic stress disorder in children* (pp. 19–43). Washington, DC: American Psychiatric Press.

Queloz, N. (1988). La justice pour mineurs dans

l'optique récente des Nations Unies et la question de son développment en Afrique [Justice for minors from the perspectives of the United Nations and African development]. *Revue Internationale de Criminologie et de Police Criminelle, 1,* 38–43.

Raffaelli, M., Campos, R., Merritt, A., Siqueira, E., Antunes, C., Parker, R., Greco, M., Greco, D., Halsey, N., & Street Youth Study Group. (1993). Sexual practices and attitudes of street youth in Belo Horizonte, Brazil. *Social Science and Medicine, 37,* 661–670.

Randal, J. & Boustany, N. (1990). Children and war in Lebanon. In C. Moorhead (Ed.), *Betrayal: Child exploitation in today's world* (pp. 59–82). New York: Doubleday.

Randall, G. (1988). *No way home: Homeless young people in central London.* London: Centerpoint Soho.

Raphael, B. (1986). *When disaster strikes: How individuals and communities cope with catastrophe.* New York: Basic Books.

Raviv, A. & Klingman, A. (1983). Children under stress. In S. Breznitz (Ed.), *Stress in Israel* (pp. 138–162). New York: Van Nostrand Reinhold.

Rayhida, J., Shaya, M., & Armenian, H. (1986). Child health in a city at war. In J. Bryce & H. Armenian (Eds.), *Wartime: The state of children in Lebanon* (pp. 11–26). Beirut: American University of Beirut.

Ressler, E., Boothby, N., & Steinbock, D. (1988). *Unaccompanied children: Care and protection in wars, natural disasters, and refugee movements.* New York: Oxford University Press.

Ressler, E., Tortoricci, J., & Marcelino, A. (1993). *Children in war: A guide to provisional services: A study for UNICEF.* New York: UNICEF.

Ritchie, J. & Ritchie, J. (1981). Child rearing and child abuse: The Polynesian context. In J. Korbin (Ed.), *Child abuse and neglect: Cross-cultural perspectives* (pp. 186–204). Berkeley: University of California Press.

Richman, N., Kanji, N., & Zinkin, P. (1988). *Psychological effects of war on children in Mozambique.* London: Save the Children Fund.

Richter, L. (1991). South African "Street Children": Comparisons with Anglo-American runaways. In N. Bleichrodt & P. Drenth (Eds.),

Contemporary issues in cross-cultural psychology (pp. 96–109). Amsterdam: Swets & Zeitlinger.

Richters, J. & Martinez, P. (1993). The NIMH Community Violence Project: I. Children as victims of and witness to violence. *Psychiatry, 56,* 7–21.

Rizzini, I. & Rizzini, I. (1991). Menores institucionalizados e meninos de rua: Os grandes temas de pesquisas na decada 80 [Institutionalized minors and street youth: The great research topics of the 80s]. In A. Fausto & R. Cervini (Eds.), *O trabalho e a rua: Criancas e adolescentes no Brasil urbano dos anos 80* (pp. 69–90) [Work and the street: Children and adolescents in urban Brazil during the 80s]. Sao Paulo: Cortez.

Rohner, R. P., & Rohner, E. (1980). Antecedents and consequences of parental rejection: A theory of emotional abuse. *Child Abuse and Neglect, 4,* 189–198.

Ronstrom, A. (1989). Children in Central America: Victims of war. *Child Welfare, 68,* 145–153.

Rosa, C. S., de Sousa, R., & Ebrahim, G. (1992). The street children of Recife: A study of their background. *Journal of Tropical Pediatrics, 38,* 34–40.

Rosenblatt, R. (1983). *Children of war.* New York: Doubleday.

Rouhana, K. (1989). Children and the Intifada. *Journal of Palestinian Studies, 18,* 110–121.

Rushwan, H. (1984). Female circumcision: A reproductive health problem. In J. Mati, O. Lapido, R. Burkman, R. Magarick, and D. Huber (Eds.), *Reproductive health in Africa* (pp. 178–180). Baltimore: Johns Hopkins.

Rutter, M. (1986). Bereaved children. In M. Rutter (Ed.), *Children of sick parents* (pp 66–75). London: Oxford University Press.

Rutter, M. (1990). Psychosocial resilience and protective mechanisms. In J. Rolf, A. Masten, D. Cicchetti, K. Neuchterlein, & S. Weintraub (Eds.), *Risk and protective factors in the development of psyhopathology* (pp. 181–214). Cambridge: Cambridge University Press.

Sack, W., Angell, R., Kinzie, D., & Rath, B. (1986). The psychiatric effects of massive trauma on Cambodian children: II, The family, the home, and the school. *Journal of the American Academy of Child Psychiatry, 25,* 377–383.

Saraswathi, T. S. & Dutta, R. (1988). *Invisible boundaries: Grooming for adult roles.* New Delhi: Northern Book Centre.

Saylor, C. (Ed.). (1993). *Children and disasters.* New York: Plenum Press.

Scharf, W., Powell, M., & Thomas, E. (1986). Stroller-street children of Cape Town. In S. Burman, & P. Reynolds (Eds.), *Growing up in a divided society: The context of childhood in South Africa* (pp 262–287). Johannesburg: Raven Press.

Scheper-Hughes, N. (1987). *Child Survival: Anthropological perspectives on the treatment and maltreatment of children.* Dordrecht, Holland: Reidel Publishing Co.

Scheper-Hughes, N. & Stein, H. (1987). Child abuse and the unconscious in American popular culture. In N. Scheper-Hughes (Ed.), *Child survival* (pp. 339–358). Dordrecht, Holland: Reidel.

Segall, M. (1983). On the search for the independent variable in cross-cultural psychology. In S. Irvine & J. Berry (Eds.), *Human assessment and cultural factors* (pp. 122–137). New York: Plenum.

Seitz, S. & Davis, D. (1984). The political matrix of natural disasters: Africa and Latin America. *International Journal of Mass Emergencies and Disasters, 2,* 231–250.

Shah, B. (1983). Is the environment becoming more hazardous? A global survey 1947 to 1980. *Disasters, 7,* 202–209.

Shisana, O. & Celentano, D. (1987). Relationship of chronic stress and coping style to health among Namibian refugees. *Social Science and Medicine, 24,* 24–157.

Simpson, M. (1993). Bitter waters: Effects on children of the stressors of unrest and oppression. In J. Wilson & B. Raphael (Eds.), *International handbook of traumatic stress syndromes* (pp 601–624). NY: Plenum Press.

Soloman, S. (1989). Research issues in assessing disaster's effects. In R. Gist & B. Lubin (Eds.), *Psychosocial aspects of disaster* (pp. 308–340). New York: John Wiley.

Spencer, E. & Pynoos, R. (1985). *Post-traumatic stress disorder in children.* Washington, DC: American Psychiatric Society.

Stöcklin, D. (1992). Note sur la statistique des naissances en Chine [Note on birth statistics in China]. *Population (INED),* Paris, (1), 223–233.

Stöcklin, D. (1993). *Socialization of children in contemporary China: A sociological search for the unvisited.* (Working Papers, No. 230). Fribourg, Switzerland. University of Fribourg.

Straker, G. (1991). *Faces in the revolution: The psychological effects of violence on township youth in South Africa.* Cape Town, South Africa: David Phillip.

Straker, G. & Moosa, F. (1988). Post-traumatic stress disorder: A reaction to state-supported child abuse and neglect. *Child Abuse and Neglect, 12,* 383–395.

Suarez-Orozco, M. (1987). The treatment of children in the "Dirty War": Ideology, state terrorism and the abuse of children in Argentina. In N. Scheper-Hughes (Ed.), *Child survival* (pp. 227–246). Dordrecht, Holland: Reidel.

Subrahmanyam, Y. & Sondhi, P. (1990). Child porters: Psychosocial profile of street children. *International Journal of Social Work, 51,* 577–582.

Suda, C. (1993). The impact of changing family structures on Nairobi children. *African Study Monographs, 14,* 109–121.

Swart, J. (1990a). Street children in Latin America, with special reference to Guatemala. *UNISA Latin America Report, 6,* 28–41.

Swart, J. (1990b). *Malunde: The street children of Hillbrow.* Cape Town, South Africa: Witwatersrand University Press.

Tacon, P. (1982). Carlinhos: The hard gloss of city polish. *UNICEF News, 111,* 4–6.

Terr, L. (1990). *Too scared to cry.* New York: Harper and Row.

Terr, L. (1991). Childhood traumas: An outline and overview. *American Journal of Psychiatry, 148,* 10–20.

Thireau, I. (1989). Les résistances à la politique de l'enfant unique en milieu paysan [Resistance to the one-child policy in rural settings]. *Revue Européenne des Sciences Sociales, 27,* 227–238.

Toner, I. J. (December, 1994). Children and political violence. *International Journal of Behavioral Development.* Edited special edition.

Townsend, P. (1985). *The situation of children in Papua New Guinea, Port Moresby.* New Guinea:

Papua New Guinea Institute of Applied Social and Economic Research.

Tsoi, M., Yu, G., & Lieh-Mak, F. (1986). Vietnamese refugee children in camps in Hong Kong. *Social Science and Medicine, 23*, 1147–1150.

Tyler, F., Tyler, S., Echeverry, J., & Zea., M. (1991). Making it on the streets of Bogota: A psychosocial study of street youth. *Genetic, Social, and General Psychology Monographs, 117,* 395–417.

UNICEF. (1985). *Borrador del plan para un programa regional de niños abandonados y de la calle* [Worksheet for the Regional Operating Plan for Abandoned and Street Children]. Bogota: United Nations Children's Fund.

UNICEF. (1986). *Children in especially difficult circumstances. Supporting annex, exploitation of working and street children.* New York: United Nations Children's Fund.

UNICEF. (1990a). *Children and development in the 1990s: A UNICEF sourcebook.* Proceedings of the World Summit for Children, September, 1990. New York: United Nations Children's Fund.

UNICEF. (1990b). *Children in situations of armed conflict: A UNICEF Perspective.* New York: UNICEF.

Valverde, L. & Lusk, M. (1989). *Los ninos de la calle de San Jose, Costa Rica* [Street children of San Jose, Costa Rica] (Research Monograph No. 2). Logan, UT: Utah State University Department of Sociology and Social Work.

Vanistendael, S. (1987). *Street children: A brief overview.* Geneva: ICCB.

Veale, A. (1992). Towards a conceptualization of street-children: The case from Sudan and Ireland. *Troaire Development Review, Dublin,* 107–128.

Verma, S. & Dhingra, G. (1993). Who do they belong to? A profile of street children in Chandigarh. *People's Action, 8,* 22–25.

Visano, L. (1990). The socialization of street children: The development and transformation of identities. *Sociological Studies of Child Development, 3,* 139–161.

Vittachi, T. (1986). Droits de l'enfant, devoirs envers l'enfant [Rights of the child and responsibilities toward children]. *Tribune Internationale des Droits de L'Enfant, 3,* 14–23.

Wagatsuma, H. (1981). Child abandonment and infanticide: A Japanese case. In J. Korbin (Ed.), *Child abuse and neglect* (pp. 120–138). Berkeley: University of California Press

Wagner, D. (1986). Child development research and the Third World. *American Psychologist, 41,* 298–301.

Wainaina, J. (1981). The "Parking Boys" of Nairobi. *African Journal of Sociology, 1,* 7–45.

Weiner, M. (1991). *The child and the state in India.* Princeton: Princeton University Press.

Weisaeth, L. & Eitinger, L., (1993). Posttraumatic stress phenomena: Common themes across wars, disasters, and traumatic events. In J. Wilson & B. Raphael (Eds), *International handbook of traumatic stress syndromes* (pp, 69–77). New York: Plenum Press.

Weisner, T. (1989). Comparing siblings relationships across cultures. In P. Zukow (Ed.), *Sibling interaction across cultures* (pp. 11–25). New York: Springer-Verlag.

Werner, E. (1990). Protective factors in individual resilience. In S. Mesiels & J. Shonkoff (Eds.) *Handbook of early childhood intervention* (pp. 97–116). Cambridge: Cambridge University Press.

Wertleib, D., Weigel, C., Springer, T., & Feldstein, M. (1990). Temperament as a moderator of children's stressful experiences. *American Journal of Orthopsychiatry, 57,* 234–245.

Wilkenson, B. & Vera, E. (1985). The management and treatment of disaster victims. *Psychiatric Annals, 15,* 174–184.

Williams, C. (1993). Who are "street children?" A hierarchy of street use and appropriate responses. *Child Abuse and Neglect, 17,* 831–841.

Williams, C. & Westermeyer, J. (1983). Psychiatric problems among adolescent Southeast Asian refugees: A descriptive study. *The Journal of Nervous and Mental Disease, 171,* 79–85.

Wolfner, G. & Gelles, R. (1993). A profile of violence toward children: A national study. *Child Abuse and Neglect, 17,* 197–212.

World Health Organization. (1987). *Evaluation of the strategy for health for all by the year 2000.* Geneva: World Health Organization.

World Health Organization. (1992). *International classification of diseases and related health prob-*

lems, Tenth revision (ICD-10). Geneva: World Health Organization.

Wortman, C. B. (1983). Coping with victimization: Conclusions and implications for research. *Journal of Social Issues, 39,* 195–221.

Wortman, C. & Silver, R. (1989). The myths of coping with loss. *Journal of Consulting and Clinical Psychology, 57,* 349–357.

Wright, J., Kaminsky, D., & Wittig, M. (1993). Health and social conditions of street children in Honduras. *American Journal of Diseases of Children, 147,* 279–283.

Wu, D. (1981). Child abuse in Taiwan. In J. Korbin (Ed.), *Child abuse and neglect* (pp 139–165). Berkeley: University of California Press.

Yopo, B. (1989). Derechos humanos y niños abandonados [Human rights and abandoned children]. *Revista Chilena de Derechos Humanos, 10,* 6–15.

Yuder, W. (1992). Resilience and vulnerability in child survivors of disasters. In B. Tizard, & V. Varma (Eds.), *Vulnerability and resilience in human development* (pp. 182–198). London: Jessica Kingsley.

Yule, W. & Williams, R. (1990). Post traumatic stress reactions in children. *Journal of Traumatic Stress, 3,* 279–295.

Zahava, S. (1988). The effect of combat-related posttraumatic stress disorder on the family. *Psychiatry, 51,* 323–329.

Zeidner, M., Klingman, A., & Itzkovitz, R. (1993). Anxiety, control, social support and coping under threat of missile attack: A semi-projectile assessment. *Journal of Personality Assessment, 60,* 435–457.

NAME INDEX

SUBJECT INDEX